THE BUILDING
OF THE HOUSE

THE BUILDING

OF THE HOUSE

Houghton Mifflin's Formative Years

ELLEN B. BALLOU

ILLUSTRATED WITH PHOTOGRAPHS

TOVT
BIEN OV
RIEN

1970

HOUGHTON MIFFLIN COMPANY BOSTON

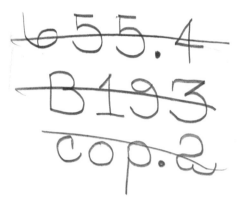

FIRST PRINTING   R

LIBRARY OF CONGRESS CATALOG CARD NUMBER: 69–15006
PRINTED IN THE UNITED STATES OF AMERICA

PREFACE

Early in my research for this history, Henry Oscar Houghton so dominated the stage that I considered using as an epigraph Emerson's aphorism, "An institution is the lengthened shadow of one man." As more and more individuals entered the scene, however, I realized that such a generalization would do an injustice to the company whose past I intended to recreate. Indeed, the founder himself would have rejected so compact a summary, for he regarded his publishing house as a republic, recognizing that without the contributions of the many there would have been no house. Especially dear to him was the Riverside Press, the parent of his publishing firms, and he would have been gratified had he overheard one of his senior pressmen say, in recalling his apprentice years at Riverside, "In my day those Cambridge boys who were looking for real security in their jobs went either to the United States Government or the Riverside Press. One was as strong as the other and there was nothing better anywhere!" Yet H. O. Houghton, being a man of large vision, probably would have agreed with Emerson that "all history resolves itself very easily into the biography of a few stout and earnest persons." To select from the many the significant few is the privilege and responsibility of the historian. To those who have not been admitted to these pages, my sincere apologies. I believe they would understand the physical limitations imposed if the book is to be comfortable to the hand and perhaps interesting as well.

In 1914 George Mifflin, at the urging of his associates, undertook to prepare a memorandum of the history of the firm with which he had been associated for more than forty years. After reaching 1878 and the founding of Houghton, Osgood & Company, he put his work aside. Two years later, he again took up his narrative and brought it up to date. The document, composed originally in shorthand, comes to slightly over seventeen typewritten pages. Appended to it is a sheet headed "Dramatis Personae." This is a list of ninety-eight men and women whom Mifflin thought should figure in any detailed account of the firm. My story, although replete with names, includes only thirty-nine of those in Mifflin's cast of characters, and missing from his list are the names of the young men who became directors after the firm incorporated in 1908; yet these were men who by 1916 had made their presence in the company vividly felt and who, after Mifflin's death in 1921, would guide the house on its historic way. Mifflin, who was seventy-one when he completed his memorandum, was absorbed in recalling the past rather than in focusing on the present or in anticipating the future, and his recollections have been chiefly valuable to me for their revelation of the man and the light they throw on the struggle with James R. Osgood which followed the founding of Houghton, Mifflin & Company in 1880.

Also missing from Mifflin's informal record are authors and their books. His concern was with the company's "business story," and the *Atlantic Monthly* is the only literary asset of the firm which he mentions. Numerous publishing house histories err perhaps in the opposite direction, centering their attention on literary successes rather than on financial achievements or failures, as though a publishing firm's fiscal stability played no part in the realization of its highest objectives in literature. Moreover, few of these house chronicles relate their stories to the accomplishments of their contemporaries.

My purpose has been to place Houghton Mifflin in the larger publishing scene of which it was a part in the years with which this narrative is concerned, the last half of the nineteenth century and the first two decades of the twentieth. Although Houghton Mifflin is the chief actor, many other publishing houses play important parts. Some of them have vanished from the contemporary scene. Others are still creating publishing history, although under somewhat altered names because of new alliances. Still others, even as Houghton Mifflin, retain the imprint of their originators. Since publishing is a profession of gentlemen, I have found only an occasional reticence in the interest of good taste necessary.

When authors and their books are the subject, the selection of the significant few from the many is especially troublesome. Of the thousands of titles the firm has published since the founding of Hurd & Houghton in 1864, relatively few can be introduced. My choices have been governed by what has seemed interesting to me and by available source material. When these sources put in perspective certain curious and complicated questions in publishing history, I have chosen to treat the subject in depth. This is the reason for my detailed examination in Chapter IV of Charles Dickens and his authorized American publishers. This is also one of the reasons for my choice of the *Atlantic Monthly* from the numerous periodicals Houghton Mifflin published in the last century. My hope is that the story will interest not only the specialist but also the general reader. That the *Atlantic* was of singular importance to Houghton Mifflin during the more than thirty years in which the firm was its owner and publisher is evidenced by the editorial letter books for the period. They are dominated by *Atlantic* correspondence. Such letters frequently served as directives. In January 1882 an *Atlantic* review of *The Portrait of a Lady* and *Doctor Breen's Practice* noted, "The Atlantic may fairly claim to have exercised its critical function upon the just completed novels of Mr. James and Mr. Howells before the reader had begun to enjoy them . . ." This creative function of the magazine's editors perhaps deserves more attention from scholars than it has so far had.

Hardly touched in this history are certain Houghton Mifflin undertakings important to its growth, among them its distinguished list of law books of the past century, its twenty-year devotion to lithography, and its continuing production of books for the young. This last subject I have presented frequently in the context of various chapters. Considerations of space and available sources have prevented me from developing the topic separately.

In transcribing the many letters which have provided the basis for my text, I have found a certain amount of standardization in spelling and punctuation convenient; however, in no case have I altered the content or sense of the original. In a few instances when errors in spelling, punctuation, or grammar are essential to the flavor of the original, I have retained them. Usually these mistakes are so evident that I have not thought a warning *sic* necessary. That I have escaped committing a number of similar solecisms is due to the wise and sympathetic guidance of my copy editor, Mrs. Sylvia Cleveland. Errors in fact are my own. These I offer to the discoverer for his delight.

This book would not have been possible without the help of many people. My debt of gratitude begins with Virginia Houghton Dole (Mrs. Alexander W. Dole), granddaughter of Henry Oscar Houghton, who more than a decade ago made available to me his family letters and private papers. For the privilege of consulting and quoting from these papers my thanks go also to the late Rosamond Houghton Whitney (Mrs. Henry L. Whitney) and Henry O. Houghton. I am further grateful to Mrs. Dole for introducing me to the late Mrs. Ingersoll Bowditch, Horace Elisha Scudder's daughter, who loaned me her father's diaries, notebooks, journals, scrapbooks, financial records, and a number of letters. For this kindness and her permission to quote, I am deeply in her debt. These Scudder and Houghton papers are now in the Harvard College Library.

Others whose assistance I take pleasure in acknowledging and whose particular contributions, when used, will be cited in the notes are T. D. Seymour Bassett, Roy P. Bassler, Mrs. Herbert R. Burgess, Mrs. Everett W. Cady, John Chipman, Mrs. Theobold F. Clark, Eugene Exman, Mifflin Frothingham, Harold A. Hatch, Ralph Hidy, Hamlin Hill, David W. Hirst, the late Mark Antony DeWolfe Howe, John Coolidge Hurd, Miss Marjorie Hurd, William T. King, Mrs. George F. Lawrence, the late Robert Newton Linscott, Macmillan & Co. Ltd., the late Frederic Melcher, George Montiero, Stephen Phillips, John K. Reeves, John B. Reigeluth, Miss Elizabeth Richardson, Claude M. Simpson, Jr., John Taylor, Thomas Whiteside, Alexander Williams, Mrs. Harold L. Williamson, and Albert B. Wolfe.

For the privilege of quoting from a wide variety of sources, I take pleasure in acknowledging the cooperation of a considerable list of institutions and individuals: the American Antiquarian Society; the Beinecke Rare Book and Manuscript Library, Yale University; Berwick Academy; the Boston Public Library; Mrs. Helen K. Bradbury; the Brown University Library; Mrs. Lilian A. Chapin; Conrad Chapman; Thomas H. de Valcourt; Mrs. Doris E. French; Gelston Hardy; Harper & Row; Lawrence K. Bret Harte; Quincy Howe; William White Howells; the Indian Arts Fund Inc.; John James; Mrs. Elizabeth Burroughs Kelley; Lloyds Bank Limited as Trustees of the Thomas Hardy Estate; Mrs. Ursula Burroughs Love; Conrad Oberdorfer and Don Belin as Trustees of the Amy Lowell Estate; Michael Putnam; the Estate of the late Francis Hopkinson Smith; Lord Tennyson; the Theodore Roosevelt Association; the University of Vermont; and A. P. Watt & Son.

The majority of letters from which I quote are in the Houghton Library in the Harvard College Library, and had it not been for the interest of the late William A. Jackson, an interest continued by his successor, William H. Bond, my work for this book would never have been completed. For permission to consult and quote from the Library's numerous collections related to my subject I am most appreciative. To Miss Carolyn Jakeman of the Library's staff and her assistant Joseph McCarthy, I can never adequately express my gratitude. Much of the material included in Chapter V appeared originally in the *Harvard Library Bulletin* XIV, Autumn 1960, in my article, "Horace Elisha Scudder and the *Riverside Magazine*," and Chapter XVII, "Scudder's *Atlantic*," was published in the same *Bulletin* XVI, October 1968. George W. Cottrell, Jr.'s wise and sympathetic editing of the first and Mrs. Rene K. Bryant's of the second have been of inestimable value to me.

One of my greatest obligations is to the officers of Houghton Mifflin Company who over the years have cooperated in making documents available to me. The first to show interest in my project was the late Ferris Greenslet, who made possible my examination of files, readers' reports, letter books, and account books stored at the Riverside Press. During the many months I worked at Riverside, the unfailing courtesy and consideration of the late Stanley

French, former head of the Press, of Morgan Smith, present head, and of Charles Rheault, production manager, made the experience a continuing pleasure.

Henry A. Laughlin, president of the company from 1939 to 1957, has been generous of his time in giving me his recollections of his early days with the firm and his reading of the completed manuscript has saved me from making a number of egregious errors. Stephen Grant, the present president, also took time from a heavy schedule to read the entire text. For his kind and considerate comments I am in his debt. William E. Spaulding, president from 1957 to 1963, gave me invaluable help both in conference and in his comments on those parts of the text related to the Educational Department. I am particularly grateful to Franklin K. Hoyt for his unfailing interest in this history. He has given many hours in helping to locate documents essential to the development of my narrative. Other members of the company to whom my thanks are due include Lovell Thompson, Henry O. Houghton, Craig Wylie, and Richard B. McAdoo.

In conclusion I take the opportunity to thank my husband to whom this book is dedicated. My odyssey through Houghton Mifflin's files would not have been possible save for his humor, understanding, and patience.

E. B. B.

Dublin, New Hampshire
June 1, 1969

CONTENTS

xii CONTENTS

ILLUSTRATIONS

THE BUILDING
OF THE HOUSE

I

A PRINTER'S PREPARATION

THIS IS THE STORY of a publishing house, of the men who built it, and who through financial panic, civil struggle, and international conflict kept the house in repair and continually enlarged it. Since this account ends in 1921, it is incomplete. In the close to fifty years that have elapsed since that date, succeeding administrations have repeatedly added dimensions and modernized the structure. The principals in my narrative are Henry Oscar Houghton and George Harrison Mifflin. Their achievements would not have been possible, however, without the contributions of many men and women. The combined lifetimes of the partners span almost one hundred years. Two of the editors for the house, Horace Elisha Scudder and Ferris Greenslet, through their lives in publishing provide continuity for these years and a projection of the future that this history might not otherwise have had. Scudder entered the service of the house in 1864. In 1902, the year of Scudder's death, Greenslet started his forty-year editorial journey. Through the work of these men and their associates, part of the miracle of the book, the mystery of the printed symbol is made manifest.

The nominal date of origin for the publishing house of Houghton Mifflin Company is 1864, when the firm of Hurd & Houghton, its precursor, was originated. However, the founder's connection with the Boston trade began in 1849, when as printer, not publisher, he bought John D. Freeman's interest in Freeman & Bolles, a Boston "book-office" founded in 1828. If right to ancestors inheres in purchase, Houghton Mifflin may claim an even earlier date of origin, for in 1876 Hurd & Houghton acquired the stereotypes and publishing rights of Crocker, Brewster & Company, a firm organized in 1818. Indeed, on occasion Houghton facetiously claimed for his house descent from the first printing establishment in Colonial America, pointing out that his great-grandfather Jacob Houghton had married Mary Willard, a descendant of Harvard's first president, Henry Dunster. In 1640, Dunster had married the wealthy widow Glover, thereby acquiring the printing equipment which José Glover, Elizabeth's first husband, who had died on the crossing from England, had destined for Cambridge and the service of the recently founded college there. In Houghton's view the owner of the press, rather than the artisan who sets type, is the printer.[1]

Claims to antiquity have small merit. Descendants increase by almost geometric progression. Adam is the father of us all. The widow Glover's press is the mother of the printed word in the United States. In ink and type at least all American presses are children of that first Cambridge press.

A cornerstone of Henry Oscar Houghton's business philosophy was his faith in partnerships. He approved of the mutual responsibility inherent in such an association. To share and share alike the risks, the profits, and the losses of an undertaking made for intelligent business relations. He first envisioned the rewards of partnership when as a boy of eight he contemplated a maple-sugaring operation. Later, when his ambition shifted from trees to type, since he had no money he could realize his purpose of becoming a printer, that is, the owner of a press, only through such an arrangement. No widow Glover stood ready to his hand. His capital had to be won from men. In return for their trust, he could contribute his passion for detail, his knowledge, skill, and driving ambition. Many men found these attributes sufficient to balance their investments.

During his more than forty years in business, Houghton showed exceptional astuteness in securing partners in his enterprises. At least eighteen assisted him in this way. Five of these lent their names to his successive companies: Charles Bolles of Bolles & Houghton, Rufus Haywood of Houghton & Haywood, Melancthon M. Hurd of Hurd & Houghton, James R. Osgood of Houghton, Osgood, and George H. Mifflin of Houghton, Mifflin. The other thirteen — Edmund H. Bennett, Marshall Whitney, William Veazie, Lawson Valentine, Horace E. Scudder, James D. Hurd, Thurlow Weed Barnes, James Murray Kay, Albert G. Houghton, a brother, his nephews Albert F. and Oscar R. Houghton, and his son Henry O. Houghton, Jr. — are concealed in the anonymous "& Company." The majority of these men, if for one reason or another they withdrew from the responsibilities of active partnership, left their investments in the company in Houghton's hands, nor did they ever have reason to regret such trust. Three of these partnerships, those with Haywood, Whitney, and Veazie, were clearly limited, marriages of convenience, lasting a brief time only. Of the other men included in the "& Company," only Thurlow Weed Barnes, who became a partner in 1888, tired of the experiment, withdrawing his money after three mutually unsatisfactory years. Another mésalliance was that with James R. Osgood. In this turbulent union Osgood lost where he had expected to gain; Houghton, Mifflin succeeded to the great Ticknor & Fields list and thus became the authorized publishers of Longfellow, Lowell, Whittier, Thoreau, Hawthorne, and many others.

The most enduring partnerships were those with Melancthon M. Hurd and George H. Mifflin. Hurd, retiring in 1878 because of poor health, left his money in Houghton's care and maintained a lively interest in the business up to the time of his death. Mifflin, who came to work for Henry O. Houghton in 1868 and assumed an active partnership in 1872, never wavered in his affectionate loyalty to his senior partner. Yet both these men were vastly different from Houghton in inheritance, education, and experience. Born to wealth, Hurd and Mifflin were heirs to the assurance money sometimes gives. Houghton's equal assurance was the product of an iron will.

In less dependent associations as well as partnerships, Houghton enjoyed the trust and support of a wide variety of men: John D. Freeman, the printer; Samuel D. Warren, the paper-maker; the brothers George and Charles Merriam, publishers of Webster's dictionary; and James Brown of Little, Brown & Company. Many writers trusted Houghton too: Oliver Wendell Holmes, James

Russell Lowell, Kate Douglas Wiggin, Margaret Deland, and Woodrow Wilson are but five among a host. There were a number, of course, who found him hard, sharp in his firm's interest rather than in theirs. He would be a rare man indeed to live seventy years without exciting the malicious quips of some, the lasting enmity of others.

As chief architect of his publishing house, Henry Oscar Houghton left the mark of his character on the firm which still bears his name. So pervasive was his personality that a devoted worker in his vineyard wrote him once when he was abroad, "Although you are thousands of miles away your influence over us is as strong as if you were here."[2] The shadow of this influence prevailed long after his death. George Harrison Mifflin, as junior partner, was first his pupil, then trustee of the traditions and reputation of the firm. The younger man made his particular contributions to the fame of the house, but these derived from his master's instruction. As the tale will show, Mifflin was a superior student and a devoted disciple.

The secret of Houghton's dominance lies in part in his time of growing up. He was a man schooled by poverty. Early in life he acquired the courage to assume debts. One debt discharged, he assumed another, larger than the first. Men were willing to lend him money, recognizing in this son of a Vermont tanner a relentless determination to succeed, a determination which assured that the money would be returned with interest. He was a good investment.

Henry Oscar Houghton was born in Sutton, Vermont, on April 30, 1823, the eleventh child and sixth son of Marilla Clay and Captain William Houghton. Two years later, when she was forty-five, Marilla Clay gave birth to a daughter, who perhaps in honor of the mother's twenty-three years of childbearing was also named Marilla. One of the William Houghton children lived but a day; the eleven others at least reached maturity. Yet, before Marilla Clay Houghton died in 1858, six of her sons and daughters had preceded her to the grave. No child achieved either her seventy-eight years or those of their father the Captain, who, a failure in almost everything else, was in his ninetieth year when he died in October 1863.[3]

Marilla Clay Houghton, a native of Putney, Vermont, was the daughter of James Clay, who had served as Captain in the American Revolution. Her husband William's title of Captain was of a different order, simply indicating some years of service in the militia of Lyndon, Vermont, where he settled with his bride shortly after their marriage in February 1802, a year earlier having taken up a claim with ten other men in this northern hill town. The Captain had been born two years before the Revolution in Bolton, Massachusetts, originally a part of Lancaster, a town settled by a group of emigrants from Lancaster, England. Henry Oscar's first American ancestor, John Houghton, was one of these emigrants who had arrived in this country on the *Abigail* in 1653.

Horace Elisha Scudder, Henry Oscar Houghton's biographer, characterized Captain William as a rover. Perhaps inevitably, he seemed so to Scudder, who had lived his entire life in Boston or its environs. However, the Captain stayed in Lyndon for over sixteen years, striving to support his growing family by practicing the tanner's trade. Here with something less than two-year regularity were born nine of his twelve children, and here one died. In 1818, he took his family but a short distance north from Lyndon to the maple-sugar town of Sutton, where abandoning his work as a tanner, he hired himself out as a farmhand. Here three more children were born, one of them Henry Oscar. The Captain's work as a hired hand brought in a pittance only, and "many a time" his wife was hard put to say "after one meal was served . . . where the next was to come from." In her youngest son's recollection, "the best meal he ever ate" was one he cooked himself, "a bit of brown bread fried with a strip of fat," on a forked stick over an open fire.[4]

The driving poverty endured by this numerous family is implicit not only in Henry Oscar's few recorded recollections of his youth but also in the strong bonds that held the Houghtons in devotion to each other after the grown children scattered to the south and west in search of richer rewards than the Vermont hills seemed to afford.

The breaking up of the family began in the Sutton years; Stella, the first-born, going to Alabama to teach and then to marry in 1830 a merchant of Tuscaloosa, David Scott; Harriet, the next in line, to Bradford, Vermont, to marry Barton M. Tyler in 1831. Within the decade, the Tylers left for Alabama urged thither by Albert, the third son, who had followed his sister Stella south and assisted by her husband David was able to report to "Brother Tyler" that he was fat and well and doing a $13,000 gross business in cotton and importing. Diantha, the third Houghton daughter, shortly afterward followed the Tylers to Tuscaloosa. William Junior, the oldest son, in 1833 migrated to western New York. The year before, James Clay Houghton, the second son, had entered Amherst and thus set a pattern for his two younger brothers, Daniel and Henry Oscar. For these three Houghtons, and Marilla too, education became poverty's panacea.[5]

In the same year that William Junior left for New York State, the senior William decided on a move also, packing up his wife and remaining five children to travel down the borders of the Passumpsic and Connecticut rivers to Bradford, Vermont, where the Captain found a house on Back Street. The house had an orchard and a clover patch. The Captain bought a cow and Oscar was put to school at the Academy.[6]

Three years later, in 1836, Daniel decided to follow James Clay's example and earn a college degree. His choice was the University of Vermont. Still working as a farmhand, William Senior continued to provide for his wife and children the meagerest of livings. Soon it was decided that the youngest son must "cut corners to security" by learning a trade, and Daniel, who to pay his way through college had secured work on the Burlington *Free Press*, arranged that his brother be apprenticed to the paper's owner, Henry B. Stacy. In October, Henry Oscar, now thirteen, and his father set off at four in the morning in a "lumbering old stage" to make the eighty-mile journey from Bradford to Burlington. Mr. and Mrs. Stacy welcomed the Houghtons hospitably and assured the father that they would keep a parental eye on his young son.[7]

Oscar and Daniel kept in close touch with their parents during these Burlington years, filling their letters with homely detail and affectionate concern. Oscar wrote of his pleasure in his work. Mrs. Stacy he thought an excellent cook and he urged his mother to try her "receipt" for potato bread (one-third potatoes ground fine, two-thirds flour). "I will leave it to father if that was not good bread he eat when he was here," he urged. Within a year the country was in the throes of a financial panic and times were hard in Burlington: flour $10 to $11 a barrel, corn $1.25 a bushel. The two boys were concerned whether their parents were getting enough to eat. Daniel's work at the *Free Press,* mostly during vacations, earned him $5 a week plus board. Oscar's indenture assured him board, bed, and clothes. By this time Daniel had made up his mind that his brother should prepare for college and to this end he started a school for the apprentices of the *Free Press.* Under Daniel's supervision, the boys studied Greek, Latin, and mathematics. To realize their ambitions, the brothers set themselves a rigorous schedule, rising at five in order to have two hours for study before the working day began.[8]

Times were hard in Bradford as well as Burlington. A man named Pomeroy had fleeced the Captain of $300, absconding to Canada. Employment was sporadic and uncertain. William Junior, who now owned a boot and shoe store in Nunda Valley, New York, urged his father to come west. As for the $300, he wrote, "let it all go to the Bugs for what I care if I can get him this side of the Line I will show him how the Cat eat the Butter. Do as you think best." The Captain thought best that he remain in Bradford on the chance of Pomeroy's return, but he accepted his son's hospitality for his wife, his son Justin, and his daughter Maria. Marilla, the youngest, had set her heart on an education, so she was to go to Burlington to be watched over by her brothers. Marilla Clay, with but two children of what had once been so large a family, set out by wagon on the arduous sixteen-day journey to western New York, and the Captain arranged to sell the house on Back Street, the clover patch, and the cow. Oscar came down from Burlington to assist at the auction and to take his sister back with him. The cow, Oscar reported to his mother, sold for $19.[9]

After a three-year apprenticeship with the *Free Press,* Henry Oscar, urged by his mother, left Burlington for Nunda, taking Marilla with him. On their westward journey, according to his journal, although at times his "cake seemed all dough," he made the most of his trade, securing passage down Lake Champlain at half-price because of his connection with a newspaper. Arrived at Whitehall, the brother and sister were "economically stowed away" aboard the canalboat *Illinois,* their destination Rochester. At every stop on the eight-day trip, the young man visited the local printing shops, where he was given the towns' papers free of charge. Because he shared these with his fellow passengers on the *Illinois,* he won "the cognomen" of "the Printing Office," he noted proudly. After a one-night stop in Rochester, he and his sister took stage for Geneseo and again his apprentice experience paid off, for traveling with him was the owner of a printing establishment who promised him employment. Thus when he finally reached Nunda, he was able to assure his mother that he would be no drain on her meager resources. However, an education was his lodestar, so in addition to serving sporadically as apprentice printer, he also attended school, first in Nunda, then at Middlebury Academy in Wyoming, New York. By early 1842, he was back in Burlington, spending "long old-fashioned days" in Stacy's composing room, before and after hours pouring over his books so he could enter the University of Vermont with the class of 1846.[10]

Henry Oscar Houghton's education so far had been laboriously acquired, nor was it an education through books alone. In addition to elementary Greek, he had learned that in hard times, it is the man with the ready cash or easy credit who buys the cow in the clover patch. More important, his work for Stacy's *Free Press* had made him aware of the larger world of which Vermont was a part, for ". . . the printers' apprentice, however humble, stands as it were, in the focus of the great events which are shaping themselves in every part of the known globe. He is a looker on. Each day he sees the whole world march in procession before him, & he listens to the fierce debates, the stirring appeals, the conflicts which are raging the world over; & while apparently not a participant, he is stirred by the influences which he sees & feels, & becomes a broader & perforce, a more useful man than those attached to other professions." Thus, in later life, Henry O. Houghton evaluated his apprentice years.[11]

The University of Vermont, during the years that Daniel and Henry Oscar lived and studied in Burlington, was an exceptional institution for its time and place. In the year of Daniel's graduation its student body numbered 109, its professors six. Despite its smallness, according to its historian Julian Ira Lindsay, the University had acquired the reputation of being "a nursery of American transcendentalism and the acknowledged source of the most advanced thought of the time in America, though not universally commended in all educational circles." This reputation was in the main the result of the work of its fifth president, James Marsh, who through his editing of Samuel Taylor Coleridge's *Aids to Reflection* in 1829 introduced the English poet and philosopher to American readers. Although Marsh resigned his presidency in 1833, he continued to teach his course in Intellectual and Moral Philosophy until 1842, the year of his death. His theories of education were carried on by his successors, John Wheeler as president and Joseph Torrey as professor of Moral and Intellectual Philosophy. These theories did much to shape Henry Oscar Houghton's character.[12]

Marsh's advanced ideas on university instruction are embodied in an early faculty report, which reads in part:

> We do not think the system at present pursued in our Colleges as practical and efficient as it should be, considered merely as a system of discipline and in relation to the purposes for which it is more specifically designed. Practically there is far too little of actual teaching and too much is left to depend on the text book. The scholar for the most part is required merely to exercise his talents in apprehending the ideas of others instead of having his mind brought in contact with those of his instructors and freely employing his own powers of thought and judgment in the various methods which a proper system of discipline would require. There is not enough *of free and familiar discussion* and of the actual trial of the scholars' powers to give the habit of applying them with promptitude and effect in the business of life and to impart that practical knowledge of one's own resources which is so important.

In 1843, Henry Oscar's sophomore year, the University reaffirmed this "dynamic progressive principle of Marsh's educational scheme." President Wheeler also intended that a student's four years of coordinated study would so prepare him that he might "be, with safety, left to his own guidance in his subsequent career."[13]

In these years the University of Vermont graduated a number of men who would amply demonstrate their ability to guide their subsequent careers: William Greenough Thayer Shedd, class of '39, first to hold the chair of Vermont's newly established Department of English Literature, and editor of Coleridge's prose and poetry in seven volumes to be published by Harper in 1853; Henry Jarvis Raymond, '40, first editor of *Harper's New Monthly Magazine* and founder of the *New York Times;* James R. Spaulding, also '40, founder of the New York *World;* William A. Wheeler, '42, future Vice President of the United States; Edmund Hatch Bennett, '43, future dean of Boston University's Law School; and Henry Oscar Houghton, '46, printer and publisher extraordinary.

According to his classmate Neziah Wright Bliss, Henry Oscar Houghton was so poorly prepared for college that he "could barely squeeze in." He had attributes, however, to compensate for his spotty preparation; chief of these was a granite determination to succeed. This determination showed in his rugged Lincolnesque features as he walked up the hill from the offices of the *Free Press* to his room in South College with 37½¢ (three York shillings) in his pocket to meet the academic and social competition of his twenty-nine classmates. It shows also in the careful record he kept of his and his competitors' academic standing. This record reveals that at the end of his freshman year on a scale of 20 his average was 14.9; his best subject, geometry with a straight 19. His poorest, algebra with 10. For all the students, the sophomore year was hard and Henry Oscar slipped to 11.4, an average which he raised the following year to 12.6. By his senior year, eight of his companions had dropped from the ranks and Henry Oscar tied for third place in a class of twenty-one, his general average 12.[14]

Had he not had to spend all his spare time working either at the *Free Press* or at the printing office of the Burlington publisher Chauncy Goodrich, "where he set type, read proof, etc., in fact did almost everything at times," his academic record might have been superior. That he was obliged to work as hard as he did was in part the fault of a man for whom he had labored who had assured him eighty dollars to pay his way through college. Unfortunately, the money was in promises only; "at a convenient time" his employer failed and all Henry Oscar had to show for his work was "a pair of boots which he afterward sold for a five-dollar gold piece." To one of his classmates Henry Oscar's achievement in earning his way through college was wonderful. That he "should be able to set type all day at the case, and still find time to study and make the three trips from down town and back again and have any vitality left" required nerve and an "iron will." To other classmates he appeared an "earnest, honest, unsophisticated Yankee boy," somewhat awkward and ungainly but genial and warmhearted.[15]

Neziah Bliss described his classmate as "stammering," "hesitant," and "lumbering" in speech. Even so, he was soon doing his share of "speechifying," both in class exhibitions and as a member of Phi Sigma Nu, an organization of which he became treasurer in his sophomore year. Membership in Phi Sigma Nu contributed as much to the making of Henry Oscar Houghton as did the free exchange of ideas in the classroom advocated by President Marsh. According to one graduate, and subsequently professor of Rhetoric and English Literature, "no private fraternity, and no debates or other exercises devised by the professor of Rhetoric, ever contributed so unmistakably to the making of thinkers, writers or speakers as did the disquisitions, and criticisms of the Phi Sigma and the University Institute. The former was the older society, and had the more valuable library. Both supplied the more important periodical literature of the United States and England, — a department in which the general library was weak. Membership was determined by lot, and Freshmen generally cherished a hope that fortune would assign them to the fraternity first named."[16]

Although Phi Sigma Nu was a literary society, its minutes reveal that Henry Oscar Houghton was primarily interested in political subjects. Among the topics for discussion in which he took part appear such questions as "Is Henry Clay a consistent politician?"; "Does our government tend more to a democracy than an aristocracy?"; "Ought Congress to abolish the Military Academy at West

Point?"; "Is the course of Massachusetts in seeking to protect her citizens against the laws of South Carolina justified?"; "Is the doctrine of Mr. Polk, with reference to foreign colonization on this continent, consistent with sound policy?"; and, perennial subject of the collegiate debater, "Ought capital punishment to be abolished?" These debates within the society sharpened Henry Oscar Houghton's wits so that they might be displayed to advantage in written exercises, general debates, and class exhibitions. The University of Vermont afforded its students opportunity to acquire fluency in the spoken word, an opportunity of which young Houghton took advantage. In later life in private discussion and public debate, he would prove himself persuasive.[17]

His poverty notwithstanding, Henry Oscar was a conservative, in his student days a Whig. The Whigs, according to his lights, advocated "a sound national currency, protection of home industry, and an equitable distribution of the sales of public land," while the Democrats had no definite principles. Theirs was a party of promises. They would "do everything well," provided the people gave them the power. However, he was no stereotype conservative. In education, his open sesame, he was a liberal. In one of his undergraduate debates in favor of enlarging educational opportunities, even for women, he opposed the "commonly received opinion."

The old men lament, 'that the times, aint as they used to was,' since, now-a-days the youth are allowed to go to school, and to get such silly notions into their heads instead of being brought up to work all their life time, as they were. The old women exclaim: 'O My! What will these addle-pated youngsters come to — they'll get so by and by that they will be good for nothing.' And the young, very generally express the sentiment that they do not need any more education than is necessary to transact the common business of life, that is, merely to know how to read, write and cypher. . . .

We often hear the farmers and mechanics styled by political demagogues the 'bone and sinew' of the country,' and to be sure they have as many bones and sinews as other men, and as there are a great many of them in this respect they may be considered 'the bone and sinew of the country,' but politically they are the mere tools of the party leaders (with some noble exceptions) but let them be educated and enlightened to the degree that I contend for, and then truly, they will be 'the bone and sinew of the country.'

What Henry Oscar contended for was a college in almost every community "so that a person might take care of his own farm, if he has one, and be going through college at the same time." Houghton was in advance of his time. Not until 1862 did President Lincoln sign the Land-Grant College Act, sponsored by Justin Smith Morell, another Vermont man.[18]

Henry Oscar's work on the *Free Press* and in Goodrich's printing office failed to pay his way. His family letters are filled with worries about his debts, and various relatives, as they could afford it, sent him funds — his brother James Clay, then a minister in Dana, Massachusetts, his parents from their small store, and his brother-in-law David Scott of Tuscaloosa. But $30 here, $20 there, proved insufficient and on graduation young Houghton was $300 in debt to his university. His business was to make good this obligation, but how? His first thought, characteristically, was to form a partnership, his talents and capacity for work to be his investment. These he offered to H. B. Stacy. His offer was a day late. The owner of the *Free Press* had signed a contract with another man the day before. Next he considered following his brothers and sisters to Alabama, but three of them (Justin, Diantha, and Stella) had by now died. Although David Scott had taken a second wife, he remained loyal and ever helpful to his Houghton in-laws, but of the young man's Southern blood kin, only Albert and Harriet remained. His closer ties were in the North, to his parents, to Daniel, to James Clay, to Marilla. (Maria, so long the companion of her mother, had married and was shortly to depart as missionary with her husband to the Dakota Indians in the Northwest Territory.) A teaching career tempted Henry Oscar and he wrote to a variety of friends and relatives, including his mother's cousin, Rufus Haywood of East Jaffrey, New Hampshire, but nothing eventuated save for a temporary post in nearby Charlotte. By fall he was in Dana, where his reunited parents were now

living with their son James Clay. Here he heard of an opening
in Worcester, but when he reached that city the position had been
filled, so he went on to Boston. On his arrival there he found his
university's president, John Wheeler, stopping at the very hotel in
which he too had found a room. President Wheeler gave Houghton a flattering recommendation and in short order the young
man had secured a temporary reporting job with the newly founded
Daily Evening Traveller at $5 a week. He also managed to pick
up a little extra cash by working in a printing office, possibly the
University Press in Cambridge. At least he had a letter of introduction to that establishment as well as to the *Traveller*. He
found other friends besides President Wheeler in Boston and
clearly hoped the reporting assignment would prove more than
temporary, for he asked his mother to send him more stockings
and his two best nightshirts. His hopes did not materialize, and
in late November he was back in Dana, teaching school in adjacent Hardwick.[19]

His brief taste of metropolitan life had spoiled him for rural
teaching. At the end of the first term at Hardwick he was off for
Worcester. This time he found stopgap employment in the Worcester *Transcript* office at $1.33 a day. This job proving a dead
end, he returned to Boston. Here he shortly found himself a place
in a "Book-office," that of Freeman and Bolles at 26 Devonshire
Street. "The work in a Book-office is more uncertain than in
a Newspaper office but far more pleasant," he told his parents.
Freeman & Bolles's hold on its journeymen was also uncertain.
Within a few months Houghton was offered a situation in the
offices of Samuel Nelson Dickinson, one of the celebrated printers
of his time. Although urged to stay at 26 Devonshire Street,
Houghton, recognizing the chance to better himself, transferred to
the Dickinson Type Foundry at a weekly wage of $9. Here by odd
chance also worked John Wilson, recently arrived with his son
from Scotland. So it happened that two men labored side by side,
one as proofreader, the other as compositor, both of whom were
to become acknowledged leaders in their craft, owners themselves of printing establishments, Houghton of the Riverside Press,
Wilson of the University Press. Their experience under Dickin-

Henry Oscar Houghton in 1846 when he took a reporting job with the Boston *Daily Evening Traveller*.

son was invaluable, for the work done at his plant was more than routine. This employing printer was a student of his art.[20]

Houghton's experience in the Dickinson plant proved at once the value of his dual training. His trade skills and his academic discipline were put to the test when he was given the job of setting in type the work of one of his professors, Joseph Torrey's translation from the German of Neander's *Church History*. The text contained a good deal of Greek. His knowledge of the language gained him a promotion from compositor to proofreader, "about the highest notch as to dignity in a Printing office," he noted proudly.[21]

The uncertainty of a book office ultimately caught up with Henry Oscar Houghton. Business declining, in the fall of 1847, Dickinson sold his establishment on Washington Street, moving to smaller quarters at 4 Wilson Lane. A number of workers were dismissed. To his pleasure, Houghton was retained, but a year later business had so far fallen off at the Dickinson office that, as Henry Oscar wrote his mother, "They thought they could not afford two proof-readers, and of course I was discharged."

Mr. Dickinson, however, had given him an approving recommendation and before long he had desk space in the office of G. C. Rand at 3 Cornhill. From this address he sent out a card to "Printers, Publishers, and Authors" announcing his availability as an independent proofreader. Included in his list of references were the names of his first Boston employers, the editors of the *Daily Evening Traveller*, Ferdinand Andrews and George Punchard. To supplement his uncertain income from the trade he had by now accepted as his own, he had again taken on reporting for the *Traveller*, writing articles on such various subjects as the Democratic Convention in Worcester, Daniel Webster's speech at Abington, Professor Wine's lectures on the Hebrew Commonwealths, and the burning at sea of the *Ocean Monarch*. This last was in fact an editorial rather than a report. Punchard was ill and he called on his cub reporter to pinch-hit for him. Had the cards fallen differently, Henry Oscar Houghton might have become a newspaperman. He was on the threshold of opportunity. Also included in his list of references were John D. Freeman and

A CARD.

TO PRINTERS, PUBLISHERS, AND AUTHORS.

THE undersigned, formerly Proof Reader in Mr. S. N. DICKINSON'S Stereotype Foundery, has taken a desk in the office of G. C. RAND AND COMPANY, for the purpose of accommodating those Printers who may need extra assistance in proof reading, or whose business will not warrant the constant employment of a professional reader. By this arrangement, it is believed, proofs can be read with promptness and despatch, and at about the same expense as in the office where the work of composition is performed.

If a long and varied experience, the facilities afforded by a regular collegiate education, and a thoroughly practical knowledge of printing, may tend, in any degree, to inspire confidence, it is hoped the undertaking may meet with encouragement.

Attention given, also, to the preparation of manuscripts for the Press, when desired.

REFERENCES. — Mr. S. Phelps; James M. Shute, Agent of the Boston Type and Stereotype Foundery; C. C. P. Moody, former partner of Mr. Dickinson; Messrs. Freeman and Bolles; Messrs. Andrews and Punchard, Editors of the Daily Evening Traveller; and a large number of Authors and Publishers.

N. B. For reading first proofs, an intelligent boy provided to read copy, without extra charge.

H. O. HOUGHTON.

No. 3, CORNHILL, BOSTON,
August 29, 1848.

In addition to sending out this Card to the Trade, Houghton advertised his services as proofreader in the Boston *Daily Evening Traveller* for August 30, 1848.

Charles Bolles, his second Boston employers. Freeman and Bolles were among the best printers in Boston, relied on for good work by such notable publishers as Little, Brown and William D. Ticknor. Freeman, the senior partner, was looking toward retirement.[22]

In a little over two years Henry Oscar Houghton, by working ten hours a day and more, had paid off his debt to his university. Freed from that obligation, he was ready to assume new ones.

These two years in Boston had been rich in experience for young Houghton. He had liked the town and its people from the first. He had found a boarding place at 47 Hancock Street, near the State House, just over the hill from 4 Park, an address he was ultimately to make synonymous with his final partnership, that of Houghton, Mifflin & Company. Hancock Street, he assured his parents, was "one of the pleasantest parts of the city." Whenever he was free from the obligations of his trade, like any outlander, he savored Boston and its environs. He climbed Bunker Hill; he went to Cambridge, where he was impressed by Harvard's library with its 52,000 volumes; he went to Andover to see some of his Burlington friends in search of a ministry. At Plymouth he put his foot on the rock of the Pilgrims. He took delight in Boston's celebration of the Fourth, the procession of flower-decked children, the fireworks on the Common in the evening. Once when his brother James was in town, he visited the exhibition of J. N. Banvard's panorama of the Mississippi. The brothers were thrilled by the 1200-mile view of the river. It had a special meaning to them, for Maria would soon cross the Mississippi on her way to the Dakota Indians, and death. Albert came up from Alabama to lay in a store of New England edibles and Henry Oscar helped with his purchases — chickens, cranberries from the Cape, and sage cheese from Vermont. Boredom was beyond his knowledge. Boston contained the continent. In addition to the wonders of the world, he had his weekly Sabbath School at the Bromfield Methodist Episcopal Church, where he taught a class of young ladies. The future held promises.[23]

Boston, despite its decapitated hills, would be his peak in Darien. In January 1848 gold had been discovered in John Sutter's mill-race in Sacramento. In the winter of that year Henry Oscar

Houghton began sifting for a different metal at the foot of Beacon Street.

For a man whose devotion was to the printed word, the time of young Houghton's start could scarcely have been more propitious. During his lifetime typographic techniques made their first great advances since the invention of the printing press and movable type. First of these was stereotyping, introduced to this country in 1813, which by mid-century, together with electrotyping, had become sufficiently perfected to be in general use, especially for books for which repeated printings were anticipated. For one who was to devote much of his energy to producing Bibles, dictionaries, and classics, both English and American, this development was of the utmost importance, for by this device a solid page could be cast in metal. These stereotype plates after printing could be compactly stored in boxes pending a new call for the book they represented, thus freeing the standing type from which they had been made for reuse on a different printing job. In the 1860s an improvement in their manufacture provided curved stereos to fit the rotary presses invented by Richard March Hoe in the 1840s. Another technical advance made during Houghton's life was Ottmar Mergenthaler's linotype machine, introduced to the trade in 1885. These three innovations, with their subsequent refinements, contributed to the speed with which books could be manufactured and changed printing from an art to an industry.[24]

That speed, and quantity too, was a matter of concern to the nineteenth-century printer was due to the tremendous growth in the market for books after 1850, the improvement in the nation's school systems under the leadership of Horace Mann and Henry Barnard, the Chautauqua and other movements directed at adult education, the westward expansion of the nation and the development of railroads. All these played a part in the building of the house which today is known as Houghton Mifflin Company.

II

PREPARATORY PARTNERSHIPS

JOHN D. FREEMAN and Charles Bolles had been in business as printers since 1828, executing contracts for a host of Boston publishers. Notable books printed by the firm in its twenty-year career include Hawthorne's *Twice Told Tales* for the American Stationers Company in 1837, Emerson's *Essays* for James Munroe in 1841, the three issues of James Russell Lowell and Robert Carter's periodical the *Pioneer* for Leland & Whiting in 1843, and for William D. Ticknor, the *Poems* of Tennyson in 1842, of John Greenleaf Whittier in 1843, and of Oliver Wendell Holmes in 1846. Their largest customer was Little, Brown & Company, since 1837 publishers of distinguished law books and a variety of standard works. Now in the winter of 1848, Freeman offered his share in the business to Henry Oscar Houghton, the Vermont tanner's son, who reported the golden opportunity to his parents.[1]

I have recently had an offer to go into business here which seems to me very favorable. Mr. Freeman, of the firm of Freeman & Bolles, who are among the best printers in the city, if not the very best, has offered to sell me one half of the office for $100 down and the rest in yearly payments of $250 each. He estimates that half of the office will be worth about $3000, which is to be left to the referees to say. Messrs. Little & Brown, who are the most extensive publishers of law books in New England, if not in the United States, propose to make a contract with us to do all their printing that we can do, at a stipulated price, which will probably of itself be sufficient to keep a large establishment in operation. They are building a large office in Cambridge, the rent of which is about half what Freeman & Bolles are now paying in the city. Mr. Bolles has been in business here about twenty years, and offers to put his experience on a par with my education, if I will go in with him. Gentlemen here in the city have agreed to sign a note for me, by which I can raise $500 or $600. Persons here who are acquainted with the business tell me that it is a good opportunity, and that we can probably make $2000 a year clear of expenses . . .[2]

The referees established half the partnership's value at $3200 rather than $3000. For the expense of moving the office from Boston to Cambridge, Freeman deducted $100 and on January 10, 1849, signed the following release: "In consideration of thirty one hundred dollars paid me by Henry O. Houghton, I hereby relinquish all my right title & interest to the printing material apprised [sic] by George Coolidge & James M. Shute located in building No. 26 Devonshire Street Boston." From Charles Bolles, whose ownership in the office amounted to $1247.44, Freeman collected $1952.56. Charles Bolles and Henry Oscar Houghton's investments were equal. So were their responsibilities. They would share and share alike profits, losses, and ventures.[3]

Freeman's terms to Houghton were generous, but acquisition of partnership status was not enough to run a business. To operate, the young capitalist must have some cash in hand. The assurance that a few gentlemen of Boston would sign a note for $500 or $600 was far from sufficient. To meet his weekly payroll and other exigencies, he must have more in the till. His relatives were ready to back him. From Alabama came promises of $1200 and more was offered should he require it. His cousin, Rufus Haywood, from whom he had so recently sought a teaching post, ventured $500 on a demand note. These funds did not come in until some months after the Bolles & Houghton partnership had been announced and the firm's headquarters established in Little, Brown's new building on Remington Street in Cambridge. With that publisher's assurance that he could have all of its business he could handle, Houghton had not hesitated to become an employing printer.[4]

To move the Freeman & Bolles printing plant from Boston to Cambridge was a practical step not alone because of cheaper rent.

Competition in the metropolitan area was keen and chaotic. The *Boston Almanac* for 1849 lists ninety printers. Cambridge had only one of importance, the University Press. Publishers in those days commonly did much of their own printing, farming out to neighboring presses such assignments as their small establishments might not be able to execute. This was a time of transition for the printing industry. The hand press was slowly being supplanted by the power press. In March 1893, Timothy Harrington Carter, printer, publisher, bookseller, and founder in 1829 of the Old Corner Bookstore, recalling the times, wrote Houghton:

> When my mind turns to the subject of printing in Cambridge, it reminds me of much curious and interesting experience. There was a time, not seeming long ago, when it devolved on me to keep the University Press, then of Hillard & Metcalf, and Cummings, Hillard & Co. in press work. There were four or five hand presses, each manned with two strong men, one of them furiously beating a type-form with printers' balls and Hastings' best (the crack book ink maker of the time,) and the other with a socking pull, bringing down the plattin and accomplishing one impression on a demy sheet of 18½ x 25½ inches, 500 of them making a token. A few years after this, the Treadwell Machine Press came into the market and Mr. Hale of the Boston Daily Advertiser, and myself, purchased exclusive right of use for this part of the country, and in a short time Mr. Hale had four of them running in his office by horse power and then by steam power, and we also had four jointly owned, running on the Mill dam by water power.
>
> The Treadwell Press did fine work but required much room and much power. Adams, a hand press manufacturer, stimulated by the Treadwell success, got up a machine press that could be run by man power in an ordinary printing office which took the market and Treadwell's press ceased to be profitable.
>
> My four went to Brattleboro to be run by the Connecticut River; Mr. Hale's four, in a few midnight hours, were reduced to ashes by fire, and those owned by us jointly on the Mill dam, went in the main for old junk, and as a whole whether we made a gain, or whether we lost I never knew. Treadwell's invention was to him a success as he had sold the rights of use in Washington, Philadelphia, New York, and perhaps other places.
>
> Now to turn again to your office and the University Press, a

few years later of Messrs. Wilson, what do I behold, in both offices [but] half a hundred or more truly noble and beautiful printing machines, each equal to a dozen or more of the improved Franklin hand press as made but a few years ago, all running in high activity by steam, multiplying the words of God to Man, and the thoughts of his children in aid to each other. It is truly wonderful to contemplate.

Will there be offered at the World's Fair an illustration of progress of deeper import than these facts?

In 1849 the labor force destined to operate these "noble and beautiful" machines was also going through a transition. Bolles & Houghton was, once more, fortunate to be in Cambridge. In Boston labor troubles were in the wind. The average pay for journeymen printers was 25¢ a thousand ems. A skilled compositor could set 8000 ems, or about 24,000 letters, in a ten-hour day. However, few were so dexterous. The standard weekly wage was $7.50 — the range from $5.00 to $11.00. Furthermore job tenure was precarious partly because of the apprentice system and the willingness of women to work at the case. To combat the uncertainty of their employment, the printers of Boston had organized themselves in a union in December 1848, their purpose to assure a wage of 28¢ a thousand ems, to limit the number of apprentices employed, and to banish women from the compositors' room.[5]

The objection to women as compositors was in part economic. The female willing to work for a pittance threw men with families to support out of work. According to the *Protective Union,* a weekly published by the Boston printers, the newspaper and book offices of the city had in their employ eighty-eight women, each one of whom had been diverted from her appropriate duties as "daughter, wife, and mother." Even the religious presses were guilty of introducing the weaker sex "into a printing office, where with sleeves rolled up, she works side by side with some poor journeyman . . . a journeyman whose wage will hardly keep him out of the poorhouse." The union had moral as well as economic reasons for protesting women working in a book office. Setting up a book was "calculated to operate detrimentally upon the morals of those so employed," it declared, "especially on account of the execution of many medical and other scientific works . . . which contain matter eminently unfitted and highly improper for the perusal of modest young women."[6]

The union's stand on apprentices had no such elevated overtones. It was economic solely. In Boston there were 166 apprentices and in some offices nearly all the work was done by these boys. "Formerly," the *Protective Union* said, "six or seven years were considered necessary to learn the 'Art'; now, generally not more than two or three are given — perhaps less. Having spent a portion of this time in some country printing office 'away down east' and learned to 'roll behind the press' and stick type a little on a country newspaper, our apprentice considers himself a 'competent workman,' puts on his Sunday clothes and starts for the 'city of notions,' without perhaps bidding his employer good-bye!" Bolles & Houghton at this time had three apprentices. Its regular employees in January 1849 numbered sixteen, one of whom was a woman. Business flourished in Little, Brown's new building and by May the payroll had almost doubled. According to the *Daily Evening Traveller* the "New Bookmaking Establishment at Cambridge" was "very perfect,"

> pleasantly and conveniently located between Main and Harvard Streets, about a quarter of a mile outside the Colleges. It consists of a large and handsome wooden building, for the printing office and bindery [Nourse & Remick were the bookbinders], and two smaller brick buildings, one for the steam engine and the safe, and the other for a fireproof warehouse [to be used by Little, Brown for storage of its stereotype plates and sheet-stock]. The two lower floors of the main building are occupied by the press room and composition room of the printing office and bindery, and the two upper by the folding and binding rooms. These are all of them the most convenient and pleasant rooms for the purposes to which they are applied, that we ever remember to have seen . . . The composition room will accommodate from forty to fifty compositors . . . Messrs. B. & H. run four power presses, three of them of Adams' patent with his recent improvements attached, and these with good ink and good paper, together with the care and attention which they personally bestow upon this part of their business, enable them, we think, to come as near perfection

as possible in this difficult art, as the works which have issued from their presses will abundantly testify.

The presses are driven by a steam engine of six horse power, built by Otis Tufts Esq., after a new model, which for compactness, beauty of finish, and economy of steam well deserves the attention of connoisseurs and economists of fuel . . .[7]

This account might well have been written by young Houghton himself. He was now living on Dana Street in Cambridge. Ferdinand Andrews of the *Daily Traveller* lived nearby and at his house Henry Oscar took his meals. During the summer, business drove the two partners "like fury," and continued to do so through October. In November, the new capitalist was faced with labor's demands. Boston printers, at a meeting on November 4, 1849, resolved to strike, all of them leaving their places of employment simultaneously. Employing printers, many of them but shortly before themselves journeymen, regarded the union's terms as "degrading," its action "coercive." Not only was it standing out for a 12 percent increase in wages (25¢ to 28¢ a thousand ems), but also it presumed to dictate shop practices, demanding that the number of apprentices be reduced and that no women should work as compositors. The *Daily Evening Traveller* was particularly angered that men who for a quarter of a century had worked contentedly at one wage should now demand an increase. In the same twenty-five years, the paper maintained, employers' profits had been reduced by at least 20 percent.[8]

The strike continued through November and December. Daniel was in Boston at this time and when he left for Dana, Henry Oscar feared he would carry a "sorry story" to his parents. And indeed it was a sorry story. The University Press and Bolles & Houghton shops were outside union territory. On November 24, a committee of fifty Boston printers went in a body to Cambridge "to molest the business of the two book printing offices there by waylaying and annoying, and if possible enticing away, the workmen who were there employed at the highest wages which they ever sought to obtain." At Bolles & Houghton a "Disgraceful Outrage" occurred. A young woman employed as a reader before the strike began had taken upon herself to work at the case. The delegation of Boston printers waylaid her as she was going home from work and offered to pay her board if she would leave her employers. She refused to do so. The committee then threatened her with a coat of tar and feathers, and in the days that followed, both she and Bolles & Houghton received obscene and threatening letters. In the streets she was assailed by vile taunts. Rocks too were hurled and finally this nameless heroine to the cause of female equality lay in the streets seriously injured. This was the sorry story Daniel bore to the old people in Dana. To compensate for the sad report of his tawdry Eldorado, Henry Oscar sent his mother a golden dollar.[9]

When the strike finally petered out, the wage demands of the union had been met. According to the *Protective Union,* even the *Traveller* was "doing the handsome thing" in that regard. However, women as compositors continued to operate. By 1857 the Boston Typographical Union had accepted the female, advocating equal pay. In this revolution (New York did not accept women in its union until 1883), Henry Oscar Houghton played a part. During these troubles, according to his biographer:

> He quietly went about amongst some teachers and other well-educated young women in Cambridge, persuaded them to put themselves under his tuition, privately trained them to set type, and, when the battle seemed to have gone against him, suddenly appeared with his reinforcements, established them in his composing-room, and from that day to the end not only had no further strike, but gave to the entire composing-room a character for industry, skill, and courtesy. He was one of the first to demonstrate on a considerable scale the practicability of the employment of women in this capacity; and it was characteristic of him that he should draw to himself the best-educated and best mannered girls, and not be aiming for the lowest-priced.

No liberalism should be attributed to Houghton here. As he reported to his parents, he intended to make the strike work to his advantage. By employing women, he was able to keep abreast of his printing orders during these turbulent months and his office was "full up."[10]

Full up as his shop might be, he was shortly faced with a new problem. Charles Bolles wished to retire and Houghton must find a new partner, a man willing to invest in the uncertain business of a book office. In this emergency, he appealed not to his Alabama relatives but to his New Hampshire cousin, Rufus Haywood. To this suggestion of partnership, Haywood replied:

> In regard to business matters I hardly know what to say. Your business is of a nature that I have but little knowledge Although it will be no harm for us to talk the matter over between ourselves
>
> Therefore I will enter in to some enquiries in regard to it If I were to connect myself with your business what part would there be that I should or could make myself capable of attending to About what amount of Capital should you want me to invest What do you think you are receiving or what do you think I should receive for my time after deducting 6 per cent on the *amt* of capital invested[11]

In answer to Haywood's questions, Henry Oscar reported that for the first six months of 1851 Bolles & Houghton's gross earnings had been $34,263.84; expenses, $33,239.92; notes payable, $9084.27; available cash, $2723.92 and a stock account of $12,219.57. His cousin found the picture attractive and before the end of the year he had assumed Charles Bolles's half interest. The new firm of Houghton & Haywood almost at once moved from their Remington Street quarters to other property, also owned by Little, Brown — the Cambridge Alms House Estate. The publishers had found the building on Remington Street too small to meet all their storage requirements. The printers looked forward to expansion.[12]

The land in Cambridgeport on which the Alms House stood had been acquired by the city of Cambridge in 1838 for $5600. The small (60' x 40') three-story, dormer-windowed, brick building had been erected at a cost of approximately $7500. Built to accommodate seventy-five of the town's paupers, within ten years the structure was crowded to the rafters. In consequence, Cambridge decided to abandon this "pleasant spot," bordering the Charles River between Western Avenue and River Street. The decision was a wise one for the value of the property had increased considerably. On May 22, 1851, Little, Brown agreed to buy the land and its buildings for $24,000. With its profits, Cambridge was able to purchase thirty-two acres in a less crowded section of the city and there to build a more commodious Alms House with sufficient land for farming.[13]

Little, Brown set about at once converting the twelve-year-old poorhouse into a printing plant. Included in the plans was ample storage space for the publisher's plates and sheet stock. So that Houghton & Haywood could add two new Adams presses to the equipment moved from Remington Street, the manufacturing area was also larger than in Little, Brown's other Cambridge building. As before, power was to be supplied by an Otis Tufts engine, but of twenty horsepower rather than six. The conversion completed, in February 1852, Houghton & Haywood moved into the Alms House, having agreed to pay an annual rent of $575, plus a portion of the taxes. Little, Brown continued to give assurance of business by extending its printing contract for five years.[14]

The Riverside Press in 1852. In converting the Cambridge Alms House to a printing office, Little, Brown added an engine room and a coal shed.

Even though Bolles & Houghton had not been spared labor troubles, the change of location from Boston to Cambridge had been an intelligent move. Even wiser was this shift to the banks of the Charles. The plant now consisted of the converted Alms House, a shed for coal, and a new brick building to house the Otis Tufts engine and provide storage space for stereotype plates. The main building stood with its back to the Charles, a navigable water-way in those days, providing a ready and inexpensive mode of distribution for the Riverside, as the press, on the suggestion of James Brown, was called. The ample space, over eleven acres, gave the impression of almost open country and provided pastur-age for the firm's dray horses and the partners' more spirited ani-mals.

The Houghton & Haywood partnership came to an end on May 10, 1852. Just why Rufus Haywood decided to withdraw is not clear, since an old payroll book indicates that the business was prospering. In its first two weeks of operation Bolles & Hough-ton had paid its sixteen employees a total of $74. The last bi-weekly payroll for Houghton & Haywood totaled $608.31 paid out to fifty-nine employees. That something was in the wind be-fore May appears in a letter from Edmund Hatch Bennett, with whom Henry Houghton had kept in touch ever since his gradua-tion from the University of Vermont. Bennett, now a lawyer in Taunton, at the time Charles Bolles was planning to retire had lent his Burlington friend $750. Now he was prepared to do more.[15]

Boston, April 16, 1852

Dear Houghton

I have seen Mr. Hatch, and he is engaged this evening and will not be able to see you — He is obliged to go to New Hampshire tomorrow. I have stated to him however all my information of the business & what he would have to do as an active partner. He is favorably disposed toward the plan & will consider it — & let us know the result. He has made application for another place, which if he should obtain, he would feel obliged to accept. In the meantime however he says go on & if we can find the neces-sary capital, not wait for him. I shall therefore continue to make efforts to raise the sum in some other way. Perhaps we shall be

obliged to fall back on our original proposition. I must go to
Taunton tonight — but will either see or write you soon. If anything new turns up, let me know —

Truly yours,
E. H. BENNETT

Within a month Bennett had raised the required capital and a
new firm in which he and Houghton were "joint & equal partners"
resulted. Little, Brown transferred its Houghton & Haywood
contract to H. O. Houghton & Company, as the new firm was
called, and John D. Freeman, who had arranged generous terms
in 1849, reaffirmed his trust by renewing notes for another ten
years.[16]

In the first year of the Bennett-Houghton partnership the employing printers of Cambridge — the University Press, the Riverside, the Cambridge *Chronicle,* and Allen & Farnham, successors
to the Bolles & Houghton space in Little, Brown's Remington
Street building — joined with their workers in forming the
Printers' Literary Union. In the light of Houghton's later effort
to found a labor magazine and his pioneer achievement in establishing a profit-sharing plan for his employees, his interest in this
cooperative venture is understandable. That the individual could
improve himself was to him an article of faith. In his university
debate, "Ought Farmers and Mechanics Go to College?" he admitted that his affirmative answer was an ideal rather than an immediate, practical possibility. Nonetheless, the hired hand or the
blacksmith might achieve a "height of mental cultivation" through
his own efforts. This was the large purpose of the Printers'
Literary Union. Its hall was to be "an arena for the free debate of
literary, scientific, and social questions, and a college for essays
and elocutionary performances." Like the University of Vermont's
two societies, it was to have a library and a reading room.

> Beyond these ideas of a forum and athenaeum [the Union de-
> clared], we shall, as soon as advisable, take measures to influence
> master printers, proof-readers, publishers, editors, and authors, at
> home and abroad, to unite with us in remedying the vexatious in-
> conveniences, and preventing the positive pecuniary loss to all
> compositors, arising from the want of universal standards in the
> use of capitals, in spelling, division, and punctuation. We main-

tain, that if uniform rules can be adhered to in one work or in one office, the same may be introduced with equal propriety into all offices; and it is possible, under sanction of this and kindred societies, certain authorities may, hereafter, be recognized and received wherever the English text is printed.

We shall also endeavor to surround our calling with such safeguards as may entitle those who shall succeed us to the acknowledgement of higher respectability in the social scale than is accorded printers of this generation. And with this in view, we shall devise, recommend, and, with the concurrence of the like-minded, morally and by associative effort enforce, certain reasonable laws of apprenticeship; foremost among which shall be the imperative requirement of at least a decent grade of scholarship, before permission can be given to learn a trade the most useful, and which two centuries ago was esteemed the most honorable of all professions.

And in order that this lyceum may fill the place which is its due in swaying the opinions of others, and as a stimulus to emulation in literary pursuits, we intend, when as a body we shall deem it expedient, to commence the publication of a periodical, as a specimen of good typography and the reliable exponent of our principles

In thus founding what we believe to be the only institution in the world of men of one craft combined for mental improvement and consequent social elevation, we make this

DECLARATION OF PRINCIPLES.

We have faith in the religion of brotherhood; that knowledge is the golden key that will admit us to the Temple of Equality, whose curtains fall wide as the mystic boundaries of human thought.

We believe that grand and permanent revolutions are of gradual achievement; that there is resistless power in the sublime march of the Theban Brothers of Reform, when the ranks are filled with those who toil, and toiling think.

We hold that there is much to be done in free America before the last rivet is sprung in the gyves that have bowed the mass since time began.

Labor must have its meet reward; marble halls must be for the builders, and hovels cease to be built; those who plant must gather in the yellow sheaves; man must be developed in his twofold nature, and constrained to labor with the mind as with the body, and with the body as well as the mind.

— And to this consummation we look. — Thus shall the race grow vigorous, strong in nerve and beautiful in soul, as in the glorious Grecian age, with invincible will, and head to plan, and heart to dare, and hand to execute, . . . and humanity become once more what GOD intended.

Henry O. Houghton's name appears among the list of founders of the Cambridge Printers' Literary Union. So do the names of a number of his employees. One of these, Charles Coolidge, would serve the Riverside Press for over sixty years.[17]

Edmund Hatch Bennett terminated his active partnership in September 1855, selling his interest to Houghton for $3674.32, to be paid in a series of notes. Actually he had become an investor rather than an active partner. In the years to follow he maintained his interest in the business, frequently acting as legal adviser. Ultimately, his investment in Houghton's printing-publishing activities was worth $50,000. However, for a year or so, Houghton was on his own. At least he had no active partners. If financial obligations may be taken as a measure of success, Henry Oscar Houghton had gone far. In 1846 he owed his university $300. Ten years later he was carrying notes in excess of $7000. More than once he received help from Little, Brown, their notes to be paid off in work done. With James Brown of that firm he enjoyed a close relationship.[18]

By 1855 Houghton had earned a reputation as a printer of discrimination who perceived the essential relationship between the author's words and the paper, page, and type through which thoughts conceived in isolation would become public property. Brown was interested in improving the typography of books published by his house. As a large importer of English and European books, he was aware of the best work being done abroad, and on one of his trips to London he purchased some fonts for experiment. Following Brown's sudden death in 1855, Houghton acquired these fonts, and James Russell Lowell, charmed by the "unique beauty" of some sample pages the printer showed him, engaged the Riverside Press to print a private edition of his dead and dearly loved wife Maria's *Poems*. That Lowell should choose the Riverside for so devotional a work was logical enough. He had known the firm and its precursors ever since Freeman & Bolles had done the *Pioneer* for him. Little, Brown had published his first book, *A Year's Life*. Since 1853 he had been closely associated with Riverside as he assisted Francis James Child and Charles Eliot Norton in their editorial work for Little, Brown on *British Poets*.[19]

Houghton's spatial sense, his geometric perception were among his many assets as a printer. Without other guide than his eye, he could judge a page and its type, the delicate relationship between the black vehicle of thought and the white fruitful space for reflection. He was, as all great printers have been, a student of his craft and a demanding perfectionist. He was no executive agent for his client, whether individual or publishing house. In his view, to press for his standards of the book's form was his responsibility. These standards were simplicity, clarity, and uniformity. By 1860, the reputation of Riverside for excellence had crossed the Atlantic. Of Richard Grant White's edition of Shakespeare, published by Little, Brown and printed by Houghton, the English periodical the *Athenaeum* said, "We have in England, among books regularly published, nothing to compare with it for goodness of paper and beauty of type. It is a credit to the American trade."[20]

However, Houghton was a businessman as well as an artist. The printed word must pay not only him but also the men who trusted their money in his hands. His artistic success depended on his business success and this had been threatened in 1857.

Sober economic analysts had anticipated disaster as early as June, noting "the amount of indebtedness incurred by railways, manufacturers, and promoters of all kinds to the banks of the country and to each other . . ." The precipitating act came on August 24, when the New York Branch of the Ohio Insurance and Trust Company suspended payment. Chaos ensued, a chaos vividly pictured by a young lawyer who would shortly have his day in court representing Houghton in a contest with a publishing house determined to destroy Hurd & Houghton. On October 12, 1857, Joseph Hodges Choate wrote his mother:

There is nothing to speak of this week. Nobody talks of anything else but the hard times.

The money panic rages like a hurricane or a devouring fire, and sweeps off everybody that stands in its way, without regard to their strength or respect to their persons. Everybody predicts a most extensive destitution among working men and women the coming winter, and really it does seem inevitable, such vast numbers in every department of trade and manufactures are daily losing their employment, and being cast upon the world penniless and starving. Their wages in the best times are no more than enough to supply daily bread and very few of them would lay up anything if they got more. This is the most grievous part of the present calamities and in comparison with it the distresses of the great operators and the 5th Avenue Nabobs are insignificant, although, to be sure, we have seen and are seeing some proud heads in those quarters brought very low.

This was the time ". . . during which the great firm of Harper & Brothers with assets to be reckoned only by millions, was forced into suspension for lack of $100,000 in ready funds at a critical moment of the whirlwind." It was also the time when Henry O. Houghton formed a new and limited partnership with his brother Albert Gallatin Houghton, who put up $6000. For this largesse he was to have 5 percent of the net profits of the business. If the press incurred losses, he would have no responsibility beyond his $6000. His younger brother's stock-in-trade was valued at $25,000, his services as executive at $1500. This was no joint and equal partnership, in which the participants share and share alike, profits and losses, which was Houghton's understanding of a responsible business arrangement. Still, desperate times demand desperate remedies. And times were desperate in Boston as well as New York.[21]

Theodore Parker, writing to an English correspondent, described the unhappy situation, seeing a "terrible logic" in the crash:

Now a word about Boston and its affairs. There was never so much mental suffering in any two months as in the last five weeks. Think of men who never thought of want . . . now left without a dollar! The man who refused thirty thousand dollars for his house in Temple Place, when he wanted to sell before he went to Europe saw it knocked down at auction for nineteen thousand dollars. Michigan State bonds, seven per cent, have gone down from a dollar twenty-five to sixty-six cents. Our banks have been forced to suspend specie payments. All property is depreciated. My income will not be half this year what it was last. But 'I still live'; only I shall buy no books.[22]

"I shall buy no books!" Augustus Flagg of Little, Brown recalling the Panic some ten years later said, "At that time most every prominent house was obliged to take up both sides of the bill-book." H. O. Houghton & Company, although still only printers, found itself in such a position. So did its Cambridge rival, the University Press. When the whirlwind had subsided Eliab W. Metcalf had been bought out by A. K. P. Welch and Marshall T. Bigelow. The Riverside Press still belonged to Houghton. So did a number of stereotype plates left in the Riverside vaults in lieu of unpaid bills. They were as good as gold. Henry Oscar Houghton could terminate his limited partnership with his brother.[23]

The financial chaos of 1857 was ostensibly over by the end of the year, the New York banks resuming specie payments on December 14, the Boston banks shortly thereafter; but its depressive effects lingered, producing in the four years following a series of business failures. In publishing, the most notable Boston collapse was that of Phillips, Sampson & Company, originators of the *Atlantic Monthly*. Houghton had been doing some of the printing for Phillips, Sampson: Emerson's *Miscellanies,* Holmes's *Autocrat,* the *Atlantic Monthly*, and a variety of works by lesser known authors. In the process of Phillips, Sampson's liquidation, William D. Ticknor, senior partner in Ticknor & Fields (James T. Fields, the junior partner was abroad), bought the magazine from assignees for $10,000, Riverside continuing as printers. In lieu of the $4097.01 owed him by the insolvent firm, Houghton found himself in possession of such Phillips, Sampson plates as were in the Riverside safe, their value a trifle over $2600.[24]

In this same year, 1859, Houghton paid Little, Brown over $3000 for the plates of the thirty-nine-volume *English Law and*

Equity Reports. In this acquisition of plates a process had begun which would eventually force the printer to turn publisher. Stereotypes, like gold, cannot be productive in a safe. To be worth their metal, both must be put to work. Stereos once translated into paper, type, and binding must be distributed, must have outlets, must find a market — the responsibilities that distinguish the publisher from the printer. Houghton was not yet ready for the risks of publishing, the times being still out of joint. The afterwash of the 1857 Panic was followed by rumors of war and war itself. He must proceed with deliberation. On November 8, 1860, Albert wrote him from Alabama:

> Since the Report of Lincoln's Election Our best Citizens are all excited & determined on resistance So we go all out. Without some miracle or something is done Our Country is gone. South Carolina will go out if the Government undertakes to [illegible, force?] her back every Man South will go to her rescue I am no politician nor alarmist but this the universal talk Massachusetts has already nullified by passing laws refusing to give up fugitives I do not suppose this will interest you but I write merely to let you know the feelings here I presume it will not affect your business much but mine is in a fair way to ruin Our Banks have all stopped discounting today Moneyed Men have all withdrawn from the market.[25]

Albert's forebodings were shortly realized. In February 1861 delegates from seven Southern states gathered in Montgomery, Alabama, to form the Confederate States of America, naming Jefferson Davis as President. On March 4, Lincoln was inaugurated, and on April 12 the Civil War began with the Confederates' bombardment of Fort Sumter. The printer decided to let his plate investment wait on the times. Since the Riverside Press had an impressive list of clients, change was not imperative.

In the light of subsequent events, the most crucial of Houghton's printing associations at this time were with Sheldon & Company and O. W. Wight. Orlando Wight, teacher, lawyer, sanitarian, translator, and author, in the years just before the Civil War was living in New York, where he wrote for both the *Democratic Review* and the *Whig Review*. In addition to his writing and translating, he prepared standard authors' works for stereotyping. Wight and Houghton had met in 1856; thereafter Riverside prepared Wight's plates, doing the printing for a variety of publishers to whom Wight, for a royalty on the retail price, gave the privilege of using their imprint on the title page.[26]

Among the plates which H. O. Houghton & Company made for Wight were his editions of Carlyle's *Essays* in four volumes, Bacon's *Works* in eight, Macaulay's *Essays* in six, and a series of French Classics in twelve. The largest Wight undertaking was a forty-six-volume Dickens. In this, the Household Edition, Houghton secured half interest by assuming half the cost of the plates at $25 a volume. Carlyle's *Essays* and Bacon's *Works* were published by Brown, Taggard & Chase. When that firm failed in 1860, Wight lost his royalty returns and as a result was unable to pay his Houghton bills. The pattern repeated itself when Derby & Jackson, publishers of his French Classics, went to the wall in 1861. Wight's Household Dickens, "elegantly printed on fine calendard paper," illustrated by F. O. C. Darley and John Gilbert, was announced for publication by W. A. Townsend on January 1, 1861. Two months later, Townsend was taken over by J. G. Gregory and on October 8, Wight, "for value received" transferred ownership of his plates and the right of publication to Houghton. So far only a few of the planned forty-six volumes of the Household Dickens had been manufactured. If the great project were to be completed, the printer required a distributor. Sheldon & Company were publishers of Wight's Milman's *Latin Christianity* and his Macaulay's *Essays,* the plates now owned by Houghton as part payment of Wight's unpaid debt. In December 1861, Houghton signed an agreement with the Sheldons, giving them exclusive publishing rights for the Household Dickens.[27]

In the firm of Sheldon & Company was a young man, Melancthon Montgomery Hurd, who after a number of years as a bookseller in Bridgeport, Connecticut, had joined the Sheldons in New York. Tall, handsome, outgoing, Hurd, in contrast to Houghton, had been born to wealth. His father Philo was a real estate speculator and railroad man, first superintendent of the New York & New Haven, then, just before Vanderbilt took over, president of the Harlem. When Melancthon was but seventeen, he had served in the Bridgeport bookstore of Birdseye Blakeman. Subsequently he had had a brief fling at railroading. By 1854, now twenty-six, he was back in Bridgeport running a bookshop of his own. In his first year, he cleared $800 and the venture was considered a success. Birdseye Blakeman, meanwhile, had gone to New York and there formed a publishing partnership with Isaac and Smith Sheldon. A year after Hurd's successful Bridgeport venture, Birdseye invited him to become a member of Sheldon, Blakeman, a firm shortly to become Sheldon & Company, booksellers and publishers primarily of religious and educational texts. During the course of the negotiations between the Sheldons and Houghton for publishing the Household Dickens, Melancthon M. Hurd and Henry Oscar Houghton met. Shortly they became fast friends.[28]

One of Houghton's unsolved problems was how best to make his stereotype plates, acquired largely because of the failure of others, work for him. By now he had the skeleton of a general publisher's list: law books, fine standards, and an educational gold mine, Warren Colburn's *First Lessons: Intellectual Arithmetic upon the Inductive Method of Instruction,* a text he had secured a half interest in at the time of the Brown, Taggard & Chase failure in 1860. Hurd, for his part, was bored with his Sheldon partnership. He had money, he wanted to travel, he liked people. His pleasure was the contemporary swim. A friend of the Cary sisters, of the Piatts, of the illustrator Darley (whose wife was Warren Colburn's daughter), he hoped to work with living authors. The union between Hurd and Houghton matured slowly. They saw each other a number of times in New York, then in 1863 Hurd came to Cambridge, where the two discussed "the merits of many enterprises."[29]

Still Houghton, by nature deliberate, hesitated. Hurd could guarantee large financial assistance, but how would a New York publishing partnership affect his Riverside Press, its equipment now worth more than $30,000? Little, Brown had just renewed its printing contract. Would trouble ensue if he went into publishing competition with this important client whose patronage since 1849 had played so significant a part in his achievement as a printer? How would such a venture affect his profitable association with other clients, Ticknor & Fields, for example? Before 1863 had run its course, Henry Oscar Houghton had negotiated a contract which briefly confirmed him in his inclination to remain printer. He was to have the job of printing and binding the fourth revision of G. & C. Merriam's unabridged Webster's dictionary.[30]

Hardly had the Houghton-Merriam contract been signed, than cancellations of certain long-standing printing agreements forced Houghton to turn publisher. For such an undertaking he was in need of capital. Melancthon M. Hurd was ready to supply it.

III

FROM PRINTER TO PUBLISHER

IN LATER LIFE, Henry O. Houghton liked to tell a story of his apprentice days when, working at the case in Burlington, he was visited by Noah Webster, the "schoolmaster to America," who was traveling from one country press to another leaving a list of words spelled in his American way, requesting in the name of emancipation from English domination that his orthography be adopted — aker for acre, lether for leather, melasses for molasses, turnep for turnip, bild for build, tung for tongue, thum for thumb, thred for thread, and so on. Of our native bird, he advised, "as the fowl was not brought from Turkey, it would be more correct to write turky." Webster at this time was at work on a revision of his 1828 two-volume *An American Dictionary of the English Language,* a revision which would appear in 1841. He had undertaken such a proselytizing journey not alone to present his particular declaration of independence. He was in search of current words, new spellings, and variations in pronunciations to be added to his original work. This meeting with the elderly lexicographer took on particular significance for Houghton when in 1863 he secured the contract for printing the G. & C. Merriam fourth revision of Noah Webster's *Unabridged Dictionary,* a contract destined to run for over one hundred years.[1]

When Houghton secured this contract, Noah Webster had been twenty years dead. In 1844, the brothers George and Charles Merriam, printers-booksellers-publishers of Springfield, Massachusetts, acquired from Webster's heirs the right to revise and publish this first significant American dictionary. The right of revision was of definitive importance. Had this not been part of the agreement, Webster's dictionary would have suffered the fate of Samuel Johnson's, becoming, as the years passed, of interest only to antiquarians and students of styles in lexicography. By the 1840s a limited number of Webster's American spellings had been grudgingly accepted — center, theater, and honor instead of centre, theatre, and honour, for example, but in the main his passionate patriotism, his wish "to invest his countrymen with a high protective tariff in thought," at least as evidenced by his extremes in orthography, had been laughed out of court. The Merriams almost at once planned a revision to appear in 1847. It would sell for $6 instead of $15, the price of the two-volume 1841 Webster. (The two volumes of the 1828 edition had sold for $20.) The 1841 volumes increased the entries of the original from 70,000 to 75,000. For its preparation, Webster, a Yale graduate, class of 1778, chose a group of specialists to work under him, including one Chauncey A. Goodrich, his son-in-law and also a Yale man of the class of 1810. The Merriams for their revision appointed Goodrich as editor-in-chief. Under his direction worked at least eleven assistant editors, the majority Yale men. This Merriam-Webster dictionary increased the entries of its precursor by 10,000. Save in Boston and Cambridge, it proved a success, realizing for Webster's heirs a quarter of a million dollars in twenty-five years.[2]

In the Bay State the Merriams had a rival in lexicography, a Cambridge man and at one time a schoolmaster of Nathaniel Hawthorne's. This maker of dictionaries, Joseph E. Worcester, had worked under Webster on the first edition, making with Webster's approval an abridgement of it in 1829. The trouble started when Worcester produced two dictionaries of his own, *A Comprehensive Pronouncing and Explanatory Dictionary* in 1830 and *A Universal and Critical Dictionary* in 1846, one year before the Merriam revision. A well-publicized Battle of the Dictionaries followed which culminated in screams of vituperative rage when the Merriams brought out an enlarged and illustrated Webster in 1859 in anticipation of Worcester's major revision of his opus scheduled to appear in 1860. In this battle Bostonians more or less favored their Cambridge son, Worcester, to whom various college presidents had given their blessing — Felton of Harvard, Wheeler of Vermont,

Hopkins of Williams, Hitchcock of Amherst, and Ballou of Tufts. The rest of the nation, well-saturated with Merriam agents and press releases, stood by Webster. Worcester's 1860 *Dictionary of the English Language* was published by Hickling, Swan, and Brewer of Boston, and printed by H. O. Houghton & Company at the Riverside Press.[3]

James Russell Lowell, at this time editor of the *Atlantic Monthly* with offices at the Riverside Press, where the periodical was printed, set his seal of approval on the new Worcester when it became available, declaring in a review of the two dictionaries that Joseph Worcester had won the battle, that his picture of the English language was the true one. Webster he thought had been a Hotspur, too eager to introduce the current and contemporary. "A dictionary," Lowell wrote, "is not a drag-net to bring up for us the broken pots and dead kittens, the sewerage of speech, as well as its living fishes." Lowell concluded his review with special commendation for the printing of Worcester, commenting on the size of type, the clarity of the page, and the freshness of the stereotype plates. Such praise for the work done at the Riverside Press endeared Lowell to Houghton.[4]

The enlarged and illustrated Merriam-Webster of 1859 was a stopgap measure, a transparent stratagem to hold the line. The Merriams knew that to meet the competition complete revision was essential. They engaged Noah Porter of Yale, a subeditor under Goodrich in 1847, as editor-in-chief. Thirty distinguished specialists were chosen to work under him. These plans antedated the Civil War; its outbreak did not deflect the Merriams from their purpose, although it had the effect of creating new words which became part of the revised work even as stereotyping and printing went forward. Thus after the *mis* section had been stereotyped, the new word *miscegenation* demanded inclusion and a line of citation for *miscarry* was deleted. This inclusion of new words was in the spirit of Noah Webster. For citations, the Merriams intended a change of policy from that of the original lexicographer. Webster, as Johnson before him, in his definitions and citations had allowed personal opinion and parochial preference to enter. In his illustration following the definition of *scenery,* for example, he had written, "Thus we may say, the scenery of the landscape presented to the view from Mount Holyoke . . . is highly picturesque, and exceeded only by the scenery of Boston and its vicinity, as seen from the State House." *Slave-Trade* he defined as "The barbarous and naked business of purchasing men and women, transplanting them to a distant country and selling them for slaves." The ideal definition, the Merriams thought, should be objective both in statement and illustration and George Merriam wrote his editors at Yale, "We do not hesitate at all proper times and places to express our abhorrence of slavery, but this . . . is not the proper place."

Sometime during 1863, H. O. Houghton and the Merriams met, possibly through associates at the Boston Stereotype Foundry, where the plates for the 1860 Worcester had been made. The Merriams were also employing the Boston Stereotype Foundry. Or perhaps they met through Samuel Dennis Warren of Grant, Warren & Company, paper manufacturers with whom both Houghton and the Merriams were doing business. Certainly Lowell's favorable review of Worcester in the *Atlantic* must have come to the Springfield publishers' attention. In any event, on December 14, 1863, H. O. Houghton & Company signed a Memorandum of Agreement to both print and bind the 1864 Merriam-Webster *Unabridged Dictionary*. The contract was to run for three years "and then run on unless either party shall have given twelve months previous notice, at the expiration of which it may be terminated." Prices were to be renegotiated each year in relation to those estimated for 1863. These ranged from $1.10 for "Rough Sheep marbled edged" to $4.75 for "Turkey Morocco gilt edged, best style work." Houghton had committed himself to print and bind the largest single volume so far produced in quantity in America. This Merriam-Webster was to have "upwards of 114,000 words" and 3000 illustrations. When he signed the contract, Houghton had no bindery.

On the appearance of the Merriam-Webster unabridged dictionary in October 1864, the editorial policy of the *Atlantic Monthly* shifted dramatically from the position taken by Lowell in 1860. The review of this new dictionary in the November number of the periodical noted that up to this time Webster's peculiar spelling had never found favor in the magazine's pages, but in praise of the Merriams, the review observed that "Dr. Webster's 'Old Curiosity Shop' " had had a thorough overhauling. As a result, in the entire English-speaking world no volume could compare with this new dictionary. The reason for the contrast in tone between Lowell's review of 1860 and this new one is not far to seek. The latter was written by William A. Wheeler, the Merriams' "Boston contact with the printers," a "wheel horse" according to the firm's official historian. Wheeler spoke with the authority of an initiate. Before signing on with the Merriams, he had worked for Worcester on his 1860 dictionary.[5]

For Houghton, the Merriam contract was the peak in a year rich with printing assignments. One of his notable jobs was for Roberts Brothers of Boston. This firm, which had developed as publishers from a house primarily concerned with producing photograph albums, had but recently undertaken literature. Thomas Niles, Jr., editor, whose training for a career in publishing had begun in 1839 when he started work for William D. Ticknor, had only this year come to Roberts Brothers. He at once moved the firm from the doldrums of undistinguished work to the forefront in this competitive and speculative business by taking a gamble on an unknown English author. Attracted by a review in the London *Athenaeum* of July 25, 1863, of Jean Ingelow's *Poems,* he persuaded the firm to order the book with a view to publishing an American edition. On August 7, in the Boston *Transcript,* Roberts Brothers announced the book as in press, a white lie, for the book had not yet arrived from England. Subsequently, Appleton of New York printed a notice of its intention to publish the book. An unwritten custom of the book trade, at least for houses which cultivated a reputation for honorable dealings, was that a firm which first announced a foreign work for publication in the United States had a pre-emptive right not only in the announced book but in all subsequent ones by the same author. This practice was known as publishers' courtesy or courtesy of the trade. Roberts Brothers drew Appleton's attention to its prior announcement and the New York firm canceled its plans for publication of Jean Ingelow's *Poems*. Roberts, however, fearing less scrupulous competitors, wished to rush its edition through the press as rapidly as possible. The firm's choice had fallen on Riverside. Within three weeks, on October 21, 1863, the first edition of 1020, beautifully printed on fine paper, was on the booksellers' shelves. The book was remarkable for its use of decorated initials and vignettes, recalling the work of the English Chiswick Press which Houghton admired and which he would shortly visit. (The *Poems* were exquisitely bound, too, but not at Riverside.) The first edition was shortly sold out and the Press drove forward to produce sheets for the next edition.[6]

One of Houghton's most gratifying printing associations was with William D. Ticknor and the various firms which from 1832 had always borne his name, Allen & Ticknor (1832–1834), William D. Ticknor (1834–1843), William D. Ticknor and Company (1843–1849), Ticknor, Reed and Fields (1849–1854), and Ticknor & Fields, which came into being in 1854. Ever since his Bolles & Houghton days, Houghton had done work for Ticknor. By 1863, most of Ticknor & Fields' printing was executed either by Houghton or his nearest rival, Welch, Bigelow's University Press. Of the many printing jobs Houghton did for Ticknor & Fields, none gave him greater continuing satisfaction than the *Atlantic Monthly*, which Ticknor had bought from Phillips, Sampson's assignees in October 1859, two years after its founding. Lowell, as editor, had been kept on, and for a short time longer, following a little footpath along the bank of the Charles, he would continue his walks from his house in Cambridge to the Press in Cambridgeport.[7]

These walks in winter and in summer compensated Lowell to a degree for the arduous task of rewriting contributions according to Worcester. "I was happy yesterday on my way to Riverside," he wrote. "I indulged in my favorite pastime of sitting on a fence in the sunshine and basking. The landscape was perfect . . . Sweet Auburn pink with new-leaved oaks, Corey's Hill green in the hayfields and brown with squares of freshly turned furrows . . . the orchards rosy with apple-blooms, the flowering grasses just darkening the meadows to set off the gold of the buttercups, here and there pale splashes of Houstonia [bluets or Quaker ladies] dropt from the Galaxy, and the river all blue and gold." Surely this was an idyllic setting for a manufactory even in 1860. Determined as Houghton was in working toward a goal not yet clearly defined, he cherished this poet-scholar-editor who on occasion went "bobo-linking instead of attending to business." He undoubtedly sensed, even as Lowell did, that he would not have his editor's genial presence at the Press for long. "I suppose," Lowell said on hearing of Ticknor's purchase of the *Atlantic,* "that he will think that Fields will make a good editor, beside saving the salary, and F. may think so too."[8]

Fields did indeed think so. Because he was abroad at the time, he had had nothing to do with the arrangements for purchase. Possibly he at first disapproved of his partner's extravagance but by the time rumors of the sale had reached London, he must have changed his mind. Authors there were his chief quarry and one, Charles Reade, assured him, "I could do *great things* for you if you had such a vent." Fields saw the acquisition of the *Atlantic* as thrusting upon him "an ocean of labor," but he welcomed the opportunity it afforded to establish continuing and cordial relations with authors.

Thirty years had elapsed since James T. Fields had first come to Boston to be an apprentice in the bookstore of Richard B. Carter and Charles J. Hendee at 135 Washington Street. Then he had been thirteen; now he was at the height of his powers, known and loved by authors in America and England for his generous, genial ways, a Maecenas with a nineteenth-century difference. The Roman had not expected material profit.[9]

Fields returned to America in June 1860. Lowell continued as *Atlantic* editor for just one more year and during this time he was under pressure to popularize the magazine. Finally in December, Lowell heard from George Nichols, proofreader at the Riverside Press, that Fields was complaining again, sighing over the heavy articles that Lowell too frequently accepted. The *Atlantic* was in danger of rivaling Crosby, Nichols & Company's *North American Review* in dullness. The essay which made Fields heave so deep a sigh this time was Charles Eliot Norton's "Fr. Rogeri Bacon Opera," hardly a title to encourage the average magazine reader. In answer to George Nichols' report, Lowell wrote Fields in defense, "If we make our Magazine merely entertaining how are we better than those Scribes and Pharisees the Harpers?" These New York Scribes and Pharisees in 1861 could claim a circulation of 200,000 for their *Monthly*. *Atlantic* subscribers numbered a mere 30,000. Ticknor on reading Lowell's letter may well have opened his eyes. Inevitably their glance fell on his junior partner.[10] In June 1861 James T. Fields succeeded Lowell as editor of the *Atlantic Monthly,* and the editorial offices were moved from the Riverside Press to the Old Corner Bookstore. Houghton continued as printer but he had lost an intimate and exciting association, more characteristic of publishing than printing. He was not one to forget, nor could he look with equanimity on working with the junior partner of Ticknor & Fields. Between Henry Oscar Houghton and James T. Fields there could be little sympathy. Fields, the senior by six years, of heavy build but a dandy in dress, genial, generous, relaxed; Houghton, taut, unpressed, guarded, imperious, forthright, and implacable. Charm was one of Fields's stocks in trade; integrity was Houghton's. James T. had a short memory; Henry Oscar a long one.

Although Fields as editor did not achieve for the *Atlantic* a circulation approaching that won by the Harper Pharisees for their *Monthly,* he did increase the number of subscribers, reaching possibly 50,000 between 1864 and 1866. By April 1864, Ticknor was well pleased with his junior partner, whose direction of the magazine was attracting new authors to the house as well as keeping content the established ones: Longfellow, Lowell, Whittier, Emerson, Hawthorne, Holmes, and many a lesser light in the New England mid-century galaxy, the majority won from other publishers, either because of business failure, as in the case of Holmes and Emerson (both formerly published by Phillips, Sampson), or by persuasion, like Longfellow, taken over from John Owen, a Cambridge publisher. Holmes and Longfellow had earlier been published by Ticknor, but in the continual dance of publisher and author had more than once changed partners. Now they were back in their proper stations, held to their publisher's uneasy chair by the glittering chain of royalties. Houghton was aware of the

James T. Fields, photographed probably in the 1860s, the decade in which he was editor of the *Atlantic*.

fascinating figures in the author-publisher quadrille. As printer he was an observer. Why dance or even play the pipe?[11]

Houghton's printing for Ticknor & Fields, as for the majority of publishers for whom he worked, was on a job basis; that is for one assignment only. Thus he was subject to the competitive pressures of other printers. A rival with a slack program could and would guarantee promptness in production at a lower price. An idle press does not earn its keep; better to secure work at negligible profit than let the machine stand unused; better to keep skilled pressmen active than be forced to let them go. In adjusting to the printer's perennial problem, the peaks and valleys of job demands, ever since the Bolles & Houghton days, Houghton had depended in part on his continuing contracts with Little, Brown which kept his machines running in times that otherwise might be dull. To Little, Brown, indeed, he was largely indebted for the success of his venture. Since 1849 these contracts had run for five years and were renewed. Now, in May 1863, Little, Brown negotiated a new agreement: H. O. Houghton & Company were to be their exclusive printers, provided always the work was executed promptly and according to established standards. However, instead of the former five-year term, this contract was for a year only, terminable on three months' notice. On December 16, 1863, two days after Houghton had signed the Merriam contract, Little, Brown wrote to inform him that "in view of the unsettled condition of the various branches of book-manufacture, by which great delay is occasioned in the publication of books, we beg to notify you, in accordance with the terms of the agreement made between us last May, that said agreement will cease at the expiration of three months from this date."

Here indeed was the end of an era. The excuse Little, Brown gave — the unsettled conditions of book manufacture — would have been more convincing in May; then the Civil War was going badly for the North and the future of the book business was as uncertain as that of any other industry. But in the summer of '63 the course of the war had changed. The victories at Gettysburg and Vicksburg had more than balanced rising production costs and industry was operating at peak. The future of the Northern book trade was brighter than ever before. Little, Brown was not curtailing its activities in any way. All it was doing was transferring its work from the Riverside Press to Welch, Bigelow, owners of the University Press.

For some time Houghton had been aware of a subtle opposition, even antagonism, in the Little, Brown organization. His good friend James Brown was dead. Others in the establishment were less interested in the welfare of H. O. Houghton & Company. The Merriam contract possibly equaled that of Little, Brown, but what assurance had the printer that this too might not be terminated at the end of three years? He must provide stability for his Press and his workers. Excellence of the product had not proved a sufficient anchor in the shifting sands of competition.[12]

In this year of '63 Houghton had learned again that his workers could jeopardize the fulfillment of any contract to which he had signed his name. In January, all his compositors had gone out on strike. The Press was loaded with work. Memories of the protracted strike of 1849–1850 must have been still vivid. The force at Riverside now numbered ninety, their biweekly payroll $860.68. He met his compositors' conditions and within three days they were back on the job. The presses were running again but labor costs had risen. By October the payroll had grown to $1506.09, distributed now to ninety-six men and women. These workers must be secured to the Press, must be made to feel loyal to it as their institution. This ideal could be achieved only through assurance of steady employment. Yet how could Houghton give such assurance, subject as he was to contract loss on three months' notice, to job loss with no notice at all? If he became publisher, perhaps as printer for himself he could so gauge the work as to achieve a continuous operation. Other eminently successful firms, Harper and Appleton of New York, Lippincott of Philadelphia, combined printing with publishing. Why should he not do likewise? Such expansion would require capital, but this he had been guaranteed. Since 1861 Melancthon Hurd had been urging a publishing partnership. However, if Hurd withdrew his partnership capital from the Sheldons, that firm would be seriously embarrassed. Since the Sheldons were the exclusive publishers of

Houghton's Household Dickens, the situation was a delicate one.
The printer continued to make haste slowly.[13]

At the time Houghton had signed his agreement with the Sheldons, seventeen volumes of the Household Edition of the works
of Charles Dickens had been manufactured. By 1863 the edition
had grown to forty-four volumes. The Sheldon-Houghton 1861
contract was to run for three years and thereafter until terminated
by a year's notice. Insolvency of either party would be sufficient
cause for annulling the agreement at any time. In such an event,
if the contractors were unable to reach agreement as to the value
of their respective interests in the association, provision was made
for arbitration. Costs of advertising were to be shared equally, as
were the profits, after expense of manufacture had been met.
Houghton, in order to make some of the stereoplates he had acquired as a result of the holocaust of 1857 bring in a return to him,
had entered into a limited publishing agreement.

The arrangement proved uncongenial, at least for him. He
liked Hurd, but the Sheldons, Smith the father and Isaac the son,
he increasingly came to detest. Ironically, for a nascent publisher,
some of Houghton's criticisms were of the kind he would only too
frequently hear in days to come from his own authors. The Sheldons' advertising was half-hearted; they didn't push the edition
enough; they didn't send out sufficient press copies for review. As
a result the edition failed to sell as it should. In support of his
contention, Houghton was able to point out that when Townsend
had been publisher, the average monthly sale had been 5475 volumes, under Townsend's successor Gregory, 3886. Yet, despite the
increase in the number of volumes available, the Sheldons' average
monthly sale was only 2698. That the Sheldons in their shop were
selling a rival edition infuriated him. Moreover, they hesitated to
include in the Household Edition Dickens' *American Notes*.
Houghton wanted his edition to be complete, "one that would
be of permanent value, that would be sought after by libraries
both public and private." He was convinced Dickens' strictures
on America would not discourage purchasers. "Next to praise of
oneself people like to read abuse," he argued. In his eagerness to
have the Household Edition as inclusive as possible, he proposed

"to employ a person to collect the stray pieces of Dickens' Works and send him a list of them with the request that he acknowledge such as are his, and he would like to have go into a Complete edition of his work . . . What do you say?" The Sheldons said, "No."[14]

Houghton next proposed that Dickens be paid a royalty, the expense being charged to the cost of manufacture. "What do you say to my offering him a copyright on future Editions of the whole series, provided he will give us early sheets on the new vols," he wrote the Sheldons. Again, the Sheldons said no. Why should they say yes?[15]

Since the United States offered no copyright protection to foreigners, English authors proved rich veins for American publishers to work, none richer or more rewarding than Charles Dickens, who made his first appearance in print in this country when "Mrs. Joseph Porter Over the Way" appeared in *Waldie's Select Circulating Library* in August 1834. From that day forward he was any energetic publisher's pay dirt.[16]

Carey, Lea & Blanchard of Philadelphia were the first publishers in the United States who offered Charles Dickens, if not a royalty, at least payment for advance sheets. These payments during a six-year period, 1836–1842, came to $1650, a small sum for *Pickwick Papers, Oliver Twist, Old Curiosity Shop,* and *Barnaby Rudge.* However, Carey, Lea & Blanchard themselves had no protection. Newspapers published the stories, so did magazines. Rival bound volumes and "complete" editions appeared at once in New York and Boston without a bow either to Dickens or to Carey, Lea & Blanchard. After 1842 and Dickens' first visit to the United States, the author refused to negotiate with the Philadelphia publishers. He had made a more lucrative arrangement for advance sheets with Harper. Angered, Carey, Lea & Blanchard printed *David Copperfield* and *Dombey and Son* without his authority. In 1851, discouraged by the viciously competitive market, Carey, Lea & Blanchard sold their plates to Getz, Buck & Company, who in turn sold them to T. B. Peterson. This firm made arrangements with Harper, who undertook to pay Dickens for advance sheets so that his future novels might appear in either Harper's *Weekly* or *Monthly* "almost simultaneously" with their London publication, Peterson sharing the cost of these payments with Harper, payments which by 1867 totaled nearly $29,000. Yet Harper and Peterson were as subject to rival reprints as Carey, Lea & Blanchard had been. Courtesy of the trade might protect Roberts Brothers when they undertook to publish the unknown Jean Ingelow; it failed when the author was an established, popular one.

By 1864 at least twelve publishers in clear violation of their boasted courtesy were publishing Dickens in volume form. The Sheldons and Houghton's Household Edition, illustrated by F. O. C. Darley and John Gilbert, was "copyrighted" in the United States though in fact Darley's illustrations were all that was copyrightable. Gilbert was English. Houghton's proposal to pay Dickens a royalty indicates that he wished to establish an honorable relationship with Dickens. However, his proposal was naïve and shows him to have been unaware of the business acumen of the author he hoped to engage.[17]

In just a trifle under four years 139,754 volumes of the Household Edition had been sold. Houghton's offer was 10 percent on each $1.25 volume, providing the author would assure him advance sheets. On the basis of sales so far, Dickens' return on the venture might average something over $4000 a year. Since Dickens could now command $5000 for advance sheets of a single novel, he would hardly be tempted by Houghton's offer, even though Harper paid no continuing royalty. More than one person has thought $5000 in hand more rewarding than the slow dribble of semiannual returns, especially in a thoroughly saturated market. Houghton blamed the Sheldons for the diminishing sales of their Dickens. The length of time that volumes of *Pickwick* and other novels had been available singly as well as in competing sets must also have had an effect on sales. Houghton would have won fame in publishing history had he offered Dickens a specified sum for advance sheets plus 10 percent on sales. Within a few years, James T. Fields, alerted by the public squabble between the Sheldons and Houghton, would do just that.[18]

At the time Houghton proposed to the Sheldons that they pay Dickens a royalty, the Hurd & Houghton partnership was some months in the future. He was still printer only. In this department, he had some unfinished business to attend to. He had undertaken to both print and bind the Merriam-Webster *Unabridged Dictionary* although he had no bindery.

On the grounds of the Cambridge Alms House Estate, in addition to the quarters H. O. Houghton & Company rented, was a bindery also owned by Little, Brown and rented first to Nourse and Remick, the firm that had shared space with Bolles & Houghton on Remington Street, and then to Lemon, Fields & Company, organized in 1859. The partners in this firm were Augustus F. Lemon, George Fields, younger brother of James T., and John Remick. Word now came that Little, Brown had plans to build a larger bindery and that Lemon, Fields were to move to the new structure. The vacated plant with its equipment was available to Houghton. On February 5, 1864, he signed an agreement with the binders to assume their lease, to purchase their equipment for $600, and to furnish steam at $840 a year for the new building which was being erected. Lemon, Fields agreed to vacate the premises by May 1.[19]

For a man who conceived of a book in terms of the whole, whose ideas on a book's outward form were as clearly defined as his ideas on paper and type, the addition of a bindery to his plant was gratifying. Now Houghton could clothe his Riverside signatures, carefully designed and meticulously printed, in appropriate dress, provided the publishers and individuals who employed him would pay attention. To the extent his Press achieved a reputation for fine work, he was in a position to be listened to, but his was not the final word, as he found when he attempted to tell James T. Fields what was wrong with the appearance of Ticknor & Fields books. Fields's taste was for elegance; he considered himself an American Moxon. The typical Ticknor binding up to 1856 had been of a fudge color. In that year Fields decided on a new format, handy volumes, pocket-sized, bound in an intense blue with heavy gilt overlay on the spine and with gilt edges. This Blue and Gold Edition, as it was called, according to the poet Stedman looked "like cheap gilt children's books."

Houghton's taste was of a different order. Of the gift book for exhibition on the parlor table, he was contemptuous. ". . . the book to be loved & cherished and carried nearest the heart," he said, "is the favorite author, printed with a type clear and round, on paper thin, but opaque, of an utterly neutral tint, with close margins, & ink of a nut brown or ebony color, & with a binding whether of purple, crimson, green or brown, as plain & simple as the dress of a Quaker maiden." "Simplicity without barrenness, ease without slouchiness, comeliness without foppishness, an attire suited to the use intended, — these are the marks of good breeding in book manufacture." Between James T. Fields and Henry Oscar Houghton little sympathy existed either in personality or in taste.[20]

Two days after Houghton had signed the lease for his bindery, Melancthon Hurd resigned from the Sheldon firm. On March 1, 1864, the Hurd & Houghton partnership papers were signed. Houghton was now in a position to control the book from its selection through its manufacture to its distribution to the bookseller and even beyond, since publishing in those days included retail selling. He was thoroughly schooled in the art of printing. Because of his experience with the Sheldons, he had clear ideas on advertising. Of authors, manuscripts, and editing, he knew little. These were to be Hurd's province. The new publishing house was to have a New York imprint.

On the day that Messrs. Hurd and Houghton signed their partnership agreement, Sheldon & Company wrote the new firm, "We will agree for One year from this date to give you all the 'Dickens' you want for your sales at our regular 'Trade-List' net prices & take in exchange for the same selections which we may make from the Riverside books which you publish or which have your imprint in, at your Trade List net prices." Apparently Hurd's shift from the Sheldons to Houghton had been accomplished without friction. The new firm of Hurd & Houghton was able to announce it would be ready to supply the trade with the Household Edition of Dickens, published by Sheldon and manufactured at the Riverside Press. *The American Literary Gazette* on April 1 commented on the new house, noting ". . . it is the intention of the firm not to be satisfied with past excellence, but deliberately to undertake to advance as far as in their power the standard of book-making

Houghton in 1864, the year he turned publisher
in partnership with Melancthon M. Hurd.

in this country, so that the American public may not be as dependent on England for handsomely printed books as has been the
case heretofore." Houghton, the *Gazette* reported, had already
sailed for Europe, whence he would return "well laden with all
the latest improvements in the typographic and mechanical departments of book-making."[21]

Melancthon Hurd brought to the new company $50,000; his
father Philo added another $20,000 in the form of a 6 percent
loan. Houghton provided no cash. The Riverside Press represented his investment, Hurd acquiring a half interest in the plant.
Profits were to be shared equally. In case of a deficit, each partner
was assessable. Each was to have a salary of $5000. Ticknor &
Fields's capital stock at this time was $200,000. By comparison,
Hurd & Houghton was a small undertaking. However, it probably
did not seem so to the man who fifteen years before had acquired,
largely on credit, a half interest in Freeman & Bolles, his share
valued at $3200.[22]

The Sheldons were not as content with the arrangement as their
letter of March 1 may have led Hurd & Houghton to assume. The
loss of Hurd's capital had proved serious. Sheldon & Company had
been forced to dissolve and reorganize, and in the days to come
Houghton would have a taste of their antagonism. On May 2, the
Sheldons issued an angry "Card to the Trade" insisting they were
still the exclusive publishers of the Household Dickens. "We supply Messrs. Hurd & Houghton with the books just as we do all
other houses in New York, Boston, or Philadelphia," they asserted.
Two weeks later Hurd & Houghton issued a card in reply. The
new house, even though it owned the plates and copyright of the
edition and even though it was manufactured at the Riverside
Press, made no claim to being publishers of the Household Dickens.
Hurd & Houghton was simply ready to supply the volumes to the
trade just as it was ready to supply the books of other publishers.
The card said in part, "When the firm of Sheldon & Co. was dissolved and our co-partnership formed some difference of opinion
arose in regard to the 'Dickens' contract. The matter was compromised by the offer of an agreement . . . By this agreement we
were enabled to supply books on the same terms as Messrs. Sheldon

& Co., they continuing as publishers for a short time longer." Hurd & Houghton encouraged the trade to order from either company, but pointed out its competency in this department, since "nearly all" its assistants had had "many years experience with the house of Sheldon & Co. when our Mr. Hurd was a partner in that firm." Hurd had not only withdrawn his capital, he had also taken with him a few loyal servitors. The mounting anger of the Sheldons is understandable. The "short time longer" in which the Sheldons could continue as exclusive publishers of the Household Dickens was approximately a year and six months, ample time for planning revenge.[23]

Immediately following the announcement of the Hurd & Houghton partnership, Houghton sailed for England and the Continent, his purpose being to engage skilled craftsmen for his new bindery, to visit various printing establishments, to study the English and Scottish markets for imports, and to confer with Dickens on the question of royalties for the Household Edition. Hurd remained in New York to placate the angry Sheldons and find permanent offices for the firm, housed temporarily at 46 Walker Street in quarters recently vacated by James G. Gregory, the publisher who had preceded the Sheldons in selling and distributing the Household Dickens.

IV

THE MYSTERY OF EDWIN DROOD

THE CHIEF ITEMS in Hurd & Houghton's virgin catalogue were books in sets made from stereotype plates acquired from others. Although few American titles graced the list, one of singular importance was Warren Colburn's *Intellectual Arithmetic upon the Inductive Method of Instruction,* on the market since 1826. In 1862, Mr. Houghton had secured from Colburn's heirs a half interest in the text. Profitable as this investment would prove, *Intellectual Arithmetic* was hardly a title to put a general publisher in the vanguard of his competitors.

A Boston house which by 1864 had achieved such distinction was that of Ticknor & Fields. Through tact, discrimination, and generous royalties to English as well as American writers, this publisher had developed a list of authors the envy of other houses. Obviously, one ship cannot carry all the cargo. Distinguished American writers sailing under other flags include Irving, Cooper, Melville, Whitman, and Poe. But the Ticknor & Fields manifest is impressive — Emerson, Hawthorne, Holmes, Longfellow, Lowell, Thoreau, Whittier, and many a lesser light. Moreover, by paying royalties when not legally required to do so, the firm had won the loyalty of many an English author. Tennyson and Browning, De Quincey and Leigh Hunt, Thackeray and Thomas Hughes, and others of comparable fame starred Ticknor & Fields's catalogue. One writer notably absent from the roster was Charles Dickens, represented so far only by an expensive edition imported from the London publisher Chapman & Hall.

Shortly after Houghton had departed for England, Ticknor & Fields's senior partner, given a clean bill of health by his neighbor, author, and doctor, Oliver Wendell Holmes, who declared that Ticknor, in spite of a persistent cold, had at least twenty years in him, left with Hawthorne, who was disturbingly unwell, for what was hoped would prove a rejuvenating trip to Philadelphia and points south. The concern was for Hawthorne, but it was Ticknor who died in the city of brotherly love. He was fifty-three. Thus was lost to Ticknor & Fields and its authors the conservative manager of one of the outstanding bookseller-publishers of his time.

Ticknor had been trained in the mysteries of money, first in an investment house, then in a bank. In the latter establishment, his business acumen recognized, he had been urged to make finance his career. However, at twenty-two (he had come to Boston from Lebanon, New Hampshire, at seventeen), perhaps feeling he could combine his bookish interests and his skill in managing money, he shifted from banking to publishing and bookselling as a more congenial profession. To realize his purpose, in 1832 he united with two men experienced in the trade, John Allen and Timothy Harrington Carter, the latter a silent partner. For $25,000, the new firm of Allen & Ticknor acquired from Richard B. Carter, younger brother of Timothy, and Charles J. Hendee the stock and goodwill of the Old Corner Bookstore at 135 Washington Street. Yearly rental for the property, which was owned by Timothy Carter, was $1325, payable quarterly. In the spring of 1834, Allen & Ticknor purchased Timothy's interest for $5000. Seven months later, William D. bought out his partner John Allen for approximately the same price. For the next nine years the firm name was simply William D. Ticknor. The young man from Lebanon was proving himself as able in managing a bookselling-publishing enterprise as he had been in banking. Beyond doubt his financial connections provided a ready source of credit, an essential for progress in the trade.[1]

When Ticknor bought the stock and goodwill of the Old Corner Bookstore, in addition to books and stationery, he secured an asset of which at the time he was perhaps unaware, a young apprentice, James T. Fields, who had started working for Carter and Hendee in 1831. The story of James T.'s rise is too well-known to rehearse save briefly. Apprentice, clerk, then in 1843 a member of Ticknor's firm, his name irritatingly concealed in the anonymous & Co. when the name of the organization changed to William D. Ticknor & Company. Another young man, John Reed, Jr., was his companion in anonymity. Reed had $8000 to invest; Fields, charm and energy. Ticknor was no master builder fearful of youth's imperious knocking, but he did take a fair time to open the door. Six years elapsed before both young men made the firm's imprint. Throughout Ticknor's life Reed shared financial interests with William D., but in 1854 he transferred to banking. At that time Ticknor paid Reed $22,000 ($14,000 in notes), a considerable profit on an original investment of $8000. Fields had also made gains. In the partnership of 1843 he had invested nothing but himself. In the reorganization following Reed's retirement, he was prepared to put up $4000 in cash and an additional $7000 in notes. Ticknor himself was feeling no stringency. Not only was he able to purchase Reed's share, but also to the new firm he contributed an additional $8000, and the publisher-booksellers were capitalized at $52,000. The firm's name now was Ticknor & Fields, an imprint which James T. took effective care should go down in publishing history, planting himself well before the "titular screen," as Henry James recalled.[2]

On his partner's death in April 1864, James T. Fields had been an underling for over thirty years. Like many a junior before and since, he must have wondered occasionally, "How long, oh Lord, how long?" Ticknor had been kind enough, first taking the apprentice to live in his own household and subsequently forwarding the young man's interests in the expanding business. After Fields's marriage in 1854 to the charming Annie Adams, Ticknor saw to it that the couple had the house of their hearts' desire at 37 Charles Street, arranging for the firm to buy and in turn rent it to the Fieldses. But kindness does not ensure gratitude. The restraining hand of seniority can be frustrating, especially to an ebullient nature whose vision prefigures spectacular accomplishments.[3]

In many ways both William D. Ticknor and James T. Fields must have recognized that despite the contradictions in their natures, theirs was a business association that approached perfection, especially in the last ten years of the partnership. Ticknor, the eldest son of a numerous family, was a home-loving man, devoted to his wife and children, a reverent Baptist and confirmed Whig. When away from home, he was unhappy, filled with longing for those he had left behind. "Oh, my dear wife [he wrote when he was in London with Hawthorne in 1853], that you could have enjoyed this with me, how it would have increased my pleasure. I hope, should our lives be spared, that your eyes may yet rest on the beauties of Old England . . . I should like to tell Tommy about the Liverpool Donkeys, and Benj. about the magnificent dray horses as large as small elephants . . . Do take care of yourself and may a kind Providence in mercy watch over and keep you all in safety till the return of your loving husband, W. D. Ticknor."[4]

Fields, by contrast, had only a younger brother and had been brought up by a widowed mother. In consequence, he was self-centered, but graced with a charm that generally concealed his egotism. In religion he was a Unitarian, in politics, uncommitted until the course of events had shown the locally accepted way. He was the perfect front man for the domestic Ticknor. His marriage to Annie enhanced his value, for she shared with her husband a love of entertaining and an enthusiasm for the great and the near great whether of the hub or the universe. Both were accomplished in the arts of flattery and prone themselves to the self-gratulation that homage from others, especially from the English, gives. Having no children, James and Annie could travel, could give breakfasts, luncheons, teas, and dinners, always together.

In the conduct of the business Fields came increasingly to make the initial contacts, but Ticknor controlled the final arrangements, drawing up the contracts and signing them. Because Jamie was himself an author, albeit of minor talent, writers regarded him as one of their own, but they looked to Ticknor for the wise management of their affairs. Fields might sense that Hawthorne had the manuscript of a story in his desk, but the author relied on the senior partner to handle his income. So well did Ticknor fulfill his responsibility, Hawthorne declared he felt like one "of the monied men in Massachusetts." Longfellow relaxed in Fields's laughing company; but when Ticknor & Fields was cajoling the poet to the firm's fold, it was with Ticknor that the poet bargained both by letter and in the counting room at 135 Washington Street. The little room with its broad window seat and prospect of School Street where Fields cheered the writers of the house diffused laughter, bonhomie, and haste. Ticknor's counting room, small though it was, had the decorum of deliberation and percentages. Gay as Fields's office was, he sometimes must have wished he had more to say on the managerial side of the business, especially as the Civil War drew to its close and the undiscovered bourn of American book-buyers was tempting all publishers to enlarge production plans.[5]

With William D. Ticknor's death on April 10, 1864, James T. Fields's years of being a junior partner came to an end. Expansion would now be the watchword of the house.

In the employ of the firm for the past nine years was a young man entirely sympathetic with the junior partner, a short, plump young man with spindle legs — drumstick legs Dickens called them — James Ripley Osgood, who had come up to Boston from Maine, having graduated from Bowdoin in 1854 and then read law briefly in a Portland attorney's office. He had had no other introduction than a letter of his own which he had written to Fields. James T. liked the letter and even more he liked the young man when he arrived for an interview. Osgood found himself promptly hired as a clerk at $375 a year. Within the next five his salary was more than tripled. Osgood's talents, like those of Fields, were of the entrepreneur. He was creative, expansive, imaginative.[6]

Business cannot stop for death even when that business is literature. A new firm was at once organized under the old name, the estate of William D. being represented by his oldest son, Howard Malcolm. James T. Fields was now senior and James R. Osgood, without benefit of investment, became the third member of the new partnership. The organization was capitalized at $200,000, a sizable increase over the $52,000 of 1854. The arrangements indicate the firm anticipated smooth sailing. Fields was to have a salary of $5000 plus his annual $2000 for running the *Atlantic* and an entertainment fund of $1000. In addition he was to have from the yearly profits an amount not to exceed $5000. If all went well, he could count on an annual income of $13,000. The articles of agreement stipulated that Fields as senior partner was to have exclusive control in making contracts, in the selection of manuscripts, and "in all matters pertaining to the style and format of books."[7]

The new firm was free of sentimental attachment to the Old Corner. The Ticknor name remained in the imprint, but William D.'s presence in the counting room was to be eradicated. The partners planned to vacate the premises at 135 Washington, selling its retail stock to the highest bidder. Except for its own publications, retailing was to be no concern of the new organization, a revolutionary step. The majority of the trade still maintained bookstores as an adjunct of publishing — Little, Brown, Appleton, Scribner, the Sheldons, Hurd & Houghton, and many more. Fields and his partners initiated other changes, although some of them did not take place immediately: an increase in the number of periodicals of the house, a New York office, a closer connection with the manufacturing side of book production, and a greatly expanded list.

During the early weeks when these startling changes were going forward, Henry Oscar Houghton was abroad. He had found no difficulty in accomplishing his first objective — to secure binders for the Merriam-Webster *Unabridged Dictionary*. When James T. Fields went to Britain his inherent worship of privilege was confirmed. He was flattered to be accepted by the English. He felt at home. To be received by people skilled in condescension was a triumph. When Henry Oscar Houghton traveled abroad his basic whiggery was reinforced. He looked on the compact island and the Continent with the experienced eyes of an employing printer. Here he saw men laboring for one third the wage paid for equivalent work at his own plant on the riverside. To secure skilled artisans was easy. Men were eager to accept his conditions: an advance of passage money for the man and his family, an assured house when they reached Cambridge, a loan to furnish it, and a wage of $15 a week. One of the binders who came to America in 1864 spoke for the group when eight years later he reported that in a similar period while working in England all he had been able to save was $62.50, whereas in the United States he had paid off his debt of $270 to Houghton, had bought life insurance, and had $617 in the bank. This contrasting economic position of English and American workers made itself felt in manu-facturing costs. The average in this country per book, including an Internal Revenue tax of 7½¢, was 59½¢. English costs, includ-ing a United States tariff of 5¼¢, came to a mere 26¼¢. At this time, Henry Oscar Houghton and his workers were certain that their sole salvation from English competition was a tariff wall.[8]

In securing binders, Houghton visited various printing estab-lishments in Edinburgh, London, and Paris. His observations proved to him that in mechanical excellence American presses had no foreign equals. In the United States the national fault in book manufacture was haste, the demand for quantity forcing sacrifice of quality. Such haste affected not only printing but also the prod-ucts on which printing depended, especially paper, which in the average plant was not allowed to rest long enough to mellow. However, he admired English type, especially the old fonts, and he imported a black letter Caxton, which he considered the most beautiful. Among the presses he visited was the Chiswick. Here he met the daughter of Charles Whittingham, the founder, and commissioned her to devise a colophon for his new publishing ven-ture. The result was a graceful interlocking of two H's.[9]

Hurd & Houghton's colophon, commissioned by Houghton in 1864, was designed by Mrs. B. F. Stevens. A similar design was used by Houghton, Mifflin until 1885.

The thirty-six-year-old printer-publisher had found his first trip abroad a rewarding experience, but he had failed in one of his missions. Dickens had refused to give authorization for the House-hold Edition. Although the author had been gracious, he had

declined to consider Houghton's proposition; he considered him-
self debarred from so doing because of his commitment to the
Harpers. That firm had agreed to pay £1250 for advance sheets of
Our Mutual Friend. By comparison a 10 percent royalty was
niggardly. Hurd & Houghton had no periodical to serve as a lure.
The Household Edition must continue to be a pirated one.[10]

Houghton returned to the United States confirmed in his whiggery. He had known poverty, but never such as he had seen in
England. He had made a decent, long-range proposal to Dickens
and had been turned down for the immediate pound. In the
larger sphere of politics he had observed England's dalliance with
the Confederacy. Southern connections though he had, Henry
Oscar's convictions were Northern. On his arrival in this country,
all seemed well in Boston, Cambridge, and New York. Hurd
had found commodious quarters at 401 Broadway, just around the
corner from 46 Walker Street, "a midway position between the up-
town and down-town publishers," according to the *American Literary Gazette,* and the Sheldons seemed to have accepted their
fate.[11]

Of singular interest to him must have been the changes going
forward at Ticknor & Fields as the result of William D. Ticknor's
death. When he learned that James T. was to have control over
the format of his firm's books, he must have anticipated that a
long and fruitful printing association would shortly come to an
end. Throughout 1864 the number of publications for Ticknor &
Fields produced at Riverside decreased significantly. By the end of
the year little work for that firm remained at the Press. Even the
Atlantic Monthly, printed since the first number by H. O. Houghton & Company, Fields transferred to Welch, Bigelow. Hencefor-
ward the University Press was to be the exclusive printer for Ticknor & Fields. Houghton's curiosity must have been piqued when
he learned through the gossip of the trade that Fields and his
partners were purchasing a new Adams power press. Not since
the days of Allen & Ticknor, when Timothy Carter had been a
silent partner, had the firm done its own press work. Then for a
brief time books were printed in a building which stood behind
the School Street extension of the Old Corner Bookstore. Here

for a year or so, seven presses had clattered, their power supplied by a team of Canadian horses. Long since, both the horses and the printers had been put out to pasture. All came clear when word came to him of the intended expansion of the University Press on Brattle Street in Cambridge.[12]

Albion K. P. Welch and Marshall T. Bigelow had acquired their plant during the depression resulting from the Panic of 1857. Both men were experienced in their craft. Welch had been engineer for the previous owners of the University Press and had shown particular aptitude for improving the operation of both the Adams presses and the Hoe stop-cylinder. A mechanic and minor inventor of considerable skill, he could take a press apart and reassemble it with ease. His partner Bigelow had been in the printing trade since the age of ten, starting as an apprentice in 1833. Eventually his skill as proofreader for the University Press earned him the title of "scholar-printer" and in 1864, an important year for Cambridge printing, Harvard awarded him an honorary degree. (The University Press, incidentally, had no connection with that first American Press of Elizabeth Glover and her second husband, Dunster of Harvard, nor was it officially connected with Harvard, although, of course, it executed many jobs for the University.) Welch, Bigelow & Company, assured of all of Ticknor & Fields's business as well as that acquired from Little, Brown, undertook to enlarge its Brattle Street premises. Such expansion was merited. Between 1862 and 1866, Ticknor & Fields increased its titles from 224 to 387, the number of volumes from 154,536 to 384,628, the retail value from $182,000 to $734,000. To cope with this volume of business as well as its other commitments, the Welch, Bigelow operation required fifteen Adams presses, five Hoe, three hydraulic, and a payroll of 300. In the process of expansion, it also acquired a bindery under the firm name of Welch & Company, an undertaking in which both James T. Fields and James R. Osgood were equal investors with Albion Welch.[13]

In addition to the expansion at the Welch, Bigelow plant, another development in 1865 increased competition amongst Cambridge printers. John Wilson, the Scottish emigrant who with his son had worked side by side with Henry Oscar in the Dickinson

Type Foundry some twenty years before, established his own press — John Wilson & Son — in the university town. This undertaking was smaller than that of Welch, Bigelow, with a payroll of only 150, eleven Adams presses and one Cottrell & Babcock stop-cylinder. In the next decade, John Wilson & Son was to acquire the University Press, but by that time James T. Fields had safely withdrawn his money and James R. Osgood sought solvency under the aegis of H. O. Houghton. However, these were events of the future.[14]

For the time being, the end of 1864 and throughout 1865, the Riverside Press was faced with stiff competition. Its payroll was under a hundred; its presses and binding equipment were housed in rented buildings. More than high standards of production was called for. Expansion of facilities was essential. Houghton was devoted to the ideal of free enterprise within American boundaries. Welch, Bigelow and John Wilson were giving him a sharp taste of the system. His new publishing activity would add more salt to the sauce.

The loss of Ticknor & Fields and Little, Brown business did not mean that the presses of Riverside ground to a halt. They were clanging incessantly on the dictionary. To complete the work, the new bindery was working efficiently, and the first huge volume was finished in October 1864. More than Webster kept Riverside busy, Hurd & Houghton's own demands as well as other jobs and contracts. From G. P. Putnam, Houghton secured the exclusive rights to the manufacture and sale of that firm's list, an interim measure for Putnam, whose responsibilities as Collector of Internal Revenue in the Eighth District of New York prevented him from devoting the necessary time to his publishing interests. A characteristic Riverside Press production which came out of this association was the Artist's Edition of Irving's *Sketch Book* in a limited edition of five hundred. Printed on special linen rag paper, the type and press work cost over $20,000, ten times standard book production costs according to the *American Literary Gazette*. For this exclusive right to the Putnam list, Houghton paid a royalty of 15 percent on the retail price of all copies sold.[15]

In line with its policy of buying the stereotypes of established works, early in January 1865, Hurd & Houghton purchased from

James G. Gregory, who was retiring from the trade, his entire
stock of books and sheets plus the woodcuts, stereotypes, and copyrights of twenty titles; included in the list were Bryant's *Forest
Hymn* and Hawthorne's *Snow Image,* the purchase price, $8700.
A provision in the Memorandum of Agreement was that Gregory,
who had acquired the publishing rights to Cooper's works through
his association with Townsend, originally of Stringer & Townsend,
retain ownership of the Cooper plates, charging Houghton a royalty of 16 percent. From this return, Gregory was to pay Cooper's
heirs their share, probably 10 percent, on such novels as were still
covered by copyright. This part of the contract was to run for
seven years. Interestingly enough, this particular edition of
Cooper had always been printed at Riverside and when it first
appeared in 1859 had been greeted as "one of the most superb
specimens of American Typography." The edition, like the
Dickens Household, was illustrated by F. O. C. Darley.[16]

Clearly Houghton and Hurd favored as a safe investment standard authors in sets. Events proved them to be right. Limited editions such as that of Irving's *Sketch Book* were for the wealthy.
Library editions were for the ever growing American middle class
whose veneration for culture would lead them to the Pierian spring
and there faced with phalanxes of volumes would purchase and
then possibly heed Pope's behest and never taste at all.

Such standard editions even though their authors had been long
dead did not excuse the publishers from paying royalties. Wight's
translations of Montaigne, Pascal, De Staël, Voltaire, Fénelon, and
La Fontaine commanded a royalty of 15 percent. James Spedding,
English editor of Bacon's works, was pleasantly surprised, since no
law required it, to receive a continuing royalty payment, writing
to Houghton in April 1867 to thank him for another remittance
"on account of my Bacon." He considered Hurd & Houghton's
edition uniquely attractive. The Riverside volumes were far more
beautiful than those of his English publisher. "I wish our English
publishers," he complained, "would consider the comfort of readers
a little more, and discover that it is to their interest to issue books
in a shape which admits of their being easily held open in the
hand. When the octavo was first introduced instead of the heavy
quarto, it was kept within moderate dimensions, and became pop-

ular because it was easier to read. But it has gradually grown
so fat and unwieldy, that it is worse than either quarto or folio."
The form of Spedding's Bacon was comparable to the Household
Dickens.[17]

And to Dickens Hurd & Houghton was paying no royalty, nor
was the course of this edition to be as smooth as had first appeared.
In December 1864 Houghton served notice that the contract between him and the Sheldons had come to an end and that they
must cease publication within a year. Following the Sheldons' initial angry reaction, an equitable solution appeared to have been
reached. Hurd & Houghton agreed to buy from the Sheldons at
net prices volumes of the edition which they, Hurd & Houghton,
wished to sell, surely an odd position for Houghton to find himself
in, since he was not only the manufacturer but also the owner of
the stereos and the steel plates of the illustrations and their copyrights, assigned to him by Darley in 1862. Despite their acquies-
cence, the Sheldons were in reality not placated. On June 1, 1865,
they notified Houghton that they were consulting counsel. On
August 30, they filed a bill of complaint in equity in the United
States Circuit Court for the Southern District of New York.
Houghton was first astonished, then indignant. The Memorandum of Agreement of December 1861 had provided for arbitration should a disagreement arise as to the value of the property
held by the respective parties, a provision Houghton regarded as
protecting the Sheldons if they had any unsold copies of the Household Edition on their hands when he should decide to terminate
the association. The Sheldons had not even considered arbitration. Instead they had engaged to prepare the bill of complaint
a lion of the bar, an authority on Constitutional law, Charles Ticknor Curtis. Houghton's first act was to draft a letter, probably
never sent, in which he accused the Sheldons of bad faith and insolvency, sufficient cause for terminating the agreement forthwith.
Cooler heads prevailed. Houghton was advised to seek legal advice. Never one for half measures, he chose an outstanding New
York firm — Evarts, Southmayde & Choate.[18]

This little known case in publishing history is worth examining
because it shows the trade in a state of transition. The transcript

of the proceedings in *Sheldon et al.* v. *Houghton* reveals that at this date publishing was defined as selling. A publisher was a distributor for the printer. To achieve distribution he advertised the books assigned to him. Nothing in the proceedings implies a publisher's responsibility to the author or the creative planning characteristic of contemporary publishing. The case has additional interest because of the definition of courtesy of the trade which it contains and because of the plaintiffs' effort to equate this custom or courtesy with the goodwill inherent in a partnership relationship. And finally it is important for the light it throws on the question of copyright in non-American works in these transitional years. The Sheldons' purpose was to establish a legal precedent for what Curtis called *"quasi* copyright"; that is, that an American publisher could acquire exclusive control of the works of a foreign author by being the first to clap them between the covers of a book manufactured in the United States.[19]

By force of the 1861 Memorandum of Agreement, the complaint alleged the Sheldons and Houghton became partners in publishing the Household Edition of Dickens' works and in consequence "the good will and right of publishing, under the custom of the trade, thereby became partnership property." Following this line of argument, the Sheldons claimed that the copyrighted Darley illustrations by virtue of the contract had been assigned to them and that they were "the equitable owners of the same, in trust for the partnership." They maintained further that they were "eminent and well known booksellers to whom the good will of the edition and the right of publication thereof, according to the custom of the trade, has become, and now is, of much greater value than before the same became partnership property, and, as is believed, is capable of being sold to others in the trade for the sum of thirty thousand dollars . . ."

The case was heard before Judge Shipman on December 4 and 5, 1865. In support of the bill's definition of courtesy or custom of the trade, Curtis had secured affidavits from William H. Appleton, Fletcher Harper, George W. Carleton, James Miller, and James T. Fields. These agreed both with the definition and with the statement that such a custom had pecuniary value, stating that "it is in consequence of the existence of this courtesy of the Trade that Publishers in the United States are often able to make contracts with foreign authors . . ." Because of the Darley illustrations and the excellence of manufacture, no other American edition of Dickens could be regarded as in competition with the Household; therefore "the right of publishing the same under said Courtesy of the Trade could be sold for a considerable sum, and after such sale and transfer to another publisher, the right of such a publisher would be respected by the Trade . . ."

James T. Fields contributed a second affidavit, which in the light of later events is significant. Fields deposed under oath that his examination of Sheldon & Company's report of sales of the works of Charles Dickens had convinced him that "while litigation is pending" to transfer the publishing rights from the Sheldons to Houghton "would [not only] affect the market value" of the right but, since it would be in clear violation of publisher's courtesy, would also "encourage" other houses to bring out rival editions.[20]

Five men prominent in the trade had joined in the attack on Houghton. Of these only Fletcher Harper had reason for particular spleen. His firm was paying Dickens large sums for advance sheets. *Our Mutual Friend* had completed its run in the *Monthly* and Peterson had announced in November its book publication from "the author's manuscript and advance proofsheets prior to its publication in Europe." James T. Fields's financial obligations to Dickens at this time were comparatively of trivial import. In the month of the hearing Dickens made his first appearance in the *Atlantic* with an article on Barry Cornwall's daughter, Adelaide Anne Proctor. Save for its imported edition, Ticknor & Fields's catalogue contained no Dickens items.[21]

Two of the members of the firm of Evarts, Southmayde & Choate were in court on the days of the hearing — William Maxwell Evarts and Joseph Hodges Choate. For both these lawyers their days of exceptional performance at the bar and in political life were ahead of them. Evarts, the senior, had yet to serve as counsel for President Johnson in his impeachment trial and as attorney for Henry Ward Beecher in his sensational legal tangle with Theodore Tilton. His distinguished work as Secretary of

U. S. Circuit Court
Southern District of New York.

Smith Sheldon
v
H. O. Houghton

City of Boston, County of Suffolk ss.
I, the undersigned James T. Fields, being duly
sworn, on oath depose, that I have examined
a table of the sales of the edition of the
works of Charles Dickens heretofore published
by Sheldon & Co annexed to a copy of the Bill
in this cause, and from my acquaintance
with the business of publishing and selling
books, I am of opinion that a sudden transfer of the right of publication of the series of
books from the hands of Sheldon & Co to the
Hand hands of another publisher, while a
litigation is pending affecting the right
of publishing under the courtesy of the trade,
would injuriously affect the market value
of that right to a large extent, and, among
other reasons, for the reason that it would
tend to encourage the introduction into the
market of rival editions, and also because
the future sales of a series of books of this
description are likely to be much larger if
carried on in the hands of the same publishing from that held it during the past
four years than they would be in the hands
of a new publisher

　　　　　　James T. Fields.

James T. Fields's affidavit in the case of *Sheldon et al.* v. *Houghton*
is on file with Houghton Mifflin's documents deposited in the
Harvard College Library.

State under Hayes and later as United States Senator from New York was yet to come. Joseph Choate at this time had no public image. His part in the Tweed Ring prosecutions, the Tilden contest, the Standard Oil antitrust cases, his notable performance as ambassador to the Court of St. James's, his work at the second Hague Conference, even his post-prandial eloquence, all were hidden in the shadow of the oncoming years.[22]

Following the reading of the affidavits for the plaintiffs, and after Curtis, with considerable oratorical flourish, had told the Court what he intended to prove, young Choate presented the defendant's answer to the charges of the bill of complaint. On his first day, December 4, 1865, he denied all allegations including the existence of such a custom as courtesy of the trade, especially when the author was one as popular as Charles Dickens. Publishers, Choate maintained, followed their own inclinations in republishing foreign authors, their decisions based on the condition of the market, on their estimates of possible profit or loss. The trade custom outlined by the plaintiffs, he declared,

> would be contrary to the public policy of the United States upon the subject of copyright which policy has always been and now is to refuse copyrights to the works of foreign authors and to encourage the free and untrammelled publication of such works in this country for the better and cheaper dissemination of learning among its people . . . such a custom would tend to prevent competition in the publication of valuable works, and, by securing a monopoly to any publisher who might first issue them, to deprive the people of the United States of other, better and cheaper editions of the same, would thus injure both the buyers and sellers of books, and diminish the circulation of such books, and establish, contrary to the said policy of the United States a quasi copyright in them in favor, not of the meritorious and original authors of such books, but of any person who might succeed in issuing a first Edition of the same of whatever style, quality or price.

To substantiate his thesis, Choate drew attention to the numerous reprints of Dickens, either in complete sets or in single volumes.

One of these competing editions, he pointed out, the Sheldons themselves had been selling.

The claim of partnership Choate denied categorically. The relationship was rather "that which usually prevails between the manufacturer of a commodity on the one hand and a person engaged to sell it for a specific compensation and at his own risk on the other." Moreover, the firm with whom Houghton had made an agreement in 1861 no longer existed. On Hurd's withdrawal it had been forced to reorganize. Hurd had not transferred his interest in the Houghton-Sheldon contract to the new Sheldon company, nor had the Sheldons at the time of the settlement with Hurd placed any value on the contract. The loss of Hurd's capital, he argued, had so seriously affected the Sheldons as to injure "their standing and credit." In consequence, under the terms of the Memorandum of Agreement, the contract "was thereby terminated and dissolved." As for the Sheldons' claim that a goodwill had developed during the course of the association which was worth $30,000, a value which they asserted had developed in the 3½ years they had been selling the Household, Choate, while insisting no partnership existed, maintained that the value of the edition derived from the excellence of its typography and its original illustrations and not from the Sheldons' management. Under the stewardship of both W. A. Townsend and James A. Gregory average monthly sales had exceeded the Sheldon performance. The Sheldons' purpose in filing the bill, Choate held, was to thwart the newly founded publishing house of Hurd & Houghton.

Choate, like Curtis, was armed with affidavits, his from sixteen publishers, among them George Palmer Putnam, Charles Scribner, A. D. F. Randolph, Osmas Brewster, Joseph Crosby, Charles Merriam, Charles C. Little, and curiously, Fletcher Harper. The tenor of these affidavits, if that of Charles C. Little, the only one available, may be taken as an example, was that while courtesy of the trade did indeed exist, it was no more than "gentlemanly conduct, and a feeling among respectable booksellers that one ought not to interfere with the business of another." This courtesy obligated no one to refrain from competition. No publisher trusted the custom sufficiently to "invest money on the entire faith thereof."

Courtesy of the trade had no pecuniary value, nor was it "a salable or assignable right." The value of the Household Dickens derived from its illustrations and its quality of manufacture. The work of the Riverside Press had "a high and increasing reputation." If management of the edition were put under a Court of Chancery, "a great injury to the owner" would result. So ended the first day.

The proceedings of December 5 opened with Curtis' argument in defense of the bill. As proof of partnership he submitted that the 1861 Memorandum of Agreement provided for an equal sharing of profits after costs of manufacture had been met; that the Sheldons and Houghton had been in constant communication throughout the association, that in advertising the Sheldons had spent between $1300 and $1600 and in addition had given out press copies whose value amounted to $1133.50. This advertising, Curtis maintained, had created "a great growing future demand." The arbitration clause, he argued, was further proof of partnership, giving evidence of anticipated joint interest, an unnecessary clause were the plaintiffs commission merchants only, wishing to fix a value on such volumes of the Household as remained on their hands on termination of the contract. Such value could be determined without calling on "the great machinery of three arbitrators." Answering one of the chief points of the defense that the purchase of goodwill without acquiring the materials of manufacture would be pointless, Curtis declared: "Here are these plaintiffs; they stand ready to give $15,000 for Mr. Houghton's share of the right to continue this publication, and then, in addition, to pay him a reasonable sum for what separate property he has got in stereotype plates. There is one purchaser, at least; and that is enough to answer the suggestion that is made that the court cannot make a decree which would operate beneficially."

The offer to buy the stereotype plates surprised the defense. Evarts jumped to his feet, objecting that such a proposition had not appeared in the bill. "I make it now," Curtis retorted, "to submit the valuation of these stereotype plates to any competent man, and we will pay cash for them on the spot . . ." As for the claim that the value of the edition resulted because of the work of the Riverside Press, Curtis fleered, "One might suppose that something might be due to the author; that something might have resulted from the influence of that extraordinary genius which has filled the world wherever the English language is known, with creations so life like that we are all obliged to count them as if among our actual experiences of mankind."

Finally Curtis came to what he regarded as his most telling point.

It has been charged, may it please your honor, in the answer, that this idea of a partnership relation was started to thwart the defendant in his purpose of publishing this book through the house of Hurd & Houghton, which he had established in this city. If your honor can see anything in this suit, or anything which is behind it, (if you can look behind it, or if the judicial mind is supposed to have anything like imagination,) — if you can see anything in this case but an honest purpose to try a controverted question of legal right, — you will give to that suggestion all the weight to which it is entitled.

But the most damaging part of the answer is to come. In opening the case I was restrained by my learned friend, Mr. Choate, from making any allusion to the firm of Hurd & Houghton, or assuming its existence. But it has all come out in the defense; and now it appears that there was a Mr. Hurd in this concern of the plaintiffs, and that by some inducement, or without inducement, [he] has withdrawn from this firm; and it is put in this answer that his withdrawing created a case for the dissolution provided for in the terms of the contract, — that his withdrawal so weakened these plaintiffs that they were unfit to carry on this enterprise any longer and that therefore these books are withdrawn . . . Does Mr. Houghton mean to have it understood that he created this alleged weakening of this house, for the purpose of having an occasion to give the notice and terminate the contract? I cannot help thinking that this answer was drawn in haste, to meet the exigency of this hearing . . .

Judge Shipman found the case "one of novel impression," one which could not be sustained either on principle or appeal to authority. He considered trade courtesy a reasonable practice, but without legal validity. ". . . nothing relating to the edition can come under the protection of the law, except what is new and original, and is covered by copyright or letters patent. For this court to recognize any other property in the works of a foreign author, would contravene the settled policy of Congress, and be an attempt to enter the field belonging exclusively to the national legislature. Of the wisdom of our legislative policy I have nothing to say here." He refused to appoint a receiver. He had no legal basis for so doing; moreover, he would not do it, had he the power "because it would tend to destroy, and not conserve, the property."

During the preparation of the case, Houghton had written his lawyers, "An injunction will ruin us." Now they were able to report triumphantly that Judge Shipman had declared goodwill "more intangible than anything in dreamland. All that remains is to pay the bills." Evarts, Southmayde & Choate's bill was $1076.45, a small charge compared with the value of the Household Edition of Dickens' works. During the years of this "limited and peculiar partnership," the Sheldons in meeting manufacturing costs and yielding Houghton his share of profits on sales had paid the Cambridge printer $50,000. Dickens, of course, had received not a cent.[23]

The *Sheldon et al* v. *Houghton* hearings had demonstrated that at least for authors of such popularity as Dickens enjoyed, publishers' courtesy was something of a fiction. For years to come, in fact until 1891 and the enactment of an International Copyright law, publishers as they were gentlemen would profess belief in courtesy of the trade, none with greater vigor than Houghton as his own list became increasingly vulnerable. Non-gentlemen would attack the custom in word and action, using the argument of Joseph Choate that such courtesy was in fact monopoly exercised by powerful publishers. So John W. Lovell, a notorious pirate of the next decade, wrote angrily:

> As a young publisher, I look back at the early beginnings of the larger houses, and I find no such thing as this so-called 'courtesy of the trade.' In olden times it was 'every man for himself,' and only after firmly established business had been built up, largely through reprinting foreign works, it was found a matter of policy by certain houses not to infringe upon each other. By this means legitimate or illegitimate competition has largely been done away

with, and the publishing houses, if not the public, greatly benefited.

But I can say to the younger and smaller houses from my own experience, Go in heartily for the 'courtesy of the trade' and — starve . . . As for my part, I prefer to follow the examples that led to success in the past rather than the precepts now advocated to prevent others from attaining it.[24]

Gentlemen in "firmly established business" would continue to insist that in the main the custom, for want of an International Copyright, worked well. But sometimes anticipation of profit proved sufficiently alluring to make them forget that they belonged to a profession of gentlemen. James T. Fields, in preparing his affidavits, had studied the sales statistics of the Household Edition. Within American borders, Houghton believed in trade untrammeled. His printing establishment in Cambridge was already having a taste of it. Shortly his New York publishing venture would also have its appetite whetted. Confident in his own standards of excellence, in his philosophy of all deliberate haste, he preferred competition to an injunction.

By the time of the Sheldon-Houghton hearings, the reorganized Ticknor & Fields had acquired a New York office and an elegant setting for its Boston headquarters at 124 Tremont Street. The Boston *Transcript* of September 2, 1865, described the new location as "the handsomest of stores," taking the reader on a tour of "the new apartments" from the cellar through the ground floor, to the second and James T. Fields's private office. The store area, the *Transcript* said:

is fitted up and furnished harmoniously, strictly in the Elizabethan style, and is rich in its elaborate and yet simple elegance. The pillars, arches, doors, counters, shelves, and railings are all of ash, elaborately adorned with moulding and carving; giving relief to the bins filled mainly with the well-known 'blue and gold' and other series, published by the firm. A profusion of light pours in through two large front windows, each composed of four mammoth panes of plate glass, and a glazed arched roof towards the rear. The gas fixtures correspond with the other ornaments in their chaste and massive character; and the arrangements of the counting-rooms, offices, secretaries, and closets leave nothing to be desired in the way of beauty and comfort.

In the second story, reached by a grand flight of stairs, heavily railed and balustered, just to the left of the front door, are to be found the cozy private office of Mr. Fields, another store-room for the elegantly bound volumes, and a parlor for the reception and entertainment of guests. This parlor, by the way, merits very special mention. Ample in dimensions, it is papered with velvety green hangings and wainscoted with black-walnut. The floor is covered with a soft carpet of a pattern to harmonize with the walls; and the furniture is of a luxurious pattern . . . Here authors and visitors can pass a leisure hour in reading or conversation, or hold interviews by previous appointments. The hospitality and liberality shown in furnishing this retreat will reconcile the most inveterate lover of the past to the loss of 'the Corner.'

Into this sumptuous parlor James T. Fields hoped to lure the most popular author in the English-speaking world.

Fields had been a worshiper of Dickens ever since that author's visit to the United States in 1842, but he did not meet his idol until the summer of 1859. At this time Ticknor & Fields had no periodical, an absolute requirement for publication of popular English authors in the United States. Only through periodical publication could one beat the pirates by securing, at a price, advance sheets so that the novels could appear almost simultaneously in both England and America. On Fields's return from England in the spring of 1860, he found that his senior partner had acquired a magazine. Even so he was unable to make publishing connections with Dickens until after the Civil War. Then all he secured was an essay for the *Atlantic*. Fields had signed two affidavits in defense of the Sheldon bill. His second had declared that abrogation of courtesy of the trade, at least as far as Dickens was concerned, would "encourage the introduction into the market of rival editions." Judge Shipman's denial of the Sheldon petition had made clear that there was no reason that Ticknor & Fields should not enter the Dickens steeplechase. Fields had learned that Houghton's offer to Dickens of a 10 percent royalty had failed. He had studied the sales figures of Houghton's Household Edition.

Clearly that venture was profitable. By 1866 Fields could offer not only a royalty but periodical publication with payment for advance sheets in any of three magazines — the *Atlantic, Our Young Folks,* a juvenile magazine which as part of his firm's expansion had been launched in 1865, or *Every Saturday,* a weekly the first number of which appeared in January 1866 under the editorship of Thomas Bailey Aldrich. Over the years Ticknor & Fields's generous treatment of English writers had been persistently advertised. Harper & Brothers might protest that in one year alone their house had paid in excess of £2000 to English authors. Still the credit went to Ticknor & Fields for "private honesty." The firm's observance of courtesy of the trade, its advocacy of International Copyright, set it apart from other publishers.[25]

In 1866 Fields opened negotiations for Dickens' next novel, offering the pages of either the *Atlantic* or *Every Saturday.* He assured the author that his firm was "prepared to pay for the privilege of simultaneous publication more than any other house," and he promised that any communication would be "strictly sealed from other notice than my own." Dickens replied that he had no story in hand at the moment, that he hoped to get to work on one the following summer. Of publishers, he wrote, "Regarding the choice of an American house, of course my personal feelings are with you. But I have no reason to complain of Harpers, and I have another proposal from Philadelphia. When I shall have decided on my mode of publication (having got to work as aforesaid), I will describe it to you, and to Harpers, and to the Philadelphia proposer, and my business decision shall be made according to the three replies." Despite this unsatisfactory letter, Fields went forward with plans for a cheap edition of Dickens' works to be called the Diamond, not because of its value but because of its small eye-torturing type.[26]

These plans were conducted with great secrecy, but by December 1866 some in the Boston trade at least were informed. On the eighth, Daniel Jefferson of Little, Brown wrote Houghton, "I heard today that our friends Ticknor & Fields have nearly complete & almost ready to issue an Edition of Dickens in 12 vols a trifle larger than the last Tennyson. This cannot be helped I suppose nor do I think you need be alarmed about it as I have no doubt your Edition will always be in demand on account of its good type & Darley Illustrations but perhaps it would be policy to lower the price and now I suppose you could do so without much or any loss to yourself."

If Houghton had not already suspected what was going on, he was now forewarned. He acted promptly. A news release in the *American Literary Gazette* for January 1, 1867, announced that Hurd & Houghton had in press a new complete edition of Dickens — the Riverside in twenty-six volumes (the Household had grown to fifty-three) containing all the illustrations of Cruikshank, Phiz, Darley, and Gilbert at $2.50 a volume. The race was on. On the fifteenth Ticknor & Fields advertised its Diamond Edition, twelve volumes, $1.25 plain, $1.50 illustrated, *Pickwick Papers* to be ready on the twenty-sixth. On the first of February, T. B. Peterson countered with "the cheapest edition of Charles Dickens published in the world," — seven octavo volumes at $20.00. Hurd & Houghton replied with a third edition, the Globe in thirteen volumes at $1.50. "Save your Eyes. Wait and Get the Best," the Hurd & Houghton advertisement advised. Peterson, not to be outnumbered in sets, now announced its Author's American Edition, justifying the description by saying that "they in connection with Harper & Brothers, New York, are the only publishers in America of the works of Charles Dickens that had ever paid anything for the manuscript and advance sheets of his various works." Not an accurate statement, but it was one which James T. Fields could not counter at this time. He had no hold whatsoever on Dickens' next novel, nor could he claim he was paying a royalty on the Diamond. That was as much pirated as Hurd & Houghton's Household, Riverside, and Globe editions. Something must be done forthwith.[27]

Fields dispatched his junior partner James R. Osgood to London, his purpose to nail down Dickens' next tale for one of the periodicals of the house, to secure the author's blessing on the Diamond and any subsequent editions Ticknor & Fields might originate, and to persuade Dickens in the interest of promotion of such editions to come to America for a speaking tour, a project which

Fields had been urging for some years. Osgood carried with him a check for £200 as an advance on royalties, a sum not exactly calculated to make the author rush from the arms of the New York Pharisees to those of the Boston Brahmins. However, Osgood, like Fields, had an engaging charm; to a limited extent, he accomplished his mission. Dickens accepted the £200. Dickens also drove a hard bargain. For £1000 down Ticknor & Fields might have a brief tale, "A Holiday Romance," a serial which would run for but four issues in *Our Young Folks*, hardly the twelve-number novel which Fields had in mind for the *Atlantic* or perhaps *Every Saturday*.[28]

In acknowledgment of the £200 Dickens wrote Fields, "I think you know how high and far beyond the money's worth I esteem this act of manhood, delicacy, and honor," a compliment which James T. Fields took care should circulate, first through the columns of the New York *Tribune*, then in the *American Literary Gazette*. The implication, of course, was that Ticknor & Fields alone among American publishers had paid money to Dickens. The reaction was instantaneous and angry. Editorials and letters proliferated as the trade rehearsed the publishing history of Dickens in the United States. After all twopence royalty per volume, with 5000 exempt, as was the case with the Diamond, was meager reward compared with £1250 for advance sheets of a single novel.[29]

Fields maintained a curious silence under attack. Dickens' letter of compliment had appeared in the *American Literary Gazette* on April 15, 1867. The controversy raged through the rest of April and May with no riposte from Boston. At last in June, Fields took two full pages in the *Gazette*. There he announced that Ticknor & Fields were "the only authorized representatives in America of the whole series" of Dickens' works. To validate his claim, he released four letters from the author. Two were dated April 2, one April 8, one April 16. Why did he wait so long? Did James R. Osgood think the letters so important he must needs bring them from England in his pocket? The fault may have been with the mails. However, a letter from Dickens to Benjamin Wood pledging a story for Wood's New York *Sunday News* and written on April 9 was printed in the *Gazette* on May 15. The first letter in the Ticknor & Fields June advertisement was the one of authorization, the second complimented the firm on its illustrations, the third, that of the eighth, the day before the letter to Wood, acknowledged receipt of advance royalties. Such liberality, Dickens declared, "binds me to you as my American Publishers, whose interests are identical with my own."[30]

In his letter of the sixteenth, Dickens admitted that Harper had paid him for advance sheets "for his three latest novels," and that Hurd & Houghton had recently bought from his English publishers a hundred impressions of illustrations for *Pickwick Papers*. These transactions he considered "irrelevant," concluding, "In America, the occupation of my life for thirty years is, unless it bears your imprint, utterly worthless and profitless to me."

These letters as published in the *Gazette* clearly show that Dickens regarded his engagement with Ticknor & Fields as one for his collected works. It had nothing to do with advance sheets for magazine publication, not a very satisfactory arrangement for an "authorized" publisher. Perhaps if Dickens would come to America for a reading tour, the situation might be remedied. Fields guaranteed him £10,000. Dickens was not to be won by such a promise only. A similar amount had been promised him in 1859 by a group of New York publishers. He must know what the conditions were in the United States in 1867, what audience he could expect, what comfort. He dispatched his agent George Dolby to scout the possibilities. Dickens was tempted. Such a tour would give the needed push to Ticknor & Fields's announced Charles Dickens Edition of his works. He didn't need the money and he was not well. "Still [he wrote], at 55 or 56, the likelihood of making a great addition to one's capital in half a year, is an immense consideration." In September, having received glowing reports about the United States from Dolby, Dickens cabled Ticknor & Fields, "Yes." The tour was on. Any unfavorable image created by his published letters to Ticknor & Fields must be destroyed. The controversy, although it had subsided, still simmered. In July, the *London Bookseller,* paying no attention to the fourth letter in the Ticknor & Fields spread of June 1, attacked the American firm for its boast about paying royalties, noting that Hurd & Houghton had paid Spedding for its reprint of his Bacon and that it had offered some years before to pay Dickens a royalty. "There is, therefore, nothing very singular in finding that an American publisher can act honorably," the *Bookseller* concluded.[31]

To smooth the way for his tour, knowing that his statement would reach the press, Dickens wrote Fields:

> For twenty years I am perfectly certain that I have never made any other allusion to republication of my books in America than the good-humored remark, 'if there had been international copyright between England and the States, I should have been a man of very large fortune, instead of a man of moderate savings, always supporting a very expensive public position.' Nor have I ever been such a fool as to charge the absence of international copyright upon individuals. Nor have I been so ungenerous as to disguise the fact that I have received handsome sums for advance sheets.

Those advance sheets were what James T. Fields wanted, or his announced position as Dickens' authorized American publisher would be suspect. By good fortune, just a month before the author sailed for America, the Honorable Benjamin Wood was unable to pay his £1000 for the story Dickens had promised him. The author was happy to "regain undisputed possession of it." Fields could have it. In consequence, two Ticknor & Fields periodicals presented Dickens stories during part of the time of the writer's American tour — a juvenile, "A Holiday Romance," in *Our Young Folks* and "George Silverman's Explanation," originally intended for a newspaper, in the *Atlantic*. The first ran for four months, the second for three. Each had cost Ticknor & Fields £1000. For a few months the Boston house could appear to rival Harper in periodical publication of Dickens.[32]

Dickens' reading tour was a staggering success. A young man who was soon to cast his lot with Henry Oscar Houghton, Francis Jackson Garrison, described the crush for tickets at 124 Tremont Street in a letter to his sister:

> All the tickets for all the four readings were sold in one day. People went as early as 6 o'clock in the morning, although it was

bitter cold. Josiah Munro went at quarter of eight in the morning & didn't get his ten tickets until quarter of six in the evening, after standing for ten hours without breakfast or dinner. Seven hours out of the ten he was outside in the cold & it was only for the last three hours that he had the warmth and shelter of the store. Theo Conant bought forty-two tickets for various parties. The price for a reserved seat was two dollars; standing room, $1.50. Of course there was much speculation, and you can easily get tickets now, provided you are willing to give five or ten dollars a piece for 'em.[33]

Dickens' profits exceeded all expectations, a clear £20,000. Ticknor & Fields profited too, receiving a commission of £1000 and 5 percent of the Boston receipts. All editions of Dickens, whether of Ticknor & Fields or of other publishers, were given an immense impulse, so much of an impulse that Appleton, who had signed an affidavit in support of the Sheldons, even as had James T. Fields, decided to come out with an edition of Dickens' works. The free advertising provided by the author's presence in the United States was too much of an opportunity to miss. So much for publishers' courtesy. Fields, carried away by the triumph of the time, paid Dickens further advance royalties. The Harpers, while the author was in New York, naturally approached their favorite English writer for advance sheets of his next novel, offering a cool £2000. Dickens accepted the proposition. After all, Ticknor & Fields were the authorized publishers of his books only. Advance sheets were a different matter. The tour was over by the end of April, and Dickens and Fields parted the best of friends.[34]

Once Dickens had left these shores, business in books settled down to its normal course. The public, devoted to Charles Dickens as it was, was unconcerned with questions of ethics and copyright. What it wanted was the best quality for the least money. Hurd & Houghton's Globe Edition, with over 100,000 in two years, outsold the Diamond. By October 1868, Ticknor & Fields was forced to confess to Dickens that no further royalty payments could be counted on, that in fact sales had not earned the advances made. The Diamond Edition's small type had made it "practically unmarketable" and on hand were "several thousand volumes" which could not be expected "to sell for a long time." Moreover, D. Appleton's rival edition was doing Ticknor & Fields "incalculable damage." If others were not to reap the harvest, Dickens must take steps to correct "the anomalous position" of his "authorized & recognized American representatives."[35]

At the time this letter was written the Boston firm was in the throes of another reorganization, one which would lead to the complete obliteration of the Ticknor name from the firm's imprint. Fields freed himself, he reported, from "the Ticknor brotherhood." He did "not feel obliged to father upon the concern the whole family." Howard M. Ticknor, the oldest of William D.'s sons, Fields declared was "of no account ever," he was unpopular in the trade, "impossible to get on with." To the firm's titular screen in Howard Ticknor's place, Fields elevated James Ripley Osgood, "my great helper for many years," "the one on whom I have always leaned most." The new house, Fields, Osgood & Company, declared its assets as $338,000. One of the first concerns of the changed establishment was to correct its "anomalous position" as Dickens' authorized American publishers. In the spring of 1869, Annie and James set out for England at the firm's expense.[36]

In June and October, Dickens entertained his Boston friends with cordial hospitality at Gad's Hill. And reward of rewards, during their October stay Dickens read to his admiring friend the opening chapters of *The Mystery of Edwin Drood*. Fields said he hoped he would have it for the *Atlantic*. No, Dickens told him, it's promised to Harper. In the quiet of Dickens' Gad's Hill study, Fields accepted the statement. His not to argue if his charm had failed. Arriving in Boston at the end of October, Fields made a quick check with his junior partner Osgood. Then he sent off a cable which he followed with a letter stating that Fields, Osgood's files revealed that Dickens had in fact promised him his next novel, adding, "When you spoke to me on that pleasant Sunday morning at Gad's, of the work you have now in hand as likely to be offered to Harpers I thought I remembered an agreement you had entered into with us to bring out on this side whatever you would have to publish and now I am rejoiced to find on my return that you elected us as your American Publishers as long ago as 1867."

On the same day, over the signature of Fields, Osgood & Company another letter, with enclosures, was dispatched.

Boston
28 October 1869

Charles Dickens Esq
Dear Sir

Mr Fields has this day sent you a telegram concerning an agreement entered into in April 1867 under which we acquired a right to republish in America your next serial novel from advance sheets to be furnished by you. We now have the pleasure of confirming that telegram by enclosing copies of the correspondence which passed between us on the occasion, and which constituted the agreement. The original letter from us of which copy is enclosed you have no doubt on file.

Anticipating with pleasure your instructions respecting the details of publication, we are, dear sir,

Very truly yours
FIELDS, OSGOOD & CO.

(copy of our letter)

London, April 2, 1867

Dear Sir:

In accordance with the understanding reached in conversation between yourself and our Mr Osgood [Osgood was in England at this time it will be recalled], we agree to pay you for the advance sheets of your next novel the sum of one Thousand Pounds Sterling. It being understood that the sheets are to go forward to us with sufficient priority to enable us to secure in America simultaneous publication.

We are, dear Sir,
Yours very truly
TICKNOR & FIELDS

p.s.   It being understood that we receive with each installment of matter casts of any illustrations which may accompany its publication here.

(Copy of Mr. Dickens's Letter)

Gad's Hill Place
Hingham by Rochester, Kent
Monday Eighth April 1867

Dear Sirs,

I beg to acknowledge the receipt of your letter of the second of this month, reciting the terms on which I have arranged with your Mr Osgood to transmit to you advance sheets of my next serial tale for simultaneous publication in America. They are stated in that letter with perfect accuracy, and I hereby accept them as binding.

Dear Sirs
Faithfully yours
CHARLES DICKENS

(signed)
Messrs. Ticknor & Fields

Dickens did not bother to check his files. He was too busy. Unfortunately, he had a short memory. The letter he had written to Ticknor & Fields two and a half years before reads,

Gad's Hill Place,
Hingham by Rochester, Kent
Monday Eighth April 1867

Dear Sirs, — I am in receipt of your letter of the second of this month reciting the terms on which I have arranged with your Mr. Osgood to contribute to your juvenile magazine. They are stated in that letter with perfect accuracy, and I hereby accept them as binding.

Dear Sirs,
Faithfully yours.

The contribution to the juvenile magazine was, of course, "A Holiday Romance." Dickens had fulfilled his commitment to Ticknor & Fields. Perhaps Dickens wrote another letter to Ticknor & Fields on April 8, 1867, almost identical in phrasing to the one last quoted, agreeing to let the house have the advance sheets of his next novel. However, the suspicion that the copy of Ticknor &

Fields's letter of April 2 had suffered a sea change is inevitable. Here is the mystery. Had the phrase "your next novel" replaced "a juvenile story or tale?"[37]

Dickens, following receipt of the Fields, Osgood communication of October 28, 1869, wrote Harper & Brothers,

> Gad's Hill Place
> Hingham by Rochester, Kent
> Tuesday Thirteenth November 1869
>
> Dear Sirs, — As I had fully intended communicating with you in reference to the early sheets of my new story (in token of my being perfectly satisfied with our past business relations in that wise) I think it courteous to let you know that I had made a great mistake in my remembrance. Messrs. Fields, Osgood & Co. have reminded me that by an agreement between us dated as far back as April 1867 I agreed to sell the advance sheets of my next story to them. The fact had altogether passed out of my recollection.
> Dear Sirs,
> Faithfully yours.[38]

The man who reveled in the market value of his genius now settled for £1000 rather than £2000 for the advance sheets of his next novel, a sacrifice made more galling by Fields, Osgood's December report on sales for 1869. They had been so insignificant that no royalties were forthcoming. Fields, Osgood hoped that *Edwin Drood*'s run in the *Atlantic* would stimulate sales of the earlier volumes. Unfortunately, publication dates presented a problem.

> Touching the date of English publication, as affecting our reprint [Fields, Osgood wrote on December 7, 1869]. We desire to use the story in the *Atlantic Monthly*. But as we always publish this on the 20th of the month; i.e. never later than the 20th, sometimes a day or two earlier. Thus the April number will be issued on or about March 20th. This is the number which should contain the first part of your story. But if you publish on March 21st we cannot print that installment in our April number without anticipating you. And we could not delay publication until the May number (appearing April 20th) as such delay will place it in the power of any other house here to anticipate us. Can you therefore fix

upon an earlier day of publication, say March 18th, in order to give us the opportunity for publishing our magazine on that day.

Dickens replied that it would be impossible to change the English publication date and suggested that the difficulty was sufficient to terminate his supposed agreement with his Boston publishers. To this letter Fields, Osgood replied in haste, "We are far from desiring to cancel the agreement. We should be very sorry to have any work of yours appear first in America under other auspices than our own." If the novel were published in *Every Saturday* rather than the *Atlantic,* dates could be arranged that would be mutually satisfactory. Ben Ticknor, youngest son of William D. (Fields was not as free of the Ticknor brotherhood as he had boasted), was dispatched to London to work out with Dickens details for simultaneous publication. Fields, Osgood's plan was "to put the story (each installment) into 3 nos. of E. S., one third to be issued here one week before English publication, one third simultaneously, and the balance a week late." This plan, Ticknor was instructed to tell Dickens, would give Fields, Osgood "everything in advance of the English edition in this market, and will not trouble Mr. Dickens' copyright at home."[39]

Ben Ticknor found considerable hostility when he reached London. Word had begun to circulate that "Mr. Dickens was much dissatisfied with his Boston publishers." Hearing of the friction, Appleton offered $12,000 for *Edwin Drood* and Harper renewed its quotation of £2000. Dickens felt himself helplessly bound and he wrote to Harper, "You may be quite sure that if I should ever find myself 'free' to make a new arrangement concerning advance sheets of *The Mystery of Edwin Drood* at any time during the issuing of the book in numbers, I will send them to you, and place myself in your hands." When Ticknor presented his firm's scheme for reprinting in which certain chapters would anticipate their English publication, Dickens was indignant. Under English law, any parts of the book appearing in the United States before they were published in Britain would cause loss of their copyright. "Imagine a copyright in Pickwick, with no copyright in the Trial," he protested. Fields, Osgood's plan would prove a fatal mistake, for him at least. He wrote at once to the Boston house, which had sent him an extra £250 for the privilege of carrying out its plan, "I positively prohibit such anticipation." To show that he meant business, he notified his authorized American publishers that he had placed the matter in the hands of his solicitor. He intended his words to be taken as "quite final and conclusive."[40]

Dickens' letter was written on the fourteenth of May. In less than a month he would be dead. His protests were without effect. *The Mystery of Edwin Drood* had started its run in *Every Saturday* on April 9, and a couple of other gentlemen publishers, angered that their generous offers had been turned down, pirated the work. *Appleton's Journal* and *Harper's Weekly* presented the first full installment of the novel on April 23, continuing the practice in a series of six monthly supplements. Faced with this competition, Fields, Osgood in its June 11 number of *Every Saturday* insisted, "Ours is the Authorized American Edition, and the only one for which Mr. Dickens receives compensation . . ." A true statement probably, but was there any searching of conscience when word arrived at the elegant offices at 124 Tremont Street that Dickens had died at Gad's Hill on June 9, leaving his novel, which some think the greatest of his works, unfinished?[41]

The Sheldon-Houghton case in equity had established that under the United States Constitution no foreign author was entitled to copyright protection and further that no publisher had a legal right to the monopoly of such an author. Its sequel demonstrated, as Choate had maintained, that a publisher's courtesy was governed by his estimate of profit and loss. The sequel also showed that competition could lead at least one respected house into practices that were suspect.

The only letter signed by James T. Fields during these murky dealings is the first, in which he wrote that on his return to Boston, he had been delighted to find that Dickens had promised Ticknor & Fields his next novel as he "thought" he remembered. Only two short years had elapsed since Dickens had authorized the Boston house as his American publishers. Queer that Fields should have been uncertain, save that between advance sheets for periodical publication and a complete collected edition there is a vast difference. The other letters are in the name of the firm. How much did James T. Fields know? Was he too carelessly trusting of his genial, bandy-legged junior, James Ripley Osgood? While Fields was abroad during the summer of 1869, he had been disturbed by the way things were going at home. "The business account you send me of 1868 is not a supremely satisfactory one," he wrote Osgood. "Please send me in your next, items of the amount [$]49,781.91 charged to my account . . . I think we have a very *loose* way of dealing with large sums."[42]

At this time, Fields himself was being pretty loose with sums. After an interview with Tennyson, he reported:

> I had a very long and interesting business talk with him and this is the result. Alexander Strahan had taken him out of the hands of his old publishers by paying him a tremendous price. These are the terms which Tennyson himself revealed. Strahan pays him four thousand pounds a year as a copyright annuity for the privilege of publishing T's poems. On all new books there is a different arrangement, but the sum to be paid is something tremendous. This arrangement of course has affected Tennyson in his demand on America. Strahan has represented to him various ways which he might receive great sums from our country and I was told before I went to Farringford by several of T's friends that I must be prepared to make large offers or run the risk of a change of feeling. So I went in boldly after considering the matter and proposed as follows; I offered him an annual payment of five hundred pounds Sterling on our sales of his poems as now issued by us, and for early sheets of any and every new work five hundred pounds sterling cash. I enclose you a copy of the paper I drew up at Farringford for his consideration. I *think* he will agree to it. I shall hear in a few days and will then let you know if all is right between us. In case he accepts I have agreed to pay him now 500 pounds for 1869 as he is building a new house & the money paid now will be a great temptation to him . . . As these letters are the only business records I make you must be careful of them.[43]

Other Fields letters reported similar successes. George Eliot, to whom he offered £300 for a single poem for the *Atlantic,* had agreed to accept Fields, Osgood as her American publishers and was coming to the house with "all sails set." Browning was considering getting out an edition of his wife's letters; Charles Reade was the same dear old fellow and Fields and Annie were in such demand they were turning down dinner invitations right and left. At some of these dinners both Annie and Jamie were overcome with embarrassment by Harriet Beecher Stowe's *Atlantic* article "The True Story of Lady Byron's Life." Both Dickens and the Tennysons regarded Mrs. Stowe's revelation of Lord Byron's incest in shocking taste.[44]

Because Osgood reported such dull trade in Boston, Fields was compelled to turn down books right and left as well as dinners. Some of Osgood's letters apparently miscarried. As a result Fields was in the dark about some of the things going on at 124 Tremont Street. Such news as did reach him was disturbing. To stop publishing the *North American Review,* he protested, would be an admission of failure; to change the *Atlantic* into an illustrated magazine would be outrageous. To do so "would seriously affect its standing as an organ of thought and literature." Fields was so troubled by what he didn't know about his home office that his tour of the Continent meant little to him. Salzburg proved an empty place. "Tell me about the Harpers," he pleaded, and their intention "to do us all possible injury." More money must be sent for him to Baring Brothers, but how were finances at home? The reports he received were upsetting in the extreme.

> In the statement of last year's business I see set down
>
> Expense a/c $59,504.97!
> Advertising   51,800.00!
>
> Now it appears to me this is enormous & profits must be prodigious to warrant this great outlay. If our great expenses go on & our profits lessen we must suffer greatly by & by.[45]

The Boston office was loose in other matters as well as accounts. On Fields's return, he found the precious Tennyson authorization had been lost and a copy had to be sent for. Because the Harpers were getting out a Tennyson and advertising it as the only complete edition, the document was essential. As he had anticipated, Fields, Osgood's profits had fallen off. No wonder Fields, although only fifty-three, was "oppressed with forebodings of mind and a disquietude of spirit." After only six years as senior partner and less than two with Osgood as second in command, James T. Fields decided to withdraw from publishing, selling his Fields, Osgood holdings for $100,000, possibly $150,000. Perhaps the muddy waters of courteous publishers' competition had become more than he could stomach. In any event at the office party on New Year's Day, 1871, given to announce his retirement, framed in the grandeur of his ersatz Elizabethan office, he served his successors peanuts.[46]

V

AN EDITOR'S EDUCATION BEGINS

SURELY no one at James T. Fields's retirement party on January 1,
1871, anticipated the disastrous decade that lay ahead for James R.
Osgood, the confident new senior partner, and his company, John
Spencer Clark and William D. Ticknor's second son Ben. Even
Henry Oscar Houghton in his Counting Room at Riverside could
not have discerned the fortunes of the '70s, and he too was celebrating. The year just passed had been the first to yield a profit to
his publishing venture, a profit resulting from seven years of experiment in this perilous business of gentlemen.[1]

In 1866, immediately after the Sheldon hearings, Hurd &
Houghton had been reorganized. The Civil War over, Albert G.
Houghton had moved North from Alabama to settle in Brooklyn.
Although he was not ready to assume any managerial responsi-
bility, he was prepared to afford $40,000 in partnership capital,
and it was agreed that profits and losses

> shall be divided share and share alike, that is one third to each
> of the undersigned partners and that Henry O. Houghton and
> Melancthon M. Hurd shall receive each a salary at the rate of
> Five Thousand dollars per annum for the present year (1866) or
> until said Albert Houghton shall give his personal attention to
> the business of the concerns at New York or Cambridge, the said
> salaries to be paid out of the net profits of the concerns. It is also
> agreed that the names and style of the firms shall remain as here-
> tofore, that is, Hurd & Houghton in New York and H. O. Hough-
> ton & Co., in Cambridge, Mass.[2]

As a result of this increase in capital, Hurd & Houghton's New
York location was changed from Broadway to Broome Street, the

Paternoster Row of Gotham, and a cherished plan of Houghton's, expansion of the Riverside Press, was put in train. First came purchase of the Riverside property. Negotiations were protracted, but in April 1867, H. O. Houghton & Company became owner of the land and buildings it had leased for fifteen years. Before the end of the year, a large four-storied, mansard-roofed brick building had been constructed, more than doubling the size of the original plant. Ten additional power presses were part of the new equipment and the employees, half of them women, now numbered 300.[3]

Such expansion was essential if the Press were to execute its orders. It was manufacturing annually one hundred "tons" of Webster's *Unabridged* and also binding the rival Worcester and printing "nearly a dozen newspapers and magazines and between thirty and forty books of a miscellaneous character." Amongst the miscellaneous books were, of course, all of Hurd & Houghton's standards, including the Globe Dickens, which had reached a sale

Side view of the Riverside Press in 1873 with the Charles River in the foreground. The main building with the mansard roof was built in 1867. In 1872 the plant was enlarged, and the following year, in celebration of Houghton's fiftieth birthday, dedication ceremonies were held on the front lawn of the Press.

of 100,000, school books, prayer books, Bibles, law books, theological works, and juveniles.[4]

On the last day of 1867, the employees of Riverside gave a party to dedicate the new building. There was a Grand March, then a Sicilian Circle, followed by Quadrilles, Contras, Waltzes, Schottisches, and Polkas, all under the gallant supervision of the Floor Director, John B. Smithers. The Press had more than a new building to celebrate, for in contrast to Houghton's publishing enterprise, his press had by now achieved wide recognition and a growing yearly profit. For examples of books produced at Riverside, H. O. Houghton & Company had won this year at the Paris Exposition the highest award given to any American book manufacturer. The volumes responsible for this recognition were Merriam-Webster's *An American Dictionary of the English Language,* Royal Quarto Edition, unabridged; *Aesop's Fables,* illustrated by H. W. Herrick; and a privately printed work, *Notes on Columbus,* a facsimile in black letter, possibly the font Houghton had imported from England in 1864.[5]

With the manufacturing side of the business in so healthy a condition, why was the publishing side sickly? Houghton's emphatic reply to such a question would have been — "The tariff!" The British could export books at an average cost per volume of less than half of American manufacturing costs. Some American publishers attempted to meet this competition by having their books manufactured in England or on the Continent, invoicing them for tariff purposes at the cost of manufacture rather than *ad valorem* as the law required. ". . . American publishers could send a manuscript to England, have a book printed and bound there, import the edition and pay a duty thereon of twenty-five percent in gold, cheaper than they could buy paper and have the same work done in the United States by American mechanics." Gentlemen such as Appleton, Lippincott, Roberts, and Holt had books made up abroad to be issued under their imprints on this side of the Atlantic. Noah Webster, the passionate patriot, would have been incensed had he been alive. His *Blue-Backed Speller,* which had been more instrumental in forming the parochial thought of America than the Bible, now under Appleton's imprint, was being printed and bound in London. In Houghton's opinion and in that of many others, including seventy-three authors, unless the tariff were raised and enforced, American publishers, and writers as well, would be driven out of business. Houghton conceded that foreign authors should have copyright protection, but he would "require English authors to publish in America through American publishers; American authors to publish in England through English publishers."[6]

Convinced as the head of the Riverside Press was that one answer to his publishing problems was a protective tariff, he must have recognized that many of his rivals were showing a profit, a profit realized not solely because some of their books were being manufactured abroad, or because like Ticknor & Fields in connection with their manufacturing interest in Welch, Bigelow, they were importing British cloth and paper. At Riverside, Houghton gave unremitting attention to book production; no volume went into manufacture until his initials had been placed on the proposed form. For all the activities of his plant he had a "supervising memory." Because he was at his press both early and late, he knew what was going on. In the New York office supervision was not as close. Hurd, who was not well, found in travel his panacea for dyspepsia, and Albert Houghton, occupied with closing up his affairs in the South, was not yet free to devote his managerial skills to Hurd & Houghton. With the Riverside Press running without interruption, Houghton perhaps regretted he had been so foolhardy as to take on the risks of publishing, especially as he examined the accounts and reflected on Hurd & Houghton's experiments in periodical publishing.[7]

In 1867 the firm had begun issuing two magazines — *London Society* and the *Riverside Magazine for Young People*. For the first Hurd & Houghton had engaged to import duplicate plates from James Hogg & Sons of London, the American edition to be printed and bound at Riverside. Hardly was publication under way when Ticknor & Fields began anticipating Hurd & Houghton's release of the magazine, an act promptly noted by the newspapers. "Ticknor & Fields are stealing a march on their rivals, Hurd & Houghton, by publishing in their *Every Saturday* all the choicer and more popular articles of the *London Society* before the American Edition of the latter is brought out by H & H," one

A coal schooner unloading at the Riverside Press wharf in 1870, when the Charles River was still tidal. Scudder, in an *Atlantic* article of 1878, anticipated the concern of today's conservationists: "Efforts are making against strong currents, to preserve this precious stream. Yet see what one or two men can do to destroy its beauty! Not far from the seat of the University, the river makes a turn around a tongue of land, and flows past what once was a lovely river-bank. The ground rose in a little bluff overhanging the marshy rim of the water, and then sloped away from the river, having on its highest point little clumps of fir trees. It

was bought as a speculation, the trees cut down, the hill leveled, great gashes made in the slopes, and now what might always have been a delight to the eye is a level piece of gravel, with scarcely a sign of vegetation . . . I have the dread of seeing in my paper, some day, a polite paragraph upon some enterprising land company which proposes to utilize the flats by making them the place of amphibious manufactories, belching forth smoke, and fouling the river with their chemical waste. I doubt not that there are many timid people like myself, who find it hard to look on and see our cities spreading desolation around them."

reporter noted. *"Every Saturday* for the current week has, for instance, three articles from *London Society* for February, which Hurd & Houghton have not yet issued. A rather rough joke, but still fair among enemies, we suppose." During the Sheldons' case in equity James T. Fields had submitted affidavits in defense of publishers' courtesy. Judge Shipman having ruled that the practice had no legal standing, Fields used the custom when it suited his convenience and not otherwise. As a result of this discourteous anticipation, Hurd & Houghton soon ceased publishing the British magazine.[8]

A further drag on the publishing resources of the business was its magazine for juveniles, edited by Horace Elisha Scudder. Since Scudder was to be associated with Houghton and his various firms for almost forty years, and since his standards for book selection were to have much to do with the character of the list the house developed between 1864 and 1902, something about his personality and the influences which formed his critical criteria is an important part of this publishing story. Scudder's diaries reveal that Houghton frequently confided in his junior. That Scudder's comments on the business of publishing reflect the theories of his superior may be taken for granted. That his editorial comments mirror in part at least the standards of the house for which he worked may also be assumed. His letters to authors depict these standards. Writers eager to be published by Scudder's firm probably regarded both his letters to them and his published criticism as practical directives. Intrinsically humble and self-effacing, he has in these latter days been ignored. The writers whom he encouraged are his best memorial. He would be the first to admit that he made errors in judgment. He would also agree that the financial tides of the time played a large part in the fortunes of the house he served. Houghton saw to it that his editor was instructed in these matters.

Scudder was in court on the final day of the Sheldons' case in equity. Just a year before, he had accepted the position of Hurd & Houghton's "literary advisor," a pretentious title for the small, shy man who bore it. He listened to Curtis' oratory and Judge Shipman's measured opinion with his head turned to the left and slightly drooped, with the puzzled, intense concentration peculiar to the deaf. The outcome of this case was of consequence to him not only because his fortunes were bound with those of Houghton but also because as an author the question of copyright protection was a matter of personal concern. Although only twenty-eight, he had already published three books, one of which had merited the compliment of British piracy. He knew at first hand that the precarious position of publishers and authors being revealed in the United States Circuit Court for the Southern District of New York in December 1865 was to be found in England as well as America. On his six-month tour of the British Isles and the Continent from which he had just returned, he had seen for sale pirated editions of Longfellow, Whittier, and Lowell, of Webster's dictionary, and of his own small book for children, *Seven Little People and Their Friends.*[9]

If to be Bostonian is to be born and bred in Boston, Horace Elisha Scudder could properly claim the title. His mother Sarah Lathrop Coit traced her American lineage through the Manwarings and the Saltonstalls to Governor Winthrop. His Scudder ancestors although not as distinguished were equally indigenous, having arrived from England early in the days of the Massachusetts Bay Colony and settled on the Cape, remaining there in the generations that followed, seafaring by inclination and profession. Charles Scudder, father of Horace, broke with family tradition, coming to Boston in the early days of the nineteenth century to work first as an apprentice, then on his own as a hardware and commission merchant. The family's inheritance was Puritan; its religion devoutly Congregational. Yet Scudder's recollections of his youth were of the happiest. Orthodox as the household was, Charles the father was of a sunny, genial, generous, understanding temper. Horace, the youngest of seven, was born in 1838 on Temple Place, close to Park, the street he was later to know so well as he went back and forth to his editorial offices at number four. A family of six boys and one girl made for a spirited childhood. In 1846, the year their son's future employer came down from Vermont to seek his fortune at the foot of Beacon Hill, Scudder's parents in search of open spaces for their energetic brood moved to a Roxbury farm surrounded by thirty acres of open country. Here the children, when not attending Roxbury Latin School, savored the joys of their fields and wood lots as well as the discipline and instruction of casual farm life. This idyllic existence came to an end in 1853, when Charles Scudder, because of temporary business reverses, sold the Roxbury property. The family returned to Boston, and here Horace completed his pre-collegiate training in the Boston Latin School in the same class with Henry Adams.[10]

Adams continued his education at Harvard, an institution he later recalled without love. Williams was the college the senior Scudder chose for his sons, chiefly because of its reputation for religious orthodoxy. In 1854, Horace followed his older brothers, Evarts, David, and Samuel, there. The choice was a wise one. The students numbered less than 250, some from backgrounds far less privileged and urbane than Scudder's. In such an environment, he attained distinctions which might not have been his in a university. Scudder always recalled with quiet affection the college and the gracious village of Williamstown with its valleys, streams, and embracing hills.

The greatest intellectual resource Williams had to offer in the '50s was its president, Mark Hopkins. Every student in his senior year took Mark Hopkins' course in Intellectual Philosophy. Here the boys had the electric experience of being asked to use their powers of analysis rather than memory. What do *you* think? was Hopkins' question. His students must use their own minds, but this was not enough. This was in the days of what Henry Adams called *"a priori* morality." Men were sure they knew the difference between right and wrong. Mark Hopkins expected his boys to use their developing intellects after they had graduated, their purpose to mold moral character. Many have borne testimony to the effectiveness of Mark Hopkins' teaching. Scudder was but one of a score when six years after graduation he wrote:

> I do not hesitate to say that the one value which attaches preeminently to Williams . . . is the power which belongs to it of inducing independent, vigorous thought. Culture, in its ordinary sense, there is none; men leave the college frequently with as little

grace as they entered; of acquaintance with general literature there is scarcely anything; the libraries are scantily supplied; thorough scholarship in the classics is quite unknown . . . but after all there remains a substantial success, of which the college may justly be proud, in the ability of the graduates to use themselves.[11]

Mark Hopkins' emphasis on creative, independent thought, his behest that his men use their influence in behalf of morality perhaps explains why Williams produced so many nineteenth-century editors: Chester P. Dewey of the *Commercial Advertiser,* Samuel I. Prime of the New York *Observer,* Henry Martin Field of the *Evangelist,* Washington Gladden of the *Independent,* Henry Mills Alden of *Harper's New Monthly Magazine,* and Horace Elisha Scudder; an impressive galaxy whose influence on American thought of the last century is difficult to gauge. Awkward as some of the Williams undergraduates may have been in those days — one of them was James A. Garfield — upon graduation they took with them a sense of dedicated responsibility.[12]

A practical experience that Williams afforded Scudder was that of editing the college *Quarterly.* He took part in a variety of extracurricular activities — in the Logia, a debating society; in the choral group; in work for the Natural History Museum; in the Art Association, of which he was one of the founders and first president. But it was his position in his senior year as editor of the *Quarterly* that determined his career, for in that year (1858) he engaged Henry Oscar Houghton and his Riverside Press to print the college periodical. However, as graduation approached no such clear pattern as his life was eventually to follow appeared to him. Anticipating the end of his college career, he wrote his father, "It all looks blank to me ahead . . . It is a shock to pass from the entire freedom from care which marks the college-life to the bustle & work of human life. And I of all men most feel it. A Student-life is so congenial to me and seems so entirely adapted to my nature, that I cling with tenacity to its last hours and half sigh whenever I think of giving up this dear quiet room where my last three or four years have been spent and which contains so much that seems almost a part of myself."[13]

Fortunately, his father asked of none of his sons that he enter upon a career immediately. His two oldest, Charles and Marshall, had become Boston businessmen; he preferred that his four remaining sons enter professions. ". . . it has been the height of my ambition," he wrote, "to give all my dear boys a good education, because I have seen in the experience of many years, that boys, when well educated, make men, and men that can make their way in the world somehow." To find that somehow, after graduating from college, each should have a probationary period at his father's expense. Yet the youngest was restive; he craved independence.

> Not, my dear father, that I am in any hurry to escape from your immediate care, but because I cannot think it right for me to be longer a burden to your purse . . . But the particular way in which I am to earn enough to keep me in decent circumstances is hard for me to see. I naturally think first of teaching. Everybody teaches, and everybody says it is an excellent discipline. I should apply for the most laborious and profitable place I could find, if it were not for my deafness. I hardly know what to do. It seems to grow no better and it is a very serious impediment in the way of active employment which contains a large element of hearers and speakers. You do not know how little I hear in ordinary matters. The conversation at the dinner-table — I hear just enough to vex me with its meager suggestions.

A terrifying aspect of his disability was that it varied in intensity. At times he could hear almost normally. Then suddenly would come the onslaught and he would be muffled in a blur of undistinguishable sound.[14]

In addition to teaching, Scudder also considered the ministry, a calling in which he might exert the influence Mark Hopkins had suggested as his responsibility, but quite aside from his deafness, he was uncertain he had the call, that he was suited to follow his brothers Evarts and David and his friend Henry Mills Alden to Andover Theological Seminary. A period of evaluation was essential. "I *like writing very much*," he wrote his father, "and all collecting, consulting books, compilation or patient literary work. My experience with the Quarterly this last year has been very valuable & has given me some reason to suppose that some such work may very well be adapted to my faculties." In considering his probationary years, he estimated five to six, and six was exactly what he took.[15]

That the years were probationary does not mean they were nonproductive or unremunerative. Within a few months of graduation he was off for Texas as tutor and cicerone for Theodore Gilman, a Williams freshman and younger brother of Arthur Gilman, who in the future would be salesman and author for Hurd & Houghton, treasurer of the American Tract Society, nephew-in-law of Henry Oscar Houghton, and one of the founders of Radcliffe. Scudder, returned to Boston from his Texas adventure, set himself a stringent course in the classics, concluding as he progressed that Homer was his man, "that one may safely leave unread most everything else, rather than him." His interest in music he continued to cultivate, becoming a member of the Apollo Society and attending concerts whenever he could. He also set himself a variety of writing tasks — one, fairy tales for his nieces. This independent study he seasoned with a little tutoring, but to live at home was not his wish. Before the end of the year he had left for New York. From there he shortly wrote his mother, "This is my last day of non-professional life for the present. I have sold myself body and mind — I hope to say my soul's my own — to a small brat of eleven years, for six hundred dollars a year . . ."[16]

The brat, a bright, roguish boy, but spoiled, Scudder thought, was Henry Brevoort, son of J. Carson Brevoort of Brooklyn. Scudder was unwilling to relinquish his New York life and he planned to travel daily from his rooms on 12th Street to the Brevoort mansion on the corner of Fulton and Bedford Avenues, a round trip of nine miles.

I shall start from here by seven [he reported to his parents] so as to breakfast downtown, making all allowances for ferry detentions, & reach his house a little before the hour. Then I shall be in my room again, having dined downtown at three o'clock, after which I shall have six hours to myself, exclusive of an hour for tea and loitering . . . Moreover, Mrs. B. tells me that in the dead of winter they mean to come to the city & take a furnished house for a couple of months; and besides they will probably go to Washington for a fortnight, in which case I am to go with them, expenses all paid.

Scudder was understandably delighted with his position. Mr. and Mrs. Brevoort were people of charm and culture. "Both of them," he told his mother, "have such perfect manners that the very contagion made me a gentleman for the evening and I felt perfectly at ease." Better than his employer's charm or his background of European education, travel, and diplomacy, was his library of several thousand volumes. Moreover, Brevoort, who was one of the trustees of the Astor Library, guaranteed Scudder's access to that incomparable collection.[17]

Scudder's hours of independence he filled with activity. Arthur Gilman was a frequent companion — so was Henry Mills Alden, who had concluded that the ministry was not for him and had come down from Andover in April 1861 to share Scudder's quarters for a few months before he married and set up housekeeping for himself. Both young men had by now set their hearts on literature as a profession. Both had had articles accepted by the *Atlantic.* Scudder also made the *North American Review,* the *National Quarterly,* and the *New Englander,* and a variety of newspapers and religious journals. Then came Scudder's *Seven Little People and Their Friends.* Alden wrote an enthusiastic review which Fields published in the *Atlantic* and a pleasant celebration in Scudder's rooms ensued. Next, Alden was commissioned by the Pennsylvania Central Railroad to write a guidebook, an engagement which led to Alden's fifty-year association with the Harpers, for the book was published by their firm.[18]

After Alden's marriage the young people continued to meet frequently, reading to each other their literary efforts. When Ticknor & Fields reported to Scudder that his manuscript had been lost, there was consternation; when another was returned as "not available," commiseration, and certainly speculation about an Alden article submitted to the *Atlantic* about which after a number of months no word had come. Such neglect was compensated for one day when Fields himself arrived at Scudder's rooms in search of Alden to apologize for his firm's oversight and to suggest that Alden might find his future with the Boston house. Fields was a day or two late. Alden had by now cast his lot with Harper & Brothers.

Scudder's halcyon New York years came to an end in January 1863, when he was summoned to Boston by the death of his father, his responsibility now to be the man in the house for his mother and sister Jeannie. One of the senior Scudder's requests had been that his literary son write a memorial biography of his brother David, who on completion of his course at Andover had sailed for India as missionary with his bride, Harriet L. Dutton, sister of E. P. Dutton, the Boston publisher-bookseller. David's brief tour of duty had ended tragically by drowning. Horace set about his task with pleasure. He had loved his brother and had received many letters from him. From these he could recreate the people and the atmosphere of the distant stations in which David had served. As Scudder wrote of his brother he looked about for a publisher. His experience in the trade had already taught him much.

Seven Little People had been published in November 1862 by A. D. F. Randolph of New York, but before achieving acceptance it had gone the rounds — Ticknor & Fields, Scribner's, Harper's, Appleton, and James Miller. Randolph's terms were 15 percent on the retail price of all copies sold, the author to pay the cost of the stereos and illustrations. The first edition of 1100 was sold out in less than two months, a second appeared in February 1863, a third in January 1864. In spite of this excellent record Scudder was not satisfied with his publisher, who he thought had been negligent in seeing the book through the press. The text was full of errors, and worse, after the book was out Randolph's advertising was half-hearted. So for his second book, *Dream Children,* Scudder accepted an offer from Sever & Francis of Cambridge, who assumed all expenses on an edition of 3000, the author to receive 10 percent of the retail price on all copies sold. For the memoir of his brother, Scudder sought yet another publisher. Although he hoped for a New York imprint, he planned to have the book manufactured in Cambridge. Since the book was a family affair, he was prepared to guarantee production costs. Quite naturally, recalling the superior work the Riverside Press had done for him on the Williams College *Quarterly,* he sought out Houghton, not knowing that the printer was about to turn publisher. No need to seek further once the printer and author were joined. *The Life and Letters of David Coit Scudder* appeared on Hurd & Houghton's list for 1864. To publish the book was not much of a gamble for the new house; Scudder paid all the costs, rendering Hurd & Houghton a 10 percent commission on the wholesale price. Since Hurd & Houghton's imprint was New York, Scudder made a similar arrangement with E. P. Dutton for Boston distribution.[19]

While negotiations were progressing for the printing of his brother's biography, Scudder was making successful entrée into Boston's literary enclave. Charles Eliot Norton accepted his offer to write an article on William Blake for the *North American Review* and in addition requested he write for the *Review* a critical paper on literature for children. Fields purchased for the *Atlantic* Scudder's story "Five-Sisters Court at Christmas-Tide" and urged him to become a monthly contributor to his firm's projected juvenile magazine, *Our Young Folks,* for Scudder by this time, because of his two books and his numerous tales for young people appearing in a variety of periodicals, had acquired the sobriquet of the American Hans Christian Andersen. E. P. Dutton, who used a number of Scudder's juveniles in his *Church Monthly,* gave the young man further employment as an adviser on manuscripts submitted for book publication. Although Scudder was busy enough with these various assignments, before the end of 1864 he had added to his schedule the post of literary adviser to Hurd & Houghton, his salary $150 a quarter, "with extra pay for extra work," his duties defined as the reading and judging of manuscripts. The arrangement was a loose one and the novice hoped he would have time to continue his independent writing. He soon learned that independence is not the lot of an editor. In his first three months with Hurd & Houghton, he not only read manuscripts and wrote judgments, but also he collated an edition of Macaulay, wrote advertising copy, and produced as part of his extra work for extra pay — $50 in this case — a topical book, *The*

Game of Croquet; Its Appointments and Laws; with Descriptive Illustrations. For this effort he used his pseudonym R. Fellows. More absorbing to him than this sort of work was Houghton's interest in starting a magazine.

The close of the Civil War was marked in the book trade by a rush of general publishers into periodical competition. Up to this time the field for mature readers had been led by Harper with its *Monthly,* begun in 1850, and its *Weekly,* begun in 1857, and by Ticknor & Fields with the *Atlantic.* In the last five years of the '6os, publishing houses took to the course in numbers — Scribner's with *Hours at Home,* the Sheldons with the *Galaxy,* Lippincott, Putnam, and Appleton with magazines named for their houses. The most prolific of publishers in launching periodicals was Ticknor & Fields. Indeed before the Civil War had ended and as part of the expansion following William D. Ticknor's death, the house acquired in October 1864 "that singular fossil," the *North American Review.* Even though their accounts were now burdened with a megatherium, Fields and his partner Osgood had no intention of becoming fossilized. Three additional periodicals shortly came into being under their imprint — the *Atlantic Almanac* (an annual), *Every Saturday,* and *Our Young Folks.* Even the great house of Harper was left behind.[20]

The problem confronting Hurd & Houghton in 1865 was hardly whether or not to start a magazine. Any house worth the name had one. The question was what kind — a weekly, a monthly, a quarterly — for grown-ups or for children? Periodicals for parents were proliferating; so were journals for juveniles. At least fourteen originated in the '6os, and the *Youth's Companion,* founded in 1827, under its new editor Daniel Sharp Ford had changed its tone. In its early days the *Companion* had warned children that they were "dying creatures, whose souls must be saved or lost, according to the deeds done in the body," an admonition scarcely calculated to encourage a devoted band of little readers. Yet this ever growing audience was one for publishers to cultivate. Make the child a browser in books and perhaps the habit will persist into manhood. From the 1860s on, the child as an enfranchised member of the republic of letters with a constitutional claim

to joy figured importantly in the plans of both authors and publishers.[21]

Houghton as a businessman perhaps contemplated this audience
with an avid eye. However, he also had clear-cut theories on what
American children should read. The namby-pamby English juveniles, even though Hurd & Houghton imported them, infuriated him. Cheaply made, from worn-out stereos, they pictured a
world foreign to the American child's experience. Their assumption of "the unalterable relation of classes" was repugnant to him.
Moreover, he knew his New England countryside. When Louis
Agassiz criticized English exports of books for children because
their illustrations pictured flora and fauna never to be found in
the United States, the scientist only confirmed his prejudice. The
tariff was one way to curtail this "unwholesome" reading matter.
Another way was to encourage in native writers the observing eye
rather than the imitative facility. In Scudder, he trusted, he had
found his man. Together in the early months of 1865 they discussed the possibilities of a magazine for young people. They
studied Ticknor & Fields's *Our Young Folks* as its issues appeared
and Scudder, with a view to its use in a magazine of his own, withheld the story he had written at Fields's request. Houghton,
however, was not a man to be hurried. He moved with all deliberate speed. Scudder must work out a prospectus, an assignment
which he completed promptly.[22]

Just at this time Hurd was planning to go abroad and he and
Houghton agreed that six months of travel would be excellent
preparation for an editor. The start of the magazine was postponed and at the end of April Scudder and his superior left for
England. From this joint trip two interesting publishing connections resulted. Scudder's *North American Review* article on William Blake had led to correspondence with the Rossetti brothers.
Through them he met Algernon Swinburne, to whose *Atalanta in
Calydon* Ticknor & Fields had recently acquired American rights.
Swinburne was in a fury with the terms arranged by his English
representative, who was to pocket half the profits from American
sales, and one night when Scudder dined with him the poet got
"drunk and ranted horribly." Apparently Scudder was able to

stomach the rant, for as a result of this meeting Hurd & Houghton secured Swinburne's next play, *Chastelard*.[23]

Hurd's acquisition was to be of more lasting significance to the new publishing house. Assigning to Scudder the responsibility of developing cordial relations with various English publishers and selecting books for Hurd & Houghton's list, he returned to the United States in July aboard the *Asia*. A fellow passenger was William D. Howells, who had just completed a four-year tour of duty as United States consul at Venice. In his pocket Howells had a contract with the London publisher Trübner for his *Venetian Life*. Although the two men played ringtoss and shuffleboard together, probably Howells said nothing to Hurd about his book at this time even though an American publisher was essential to him. Trübner's condition for issuing the book was that an American house take 500 of an edition of 1000. Howells hoped for an established publisher, not a new one such as Hurd & Houghton. His lodestar was Ticknor & Fields. As soon as he reached Boston, he wrote James T. Fields, trusting his letter to his friend James Russell Lowell for delivery. Lowell was dilatory and six weeks went by. Howells, now in New York, met Hurd by chance on the street and the two men lunched together. Since he had had no word from Fields, he told Hurd of Trübner's proposition. Thus by chance Hurd & Houghton acquired a "first" that in the years to come would become a standard. The firm had also initiated a publisher-author relationship that would become increasingly complicated in the years ahead.[24]

Scudder returned to the United States in November eager to begin work on his periodical. However, plans for the magazine did not come to fruition for almost a year. Meanwhile he was kept busy enough. Houghton had concluded he must have a Boston as well as a New York office for the publishing side of his business. Desk space would be sufficient to begin with, he thought. This Scudder found for him at the Old Corner Bookstore, now the property of his friend E. P. Dutton rather than Ticknor & Fields. Here Houghton and his adviser met frequently. Here Scudder left bundles of manuscripts with his written judgments; here he left advertising copy. At home and at the Riverside Press he worked

William Dean Howells at the time
Hurd & Houghton agreed to publish an American edition of his first
book, *Venetian Life*.

on Hurd & Houghton's 1866 catalogue, of which when it appeared the Boston *Evening Transcript* noted: "Hurd & Houghton bid fair to do for New York what Ticknor & Fields have done for Boston," adding that to Houghton "is due the honor of having raised the style of printing and caused the publishers and reading community to recognize its claims and capabilities as a fine art, as well as a special economy."[25]

Occupied as he was, for Scudder the absorbing question was that of the magazine. Endless conferences took place in Boston at the Old Corner, at Houghton's Cambridge house, on long drives the two men took together, at the Riverside Press, at Hurd's in Brooklyn, and at the New York office in Broome Street. By May 1866, the partners had "quite concluded to begin it," and Scudder set about lining up contributors even though the first number was not to appear until January 1867. By September a Memorandum of Agreement had been worked out. According to its specifications the editor was to have "absolute control" of the *Riverside Magazine for Young People,* his salary $1800. In addition, as soon as the magazine began to show a profit, he was to have 1 percent on the retail price of all copies sold.[26]

In writing his prospective contributors, Scudder was able to assure them that "Mr. HO is heartily engaged in the matter! So is Mr. Hurd. There is capital enough to give a cheerful boldness and now all that I want is a spirited corps of contributors." At Houghton's direction, he advised his authors that "publication first in the magazine would not interfere with a subsequent publication in book form but would rather help the latter." To secure for the house and the magazine distinguished contributors, the partners agreed rates should be generous. They must at least equal those of *Our Young Folks.* The *Riverside Magazine* was to have about 1000 words to the page, or half again as many as *Our Young Folks.* Since Ticknor & Fields paid their contributors $4 a page, Scudder announced his rates as $6 if the copyright were sold to the publisher, or $5 if the author retained the copyright, payment on publication. These rates were for prose; for verse Scudder suggested $5 "for the shortest piece" and as much more as he could afford for longer poems. The magazine was to have a gay, variegated cover, excellent paper, and numerous illustrations. That the way of the new periodical must be prepared was agreed. Its editor was "to give first a 'literary item,' then 'an announcement,' and finally a 'standing advertisement.' " Scudder, backed by Hurd & Houghton and with the facilities of the Riverside Press at his command, hoped to make his juvenile journal the best of its kind.[27]

Because it was "so grave a matter to direct the reading of thousands of children's minds," Scudder assumed his duties with a sense of dedication. He considered the magazine an instrument through which he might wield moral influence; through it he could aid "in the real education" of children. However, he wished to be a genial teacher, not a pedagogue and he pointed out to his contributors the "difference between being moral and making morals." Example rather than precept should be the writer's aim. As heroes, "audacious little divines" betray the purpose of the story. "Gentle lessons of forebearance, charity, and unselfishness" should be impressed by the narrative rather than direct teaching. Scudder regarded his editorial work as comparable to that of an architect. "I have to build up by detail a facade, having in mind a general effect and yet noting each stone and carving," he thought. Text and illustrations must combine to produce a unified impression.

Illustrations figured largely in his plans; they would serve his educative purpose providing they had charm and reality, qualities lacking in the general run of pictures in books and magazines for children. He hoped that each issue of his periodical would have at least one original work of art, "a picture for its own sake and not for the good of something in the text." He wanted *good workmen* in *art* with whom the subject and not their personal distinction would be the main thing"; at the same time, he was on the "alert to find and use men of original power." He did not wait for artists to come to him; he sought them out in Boston, New York, and Philadelphia. As a result he secured work from such established illustrators as Winslow Homer, Thomas Nast, and F. O. C. Darley. He also found and developed new artists; two of these were John La Farge and a Williams classmate S. G. W. Benjamin. For these unknown men Scudder made an especial effort, soliciting "puffs" in other periodicals, calling attention of friends to the illustrations and discussing them with his young readers in his editorial column, noting implicit movement, the details, the significance. Thus for John La Farge's dramatic frontispiece in the December 1868 *Riverside Magazine* he wrote:

> Here, to begin with, is Mr. La Farge's picture of the "Wise Men out of the East" following the star that is to lead them to where the young child lay. See! the fresh wind is blowing on the little knoll, stirring the horses' manes, and cooling the faces of the Wise Men. They have stopped, and let the caravan go on a little while they take a new observation of the star. Perhaps it is the morning after the Shepherds have heard the song of the Angels. Nowadays even humble watchmen in city streets may see sights that show them the light of the world.

As with artists, so with writers; the *Riverside Magazine*'s liberal rates enabled Scudder to secure men and women of recognized achievement. He did not wait for unsolicited contributions to drop through his letter slot but was active in solicitation, securing commitments well in advance of printing. In fact, so generous was the response to his appeals during 1867 that by the end of the year he had more than sufficient inventory for all of 1868, a matter of genuine concern. "It is really alarming," he wrote. "Must decline everything hereafter that I possibly can." His most provocative promise of a story came from Herman Melville — a promise that never materialized. Others were happy to respond to his invitation. Jacob Abbott, Christopher Pearse Cranch, Rose Terry, the Cary sisters, Celia Thaxter, Edward Everett Hale, and Lucretia Peabody Hale appeared in the *Riverside Magazine,* but these writers contributed to many other juvenile magazines. One who was exclusively Scudder's and Hurd & Houghton's was Hans Christian Andersen.

Long an admirer of the Danish author, who had been known in America since Mary Howitt's translation of 1847, Scudder had attempted unsuccessfully to establish friendly relations with Andersen as early as 1862. Another effort the following year also failed to win a response. Even so, in 1866, seeking contributions for his magazine, Scudder made a third try. Again no word from Denmark, but patience and persistence are attributes of an editor. At last in 1868, Scudder was able to announce that Hans Christian Andersen had agreed to contribute regularly to the *Riverside Magazine for Young People.* Scudder's rates were generous — $500 for twelve contributions, Hurd & Houghton to be the authorized American publishers, Andersen to receive 5 percent on the retail price of all volumes sold of a proposed collected edition of his writings. On receipt of his first payment, Andersen feared some mistake might have been made. His *Fairy Tales,* published by Wiley & Putnam in the 1840s, had been in circulation for years, but Hurd & Houghton's draft was the first money he had ever received from an American publisher. In 1874, the year before his death, Andersen expressed his continuing satisfaction with Hurd & Houghton, writing, "The Americans are commonly called covetous, selfish and I know not what, and yet the only compensation which I have ever received from a foreigner has come to me from an American publisher. I have never seen or known the man, and he sent me a short time ago of his own accord 800 Danish rix-dollars."[28]

Important as Hans Christian Andersen was to Hurd & Houghton's list and the *Riverside Magazine,* he was nonetheless, even though living, already a classic or standard author. In anticipation of future performance, of books to come, Scudder knew he must seek the recently emerged writer or one yet untried. Because of Scudder's efforts Mary Elizabeth Mapes Dodge, whose *Hans Brinker; or the Silver Skates* had been published by an obscure New York house in 1866, became contributor to the magazine and Mrs. Dodge, in preparation for her work as editor of a juvenile magazine, learned much from the editor of the *Riverside Magazine,* both through his criticism of her stories and later through his active participation in drawing up plans for *St. Nicholas,* in many ways an obvious successor to the *Riverside.* Moreover, it was through Scudder that Mrs. Dodge acquired her *St. Nicholas* editorial assistant, Frank Stockton.

Stockton was one of two writers unknown in 1867 who profited by Scudder's criticism and guidance. The other was Sarah Orne Jewett. Scudder's standards are relevant to any estimate of the development of these authors.

As manuscripts, both requested and unsolicited, began pouring in, Scudder was shocked at their quality.

You know of course how much has to be rejected [he wrote Charles Eliot Norton, editor with Lowell of the *North American Review*] . . . but do writers for reviews send *bosh?* I suppose you have tedious, lumbering papers, but I hope you have no contributors answering to the great herd of writers for the young, who make me daily wonder how they could suppose I should print their work: but I suppose that the mind which conceives such trash has a depth which appreciates it. If I were to make a Swamp Magazine for People who never will be Young out of my rejected articles, I think my friends would begin to wonder how the Riverside was even as good as it is.[29]

Through his letters to contributors and in the editorial department of the magazine, he tried to show what his criteria for selection were.

In his opinion a novice could have no better preparation for "bolder flights" than to write for children. Because to achieve clarity, he must understand his subject thoroughly, a juvenile audience acts "with a very clarifying power" upon an author. Stories of imagination as well as biography, history, and science require comprehension of detail in depth; otherwise the product will be neither illuminated nor illuminating. The narrative must move rapidly. The style must be simple and straightforward. In requesting a series of articles on Arctic life from the explorer Isaac Hayes, he advised, "Good strong stuff in forcible Saxon English is what we want for boys: such writing in fact as their fathers want if they have not lost their freshness of life." Provided the style is free of condescension, almost any subject will do. To the Honorable George Perkins Marsh, at this time United States minister to Italy, Scudder suggested, "History and biography afford a very wide field and even politics may be admitted for I should like to open the way for making our boys good citizens as well as good men. If I could give them an idea of what a town meeting means and show how it differs from an Athenian Agora I think they would read it." The young writer, he advised, should observe his surroundings and write about what is near at hand. Such was the method of Hawthorne, the genius of the nation as well as its conscience, a tortured conscience because of the blight of slavery.

But now the Civil War was over and the divisive effect of sectionalism must be submerged in the new nationalism.

> I am unwilling [he wrote John Esten Cooke of Virginia] to introduce in the education of the coming generation any element which will serve to keep alive sectional hostility. In the recent war I was as hearty and uncompromising an adherent of the Union as I know you have been to the cause of Southern Independence. The old questions then fought over on the field will doubtless in one form or another be fought over again in words before we shall regard them as historical and beyond the pale of practical concern, but I do not think it necessary to make them play a part in our magazine. American ideas I shall hope to inculcate with a view to making good citizens of our children, but these I conceive to be equally applicable in all parts of our country.

Accordingly, "Frank Gordon," a serial about the life of some children in Georgia appeared in the first volume; a sequence on "The Young Virginians" followed in the second. Anticipating the work of Joel Chandler Harris by a few years, the *Riverside Magazine* presented some stories in Negro dialect about Br. Rabbit and Br. Fox. Scudder drew particular attention to these tales in his editorial column, saying they were familiar to Southerners, but that as far as he knew, they had never been printed before.

Other sections of the country were also represented in the magazine. The usual contemporary stories of the West, Scudder thought sensational, vulgar, and full of slang, seeming to be "a succession of shouts," but Martha M. Thomas and Helen Campbell Weeks satisfied his requirement of decorous realism with true accounts of life among the Indians and other tales of the frontier. Rebecca Harding Davis told the children about life in Pennsylvania "A Hundred Years Ago," and New England, of course, was more than adequately represented by a variety of contributions that included Scudder's own Bodley series, Jacob Abbott's instructive stories, and Sarah Orne Jewett's "The Shipwrecked Buttons," "In a Hurry" (a poem), and "The Girl with the Cannon Dresses."

Sarah Orne Jewett had just turned twenty when she had two of her stories accepted by Boston periodicals — "Mr. Bruce" by the *Atlantic* and "The Shipwrecked Buttons" by the *Riverside*. For the former she used the pseudonym "Alice Eliot." In submitting the latter she signed her name "S. Jewett." When both were accepted, she was in a quandary and wrote at once to the editor of the *Riverside Magazine* requesting that her story to be printed there appear over the name "Alice Eliot." Scudder followed her directions but advised that in the future she use her own name. He also wrote her judicial comment not only on her contributions to him, but also about her narrative in the *Atlantic*, for he recognized in this appealing girl a writer of promise who deserved being cultivated. She was doing as he had advised. Although her sketches lacked incident, she was using her eyes to see that which was close at hand; she was writing simply and directly. He intended she should feel free to call on him "for any possible service" he might render "in the matter of literary labor," and offered to write a letter of introduction to the editor of *Scribner's Monthly*. He hoped his literary connection with Sarah Orne Jewett would be an enduring one.[30]

Of all the types of literature written specifically for the young, that which drew Scudder's keenest analysis was the fairy or wonder tale. Hans Christian Andersen he regarded as the greatest practitioner of the form because he "depends for his material upon what he has actually seen and heard, and for his inspiration upon the power to penetrate to the heart of things; so that the old fairy tale finds its successor in this new realistic wonder-story, just as the old romance gives place to the new novel. In both . . . is found a deeper sense of life and a finer perception of the intrinsic value of common forms." This secret of penetrating the heart of things gives Andersen's stories an appeal that transcends difference in age. Andersen speaks to the reader on a variety of levels. The young read him for the charm of the story, for his provocative, imaginative detail. Adults find in the tale something that escapes the limits of the page, a hint of the inexpressible. Andersen believes in his creations; he does not talk down to children; he does not stand outside the frame of his narrative and laugh at his own inventiveness. Writers attempting the wonder story should study Andersen. On receipt of Frank Stockton's first manuscript for the *Riverside Magazine* in 1867, Scudder wrote him:

> I am struck with the fertility of your invention and with the quick turns and sudden surprises which you present and I wish you would try all this on some story which is entirely human. I am aware that you have an advantage in dealing with creatures that allow such fanciful contrivances as fairies and giants, but I think you take unfair advantage. These people belong to children and are the small remnant of what is left to them in a purely imaginative field. It is really too bad to make fun of them and turn them into burlesque . . . A small child who pretends to himself that he believes in the pretty superstition of fairy-life is to be pitied when the domain is rudely invaded and his creatures dragged out to be made fun of. Fairies are something more than diminutive men and women, giants something more than exaggerated mortals and to make a puppet show of them for a mimic stage of humor . . . is robbing children of a certain fine imaginative possession that we ought to respect. The same argument applies though with less force to kings, queens, princes and princesses, for children are by nature not republicans but royalists and take most kindly to those naive representations of royalty which Hans Andersen for one produces with so much quiet fun.

Although Scudder had worked with almost single-minded devotion to the preparation of his magazine, the first number when it appeared on December 20, 1866, fell short of his hopes. The cover dissatisfied him; so did the illustrations. He especially disliked "these weak attempts at investing animals with human nature by putting a coat and hat on them . . . if a man is a man only as he wears a hat or smokes a pipe, then a dog would better remain as he is and leave the hat and pipe to his superior." "And what disciple of what school drew that Irish child holding a squash as if it had an explosive powder in it and might go off at any moment!" As for the engraving of the Belfry of Bruges, what possible interest could it have for a child? The printed matter appeared to him even worse than the illustrations.

We seem to get down one more step when we come to read the

number, if we can manage to read it [he wrote Norton]. Is there to be no downright fun for children in it, or is the material all to be of this seriously cheerful cant? . . . I used to think that the editor could at least appreciate other people's fun, but has he fallen so low that he thinks Mr. Jacob Abbott funny? And yet I confess to a lingering fondness for Jacob. I feel the ground so firmly under my feet when I read his writings . . . I go along with his characters so calmly, with the enquiring Rollo, the wondering Lucy and the philosophic Jonas . . . I believe again in the great laws of nature, in the tendency of heat to ascend and I am charmed at my own intelligence as I listen to the explanation of the fact that a chimney will draw better when it is upright than when it is lying down . . .

After Mr. Abbott comes the editor who is, I am glad to see, getting more matter of fact in his treatment of subjects . . . But is he not sometimes disturbed when he opens the magazine . . . to find that what he thought he said in a whisper was really spoken very loudly on a house top? . . .

But I am tired of criticising . . . There is only one person whom I can trust to find more faults than I, and that is the Editor of the Upper Half of the Western Hemisphere Review.

Truthfully yours
HORACE E. SCUDDER

I am going to one of the islands of the South Seas next week. They eat all the children up there. I am going to edit a Juvenile Magazine for parents.[31]

Others were not as critical. Toward the end of the first year the *American Literary Gazette* noted, "*The Riverside Magazine,* with its beautiful cover, its charming illustrations, and its capital prose and verse, is one of the most attractive magazines which we have. It is edited with good taste, and published with a liberal, enterprising determination to excel." True perhaps, but Houghton and Hurd had further noted that the magazine, even though its editor had secured gratuitous puffs in the *Post,* the *Transcript,* and other papers, was not paying its way. It looked as though the periodical would die after one abortive year. Even though the future looked gloomy, Scudder was by no means ready to give up. He

studied those costs of the magazine over which he had control —
payments to authors, designers, engravers, and his own salary. The
results of his analysis he outlined to his firm. The cost of illustrations could be reduced to $400. Payments to authors must remain
high, but he could lessen the monthly outlay by writing about ten
pages himself without charge. The cost for contributions would
thus come to $200 a month rather than $260. As a final item in his
economy measures, he offered to trim his own salary by 50 percent.
If his suggestions were followed, he thought the monthly outlay
for the magazine would come to within $700.

> I am too much interested in the magazine [he concluded] &
> have too much pride to let it stop, without using every effort in
> my power to carry it through. I would gladly sacrifice more: I
> would relinquish my entire salary if I could: but it is my only re-
> source and it would be impossible for me to give all my time or
> even half for nothing.
>
> But if our united efforts are not sufficient to keep the magazine
> out of debt, then let us stop at once and inform the world . . .
> with as good grace as possible that we cannot do what we ought
> to do.

Houghton and Hurd accepted the first part of Scudder's offer —
that he write ten pages a month for the magazine for nothing, but
his operating budget was cut to $600. However, his salary was
maintained.[32]

Despite Scudder's efforts the *Riverside Magazine* continued to
lose money. One reason was that rather than sticking to his announced rates, he frequently increased the scale for a particular
author. Hans Christian Andersen, George Perkins Marsh, and
Rebecca Harding Davis all received well over $6 a page. To other
writers he guaranteed an increase once the magazine was prospering. As far as they could see the magazine was doing just that and
they complained that rival periodicals were more generous. Helen
Weeks wrote angrily, "Three years ago you told me the Riverside
designed to give seven dollars a page when safely established, and
more if possible. The establishment is a fixed fact, but where is
the money?" The establishment was not as fixed as Mrs. Weeks
supposed.

When Scudder did try to economize on authors' rates, he met rebuff. Phoebe Cary had submitted a poem, "Griselda Goose," which would fill approximately four pages of the *Riverside*. Scudder had held it over six months waiting for space in the magazine. Faced with the need to cut costs, he wrote her:

> When you sent G. G. last spring I engaged to pay $75. for it, the price you named. Since then — when I had had but short experience — I have been made aware of the great expense attending the publication of the magazine, & I am exceedingly desirous of easing the load which the publishers have to carry, as much as possible. Will you think it ungenerous in me to ask you to name a lower sum now? I enclose an order for $50: at the same time I wish to say unmistakably & emphatically that I will at once send on an additional order for 25. if you say so. This is my proposition. The publishers know nothing of it & have not asked me to do anything of the sort. I am only assuming that my contributors feel that kind of interest in the magazine which would lead them to make such a sacrifice if it were reasonable.

An assumption which found no warrant in gentle Phoebe's heart. A week later Scudder wrote in his journal, "Sent Phoebe Cary a jocular letter and twenty-five dollars additional."

Scudder's magazine was not the only one having financial troubles. Of the fourteen juvenile periodicals originated in the 1860s, three ceased publication in 1870, eight in the following years of the decade. Even Ticknor & Fields's *Our Young Folks,* though it claimed a circulation of 50,000, was in trouble. Pleading with its youthful readers to secure more subscribers, it said, "We have given authors and artists the highest prices to work, not for us, but for you, that you might have only the best; and the magazines which grown-up people read have not been prepared for them at a cost nearly so great in proportion as this little monthly of yours." The *Riverside Magazine for Young People,* with its bright cover of heavy stock, its generous rates for authors and artists, and a yearly subscription price of $2.50, could not maintain the standards set by its editor and pay for itself. Hurd & Houghton decided to transfer the *Riverside*'s subscription list to the new *Scribner's Monthly,* and in December 1870, Scudder said goodbye to his young readers, saying that the years he had devoted to the magazine would be among his happy recollections. At the same time Josiah Gilbert Holland, editor of *Scribner's*, welcomed the "thousands" of readers of the "charming Riverside." Of its editor Dr. Holland wrote, "Mr. Scudder has few equals and no superior in originating and selecting literary material," assets of which Houghton was aware. He had no intention of permitting Scudder to go elsewhere. Moreover, the idea of having his house publish some sort of periodical still interested him.[33]

Financial failure though the *Riverside Magazine* had proved, it had brought to the firm a number of authors for book publication, among them, in addition to Hans Christian Andersen, Helen Campbell Weeks, S. G. W. Benjamin, and Frank Stockton. It had also served as a subtle advertising medium, a function which Scudder thought the chief reason a publisher assumed such responsibility,

> for the magazine rarely fails to symbolize the house from which it issues. This is, in fact, its great charm with the publisher. He is always wishing to impress his business upon the public mind, and though he may issue book after book, no single one quite expresses what he conceives to be the character of his house, while a magazine with its flexibility, its power of presenting many sides, and its magisterial function also of accepting, rejecting, and criticising, becomes a very exponent. It is indeed much more likely to reflect the character and taste of the house than of its editor, and is most likely to succeed when it is a genuine representative of the concern whose name it carries. For this reason a publishing house will, as a rule, publish a more honest magazine than a company of gentlemen, since its responsibility to the public is more clearly recognized and more sharply defined and its interest in success more weighty.[34]

Scudder's reference to "a company of gentlemen" was to Edward Everett Hale and his associates, whose periodical *Old and New* Houghton had undertaken to publish in November 1869. At just about the time Hale had made his alliance with Houghton, James T. Fields, home from his European trip, approached him to suggest that he and his friends buy the *North American Review*.

The *North American* had proved a burden to Fields ever since he had purchased it, and before sailing for Europe in the spring of 1869, he wrote Charles Eliot Norton, who had resigned as editor of the *North American* so that he also could go abroad, that since the *Review* was "an out of the pocket certainty of five or six thousand a year," he intended "to let it die with the October number of this year. Let us mourn over it when we meet in London." Fields and Norton may have mourned the *North American* in England, but by the time the former had reached Switzerland, he was loath to give his partners at home permission to end its career. Such an act would be an admission of failure. However, back in Boston in late October, his worries about his firm's precarious financial condition intensified, he looked about for a purchaser. Edward Everett Hale, who was known to be starting a magazine intended to combine the virtues of *Blackwood's* and the *Atlantic,* was a logical choice. He had an inherited interest in Fields's quarterly. His father had been one of the company of gentlemen who sustained the *North American Review* in its early days. Fields offered "favorable terms" for purchase and Hale was tempted, but when he discussed the proposition with Houghton, he met with ridicule. Why should anyone waste money on a periodical with a circulation of four or five hundred only? Hale forwent his temptation, and Fields, Osgood was left with its prestigious *Review*.[35]

Although Hurd & Houghton assumed the publication of *Old and New* with little risk (the contract was a 10 percent commission one), the association with Hale proved difficult. According to Scudder, he had a kangaroo mind. Certainly he was not businesslike. The announcement of the magazine appeared in the *American Literary Gazette* on December 1, 1869; yet on December 4, Hale was writing to his brother that he might put off publication until March. For Houghton, announcement meant publication. What force he exerted must be imagined. The first number, dated January 1870, appeared on schedule, December 15, 1869. Obviously the Houghton-Hale association was not one to last. By May the breach was complete. Hale transferred his business to Roberts Brothers and Houghton left for California. Before he left he directed Scudder to outline plans for a periodical that would have greater chance of success than the *Riverside Magazine for Young People* had had.

This trip to California was ostensibly for pleasure. "Our Mr. Houghton," Scudder reported to Andersen, "is just now travelling to California. Think of it! only a week from Boston to San Francisco by the great Pacific Railway. He takes his wife with him and they travel with a party of ladies and gentlemen in superb cars, where they have state rooms as in a boat, and sit down to elegant dinners in a travelling dining room! The Arabian Nights can show few things more wonderful." But "Our Mr. Houghton" took with him something besides his wife. In his pocket he had Colburn's *Intellectual Arithmetic upon the Inductive Method of Instruction,* which he hoped to place with various school boards across the country.[36]

Scudder meanwhile continued to edit his dying periodical, writing ten pages for free, reading manuscripts, inventing advertising techniques, which produced "a perfect waterfall" of replies, and considering what form Hurd & Houghton's next periodical should take. He reported his conclusions to Houghton in a detailed letter.[37]

Houghton, back from California, praised Scudder's report. However, he had no intention of originating a periodical once the *Riverside Magazine for Young People* was safely out of his hands. To pick up one in being was the safer way. For that he was prepared to wait. In the meantime, he required an editor educated in the intricacies of printing and publishing. Literature had its place on his list, but the best requires more than the pennies of praise. What Houghton needed was someone in Boston and Cambridge to act as his lieutenant when business or politics required that he be on the road.

In January 1871 Scudder found himself engaged as Houghton's adjutant, "to act for him in his absence, to be second in command in his establishment and to represent there as completely as possible the interests of Hurd & Houghton. I am a publisher of books actually, as far as I can discover, without the name or direct responsibility . . ." he wrote in his private journal. Somewhat overwhelmed by the position, he had been tempted to refuse, but Houghton had taken him so much into his confidence that he feared, "I should feel treacherous to turn away from him now."[38]

One of Houghton's confidences was that he had undertaken to act as publisher for the American Tract Society, a nonsectarian group dating from 1814, engaged in distributing tracts and other religious literature. Although the organization was a nonprofit one, its sales were intended to cover expenses. The organization's financial report for June 1870 revealed that expenses had exceeded receipts by something over $800, not a serious imbalance, but still one to be rectified, and it was concluded to make a standard business arrangement, that is, a 10 percent royalty on all publications, with Hurd & Houghton and H. O. Houghton & Company. Since the society's manufacturing expenditures annually exceeded $300,000, Houghton was understandably pleased with this addition to the commitments of the Riverside Press. Another secret Houghton told Scudder at this time was that his firm was also to become publisher of the *Journal of the American Social Sciences.* So much for Scudder's speculations about a magazine over which he might have control. As a sop to his disappointment, his employer told him he could have a four-page monthly sheet to be called the *Riverside Bulletin.* Scudder was determinedly cheerful. Even four pages could be a source of influence for good. The future looked bright, he said, and he bought himself a pony whom he named Sparkle and stabled in Charles Street not far from his mother's house on St. James.

> . . . she is brought around every morning just after breakfast [he wrote his little niece Vida]. I put on a pair of leggings, a reefer and an astrachan cap and with a satchel slung over my shoulder I mount and ride off in gay style. There is a stable close by the Press, where I have a stall. I have a key and let the horse in, off saddle her and blanket and halter her. Then at noon I run over and give her some oats, and at night, I saddle her, jump on and race into town. It's a fine thing and keeps my color up.

Scudder had joined the commuters.[39]

The year ran its course. The presses at Riverside clanged away without interruption. Hurd, on doctor's orders, left for eighteen months abroad. For the second year Hurd & Houghton showed a profit. Scudder's apprenticeship had come to an end. In lieu of his salary Houghton offered him a partnership at $15,000, share and share alike, profit and loss. The atmosphere was filled with the delightful sound of dollars ringing in coffers. The Scudder family had a conference and since all the brothers agreed this was a rare opportunity, Scudder's widowed mother provided the cash. No longer was he a publisher's adjutant without responsibility.[40]

To find a decade more fateful than the 1870s for the speculative business of book production would be difficult, as Mark Hopkins' boy was to learn. A Bowdoin graduate, James Ripley Osgood, was to learn the lesson also. So was a Harvard man, George Harrison Mifflin.

VI

THE BATTLE OF THE BOOKS

GEORGE HARRISON MIFFLIN, Scudder's junior by five years, also became a partner in Hurd & Houghton in 1872. His parents at the time their son was considering Houghton's proposition may have held a family conference, but the $15,000 they afforded for his share in the company was no widow's mite. His mother was a Boston Crowninshield, one of the wealthiest families in the East. Curiously, Mifflin's paternal line was in reality not of the Mifflin name at all; rather it was Francis. Tench Francis, a British colonel who emigrated to America in 1724, was his first American ancestor in the male pedigree. Tench's son Samuel fell in love with Sarah, daughter of Samuel Mifflin, a Philadelphia merchant. To please his father-in-law, young Samuel Francis assumed his wife's family name. By this translation he acquired for himself and his descendants a "princely fortune" and a romantic strain of Portuguese blood. Sarah Mifflin's grandmother on the maternal side, when a baby, had been miraculously saved at the time of the Lisbon earthquake by an American sailor who brought her to this country, where she was adopted. Here she grew up and married, and one of her daughters became the bride of the Quaker Samuel Mifflin.[1]

George Harrison's father, Charles Mifflin, might have had a distinguished medical career had his lines been other than to Mary Crowninshield. Graduating from the University of Pennsylvania's medical school, he remained there as resident physician until he was assigned as surgeon on the corvette *Kensington* destined for Russia. During his stay in Saint Petersburg, cholera broke out in epidemic proportions, and the young doctor made it his business to study the affliction. After his return to the United States, the disease breaking out in Montreal, Dr. Mifflin was appointed to a commission and dispatched to Canada. When the plague swept southward, the doctor returned to Philadelphia and there put the knowledge he had acquired to such good effect that his city was far more lightly stricken than was New York. His medical career, as far as it had been exceptional, came to an end when he met Mary Crowninshield at Saratoga. They were married in 1835 and Mary's parents persuaded their son-in-law that life in Boston would be far more attractive than in Philadelphia. From that date forward he practiced his profession only in Nahant, where the Crowninshields had a summer home.

In contrast to Henry Oscar Houghton, George Harrison Mifflin's growing-up was blessed with the pleasures of affluence, winters in the family house on the corner of Beacon and Somerset and summers at Nahant, varied by frequent travel abroad. Mifflin, like Scudder, went to the Boston Latin School, graduating in 1861, and then to Harvard. Here he was one of the gilded youth of his day and according to his recollections learned nothing. Receiving his degree in 1865, he left for Europe with his parents, who in the year and a half that followed allowed him considerable independence. In Greece, with *Childe Harold* as his guide, he had a horse and a boat to make expeditions; in Paris, an apartment done in red with an alcove for a bed. To keep him busy, he had a number of gay companions and once, the waiters mistaking him for Robert Lincoln, he and his friends "had a nice supper" with "a band of music — and all without cost" because he was thought to be the son of the martyred President.[2]

This was mid-September 1867; in November, he was due to sail for home. All summer he had been wondering what he could do, for he had decided his father's kind of life was not for him. His older brother Ben, who was in State Street, advised him to steer clear of investments as a profession. An opportunity in Kentucky offered. Then a couple of other openings appeared available, but each came to nothing. Though friends warned him that a life in trade would be degrading, he was certain that in some form of business he would find his future. "I do not feel as strongly as

George Harrison Mifflin in 1865, on graduation from Harvard.

you do about the common place of business," he wrote. "Business itself, yes; but the means one takes to succeed in it no. Provided a man *works* in earnest — no matter what . . . " Just where he was to work was the question.[3]

During his weeks in Paris, he was a frequent visitor at the Exposition. He was in attendance, wearing a dress coat and a white cravat, on the day the prizes were distributed. When the Riverside Press received its award, he must have been vividly reminded of a home industry. Even as a boy he had loved beautifully made books and he cherished those in his library which came from Houghton's Press.

On his return to Boston in late November, he at once sought an interview with Henry Oscar Houghton. Across "a tiny old pine desk in the farthest corner" of the Old Corner Bookstore, the two men faced each other — the tanner's son from Vermont and this scion of Beacon Street. Houghton needed help. Scudder he had for the literary interests of the firm, but so far he had no one to relieve him in supervising the intricate, ever expanding business of the Press. Just elected Cambridge Common Councilman, he was becoming something of a public figure. The future, he knew, would take more of his time in community service. However, he doubted this product of the Boston and Philadelphia Gold Coasts could be of assistance. Houghton had already had experience with the privileged. Hurd had proved congenial and interesting, with literary connections and important capital, but his financial security allowed him to indulge a vague stomach complaint which responded favorably to travel. What Houghton required was a devoted representative, but he questioned that this tall, eager young man with the smiling eyes could master the mysteries of profit and loss, the mechanics of the clattering presses, the techniques of binding, the necessary knowledge of leather, paper, and cloth. He discouraged the applicant from seeking further.

Mifflin, however, was persistent. He liked the gaunt printer whose behavior and appearance made him think of Lincoln and he made repeated calls at the Old Corner. Houghton at last yielded so far as to make a test, giving Mifflin an appointment at Riverside for seven-thirty in the morning. Mifflin's siege finally bore fruit,

The Old Corner Bookstore as it appeared after Ticknor & Fields had moved to more spacious quarters at 124 Tremont Street. Here Houghton came to conduct the Boston end of his business, and here he interviewed young Mifflin across a tiny old pine desk.

for this last interview resulted in employment. On February 1, 1868, he was put to work in the Riverside Counting Room, copying bills under the direction of the head bookkeeper, and it was here he acquired an enduring love of figures as they marched down the page to a neat footing. Next he was put in charge of the Bindery, and presently Houghton was taking him as a companion on some of his trips to New York. The novice took to his work with enthusiasm, feeling within a year he had already become a fixture at the Press. "My work is really interesting," he wrote, "and beside the life I led abroad it is *glorious.*" By November 1871, Houghton had concluded that the young man whom he had been so deliberate in hiring would serve his purpose, and he offered Mifflin a partnership. Scudder had assumed his responsibilities with a certain reluctance, hoping he would find time to write. George Harrison Mifflin had no reservations; his commitment was complete.[4]

A third new partner joined Hurd & Houghton at this time — Edmund Hatch Bennett, the friend of Henry Oscar's Burlington days who had played a part in the founding of H. O. Houghton & Company in 1852. This time, as before, he was a silent partner, and his investment was but $5000. During the time of reorganization preceding the announcement of the new partnerships, since Hurd on doctor's orders was to be away for at least eighteen months, the question of how the New York office (now 13 Astor Place) was to be run had to be resolved. For a time Scudder feared he would be asked to take on the job. Fortunately, Albert Houghton had at last wound up his Southern responsibilities and was free to assume direction of the New York side of the business. As in the earlier organizations, partners were to share and share alike, profits and losses, according to their contributions: Hurd 25 percent, Houghton 25 percent, Albert 25 percent, Scudder and Mifflin 10 percent each, Bennett 5 percent.[5]

A year before this 1872 reorganization another young man had come to the Riverside Press, one who would not have a widow's mite to invest were he given the opportunity — twenty-three-year-old Francis Jackson Garrison, youngest son of William Lloyd Garrison, and brother of Wendell P. Garrison, at this time on the staff of the *Nation* and soon to become its literary editor. Now that George Mifflin had graduated from bookkeeping and was in charge of the Bindery, Houghton was in need of yet another lieutenant. His plant was running without interruption. Francis Garrison was just the man he was looking for. He was familiar with the printer's craft, for he had assisted his father in getting out the *Liberator* and had stood by when his father prepared his valedictory, set it up, locked the forms, and put the final number to bed.

Francis Garrison, like Scudder and Mifflin, was a product of the Boston Latin School, class of 1865. A college or university was the logical sequel for one so prepared, but Frank questioned this easy assumption. His brothers gave him the familiar advice that under collegiate instruction he would learn how little he knew. Of this deficiency, he retorted, he was already aware. He preferred to go abroad with his father, especially since his sister Fanny, whom he adored, was there with her husband, Henry Villard. In October 1866, he and his father left for a triumphal year in Europe, and they, even as George Mifflin, were in Paris at the time of the International Exposition. The spectacle failed to clarify Frank's purpose as it had Mifflin's. On his return to America in November 1867, he was still uncertain. All he knew was "My head-centre is Boston, the hub of the Universe, and in it I wish to spend and end my days." That object might be accomplished if he could help his father in writing his memoirs.

Ticknor & Fields had made a definite proposition for a two-volume work: $5000 on completion of the first volume, the same for the second, with 10 percent on sales. However, the elder Garrison was not capable of sustained composition. In January 1868, Frank reported to Fanny, "It is useless to talk about the HISTORY. He will never write it." As a result he decided to follow a "Hunky dorum" plan, taking a special course at the recently established Massachusetts Institute of Technology. On completion of his studies at M.I.T., he found employment on the *Journal of the American Social Sciences*. During the negotiations for the transfer of the periodical from Leypolt, Holt & Williams to Hurd & Houghton, young Garrison met the owner of Riverside, and here in 1871 to his pleasure and that of his family he found his place in business.

Hardly had a month passed when Wendell Garrison was writing from his *Nation* office to Scudder, "My brother seems to be very happy in his new vocation, and that his association with you will add both to his pleasure and his knowledge, I am well persuaded. For him I will say — what I hope is true in a degree of all his father's children — that he is faithful and trustworthy as few are: *e più non dimandare.*" Henry Oscar Houghton once again had found his man and he proceeded to bind him to his house by raising his salary from $1000 to $1200 and making him his confidential clerk.[6]

After twenty years in the trade and a variety of partnerships, Houghton had at last found three men who would never desert him — Scudder, the Mark Hopkins man, shy, reserved, self-effacing, but with a missionary zeal for "pure literature"; Mifflin, Harvard, Porcellian, energetic, boisterous, warm-hearted; and Garrison, liberal by inheritance, devoted to the causes for which his father had worked — the plight of the Negro, rights for women, pacifism, and temperance. Each of these men played his part in creating the public image of the house as it developed from Hurd & Houghton through Houghton, Osgood to Houghton, Mifflin & Company. Between Garrison and Mifflin there was an immediate affinity. They, together with Houghton, had much to do with the tight financial administration which helped the firm ride the turbulent economic tides of the ensuing years. Scudder, devoted though he was to the noble in letters, learned from his associates that a publishing house is not an eleemosynary institution, that to survive it must produce utilitarian books as well as masterpieces. On him in large measure fell the responsibility of developing a balanced general list for his employers. There would be other partners who would put more money in the business, other associates to stand by Houghton in times of stress, other editors of distinction, but these three — Scudder, Mifflin, and Garrison — are central in any picture of Houghton's companies.

In Houghton's history reorganization may be taken as a sign of expansion. The January 2, 1872, number of the *Riverside Bulletin,* in addition to announcing the Scudder and Mifflin partnerships, heralded a new building plan for the Press which would enlarge by three times its existing capacity, an announcement which possibly surprised other publishers, for the year just closed had been a poor one for the trade, especially in Boston. According to the *American Literary Gazette,* "In the month of February, only four books (excepting law, and perhaps two or three 'juveniles' of little note) were issued in that city, which claims to be the fountain-head of American literature." This was not for want of manuscripts. Rather publishers were withholding new books, awaiting "better times." Among the publishers' worries were the printers, who were becoming restless once again. Edward Everett Hale in his *Old and New* took it upon himself in an article called "Printers' Suicide" to deliver a lecture to the craft.

> No working-man gets too much pay [he wrote] . . . But there have been occasions when working-men have exacted more pay than their employers can afford . . . None of the six parties in interest in book-making [publishers, booksellers, authors, paper makers, bookbinders, and printers] gets too much money. But as things are now, none of them can afford to lessen his own share, in order to increase the others. If . . . the printers shall insist on any important increase of their wages at present, they will cause the publishing business of the United States to be stopped here, and transferred to England, faster than is already happening. And then they themselves can, if they will, "go West" — or go to Jericho.

Of the parties involved in book production, the publishers run the greatest risk, workingmen the least, the Reverend Mr. Hale pontificated.[7]

Houghton's approach to labor's dissatisfactions differed radically from Hale's. He had himself been a laborer, a worker in a craft he esteemed, believing it to be one of the most educative of callings. For a boy unable to afford a college education, work at the case — the very center of ideas as they are transferred from script to type — was an excellent substitute. But many in his plant lacked his dedication. This he knew. He had had already bitter experience with two strikes, one protracted, the other brief because he had met the demands of the compositors. That his men might consider walking off the job if their demands for higher pay were not met, he attributed to lack of instructive information which would lead them to understand that profitable management meant their security in hard times as well as lush. What better way to make his printers and compositors aware of this than to take them into partnership? He already had five partners. Why not three hundred and five?

On May 19, 1872, Garrison reported to his sister:

Harry [Henry Villard] is so much interested in co-operative matters that he will like to hear of a scheme which we are just putting into operation at the Riverside, & of which your correspondent will have charge for the present. Any of the people who work at the Press can deposit money with us in such sums as they are able & receive six per ct. interest on it as long as it remains, but they are entirely at liberty to draw out whenever they need or want it. When their deposit reaches the sum of $100.00 & remains as much as that for a year, Jany. to Jany., they will be entitled to a proportionate share in the profits on the entire business, both here & in New York, as their deposit is proportioned to the entire capital, but such proportion of the profits shall not exceed four per cent. of their deposit, that is to say, they shall not receive more than ten per cent. in all, interest and profits, but the interest of six per cent., on whatever money they place with us, shall be absolutely guaranteed. As Mr. Houghton only broached the thing to the people yesterday, it remains to be seen how they will go into it, but it will probably be a thing of slow growth.

Two days later Garrison was writing that the people were "excited" about the plan, that probably "a very considerable number will invest their earnings with us." The first depositor proved to be a reformed drunkard, who trusted the plan would save others from the grog shop. "A shrewd & canny Scotchman" put down $150 as his "first nest-egg." Others followed suit and within three months the Riverside's Savings Department had over $3000 in deposits, in sums varying from $5 to $500. During the rest of Houghton's life, the Riverside Press, in part due to this cooperative plan, was spared serious labor troubles.[8]

Houghton had made his workers partners in his printing business. Was such a relationship possible with the laborers on the publishing side, the authors, the living ones, those who might themselves produce standards, providing in the years to come a valuable, reworkable backlist, one that would create for Hurd & Houghton a public image of Ticknor & Fields's distinction? Compositors, printers and binders, although individuals, could be treated as a group. Uniformity of contractual arrangements was possible, even essential. Could authors and their publishers agree on universal, standard practices? Or were authors too singular, publishers too competitive?

Though honored as a profession of gentlemen, publishing had always been a business. In the nineteenth century authorship also entered the marketplace. In the beginning the publisher was but a middleman, a distributor, operating between the printer, the author, and available markets. As the possibility of distribution outlets multiplied, a multiplication inherent in population growth, the publisher's value to the author increased; so did the publisher's speculative investment. The incidence of a successful book, in the general field, defies analysis. The contract embodies the publisher's effort to cover contingencies, the author's to secure a proportionate profit. Through memoranda of agreement each party attempted to secure his just return. Since the author's rights in his book are not only income producing but also assignable assets comparable to stocks and bonds in another's portfolio, he seeks a publisher who, recognized for his integrity, seems to assure the most substantial continuing return. William Dean Howells wrote that it is "a sin and a shame" that a writer feels besmirched when he is forced to put a price on his wares. "Business," he protested, "is the opprobrium of Literature." Nonetheless Howells early mastered the techniques of selling his product. So did a number of other authors, among them Mark Twain and Henry James, Jr. Other writers were not as successful.[9]

Broadly speaking there were three forms of contracts between authors and their publishers: the commission, the half-profits, and the percentage. Under the first, the author assumed all costs, paying his publisher a commission, usually 10 percent of the retail price of all copies sold. However, under this arrangement, publishers concerned with the reputation of their imprint did not take any book offered. Valuing their colophons and what they stood for, they took only those books which met their standards. An author who could afford the initial cost was apt to prefer this arrangement, for after expenses had been met, all but 10 percent of the return was his. Moreover, if he were dissatisfied with the publisher's handling of his book, he could readily transfer to another since everything belonged to him — the copyright, the stereotype plates, and all stock, bound and unbound. The second type of contract — the half-profits — provided that author and publisher share alike costs and profits. This was the system preferred by the English and the one used by the British publisher Trübner for William Dean Howells' *Venetian Life*. Though less commonly employed in the United States than Britain, the form did occur here.

The most generally used contract was based on a percentage of retail sales. Usually 10 percent on the retail price of a specified number of copies sold was guaranteed the author. Wide variation was possible within the form. The simplest arrangement was that the publisher promised the agreed percentage on all copies sold, exempting from royalty only volumes intended for publicity distribution, review copies, and the like. However, a new writer might accept an exemption of the entire first edition. Sometimes even established writers agreed to such exemptions, or perhaps smaller ones. Another variation, rather than exempting a specific number of copies, was for the publisher to ask the writer to forgo royalty returns until costs of manufacture had been met.

If the relationship between author and publisher were to be comfortable, complete trust on the author's part was requisite. Yet when an author became aware his royalty returns were diminishing, that he fed on corroding suspicion was perhaps inevitable. How could he believe his books were not selling like hotcakes when he was assured by friends that his word was in demand from coast to coast, or at least from Boston to New York? He could of course demand to see his publisher's accounts. On examining them, he would find what he already knew, that his returns were less than they had been. He might also find out that his contractual arrangements were not what he had thought they were.

In the fall of 1869 a writer of established reputation came to Hurd & Houghton with a manuscript which the firm agreed to publish on a 10 percent commission. The writer was Mary Abigail Dodge (Gail Hamilton); her manuscript, *A Battle of the Books.*

Up to this time, with the exception of a memorial to her mother, which she had had privately printed at the Riverside Press, Miss Dodge had been published exclusively, and at James T. Fields's urging, by Ticknor & Fields. She had first appeared in the *Atlantic* in 1860. Thereafter she had been one of Fields's favored authors, or so she thought. By the end of 1868 his house had published nine of her books, she had appeared frequently in the *Atlantic,* and for an annual $500 she had acted as consulting editor for *Our Young Folks.* Her first book, *Country Living and Country Thinking,* had been an outstanding success, earning her in two years something over $3700. Understandably pleased, she paid small heed to subsequent arrangements for her books. Fields was so handsome, so "straight-forward, genial, simple-hearted," she accepted as beyond question his assurance that he had her welfare at heart. He was so generous in praise. "He says very fine things of my paper," she wrote, "and he is constantly asking for more. He gets my books up himself, — proposes to have them as books, I mean — and is strenuous that I write only for them, to which I am myself strongly inclined." At the time she wrote in this vein, although she had written three books, *Country Living and Country Thinking, Gala-Days,* and *Stumbling-Blocks,* she had a contract for the first only. This contract specified 10 percent of the retail price ($1.25) after the first edition had been sold. However, the size of the edition, which turned out to be 1500, was not mentioned. Two years later, in September 1864, Fields drew up a new contract to cover her forthcoming *A New Atmosphere.* Included also in the Memorandum of Agreement were her already published *Gala-Days* and *Stumbling-Blocks.* This contract instead of guaranteeing a percentage substituted a fixed sum on all copies sold, 15 cents. Since her books were now selling for $1.50, to Mary Abigail this just seemed another way of saying 10 percent. Fields in his letter of explanation was clear enough.

... as the business times are fluctuating the prices of manufacture
so there is no telling to-morrow, or for a new edition, what may
be the expense of publication. So we reckon your percentage in
every and any event as fixed at fifteen cents per volume on all
your books. If it should cost $1.50 to make the volumes you are
sure of your author profit of fifteen cents. The price at retail
may be $1.50, $2.00, or $3.00, as the high or low rates of paper,
binding etc., may be, but *you* are all right. This arrangement we
make now with all our authors.

Shortly after this letter, the price of all Mary Abigail's books went
up to $2.00.[10]

Although *Country Living* was not included in the fixed sum
Memorandum of Agreement of 1864, Fields subsequently maintained that the 10 percent on that book had been abrogated under
the new arrangement and that he had explained the change to
Miss Dodge in an interview. This assertion Miss Dodge flatly
denied, admitting however that in her stupidly trusting mood
of those days, she would have made no protest. If Fields had
said, "Owing to the state of the trade and manufactures, all the
trees are now going to be bread and cheese, and all the rivers ink,"
she would have believed him. After all, under Ticknor & Fields's
management, her income from trivia, sprightly essays of observation on people and places, was better than she had originally
hoped. Hers not to question. For her next three books Miss Dodge
asked no contract, allowing that of 1864 to prevail. Not until 1867
did she find cause to complain. Then an article in the *Congregationalist* fired the first shot in this Battle of the Books. Here she
read that the standard pay for beginning authors was 10 percent.
It didn't take much figuring on her part for her to realize that
15 cents on a $2 book was anything but 10 percent. However, long
before she picked up the *Congregationalist,* she must have looked
at her semiannual reports in some mystification. Her income from
her books began to plummet in 1865: $2500 plus for that year,
$1731 in 1866, and $868.55 in 1867. Yet she now had eight books
in the Ticknor & Fields catalogue. Could she believe that seven
failed to earn the return of one; that popularity in 1864 did not
assure popularity in 1867? A diminishing audience is hard to

stomach; so was 10 percent for novices. She was by now a writer of repute.[11]

She wrote Fields in a friendly enough spirit requesting an explanation. In his replies, Fields was first dilatory, then abrupt, suggesting if she were unhappy with him she transfer her books to another publisher. He refused to discuss the firm's rates for other authors of her experience. Ticknor & Fields had no uniform scale. "What we pay any individual author is a matter quite between him — or her — and ourselves," he told her. The answer did not satisfy the Gail from Hamilton. The more she thought, the more indignant she became. She had regarded Fields as her friend. She had been unwilling to color their association with "mere business." Angry, contemptuous of herself, she realized she had been naïve. "Mr. ——— [Fields] had the matter entirely in his own hands," she complained. "I never questioned, or proposed, or bargained, and that he could have gone on, year after year, paying me less than a new author has, paying me from one-third to one-half less than the lowest market price, is not a thing to be overlooked." Still, she wished the matter kept private.[12]

So did Ticknor & Fields. Arbitration was the solution. Negotiations begun early in 1868 were protracted. Neither side could agree on choice of arbiters nor on what form the reference should take. The transformation of Ticknor & Fields to Fields, Osgood & Company at the end of October further delayed matters. Arguments about referees continued and finally on November 28, 1868, the new firm wrote in exasperation that the estimated cost of such a proceeding was $500. Fields, Osgood would gladly write a check for this amount, and in the future pay 10 percent of the retail price on all Miss Dodge's books. The offer came too late. What Gail Hamilton now wanted "was indemnity for the past, not security for the future." Moreover, during the summer what had started as a "mere personal altercation" had now become a crusade. She had made it her business to inquire of other authors in the Ticknor & Fields stable, "Have you any objections to telling me in what manner you are paid by your publishers for your books — whether by percentage or by fixed sum — and whether in or near the autumn of 1864 a change was made from a percentage to a fixed sum — also what was the percentage and what was the fixed sum. If these questions seem to you impertinent it will only show how deceitful are appearances!" Her researches "unearthed venomous creeping things and revealed nests of unclean and hateful birds." Ticknor & Fields, she discovered, was paying Hawthorne's heirs, Sophia and her three children, less even than she was receiving — only 12 cents a volume. Now she was willing to talk to anyone and everybody. Her own experience was of small import compared to that of the widow of an author who was one of Ticknor & Fields's proudest boasts. "The case was more aggravated than mine," she wrote, "not only because the author in question had been of an immeasureably higher standard than I, but also because he was dead, and the apparent exactions were made upon those who were dearest to him in life, and who were dependent upon the fruits of his genius."[13]

Hawthorne's Sophia had been aware of diminishing royalties ever since her husband's death in 1864, especially since two banks in which George Hillard, Hawthorne's friend and administrator, had deposited the inheritance had had financial difficulties and were not paying the expected return. After Hawthorne's death, Fields had arranged with Hillard for the fixed sum of 12 cents rather than continuing the percentage arrangements William D. Ticknor had made verbally with Hawthorne over the years, for some books 15 percent, for others 10 percent. With the exception of *The Wonder Book, Tanglewood Tales,* and *Twice-Told Tales,* which sold for $1.50, all of Hawthorne's books were now priced at $2.00. During the summer of 1868, when Fields had been struggling to placate Gail Hamilton, he had word from Hillard that Sophia Hawthorne was dissatisfied, vocal in her displeasure. Her complaints might have serious repercussions. If they became public property, Ticknor & Fields's cultivated reputation for munificence would suffer serious diminution. When Sophia, through Hillard, sent word that she would not allow Ticknor & Fields the posthumous possibilities in her store of Hawthorne manuscripts and notebooks and that she was considering transferring all her husband's books to another publisher, Fields acted promptly, writing her on August 13, 1868:

As far as we are advised, we are led to believe that you are under the impression that we have for some time wrongly and purposely withheld from you a certain percentage of the copyright we should have paid you . . .

The relations between us are simply these: By virtue of a contract duly executed by your administrator on the one side, and by ourselves on the other, we hold the exclusive right to the publication of Mr. Hawthorne's works during the time of the copyright therein. One of the conditions of this contract is that we shall pay as copyright in the said work the sum of (12) twelve cents per volume of each copy of the said work which we shall sell.

This stipulation we have faithfully performed; and our right to the future publication of the said works is therefore incontestable.

With reference to the rate of copyright as expressed in the contract we can say; that at the time it was agreed upon, it was a fair one for both parties. Certain it is that it made the aggregate copyright on the works considerably larger than it had hitherto been; and the change from a percentage copyright to a specific one, was made because the fluctuation in the prices of books made such a change necessary.

To prove his point Fields compared the percentage copyright and what it had equaled in cents with the specific return under the new contract. On all Hawthorne's individual works, the heirs were receiving 12 cents a copy. With the exception of two books, this amounted to an increase in revenue. However, for *The House of Seven Gables* and *Our Old Home* the reverse was true. Their original 15 percent copyright had earned 15 cents a volume.

This exhibit [the letter continued] shows that the change from a percentage copyt to a specific one was not made for the purpose of evading any portion of it. We can truly say that in our possession of the right to the publication of Mr. Hawthorne's works it is far from our desire to deprive his family in the slightest degree of any returns to which they may be entitled to receive therefrom.

Indeed our feelings toward them prompts us to a very different conduct; and we would err if err at all on the side of kindness and consideration rather than on the side of injustice.

Permit us then to offer a suggestion for your consideration:

that you choose some person, wholly disinterested — say Judge Hoar, or Dr. Holmes, or both, and have them examine fully into all matters between us. We will agree in case you consent to this reference to submit on our part all matters into their hands, and to accept their decision and abide by their recommendations whatever they may be.[14]

Until her husband's death, Sophia Hawthorne's financial experience had been confined to domestic accounts. Even so, she could figure percentages. Five of her husband's books had been engaged for at 15 percent, the others at 10 percent. Under the old system she would have benefited by the increase in the retail price of his books. Whereas under the fixed sum scheme Ticknor & Fields reaped the harvest. She refused to consider any sort of arbitration, and demanded further details on her husband's original arrangements with William D. Ticknor. In reply to this demand, Fields protested that Ticknor, acting as Hawthorne's attorney, had "obliged the firm to pay the highest rate of copyright it ever paid." "With reference to contracts for copyright on Mr. Hawthorne's works we have to say, that previous to the present one, none existed. The arrangement for copyrt. on the volumes consisted simply of mutual agreements made by Mr. Hawthorne or his attorney, at the various times of publication of the various works." As for her charge that the fixed sum copyright worked for the benefit of Ticknor & Fields rather than Hawthorne's estate, Fields explained:

> You doubtless are well aware of the great increase in the prices of all commodities that took place in 1863-4-5. This advance in the cost of all materials affected the business of publishing as much as any other business & publishers were obliged to advance the prices of their books accordingly. They were obliged however to move cautiously; as books not being articles of necessity, people were not obliged to buy them, and would not purchase them at all if the prices were too high. Without waiting to see if the public would stand the necessary advance in the prices of books the cost of manufacturing them went rapidly upwards, until we found ourselves obliged to pay nearly double the cost of manufacturing, without a corresponding increase in our returns.
>
> On representing the circumstances under which we were placed

by the condition of things in '63 & 4 to the various authors for whom we then published, the justice of our claims for modification of the rates of copyts heretofore existing was in every case readily admitted, and new arrangements were made to meet the altered condition of affairs.[15]

Ticknor & Fields, shortly to become Fields, Osgood & Company, was eager to placate Mrs. Hawthorne. Again a proposal for arbitration was tendered. Would she select two from four names presented: Francis E. Parker, George S. Hale, Richard H. Dana, and the Reverend E. E. Hale? Moreover, since paper and binding costs had recently fallen, the firm could manage to carry a percentage contract of 10 percent if it included forthcoming volumes as well as those of Hawthorne's books already in the catalogue. The letter containing these proposals concluded with a gratuitous warning. The prices of books were not fixed. They might go down. If this should happen, her return on the percentage basis would be less than that under the fixed sum arrangement. Sophia repudiated the proposals. The price of her husband's books must drop below $1.20 before 10 percent would yield less than the fixed sum of 12¢. She threatened to transfer her husband's books to G. P. Putnam of New York. If Fields, Osgood insisted on her adherence to the Hillard contract, she intended an investigation of its accounts by her sister Elizabeth Peabody.[16]

The publishers went to extraordinary lengths for Mrs. Hawthorne and Miss Dodge. Both were given the courtesy of the contracts and the benefit of the books. From the latter Miss Dodge chose to steer clear, declaring only a Solomon could understand them, but Miss Peabody went courageously on course, undertaking not only a study of the contracts, "a most perplexing medley — a sort of contra dance between written contracts and verbal agreements with the rattling of stereotype plates for tambourines," according to Mary Abigail, but also the firm's ledgers, daybooks, accounts of sales, and all the other paraphernalia of business accounting. "One can imagine Miss ——— [Peabody] hunting up Messrs. Hunt, Parry & Co.'s [Fields, Osgood, & Co.'s] account books in pursuit of knowledge!" exclaimed Miss Dodge. In any event, Elizabeth Peabody's pursuit led her to the guarded conclusion

This Indenture, of two parts, made this Sixteenth day of March in the year of our Lord, Eighteen Hundred and Fifty Four. by and between Henry D. Thoreau, of Concord, in the County of Middlesex, and State of Massachusetts. of the first part, and William D. Ticknor, John Reed Jr. and James T. Fields of Boston. Booksellers and Copartners under the firm of William D. Ticknor and Co. of the second part. Witnesseth, That the said Thoreau agrees to give, and does by these presents give to the said Ticknor & Co. the right to publish, for the term of five years, a certain book. entitled "Walden, a Life in the Woods." of which, said Thoreau is the Author and Proprietor.

And in consideration of the premises. the said Ticknor & Co. on their part, agree to cause said work to be printed, and to publish at once. an Edition of Two Thousand copies. and to pay to the said Thoreau, his heirs and assigns. Fifteen per cent on the retail price of said work

Thoreau's agreement with Ticknor & Fields for *Walden* is in Houghton Mifflin's contract files. Following Thoreau's death in 1862, Ticknor & Fields arranged with Thoreau's sister and heir Sophia to publish her

on all copies which shall be sold,
payable semi-annually, commencing
at the expiration of six months from
the day of publication, at which
time, an account of sales shall be
rendered, to the said Thoreau.

It is understood and agreed
that the said Thoreau shall receive
Twenty Five copies of the first
Edition without charge, and
that any additional copies
that the said Thoreau may desire,
he shall have the right to purchase
at a discount of Twenty five per
cent from the retail price

Witness
J. B. Neill

Henry D. Thoreau
W. D. Ticknor & Co.

brother's books on a fixed sum royalty of twelve and a half cents for all
but *Walden,* which was allowed fifteen cents.

that Ticknor & Fields, and Fields, Osgood's books and bills were consistent with themselves and that the firm's conduct had been "legally righteous, that so small had been the actual demand & sale of Mr. Hawthorne's works, that neither publisher nor author had received since the firm had been publishers on an average even one thousand a year." Nevertheless Mrs. Hawthorne still felt "aggrieved that a new contract was made with the firm by one of its own members, without her knowledge; & without telling her administrator that she had not been consulted, that for several years she did not receive what the original contract would have given her." Miss Peabody concluded by assuring Fields, Osgood that since Mrs. Hawthorne now had the facts "respecting the income of Mr. Hawthorne's works" she had no illusions. In the future, she hoped, the publishers would take "special care to guard against all carelessness and misunderstandings."[17]

Limited vindication surely, scarcely one to be released to the press. As a result, innuendos reflecting on Fields, Osgood's integrity persisted. Mrs. Stowe demanded an accounting of her sales; so did Anna Dickinson. Possibly there were others.[18]

Even though Elizabeth Peabody's report was hardly what Fields had hoped for, at least the Hawthorne chapter was closed. Sophia, preferring "peace to pence," accepted the firm's 10 percent offer. Fields was to sail for England on April 29. All that remained was to settle with Mary Abigail Dodge, whose case had dragged on for almost a year and a half. In latter-day haste, the hearing before referees was arranged for the twenty-second. Here, Mary Abigail presented her case in damning detail. She knew her popularity was ephemeral, that she was but an average writer, only a cut above Hawthorne's scribbling women who put their hearts on the counter; but she was a fighter. A penalty of pence not peace was her demand — $3000 plus costs, a demand the referees compromised at $1250. This was on April 30 and James T. Fields and Annie had already sailed for England and a rendezvous with Dickens which would result in the controversial appearance of *Edwin Drood* in *Every Saturday*.[19]

Fields's conduct in this battle with the ladies is curious. The August 1868 letters to Sophia are written in the name of the firm, rather than his. Yet as senior partner, he must carry the burden of the blame. As far as Mary Abigail Dodge was concerned, he may well have felt she had small cause for complaint. Within six years his firm had paid her over $10,000 in royalties alone. He may have concluded that Gail Hamilton had shot her bolt, that he had had the best of her. He may not have cared whether she stayed in his stable or strayed to some parvenu's apparently greener pasture. From his point of view, the firm's increase in book prices was to cover rising costs. Why should authors share collaterally in price increases? Gail Hamilton's retort was that her living costs had also gone up. So had Sophia Hawthorne's. Even though women had few rights in these days, was Fields's behavior that of a Maecenas, a patron of American letters?

Fields's partners, James R. Osgood and John S. Clark, were not in the least confident that the gadfly Dodge would be content with her limited victory. ". . . what does she say about the conclusion of the matter?" they anxiously inquired of Mrs. Stowe. The Gail from Hamilton's say is embodied in her *Battle of the Books* and her conclusions set the tone for the author-publisher relationship for the next hundred years. Sophia Hawthorne's was the most dramatic case that came to light during the course of her investigations. But she discovered also that writer after writer whom she queried hadn't the foggiest notion of what his returns were, had no idea whether he was on a percentage or a fixed sum basis, or whether the figures in his semiannual reports were accurate or not. Many appeared to feel that there was something ill-bred in an author's being concerned with money, that lucre and letters were somehow antithetical. She admitted that she had been stupidly trusting. Her researches showed that many of her peers had been equally ingenuous. In concluding her diatribe, she exhorted the craft "to deal with publishers, not like women and idiots but as business men with business men." Moreover, a woman "has no right to demand a favorable judgment of her work because she is a woman . . . Trade laws know no more of gallantry than trade winds . . . There is nothing but supply and demand; nothing but buy and sell. To him who understands it, it is a chariot of state bearing him on to fame and fortune. To him who does not comprehend it and flings himself against it, it is a car of Juggernaut, crushing him beneath its wheels, without passion, but without pity."[20]

In her dealings with Hurd & Houghton for *Battle of the Books,* Gail Hamilton intended to practice what she was preaching. But the course of publication did not run smoothly. Her commission contract stated that the book was to be on sale by February 1, 1870. She was prompt in sending copy, but the Press was slow in returning proof. Next, production was held up two weeks because of difficulties in getting out Hale's *Old and New.* However, Houghton promised to delay other books so that hers "should be baked in the first batch." But this was a promise only and shortly he put her off for another two weeks, telling her that March was the best month for publication, that the delay would afford time for advertising. What had her being prompt and businesslike proved? In frustration, she wrote, ". . . I don't know what else to do, and because Mr. H. looks honest and talks reason, I say yes, yes, but coming home and thinking it all over it seems to me that contracts or no contracts, these men do pretty much as they please . . ." The book failed to appear on the first of March, but the bills came, $600 worth. "Think I am going to fulfill my part of the contract when a man has failed in his?" Gail exclaimed. "I don't mean to pay a cent until next summer and hope meanwhile the book will pay for itself, and if it does I think Mr. ——— [Houghton] better have the next book." By the middle of the month *A Battle of the Books* was in the shops and selling well, reaching a third edition before the thirtieth. Gail was gay; now her publishers were "everything that is civil and obliging . . . I have plenty of money, and no end of a good time," she boasted. Even so, Hurd & Houghton was not to have her next book. Its methods of accounting satisfied her no more than had Ticknor & Fields's. She asked her good friend James Blaine to examine the accounts. His report proving unsatisfactory, she presently transferred her business to Harper.[21]

In all probability Houghton was no more content with Gail Hamilton than she with him. The declared purpose of *Battle of the Books* was to make authors more businesslike. Although its particular targets were Ticknor & Fields and Fields, Osgood, its shafts struck all publishers in a vulnerable spot, the integrity of their relationship with authors. A publisher is a man of many wives. With each he must establish a marriage secured by trust. If the private quarrel becomes public property, the repute of the publisher is threatened far more menacingly than is that of the writer, for the public image of the publisher in part determines what new authors will come to him. It also influences those who buy books. To counteract behind-the-hand gossip of suspicious authors and more formidable attacks such as that launched by Gail Hamilton, the publisher can take to the periodicals, his own and those of his allies. There he can create the facade in which he wishes the public to believe.

Houghton, at the time he published Gail Hamilton, had only a dying juvenile magazine wherewith to create a picture of his establishment. True, he secured space for puffs of praise, many written by Scudder, in an assortment of magazines and newspapers, but he had no periodical to serve him as those of Fields, Osgood served that house. At the time of the Dodge–Sophia Hawthorne fracas, the *Atlantic* could be relied on to paint a fair picture of publishing in dignified, objective phrases:

> There are no business men more honorable or more generous than the publishers of the United States, and especially honorable and considerate towards authors. The relation usually existing between author and publisher in the United States is that of a warm and lasting friendship, — such as . . . now animates and dignifies the intercourse between the literary men of New England and Messrs. Ticknor & Fields . . . The relation, too, is one of a singular mutual trustfulness. The author receives his semi-annual account from the publisher with as absolute faith in its correctness as though he had himself counted the volumes sold . . . We have heard of instances in which a publisher had serious cause for complaint against an author, but never have we known an author to be intentionally wronged by a publisher . . . How common, too, it is in the trade for a publisher to go beyond the letter of his bond, and after publishing five books without profit, to give the author of the successful sixth more than the stipulated price.

Amen, exclaimed Gail Hamilton, let all publishers keep historians to record their royal deeds![22]

James T. Fields and his pupil James R. Osgood were masters in the ancient art of puffery. In 1866 their own genuine skills were reinforced when Azariah Smith, a Greek scholar, came to the house, his special function to write bulletins, trade releases, and advertising. Smith's "candid and clever" dispatches from Boston, which he signed "Fritz," appeared frequently in the *American Literary Gazette,* the New York *Mail,* and other newspapers. At a later date the *Publishers' Weekly* noted that Smith's skill was "to be envied by less artistic workers in the same line." Azariah and his superiors saw to it that the merited reputation of their house for munificence and honest dealing was widely bruited. As publication date for *Battle of the Books* approached, Houghton could not help but notice that literary paragraphs and editorials in praise of Fields, Osgood proliferated. A substantial public image cannot be created of thin air. The facts are there, supported by contracts, cost-books, and the testimony of authors. Ticknor & Fields and its successor, Fields, Osgood, were liberal in their terms, energetic in pushing their publications, creative and munificent in securing new names for the list. So successful were Smith, Osgood, and Fields in insisting on these virtues that their largesse is today remembered. Their questionable treatment of widows and old maids has been largely forgotten. Perhaps that is as it should be.[23]

Public opinion was as important to Houghton as it was to Fields and Osgood. He had defined Scudder's duties in part as "choice of books to publish and formation of public opinion." The diaries Scudder kept in connection with his editing of the *Riverside Magazine for Young People* are replete with notations as to puffs sent in praise of the magazine, its authors and its artists. The most powerful yet subtle instrument with which to create the publisher's image, Scudder believed, was the magazine. Yet after the demise of the *Riverside Magazine,* he had none. To be sure, the house was acting as publisher for the American Tract Society, which issued a variety of periodicals, especially juveniles, and for the American Social Sciences Association, which had a *Journal.* It had also undertaken another periodical for specialists, Hall's *Journal of*

Health. From these publishing associations the firm might well acquire books for its list, might establish rewarding connections with authors, but none of these periodicals reflected the character of Hurd & Houghton as Harper's magazines created an image of that house, carrying the firm's imprint into homes across the land, as the *Atlantic* kept constantly before its readers the achievements of its publishers. Moreover, these magazines served as a lure. Authors came to these houses not only because of the chance to appear among the elect in their magazines but also because of the opportunity to make a piece of writing do double duty, first in the pages of the periodical, then between covers, each appearance at its own price. The serious writer valued periodical publication for yet another reason. After its first appearance he had further opportunity to revise his text before its final publication as a book.[24]

Houghton, having had an expensive lesson from his periodical ventures so far, was loath to launch a new one. Yet Gail Hamilton's *Battle* and the consequent flurry of items in newspapers and magazines had amply demonstrated the power of the strategically placed paragraph. If Scudder were to form public opinion, Houghton recognized the necessity of a vehicle. And so the *Riverside Bulletin* came into being, a trade sheet rarely of more than four pages, its circulation at its height of popularity just over 4000. Insignificant in circulation and size as the *Riverside Bulletin* was, its sphere of influence was comprehensive for it was frequently quoted in the *Publishers' Weekly* and other publications. Scudder made of the *Bulletin* a sprightly journal of critical comment on both the firm's books and those of other houses. Here also appeared statements of publishing philosophy which reflected his ideas and those he was acquiring from his associates as he struggled to become a man of business as well as a man of letters.

As though to counteract such harm as Gail Hamilton's *Battle* may have done to the repute of all publishers, Scudder's effort in his small sheet was to elucidate the problems of publishing rather than to render high praise to the house of which he was a member. The publisher, he wrote, is the true ally of the writer, rather than those friends who of his new book ". . . wonder it is so long coming out; they are surprised after it is out that they do not see it in the bookstores; it is singular how little it is advertised — their wonder never ceases on this point; it ought to be pushed more; why is it not noticed? Invidious comparisons are drawn between this and other books by the same house as regards the energy shown in bringing them before the public, when one is an oak and the other a bean-stalk." The publisher is the author's true friend because he provides the opportunity for "a sober second thought"; perhaps the book should not be published at all, perhaps it should be revised. Once the die to publish has been cast, the publisher carries the final burden for the book's accuracy, for its index, for its other equipment.[25]

The publisher is responsible for the book's appropriate dress. Under his hand "a book grows and has unity and integrity . . . He educates the eye to see what is graceful and becoming, and makes a thing of daily use beautiful. It is the excellence of the average publications of a house, and not its occasional bursts in the way of gift-books, that establishes a sound reputation for good taste." However, "a vast number of useless books owe their continued miserable existence to the sort of divinity with which they are hedged by their substantial covers." Books in paper, in imitation of the Continental manner, might be the answer. And Scudder in prophecy looked to the day when "we shall hit upon some cheap substitute for cloth and boards, which will avoid the expense and stiffness of our present covers, and obviate the patent difficulties of destructible paper covers."[26]

The publisher is the author's friend because it is he who devises the advertising. Such advertising should describe the book accurately and in conservative terms. False claims harm a book. "There was a publisher once who fired off twenty guns, we believe, when he published his first book. The guns went off better than the book."[27]

The publisher has problems unknown to the author. He must make judgments and devise projects in which the writer takes no part. *The Arabian Nights* has no more miraculous tale to tell than has the publisher "who is constantly transforming books from pieces of manufacture into incarnate ideas, and from ideas into items on a profit and loss account." The profit and loss account is a further burden for the publisher. "When one sees the load which every book has to bear of expense before the first return begins, one is tempted to say — Go back, poor little book, into the brain of your author, and venture not again into this groaning world . . . There should be attached to every publishing house a little cemetery, with headstones made of stereotype plates, in which the author should be invited to walk while the publisher is reading his book."

Those who have some romantic idea that the trade lives by belles lettres are ignorant whereof they speak. ". . . the great bulk of the publishing business of the world is engaged upon what, properly speaking, is not literature at all." The house which has a backlog of one or two specialties — law, education, medicine — or which produces technical books of some kind, "tool-books" and "servant-books" Scudder called them — dictionaries, cookbooks, travel guides — is apt to be successful because the demand for such books can be accurately gauged and is continuing. Books which may qualify as literature, on the other hand, are a speculation. If there are any laws governing their sales, they cannot be determined. "As in all other kinds of speculation, the outside public hears of the grand successes, and takes little account of the miserable failures . . . the books which are tools must be the reliance of the book-making class."[28]

There comes a point when certain books because they are literature become tool books. These are the so-called standards, the type of book which dominated Hurd & Houghton's list. The standard book Scudder defined as one which has life and therefore promise of growth:

> not in material bulk, but in certain spiritual qualities . . . Thus, by the growth which time permits, a book becomes a standard by which books with like purposes are measured. Again the power of a book to produce other books is a test of its standard qualities . . . But perhaps the most comprehensive account of the matter is reckoned when we see, in a standard book, not its individuality, but its capacity for holding the juices of a period of thought or action, its power to renew for us the experience of a race of men, the throes of a travailing generation, the days of the Son of man.

Then it is we see in it a standard by which to measure the flow of our own thought, to weigh our endurance, to register the heights to which we may rise and haply pass.

The publisher cannot add to the number of standards, nor can he determine that a book will become one. He only looks on, and, as a servant of the public, sees they are never left in want. In this capacity he takes no risks, but receives from one generation, where the risks were taken, and passes on to the next, which enters upon possession as upon its just inheritance. Yet no generation, however rich in inheritance, can live and not be formulated in books which shall by and by also become standard books.[29]

Since a publisher with a solid list of standards must find purchasers more numerous than individuals building private libraries, Scudder wrote of the new public library movement and of "Reading in the Schools," advocating courses in graded reading based on great literature — Homer, Dante, Shakespeare, Spenser — "innocent of foot-notes." Too many grown people read books about literature, rather than the works themselves. A new generation must be brought up to love reading for itself.

As for the author of scholarly books, based perhaps on the very standards Scudder had so adequately defined, where was he to find a publisher whose profit and loss sheets could bear the burden? Cornell University had originated a Press in 1869, but it was to be short-lived. Scudder envisioned one function of the publishing house as that of a "Minor University," writing:

It may be that the University will one day be a trader in books as it is now a trader in personal learning, but we are disposed to think that there is an equal justification and probability also in the publishing house assuming this legitimate function of the University. That is to say, the University being bound by its high calling to set learning first, and material prosperity second, we can conceive of a publishing house, which, never departing from the sound laws of economy which govern right mercantile transactions, should also never rest in the acquisition of material prosperity, but should, first and last, hold such position and wealth to be but the means toward the real end set before it of projecting substantial works in the interest of sound scholarship and good literature.

The conception of this minor University is of a society of educated men, possessed of the apparatus of book manufacture, and engaged in the supply not merely of existing intellectual demands, but also of demands which it has in a measure created. . . . It may as properly organize an Encyclopaedia, sound in learning and fresh in statement, as a major university plans a curriculum for its students; it may busy itself with the accuracy of the books it publishes as well as with the correctness of the types. It may and must maintain itself firmly on the sound footing of business integrity, sacrificing courageously its fancies to the stern logic of the balance sheet, but it may not, it must not forget the obligation upon it to fulfill its highest calling in the defense of sound learning and the construction of pure literature.[30]

It is not by chance that Houghton Mifflin over the years has published many books notable for their scholarship. Scudder enunciated a principle. Garrison, Mifflin, and Houghton enforced the stern logic of the balance sheet. The four formed Scudder's society of educated gentlemen.

The *Riverside Bulletin* ceased publication in December 1873. Through its columns during its brief existence, Scudder had begun the careful molding of the public image of the house. Like Ticknor & Fields's image, it was carved from facts. Scudder's emphasis, however, was not on liberality, creative discovery, and adulating acclaim from satisfied authors. Rather, the logic of the balance sheet provided the frame within which might be produced the types of books Scudder discussed, types to be found in Hurd & Houghton's catalogue: the standards — Dickens, Bacon, Macaulay, Andersen; tool books — Colburn's *Arithmetic,* Smith's *Bible Dictionary,* law books, and Rolfe's *Satchel Guide.* This last amply illustrates Scudder's definition of the type. The *Satchel Guide,* constantly revised, was still being published by Houghton Mifflin as late as 1941.

As for speculation in literature, risks taken for the just inheritance of future generations, the Hurd & Houghton list in 1872 was thin indeed. William Dean Howells, on his accession to the post of editor-in-chief of the *Atlantic Monthly* in 1871, had transferred his loyalty to James R. Osgood & Company, even though his first

American publishers had successfully forwarded three of his books
and had met his demands for 10 percent on all copies sold with no
exemptions after the first edition of *Venetian Life* had run its
course. In 1867 the firm had published another first, Sidney Lanier's novel *Tiger Lilies,* Lanier paying the costs of manufacture.
The venture had not proved sufficiently profitable to encourage
either the poet or the publisher to further association. Lately
secured were the Cary sisters, surely not immortals, sweet singers
though they may have been. Up to the time of their deaths in 1871,
their books had not returned enough to pay for the stereotype
plates. But Houghton, having taken them on, made them standards in spite of themselves. By dint of memorials and successive
editions, he put the frail pair on library shelves. Before the decade
drew to a close, Hurd & Houghton had paid the Cary heirs over
$4000. Also in Hurd & Houghton's catalogue was John J. Piatt,
but he was on another publisher's list as well. Celia Thaxter with
her "fugitive pieces" was in the Houghton stable, but she was far
from secure, for James R. Osgood, at almost the same time, was
bringing out her *Among the Isles of Shoals.* Another poet was
Emma Lazarus, whose lines

> Give me your tired, your poor,
> Your huddled masses yearning to breathe free,
> The wretched refuse of your teeming shore.
> Send these, the homeless, tempest-tost to me.
> I lift my lamp beside the golden door!

certainly echo "the throes of a travailing generation," even though
her name is today but hazily remembered and all her other poems
forgotten.

In the Hurd & Houghton catalogue of 1872, only John Burroughs perhaps was destined to stand the test of time and the balance sheet. The first Burroughs submission had come in the form
of proof sheets rather than manuscript and the covering letter,
dated February 26, 1867, from the Treasury Department, Washington, D.C., demanded to know within a week whether Hurd &
Houghton would publish a small book, "Notes on Walt Whitman
as Poet and Person." The letter stated that "4000 copies of *Leaves*

of Grass have been sold in the United States, and there can be little doubt if this criticism was brought fairly before the public at least that number of copies could be sold." Scudder was more understanding of the poet than were many of his contemporaries, finding in his poetry a "comprehensive sympathy." However, he distrusted the poet's effort "to escape from eternal laws into vague regions of windy freedom." The proof sheets were returned to Burroughs. Even so, the firm's letter of rejection was sufficiently gracious to encourage Burroughs, and a long, fruitful association between the naturalist and Houghton's various firms began. None of his books, however, qualified as one of the "grand successes" of which Scudder wrote. Indeed in 1871 so doubtful were the publishers of the financial future of *Wake-Robin* that at first only 750 copies were printed, these from type rather than plates.

So far no sensational seller had fallen to the firm's lot. Perhaps for a gamble the partners put their money on Thérèse Yelverton, whose *Zanita, A Tale of the Yosemite* appeared in the fall of 1871. At least she was given 10 percent on all copies sold with no exemptions.

Interesting as Scudder's theories are to the student of publishing, the most important item ever to appear in the *Riverside Bulletin* was the announcement in the December 15, 1873, number of Hurd & Houghton's purchase from James R. Osgood & Company of the *Atlantic Monthly* and *Every Saturday*. Henry Oscar Houghton had waited a long time. He had printed the *Atlantic* from 1857 to 1865. Then James T. Fields had taken it away from him. Now he had it back, not only as printer but also as publisher. He had had staying power; he had been able to wait. The stern logic of the balance sheet observed, he had ridden above the moils of the great Boston fire of 1872 and the financial holocaust of 1873. Now the *Monthly* was his. "The *Atlantic* is a great acquisition for us, and will add prestige to the house," young Garrison celebrated. The story of how this purchase came about must be reserved for another chapter.[31]

VII

JAMES R. OSGOOD & COMPANY —
BEFORE THE CRASH

A YEAR BEFORE the 1872 reorganization of Hurd & Houghton, a
new firm had appeared on the roster of Boston publishers, that of
James R. Osgood, the inevitable product of the short-lived Fields,
Osgood. Although Fields as early as August 1869 had indicated his
intention of retiring, the execution of his purpose took more than
a year of negotiation. That the event was imminent was the gossip
of the trade by the fall of 1870. Osgood and Clark had been carrying the burden of administration for some months before public
announcement of the company, organized as of January 2, 1871,
appeared in the press.[1]

Henry Oscar Houghton had early learned that the man with
ready cash buys the cow in the clover patch. James T. Fields had
had the cash and played Maecenas. His pupil James R. Osgood
was to search in vain for the miracle of Midas.

Osgood's partners were the juniors of the previous firm — John
Spencer Clark, who like Osgood had come to Ticknor & Fields in
1855 and who had been admitted as partner in 1866, and Benjamin Holt Ticknor, clerk since 1860 and partner since the spring
of 1870. The traditions of the new house were almost as old as
those of any existing Boston publishing company; the partners
were sagacious and experienced. Youth was on their side. Osgood
and Clark were thirty-five; Ticknor, twenty-eight. Even though
the trade, especially in Boston, seemed at a dead level, even though
some wiseacres looked on the economic scene with jaundiced eye,
among them the economist David Ames Wells, predicting disaster,
the entrepreneurs were sanguine. As heirs to the Ticknor & Fields
list, they would surely prosper. In their catalogue were repre-

sented 250 authors whose titles numbered a thousand. The roll rehearsed the names of England and New England's great: Tennyson, Browning, Charles Reade, and Dickens; Hawthorne, Emerson, and Thoreau; Longfellow, Lowell, and Whittier. It also included new names of promise. From England, George Eliot, and in America, Thomas Bailey Aldrich, Henry James, Jr., and Bret Harte. In addition, among their standards was the 130-volume *British Poets,* edited by Francis James Child, purchased in 1866 from Little, Brown, the original publishers. The firm's stereotypes the partners valued at $200,000; their business for the month of December 1870 at $120,000. Osgood, Clark, and Ticknor were more than eager to assume Fields's capital stock. For half his interest they paid cash, the remaining $52,000 they guaranteed in twenty-one notes to be paid off with interest at 7 percent in eight years. Osgood and Clark carried the larger share of the purchase; Ben Ticknor's contribution to the new company, like Mifflin's and Scudder's to Hurd & Houghton, was $15,000.[2]

James Osgood could boast not only his distinguished list but also his impressive facilities which he and Fields had acquired in the years following William D. Ticknor's death. First had come the handsome quarters at 124 Tremont Street. Then, in 1868, Fields and Osgood had formed a partnership with their Cambridge printers, Welch, Bigelow. To the new organization, known as Welch & Company, its purpose bookbinding, each partner contributed $10,000 in capital stock. The venture proved profitable; within two years each partner had realized 100 percent on his investment. In 1869, so busy was Fields, Osgood, and so great was the need of speed, that a telegraph line, which required an act of the Massachusetts Legislature, was erected between the Tremont Street offices and those of Welch, Bigelow in Cambridge.[3]

Another expansion had been the opening of a small New York office. This proving inadequate, in April 1869, just before Fields left for Europe, his firm negotiated an agreement with E. P. Dutton. The latter was to leave his Boston location at the Old Corner Bookstore and open in New York at 713 Broadway a "first class bookstore." This done, Fields, Osgood would transfer its New York operations from 63 Bleecker Street to the Broadway building,

James R. Osgood, called by some of his friends the
"Boston Bantam," by others "Jamaica Rum."

Dutton to market Fields, Osgood publications, giving "special prominence to them and the firm-name . . . in their advertisements, show-bills, circulars, bill-heads, letter-heads, etc., and in the sign upon the building . . ." Fields, Osgood's stock to "occupy the most prominent place in said store." In addition Fields, Osgood was to have a ground floor office at an annual $2000 and Dutton was assured Fields, Osgood would keep him supplied with its publications, "not to be less than $10,000 net prices" at a 40 percent discount. Once Osgood was in control, he added to his firm's responsibilities by opening an office in Philadelphia.[4]

Another extension of interest of the new house was that of pictorial reproduction. In this Osgood and his partners were men of their times. Illustrations had become the concern of many publishing houses. Advances were being made in methods. Photographic processes were emerging for both lithographic stone and wood block which made possible mechanical rather than hand-copied work. The sometimes unsatisfactory efforts of the engraver or wood-carver in copying the original were being obviated. Concomitant with these improved techniques was public interest in art, an interest signalized in Boston by the establishment of the Museum of Fine Arts in 1870, and reflected in Fields, Osgood's publication of Thomas Bailey Aldrich's "Among the Studios" in *Our Young Folks*. Scudder's discussions in the *Riverside Magazine for Young People* of William Blake and the emerging American artist John La Farge also mirror this preoccupation. The public was "greedy of art knowledge," according to the *Literary World*.[5]

Among Osgood's artists was the engraver A. V. S. Anthony. Anthony and his wife rented Osgood's house at 71 Pinckney Street, the publisher retaining bachelor quarters there. During the Fields-Osgood partnership, illustrated books had begun to receive increasing emphasis. Following Fields's retirement, Osgood and Anthony organized the Chemical Engraving Company with offices also at 124 Tremont Street, Osgood as president, Anthony as treasurer. To supervise their process, they employed a Philip H. Mandel, binding him in a rigid contract which set a value of $20,000 on such knowledge as Mandel might acquire. The firm advertised, "By uniting and practically applying the various arts of Photography, transfer-etching, Zincography, Heliography, each of which has its separate use, this Company is able to produce artistic and commercial results in illustrations, which, for Quality, Rapidity, and Economy, are unequaled." Within three hours of receipt of drawings, reproductions could be completed.[6]

This process, to which Osgood claimed he had "devoted a large amount of capital," must earn its way. He made a careful survey and decided an educational series would afford the most profitable return and as a result he undertook to publish the Massachusetts Director of Art Education's drawing books. In his proposal to the author, Walter Smith, he wrote:

> And I will say to you *confidentially* that I have been for more than a year thinking seriously about going into the business and have been quietly looking over the field. In my judgment, the schoolbooks of the future have yet . . . to be made. Hitherto the books have all been controlled by the interest of the publishers and not the learners. Strong symptoms of a reform in the direction of common sense are apparent everywhere, and the publisher who recognizes it first and most readily profits by the recognition will be "in the first boat." A publisher untrammeled by any ties or traditions will not be at a disadvantage in such a case. Now I look on Walter Smith's Common Sense Series of Drawing-Books as a good pioneer in this ideal series.[7]

While negotiations were going forward for the Art Education Series, Osgood heard from Ben Ticknor, in London once again, that Gilbert & Rivington controlled a competing photomechanical process. For its exclusive use in the six New England states, the British firm asked an annual £250. An artisan skilled in photomechanics would be sent to Boston for an additional £50. Osgood accepted the offer of this Heliotype Process, as it was called. Its acquisition meant that he must secure steam presses for its operation. Since 124 Tremont Street was not suitable to handle heavy equipment, a new location must be found. During the months of search for an appropriate building, temporary quarters in Boston's warehouse district served Osgood's purpose.[8]

Perhaps the most rewarding contract Osgood secured for his heliotype was with the President and Fellows of Harvard College

for the exclusive right to reproduce the Gray Collection of Engravings. The object of President Eliot and his Fellows was "to
multiply faithful and cheap copies of those prints which by reason
of rarity or costliness are beyond the reach of most people, or which
are specially instructive as regards the development of the art of
engraving, or the personal history of engravers, or which, in general, would be of service in cultivating and refining the public
taste, if they were widely diffused." Osgood looked forward ex-
uberantly to "a democracy in art" and to that end promoted
"Heliotype Galleries," his hope — to place them in cities of the
North and West with populations in excess of 10,000.[9]

Such enthusiasm did not eliminate problems. His limitation to
the six New England states hardly afforded protection. Moreover,
his patent rights were open to contest. The owners of a competing
method, the Albertype, threatened suit for infringement. Then
other methods appeared which outclassed the heliotype in cheapness, clarity, and speed of reproduction. Osgood's pictures, while
excellent if the original had been vigorously engraved, were unsatisfactory if delicacy was characteristic of the subject. The Heliotype process thickened the lines. For the duration of his independence as publisher, Osgood remained faithful to his hard-won
method. To maintain it in the face of increasing competition
militated against his success as a publisher of belles lettres.[10]

The legal complications, the plant expansion, and the advertising costs resulting from Osgood's devotion to his heliotype required large capital outlay, secured either by cash or credit. So did
commitments to authors, among them those made by Fields during
his 1869 European holiday. When one considers that the pound in
these years was valued at $7, his promises appear exorbitant.
To Tennyson an annual retainer of $3500 with an additional
$3500 "for early sheets of any and every new work," regardless of
length; to George Eliot $2100 for a single poem which would run
eight and a half *Atlantic* pages. Nor did his munificent rates protect the authorized American publishers. Both Harper and Appleton ran *Edwin Drood* in their periodicals and hardly had Fields
returned to Boston than Harper brought out an edition of Tennyson, claiming it to be the only complete one. James T. Fields had

made a number of extravagant engagements. James Ripley Osgood, his apt pupil, was prepared to make even richer promises. Some he was unable to keep.

A number of these unkept promises are related to the four periodicals of the house (five if the annual *Atlantic Almanac* is counted). *Our Young Folks* had been launched by Ticknor & Fields in 1865; *Every Saturday* in 1866. The other two the firm had purchased, the *Atlantic Monthly* in 1859, the *North American Review* in 1864.

Our Young Folks had at its command that exceptional group of writers so often rehearsed. Longfellow, Lowell, Whittier, Higginson, and Harriet Beecher Stowe all wrote at least occasionally for the magazine. Less well-known writers, especially women, were eager to appear in its pages. Perhaps its most notable contributions to classic literature for children were Lucretia Peabody Hale's stories about the Peterkin family and the lady from Philadelphia, Dickens' "Holiday Romance," John Townsend Trowbridge's Jack Hazard series, and Thomas Bailey Aldrich's "Story of a Bad Boy."

By 1870, despite its repeated boasts of 50,000 or more subscribers, *Our Young Folks* was in trouble and when it came under Osgood's control he at once considered getting rid of it. Its subscription list was declining and in contrast to Hurd & Houghton's *Riverside Magazine for Young People,* its editorial arrangements were divisive and a constant headache to the partners. Howard M. Ticknor had been its managing or office editor from the start. Its announced editors, however, were John Townsend Trowbridge, Gail Hamilton, and Lucy Larcom. Gail's description of her duties makes clear her association with the periodical was loose indeed. "My connection with the 'New Magazine' will be as close as I choose to make it," she wrote a friend. "I shall have none of the labor to do, the scissoring, selecting, etc. . . . advice, you know, and opinion I am always ready to give without much urging." For these trivial duties, Fields first suggested a salary. Upon her refusing this, he offered and she accepted a yearly retainer of $500. That Gail took her duties lightly is apparent. She didn't even know that her name had been removed from the cover at the beginning of her quarrel with Ticknor & Fields. Howard Ticknor's justification was that when the agreement for the magazine had been drawn up, he had understood "that its ostensible editors were to be regular contributors, — supplying for its pages articles whenever wanted, as often as monthly." Gail retorted that at first she had made such contributions, but finding Ticknor held them for two or three months without printing, she thought he had better things on hand and therefore waited to be asked.[11]

Clearly by the time the new firm of Fields, Osgood was being contemplated, some changes were in order. Lucy Larcom was given a salary rather than a yearly stipend, Trowbridge was asked to assume Ticknor's managerial responsibilities, Elizabeth Stuart Phelps was offered $500 a year, provided she contribute to no other juvenile, and Mary Elizabeth (Mapes) Dodge, future editor of *St. Nicholas*, was announced as a contributor, "a little game," Gail thought, "to hush me up as much as possible, and show how hard it is to climb Fame's rugged steeps without their helping hand." The move to have Trowbridge assume the managerial post was initiated by Ticknor, who possibly sensed that Fields intended to rid himself of his Ticknor incubus. On September 8, 1868, he wrote:

My dear Trowbridge:—

Let me give you in writing the points which I suggested during our last interview, that they may be perfectly clear between us.

You to resume your connection with "Our Young Folks" on the old terms, and to be not only a contributor as constant as the wants of the magazine may require, but also to be — as you tell me you first anticipated being — an editorial assistant. In this latter capacity I should look to you not only to give me such suggestion & counsel as your observation and experience should dictate, but also to be so conversant with the general routine of the magazine after the acceptance of Mss that you could be my *locum tenent* during any absence of mine whether for a few days or a longer period. Of course, if I should, by any chance, make a long vacation, you might be called upon for a final decision in regard to some articles concerning which there was doubt after the first reading.

Here, I think, I have given you all the points succinctly, and you will soon be able, I hope, to let me know how you regard them.

Very truly yours
H. M. TICKNOR[12]

In October Howard Ticknor went on his long vacation, the firm changed to Fields, Osgood & Company, and Trowbridge became office editor with Miss Larcom his superior in judging manuscripts. The relationship was unsatisfactory. Miss Larcom rarely came to 124 Tremont Street. Indeed, by her own say, she "never met with Mr. Trowbridge." Neither Trowbridge nor Miss Larcom knew exactly what the responsibilities of each were. Fields and his partners found they must frequently exert themselves to secure contributions. In exasperation, they gave Trowbridge supreme authority in 1870. Miss Larcom, angered at her demotion, took offense that she was not consulted on matters of acceptance, illustrations, and layout. Trowbridge, for his part, found Miss Larcom's work less than competent. Her comments on manuscripts were so vague as to be of no help. He had to reread the submissions. Finally, in spite of the firm's pleas for economy, he felt himself forced to hire a third person (his wife) at an annual $1000.[13]

By the time *Our Young Folks* came under the imprint of James R. Osgood, it was a liability rather than an asset. Its cost of production almost equaled that of his adult magazines; yet it sold for only $2. Unable to rid himself of it, he tried to place it in the schools as a reader but that scheme failed. Not until the end of 1873 was he able to unload the burden. At that time he confessed to Roswell Smith of Scribner's that *Our Young Folks'* subscription list was only a hundred or so over 8000. And so it was that *Our Young Folks* readers combined with the *Riverside Magazine*'s "thousands" contributed to the affectionately recalled long success of *St. Nicholas*. Another of Osgood's periodicals met a less distinguished demise.[14]

Every Saturday was the brain child of Osgood and it was at his invitation that the "little New York poet" Thomas Bailey Aldrich came from Gotham to the fading Athens of America to serve as editor. Although Aldrich was only thirty, he had already acquired during ten years in New York considerable editorial and literary experience. He had seven books to his credit, four of verse, three of fiction, and he had served as assistant reader to two different publishers — Derby & Jackson and Rudd & Carleton. He had written bright paragraphs for that "Night-Blooming Serious," the

Saturday Press, served briefly as a war correspondent for the *Tribune,* acted as literary critic on the *Evening Mirror* and the *Home Journal,* and as managing editor of the *Illustrated News.* He had been accepted by New York's literary Bohemia. Even so, throughout his Gotham years he remained uncommitted, for as with Howells, Boston was his literary lodestone and he had laid siege in the beginning of his maturity. Even though he was acting as literary adviser to J. C. Derby, his first publisher, his second book he offered to James T. Fields, saying he was coming "to headquarters, for good advice," and suggesting that in his position as critic for the *Home Journal* he could "do more for the books which you so considerately send me than hitherto." Fields was not to be so won, and Aldrich's next six productions were published in New York, one by Derby, the others by Carleton. In 1860, encouraged by Lowell's acceptance of a poem for the *Atlantic,* Aldrich approached Fields a second time, pointing out that his two latest Rudd & Carleton volumes had sold 3000 and 2200 respectively. "What Cheer?" he asked. "It would be of such service to me." But no cheer came from the Old Corner, at least for a number of years.[15]

At last, in the spring of 1865, Ticknor & Fields agreed to publish a collected edition of his poems, the author to have 10 percent on sales, 250 volumes being exempt. Now Aldrich was heart and soul for the Boston house, reporting Gotham gossip as it might affect the interests of his new publishers. On June 2, 1865, he wrote Osgood of rumors of a new periodical which was expected to "dry up the 'Atlantic' in about two calendar months, the time to be measured by the clock in Messrs Hurd and Houghton's office."[16]

If New York planned a periodical which would cause an *Atlantic* drought, why should not Boston anticipate with a sprightly weekly and who better to serve as editor than the witty, sophisticated New Yorker, Thomas Bailey Aldrich? Fields was reluctant; Osgood persuasive. The nimble sixpence of the monthly could be quadrupled. The *Atlantic* was too slow in its course of being laid out, printed, proofread, bound, and shipped to compete effectively with its New York peers. Fields gave grudging consent but, at least until success was assured, the proposed weekly must be an eclectic, comparable to *Littell's Living Age,* with only an occasional poem or serial paid for. Early in November 1865, Aldrich was invited to Boston for an interview, and on the seventeenth, Osgood reported triumphantly the matter had been decided, T. B. A. was to be editor of the new weekly, his salary $1500. The New Yorker by way of Portsmouth, New Hampshire, with his finely waxed mustachios, his remote blue eyes, and his bride Lilian, moved from Carthage to Athens to live first on Hancock, the street from which Henry Oscar Houghton had once looked on Boston with wondering eyes, and then Pinckney in a little "cocked hat of a house." From here to 124 Tremont and his office next to William Dean Howells' was less than a ten-minute walk.[17]

For the first four years of his editorship, Aldrich felt himself a writer of perpetual leaders. At Osgood's request, he dutifully manufactured puffs *ad seriatim* and accepted with resignation articles, stories, and poems which Howells found "unavailable" for the *Atlantic.* Aldrich's selections from "the floating literature of Europe" proved caviar to the general. On the appearance of the first number, Richard Grant White wrote Houghton, " 'Every Saturday' promises to be a failure. It is neither fish, flesh, nor good red herring. Too heavy to be read as a paper not substantial or of permanent interest either in subject or style of article to be read as a review. What say you? The field is open. I am ready. I shall talk to Mr. Hurd. We should decide at once." Houghton was not a man to be so ordered. Moreover, he had in train plans for a juvenile magazine to rival Ticknor & Fields's *Our Young Folks.* That and his imported *London Society,* for the time being, would be enough for him.[18]

Although *Every Saturday* was not good red herring, in its first phase it achieved the respectable circulation of 25,000. However, Osgood and his partner John Spencer Clark appear to have agreed with White and other critics that the periodical lacked character. They wanted to have at least one adult magazine with pictures. When Fields gave a horrified "No!" to their proposal for the *Atlantic, Every Saturday* was their inevitable second choice.

During the time Osgood and Clark were scheming for *Every*

Saturday's change in format, Fields was still abroad. Their letter detailing plans was lost with the *Germania* when she went down at sea. In consequence the senior partner was in the dark until he arrived in London in the fall following his European tour. Then he learned from W. L. Thomas, publisher of the new London *Graphic,* what was afoot. The project was too far advanced for Fields to make changes had he wished to. Beginning with the first number for 1870, to appear in mid-December 1869, *Every Saturday* was to be of large quarto size, illustrated by such American artists as W. J. Linton, Winslow Homer. F. O. C. Darley, and Sol Eytinge, and advertised as an art journal. It would also carry illustrations from the *Graphic,* to be published simultaneously in England and America. To achieve this, the English publisher must send his casts from four to six weeks prior to publication. Trouble, perhaps unavoidable, resulted. Thomas failed to send a prospectus of his new magazine and Osgood had no idea what the plans for the British periodical were. A week before *Every Saturday* was to appear, some of the expected casts and none of the letterpress had arrived. Fields, Osgood had not the foggiest notion of the pictures' subjects and out of ignorance titles had to be invented. In desperation, Osgood ordered Ben Ticknor to add Thomas and his *Graphic* to his London responsibilities. More than Dickens hung in the balance.[19]

A weekly must be put together with more haste than a monthly. To speed production, Osgood ordered three machines in the process of development by Chambers Brothers of Philadelphia, each of a different size, the largest capable of folding twenty-four pages at once, sixteen printed on one sheet, eight on another; then it would "paste, trim, and inset same," producing in an hour 1800 copies. The invention, according to the *American Literary Gazette,* marked "an era in the publication of mammoth illustrated newspapers."[20]

In addition to illustrations this new *Every Saturday* was to have more English fiction than its predecessor had had, paid for at current prices for advance sheets. To follow *Edwin Drood,* Osgood secured from Charles Reade *A Terrible Temptation* at £5 an *Atlantic* page. He must have been aware of his gamble in asking

Reade for a serial. His *Foul Play,* which had appeared in the smaller *Every Saturday,* had been promptly pirated, and earlier his *Griffith Gaunt,* a tale of jealousy and bigamy, had caused a sensation in the *Atlantic,* demonstrating the "critical cackle" of which America was capable when its sense of propriety was pricked. In *A Terrible Temptation* Reade told the truth as he saw it: "that young men of fortune have all mistresses; that these are not romantic creatures, but only low uneducated women bedizened in fashionable clothes." The novel was at once attacked as indecent. It was nothing more than a "mass of brothel garbage." Such censure stimulated the pirates. Even as the tale was appearing in *Every Saturday,* Harper ran it in the *Weekly* and three other publishers sold 370,000 copies of the book. However, the effect on *Every Saturday'*s circulation was adverse, and in November 1871, Osgood wrote Reade that his *Terrible Temptation* had lessened his value to James R. Osgood & Company. In the future his rate would be but £3 an *Atlantic* page.[21]

This reduction of Reade's page rate was an economic necessity rather than a moral judgment. In the first year of his independence, Osgood had found the Maecenas was not the Midas touch. Fields's largess had foisted on his successors a number of liabilities. Osgood and Clark had created others. For survival retrenchment was essential.

Another intended attraction for *Every Saturday* was to have been George Eliot's *Middlemarch,* which Osgood had engaged in June 1871 for £1200, planning to have the novel start in November. However, by the time that drear month had arrived, the weekly's expense of production, its falling circulation, and the recession caused by the Chicago fire of the month before forced a change. Osgood cabled George H. Lewes, George Eliot's husband, that he had transferred the *Middlemarch* contract to Harper. *Every Saturday* was to return to its original format with the January 1872 issue. In Boston, he explained, experience had proved there was no demand for an illustrated journal. In New York, however, Harper claimed a circulation of 160,000 for its *Weekly* and at the time it picked up *Middlemarch,* it also bought *Every Saturday'*s wood blocks. "You know," Osgood wrote Trübner, "there has always been a warm rivalry between the two houses, and the transfer is as you will readily perceive one of the steps towards extinguishing any bad feeling." So much for Osgood's flier in illustrated journalism.[22]

Elinor Howells, in reporting the events to her sister-in-law Annie, wrote:

> I'll tell you a few particulars of the ending of *Every Saturday* — though I don't know certainly whether Will will like it. Don't tell anybody! Mr. Clark undertook to manage the paper, much to Aldrich's disgust, and managed it very extravagantly, — paying enormous sums for original illustrations, many of which he threw aside because they did not suit his fastidious taste — and besides the pictures he paid for a great deal of original writing for the paper — when the idea it was started on was that the plates of the English *Graphic* were to be used, and the reading was to be selected matter. Aldrich is thrown out of his place, his salary reduced one half, and he is now after January 1st to edit something like the old *Every Saturday* for Osgood and Co. Of course the Chicago crash was what finally killed the paper — but if it had been in good health it needn't have died. Will's account of Quebec which he wrote for E. S., and Shepard's illustrations, are on the firm's hands, and they don't know what to do with them. Everybody is disgusted with Mr. Clark. Anthony, the engraver, who received a large salary, and with whom Osgood boards, has also lost his place. Aldrich is now editing the paper alone until the first of January which closes its existence.[23]

Osgood's reduced *Every Saturday* ran for two years, its circulation when he finally rid himself of the burden something over 7000. Yet this was a respectable distribution compared with the three or four hundred of the *North American Review* with its annual deficit of $5000 to $6000. When Fields had failed to unload the quarterly on Edward Everett Hale and Henry Oscar Houghton in the fall of 1869, his next step had been to try to secure Henry Adams as editor to relieve the restive Lowell and ailing Gurney. Although Adams at first turned down the opportunity, by October 1870, urged by his family, he reluctantly indicated he would take on the *Review,* a bit of good luck for Osgood, who, already looking forward to becoming senior partner in his own firm, wrote his prospective editor:

> We gladly avail ourselves of your offer to assume the editorial contract gratuitously. There are two points however upon which we should like to come to an understanding with you before the matter is definitely settled. These are
>
> 1st   As to the payment of contributors during the present year. The gross amount paid to contributors has been $1994.50 or $664.83 per number. [For three numbers Ap–Oct.] We should prefer to place a stated sum at your disposal for each number. We suggest seven hundred and fifty dollars as the amount we are willing to appropriate in this way. We should send our checks, as now, to each contributor, taking your instructions as to apportionment of each.
>
> 2nd   Copy must be in our hands by the first day of the quarter. The number of pages limited to 240, or 15 sheets of 16 pages each.

Once Adams had accepted these conditions, Osgood notified James Russell Lowell, requesting he continue to act as adviser to the quarterly.[24]

From the start Adams offered his contributors $5 a page. This meant that to stay within Osgood's specified $750, in addition to editing, he must write many pages of the *Review* himself. He hoped ultimately to make the journal self-supporting. If that happened, he promised to quadruple his rates. He might possibly have realized his purpose had he not fallen in love, married, and gone abroad for a year's honeymoon. Before he left in 1872, the first three numbers of the *North American* were out, and he had "planted" the October issue. Lowell, too, departed for Europe, and Howells, now editor-in-chief of the *Atlantic,* was left with the onerous duties of layout, proofreading, and hounding authors for manuscripts. For future numbers, pending Adams' return, he looked for a subeditor. His choice was Thomas Sergeant Perry who, unfortunately for Osgood, was in no position to work for free in getting out the five issues required during Adams' absence. Perry's salary was probably small, but any additional call on Osgood's resources added a straw to the load of an already overburdened camel.[25]

The magazine most valuable to Ticknor & Fields in maintaining the reputation of the house and in securing authors for its list was the *Atlantic Monthly,* its circulation in 1869 at least 50,000. During 1870 that figure plummeted to 35,000. One reason for this dramatic drop was the competition from New York with its illustrated magazines, especially those of Harper. Even in Gotham the determination of this house to dominate took its toll. The weekly *Round Table* with a circulation between 4000 and 5000 folded in 1869; *Putnam's Magazine,* after a three-year struggle, its circulation never over 15,000, succumbed in November of the following year. Another reason for the *Atlantic's* ailing circulation was Harriet Beecher Stowe's "The True Story of Lady Byron's Life," which appeared in September 1869. That Mrs. Stowe should have been responsible for so great a falling off was ironic, for in 1857 at the time of the magazine's founding, the senior partner of Phillips, Sampson had been unwilling to give his support to the proposed periodical unless the firm's most popular writer could be secured as a contributor. Her cooperation assured, the *Atlantic Monthly* made its appearance in October of the panic year 1857, James Russell Lowell its editor, Henry Oscar Houghton its printer.[26]

Phillips in stipulating that Mrs. Stowe be secured as a contributor to the *Atlantic* hoped for a serial novel. Although she fulfilled the letter of her assent with two short pieces for the first volume, not until December 1858 did her next novel, *The Minister's Wooing,* begin its run. Phillips, Sampson were the logical American publishers for the book, but before Mrs. Stowe left for England to secure her English copyright in *The Minister's Wooing,* she had made arrangements with Derby & Jackson of New York and Brown, Taggard & Chase of Boston to issue the novel jointly. Perhaps she was aware of Phillips, Sampson's impending failure. On October 20, 1859, the day William D. Ticknor bought the *Atlantic* from the assignees of Phillips, Sampson, *The Minister's Wooing* appeared under the imprint of her new publishers.[27]

In her intention to secure English copyright for *The Minister's Wooing,* Mrs. Stowe failed. Sampson, Low & Company had anticipated book publication by issuing the novel in uncopyrighted monthly parts. However, to compensate for this failure, she had the fortune to meet James T. Fields, a meeting significant enough in her eyes to merit a change in her planned itinerary so that she could return to America aboard the *Europa* with the Fieldses and the Hawthornes. She quite frankly told Annie she wished to discuss business with Fields. Her reasons are obvious. So far, despite her popular acceptance, her experience with publishers had been nerve-racking. John P. Jewett, publisher of *Uncle Tom's Cabin,* despite the book's sensational sales, had failed. Phillips, Sampson had failed. Perhaps she sensed that both Derby & Jackson and Brown, Taggard & Chase were about to repeat the pattern. In any case, Ticknor & Fields now owned the *Atlantic* and she was a contributor. Fields, for his part, welcomed establishing rapport with this foremost of American female authors who to date had missed the protection of a solvent, well-managed house. As a result of this shipboard association, Ticknor & Fields secured the publishing rights to *Uncle Tom, Dred* (a title which Fields specified must be changed to one "more taking"), *The Minister's Wooing,* and other of her published works. On these, since she now owned the plates purchased from the assignees of the failed companies, Fields promised 18¢ a copy on sales; for new fiction, half profits. Under these arrangements her returns proved disappointing, as she found out when, piqued by Gail Hamilton's revelations, she requested a report on earnings. In five years (1863–1868) her share of profits on her books amounted to only $4515.14. However, even though the report included two new books, *Agnes of Sorrento* and *The Pearl of Orr's Island,* she was content. Fields had been generous both in rates for her contributions to the *Atlantic* and *Our Young Folks* and, "that she might write with a mind at leisure," in advances for her novel *Oldtown Folks,* paying her between 1865 and 1869 possibly as much as $13,000.[28]

When *Oldtown Folks* was to appear in 1869, Mrs. Stowe again wished to secure her English copyright and now, because of a change in English law, she could accomplish her purpose by being resident on British soil when Sampson, Low took out the copyright in London. A trip to Canada would suffice. For something to read during her brief exile, she took Countess Guiccioli's *Recollections of Lord Byron,* recently published in London and reprinted in this country by Harper.

In the United States, in consequence of the Fourteenth Amendment with its introduction of the phrase "male citizen," the years 1868–1870 were in ferment over Women's Rights. In January 1869 the first National Suffrage Convention was called in Washington. Thereafter local conventions were held in New York and other cities, including Hartford, where the Stowes lived. Also living in Hartford was Harriet Stowe's half-sister Isabella Hooker, who persuaded Harriet and her husband to act as delegates to the Hartford convention. To many, a woman's right to vote was of minor importance. At the heart of the struggle was a married woman's subjugation to her husband, be he sinner or saint. She had practically no control over her money earned or inherited. Her children belonged to her husband, drunkard though he might be. In the passing of the Thirteenth Amendment, Harriet had seen a paper victory at least for Uncle Tom and his descendants. The Fourteenth gave her a new crusade.[29]

Gail Hamilton in her *Battle of the Books* had chosen Sophia Hawthorne as her heroine, but all she had dramatized was that women should be more intelligent about their business affairs, that in these matters they should not trust to the chivalry of the male. Harriet Beecher Stowe intended a stronger message and la Guiccioli's adoring recollections of Byron gave her a case for her point, a mistress glorying in memories of an adulterer and waxing "eloquent in denunciation of the marble-hearted, insensible wife." Mrs. Stowe believed that Lady Byron had been justified in seeking separation from her profligate husband and in insisting on custody of their child. She wished to make clear that no young girl should entertain the romantic notion that in marriage her virtue would reform a wastrel. The Byron marriage proved her thesis. So universal was the double standard that a man taken in adultery served no warning. Perhaps a man taken in a worse crime would. She intended to show "the reasoning by which he [Byron] justified himself in incest." Her authority she regarded as impeccable, Lady Byron herself, who had confided in her years before.[30]

Mrs. Stowe expected her revelation to be a sensation and therefore wished it to be in the most telling form possible. She sent proof to Dr. Holmes, not for advice on content, but that he might study it to be sure her narrative was effective. She relied on William Dean Howells, in the *Atlantic*'s editorial chair during Fields's absence abroad, to take care of punctuation and other details of excellence which she held in contempt. Howells was harassed. The printers were at his back. He must get sheets off to England in ample time for Macmillan, with whom Fields had arranged for simultaneous publication, to prepare the article for its English audience. None of those experienced in publishing, none who had witnessed the shrieks of the proper raised by Reade's *Griffith Gaunt*, none knowledgeable in the taste of the times warned Harriet that her exposé would besmirch the skirts of a daughter of Lyman and a sister of Henry Ward Beecher. No one anticipated that proof would be asked. Indeed, Dr. Holmes thought her quotations from Byron's *Don Juan* and *Cain* sufficient substantiation. Howells, though weary of Mrs. Stowe's careless writing, her exasperating inaccuracies, thought the article ought to be published because "the world needed to know just how base, filthy and mean Byron was, in order that all glamor should be forever removed from his literature, and the taint of it should be communicated only to those who love sensual things, and no more pure young souls should suffer from him through their sympathy with the supposed generous and noble traits in his character." Fields, even though abroad, knew all about the article and had ample time to ward off the whirlwind had he thought printing unwise. Instead he wrote to Osgood:

> Mrs. Stowe's article on Byron which is to appear in the September No. should attract considerable attention, though the main fact of that paper has been for a long time known to certain circles in both Europe and America. Wendell Phillips many years ago revealed it to me as having been imparted to him by Lady Byron herself. I wrote you sometime ago that Macmillan will publish the article and pay £50 sterling for it. As I wrote this some letters back I hope you have sent him the corrected proofs already. He also and his particular circle knew all about the matter of Byron's guilt long ago.[31]

The September *Atlantic* and *Macmillan's* appeared in mid-August. The English magazine carried a foreword which concluded, "Towards so pure and lofty a character [as Lady Byron], *compassion* would be out of place but *justice* may be rendered, even after this lapse of time; and it is peculiarly gratifying to the Editor of *Macmillan's Magazine* that it should be rendered through these columns." Not Fields nor Macmillan, Holmes nor Howells, nor James R. Osgood was prepared for the virulent attacks on both Mrs. Stowe and her publishers which followed the appearance of the article. Osgood could find only three notices which mentioned "The True Story of Lady Byron" favorably and even these de-demanded proof. Worriedly, he urged Mrs. Stowe to produce a vindicating pamphlet as soon as possible, explaining that ". . . as the *Atlantic* has been assailed quite vehemently, I should like to be able to reply understandably for its sake as well as yours." Fields, in London, must have winced as he read the weekly attacks in the *Athenaeum,* in which the central thrust was the money both pub-lisher and author were making from the tasteless revelation. Piously the magazine prayed the author of *Uncle Tom's Cabin* had received no "honorarium," such money would be "filthy lucre," as tainted as Judas Iscariot's thirty pieces of silver. As for the thirty pieces, Osgood wanted his share and he wrote Fields suggesting a percentage of the sum Macmillan was to pay Mrs. Stowe belonged to Fields, Osgood as agents.[32]

Fields's worldly acceptance of Mrs. Stowe's "True Story" had by now suffered eclipse. He was staying at Gad's Hill, where he had heard Dickens declare Mrs. Stowe ought to be pilloried. He devoutly wished James T. had had nothing to do with the scandal. Fields replied in haste to Osgood's suggestion:

> It is imperative that Mrs. Stowe be paid all the sum which Macmillan paid for the Byron paper. A great point in the history of the affair will be made of the money she got for the story both from us & England & it will never do for us to appear as having divided the spoils. So do not fail to set this all right for ourselves. I dined with Motley last week & he fired up warmly against Mrs. S. & the money part of it. I can do nothing to help Mrs. S. out of the affair. Lushington will not speak and I have not heard any way devised for Mrs. S. to clear her skirts. At table the Tennysons who had all known Lady Byron and the Leighs were very hard in

their condemnation of Mrs. S. We come in of course for a great share of abuse and I fully believe we shall not go unscathed in certain circles. At breakfast a few days ago a daughter of Lord Elgin told me the children of Mrs. Leigh were heartbroken over the article.

If Stephen Lushington, Lady Byron's counsel at the time of the separation, would not speak, who could submit proof? Macmillan cabled that he would but in the end failed his promise. In her book *Lady Byron Vindicated*, Mrs. Stowe attempted proof, but all she could offer was a perfervid expansion of her *Atlantic* "True Story." The sophisticated, the men to whom the allegations were old hat, the after-dinner gossip of their clubs, remained aloof, even her publisher, James T. Fields.[33]

In *Uncle Tom's Cabin*, Mrs. Stowe had achieved a purpose larger than she had expected. She had set a nation on the march. With her Lady Byron article she achieved a result the reverse of what she intended. Blissful maidens continued to marry wastrels, editions of Byron flooded the market, and subscribers to the *Atlantic* stayed away in droves, a bitter fact which Fields and James R. Osgood had to face throughout 1870.

As plans for Fields's retirement took form, Osgood must have been troubled by the state of all the firm's periodicals and in particular that of the *Atlantic,* which for ten years had been serving as a subtle advertising medium for the firm. Fields agreed to continue as editor until July 1871 and the plans he and Osgood made for the year's volumes were calculated to bring it out of its Byron slump, were to contradict the New York sneer that only New Englanders could find space in its pages. In later years, William Ellsworth recalling his experience in the trade wrote that in 1871 ". . . of the three magazines, Harper's, The Atlantic, and the new Scribner's Monthly, certainly the Atlantic ranked first in literature." The two volumes were in truth impressive in promise. Writers whose names were associated with the periodical's beginnings were there — Holmes, Whittier, and Longfellow, but there were new names too, young writers just starting the long ascent: John Fiske with his studies of folklore and myth, Clarence Rivers King with his series on the high peaks of the west, John Hay with

Castilian Days, and in fiction, Howells with his first novel, *Their Wedding Journey,* Henry James, Jr., with "A Passionate Pilgrim" and *Watch and Ward,* and Bret Harte with three short stories. In this last was surely a writer to recover the *Atlantic's* lost subscribers and give the lie to the canard that the periodical was living on its past.[34]

Harte had first appeared in the *Atlantic* in 1863, recommended to Fields by Jessie Frémont, wife of the General. For the next six years as far as Boston was concerned, Harte ceased to exist. Then Susan Francis, office factotum for Fields, noted a story in the Californian *Overland Monthly* — "The Luck of Roaring Camp," and Fields shortly began angling, writing to Harte that if he had several more stories by him like "The Luck of Roaring Camp," Fields, Osgood would be pleased to make a volume, the terms, which Harte accepted, 10 percent on sales after 1000. *The Luck of Roaring Camp and Other Sketches* appeared in May 1870 and a second edition was promptly necessary. Fields now offered to publish Harte's poems at 10 percent, none exempted. He further suggested Harte write an *Atlantic* serial for $2000 with 10 percent on the resulting book. By this time, however, Harte had become a national figure. His "Plain Words from Truthful James" had appeared in the September *Overland Monthly* and Ah Sin, the Heathen Chinee, had entered the American idiom. To Fields, Osgood's offer, Harte countered with a request for an annual $6000, Fields, Osgood to have exclusive right to his periodical contributions. The firm protested it could not afford the price. Harte's *Poems* came out on December 22. Within five days Osgood reported, "We have already sold two editions of about 1100 each and have worked our way well into a third edition, which has some 1800 copies." By this time, Harte, dissatisfied with the *Overland Monthly,* had decided his fortune lay in the East. Receiving the news, Osgood urged Harte to make his first stop after the Berkshires in Boston. He hoped to boast of James R. Osgood & Company as Harte's exclusive publishers and to this end had started negotiating with G. W. Carleton of New York for Harte's *Condensed Novels,* published in 1867. Carleton's first proposition Osgood had thought too high, but now Harte was coming East, he reopened negotiations. Carleton replied to Osgood's new proposal in the language of Truthful James:

New York Dec 28 1870

My dear Osgood —
Yours of the 27th is recd. — My views upon the "Condensed Novel" question are "pensive and child-like, but plain
"Which the same I would rise to explain":
— When I first offered to sell you the plates of this book I did not much expect to print any more, & their value was comparatively trifling — so trifling that even *you* did not see fit to accept the first ridiculously low offer.

I waited a reasonable time for you to accept or decline the thing, and then, as Harte's reputation suddenly, almost rocket-like flashed out, I saw my property rapidly increasing in value, and very justly & honestly took advantage of it by withdrawing my offer, as you had not seen fit to accept it . . .

A bargain is a bargain only when both parties are contented at the time. If I sold you these plates now at the bagatelle price (which you evidently didn't consider them worth, or you would have jumped at them) I would be losing, and you gaining, enormously. The book is a real good book, & Bret Harte's popularity is so great just at this time, that either you or I could print from 3 to 5,000 at once, advertise it strongly as by the author of "Heathen Chinee" etc., and sell the whole edition in less than a month, at a profit of 1 to 2000 dollars — and with Harte's increasing reputation the plates would be a good paying property for a long time. There is an author's copyright of only 10 cents on each copy sold.

I prefer keeping the plates, but if you want them for $1000. *cash,* you may have them! This offer I keep *only three days.*

"— and my language is plain, which the same I am free to maintain."

Faithfully yours,
GEO. W. CARLETON

N. B.
I don't want you to think my estimate of value unreasonable — a precisely similar case is that of Loring's selling last summer over 10,000 of "Moods" (an apparently dead & buried book) on the strength of Miss Alcott's sudden popularity as author of "Little

Women" etc! My dear Osgood — the only thing I have to add to my long story . . . is, that I want your decision within 3 days, so if you decline, I can take advantage of the *tidal wave* and rush out a big edition of the book & *sell it* while your splendid book of Poems is making such excitement. You've made a *hit* with the Poems, & I hope you will make many hundreds of them as *J. R. Osgood & Co* Three cheers for J. R. O. & Co ! ! !

Although Osgood thought Carleton "peremptory" and "un-handsome," he met the terms, securing for his $1000 the stereotype plates, woodcuts, back stamp, and seventy-four copies of the book. The deal completed on January 3, 1871, Osgood was prepared to talk business with Harte.[35]

During the Harte family's two-week stay in Boston, conferences went forward in moments spared from a ceaseless round of parties. To his chagrin, Osgood found the man who the previous September had been willing to sign on for $6000, now, because of over-tures from New York, had grander ideas. Osgood had learned from Fields that the way to win was to pay and fearful of losing his prize he made an extravagant offer — $10,000 for the exclusive right to publish in his periodicals for one year twelve of Harte's poems or sketches, the year to begin March 1, 1871. Such munificence failed to startle Harte into immediate agreement. Rather he kept Os-good on tenterhooks, leaving for New York without committing himself. Not until March 8 was Osgood able to celebrate that Harte had decided "to join hands" with his new firm. Under-standably, he requested the terms be kept secret. However, such a sensational engagement could not be kept under wraps for long. The April 1 *American Literary Gazette* carried a note that Osgood had promised Harte $15,000 for the exclusive right to his work. "On dit," the *Gazette* reported, "that Harper offered Mr. Harte $10,000"; but that Osgood "went better" by $5000, this extra being guaranteed in royalties from his books.[36]

Osgood found he had signed on a procrastinator. Harte's first contribution, "Poet of Sierra Flat," did not appear until the July *Atlantic*. When nothing arrived for the August number, Osgood wrote in desperation, "I have forborne until now to press you, thinking that you must have cogent reasons for your silence. But we kept the August *Atlantic* open at considerable inconvenience and no small loss, and we're compelled after all to go to press without you . . . We must have whatever is intended for September before August 1st . . . It is a serious damage to both of us that you should not appear in the August number. We have announced you, and now the 'swing' will be broken and the effect bad." By the end of 1871, Osgood had received seven Harte contributions (but only after repeated letters and telegrams), five for the *Atlantic,* two for *Every Saturday,* for which he had paid $8333.33. More delays followed in 1872 and Osgood refused to make further payments until Harte came to Boston for a face-to-face talk. Not until September, six months after his contract had run out, had Harte fulfilled his engagement. Moreover, the quality of some of his contributions was not comparable to the writing which had earlier won him fame. The Maecenas touch had not served the *Atlantic* or Osgood as it had served James T. Fields.[37]

In the old days, it would have been the Fieldses with whom the Hartes would have stayed during their Boston sojourn; it would have been at Charles Street that the grand dinner of February 27 in the writer's honor would have been given, paid for out of Fields's expense account. But now things were different. Osgood kept bachelor quarters. The responsibility for this phase of the conquest of Harte fell to William Dean Howells and his wife Elinor. Howells had anticipated meeting Harte ever since the previous May when he had reviewed *The Luck of Roaring Camp* for the *Atlantic.* The two couples took to each other at once. The Howellses were delighted to find others of their own age with whom they were congenial and Elinor prepared with pleasure for the big party. To lighten the burden, she had a caterer, who for $1.50 a head provided linen, silver, and dishes as well as food. "Afterwards," she reported, "he and another man washed up the dishes and took them off — and by twelve o'clock all was quiet."[38]

Howells, still only assistant editor, was clearly preparing to assume command; playing host to Harte was but one sign. The announcement that he was to succeed Fields as editor of the *Atlantic* on July 1 appeared in the May 1 issue of the *American Literary Gazette,* which commented, "It seldom happens that a Western man emigrates to New England to instruct the inhabitants of that advanced region in purely aesthetic matters." Ten years before as an emigré from Ohio, Howells had thought he would be content to be "a linch pin in the Hub." Now he was to captain the *Atlantic* under the imprint of James R. Osgood. Yet his books were in the hands of another house — Hurd & Houghton of New York.[39]

Howells' relationship to his publishers had been anomalous ever since he had come to Boston as assistant to Fields in 1866. At that time he had just arranged with Hurd & Houghton for publication of his *Venetian Life*. When this proved a success, Hurd feared his new author might be won to another house, Ticknor & Fields, possibly. Howells, however, was reassuring, protesting he had no intention of leaving the Houghton establishment, and the firm brought out his next two books, *Italian Journeys* and *Suburban Sketches,* both made in part from his contributions to Fields's *Atlantic*. His relationship with Hurd & Houghton was however an uneasy one. He was critical of their sales accounting for *Venetian Life*. Then when he offered a long poem, which since it had been stereotyped he thought should bring him 20 percent, the firm, at first interested, then dilatory, finally decided against the venture. Next Hurd was critical of his title for his second book which Howells proposed to call "The Road to Rome." Howells thought his publisher stupid not to realize it had nothing to do with Catholicism but came from the proverb "All Roads Lead to Rome." Not until some of his Cambridge friends, one of them Longfellow, had convinced him that his title would certainly suggest religion, did he reluctantly substitute "Italian Journeys" as the title. Finally, Hurd took exception to a passage in "Como," a chapter of the book, in which Howells wrote with passion of a small boat in that far lake flying in 1862 the "insolent banner" of the South. Hurd wished the passage deleted. Howells refused, writing:

> . . . I would very willingly exclude from the book the passage you think disadvantageous, if I could conscientiously do so. It is pretty well known, wherever I am known, that I am an abolitionist of the most deadly sort, and I am afraid it is too late to reform. I do not believe you will sell one copy the less because of the

paragraph, and I trust our literature will never again be subject to the ignorant prejudices of the South. In fine, I cannot do what I should do my best to destroy another writer for doing, and I hope you will look at the matter in another light.

In the end it was Howells, not Hurd, who looked at the matter in another light. Three days later he modified his position, sending a revision and writing, "In this, without changing the sentiment as to the rebellion, I remove what refers to the private troubles of the Southerners, and I think this is all that can be asked. The allusion to the Southern flag is not dragged into the article, according to my thinking, but is a part of the history of the time, and ought to stand for a record of the universal feeling among loyal Americans abroad in that year." Despite these evidences of friction, Howells allowed Hurd & Houghton to publish *Suburban Sketches.* This was in 1871 and certain Osgoodian changes were in the making.[40]

Fields had engaged Howells as assistant on the *Atlantic* because of his experience as printer and consequent skill in reading proof. By 1868 Howells had shown he could do proof, punctuate and spell for Mrs. Stowe, write reviews for the *Atlantic,* and at the same time produce two successful books for a rival house. Fields raised his assistant's salary from $50 a week to an annual $3500. Although this amount covered his contributions to the magazine, Howells was pleased, feeling his ability as a writer had been recognized. Yet he was in no sense in control of the periodical, even when Fields was abroad. In a general way everything had been laid out before the publisher left for his holiday and Howells was expected to send a diary of his execution of responsibilities.[41]

From any point of view Howells' position was unsatisfactory, not only for him but for the publishing houses with which he was associated. Osgood intended that under his aegis affairs would be conducted differently. He raised Howells' salary to $5000 and in May 1871 proposed to Houghton that the plates and publishing rights for Howells' three books be sold to him. Henry Oscar Houghton was slow to respond. Fields had taken the printing of the *Atlantic* from him in 1864. Now, seven years later, Fields's successor sought to capture his most distinguished living author. Not until September was the imminent loss of Howells known to

Houghton's intimates, not until March 1872 had the details of purchase and contract been worked out. Long before, however, the
printer had probably accepted the inevitable. Howells' first novel,
Their Wedding Journey, had started its run in the July 1871 *Atlantic.*[42]

In November Howells engaged with Osgood for the novel's publication. The conditions of the contract, with one exception, were
standard, 10 percent on all copies sold. The exception is curious, if
not prescient. Introduced into the printed contract was a hand-
written clause specifying that if James R. Osgood & Company went
bankrupt, Howells would have the right to purchase the stereotypes at fair valuation. If Howells did not wish to purchase, the
plates could be sold for mutual benefit, a curious provision since
Howells had had no experience with bankrupt publishing houses.
He was aware, however, of the experience of other writers, Mrs.
Stowe among them, with failing houses. He also had seen James R.
Osgood's startling participation in the New York Trade Sale of
September 1871.[43]

Osgood's position in the first two years of his company's existence was rich with promise. He had a unique list of established
authors, both English and American; gifted youthful authors were
also his. He had commodious offices at 124 Tremont Street, a
happy arrangement in New York with E. P. Dutton, and in Philadelphia another distributing center. His company was not cozily
sitting on its inheritance. Rather it was pressing ahead with the
vigor of a new firm. As well as the essential standards, it had a
new line of educational books and one of the most advanced
methods of pictorial reproduction. For editors it had men of remarkable gifts, two — William Dean Howells and Henry Adams
— destined to leave their ineradicable mark on their own generation and those to follow. In the 1870s neither Harper with its
Henry Mills Alden and George William Curtis nor Scribner with
its Josiah Gilbert Holland had men of comparable stature. These
houses however had something which Osgood had not — large financial resources. At 124 Tremont Street the need for ready cash
was pressing. One way to raise it was to sell the firm's publications
at excessive discounts.

Trade Sales, a part of the publishing scene since the early days of the century, by the time of the Civil War had become an accepted method of circulating books beyond the centers of their origin. Ticknor & Fields had taken part in them for years. In 1835 William D. Ticknor had joined the Boston Publishers and Booksellers organization, one purpose of which was to regulate the conduct of such sales held at that time in Philadelphia, New York, and Boston. By 1870 New York had become the center. To take part was not unusual. The custom offered a ready way to move stock and raise cash. Osgood's participation in 1871 would hardly merit comment, save for his spectacular invoice, "of a magnitude never before offered," according to the *American Literary Gazette*.[44]

In retail value this invoice amounted to at least $130,000, possibly more. Osgood revealed his excited concern to George A. Leavitt, the New York auctioneer, in his letter of July 13, 1871. Across the top of his letter, Osgood scribbled in haste, "Our sales ought to nett $60,000."

Whatever this sale, and another in April 1872, netted his firm it was not enough, any more than were his economies in returning *Every Saturday* to its original size and eclectic purpose. Particularly troublesome were his English interests. Spalding & Hodge, from whom he imported paper, were demanding more than 5 percent on his £15,000 debt. His limited control of the heliotype process was far from satisfactory, and, worst of all, the reputation of James R. Osgood & Company as heirs to Ticknor & Fields was in eclipse. As Fields had feared, Mrs. Stowe's article had tarnished the reputation of the house. Moreover, Julian Hawthorne had been talking. Knowledge of the firm's niggardly treatment of Nathaniel's heirs was common gossip. "Several leading authors and publishers" had assured Julian and his sisters (Sophia had died) that 12 cents a volume had been much too low. Alexander Strahan had expressed "indignation, rather than surprise . . . at the few details related of the action of your late Partner in Business, Mr. Fields," Julian reported, demanding 15 percent on the remains of his father's writings. Tennyson too was restive. James T. Fields had more than once demonstrated the miracles worked by the personal touch. For Osgood, in 1872, a trip to England was indicated.[45]

He left in midsummer to return by the end of September, pleased with his accomplishments. He had reached an understanding with Spalding & Hodge, had secured United States control of the heliotype at an eventual cost of over £1900, and just before he left, Tennyson had written, ". . . I am glad to assure you that our arrangements of today seem to me to be satisfactory, & that the small cloud which lately hovered over us has been altogether dissipated." Osgood was hopeful as he looked forward to the closing quarter of 1872. November and December were Midas months for the trade.[46]

VIII

"THE ROUND TABLE IS KINDLING WOOD"

FOR HOUGHTON, the five years following the 1872 reorganization of his company were years of acquisition and expansion. For James R. Osgood, except for his heliotype, they were of divestment and contraction. As a salute to the future and in celebration of the past, in 1873 on Houghton's fiftieth birthday a fountain in his honor was unveiled on the front lawn of the Riverside Press. In September of that year he became publisher of the *Law Times*. Two months later he acquired Osgood's *Every Saturday* and *Atlantic Monthly*. At the same time Osgood sold *Our Young Folks* to Scribner. In 1874 Houghton negotiated a printing contract with the Federal Government and took over the list of the New York publisher Albert Mason. In 1875, a crucial year, Osgood sold to Louis Prang his stereotype plates and publishing rights to Walter Smith's drawing books and to C. J. Little his shares in Welch & Company. Houghton, on the other hand, won another government contract, added the *American Naturalist* to his collection of periodicals, bought from J. B. Ford & Company the rights to Knight's *Mechanical Dictionary,* and purchased additional acreage for Riverside, a purchase made necessary by his contract with the lithographers Armstrong & Company. At the same time Osgood, in an effort to stop competition in heliotype methods, bought from its owner the rights to the Rockwood Photo-Engraving Process. In the following year he started the *American Architect and Building News,* a weekly with numerous heliotype illustrations. In this year of national celebration, Houghton secured the contract for the program of the Centennial Exhibition at Philadelphia, a million being estimated as the number required.

The Centennial over, he acquired the stereotype plates, publishing rights, and goodwill of Crocker, Brewster, thus gaining for his firm a strong line of educational books and a lineage dating from 1818. The following year he added the *Boston Medical and Surgical Journal* to his periodicals, bought from Osgood the plates and publishing rights to the many-volumed *British Poets,* and from the Church brothers of New York, the subscription list, goodwill, and rights of the *Galaxy.* During these five years Houghton also purchased at the semiannual Trade Sales, in which Osgood participated with increasing desperation, numerous of Osgood's rights and stereos. In 1878, James R. Osgood Company and Hurd & Houghton merged to become Houghton, Osgood. The tanner's son had become successor to William D. Ticknor and James T. Fields.

This shift in the balance of publishing power was in part inherent in the character of the two men. Houghton, the older, tall, gauntly handsome, severe, yet humorous, was the epitome of a man of substance. Happily married and religious, he was devoted to his family and his church. He had served his community as well as his business, rising through lesser offices until elected Mayor of Cambridge in 1872. His part in the founding of the Boston Museum of Fine Arts and his trusteeship of the Boston University Law School further revealed interests wider than his press and publishing house. As his business grew, "his native passion for thoroughness" infected those who worked with him, as did his understanding of the meaning of loyalty. Because of his years of childhood privation and his rugged experience in the ascent from the Dickinson Type Foundry to his present eminence, he was "forearmed against . . . over confidence." Osgood lacked such armor. Bachelor, clubman, and bon vivant, so fond of parties that having no excuse he would invent one in order to have his gay friends with him, in a time of economic collapse he was vulnerable. Everyone liked him for his laughing, genial, generous ways. Although recurrently racked with rheumatism, he was persistently ebullient, impulsive, enthusiastic, optimistic. Tomorrow, he believed, would afford the golden opportunity.

Other forces also played a part in the changed relative positions of the two publishers. One was a man — Charles Fairchild — junior partner in the firm of S. D. Warren, paper manufacturer. In addition, two events contributed their weight to alter the balance — the Great Boston Fire of November 9, 1872, and the September panic of 1873 with its ensuing depression.

With unconscious irony in the October 1867 number of *Our Young Folks,* in one of those articles of entertaining and useful knowledge so characteristic of the juvenile publications of the time, James M. Bugbee described the Boston Fire Department. He wished his little readers to take pride in its ultramodern equipment, its telegraphic alarm, with central offices atop the new City Hall on School Street, its eleven steam fire engines, its ten hose carriages, its three hook and ladder companies, its "stout, good-natured horses" to whom the gong in the station house was "as the bugle to the war-horse," and its fire hydrants which supplied water "at the rate of six hundred gallons a minute." He pictured the Chief Engineer, white-hatted and rubber-coated, trumpet in hand, as monarch of the scene. "He holds absolute sway," Bugbee told the children. "He can break into buildings, smash doors and windows, blow up walls, and compel any citizen in the vicinity to help in extinguishing the fire or carrying out goods." To show the department in action, he pictured a fire as breaking out on Congress Street, "centre of a large block stored with combustible materials." Before the fire is conquered, three alarms have been sounded and the entire force of two hundred and seventy-five men is battling the blaze. ". . . the eleven engines are throwing six thousand gallons of water a minute . . . Presently the roof falls in, carrying with it the upper floors. There is a momentary pause, and then the firemen make a desperate onset, before the flames have time to gather strength again. The fire is now in a position to be played upon with full effect, and the result is no longer doubtful. After a few feeble attempts to raise its head, it falls back utterly defeated and crushed. Some of the engineers are detailed to play upon the ruins for a while, and others are sent home . . . That is the way they put out fires in Boston." Since Boston's fire alarm telegraph had been adopted by "all places of any consequence," never again, Bugbee predicted, would a fire occur to equal in destructiveness the New York one of 1835 "when six hundred and forty-eight houses were burned, with eighteen million dollars' worth of property." Bugbee's prophecy was made in 1867.[1]

Four years later, to the month, Mrs. O'Leary's cow kicked over an oil lamp and most of Chicago went up in flames. Property destroyed totaled $200,000,000. Fifty-four American fire insurance companies were ruined and the insured were lucky to be paid three cents on the dollar. A year before, Lloyd's of London had warned Chicago that because of its crowded tinderbox construction, the firm would write no insurance on property there. A similar warning, seconded by the city's board of engineers, had been given Boston. The report stressed that in the business district bounded by Washington, State, Atlantic, and Summer Streets, there would not be enough water to fight the flames should a conflagration occur. In this district, in addition to warehouses for a variety of businesses, were concentrated those of the paper manufacturers. Here also were printers, publishers, and booksellers. The city fathers paid no heed to the warning, nor to a premonitory fire that broke out in the shop of Lee & Shepard, booksellers and publishers, in March 1871, causing a loss of $10,400. In this case the fire was confined, Bugbee's faith in Boston's fire department confirmed.[2]

Neither Bugbee nor the city fathers, nor indeed the fire department itself, were prepared for a peculiar epidemic that struck the horses of the nation in 1872, a crippling but nonfatal complaint, "influenza catarrah," or "epizootic" as it was called. In Boston the disease was exceptionally severe.

For citizens unconcerned with public safety, the "epizootic" and the inconvenience it caused inspired comment, not anxiety. Gail Hamilton noted that although Hamilton was slow to follow Boston fashion, by November it was in style; all local horses were sick in their stalls. The Reverend Hale prayed for the day when American inventiveness would free man from dependence on the unreliable horse and from Roxbury Francis Garrison reported:

> This extraordinary horse epidemic puts us all on our taps, & a
> good many people are discovering for the first time that they

really have legs & are able to walk. I enjoy my morning walk over [to the Riverside Press] & never tire of the lovely views of Parker's, Aspenwall & Corey's Hills from Francis St., the woods by Longwood Creek, the glimpses of Brookline Village with its spires & Town Hall, and the quiet, retired Longwood estates with their noble trees & green lawns & hedges, not to mention the glorious bay which sparkles in the morning sun between me & the city . . .[3]

Chief Damrell of the Boston Fire Department could afford neither Gail Hamilton's sarcasm nor Garrison's pleasure in scenic walks. With all but two of his ninety or more horses incapacitated, he prepared for the worst. He doubled his force of fire fighters and to the amusement of sidewalk loiterers, put the men to work practicing drawing the steamers, the hook and ladder equipment, and the hose carriages through the narrow crooked streets.[4]

Saturday, November 9, was a beautiful day for the penultimate month of the year, clear and bright with a gentle northwest breeze. At dusk the sun illuminated the Charles with exceptional brilliance, the moon came up, and quiet settled on Boston's business district. Then at 7:24 the attendants in the fire alarm office atop City Hall were startled by a Morse Code message from firebox 52. A six-story granite building on the corner of Summer and Kingston Streets was afire. Chief Damrell was on the scene within ten minutes, but there was delay in sounding a general alarm. Finally all the church bells of Boston clanged the fearful news. Before any equipment, pulled laboriously by panting men, reached the scene, the fire was out of control, nor could it be contained for eighteen hours, even though help came from as far as fifty miles. Over seven hundred buildings, the majority brick and granite, were destroyed; property loss reached an estimated sixty to seventy million dollars. By Sunday night the area between Summer and Pearl Streets, Washington Street and Atlantic Avenue, was a mass of twisted, smoking ruins and a dun brown veil hung over the city.[5]

In Roxbury the Garrisons heard the bells of Boston. From his mother's sitting room Francis "could see the dreadful flames leaping & spreading through the night, while every now & then would come the deep boom of an explosion as some building was blown up to stay the progress of the flames . . . Distinct above all [he heard] the hoarse puffing of the multitudinous steam engines . . . The whole sky was aglow, & every object for miles around lighted by the flames."

Eleven days later Garrison described the devastation to his sister.

Think of standing on Washington St., opposite Franklin, & looking across a desolate waste of ruins to the shipping in the harbor, or at the corner of Chauncy & Summer Sts., & seeing Liberty Square & Kilby St! . . . We are not yet over our panic . . . Every time the fire bells strike people start & turn pale, stop & listen. The fire in State St. Block night before last was an ugly one & required two or three hours hard work from the entire Fire Department, with help from Charlestown & elsewhere, to subdue. Tonight as I came home three alarms were struck in quick succession, again calling out the entire force, & we could see the fire

Franklin Street view of the destruction caused by the Great Fire of 1872.

plainly from here, though just where it was we don't yet know. Somewhere downtown. The flames were subdued in half an hour fortunately.[6]

But flames can do serious damage in half an hour. The alarm Garrison heard was for Rand, Avery, whose printing establishment spared in the fire of the ninth was running round the clock to keep up with work which had devolved on it because of the burning out of 23 printers. Although the destruction caused by these November fires was less than that of the big Chicago burn, the ruin of 960 businesses affected almost everybody. Even the Riverside Press, secure in its position across the Charles, lost $5000 in plates sent into Boston because of excess business. Among the largest losers were the paper makers, their combined loss being estimated at $3,250,000. Amongst the printers, Rand, Avery's fire was the most costly, at least as far as this narrative is concerned, for here were being printed Hale's *Old and New,* various Osgood books, and his Holiday Edition of *Every Saturday.*[7]

Osgood's offices on Tremont Street were above the fire line and the bulk of his stereotype plates was with Welch, Bigelow in Cambridge. However, in the fire of the ninth he suffered a direct loss of $30,000 in presses, plates, paper, and stock located in various warehouses, printing offices, and binderies in the city. He at once sought indulgence from his creditors. The Rand, Avery fire of the twentieth forced him to more urgent appeals.

> Since I wrote you last week [he reported to his London agent, Nicholas Trübner] we have had nothing but fires, two or three *per diem* having been the rule. The night before last (20th) our largest printing office (Messrs. Rand, Avery & Co.) was almost entirely destroyed. A very large quantity of our property was burned, but as we had taken extra precautions respecting insurance since the great fire of the 10th [sic] we hope and think our loss is fully covered. — i.e. our direct loss. The indirect loss from such a fire can never be estimated in money. The effect of the great fire upon business has so far been more or less disastrous. You know that the book business is almost the first to feel a great public calamity, and this calamity is one not confined to Boston alone, but is a national calamity quite as serious in its business

aspects as was that of Chicago. It caught *us* in the season of the
year when we feel it most severely, the suspension of business for
the months of November and December necessitating our carrying over into the New Year an immensely heavy stock. At present
writing it is not possible for us to say what our position will be
in January towards our maturing obligations for the first six
months of 1873. It is certain however that we shall be compelled
to ask our principal creditors the extension of a part of our liabilities. Our present feeling is that we shall need an accomoda-
tion of twelve months on one half of our indebtedness: and our
leading creditors here are entirely willing to meet us in any reasonable request we may have to make. Will Mr. Spalding do the
same? I think he will, as our indebtedness to him has been diminished over Five Thousand Pounds, since we made a similar
request last year. In October 1871 we were owing his house between £15,000 to £16,000: now it is a little over £9,000.* If you
can arrange with him to postpone £5000 until 1874 paying
alternate notes as they mature & giving new bills at 12 months
for others we shall be glad to do so, paying seven per cent interest . . .

* exact amt £9,449.10.6.[8]

During the first six months of 1873, trade was dull in Boston,
but by June, Osgood's publicity releases belied the "nothing doing
complaint." His Mrs. Whitney's *The Other Girls* had sold over
10,000 and Howells' *Chance Acquaintance* and Celia Thaxter's
Among the Isles of Shoals were on the "top wave of success."
Despite these visible signs of prosperity, the indulgences he had
secured had postponed rather than solved his problems. His need
for cash continued harassing. Even so, he had begun negotiations
to change his location from Tremont Street to the new business
section Boston was building in its burnt-out district. Here, on improved and widened avenues, were to rise "handsome, more substantial, durable, and secure structures." He intended his offices
should be in this rebuilt area in a building which could adequately
and safely house his heliotype equipment. The heavy inventory
left on his hands because of the November fires was an embarrassment. Somehow it must be turned into cash. At the April Trade

Sale he disposed of 20,000 volumes and in September of an invoice so large an entire day was devoted to his consignment alone. Among the bidders at these sales, in addition to the regular retailers and publishers, were the "book-butchers," men intent on attracting custom to their stores by bargains in books — setting prices far below the usually accepted retail price. Two who bought largely of Osgood's publications were A. W. Lovering of Boston and R. H. Macy of New York. Six days after Osgood's 1873 September sale, the forebodings of David Wells and other dismal scientists came true. Jay Cooke & Company of Philadelphia suspended payments, twenty-three other banks followed suit, and the New York Stock Exchange closed for twelve days. Osgood was forced to seek relief in a special December Trade Sale.[9]

Osgood's authors and friends watched in consternation his behavior in this year of crisis, finding it "fearful and ruinous," but few were prepared for the late November news that he was shedding three of his periodicals — *Our Young Folks* to Scribner, *Every Saturday* and the *Atlantic Monthly* to Hurd & Houghton. At the same time he attempted to unload the *North American Review*, offering it to Godkin of the *Nation*, but his price — $10,000 — was too high and the incubus remained his for a few more years.[10]

In the *Every Saturday* deal, no money changed hands. However, according to the Memorandum of Agreement, Osgood retained the right to select and subsequently publish or dispose of fiction running in the 1874 volumes. As a result of this arrangement he was able to sell to Henry Holt Thomas Hardy's *Far from the Madding Crowd*, a "catch" for Holt according to the *Publishers' Weekly*. Aldrich, if he chose, was to remain editor for a year. At the time, he reported cheerfully to Bayard Taylor that although he felt cut adrift having been associated with Osgood for nine years, he expected his light stories would keep him afloat. All the magazines, he boasted, were after him. With this surety, he did not choose to stay with the doomed *Every Saturday* for a full year, and in September Houghton sold for $2500 the subscription list and goodwill of the magazine to *Littell's Living Age*, specifying that the periodical be continued through October. Aldrich retired to his country place in Ponkapog, freed from the editorial mill for the next six years.[11]

Osgood's price for the *Atlantic* was $20,000 cash. Hurd & Houghton did not have that amount available. The money to consummate the bargain was provided by S. D. Warren & Company through the agency of Warren's junior partner, Charles Fairchild. Such assistance was consistent with that which Warren had provided Houghton ever since they had become business associates in producing Webster's unabridged for the Merriams. Fairchild, even as his partner, S. D. Warren, admired Houghton's business acumen and integrity. On the other hand, he was a close friend and drinking companion of James R. Osgood and his knights of the quill — Aldrich, Samuel Clemens, and William Dean Howells. Osgood received his $20,000 cash all right. What he possibly did not know was that his boon companion Fairchild had supplied the purchase price. Young Mifflin, with whom Houghton discussed the matter, considered Fairchild's dealing both "curious" and "outrageous."[12]

Although Houghton now had the periodical for which he had waited, he had not by its acquisition secured the authors who maintained the *Atlantic*'s reputation. Clause 3 of the purchase agreement made a number of conditions. Osgood was neither to start nor invest in another magazine for five years, and in the words of the document, "It is especially agreed that this transfer of the magazine does not carry with it or imply any transfer of the right of publication of books by authors who write for said magazine." An additional stipulation was "that neither party without the written consent of the other party offer more than ten per centum of the retail price to authors for books growing out of articles contributed to said magazine." In other words, Houghton might hope for trade books only from *Atlantic* authors not already in Osgood's stable. The great New England group nurtured by Ticknor & Fields was to remain with James R. Osgood & Company as were the newer writers, unless of course they sought greener pastures, something Hurd & Houghton could not offer because of the 10 percent royalty limitation.

And so it was that Osgood continued to publish books that made literary history — Howells' *A Foregone Conclusion,* Henry James's *Roderick Hudson* and *The American,* and Aldrich's *Prudence Palfrey.* Because of his inherited reputation, he also readily secured of the new writers for the *Atlantic* those he wanted, among them Sarah Orne Jewett with her *Deephaven.*

Now that the *Atlantic* was Houghton's even if its authors were not, once again the periodical's offices were set up at the Riverside Press. But Howells did not relish his walks across the dreary, lonesome Cambridge flats from his house on Concord Avenue as Lowell so many years before had found joy in his strolls along the Charles. Although Howells assured his friends the change in ownership would make no difference in the magazine, that Hurd & Houghton had promised him autonomy in its conduct, an era had come to an end and he knew it. Early in 1874, Osgood's new offices at 131 Franklin Street were ready. With their magnificent plate glass windows, the rooms were "light and airy as a spring day." His floor area was one fourth again as large as that at

The new Franklin Building at 131 Franklin Street, which became the headquarters for James R. Osgood & Company in 1874.

Tremont Street; now Osgood had space to house safely his twenty-two heliotype presses and storage vaults built to accommodate $300,000 worth of stock. The building at 124 Tremont Street, which ten years before had seemed with its Elizabethan embellishment the latest thing in publishing offices, was let out for other uses. Howells, who in 1860 had said, "Better fifty years of Boston than a cycle in New York," now wrote to his former companion-in-arms, Aldrich, "Isn't it odd to see old 124 turned into a china shop? After flattening my nose against the familiar window for the more intimate inspection of a lady in Parian and very little else, I went down to the corner of Federal and Franklin, and felt myself an exile there. Aldrich, the charm is broken . . . another cycle is completed, the Round Table is kindling wood."[13]

Houghton believed in partnerships. Their usefulness had been demonstrated in his quarter century of business experience. Now, at fifty, he had four partners and his workers were sharers in the profits of his firm. He would have liked much to have his editors also sharers, believing that an understanding of profit and loss, of overhead and labor would make them even-handed in their dealings with authors, sympathetic with the side of the business which must pay the promised price for an article, the assured royalty on a book. Such understanding was to be denied him. Editors of his day looked with disdain on the money-grubbing necessity of business. William Dean Howells, astute in making his own publishing arrangements, shuddered from being on that side of the desk which seemed to require him to be in league with the managers rather than with his brothers and sisters, the writers.

During Lowell's years as editor of the *Atlantic,* this separation of literature and silver had become well established. The editor chopped off and reassembled the living words of the writer; the business office paid the blood-money. When Howells became editor-in-chief under James R. Osgood, the promise of routine rates was in his hands; for exceptional engagements, such as that made with Bret Harte, the publisher conducted the negotiations. One of the merits of such an arrangement was that the editor could throw the blame on the counting room even when he himself agreed with the money-changers that the measured word was not worth the price. One of the faults of the system was that it produced an ever widening gulf between the literary worker and those who must estimate his value in dollars and cents.

Howells' struggles with his contributors over price as related to Houghton began early in 1874. Aldrich, now a free lance, entered the lists with an eleven-stanza poem which would fill just one *Atlantic* page. He wanted more than Howells' offered $75, even though the editor explained, "I don't think I'd better ask more than $75 for it. 'H.O.' would be sure to kick at $100, and $75 is $25 more than Taylor got for ["The Two Homes"] a longer poem. Stedman's ["The Lord's-Day Gale"] was $100 — 3½ pp. — his own price." Aldrich's answer was to place his contribution elsewhere. Caught between the grindstones of Houghton's estimate of value and the author's importunity, Howells was in a painful position. Later Aldrich submitted a group of poems, asking $300 for the lot.

> My dear Aldrich: [Howells wrote]
> I spoke with the owners about the poems, and they seemed to think $300 a good deal for them, as it indeed is when you consider that Lowell got $400 for his Agassiz 11 pages long. But I don't want to beat down a brother bard, and so I suggest that you somehow eke out eight Atlantic pages of verse, and then they'll give you $300. What I have now makes five pages: you can string that next one out to three pages.
> Mr. H. said he would leave the matter entirely to me, and I wish he wouldn't. But I know you'll be good.

Aldrich was at least good enough to string the matter out to just under seven pages.[14]

Under the terms of the purchase agreement Hurd & Houghton was to fulfill all *Atlantic* engagements with authors which Osgood had made for 1874. One such engagement was with Bret Harte for two poems at $300 apiece. These sums Harte was paid but negotiations for 1875 took on a different color. Harte offered a poem for $200. All Houghton would pay was $125. Harte was angered beyond patience by what he called Houghton's "Yankee cheapening" of his work. He was further exasperated by what he considered a paltry proposal for a story.

713 Broadway, N. Y.
September 8/74

My dear Howells, [he wrote in protest]

When I tell you that, since my arrival East, I have never received so small an offer for any story as that made to me by Mr. Houghton; that the lowest offer from any magazine or newspaper was $150 *more* than his, and that before sending it to you I had already refused $450 for the *ms* that I might make it the basis of terms with the *Atlantic,* you can readily imagine that I was considerably exasperated, and I think justly so, to have waited a week for such a reply.

I do not question Mr. Houghton's right to appraise my work by its value to his magazine, but before soliciting exclusive contributions from a popular author it seems to me that he ought to have informed himself of the prices they are in the habit of receiving. I thought I had guarded against such a contingency by first giving my price to you before offering to treat with the *Atlantic* in general terms. To oblige you I sent the *ms* for examination — which I have never *ever* been required to do before by any editor or publisher. My stories have always been *contracted for, accepted* and the price *fixed* before I put pen to paper ... I do wish you lived out of a literary atmosphere which seems to exclude any vision of a broader literary world beyond — its methods, profits, and emoluments ... A horrible thought strikes me that perhaps Mr. Houghton believes that it is worth $300 to me to appear in the *Atlantic.* The *Times* paid me $600 for "The Roses of Tuolumne," $500 for "John Oakhurst." Scribner paid me $1000 for "Fiddletown" — 16 pp. long and $500 for "Monte Flat Pastoral"; 7 pp.

After 1874 Bret Harte ceased to appear in the *Atlantic.* Howells may have believed he had editorial independence. Houghton may have insisted that if he were going to do the work himself, he would not have an editor. Nonetheless, pay scale determined by Houghton, or his confidential clerk Francis J. Garrison, performed an editorial, selective function.[15]

The *Atlantic* page rate by 1874 had risen to $10. However, an author frequently was encouraged to write a few extra without measurement from the counting room. Howells told Arthur Sedgwick, for example, that Hurd & Houghton would pay him $100 for an article on the Lobby. Ten pages would do, but fifteen would be better. "$100 is not much for Life's blood," Howells apologized, "but that is a thing which in these days can be had at panic prices: it is marked down on every hand." Fiction in these years had no definite page rate and, like poetry, presented the insoluble problem of length versus worth. Aldrich for *Prudence Palfrey* received $200 an issue; Henry James for *Roderick Hudson,* only $100. Yet this amounted to more than the $1000 Scribner had offered him for a year's serial. Since *Scribner's Magazine* numbered over 850 words to the page, the *Atlantic* under 750, the rate was even more liberal than first appears. James, however, was not interested in brevity. That the number of words to the *Atlantic* page was fewer than in any of the other quality magazines was of no benefit to him. For his next novel, *The American,* Hurd & Houghton agreed to his request for $150 a number. The story was originally to appear in nine installments. Howells, finding he could not fit the text to the available monthly space, requested James to accept a year for the run. James agreed, stipulating he be paid on the original basis of nine months. His take for *The American* was thus $1350, only $150 more than he had been paid for *Roderick Hudson.*[16]

The announced custom of the *Atlantic* in these years was to pay on publication. When Howells accepted a manuscript and then held it for months, this practice was irritating to say the least, especially if an author was in need of cash. Of her articles which had been in the editor's drawer for nine months, Harriet Waters Preston demanded in frustration, ". . . please print them or pay for them, or something, before the leaves are much greener." This custom of payment on publication was frequently honored in the breach. When Hurd & Houghton took over the magazine, authors for 1874 had been paid to the extent of $2225.86. Although advance payment was not usual, all an author had to do apparently was to ask. For both *Roderick Hudson* and *The American* James sought and was granted payment before printing. William Mumford Baker requested and received $200 before *Mose Evans* began its run. For some authors the privilege proved pernicious, especially for those who won payments before they had even set pen to paper. Unable to fulfill their engagements on time, they found themselves in irksome obligation to the firm. John Fiske was one of these. In the 1870s his debt to his publisher was in the trivial hundreds; before he died it had reached astronomical proportions. Of course, in this decade, Hurd & Houghton was not Fiske's publisher. He was an Osgood author, as were the majority who wrote for the *Atlantic*. Under the terms of the purchase agreement most of the poems, essays, and fiction published in the magazine would result in Osgood books.[17]

The case was different with Samuel Clemens. Already famous because of his *Innocents Abroad* and *Roughing It,* he had not appeared in the *Atlantic* before it became the property of Hurd & Houghton. There was nothing in the Memorandum of Agreement to stay Houghton from trying to secure this Westerner for his list. That Clemens even considered the *Atlantic* as a vehicle was due to his friendship with its editor, a friendship dating from a meeting in Fields's office in 1869. In the ensuing five years a warm, laughing friendship developed. In September 1874, Clemens offered Howells two stories — "Fable for Old Boys and Girls" and "A True Story, repeated Word for Word as I heard it." On the "Fable" he set a steep price, on "A True Story," no value. "You can pay as lightly as you choose for that, if you want it, for it is rather out of my line," he wrote. Howells returned the "Fable," even though Clemens reduced the price, but "A True Story" he set his heart on, finding it "touching with the best and realist kind of black talk." But how much to pay an author who boasted that his *Innocents* and *Roughing It* sold like the Bible? "Paymaster" Houghton, as Howells called him, determined the price, $20 an *Atlantic* page. Since the tale filled only three pages, the price was worth the gamble.[18]

Shortly after "A True Story" appeared in the *Atlantic,* Houghton pressed his advantage by inviting Clemens to a dinner for *Atlantic* contributors. Then, early in 1875, he approached him for cooperation in a project close to his heart. He hoped to start a Library of American Fiction in which would be featured "the foremost American novelists." "We wish to make the series an event in American literature," he wrote Clemens. His purpose was to demonstrate that America had "an independent class of . . . fiction worthy of prominence. We mean to see what the Riverside Press can do in turning out a set of books, inexpensive yet beautiful . . ." and he urged Clemens to provide the first number in the series. However, Clemens, though dissatisfied with his publisher, Elisha Bliss of the American Publishing Company, was committed to the subscription scheme of selling books. He believed it to be the most lucrative method of distribution; he felt he could not afford the luxury of trade publication, or so he told Houghton. Even so, at this very time he was negotiating with Osgood for a trade book of his sketches.[19]

Houghton's next move was to suggest through Howells that before book publication, Clemens advertise his next story, *The Adventures of Tom Sawyer,* by running it in the *Atlantic.* But Clemens, although he "would dearly love to see it in the Atlantic" doubted that Hurd & Houghton would meet his price. He expected more than $20 a page. "You see I take a vile, mercenary view of things," he apologized. Even so, contributions on which he put less value, including *Old Times on the Mississippi,* he continued to send to the *Atlantic,* expecting to be paid at his "usual" rate. From this association in 1877, Osgood, not Houghton, secured one book — *A True Story and the Recent Carnival of Crime.* He would have others in the following decade. Houghton benefited not a whit, not even in an increase in *Atlantic* subscribers.[20]

Certain significant changes occurred in the *Atlantic* after it came under Hurd & Houghton's imprint, some attributable to Howells, others to the publishers, each hopefully designed to secure more subscribers, whose number under Osgood's management had fallen to a little under 21,000.[21]

In the early days of the magazine, although their authorship shortly became an open secret, all articles had appeared anonymously. In 1862 Fields had introduced indexes to the bound volumes of the periodical. In these indexes only writers of "body" articles were identified. In July 1870 the practice of signing such articles was initiated. However, the reviewing and editorial sections, written by various hands, continued anonymous. Houghton did not believe in the concealed name for articles of political opinion. In consequence the editorial section reserved for that subject was dropped and in its place a department devoted to education appeared. The dropping of politics from the editorial pages did not mean the *Atlantic* ceased to consider questions of national import. If anything, discussions of political and social questions were more numerous than they had been, the majority signed. Understandably, in these years of financial crisis, the money question was of critical interest and essays on the subject and related topics were provided by David Ames Wells, Joseph Wharton, Horatio Burchard, James A. Garfield, Brooks Adams, and his brother Charles Francis. Finance was also the core of Erastus Bigelow's "The Relations of Labor and Capital," in which Bigelow maintained that the cause of the continuing depression was excessive extensions of credit rather than labor-saving machinery, as some theorists were saying. Machines, Bigelow said, would benefit rather than harm the worker provided steps were taken to educate him to meet the increasing demands for technological skills. "Capital is the laborer's best friend," Bigelow concluded, "excessive credit his worst enemy." With such a creed Houghton was in hearty agreement.[22]

That Houghton's hand shows in the introduction of an editorial department for education is beyond question, considering his conviction that in disciplined enlightenment lay the salvation of the country. That its introduction was directed at an increase in the *Atlantic*'s circulation is also beyond doubt. In 1867 the Federal Government had established an Office of Education. What to do about the exploding population and the quality of its instruction had become a national concern; the book which was to carry the word, a highly competitive enterprise. Hurd & Houghton had made important investments in educational publishing. In this new *Atlantic* department, Harvard, hardly a stone's throw from the Riverside Press, found a place, as it had in earlier *Atlantic*s, but the subject was not contained by Cambridge. Daniel Coit Gilman, president of the recently founded University of California, wrote of the problem of state control of education. Other editorials considered the poverty of instruction in the South, the low standards of the common schools in general, the pitiable pay of teachers, especially in the primary grades, and increased educational opportunities for women. In this department also new texts were occasionally reviewed, some understandably Hurd & Houghton's. The innovation at least won educators as readers. Inaugurated in May 1874, by November the department had received reports from the Superintendents of Public Instruction of thirty states and four territories. Unfortunately, these Superintendents of Public Instruction failed to stem the *Atlantic*'s falling circulation. By the end of the year 4000 readers had canceled their subscriptions in favor of New York's magazines with pictures, *Harper's* and *Scribner's,* each of whose circulations topped 100,000.[23]

Three innovations that appear to be solely attributable to Howells were a briefly sustained drama department, occasional musical scores, and in 1877 the Contributors' Club, a section in which Howells encouraged his writers to be colloquial and to "spit" their "spite at somebody or something." As protection, they were promised permanent anonymity; never, even in the indexes, would their names appear.[24]

In the beginning the Club's paragraphs were written primarily by Howells, George Parsons Lathrop, and close literary friends. Soon, however, there were more than enough unsolicited items to fill the allotted pages. Nonetheless, in the interest of controversy, planted paragraphs continued to appear. One such obvious piece of bait begins with a dialogue between author and publisher. The latter, in answer to a question on the secret of a book's success, explains that publishing is a lottery, that neither well-placed criticism nor advertising assures sales. The number of volumes a new book by an established writer will sell can be fairly well predicted but sales of a novel by an untried author defy anticipation. The publisher hopes, of course, that his novice may turn out to be a "twenty-edition fellow." Encouraged by this opening, in ensuing issues of the magazine, disgruntled authors rehearsed their complaints, the editor their particular target: manuscripts rejected, manuscripts held for months, even years, checks (and paltry ones at that) arriving weeks after the matter had appeared in print, the impossibility of making a living as an author even by writing Sundays and holidays, and so on. The series concludes with the editor's reply to his critics. In this he points out that magazine production is a business embracing three separate interests, those of the publisher, the editor, and the contributor. Writers, he urges, should realize that an editor has a responsibility to the proprietors as well as to authors. They should also realize that requests for brevity, that excisions or curtailments made by the editor, are related to the available pages in the magazine. The style of the fictional editor does not suggest Howells, but these were some of the ideas he later presented in his "Recollections of an Atlantic Editorship," in 1907, writing of the "liberal Atlantic tradition of bettering the authors by editorial transportation and paraphrase, either in the form of suggestion or of absolute correction," of the burden of the "editor's month," when as it draws to a close he must hew and pare "at the quivering members of the closing pages."[25]

In this Contributors' Club exposition of the magazine as essentially a business proposition, no word is said about the importance of subscribers to a periodical's success. Yet this must have been a subject uppermost in the mind of both editor and publisher. From 1874 through 1877, Howells and his contributors maintained the status quo at approximately 17,000 subscribers. The rise to 20,000 in 1878 should not be attributed to any of the innovations of publisher or editor, but rather to a characteristic Houghton move. In December 1877, Mr. Houghton purchased the subscription list and goodwill of the *Galaxy*, the purchase price $3800, the estimated number of subscribers, 5200.[26]

Houghton's acquisition of the *Atlantic* had proved of small commercial value. To be its publisher carried prestige perhaps; yet three years of ownership had done little to alter the essential character of Hurd & Houghton's list. The terms of the purchase agreement prohibited seeking authors already in Osgood's stable, and authors new to the magazine preferred Osgood's imprint because " 'Atlantic things' " seemed to "have a natural affinity with that house."[27]

Of course, the investment had not proved entirely barren. Among the trade books that came to Hurd & Houghton from "Atlantic things" were George Cary Eggleston's *A Rebel's Recollections* and William Mumford Baker's *Mose Evans*. Another book that resulted, but not from articles in the magazine, was Howells' biography of Rutherford B. Hayes. Houghton's interest in politics had been keen ever since his university days. His career in publishing had served to whet his interest. What went on in Washington was related to his continuing success. In 1874 he had been chosen publisher of the *United States Official Postal Guide*. Congress appropriated the money to foot the bills. The following year Hurd & Houghton was chosen as exclusive agent for the *Revised Statutes of the United States*. What took place in the halls of Congress in relation to postal charges, tariff, and International Copyright were of publishing concern. After the nomination of Hayes as Republican candidate for President, Houghton recognized the opportunity to do the candidate and possibly himself a service. His *Atlantic* editor, related to Hayes by marriage, was the obvious person to write a campaign biography, and he so proposed, writing:

> Princeton, Mass
> July 18 '76

> My dear Mr. Howells
>   What do you think of a Life of Gov. Hayes? Who is better fitted to write it than the "accomplished scholar & able critic," W. D. Howells? Who knows but that it might recuperate the waning fortunes of both of us? 70,000 copies sold of the miserable Life of Fremont, when he was candidate for President, & I see that Appletons are to publish a Life of Tilden, & that would produce a healthy competition.
>   Would the usual 10 per cent. & a continuance meanwhile of the Atlantic salary be sufficient inducement for the extra work? Could it be ready & finished by Sept 1st?
>   I am staying here & trying to be lazy for this week, & this "happy thought" is the result . . .
>   Hoping that you succeed in "keeping cool" this weather I am
> Yrs very truly[28]

Howells sent off at once to Hayes enclosing Houghton's proposal and referring to him as "my 'owner.'" Hayes offered hearty cooperation, but warned that another biography was almost ready for the market. Although Howells drove his pen with all speed, producing his *Sketch of the Life and Character of Rutherford B.*

Hayes in twenty-two days, before his brief narrative appeared, the competing biography was out. Rather than 70,000 copies, at the height of the Hayes-Tilden campaign, Howells' *Sketch* had sold a bare 2000.[29]

The poet Stedman when he heard of the *Atlantic*'s transfer feared for the magazine's future; he judged Houghton and Hurd as timidly evangelical. On the evidence, Howells, however, appears as the timid one, made so perhaps by his eight-year experience. He was aware of the effect on circulation of Reade's *Griffith Gaunt* and Mrs. Stowe's Lady Byron article. Language and situations which violated his standards of decorum, he would not accept. Gentle and sensitive to criticism himself, he would not permit jibes which might hurt his friends. At no suggestion from the publishers, he deleted from Lathrop's *Waverly Oaks* ridicule of Osgood's *North American Review* and turned down an unfavorable article on Edward Everett Hale because the reverend gentleman "had just given him two or three pages of wandering praise in Old & New." Because he did not "wish to be put in pain about a woman's virtue," he turned down a play with Casanova as one of the characters even though he found the dialogue to have "great point and brilliancy." Contributions which he judged as "calculated to trouble" the *Atlantic*'s religious readers, he returned.[30]

In October 1873, Hurd, after eighteen months in Europe, had returned to his desk in New York and for the *Atlantic*'s first year under its new owners, he was active in recommending authors for Howells' consideration. However, early in 1875 his precarious health gave way again. As in other years, travel was his panacea and he departed for Florida. The fate of the *Atlantic* was in the hands of Houghton and William Dean Howells. Nothing better illustrates the contrast between Houghton's robust, uncritical heartiness and his editor's delicate sensitivity than their relationship with Samuel Clemens as dramatized in the celebrated *Atlantic*-Whittier dinner of December 1877.

Atlantic dinners had played a part in the early history of the magazine. Houghton revived the tradition in 1874 to celebrate the conclusion of a year's ownership. However, more than a year's ownership guided him in staging the affair. Ever since the magazine had been his, rumors had persisted that Howells intended to resign, that the *Atlantic* was a failing property. Now in December 1874 the *Literary World* stated unequivocally that the editor was to "abdicate" his chair, that the *Atlantic* was to be absorbed by *Old and New.* Houghton was angry. Of the *Literary World* he demanded a retraction. "We may be in error," he wrote the editor, "but we cannot help feeling that the statements in the Literary World are calculated and perhaps intended to injure the reputation and standing of the Atlantic in the community . . ." To the *Publishers' Weekly* he dispatched a denial. "Hurd & Houghton," he wrote, "were never anxious to get rid of the *Atlantic,* and never made any advances or had any desire to sell it to the proprietors of *Old and New.* On the contrary, the only suggestion for a union came from friends of *Old and New* but no negotiations, earnest or otherwise, were ever had on the subject, and no interview ever took place in relation to it. We are entirely satisfied with the condition and prospects of the *Atlantic,* and have no reason to seek union with any other magazine."[31]

The editor of the *Literary World, S. R. Crocker,* a Bowdoin contemporary of James R. Osgood, refused to retract. His information he said had come from an unimpeachable source. In January 1875 Edward Everett Hale's *Old and New* was transferred from Roberts Brothers to Lee & Shepard, a firm with which Osgood, as will be seen, was closely involved.[32]

Houghton took hasty steps to belie the rumor. A convivial dinner where a show of amity would color subsequent press reports might do the trick. Invitations for an *Atlantic* Contributors' Dinner on December 15 were sent out on December 8. Howells and his "owner" Houghton were eager that their new contributor Clemens attend, and Howells followed the firm's invitation with an urgent letter. "Don't you dare refuse that invitation to the Atlantic dinner for Tuesday evening. . . . *Come!*" he commanded. Like children preparing for a picnic, the two men planned their holiday, winning permission from their wives for a night on the town. For the anticipated post-banquet hilarity, Clemens insisted on playing host, promising Howells he would secure a room with a fireplace at the Parker House, so that after the event they could "tell lies & have an improving time."[33]

Dr. Holmes and Christopher Cranch accepted Hurd & Houghton's invitation, but other of the *Atlantic*'s Olympians refused because of illness or previous commitments. Their absence perhaps made the evening gayer than it otherwise might have been. The guests gathered at the Parker House at six o'clock, among them Aldrich, Henry James, Thomas Sergeant Perry, Frank Sanborn, Trowbridge, Lathrop, Whipple, and Scudder, twenty-eight or thirty in all. Two of the guests who were not *Atlantic* contributors were James R. Osgood and Charles Fairchild. Champagne eased the throats of the small congenial group. Dr. Holmes read his inevitable poem and Cranch, as the evening wore on, chanted one of his. At least six others took the floor. Clemens responding to the toast "To the President of the United States, and the women who write for the *Atlantic*," gave "an inimitable and utterly unreportable speech," in which he expressed surprise to find a publisher acting as though he wanted to conciliate his menials, the authors. Howells, replying to the toast "To the editor of the *Atlantic*: Such is his impartiality that he has been known to reject his own contributions," made a few oblique remarks about "the incorruptible press, which not having always a bottle of champagne at its elbow to clear its vision with — is sometimes pleased to find the magazine dull . . . They have no idea of the many pieces of inanity and obscurity which are each month mercifully withheld from them. They cannot understand what strong restraint the editor places upon his own gifts for their sake, and how continually he rejects his own contributions." He paid graceful compliment to the eminent authors who had brought the magazine to its present distinction and took credit for welcoming "the new talents throughout the country upon whose co-operation," the *Atlantic*'s future depended. The dinner concluded at a reasonable hour; then Clemens, Howells, and Aldrich, persuaded during the jolly dinner, went to their rooms above for an evening full of "play-talk," aimless and joyful, illuminated from time to time by Aldrich's "heat-lightning shimmer of wit."[34]

Since reports of the jovial dinner found their way to the papers, the dinner had served its purpose. Gossip of Howells' possible retirement and the absorption of the *Atlantic* by *Old and New* had been shown to be without foundation. Another *Atlantic* dinner was not called for until 1877. The ostensible occasion was the twentieth anniversary of the *Atlantic* and Whittier's seventieth birthday. Invitations went out nine days in advance. Clemens, recalling the high times of 1874, jubilantly accepted and set about preparing his speech with "joyous self-reliance." He anticipated "an unparalleled triumph." Houghton, too, prepared for the event. This was to be a larger affair than his first dinner and as before he had reasons other than a celebration for his public hospitality.

Ray Nash Smith in "That Hideous Mistake of Poor Clemens's" has shown that the Howells and Clemens accounts of the 1877 *Atlantic* dinner contain more fiction than fact. Smith is so convincing in his analysis that another recapitulation of Whittier's seventieth birthday dinner would be unnecessary were it not that on that evening certain publishing projects, of which Smith was unaware, were afoot. Knowledge of these projects may well have played a part in the creation of the Howells-Clemens fable.[35]

According to these masters of fiction, Clemens' speech, a burlesque in which three deadbeats impersonating Emerson, Longfellow, and Holmes impose on a Nevada miner's hospitality, fell "dead on his hands." By the turn of the century both had so embroidered the legend that their recollections, colored by the subtle undercurrents of the evening, had small connection with reality. As Howells recreated the evening, his friend's speech was near "the death of us all." It was "an amazing mistake," a "bewildering blunder," a "cruel catastrophe." The audience did not laugh and the silence, "weighing many tons to the square inch, was broken only by the hysterical and blood-curdling laughter of a single guest . . ." Clemens, for his part, recalled that his audience had been "turned to stone with horror." Young Henry Bishop, who followed him on the program, he said, was so overcome with shock, that he was unable to face "those awful deities" at the head table, Emerson, Longfellow, Holmes, and Whittier. In his embarrassment he could barely manage a sentence or two before his legs gave way and he "slumped down in a limp and mushy pile." Then, as Clemens tells the story, although the program was only a third over, no one else took the floor and "Howells mournfully and without words, hitched himself to Bishop and me and supported us out of the room."

Nothing could have been further from the truth. Clemens' jest received both laughter and applause and at first Boston's press reported the dinner favorably, some giving Clemens' speech in full. Shortly, however, alerted by provincial reporters, Boston's fourth estate changed its tune, warning Clemens that he had committed an offense which if repeated would cost him "his place among the contributors to the Atlantic, where indeed his appearance was in the beginning considered an innovation."

Such was not the case at all. Houghton had been delighted by the performance. He had no intention of shutting the door of the *Atlantic* to his new contributor. The next day he wrote him a letter of compliment. Moreover, he would invite Clemens to all subsequent *Atlantic* festivities, encouraging him to speak as well.

How was it that two realists allowed themselves a fable of such proportions? In reply to Clemens' letter of apology, Longfellow, after assuring the humorist that he had not been in the least troubled by his broad merriment, suggested that newspaper reports were murky mirrors. "A bit of humor at a dinner table is one thing," he wrote, "a report of it in the morning papers is another. One needs the lamp-light, and the scenery." True enough. One also needs to know the undercurrents of the occasion.

Nothing is ever the same. Clemens had come to Boston anticipating the innocent hilarity of 1874. Such was not to be. Rather than the accustomed and familiar Parker House, Houghton had chosen the East Room of the new Hotel Brunswick. The guests, gathered at six-thirty, numbered sixty rather than thirty. At seven-thirty they sat for dinner at a huge U-shaped table to be served a stultifying seven-course dinner with its attendant wines. At the foot of the right arm of the U was George Harrison Mifflin; at the foot of the left arm, just returned from another health trip, was Melancthon M. Hurd. At the salt, neither above nor below, on Mifflin's side was Clemens, on his left, Charles Fairchild, on his right, James R. Osgood. At ten-fifteen the doors of the dining room were thrown open and the lady guests of the house joined the stuffed and satiated men.[36]

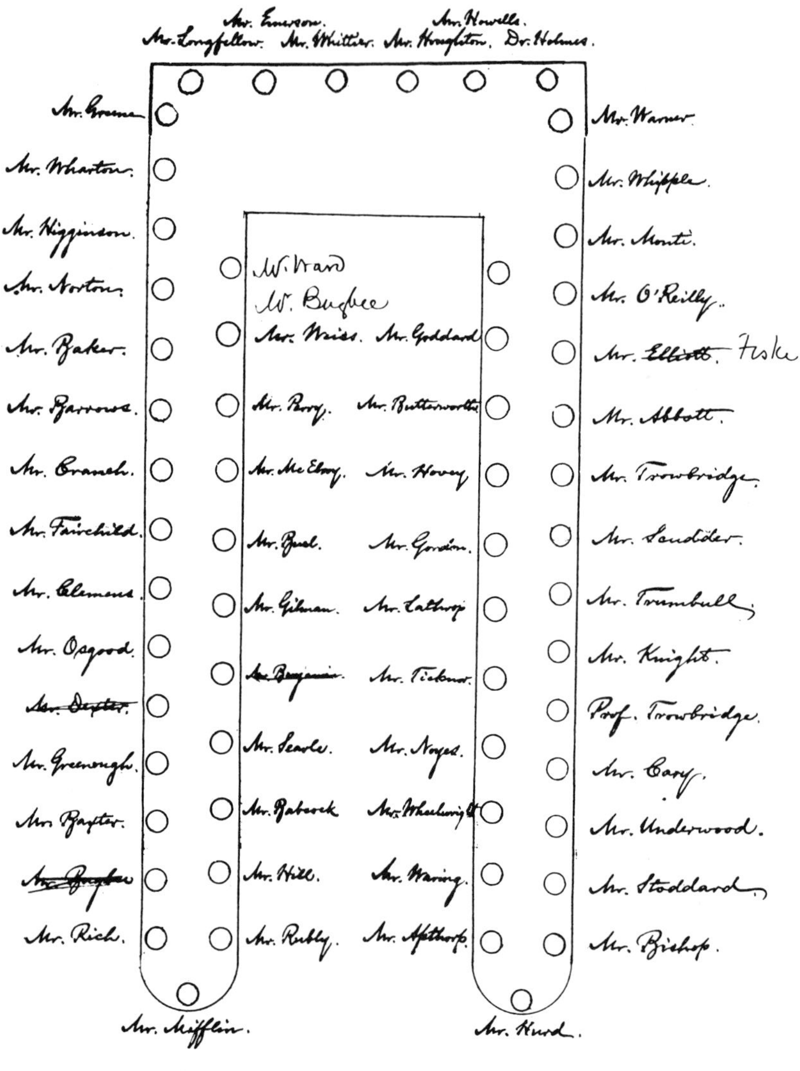
Mr. Emerson.
Mr. Howells.
Mr. Longfellow. Mr. Whittier. Mr. Houghton. Dr. Holmes.
Mr. Greene
Mr. Wharton.
Mr. Higginson.
Mr. Norton.
Mr. Baker.
Mr. Barrows.
Mr. Branch.
Mr. Fairchild.
Mr. Clemens.
Mr. Osgood.
Mr. Dexter.
Mr. Greenough.
Mr. Baxter.
Mr. Rich.
Mr. Mifflin.
Mr. Ward
Mr. Bugbee
Mr. Weiss. Mr. Goddard
Mr. Perry. Mr. Butterworth
Mr. McElroy. Mr. Hovey
Mr. Gilman. Mr. Lathrop
Mr. Ticknor.
Mr. Searle. Mr. Noyes.
Mr. Babcock Mr. Wheelwright
Mr. Hill. Mr. Waring.
Mr. Rubly. Mr. Apthorp.
Mr. Warner.
Mr. Whipple.
Mr. Monti.
Mr. O'Reilly.
Mr. Elliott. Fiske
Mr. Abbott.
Mr. Trowbridge.
Mr. Scudder.
Mr. Trumbull.
Mr. Knight.
Prof. Trowbridge.
Mr. Cary.
Mr. Underwood.
Mr. Stoddard.
Mr. Bishop.
Mr. Hurd.

Seating plan for the 1877 Whittier dinner

Houghton, in opening the proceedings, recalled his early days in the trade when poetry and pills had been produced by apothecaries. He emphasized the continuing loyalty of the *Atlantic*'s original contributors and the promise of Western writers now appearing in the periodical. Then pointing out the need for mutual trust between authors and publishers, he said:

> There is, probably, no business strictly legitimate, so speculative and so uncertain in its results as that of publishing books. The picture of the distraught author, with his massive pile of manuscript under his arm, and his 'eyes in a fine frenzy rolling,' is not more mirth-provoking or truly harrowing in its effect on the looker-on than that of the publisher, who with his own, or more likely borrowed, capital strikes hands with him and sits down and counts in advance the immense profits of the venture, sees visions of brownstone fronts, palatial seashore residences and all the paraphernalia which wealth is apt to inflict upon its possessor. But alas! the result is pretty sure to be loss of capital, unpaid printers' bills, and the manuscript which came seething hot from the brain of the poor author transmuted into cold lead and then consigned to a dungeon to await the fate of resurrection-day, unless previously brought out to be melted up in the electrotyper's furnace. Publishing and authorship must necessarily keep pace with each other. However antagonistic, they travel under the same yoke . . . the business of publishing books has its uses and its success, which are not the result of fortunate ventures, but, as in every other profession or calling, are only secured by thorough knowledge, patient labor, and a clear conception of the end to be attained.

To those in the know, Houghton's words were of devastating import.[37]

His negotiations for the *Galaxy*, under way since November, were practically complete. This failure of a magazine which had been a success was a concrete illustration of Houghton's thesis. The *Galaxy* had been an early vehicle for Clemens, and its quondam publishers, the Sheldons, publishers also of one of his books, owed him money. More fraught with implication than the transfer of the *Galaxy* was another publishing shift that involved the demigods at the head table, a shift of which Howells, at least, must have

MENU.

·————·

OYSTERS ON SHELL. *Sauterne.*

SOUPS.

Purée of Tomatoes au Croutons. Consommé Printanier Royal.

Sherry.

FISH.

Boiled Chicken Halibut à la Navarine.
Potatoes à la Hollandaise.

Smelts Panne, Sauce Tartar. *Chablis.*

REMOVES.

Capon à l'Anglaise.
Rice. Cauliflower. *Champagne.*
Mumm's Dry Verzenay.
Saddle of English Mutton à la Pontoise. *Roederer Imperial.*
String Beans. Turnips.

ENTRÉES.

Filet of Beef, larded, Sauce Financière.

Épinards Veloutés.

Vol au Vent of Oysters à l'Américaine. *Claret.*

Squabs en Compote à la Française, Tomatoes Sautées.

Terrapin Stewed, Maryland Style.

Sorbet au Kirsh.

GAME.

Broiled Partridges on Toast. Canvasback Ducks.

Water Cresses, Sweet Potatoes, Dressed Lettuce. *Burgundy.*

PASTRY.

Charlotte Russe. Gelée au Champagne. Gâteaux Variés.

Confectionery.

Fruit. Dessert.

COFFEE.

Menu for the Whittier dinner.

been aware. After all, he was Houghton's *Atlantic* editor, Osgood was his publisher, and Charles Fairchild was financing his new house in Belmont, now abuilding.[38]

That Emerson chose to read that night "Ichabod," Whittier's great poem of betrayal, was appropriate. Osgood, who had been operating mainly on borrowed capital, could no longer pay his authors. His largest creditor, to whom he owed well over $100,000, was S. D. Warren & Company, of which Fairchild was a partner. Under consideration was a Fairchild scheme to transfer the publishing interests of James R. Osgood & Company to New York and the house of Harper.[39]

Under the shadow of this possibility, Howells listened to his friend's carefully prepared bit of levity. Nor did the evening end with Bishop's collapse. Speeches and recitations followed each other in appalling sequence: Underwood, Warner, Whipple, Higginson, Stedman, and on into the night. During the stupefying deluge, Clemens had time to brood and to decide that the laughter and applause for his joke had been less than he had expected, and Howells, as the evening wore on, was distressed to see the guests at the head table, understandably wearied by the sequence of speeches, tiptoe out. Not until after one o'clock could Howells and Clemens retire to their rooms at the Parker House. There in self-indulgent masochism, they began to create a funny fable that would help them forget the shame. After all Osgood and Fairchild were their good friends. For them the round table was indeed kindling wood.

What they did not know was that during the long evening Houghton had initiated conversation that would ensure that Boston would continue as the publishing home of the New England galaxy.[40]

MEN OF LONGER PURSE AND
LONGER PATIENCE[1]

EVEN FOR THOSE UNAWARE of the possible transfer of the Ticknor & Fields list to Harper, Houghton's introductory remarks at the Whittier dinner were freighted with overtones. The depression had dragged on for more than four exhausting years. Nor was the end in sight. Simply to make ends meet was the resigned hope of some. Throughout the country bankruptcy piled on bankruptcy. Suspensions of credit seemed the rule rather than the exception. Prosperity was not for this generation, the croakers croaked. Financial and commercial solvency would never come again. In 1875 alone, 7740 business failures occurred, representing a total loss of over $200,000,000. Prophets of doom warned of national bankruptcy. Although the book business was but a part of the national scene, smaller in volume than cheap jewelry, in these desperate years it was in serious trouble. In Boston between 1875 and 1879 there were at least seven publishing failures, probably more. Some houses that didn't fail maintained a precarious balance.[2]

To many the cause of the trade's misery was price-cutting. To combat the evil, the industry in 1874 united in the American Book Trade Association. The following year, a plan of attack devised, the Association called a convention to be held in July at Niagara Falls. Here the strategy of the scheme was presented. The Trade Sale was to be abandoned. In its place was to be substituted a biannual Book Fair or Booksellers' Exchange and Clearing House, buyers not members of the Association to be excluded. As for potential purchasers outside the trade, individuals such as ministers and teachers, they might purchase their books at 20 percent off, doctors at 10 percent only. For all other customers, except jobbers and legitimate booksellers, the publishers' stated retail price was to be observed strictly. In addition the publishers and jobbers agreed not to sell their products to known price cutters for less than 20 percent off, no matter how temptingly large the order. R. H. Macy, A. W. Lovering, the Troy book-butcher, and others of their ilk were to be denied bargain counters in books. Any member of the Association breaking the price line, except for clearance sales of dead or shopworn stock and the like, would be referred to an Arbitration Committee for penalties. Some grumbled that the American Book Trade Association had the halo of a "ring," but clairvoyance was denied the trade. The Sherman Act was fifteen years in the future.[3]

At least 250 members of the profession from twenty-seven states attended this 1875 Niagara Falls Convention. A. D. F. Randolph, president of the Association, opened the assembly with a speech in praise of publishers and booksellers, great civilizing forces to whom the nation was in debt. In answer to the charge of monopoly, Randolph protested the Association's sole purpose was to assure the bookseller a profit proportionate to "that afforded on all articles of common merchandise." During the three days of the convention, report followed report and endless "experience meetings," at which small retailers aired their grievances, took up the time of day, but in the end there was qualified unanimity on the 20 percent rule and the Book Fair.

Although forty-three Boston publishers signed the 20 percent rule, few attended the convention. Conditions at the Hub were in too perilous straits. Cures more drastic than persecution of undersellers and limiting discounts were essential if certain reputable houses were to be saved from bankruptcy. Henry Oscar Houghton was there, but among the missing were James Ripley Osgood and Charles Augustus Billings Shepard, junior partner in Lee & Shepard.

The firm of Lee & Shepard was relatively new in Boston trade, having been established in 1862. The partners, William Lee and C. A. B. Shepard were no novices in books, however. Both had started as boys in the business, Shepard with John P. Jewett, *Uncle Tom*'s publisher. Lee, after experience in a variety of firms, joined Phillips, Sampson, eventually to become junior partner. Both were therefore familiar with the speculative nature of the book industry. Each had reason to know that the spectacular success of a single author was not the secret of survival. Although Lee & Shepard's original prominence derived from such now forgotten juveniles as Sophie May's Little Purdy and Dottie Dimple series, Elijah Kellogg's pious Down East novels for boys and girls, and William Taylor Adams' Oliver Optic books, it had also published in 1869 the first *Alice in Wonderland* of American manufacture. For heavier fare its list carried Charles Sumner's *Works* in eleven volumes, Francis Wayland's *Life of Dr. Judson,* and George L. Vose's *Manual for Railroad Engineers and Engineering Students* in a revised edition. In the spring of 1875 it had undertaken Thomas Wentworth Higginson's *Young Folks' History of the United States,* advancing him $1000 and encouraging in him dreams of avarice by predicting an eventual sale of 200,000. In addition to publishing, Lee & Shepard conducted a large jobbing business. In 1870, requiring a New York outlet, it formed an association with an experienced wholesaler, Charles Dillingham.[4]

Lee & Shepard, touched by fire in 1871, suffered severely in the November fires of the following year; in that of November 9 they had an estimated loss of $75,000. The Rand, Avery holocaust of the twentieth more than tripled its calamity. The Lee & Shepard store at 149 Washington Street was only slightly damaged. However, space requirements for the firm's jobbing seemed to require larger quarters, and in 1874, it took over part of one of the new granite buildings on Franklin Street at an address not far from Osgood's new location. Here Lee & Shepard had room for 500,000 volumes, and each partner had a separate office with a silver nameplate on his door. In New York, Lee, Shepard & Dillingham, not to be outdone, moved from small offices at 49 Green Street to ample display rooms at 687 Broadway opposite the Grand Central Hotel. By 1875 the firms were claiming $250,000 of stock in Boston, $150,000 their own publications; in New York $134,000 one-half their own publications. Such expansion had required extensions of notes already on the books and additional borrowed capital. Within the trade, the three partners were highly esteemed.

William Lee, gracious, polished, assured, served as chairman for many a committee. Charlie Dillingham for his generous geniality was popular with retailers looking for large discounts and credit indulgences. Shepard was deemed the financial wizard of the house, characterized by friends as "frightfully sagacious" and "relentless in judgment." With such a reputation, he secured credit easily. He gave credit with equal ease. As the depression dragged out its redundant days, his firm was nagged increasingly with demands for payment and refusals of indulgence. By the spring of 1875 many of Lee & Shepard's 300 creditors were insisting they be paid. One was James R. Osgood, who had endorsed Lee & Shepard notes to the amount of $75,000.

Osgood was himself being pressed on all sides. He was only too familiar with individuals worried about his ability to meet obligations. Following the panic of '73, James T. Fields, concerned about the money he had left with his former partner, the man he had once leaned on, asked Charles Fairchild for help. Shortly, S. D. Warren & Company, "for the better securing payment of said notes," took an assignment from Fields for Osgood's twenty-one promissory notes. Osgood, with infinite faith in the future, did not appear to be concerned. He continued to borrow on the one hand and loan on the other. Lee & Shepard was only one of the firms to secure his endorsements. Welch, Bigelow, half owners with him in Welch & Company, was another. In October 1874, on being questioned by the Bank of North America on the signed paper of the triangle, Osgood listed his assets as $645,000, his liabilities as $322,500. Among his assets he included Walter Smith's drawing books, that series that had been going to put him in the first boat, valuing them at $75,000. His heliotype he estimated as worth $50,000, claiming that "the drawing enterprise and the heliotype are now becoming very remunerative. From their standard character they will yield large profits in the future." But Osgood had neither the purse nor patience to await the future. In December, for $100,000 he sold Smith's series to the chromo-maker Louis Prang, payment, of course in notes, half to be paid off within the year, the rest not until 1877. At the same time John S. Clark, his associate since he had come as novice to Ticknor & Fields twenty years before, left to join Prang as partner. In search of further capital in January 1875, Osgood sold off his interest in Welch & Company.[5]

By such desperate measures Osgood reduced his indebtedness, at least as he reported, to $270,000. He now reached an understanding with his leading creditors that he would take care of his commitments to the amount of $200,000 within the year. Since he claimed an annual business of over half a million, he foresaw no difficulty. His list was replete with great names. His senior writers were still producing immensely popular books, in demand even in depression days. His young writers, Howells, Harte, and James, showed promise of developing into valuable properties. However, in spite of his efforts at retrenchment, by September his liabilities had increased to $396,000. By now disaster had overtaken Lee & Shepard. A series of hasty hectic notes from the sagacious Charles Augustus Billings Shepard forecast the event.[6]

1875
23 April

My dear Osgood

Yesterday when you were here I was too anxious to say anything hardly about the maturing paper this month — there is $5000 on the 26th — 2518 on the 27th — 2500 on the 29th — 2500 on the 30th; in all $15,000 and I fear tis a moral impossibility for us to meet one single dollar of it. We will do *all that we can* but I dare not promise *anything*

Yours truly
SHEPARD

Thursday A. M.

Dear Osgood

Today I shall need a cheque for $2496 — to *no ones order* — to send to N. Y. and bills amounting to 2520.40 to use here Thus far I get absolutely 0 — and am see sawing bank a/c daily

Yours truly
SHEPARD

May 14, 1875

My dear Osgood

Worse, WORSE, WORSE and more of it. How in thunder I can do anything under Heavens tomorrow at present I cannot see. I dislike to say so but tis nevertheless true — We get scarcely nothing remitted while everything is *maturing*

> Yours truly
> SHEPARD

[June 1875]

Dr. Osgood

I got worse than strapped on Saturday and have *part* made my a/cs good — I do not know where to go today to get the diff on note — I cant Kite in N/Y. for I have no cheque — Shall have to get you to give me at least 650 more today. If I can early in July make it up I will but today I CANT

> Yrs truly
> SHEPARD

I was down to see you but could not wait — give bearer cheque & I will see that tis deposited

> 1875
> 14 June

Dear Osgood

Tomorrow Tuesday there is one of our notes maturing and on the 17th one of L, S & D — I shall want at least ⅔ on *each* of them Now Charlie D will have to leave his store on the *16th* at 12 M and will not be back until the 18th and will need to arrange that cheque before he leaves — Will you therefore let me have cheque *for* him payable to *no ones* order but *blank* so that he can fill in the name — The banks in Boston will not be open on the 17th Consequently it will make no difference to you as it cant get into your bank before the 18th *anyway* and it will accomodate Charlie very much to get the note out of the way on the 16th that being his only payment on the 17th

> Yours truly
> SHEPARD

> 1875
> 3 July

Dear Osgood

I enclose herewith L. S. & D's cheque for 1285.90 and bills & currency for 4.10 Please deposit it in one bank and send me cheque on another for $1300 which last I will deposit. I do not think t'will do any harm for us to deposit it and I see no alternative thus far. I shall deposit one for about 2000 of L S D myself. Have borrowed $3000 thus far.

SHEPARD

Tuesday A. M. July

My dear Osgood

I did not observe until Dill's letter came this A.M. that the note of today is in N. Y. He has *nothing* in hand but has signed a cheque of mine which I *hope* he will be able to use. Let me know by *sending* or coming up as soon as you get in as before telegraphing him I want to see you — Tis culpable negligence in me the overlooking of it — but I was fearfully nervous yesterday and went away at noon sick — Shall have to decide early what to do in this extremity

Yours truly
SHEPARD

July 16, 1875

My dear Osgood

What time were you in — I have not been out more than five minutes to day (all told) Your conundrum is a poser. If I should guess it *now* I should say that there was *not a ghost of a chance of my ability to do anything at all* but will do everything possible — Tomorrow I have $3160.00 discounted paper to take up and bills payable amounting to $5400 more — On Monday I have $1069 paper to take up and on Tuesday $1009 — besides notes of $3500 on Wednesday $1040.00 on Thursday 5000 and so on through the month — I don't know day by day which way to turn — It is and has been the worst month I have ever had — next month is not so large by $20 to $25 M dollars but this is a screecher and nothing coming in — I shall have to re borrow to-morrow of everybody I can or throw up the sponge — Am almost disheartened Think I can weather the fall easily but this month nothing short of an interposition of Divine Providence can carry me through Tear this into minimum pieces when read — Regretting my inability to give you a more satisfactory answer I remain

Yours truly
CHARLES A. B. SHEPARD

Aug 4/75
My dear Osgood
It is not *possible* for me to do with less than $2500 today — I get no collections and my bank accounts are in a fearful condition

Yours truly
SHEPARD

Later in the month I hope matters will look differently

Saturday Aug 7, 1875
My dear Osgood
Tis too bad to crowd so hard — but I am WORSE off *even* than I was yesterday

Yours truly
SHEPARD

Aug 14, 1875
Dear J. R.
Let me have a cheque for N. Y. as early as you can and dont for God's sake make it less than $2500

Yours in a Stew
SHEPARD

Aug 25/75
Dear J. R. Osgood
My matters are worse even today than they were on Monday and I can do *just* nothing at all on that note

Yours truly
SHEPARD

p.s. If you get time come up — I can hardly move

Whether Osgood found time to go up is not recorded, but three days after this last appeal the failure of Lee & Shepard was announced, and on August 30, Lee, Shepard & Dillingham, in which the Boston firm had a two-thirds interest, was taken over by James Miller as assignee. On the same day twelve of James R. Osgood's creditors signed a Memorandum of Agreement granting him a six-month extension, with provision for an additional six-month indulgence should such prove necessary. S. D. Warren & Company led the list of signers.[7]

On September 16, a meeting of Lee & Shepard's creditors was

held in their store on Franklin Street, Charles Fairchild presiding until a chairman was elected. That honor fell to Henry Oscar Houghton. Only fifty of the 300 claimants were present. They listened sympathetically as Shepard, "the financial wizard" of the house, described the three-year heroic struggle he and his partner had made to stave off calamity. On Fairchild's motion, Houghton appointed a group of five to weigh the affairs of the firm. Three of the five were Osgood, Fairchild, and Isaac Sheldon. The meeting adjourned subject to call and Osgood, Fairchild, and Sheldon entrained for New York to attend the Lee, Shepard & Dillingham wake. Here Smith Sheldon, the chairman, chose a committee to evaluate the condition of the New York firm, which reported its assets as $93,001.82; its liabilities as $85,259.55, figures the committee revised to read, assets—$53,084.17; liabilities—$61,303.68. The recommendation, one unanimously accepted, was that Lee, Shepard & Dillingham pay 70 cents on the dollar in notes without interest at six, twelve, and eighteen months.[8]

Agreement as to the Boston house was not reached with equal speed. As in the case of the New York firm, the committee found that Lee & Shepard's reported assets of $179,433.67, plus $250,000 in stereotype plates, and liabilities of $558,809.50, did not agree with the facts. The revised estimates set gross liabilities at $625,-277.84, assets at $153,206.93, stereotype plates at $42,881.80, "providing they are not subject to any claim from authors for payment of sums now due under the contracts." Despite the radical revisions, creditors were assured that no intentional dishonesty had been discovered. The causes of the failure were insufficient margin, disregard of sources of buyers' credit, inadequate capital to cover such risks, large expenditures for small returns, omission of interest accounts in estimates of expense, and failure to allow for depreciation of stereotype plates.

As a member of the committee Osgood must have found his study of Lee & Shepard's accounts instructive. When the partners offered 20 cents on the dollar in unsecured notes without interest at six, twelve, eighteen, and twenty-four months (an offer the majority were disposed to accept), he objected. He wanted a cash settlement. Houghton supported him, indeed bettered him by offering to buy the assets of the firm for $80,000 in hard money. He would then settle with the creditors for approximately 15 cents on the dollar. Lee & Shepard, Houghton argued, would thus have a chance to go into business again untrammeled by debt. His proposal had an electric effect. The genial Lee sprang to his feet, protesting such a procedure "would be equivalent to wiping out the house." Isaac Sheldon exclaimed in pious horror that the plan savored of "speculating on a corpse." After Lee and his partner asked a two-week delay while they sought an alternative, the meeting broke up in argument.

In the meantime, Lee, Shepard & Dillingham took care of its reduced obligations promptly and Charlie Dillingham, under his own name only, was in business again. Osgood settled for 70 cents on the dollar less an additional 7 percent for cash. On the day he accepted his cash settlement, he offered Dillingham his new publications at 45 percent off, 50 percent off on such standards as Dickens, Scott, Thackeray, and Reade in all editions including Redlines and Diamonds.

At the October 24 meeting of the Lee & Shepard creditors, the partners renewed their original offer of 20 cents on the dollar, but provided security on the last three notes through endorsement. Such assurance was not enough for Osgood. The next day he petitioned Lee & Shepard into Involuntary Bankruptcy. Then by permission of the United States Court and under its direction, William Lee and Charles Augustus Billings Shepard were allowed to conduct their affairs for the benefit of their creditors. They now hoped to effect a composition at 25 percent and be on their own again by the first of December. Osgood couldn't wait. He assigned his claim to Lee & Shepard's largest creditor, accepting 25 cents on the dollar less 7 percent for cash. As a step toward solvency, Lee & Shepard announced a tremendous bargain sale of both old and new publications. Booksellers were encouraged to build up their stock to catch the Christmas trade. Among the bargain hunters was A. V. Lovering, the Boston Lottery man. No one could blame Lee & Shepard in their extremity for breaking the price line.

Yet it was not bankrupt publishers alone who broke restraint. In New York, the Sheldons, made wise by their investigation of

Lee & Shepard, decided to abandon retail selling and in consequence announced a huge closing-out sale at which their stock, including books from all the important houses, would be offered at discounts 25 percent greater than the discounts on such publications anywhere else. The book-butchers seized their opportunity, among them A. V. Lovering.

In Boston Lovering crowded his shop by offering $2 and $3 books for $1 plus premiums of $30,000 in greenbacks, $25,000 in watches, $45,000 in books, $150,000 in various other articles. How could a retailer cut prices and offer prizes as well, people asked. Lovering explained that he had in stock more than a million books bought at the recent depression sales. "Many of these books cost me less than fifty cents on the dollar; in selling them I give away in presents $250,000; I pay for advertising and expenses of selling $50,000. This leaves me $700,000, with at least $100,000 profit, and still I can sell the books at the prices named, and give away ELEGANT PRESENTS." The *Publishers' Weekly*, commenting on Lovering's business techniques, voiced a suspicion "that Mr. Lottery is counting in with his stock the contents of the publishers' and jobbers' shops in Boston, from which he expects to buy as he sells . . . So far as we have learned [the trade journal warned] no one has yet succeeded in selling valuable books at less than fifty percent off the retail price, paying expenses and paying bills. Some day there must be an accounting . . ." So Osgood found. He, for one, was doing business with the Boston book-butcher and had afforded him credit. When he asked for payment and found that it was not forthcoming, he expressed injured surprise. Lovering could not meet his obligations. Once more the Boston Bantam found himself on an investigating committee. Since all Lovering had was a depleted stock of worthless books, unpaid bills, and a bank account of 62 cents, the only solution was voluntary bankruptcy. The creditors swallowed their losses, Osgood's a mere $13,000, and Lovering was shortly back at his old stand underselling the legitimate bookseller. The American Book Trade Association's efforts to hold the price line had proved futile. So were its efforts to substitute a Book Fair for the auction techniques of the Trade Sales.[9]

Immediately following the 1875 Niagara Falls Convention, the Book Fair opened in New York's familiar Clinton Hall, George A. Leavitt, as usual, in charge. The setting was the same as that for the Trade Sales, but the atmosphere lacked the excitement of former years. However, the *Publishers' Weekly* was sanguine, insisting the hoped for reform would be realized. Ninety-seven houses took part, the majority from New York. Only seventeen came from Boston. Harper exhibited 4400 samples; Osgood, 1000; Hurd & Houghton, 606. Representatives of each house were on hand to take orders. *Publishers' Weekly* had given considerable advance publicity to the event and in its pages, the various publishing firms to be represented had run advertisements of the attractive titles buyers would be asked to consider. Both Hurd & Houghton and James R. Osgood & Company took two full pages. The layout of these contrasting appeals is instructive.[10]

Hurd & Houghton devoted an entire page to a sure-fire title — W. W. Hall's *How to Live Long*. To whet the prospective purchasers' appetites, the copy gave the savor of the good doctor's book. "In warm weather, the longer you can put off drinking water in the forenoon, the better you will feel at night." "Acids always injure the teeth, pure sweets never do." "We should go to sleep on the right side, then the food descends through the outlet of the stomach by gravity; otherwise stomach power is wasted in drawing it up as from the bottom of a deep well; after the first sleep, let the body take care of its own position." Beyond doubt people would stand in line to acquire a compendium of such sound advice. On the facing page appeared Mary Clemmer Ames's *His Two Wives,* Eggleston's *A Rebel's Recollections,* reports of the American Public Health Association, two books on art, a book in behalf of Bacon as the author of Shakespeare's works, Rolfe's *Satchel Guide,* and Celia Thaxter's *Poems.* The prices ranged from $1.50 to $2.00. Out of its 600 titles, Hurd & Houghton had chosen only eight for emphasis. The firm's reputation for its standards was sufficiently established. The virtues of library sets from the Riverside Press were too well-known to be rehearsed.

Osgood's advertisement presented seventy-five titles with a price range from 25 cents to $30. He also had a taking topical title or two — *Sex in Industry, Prohibition a Failure, Europe for Two Dollars a Day* — but the character of the list was in its recently published literature: Longfellow's *The Hanging of the Crane,* Whittier's *Hazel-Blossoms,* Emerson's anthology *Parnassus,* Aldrich's *Cloth of Gold,* Howells' *A Foregone Conclusion,* Henry James's *A Passionate Pilgrim* and *Transatlantic Sketches,* and John Fiske's *Cosmic Philosophy.* His expensive books were art works produced by heliotype, Charles Eliot Norton's *Blake's Job* at $10; the most elegant, *Specimens of the Decoration and Ornamentation of the Nineteenth Century* in half morocco at $30. With such titles, plenty of standards, and pirated editions of Jules Verne Osgood's house might well have been chosen as the one most likely to succeed. Unless, of course, one were privy to Shepard's frantic appeals being made at the very time of the Niagara Falls Convention and the Book Fair.

At the time, certainly, James R. Osgood & Company gave every impression of prosperity. Ben Ticknor was busy as a drill sergeant, and his firm was one of four to secure the majority of business, its return possibly $37,000. For Osgood, the Trade Sales had been richer in reward, and he declined to take part in the next Fair. Instead he held a special sale of his own, exhibiting his samples at his Dutton headquarters on Broadway. This scheme proved no more lucrative than the trade-sanctioned Fair. For the spring of 1876, he devised a sensational plan. Nothing in the resolutions of the Niagara Falls Convention, which he had signed, prohibited a sale of stereotype plates and remainders. He announced that following the Spring Fair, his house would have a grand auction of plates and dead stock, their value, he claimed, over $400,000, an estimate the knowing took with a grain of salt.[11]

For the sale Osgood prepared a handsome, illustrated catalogue. Here were listed the plates, their value, their copyright if any, the cost of manufacture per volume, the wholesale and retail prices and the profit per thousand copies or sets, as the case might be. Of the boasted profits many took a dim view. *Publishers' Weekly* considered them rose-colored and was thankful that copies of the catalogue had not fallen into the hands of the press. Serious harm would have resulted, misleading as the brochure was as to publishing returns. Within the fraternity of the trade, Osgood submitted to some good-natured joking about his optimistic forecasts. Even so he was in his element as generous host, providing lavish luncheons for all on both days of the sale. Pessimists prophesied the most he would realize would be $50,000. Two who were more ebullient wagered a bottle of champagne that $70,000 or even $90,000 would be nearer the mark.

The bulk of the plates to be auctioned were royalty-free English works. Under Leavitt's hammer were to go five different editions of Dickens, the great Ticknor & Fields De Quincey in twenty-three volumes, Scott in sixty-five volumes, and Thackeray in eleven. Few prospective bidders were misled by Osgood's exuberant estimates. Certainly, Houghton was not. He had made it his business to discover the average sale for the preceding three years of the sets on which he intended to bid. At his request, Osgood reported to him confidentially that the De Quincey had averaged 225 sets; the Library Edition of Dickens, 200; Scott, 375; Thackeray, 775. In his catalogue Osgood promised on 1000 sets of the Library Dickens a profit of $13,000. Houghton made his own estimate, concluding an annual sale of 200 would yield $2000.

The best-selling of Osgood's offerings, the Thackeray plates, excited the sharpest bidding. Shepard, in behalf of Harper, opened with $360 a volume. Houghton also bid but retired as the price went up and sharp increases came from around the hall. The atmosphere had more the ring of the Gold Exchange than the scratching pen of an author, his words now immobilized in lead. The eleven volumes were finally knocked down to Shepard at $515 each. Although Thackeray commanded the most money, Dickens, who less than a decade before had given his blessing to Ticknor & Fields as his authorized American publisher, aroused keen competition. The previous year Osgood had privately offered Houghton the plates of the twenty-nine-volume Library Edition (which also printed the Gadshill in fifteen) for $12,500. Houghton preferred to await a less expensive opportunity. At the auction he let the cheaper sets go to others. Lippincott bid in the Diamond in fourteen volumes for $60 each; Lee & Shepard took the fifteen-volume Household for $205 each; Porter & Coates, the Charles

Dickens, also in fifteen, for $210. Houghton secured the Library plates for $250, or $7250 for the set, a handsome reduction from the $12,500 Osgood had asked the year before. He also bid in the De Quincey for $2300; the Scott for $7457, his total purchase amounting to $17,025. Five days later S. D. Warren & Company loaned him the money to cover his investment.

Osgood on his Dickens plates and stock, all sets, took in something over $39,000. The total of his big sell he claimed amounted to $105,000 or possibly $110,000. Out of this he must pay the auctioneer Leavitt a 9 percent commission. Even though the amount Osgood realized from his auction was some 70 percent less than its announced retail value, he apparently regarded the cash in hand as sufficient compensation. At least he tried another at the conclusion of the 1876 fall Book Fair. Such auctions spelled the end of the Book Trade Association's work for reform. Osgood's stock of remainders, which included in addition to Jules Verne, his paper novels, his Little Classics, and the bound stock of all plates sold, soon found its way to the bargain counters of the book-butchers. Inevitably, the jobbers began to break the line too. Early in 1877 the *Publishers' Weekly* caroled the news. "The 'Trade Sale' is back! It sounds as familiar and cheery as to say Santa Claus is back, Barnum is back, Spring is back . . . The committees are dead, the 'Ring' is dead, the Book Fair is dead, but the Trade Sale is back! Le roi est mort; long live the king!" Osgood could now put under the hammer new volumes as well as his remainders, and he urged Howells to push ahead with his editing of *Choice Biographies* so they could be ready for the coming event.

Whatever returns Osgood actually realized in his spectacular auctions, not much went to paying off his indebtedness. Despite his agreement at the time of the *Atlantic* sale not to start or invest in another magazine for five years, in January 1876 appeared the first number of his handsome, profusely illustrated *American Architect and Building News*. Then in May 1876 he changed his address from 131 Franklin Street to the new Cathedral Building on Devonshire Street, retaining at Franklin Street the upper floor where were located his heliotype presses, an area connected to the Cathedral Building at the fifth floor. Here he set up a photographers' and heliotype exhibition room. Other floors provided him with space for retail and wholesale stock as well as offices. However, James R. Osgood was not the sole occupant of the building. Among others, S. D. Warren & Company had offices on the second floor.[12]

Osgood's commitment to the heliotype received further illustration at the Philadelphia Centennial Exhibition. In the main building he shared equal and adjacent space with Hurd & Houghton. It was Houghton, however, rather than Osgood, who won ecstatic accolades. Here under a huge bell jar was the first volume of the large paper Webster's *Unabridged Dictionary,* bound in vellum, ornately illuminated, the result of months of work by a Riverside craftsman. The emphasis of the entire layout was on fine press work, beautiful paper, limited editions, and exquisite bindings: Bacon's *Works* on India paper, the catalogue of John Carter Brown's library, *Notes on Columbus,* Worcester's *Dictionary* in full Russia calf, handsome sets of Dickens, Macaulay, and Hans Christian Andersen, and so on. Houghton had delegated responsibility for the Centennial show to his youngest partner, George Harrison Mifflin, who designed his exhibition to appeal to the bibliophile or gentleman who even in depression years could afford commission books and specially designed library sets. Ironically, since Osgood's specialty was reproductions of works of art, Hurd & Houghton received particular praise for its lithographs.[13]

As for Osgood's display, the *Publishers' Weekly* bemoaned its niggardliness — only one bookcase of eight shelves, two and a half filled with volumes of the *British Poets* (an income-producing asset Osgood was presently to sell to Houghton). The remaining shelves were filled with works of his native authors, a sufficient number to make an American proud, the *Publishers' Weekly* confessed grudgingly. Although the walls of his triangular space were hung with examples of his heliotype art, it was not here that his main efforts had been spent. He had taken space in that "Ezekiel's vision of machinery," that "nightmare confusion of the world's curiosity shop," Machinery Hall. Here were several of his heliotype presses clattering out their copies. Nor was Osgood content with Machinery Hall. To demonstrate his hope for heliotype galleries in every hamlet in the United States he had on display in the Photographic Annex examples of his art reproductions.

Houghton had instructed his partner that the binding is what sells the book. Mifflin's work for the Centennial demonstrated that he had taken the instruction to heart. Osgood's displays seem to indicate his conviction that profits in publishing were to be found in pictures.

One of the significant results of the Centennial Exhibition was that here for the first time publishing was defined as a profession in its own right, distinct from the two activities to which it owed its birth, printing and bookselling. The original proposal for the basis for awards for books had been that they must be manufactured by the exhibitor. Since by this time many houses assigned their books' manufacture to others, Holt, Scribner, and Putnam for example, violent objections were raised, objections supported by the *Publishers' Weekly,* which said, "Publishing is a business by itself, the most important of various factors in the production of a book, except the work of the author himself. It consists not so much . . . in manufacturing as in providing for manufacturing; and the responsibility, and therefore the credit, of the various details of printing, binding, etc., are the publisher's rather than his agent's." The publisher in directing his agent the printer places "the recognized stamp of his own individuality" on the work. Because of the outcry raised, the basis of the publishing awards was changed. For the purposes of the award, the publisher was held to be the producer of the book.[14]

Under these rules James R. Osgood & Company won a medal for the "exquisite taste in all the details of book-making" with a special accolade for its display of American authors. Hurd & Houghton won no publishing award, but perhaps Houghton regarded some of the prizes as his own; a number of the books chosen he had manufactured. As a manufacturer he was without peer. His Riverside Press earned medals for printing, binding, and lithography.

Following the Centennial, at his fall auction, Osgood made clear that despite his absorption in his heliotype and his furious campaign of asset selling, he had no intention of putting his native authors on the block. One or two, it is true, went under the hammer, mostly troublemakers, among them Gail Hamilton, John Trowbridge, and Julia Ward Howe. The majority of great names he kept secure. He had been binding them to him with contractual hoops, annuity contracts which assured him exclusive publication, for books only of course, since he had sold the *Atlantic.* The annuity contract was of a type created by James T. Fields, but Osgood improved on it. After the phenomenal success of Whittier's *Snow-Bound* in 1866, Ticknor & Fields paid the poet $3000 for its Diamond Edition of his *Poems,* the money to cover returns for five years. In 1872 the edition would revert to a standard 10 percent royalty. The original contract running out, Osgood offered Whittier a yearly $1000 on the Diamond for ten years. The following year Osgood devised a ten-year annuity. Under this agreement, Whittier was to receive an annual $2500, any new books to return the author a 10 percent royalty for eight months. After that the annuity would cover all returns. This Whittier contract was drawn in August 1873. Following the September panic, Osgood was driven to request the author to accept interest-bearing notes. However, he assured the poet, "Business never looked so promising with us for this season and we do not think the present disturbance will seriously affect it."[15]

For the author the advantage of the annuity arrangement with its limited exemption for new work was that he was guaranteed a minimum annual income. For the publisher, it meant he would be spared the pettifogging bookkeeping and semiannual reports on small as well as large sales. After the first months of a new book's being on the market, he would have a known yearly outlay for each author under such a contract. However, his most important gain was his exclusive right to future volumes of his most lucrative authors. For ten years at least Osgood need not worry about the subtle lures offered his poets and prophets by other houses.

When Lowell was approached on the annuity proposition, he objected, fearing he would lose "the first crop of profit" on his new books. James R. Osgood & Company explained:

> . . . this is just what we meant that you should *not* lose; but, on the contrary, intended to secure this to you in addition to the fixed sum *per annum* for all of your works in every shape . . . It was . . .

a part of our proposal of $1000 *per annum* for the old books, to pay in addition the regular copyright on every new book for (say) six months after publication: then, the "first crop" having been gathered, the book to take its place with the rest of the works under the general payment.

Our offer considerably exceeds the average returns of recent years and in making it up we endeavored to allow for all probable increase in sales hereafter, as well as for such increases of the amount as would come from the addition of new volumes to the list.

We thought we had made a liberal estimate, but as it seems to you insufficient we should be willing to make the amount $1000 besides the Diamond, (or $1300 total) [Fields, Osgood in 1869 had given Lowell a $300 annual return on the Diamond Edition of his poems for ten years]; but to go beyond that amount, would it seems to me, be too much of a tax upon the Earnings of the books, as it would come to about three times their present returns. To offset this we should have to triple the sale, which I think we could hardly hope to do, certainly not immediately.

We realize the obligation of pleasing and satisfying you in any arrangement, and desire to do what will be encouraging to you to produce new books; (as many as possible) and I trust this present proposition may appear to you in that light, and that not ten, nor twice ten, years shall be the limit of our bringing out new volumes from your pen.

Lowell continued reluctant and did not sign the agreement until his annual fee had been raised to $1500. Emerson agreed to $1500 also. Oliver Wendell Holmes accepted a lesser amount; $750 for three years, then $1000. Osgood also proposed an $1800 annuity to Hawthorne's heirs, but his efforts came to nothing because of arguments among the three children, Una, Rose, and Julian.[16]

Longfellow's annuity contract reflects both his exceptional popularity and his skill in driving a bargain. In 1874, a year before he agreed to the annuity arrangement, through the good offices of his friend Sam Ward, Robert Bonner of the New York *Ledger* offered Longfellow $3000 (plus $1000 to Ward for his "Lyrical Brokerage") for *The Hanging of the Crane*. Longfellow consulted Osgood, who was at first reluctant to permit newspaper publication of what he hoped would prove a best seller on his fall list. However, ultimately he agreed provided the poem was run in the *Ledger* without illustrations and was published in September, fully copyrighted in Longfellow's name. Osgood's *The Hanging of the Crane* would be on the market in October, possibly benefited by this advance release. He had nothing to fear about his rights in the book.[17]

The annuity contract Osgood presented for Longfellow's consideration in April 1875, postdated to January 1, specified an annual $4000 with an eight-month 10 percent on new books. The poet demurred. Matters dragged on. In the meantime Harper had entered the picture (through the agency of James T. Fields, who wished his part in the negotiations kept secret), securing Longfellow's Bowdoin anniversary poem "Morituri Salutamus" for the August *Harper's*. Longfellow set his own price — $1000. The poem was to appear under Osgood's imprint in *The Masque of Pandora,* scheduled for September publication. The Harper intrusion on Osgood's preserve was quite a different matter from that of Robert Bonner. Behind the magazine stood the house. From magazine to book might prove a logical sequence. Osgood went to Cambridge to win the poet's long withheld signature. On August 16, 1875, Longfellow recorded, "Signed agreement with Osgood and Co. for ten years' right of publishing my books for $4000. annually, in equal quarterly payments. My new book, on old arrangement at ten percent for nine months; then, on payment of $500. to be added to the others." He had won an extra month and $500 from his publisher.

That Osgood more than once regretted he had parted with the *Atlantic* is beyond question. The *North American Review* he would gladly have shed. For four years he tried to rid himself of it. In '73 his price of $10,000 had been too much for Godkin. In the spring of 1875 the chance Hurd & Houghton might take the incubus lightened his horizon. But the aristocratic Henry Adams and Henry Oscar Houghton could hardly be expected to see eye to eye. Houghton's suggestion that as a first step toward solvency rates for *Review* contributors be reduced, Adams contemptuously rejected. Nor would Adams entertain Osgood's proposal that he finance the periodical. However, despite the *North American*'s bleak prospects, he continued his irksome, unpaid editorial duties, all the time dreading it might die on his hands or "go to some Jew." The October 1876 issue proved his tombstone number. Osgood took exception to the content and Adams seized the opportunity to resign.[18]

Osgood had more than one reason for complaint. Among the book reviews appeared a slashing criticism of an Osgood book, George Parsons Lathrop's *A Study of Hawthorne*. However, this was the least offense. Unacceptable were the ideas and theories appearing in the body articles of the *Review*, especially in "The Independents and the Canvas," written by Adams and his brother Charles Francis. Here the brothers came out for Tilden as President, advocated return to specie payments, civil service reform, and "an entire abandonment of the theory of protection." S. D. Warren & Company was benefiting from the high tariff on paper. The suspicion that it was Osgood's masters rather than the genial Bantam who exploded over the Adams' attack on the Republican Party is inevitable.

Adams' fear the *Review* might go to some Jew proved groundless. That it might go to New York, for an Adams possibly the same thing, was an imminent possibility. Henry Holt, aware of Osgood's troubles, had taken an option to purchase, his intent to install Godkin as editor. He thought his option secure and was in the process of organizing a syndicate to back the project when on October 28, 1876, Osgood telegraphed: "Stop all negotiations respecting the Review. I have telegraphed Ticknor [who was in New York] to see you." To Ben he wired directing him to confirm his message to Holt, adding, "The Review is sold and money paid but this fact is not known at present."

Osgood had found a wealthy backer for the *North American*, Boston-born, Oxford-trained, brilliant twenty-three-year-old Allen Thorndike Rice. Under the terms of the agreement Rice owned the copyright and goodwill of the periodical. He was to pay all expenses of production, editing, manufacturing, and advertising, furnishing as security $10,000. Osgood, however, retained control. The *Review* was to continue under his imprint, the issues being increased from four to six a year, scale of payment to contributors not less than $3 a page, the editor of Osgood's choosing, the manufacture under his supervision, all payments over his signature. Osgood also reserved the right to exclude from publication any article he judged as injurious to his business interest. For such services, James R. Osgood & Company was to receive a 10 percent commission. Under the terms of the agreement, Osgood might resume ownership at the end of the first year. By the fall of 1877 he was in no position to do so. Rice, after paying $3000, took the venerable sheet to New York, there to rejuvenate it under Appleton's imprint by making it a forum for conflicting points of view.

By the evening of the Whittier dinner, Osgood was enough in debt to find himself in a new partnership. The house of Harper, which he had been courting ever since he released George Eliot, was one possibility. S. D. Warren & Company had a vested interest in Osgood. It also supplied paper to both Harper and Hurd & Houghton. The New York house may have been willing; Henry Oscar Houghton was reluctant. A more tempting opportunity was in the offing. Welch, Bigelow, closely associated with Osgood, was also up for bids. If he took over the University Press, his Riverside would be without rival.[19]

Houghton was still a printer at heart, and with reason. Throughout the '70s net gains of the Press had been in excess of those of the publishing house, and in the difficult year following the panic, Hurd & Houghton recorded a net loss of $2000, the Riverside Press a net gain in excess of $20,000. As publisher, the authors under his imprint who would attract others, who would perpetuate the name of Hurd & Houghton to future generations, were barely a handful; but for the long range, in addition to his standards, law books, medical texts, dictionaries, and guidebooks, he had a remarkable though short list of school books, not only Colburn's *Arithmetic* but also a solid series of classical texts acquired by his purchase of Crocker & Brewster's stereotype plates and publishing rights, the most enduring, Ethan A. Andrews and Solomon Stoddard's *Grammar of the Latin Language,* first published in 1836 and at the time of his purchase in its 65th edition. Another rugged volume that came to Hurd & Houghton with the Crocker & Brewster purchase

Houghton in 1878, the year he joined with Osgood to form
Houghton, Osgood & Company.

was Edward Robinson's *Hebrew and English Lexicon of the Old Testament,* on which the originator and his heirs would receive royalties for one hundred and ten years. Houghton's progress in publishing so far had been chiefly in the direction of tool-books and even these received praise for excellence of manufacture, as being representative of the art of bookmaking. The *American Bookseller* in 1877 selected so unlikely a title as Hurd & Houghton's *Transactions of the American Gynecological Association* to praise for its beauty, its "elegance of typography." The Riverside Press was still Henry Oscar Houghton's first love.[20]

Yet to secure the Ticknor & Fields list was an opportunity difficult to resist, especially since his youngest partner approved the plan. Houghton forwent his chance to acquire the University Press and took on James R. Osgood instead. The conversations initiated at the Whittier dinner took a month or more for formulation. The partnership papers, postdated to January 1, were not signed until February 4, 1878. First, Ben Ticknor had to be taken care of; he was bought out for $40,000 in short-term notes and given a salesman's job with S. D. Warren & Company. Then both Hurd and Albert Houghton, for reasons of health, wished to retire. Fortunately, this meant no loss of capital; both trusted Henry Oscar Houghton's skill in money matters sufficiently to leave their funds in his keeping. The Riverside Press, valued at $150,000, remained the property of H. O. Houghton & Company. For its use the new publishing house was to pay an annual rent of $15,000. A similar arrangement was made for Osgood's Heliotype Company. Since Hurd & Houghton's store at 13 Astor Place would serve adequately as an outlet for Houghton, Osgood publications, Osgood was to give up his New York Dutton headquarters. In Boston, Osgood's offices in the Cathedral Building at 220 Devonshire with a second entrance on Winthrop Square was considered as more appropriate for the new firm than Houghton's modest rooms on Beacon Street. The new firm's imprint was to be Boston and Cambridge. The poets and prophets of New England, bound by their annuity contracts, had been saved for Boston.[21]

Houghton, Osgood's capital stock consisting of "the Books, Merchandise, Prints, Stereotype, and Electrotype Plates with Contracts pertaining thereto, Good Will of periodicals and other property," was valued at $1,250,000, one third of it Osgood's. On this capital stock the partners were to receive 7 percent interest. Profits and losses were to be shared — Henry Oscar Houghton, five-twelfths, James Ripley Osgood, four-twelfths, George Harrison Mifflin, three-twelfths. In addition each had the privilege of drawing on the firm annually for current expenses — Houghton, $10,000; Osgood, $8000; Mifflin, $6000. Significantly, the partnership papers specified that stereotype plates be valued no higher than their cost of manufacture and that no partner indulge in speculation, or sign bonds or notes except in the legitimate interest of the business.

Under these conditions Houghton, Osgood & Company came into being to endure for a brief two years, years which George Harrison Mifflin remembered with horror to the end of his life, recalling that the new house "started off with brilliant possibilities but with heavy obligations, realized, as I now think, by none of us, and by the public not at all . . . It was not until the first maturing notes given by the new firm in settlement of Osgood's personal obligations, that the first real signs of danger appeared." Houghton, a man of infinite patience, with the assistance of a number of men of longer purse, survived the danger.

X

BETWEEN TWO FIRES

HAD HENRY O. HOUGHTON believed in omens, he might not have
signed the co-partnership agreement with Osgood. On January 7,
1878, fire broke out in the Dry Press Room of the Press. However,
so well trained was the Riverside fire brigade that before the Cambridge apparatus arrived, the flames were under control. Even so,
damage was considerable. The room was filled with sheets just
from the press — 70,000 of Webster's *Unabridged Dictionary,* a
large part of the February *Atlantic,* and "an immense quantity of
sheets of other works." Also, water seeping through the floor damaged books stored in bins below, the piles becoming so swelled
axes had to be used to hack them loose. However, Houghton was
not superstitious and he, with Mifflin, agreed to be yoked with
James Ripley Osgood.[1]

The announcement of the new partnership was greeted with a
blare of trumpets from the press, blazoned as a union which combined "the historical prestige of the old Ticknor house . . . with
the commercial strength and balanced enterprise of the Houghton
establishment, making Houghton, Osgood at once among the
foremost publishing-printing houses in the trade." Riverside was
pictured with its water front "protected by a stone pier allowing
ample wharf room, and a fine view of the river, meadows, and university towers." Its fire department, its library for workers, its savings department (which now had on deposit almost $25,000), "its
telegraphic communication with all points and telephonic connection with the publishing house in Boston" were all extolled.
An extensive spread in the New York *Daily Graphic* on March 4,
under the dates 1832–1878, presented pictures of the "quaint" Old

Corner Bookstore, the modern "stately" Cathedral Building, the Riverside Press, an American flag flying from its tower, and a camera, "noble" partner of the printing press and an essential tool for the heliotype. Displayed below the picture of the Press were the periodicals of the firm: The *Boston Medical and Surgical Journal,* the *Reporter* (a combination of Houghton's earlier *American Law Times* and his more recently acquired *Law and Equity Reporter*), the *American Architect and Building News,* the *Atlantic Monthly,* and the *United States Official Postal Guide.* Framing all were the signatures of Longfellow, Whittier, Holmes, Bryant, Emerson, Tennyson, Saxe, Bret Harte, Charles Dudley Warner, Bayard Taylor, Stedman, Aldrich, Agassiz, Harriet Beecher Stowe, Lowell, and William Dean Howells. In more than a column of detail the *Graphic* rehearsed the proud history of the two-branched derivation of the house, declaring that in the combination appeared "the history of half a century of the growth of American literature" as well as the striking advances made in the craft of the book. "The Riverside Press has been, not a copyist or imitator, but an originator in features of paper and type, binding and execution, that mark strides of progress that have laid widely and strong the reputation of the house," the *Graphic* declared, seeing an especial fitness in this combination by which "the Riverside Press wins and henceforth shares successes it has so largely helped." And indeed, Houghton must have taken satisfaction in having at last under his aegis authors whose books in the old days when William D. Ticknor had been in command he had printed for Ticknor & Fields. At last there would be no division between contributions to the *Atlantic* and the books which resulted. The imprint for both would be Houghton, Osgood & Company.[2]

The two-year association was an active one for the partners. Both Houghton and Osgood traveled widely pushing the interests of the firm. Mifflin stayed at the Press struggling with the increased demands for production and constantly ciphering, trying to devise solutions for the diffuse problems of bookkeeping which the union presented.

One of the first matters to absorb the attention of the house was the Paris Exposition, due to open May first. Fortunately for

Houghton, Osgood, if not for those burdened with details for arranging entries, Congress had been dilatory in accepting the French Government's invitation, tendered in May 1876. Not until December 1877 did our representatives act, then appropriating $150,000 for the undertaking, an appropriation subsequently increased by $40,000. Exhibition material was scheduled to leave this country on February 9, 1878. Had this date been insisted on, books by many writers to whom was owed America's growing reputation for national identity in literature would have been missing. Osgood, in his straitened circumstances had not intended to take part. Houghton, on the other hand, had been in the forefront of publishers active in arranging for American participation, and his Press had been chosen to prepare one of the catalogues, that of the *Collective Exhibit of the American Book Trade for the Exposition Universalle de Paris 1878*. Few industries hoping to show at the Exposition could meet the February deadline. As a result, sailing dates for the various ships assigned to convey material to France were repeatedly advanced, the last departure being set for early April. Thus it was possible for Houghton, Osgood to dispatch its books with the new imprint in time to take a distinguished place in the *Palais de l'Exposition, Section Américaine*.[3]

Mifflin, had the Exposition been the only foreign interest of the house, would have been the logical partner to represent Houghton, Osgood. He cherished affectionate memories of his months in France some ten years before; he loved her literature and spoke her language fluently. Moreover his work for the Centennial had demonstrated his skill in planning such exhibitions. However, more than the Exposition required attention. English authors and publishers must be briefed on the changes which had taken place in Boston. Osgood, with his Ticknor & Fields background and his own association with the British trade, was the obvious emissary. Also, he had a brother who for the past decade had been associated with the Parisian banking house of Drexel, Harjes. Fields, who had used Drexel, Harjes on his 1869 tour, had reported that he found young Edward Osgood both prompt and kind. "He is evidently cut out for either a Baring or a Rothschild," he joked. Six years later Aldrich related he had had a fine time with Edward, exclaiming, "*He's* a cool boy! A way-worn and battered old citizen of the world. What a soft thing he has in Paris!" In May Edward landed another soft job. So that he could watch over Houghton, Osgood's interests at the Exposition until his brother showed up, he was put on the firm's payroll.[4]

Because of the New York Spring Trade Sale and farewell banquets for Bayard Taylor, about to leave to assume his ministerial duties in Berlin, Osgood could not sail until the end of June. On board with him were two of his authors, George W. Waring, sanitary engineer, novelist, and raconteur, on his way to Switzerland, and Bret Harte, recently appointed consul at Krefeld in Germany.

Poor Harte, despite the sums his writing had commanded, was as usual in a morass of money troubles. The American Publishing Company between 1872 and 1875 had advanced him $6600. *Gabriel Conroy* had failed to earn through sales sufficient credit to eradicate his debt and he was leaving for his diplomatic post with a claim of over $2500 against him, a claim he never paid. Harte was also in debt to Houghton, Osgood. To relieve the author of that burden, Osgood, shortly before sailing, had devised a contract under which for $1500 Harte transferred to the new firm his ownership of copyright in fourteen books. In return the publishers acquitted him of "any pecuniary indebtedness appearing against him on their books." Harte further agreed to submit all his future books first to Houghton, Osgood. If the firm accepted his offering, Harte was to receive 10 percent for one year; then the publishers would have the option of buying the copyright, price to be arranged. If Houghton, Osgood did not pick up its option, the 10 percent would remain in force until expiration of copyright.[5]

The three companions reached London on July 8, Waring setting out for Switzerland at once. After Harte had checked in at Krefeld, he and Osgood planned to meet in Paris on July 22. However, taking over his diplomatic post proved more complicated than he had anticipated. In consequence, he arrived in the French capital too late to have a gay day or two with his publisher, who by the time he arrived had left for England. Osgood had not been in the least downcast by his friend's failure to appear. He had his bachelor brother to call on for convivial company. He also had another friend at court. Charles Fairchild's brother, General Lucius Fairchild, Governor of Wisconsin from 1866 to 1872, was now serving in Paris as Consul-General under United States Minister Edward F. Noyes.

Paris was filled to overflowing this Exposition summer. The display grounds on the Champ de Mars and the Trocadero were thronged with a daily attendance of over 83,000. In spite of the crowds, the city was at its loveliest, especially at night when public monuments were illuminated and Chinese lanterns swung from the windows of private residences. Americans were everywhere and the Ministry was besieged by aggressive nationals demanding invitations to official functions. Various in attendance used their connections with the Exposition, tenuous as they might be, to request influence in securing decorations. Nothing less than the Legion of Honor would do. All this and more Osgood must have heard from his brother and General Fairchild.

Surely wayworn Edward told his brother of the distressing performance of his countrymen on the Fourth of July, when the French Government set up a collation in the Bois de Boulogne at which wine was served liberally. The Americans unused to such generosity guzzled glass after glass, some even swigging from bottles. When members of the French Cabinet attempted to address the noisy audience, they were greeted with rowdy applause, then with taunts: "Speak English, Old Boy!" "Talk Yankee fashion!" "Give it to the British!" "Make the Eagle Scream!" Finally the crowd became so unruly the proceedings were cut short and for the rest of the day groups of American drunks were to be seen reeling down the Champs Elysées. Such excesses were not reserved to the Fourth. Harte recalled his three-day stopover in Paris on his way to Krefeld as "confused" and "hysterical." When he returned at the end of July some days late for his date with Osgood, again temptation proved too much for him and he became "so thoroughly steeped in iniquity and dissipation" that in retrospect the time made his hair stand on end. Perhaps if Osgood had been on hand to act the cicerone, Harte's recollections would have been less tortured. Osgood's pleasures were of a more sophisticated cast. Furthermore, he was in Paris on business, theoretically. He must have paid some attention to the Exposition.[6]

Second only in acclaim to the American exhibits of machinery were those dramatizing the remarkable progress the United States had made in developing its free educational system. As Osgood walked through the immense areas of display, he could perhaps take wry pride in the two large volumes of heliotype illustrations of Harvard buildings in the display of that institution. He must have stood long before Louis Prang's exhibit, rated as one of the most outstanding in the Educational Section. Spread out here was that series which he had once been confident would put him in the first boat — Walter Smith's drawing books. He may have noted the catalogue's paragraph which in accounting for Prang's progress in publishing said, "The educational department received a special impetus when, in the year 1874, Mr. Prang admitted Mr. John S. Clark, formerly of the firm of James R. Osgood & Co., as partner, and assumed the publication of Prof. Walter Smith's 'American Text-books of Art Education.'" Smith's texts, combined with another more advanced Prang series, formed "a well-developed systematic course of instruction, such as no other country, not even France or England," could claim. However, Osgood was not one to regret. His future was pregnant with promise.

Among the twenty-five publishing houses participating in the Exposition, Houghton, Osgood's display was outstanding. On view were not only the standards, professional works, and text-books of the Hurd & Houghton line but also the "pure literature" of those writers so long associated with Ticknor & Fields and its successors, works which gave "the peculiar flavor" of America and demonstrated that the country had "reached her maturity," that she was no longer imitative. For this exhibit, the Riverside Press received a gold medal; Houghton, Osgood, a silver one, and one of its authors, Edward H. Knight whose *American Mechanical Dictionary* Houghton had recently acquired, was honored with the Legion of Honor with the rank of Chevalier for his work on the American Industrial Exhibit. In these awards a publisher might well take pride.

During his stay in Paris, Osgood talked with his brother about the possibility of his coming home. Perhaps their plans were of longer range than the immediate. So far, Osgood's independent publishing life had demonstrated that loved as he was for his open,

Some of the medals the Riverside Press has won for its
book design and manufacture.

generous, genial ways, he had no head for figures. He was too fond of round numbers, too ready to lend and borrow. His popularity with writers was sufficient assurance he could always produce a striking list. The cool Edward, with his decade of banking experience, might be the very person to provide the calculating balance James Ripley lacked. Osgood promised his brother a berth in Boston and Edward agreed to return to America.

By July 31 Osgood was back in London. Within a week he had settled his few publishing affairs: Trübner was to bring out Holmes's *John Lothrop Motley* and Taylor's *Deukalion,* anticipating American publication by a few days in order to secure English copyright; Cassell, Petter & Galpin agreed to act as exclusive agents for Houghton, Osgood's forthcoming two-volume, illustrated, subscription edition of Longfellow's *Poetical Works.* By the time the weary Harte dragged into London from Paris, the peripatetic Osgood, combining business with pleasure, was off to Scotland for a visit with his poker-playing companion, the novelist William Black, first published in America in *Every Saturday* and now in the Harper stable. Due to sail on August 29, Osgood joined Harte at last shortly before that date. At this meeting, Harte gave Osgood "The Great Deadwood Mystery," one of the stories to appear in his next book, *The Twins of Table Mountain.* In return, Osgood promised to pay Mrs. Harte, still in America, $150 as an advance on royalties. Harte's nature was to repine; Osgood's to be gay. But both must have ruefully recalled the plush days before the fire of '72 and the panic of '73, when Harte could ask for and Osgood agree to $10,000 for twelve contributions, none of them in hand at the time of contract.[7]

Osgood reached home early in September, in time to install his brother in Houghton, Osgood's Devonshire Street offices and to take part in the fall Trade Sales. His eight-week excursion had cost the firm a little over $1500.[8]

While Osgood was happily combining pleasure with business abroad, at home Houghton was demonstrating that business was his pleasure even though travel the penalty. He was repeatedly on the road, taking his wife with him when possible, an indulgence he was sure Osgood could not understand, he told Mifflin. Because of

Hurd's and Albert G. Houghton's retirements, the New York end of the business demanded attention. The first plan of the new firm had been to abandon the store, maintaining a small office only. Mifflin, indeed, was for closing out the New York end entirely. However, Albert, because of the large sums he had left with his brother, even in retirement had a voice in the firm's affairs. He also had two sons already in the employ of the house. The store was moved from 13 to 21 Astor Place and Albert Flyer Houghton, with his brother Oscar Ready as assistant, was put in charge. Oscar Ready would shortly go on the road.[9]

Houghton had problems to solve of greater import than the New York store. For one thing, Congress had cut its appropriation for the *Postal Guide* from $20,000 to $15,000. Pressure must be applied to have the $5000 restored. Trips to Washington were therefore essential. For another, he had been appointed to a committee to confer with the Post Office Department on postal rates. His interest as a publisher was chiefly in mail charges for periodicals. His efforts in behalf of the *Postal Guide* were successful. So were those for Postal Reform. In 1879, Congress enacted legislation providing that second class matter could be sent anywhere in the country at a low uniform rate. Important as the *Postal Guide* appropriation and the periodical mailing rates were to Houghton, they were of minor significance compared to his fight for tariff protection. Early in '78 he was delegated to a committee of publishers and related manufacturers to investigate the current law and its enforcement.[10]

Henry Oscar Houghton was probably born a protectionist. Certainly, in his college years the concept that protection of home industries was a government duty had characterized his thinking. His business experience had repeatedly confirmed his youthful convictions. Now surveying the potential book markets west of the Berkshires and south of the Mason-Dixon Line, he was dismayed by apparent British preemption of provinces he assumed belonged by natural right to American publishers. In 1876 the United States had imported books from England to the value of $940,000. American books exported to England came to only $93,000. Despite this imbalance, Houghton considered the existing 25 percent ad valorem duty sufficient, even though duty on the raw material for books — paper and cloth — ran from 5 percent to 10 percent higher. The trouble was, the law was not enforced. Other publishers, especially those who were not also manufacturers, viewed the tariff differently. The most vocal of the trade in attacking existing duties on imports was George Haven Putnam, who in 1874 had become a member of the Free Trade League.[11]

To Houghton, the Free Trade movement was a perfidious Albion attempt to saturate the American market with subversive literature. American Anglophobia was general in the 1870s. Many people still remembered bitterly England's friendship with the Confederacy. The Centennial year had reawakened even more ancient hates. The chauvinism of the American drunks in the Bois de Boulogne had its source in sober men at home, one of them Henry Oscar Houghton, who protested that we had fought the Revolution so "that we might have the privilege of making our own goods and buying where we pleased." Now with our forty millions to educate, British publishers eyed us acquisitively, he asserted. "If a man owns a thousand cattle, and another man owns a thousand acres of grass, the man that owns the cattle is the free trader; he is bound to have the grass if he has to break down the fence to get it," Houghton warned. The English, including their Canadian subjects, were invading the country, especially in the West, selling their books so cheaply that a paper maker could afford to take them from the customhouse at their appraised value and grind them up for paper stock. The British were able to infiltrate the American market in a variety of ways. They used the mails, sowing their books "all over the United States . . . as thick as locusts in Egypt." Post offices were negligent in inspecting packages and exacting duty as the law required. Importers did not honestly declare goods; frequently they valued them as much as 90 percent off the retail price. Moreover, British books designed for American markets had already paid their prime cost — stereotype plates — by sales at home. Now the plates, battered and broken, were being used over and over again to produce books made of cheap and dirty paper. Because American workers were paid two to three times more than their English counterparts,

American manufacturers could not undercut the British in the initial outlay for stereotypes, seven eighths of their cost being attributable to manual labor, only one eighth to material and machines.

Houghton was further incensed because these sorry English exports failed to reflect American experience and ideals. The textbooks, widely used throughout the country because of their cheapness, pictured insects never seen on this side of the Atlantic and were full of the Divine Right of Kings. "I do not want my children to be taught that one man is better than another; that one man was born to serve another," Houghton fulminated. "These namby-pamby English books teach our children to be respectful of their masters!" Rather, children should be brought up on a literature reflecting "the great ideas that we have been living on for the past one hundred years." Publishers, he insisted, "have some responsibility as to what shall be the character of this generation." Why do we send our young men abroad for an education, he demanded. America has universities. America has teachers. Moreover, America's scholars need encouragement, he argued. "Let us call into action all the great men to investigate our original subjects here." Louis Agassiz had told him, "if we had proper protection of our literature . . . this would be the greatest country on the face of the earth for original investigation." Publishers, if given adequate protection, could afford to publish the work of such men of science.

The memorial which Houghton's committee drew up to present to Congress opposed any reduction in the duty on books or their raw materials, advised that any change to be made should be from an ad valorem to a specific duty, and requested that action be postponed to a future session. It was signed not only by publishers and manufacturers but also by authors, among them William Dean Howells. To conclude that Howells' signing of the appeal (and a later one) was a time-serving submission to his publisher's wish is a slur on the author's integrity and a disregard of his known political convictions. At this time, Whittier, Clemens, Holmes, Longfellow, Fields, Aldrich, Stedman, and Scudder were also high-tariff men.

Scudder in the 1870s had taken American literature for his particular critical province. In 1875, leaving his money with the firm at 10 percent, he resigned his Hurd & Houghton partnership, feeling he could not afford to work without salary and have his investment assessed when the company lost money as it did in 1874. For the next few years, although never far from the Press or free from Houghton's loose tether, he enjoyed relative independence, writing and lecturing on, even agitating for, academic recognition of our national literary heritage and its promise. His balanced critical approach was larger than parochial. He cherished the root as well as the branch. "So long as literature is regarded as a product which is to carry off the prize in some international exhibition," he wrote, "we shall no doubt bring forward the biggest squashes that can be shown on any latitude, but every effort to sunder ourselves violently from the common traditions of literature can only end in the production of what will create no tradition." Hawthorne, he believed, in whose "curiously experimental spirit" the sense of the past was "profoundly present," should serve as a touchstone for the times, so corroded by corruption in high places. In one of his lectures on "American Literature" in 1876, he said, "Hope and courage, bright sunshine and fresh air are indeed the birthright of Americans . . . Yet will not the time come when people will look back upon this period and see the shadow steadily creeping over the face of the nation, as the dark evil of national pride, vainglory, insolence and injustice rises portentously before the conscience? I dare say that the figure of Hawthorne then, walking his solitary way, peering, with his shaded candle, into the dark recesses of evil, will seem the truest representative of the nation's secret consciousness."[12]

More novelists, Scudder advised, should follow Howells' example in using the accidental and particular. Too many created a setting without substance, treating "their towns and railways as cautiously as if they feared a libel suit." He anticipated that writers would increasingly picture their local scenes in honest, direct speech and would find in both history and politics the stuff of fiction. Poets must find in their streams and fields the shape of their song ". . . not because they are American, but because the white-throated sparrow singing in the border of the woods has been heard by them in the very heart of their home life, and they know the English lark only by hearsay."[13]

From Bradford through Hawthorne to Howells and beyond, Scudder mastered his subject. In these years he probably knew as much as any of his contemporaries about the seed as well as the flower of his country's literature. Consequently, Representative James A. Garfield, who was intent on mastering the arguments in favor of protective tariff, may well have listened to Scudder, whom he had known in his Williams years, and to whom he had confessed that in his reading he sought surcease from the "husks of politics."

It is a very trifling matter [Scudder wrote him] whether a few bookmakers and publishers make a large or a small profit, and regarding them simply as capitalists or mechanics, I would put their personal interests . . . entirely at the disposal of the government . . .

The real question is, not how will this measure affect the revenue, but how will it affect national character and education . . . It is marvelous how rapidly our people have become nationalized, especially under the fusing of war, and with what apparent ease we receive and absorb the elements of foreign life. Certainly we Americanize foreigners who come to live with us much more positively than they Anglicize or Francise, or Germanize us; and yet our own national character is modified by the constant accessions of foreigners. Just as our country is open to visitors from all lands and the process of naturalization is made very easy, so we give easy reception to the ideas of Europe. But the men who come here are more or less predisposed to our order of life, while a great portion of the literature we receive is antagonistic to our institutions. No one who observed the tone of a large portion of the English press during the war, can fail to see that it displayed a perverted view of the relation between the government and the governed. Now it is true that we do throw off these theories and false judgments . . . but we do it only after a painful process, and just because we have so little positive literature of our own bearing upon these subjects . . .

There is another point on the subject which seems to me per-

haps even more important. The literature of a nation which af-
fects its character most powerfully is not the philosophic so much
as the romantic. You have not forgotten the Fletcher of Saltoun
saying which our college orators used to quote so regularly — I
care not etc. so men's minds are affected for good or evil by the
bent which their feelings take when they are children, by the associations which they form with images then presented to them.
But the home literature of American life is of the scantiest sort.
If you go to any theatre to see a domestic play, the entire properties down to the coal hod are English. We import historic
associations from Europe and a child may grow up fed upon a
literature saturated with English ideas until as often happened
previous to the war, he becomes ashamed of his country!
Ashamed not of her sins, but of what he thought her want of
culture.

National literature is not to be legislated into being, and it
will struggle into existence in spite of any legislative embarrass-
ments, but it is possible for Congress to act as to encourage literature and save us from being swamped by foreign notions. There
can be no doubt that in literature, as in other fields, demand will
act upon the supply. There is thought in this country, there is a
vast amount of talent, diverse and peculiar, expending itself in
more transient employment, simply because the general field of
literature, where it belongs, pays poorly and has been suffered to
fall into the hands of foreigners. I am glad when I see any new
magazine started and keep its legs. I know that it will add at least
one new author to our lit. who otherwise might leave his book
unwritten . . .[14]

The tariff question in these days was inextricably bound with
that of International Copyright. The authors who supported protection did so because they saw no chance that the United States
would reach agreement with other countries, especially England,
on methods and restrictions for an International Copyright Law.
Lacking a foreign covenant, they believed the tariff offered some
assurance that a living could be made from the published word.
They were not condoning piracy. They would have preferred the
justice as well as the rewards of International Copyright.

Houghton had always been in favor of International Copyright.
Now that his list included many of the American writers most

widely pirated abroad, he was unequivocally committed in his own interest as well as theirs. Authors had themselves only to protect. Houghton wished to foster their interests, his own, and those of his laborers as well, a class from which he had recently emerged. During the fearful railroad strife of 1877 with its contagious unrest, Riverside had had no overt trouble. His allegiance to his publishing self was hedged. He was caught between the upper and nether millstones of the writer and the mechanic, each with his justified drive for increased cash reward. He believed the existing duty on books, provided it were collected, served the three interests most equitably. If an International Copyright Law were to be negotiated, affording security for the publisher and author, some provision must be included for the protection of his press and his craftsmen. This condition delayed the enactment of an International Copyright Law for more than a decade. Then a contentious compromise would be devised, a compromise which even today forces the publisher and the printer into opposite camps. Houghton was both publisher and printer. Protective tariff was his partial answer to an unsolved question.

At this stage of the contest, victory was his. The Hayes Administration, under Garfield's skilled direction, saw to it that consideration of the Wood bill, a proposal for a general tariff reduction, was postponed. Of course, tariff adherents far more powerful than publishers, printers, and writers brought pressure on Washington, but Houghton and his associates could feel they had contributed to bringing the struggle, temporarily at least, to their desired conclusion. The battle would be repeatedly renewed.

Houghton's preoccupations in 1878 and '79 included more than tariff, his travels more than New York and Washington. In the first year he journeyed through the Middle West. In the following year he went to California. These Western trips opened his eyes to the possibilities of business beyond the Berkshires. They gave him a fresh point of view, he told Mifflin, making him realize that their list wasn't "half worked." He was concerned about Houghton, Osgood's uncopyrighted standards; there were so many competing, cheaper editions. Riverside must find ways to reduce costs yet maintain its reputation for excellence. His talks with people in Chicago and Milwaukee made him aware of unfamiliar attitudes and values. There he heard that Houghton, Osgood's medical journal would sell better if Boston were omitted from the title. People were ready to tell him what was the matter with the *Atlantic* too. It was too literary, too scholarly, too remote from the day. What the periodical needed was more articles on contemporary, controversial questions. Refreshing as these opening horizons of the West were to his publishing purpose, they did not basically affect Houghton's deliberate caution in this time of trial for the new partnership. Innovations must wait. "I think our policy should be," he wrote Mifflin from Cincinnati, "for the present not to add a thing to our list that involves risk, that we can avoid, until we get things in better working order, specially our periodicals." A point of view with which young Mifflin agreed heartily. Osgood, on the other hand, wouldn't consider himself a publisher if he didn't take risks.[15]

During Houghton's frequent times away, Mifflin kept him informed on the business in Boston and Cambridge. In the fall of '78, although people were still complaining of hard times, he was pleased to report that affairs were proceeding smoothly. The Press was running full tilt and the Merriams were going ahead with plans for a new edition of Webster's unabridged. The undertaking was to be a huge one of almost 7000 pages, including 4500 new words and a biographical supplement of over 10,000 names, an innovation in dictionaries. Later in summarizing the first year of the new partnership, Mifflin wrote that book sales had brought in $418,000; periodicals, $163,000, and outside manufacturing by Riverside, $300,000. He was worried about expenses, however. They were out of all proportion to receipts. As a step toward economy, he recommended the firm be centralized at an enlarged Press. He was convinced "that by discontinuing the New-York Store and concentrating the Business at Riverside retaining only a small Boston office, the expense A/c would not simply be reduced, but greater efficiency resulting in larger Book Sales and manufacturing product would also follow . . ." He saw no reason why the two companies — Houghton, Osgood and H. O. Houghton & Company — could not be conducted under one roof. A metropolitan location involved needless expense. "The Merriams," he reminded Houghton, "have shown their wisdom and shrewdness in remaining in their old little side street in Springfield, and yet it is clear that the wonderful success of the Dictionary is due to their never tiring watchfulness and study . . ." Such watchfulness would be possible for Houghton, Osgood were its offices at the Press. The three partners would then meet constantly for conferences and a friendly exchange of ideas. Moreover, such show of unity would improve the morale of Riverside's four hundred employees. In concluding his report on the business for 1878, Mifflin craved indulgence for its length. "But," he explained, "my mind has been engrossed with this subject so incessantly for the past year . . . it must seek relief in some shape!"[16]

If Osgood read Mifflin's report, he must have laughed at the idea of Houghton, Osgood's giving up its luxurious quarters in the Cathedral Building. The logjam of the depression had begun to shift. Although many were not aware an upsurge was on the way, the signs were there, even in the fall of '78 on his return from England. At the Trade Sales, with the exception of his heliotype books which went for more than half off, prices were up, bringing bids only a little less than the standard discount. The Merriams' dictionaries even brought offers close to their retail value. By the spring of the following year revival had demonstrably set in. Estes & Lauriat reported its business doubled over the previous year and Mifflin, footing up his figures for the first six months of '79, reported book sales were up and promising well for the months to come. By September Boston trade was celebrating signs of white water and the prospect of an expanding stream. Orders were flowing in from the West. Locally, despite the promise of sales, people complained there was little new for the discriminating reader. Publishers generally were reworking their lists, producing new issues of old titles, enlarged, abridged, illustrated, and so on. The trade as a whole was disposed to work over old plates, the *Publishers' Weekly* noted. Houghton was not alone in being cautious, in eyeing risk with suspicion. Yet anyone associated with James Ripley Osgood of necessity took risks.[17]

Houghton, Osgood, in contrast to the disposition of the trade as a whole, in its two-year existence produced many titles for the discriminating reader. With the exception of John Burroughs' *Locusts and Wild Honey,* the new "literature" of the house came from

Osgood's line. Each of his annuitants, save Lowell, who was un-derstandably preoccupied with his ministerial duties at Madrid, produced a book. Younger men also contributed to the list, most achieving acceptable sales. But none could touch Howells, whose *The Lady of the Aroostook* was published in February 1879. Be-fore the end of the year it had sold 8631 copies. Yet Scudder was outpacing Howells. His healthy juvenile, third in a series, *The Bodleys on Wheels,* sold 13,152 in a little over a year. However, the book that set the publishers' hearts pounding, the sparkler in the stable, a one-shot, was Mary A. Sprague's *An Earnest Trifler.* Published in November, its sales topped 9000 by the end of De-cember.[18]

Nor was the list weak in standards. Globe Editions of Cooper, Dickens, and Scott were being turned out "by the cord," taxing the resources of "the gigantic Riverside Press," according to the *Pub-lishers' Weekly.* Moreover, the catalogue contained plenty of an-thologies, biographies, topical and tool books. To rehearse the titles would be tedious. There is sufficient evidence that Hough-ton, Osgood, at least, was free of the depression's downward drag.[19]

In anticipation of prosperity for the country generally and his house in particular, Houghton decided to close out 1879 with an-other party for *Atlantic* contributors. The nearest excuse that offered was Dr. Holmes's seventieth birthday, which had occurred in August. Plans for the affair were laid well in advance. For one thing, Houghton wanted to be sure Clemens would be on hand. On October 24, Howells extended the invitation. Clemens both accepted and requested he be allowed to speak, writing, "If any-body talks, there, I shall claim the right to say a word myself, & be heard among the *earliest* . . ." Then, remembering Howells' misery over his performance at the Whittier banquet, he added, "but you may read what I say beforehand, & strike out whatever you choose."[20]

Houghton's first *Atlantic* dinner had been for thirty guests; at his next over sixty sat down. The Holmes celebration with over a hundred was the largest yet. One reason for the increase was that lady contributors were invited.

Shortly after the Whittier banquet a satiric squib had appeared in the press. Titled "Mr. Houghton's Mistake," it pictured various females declining invitations they had not received. In the skit, Gail Hamilton, whose feud with Houghton since he had published her *Battle of the Books* was public property, was reported to have written:

> Well, my boy, so you're going to have a dinner, are you? To Mr. Whittier, the dearest and best for whom my soul longeth? I was about to say I didn't think anything of you, but I won't. You can thank your true goodness for that. O, say nothing of that last check. Seriously, however, I don't blame you. If there's anything unpleasant in this world it is a woman in a wide house — I mean a banquet hall. I will not stop to argue the wine question; I have no liquid by me to create the necessary inspiration. I suppose it would do no good either — you men are determined to have your own way always, and ours as often as possible. I write to say that I won't come, and to insist that Mr. Whittier and the rest shall not break their hearts over it. Sufficient is it on these occasions to break bread, and, perhaps, also heads. I have just seen a circular in behalf of a new ladies' magazine. Have you seen it? . . . Do you know, by the way, that Mrs. Spofford is about to give a grand dinner to the lady contributors of the *Atlantic?*

Houghton took the hint. Ladies were invited to the Holmes celebration, but it was to be a "breakfast." And that made all the difference, or almost all.[21]

A number of august individuals attended the affair who by no stretch of the imagination could be considered *Atlantic* contributors. No line of theirs had ever been printed in the periodical. Their presence as much as that of the ladies required decorous behavior. No chanting of sonnets this time, no wildly funny satire. Augustus Flagg, managing editor of Little, Brown was there; so were Edward L. Burlingame of Scribner's and Joseph Wesley Harper of the house of Harper. Samuel D. Warren was there, and also a former Governor of Massachusetts, Alexander Hamilton Rice, founder of his state's Republican Party and senior partner of Rice, Kendall & Company, a firm second only to Warren's in extending credit to James R. Osgood & Company, obligations now carried by Houghton, Osgood. Crackling short and long term notes played an obbligato to the rustle of the ladies' bustled silks. Charles Fairchild was there too. For him the occasion had an element of farewell. He was about to leave for Europe. When he returned, he would no longer be a partner of S. D. Warren.[22]

Although they were not to sit down to their breakfast until two in the afternoon, guests were invited to forgather in the Brunswick at twelve. During these social hours, perhaps Clemens, Howells, Osgood, Fairchild, Aldrich, and others of their brotherhood fortified themselves with a dram or two; at table, out of deference to the ladies, water would be the only liquid. After all, it was a breakfast, even though no bacon and eggs affair. The guests sat at six long tables arranged in a parallelogram and the popular Phillips Brooks was on hand at the head table to say grace before the hardy diners attacked the barbaric series of courses which would occupy them for the afternoon.

As at the two earlier Houghton affairs for *Atlantic* contributors, the senior partner opened the program. After complimenting the guest of honor for his gift of showing us "what wonderful people we are" and giving due recognition of the still living originators of the magazine, he talked of the young contributors coming on, nearly a thousand he reckoned. His recent travels had enlarged his vision and so he prophesied that these new writers, having at their command a wider knowledge than those who had preceded them, would increasingly turn their attention to the country's spectacular scenery, its oppressed aborigines, its heterogeneous population, its dramatic discoveries and inventions. These would be the subjects for the coming historians, novelists, and poets. "Men and women are to come who will write of the wrongs of the Indian, of the scenery of the West, of the great problems of humanity," he predicted. Helen Hunt Jackson, a guest at the head table, listened attentively. Her articles on the American Indian were to fill many an *Atlantic* page.

Although Clemens had asked to speak early in the program, others took precedence. In waiting his turn he had no friends on his right and left as in former years to relieve the tedium. Seated at Mifflin's table on the west of the oblong, he was wedged between the impoverished Harriet Waters Preston and a Mrs. Walker. On Miss Preston's right was the nearly blind historian Francis Parkman. Somehow during the course of the long afternoon, Clemens, to his torturing regret, managed to blunder in conversation with

Parkman; otherwise his behavior was impeccable, even though he was forced to bide his time listening to speeches or recitations by his host, Dr. Holmes, Fields, Julia Ward Howe, Charles Dudley Warner, and Harvard's President Eliot. Then after Clemens had made a graceful speech paying a debt of long standing to Dr. Holmes, he had to endure further oratory. The number of speakers appalls, even as do the number of courses, at this prodigious breakfast: Joseph Wesley Harper, introduced by toastmaster Howells as one who would say something "to allay the animosity prevailing between authors and publishers," Stedman, Aldrich, Trowbridge, Cranch, and Higginson with his airs and graces, and on and on through the waning afternoon. At least there was one bit of drama to lessen the boredom. Osgood, with his flair for the vivid, had arranged that a telegram be delivered to him at table. Flourishing the yellow sheet, he jumped to his feet to announce that the charming little lady on his right from Ohio was on her way to fame and fortune. Another large, pre-Christmas order for Mary A. Sprague's *An Earnest Trifler* was in his hand.

Publishers and authors alike that night must have dreamed of oysters, broiled partridge, terrapin stew, and delicious royalties. The holiday season was on. Signs of renewing affluence were everywhere. At long last, Christmas would fulfill its promise. The depression was over. The New Year would be the first worthy of celebration in seven long years.

Early Monday morning, December 29, a note was delivered to Houghton at his Cambridge house.

Monday, 1 A M Dec 28 [29], 1879

Dear Mr. Houghton

As you may be aware our store is all burnt up. Ned & Anthony & I have just returned. We took the ledgers out of the safe and they are all right whether the safe stands or not. I have tried to raise Mifflin but cannot.

Please call at the house (196 Beacon St.) when you come in in the morning, and if I have gone downtown I will leave word where I am.

Yours
J. R. Osgood

Happy New Year!

At eleven o'clock Sunday night fire had broken out on the fifth floor of Rice, Kendall's warehouse at 91 Federal, connected by a bridge at this level with the Cathedral Building. As at the time of the 1872 fire, there was delay in alerting the Fire Department. Before the alarm could be sounded, the heat from the flames had melted the wires of the electrical system and a boy had to be sent running to City Hall. Four hours later the fire was out, the Rice, Kendall warehouse and the Cathedral Building a mass of smoking rubble, the total loss an estimated one to one and a half million; Houghton, Osgood's between $100,000 and $150,000; the Heliotype Company's between $30,000 and $40,000, both fully insured.[23]

When Houghton reached Boston the morning of the twenty-ninth, he perhaps found word at Osgood's Beacon Street house to come to 47 Franklin, for here Osgood and his brother had engaged rooms over Lee & Shepard's store. The partners took steps immediately to assure the public that their business would continue as usual. Before the debris of the once stately Cathedral Building had cooled, a secretary was put to work notifying all customers that despite the total destruction of the firm's Boston offices, all orders would be promptly filled, there being ample inventory at the Riverside Press. Although not an artist's tool, not a proof, negative stone, or press of the Heliotype Company had been saved, Osgood promptly took temporary quarters on Pearl Street. Some of the Heliotype Company's first pictures in 1872 had been of Boston's burnt out district. Eight years later, in January 1880, he had pictures of his own burnt out district on the market.[24]

In New York, a prosperous paint manufacturer and former Cambridge friend of Houghton's, learning of Houghton, Osgood's catastrophe, entrained for Boston.

XI

GENTLEMEN PUBLISHERS

In 1871 when Howells was writing *Their Wedding Journey,* he asked his sister to return his Niagara Falls guidebook. He wanted to be certain his recollections of the area were accurate in detail. In 1884 when he was writing *The Rise of Silas Lapham,* he could not rely on a map to check his memory of the years the novel mirrors. He must be his own cartographer. The time of the novel is 1875, the year of Lee & Shepard's failure and Osgood's rescue from a similar fate through the indulgence of his major creditors. The story does not include a decade of experience for Lapham, but it does for Howells. It embodies his recollections of things past; it also renders concrete his experience of things present. "An author," he once said, "is merely one who has had the fortune to remember more . . . than other men. A good many wise critics will tell you that writing is inventing; but I know better than that; it is only remembering . . . the history of your own life." In selecting the details for the *Silas Lapham* plot and the characters out of whom the plot grows, he drew not only from his well of memory but also on "the intensities" and "implications" of his day to day perceptions. The novel pictures a businessman's rise, at the expense of material well-being, from arrogant affluence to moral solvency. As he completed the novel in March 1885, he later recalled, "the bottom dropped out of everything." Possibly the reason for this sense of desolation was that reality had betrayed his subtle sermon. The facts had contradicted his ethical vision.[1]

The characters, the setting, the plot of *Silas Lapham* are the product of Howells' creative imagination working evocatively with materials of his experience. Anyone reading the novel is struck by the accuracy of particulars, by the skillful economy of selection through which Howells creates an image apprehended by all the senses. The setting and characters have both substantial reality and an aura of supersensible experience. Of all the pictures in the novel none is more vivid than Lapham's house in the course of building on the water side of Beacon Street. The skeleton staircases with their provisional treads, the floor roughly laid, the crevasses of carpentry, the narrow paths of planking over which Mrs. Lapham clambers, the trestle on which Silas sits to whittle, the smell of mortar, the fragrance of pine shavings, the carpenter with his rule sticking out of his overall pocket create the house.

Howells, at the time he was working on *Silas Lapham,* himself bought a house on the water side of Beacon Street. In reporting his purchase to Henry James, he spoke of his novel and its hero, saying he would be able to use all his experience "down to the quick." Lapham's Beacon Street house is, of course, a composite picture of Howells' various residences. The one at 302 Beacon he did not build, but simply renovated. He had had however two earlier opportunities to become acquainted with cellar holes, brick and mortar, raw boards and paint, his first when he built in Cambridge on Concord Avenue, his second with Redtop on Fairchild's land in Belmont. The reality of the Lapham house results from the mingling of details from these experiences. Lapham's office, more briefly sketched, has a comparable actuality and is an equally composite picture, derived from the Ticknor & Fields offices at 124 Tremont Street, the Cathedral Building, and the Riverside Press, from which he edited the *Atlantic Monthly* for over three years. Composite as the picture may be, to anyone who knows the Press today the similarity is startling. There on the second floor is Lapham's small den of an office with its glass door, swivel chair, and roll-top desk. Beyond the glass door is the larger den where Lapham's knowing bookkeeper watched and worked and where the beautiful enigmatic Miss Dewey beat the keys of her typewriter.[2]

Just as the setting for *Silas Lapham* is made from Howells' years of perceptive observation so with the characters. To seek similarities too closely would be a "biographic fallacy." After all,

The counting room at the Riverside Press in the 1880s.

Howells was an artist not a photographer. He had the privilege of arranging his objects according to his purpose. None of us is singular. We share characteristics with many others. The universal emerges in the particular. The individual provokes a shock of recognition because he is not unique. However, some of the parallels between the fictional characters and Howells' contemporaries are as striking as those between Lapham's office and that once used by Henry Oscar Houghton at the Riverside Press.

George Harrison Mifflin and Tom Corey, the young man who through his love for Lapham's daughter Penelope links the main plot with the subplot, have much in common. Mifflin with his aristocratic Crowninshield background reflects Corey in detail after detail. His father, like Tom's, was a dilettante. Mifflin, like Tom, was a young man of wealth with a Harvard degree, determined despite his privilege to strike out and do something for himself. Like Corey, he was persistent in securing his job from a reluctant employer. Both through their gentleness, energy, reticence, and self-discipline won the unreserved support of their superiors.

In May 1880 the *Publishers' Weekly* ran the following paragraph on Houghton's junior partner. It could serve as a pen portrait of Tom Corey.

Mr. Mifflin is an excellent specimen of a Boston boy who believes in work. Coming from an old family, he might easily have sunk into a fashionable dilettante, a gentlemanly frequenter of clubs and drawing rooms, a *nobody*. Instead of this, immediately after graduating at Harvard, he went to the Riverside Press, began at the beginning, made himself master of all the steps and processes of book-making, became a member of the firm of Hurd & Houghton, then of Houghton, Osgood & Co., and for sometime has managed the Riverside Press with ability and success. No small part of the tasteful appearance and good workmanship of the present products of the Press is due to his skill and conscientious fidelity to his work.[3]

As striking as the similarities between Mifflin and young Corey are those between Henry Oscar Houghton and Silas Lapham. Houghton, like Lapham, came from a numerous family and had been born in northern Vermont along the Canada line. He also was a man of simple, homely loyalties, devoted to his parents, his brothers and sisters, his wife and children. He, like Silas, married a schoolteacher. Both were clear, bold, straightforward, single-minded, and persevering. Beyond the sphere of the family, business was their being. In politics they were Republican. Physically they were large men, although Houghton was free of the grossness in Lapham's bearing. In speech he quite probably retained his Vermont twang; however, he was a literate, persuasive speaker, an accomplishment Howells denies Lapham. Both had emerged from poverty to opulence. Houghton's favorite extravagance was horses and their equipages; Lapham too loved the horse in harness. Houghton, however, did not think it proper "for the senior partner to be mounted on a Brewster trotting wagon with side pieces with a Kossuth hat knocked in at the side, on his head and shooting by every man on the road." Such display he left to his juniors. In this he differed from Lapham. Nor did he build on Beacon Street. He was content with his ample Cambridge residence. To this, in the early eighties, he added a spacious library done in oak and rich damask.[4]

In the novel Lapham's wife Persis is his conscience, attenuating his business common sense to the tune of about $150,000, the sum he loans his former partner Milton K. Rogers as salve to his wife-inflicted feeling of guilt for having forced the man out of the firm at the moment of promising prosperity. Although Rogers' partnership capital had made possible the development of their paint business, the man had proved himself financially incompetent. Money had run through his fingers as through a sieve. "Buy out or go out," Lapham had told him. A letter from Albert Houghton's widow to her brother-in-law duplicates the anxiety that Persis had shown. Her husband had died in 1880 and she was considering withdrawing her inheritance from the firm and putting it in Government bonds.

> I know that if Albert had lived to take care of his interest [she wrote] he would have wanted his money to remain there as you say. He was a *great balance wheel,* and had to *hold* back — he did not believe in going into such great expense for show & he did not believe in getting deeply in debt — and he always would live within his means. Now bro H. O. I confess I have felt a *little* uneasy for you. When I see the great change that has taken place since he went out of the business, but it may be you are doing an immensely larger business than when he was in the concern and you can afford it. You certainly live in the style of a Millionaire which of course is all right & no one's business if you are out of debt and "owe no man anything."[5]

Houghton was able to reassure his sister-in-law, and she left her funds, over $100,000, with his firm. Indeed, in contrast to Silas Lapham, Houghton was punctilious in money matters, precise to the fraction. Nor was he attracted by risk. Given an inside tip on "Canada Lands," he was tempted, but replied, "I have scrupulously abstained from doing anything of a speculative nature and perhaps had better continue to do so." Publishing was enough of a gamble for him. Lapham's character is an amalgam. His stock deals, his love of round figures, his perennial optimism, his loose way of overstating his resources appear in James R. Osgood.[6]

A third character embodied in Silas Lapham and one who may have supplied the crux of the novel's plot is Lawson Valentine. In the late 1860s, Valentine, Cambridge-born of well-to-do parents, having had a variety of partnerships in the paint and varnish business in Boston, established his plant in Brighton. By this time, after fifteen years of experiment, Valentine & Company was boasting that its varnish was the best in the world, largely supplanting the English product. In 1872, Valentine's Brighton factory was burned to the ground, and he transferred his business to New York, where it prospered. According to Lyman Abbott, Lawson Valentine was "a genius," "a seer in business," "an electric dynamo," "a fascinating enigma," "quick to see and bold to use commercial opportunities." "Business was to him a form of energy, not a game for money." Although paint was his business, publishing held for him a fascination. After his transfer to New York, he acquired a number of publishing activities, the most important, large shares in Orange, Judd & Company and the Christian Union Company, the latter organized after the failure of J. B. Ford and Company, the original publishers of the *Christian Union*. Valentine played a key roll in the founding of Houghton, Mifflin & Company.[7]

Eighteen eighty opened for Houghton, Osgood & Company under the slogan of business as usual, the publishing end being conducted from the rooms over Lee & Shepard at 47 Franklin Street, the heliotype from temporary quarters on Pearl Street. However, the company was operating under a staggering load, a load that had little to do with the fire of late December. Its net indebtedness totaled $838,000. When Houghton, Osgood had come into being, Osgood's capital stock, consisting of books, merchandise, prints, stereotype plates, and rights to publish, was valued at $428,208.81. His liabilities were found to exceed anticipation, amounting to $425,000.00. What went on behind closed doors during the first quarter of 1880 is a matter of surmise. Houghton, Osgood required additional capital. According to one story, Osgood was unwilling to assume his share of responsibility and the firm was dissolved on his initiative. Another has it that Lawson Valentine and S. D. Warren made their promised support of Houghton conditional on Osgood's withdrawal. Mifflin in his unpublished recollections said that the dissolution of Houghton, Osgood was a Fairchild-Osgood plot. According to Mifflin, "Osgood . . . took every legal measure to free himself from every obligation, direct or indirect, of the old firm" so that he could start business afresh free of debt. Charles Fairchild, for his part, made excessive demands on Warren. When they were not granted, he withdrew from the partnership, "released from all liabilities, and with a handsome cash balance," two or three hundred thousand, Mifflin thought. Osgood and Fairchild's "pretty conspiracy" was to be on hand to pick up the pieces when Houghton, Mifflin fell apart under the burden of its heavy debt. If this was in fact the plan of the two friends, they underestimated their opponents. Lawson Valentine guaranteed $200,000 in partnership capital; Warren $400,000 in notes.[8]

The dissolution of Houghton, Osgood and the formation of Houghton, Mifflin & Company and James R. Osgood's second company took time. First there was the possibility that Osgood might find a berth in the house of Harper, then that he would be content with his Heliotype Company. When during the course of negotiations he made clear that he intended to revive his imprint of James R. Osgood & Company, Mifflin "discerned future complications," but Houghton "was so delighted to be clear of Osgood" that he regarded revival of Osgood's imprint "as of no account." Not until May 1, 1880, was the public confronted with the accomplished fact; then the co-partnership announcements of Houghton, Mifflin & Company and James R. Osgood & Company were "the nine days' talk of the month," the chief wonder that a man in varnish was now to put a little polish on the minds of men as well as carriages! Osgood was rumored to have withdrawn "with a handsome sum," $25,000 the books of Houghton, Mifflin indicate. Various journals carrying the news stated that Osgood and his partners, John H. Ammon (an associate for fifteen years) and Edward L. Osgood, intended to concentrate almost exclusively on the heliotype business. Osgood at once denied the statement. The heliotype business would continue, of course, but he also proposed to carry on as a general publisher "for a select circle of authors."[9]

Osgood would have to woo his select circle. The Memorandum of Agreement covering his assignment of copyrights to Houghton, Mifflin read:

> Know all men by these presents, that we, Ticknor & Fields, Fields, Osgood & Company, James R. Osgood & Company and Houghton, Osgood & Company, all of Boston, Massachusetts, for

valuable considerations by us received from H. O. Houghton, G. H. Mifflin, & Lawson Valentine, partners under the style of Houghton, Mifflin & Company, do hereby assign, transfer and set over unto Houghton, Mifflin & Company all the right, title and interest now vested in us respectively in and to the copyrights of the books the titles of which are affixed to our respective names in the accompanying schedule [the schedule runs to forty-eight pages and includes all the great names responsible for the fame of Ticknor & Fields and its successors] . . . to have and to hold the assigned copyrights to them, the said Houghton, Mifflin & Company, and to their executors, administrators and assigns so long as said copyrights continue in force . . .

Included in another document, the agreement for dissolution of Houghton, Osgood, appeared the statement that

It is understood that this dissolution of co-partnership is a voluntary one on both sides, and it is the desire of both parties that their future business relations should be of a friendly character. To this end it is mutually agreed that each party shall respect the authors and enterprises belonging to the other, and shall not seek by any influence, direct or indirect, to divert or interfere with them. And neither party shall make a contract with any author belonging to the other without the consent of such other party, provided, however, that such consent shall not be withheld when such an author has determined to change his publisher.

Another paragraph in this agreement provided that James R. Osgood & Company should have the privilege of purchasing books of Houghton, Mifflin & Company at a discount more generous than allowed the trade generally. Since this condition was designed to assist the new Osgood & Company in its first months of trial, it contained a time limitation; the privilege would terminate on January 1, 1881.[10]

Houghton in the *Sheldon et al.* v. *Houghton* had seen it proved to his advantage that "Courtesy of the Trade" was legally as thin as air. The sequel to that case demonstrated that no publisher, even though paying large sums for advance sheets, as Harper had done, could secure against rivals a foreign author of Dickens' popularity.

Trade courtesy as it applied to American authors, who were of course protected by copyright, was understood to mean that reputable publishers would not offer an author discovered and developed by another house better terms than he presently enjoyed unless the writer himself indicated he was ready for a change. Even when the author did seek a new firm, the publisher usually would check with the original house to make certain no misunderstanding would result. Thus when Bret Harte in September 1873 offered Scribner a serial for its *Monthly,* Roswell Smith wrote Osgood saying his firm was willing to meet Harte's terms, $5000 in advance, providing it also had the book rights, but courtesy demanded the book be first offered to the Boston firm. In the Houghton, Osgood dissolution agreement, Houghton had embodied the principle of trade courtesy in legal form.[11]

Young Mifflin in anticipating complications proved to be right. The struggle of the next five years was hardly that of gentlemen. Houghton assumed that in Osgood's transfer of copyrights, Houghton, Mifflin had acquired in legal form first rights to the new works of authors represented in the document. His assumption proved correct for all the annuitants and also for the majority of the younger writers. However, although the contest did not begin at once, Osgood had no intention of observing either the ethics of the trade or the legal document. During the first months of his new partnership he was busy establishing himself and his Heliotype Company in new offices at 211 Tremont Street and in raising capital. This he secured in part from Charles Fairchild, now with a paper company of his own and also with Lee, Higginson, the investment house, and in part from his brother Edward, who in January 1881 married the daughter of General George Draper, wealthy textile manufacturer of Hopedale, Massachusetts. He also was busy adding partners to his roster. First Ben Ticknor returned to the fold from S. D. Warren. Then came Thomas B. Ticknor, youngest son of William D., and S. D. Sargeant, both in the employ of Houghton, Mifflin until they switched allegiance.[12]

Throughout 1880, Osgood appears to have abided by the terms of the dissolution agreement. His major publishing achievement was to secure Samuel Clemens, who constitutionally suspicious had become increasingly dissatisfied with the American Publishing Company and its manager Elisha Bliss. In September 1880 Bliss died, and Clemens decided to risk *The Prince and the Pauper* with Osgood, "the best publisher who ever breathed." The publishing agreement, of Clemens' devising, was "no fool of a contract," he boasted. The book was to be sold by subscription until that market had been exhausted, issued at his "sole & heavy expense." Osgood was to be distributor only, receiving 7½ percent on sales. In the years that remained to him as an independent operator, Osgood handled two more books for Clemens, *The Stolen White Elephant* (as a trade book) and *Life on the Mississippi.* For this last Osgood reluctantly accepted a commission of only 5 percent on the first 50,000, 7½ percent thereafter. Although Clemens was to pay the cost of manufacture, Osgood assumed the responsibility of supervising the work, promising to keep charges per copy to forty-five cents or less. "No doubt," he told Clemens, "you will save by this means $10,000 or $12,000 in manufacture over what it would have cost you under the old regime, to say nothing of getting a decent book."[13]

At first the engagement was filled with promise. For the *Prince and the Pauper,* Osgood's skill in "working the newspapers" impressed Clemens. He liked his new publisher's cheerful estimates, and even after this first book failed to achieve the anticipated sales, he continued to employ Osgood, whom he found "the dearest and sweetest and loveliest human being to be found on the planet anywhere." However, when *Life on the Mississippi* also failed to reach in the first ripe months the sales expected — 50,000 to 80,000 — he was driven to distraction. For him a sale of 30,000 was worse than nothing. He would not have agreed even to a 5 percent commission had he known sales were to be less than 50,000. After all, he was paying the manufacturing costs and they had run a third again as much as Osgood's estimate, sixty rather than forty-five cents a volume. By now he was convinced that if Osgood had "the copyright on the Bible, his gang" were "stupid enough to publish it in such a way as to lose money on it." He demanded explanations. Why had Osgood bound 10,000 in a special binding for which no sale could be imagined? Why had he employed Anthony to "approve & 'place' 300 pictures"? He wanted itemized accountings, not round figures and "omnibus" billings. Osgood must pay the overcharges or face suit. When Osgood confessed he had failed to make a copy of his letter in which he had promised such lush savings on manufacturing costs and Charles Webster, Clemens' nephew and new publisher, faced him with the original, he was forced to agree that his firm was "properly chargeable" for possibly $4000. He paid $2500 in cash, the rest in acceptances, a compromise Clemens later regretted as he became increasingly certain Osgood was on the skids. Cash was going to be "main scarce," he told his nephew. Over and over again he harassed Webster for collection. "When [are] you going to dig that money out of Osgood? Don't let him *bust* on us." "Didn't you get those acceptances out of Osgood? . . . you better make him pony up . . . He has already delayed so long that he has just about annulled any half-promise to let him give acceptances instead of cash." Later, "Osgood is about to sail for Europe — get everything squared up before he leaves." Again, "If Osgood doesn't pay that $825 instantly . . . bring suit — & do it before he gets out of the country." Where are the accounts? When is Osgood going to send his January statement? When is he going to report? "Make Osgood furnish his Jan *statement*." "I have *paid* Osgood for 50,000 Mississippis, bound & complete. — He has not accounted to me for more than 33,000 . . . Has he furnished that statement yet?" And finally on May 5, 1885, "Osgood's busted, at last. It was sure to come." A moving epitaph for "the best publisher who ever breathed."[14]

Save for the pleasure of his company, Osgood had every reason to regret he had ever taken on the eruptive Hartford humorist. *Life on the Mississippi* proved a bitter publishing experience for Clemens. It was equally bitter for Osgood. Hurt by Clemens' accusations, he wrote, "We are deeply conscious of having done everything which anybody could have done for this book. We have worked harder over it and had more trouble and anxiety in connection with it than any book we ever had to do with. So far from being a source of undue profit to us, we have done the business at an unprecedentedly low commission. If it is a failure it is not due to the lack of intelligent, conscientious & energetic effort on our part."[15]

Although Houghton would have been pleased to have Clemens on his list, he would never have bid for him by accepting so niggardly a commission. On the other hand, his estimates of costs would have been much nearer the mark. This is not to suggest that had he been Clemens' publisher, he would have had less trouble than Osgood. In these years Clemens thought he knew more about the book business than the men he hired to do the work for him.

Another noteworthy Osgood acquisition that in no way violated his agreement with Houghton, Mifflin was Lafcadio Hearn, whose *Stray Leaves from Strange Literature* he published in 1884. That Osgood did secure Hearn is probably Scudder's fault. In June 1882 Hearn submitted to Houghton, Mifflin "Dream Tapestries," in December, his translation of Flaubert's *The Temptation of St. Anthony.* Both manuscripts were returned. The rejections, however, were sufficiently generous in tone to encourage Hearn to send on his next book. This too Scudder returned. The manuscript thereupon went the rounds of a variety of publishers, finally falling to James R. Osgood. *Stray Leaves from Strange Literature* gives distinction to Osgood's list, but it was not one to make a fortune for either himself or its author.[16]

Osgood almost gained further distinction when he undertook to publish the 1881-1882 edition of *Leaves of Grass,* promising Whitman a royalty of 25¢ if the book retailed for $2.00; 30¢ if for $2.50. This was a brave venture, especially since Osgood intended "to let Whitman retain all the *beastliness* of the earlier editions," according to Stedman. The plates were made and the book announced. Then the New England Society for the Suppression of Vice scared the courage out of James R. Osgood by persuading the District Attorney to threaten legal action if the book were not expurgated according to the State's direction. Osgood was willing to meet the Attorney's demands for cleaning up the text; Walt Whitman was not. Osgood refused to tempt the law and Whitman bought the stereotype plates, turning them over to Rees, Welsh & Company of Philadelphia. At long last, *Leaves of Grass* made some money for Whitman. The Philadelphia edition sold more copies than any previous one. John Hay was incredulous that Osgood had "given up publication merely because a superserviceable official threatened to give him a magnificent advertisement." The partisan John Burroughs denounced the threatened censorship as "impoverished and illegal . . . the tool of private spite, and bigotry, and clubhouse lust, anxious about its fig-leaves." He wished Osgood had had the pluck to make a fight.[17]

The Whitman-Osgood fiasco Houghton could watch with equanimity, perhaps amusement. He was neither a clubman nor a friend of Anthony Comstock, and when Whitman had been in Boston working on proof, he had taken him on a personally conducted tour of the Riverside Press. He might even be excused for taking some private pleasure in Osgood's failures with Clemens and Whitman, for early in 1881 Osgood had begun to play a number of the cards in his questionable hand. Mifflin had expected trouble, but none of the partners could have anticipated the form some of it was to take.

During the minor business recession of 1882, Lawson Valentine suffered reverses. A man to whom he had loaned $90,000 in negotiable paper failed and that was the last Valentine saw of his $90,000. Because of this bit of chicanery, theft Houghton called it, to meet his current obligations was impossible. As a temporary measure, to pay creditors' claims, Valentine sold his interest in his varnish company. At the time both Mifflin and Houghton feared their new partner might call on his recently contributed partnership funds instead. Such an act would have seriously embarrassed Houghton, Mifflin. When Valentine gave assurance that his partnership capital was sacrosanct, the youngest partner wept. Months before Valentine's money troubles, snide paragraphs reflecting on Houghton, Mifflin's financial integrity had begun to circulate. His loss gave color to the innuendoes.[18]

The proliferation of rumor reached abroad. When Houghton went to England in 1881 and again in 1883, the word had gone before him. His firm was in danger of bankruptcy. Generally he took no action, even though some of the word he thought libelous; he relied on his reputation and conduct to give the lie to gossip.

Not until Osgood's failure in 1885 did he sharply rebuke his English agent and Vermont friend, the bibliophile Henry Stevens, for believing "the supposed fact" confided "by a disinterested person (!)" that Houghton, Mifflin "had been very unprosperous." Stevens' supposed "confidential friend," Houghton pointed out, had proved to be "the boon companion, if not the *pal,* of a man who was Osgood's *pal.*"

Yet there were times when the record must be set straight promptly. The Merriams, disturbed by a paragraph in the *Tribune,* requested an explanation and Arthur Macy, manager of Bradstreet, prepared a memorandum on the firm's financial position which Houghton considered unpardonable in its distortion of fact. To such inquiries and reports, he made angry denials. "The statement that the firm of Houghton, Mifflin & Co. were heavily in debt [he wrote Macy] . . . is only relatively true . . . much of what you call debt has always been, and still is really, capital, as a large portion of it cannot be drawn out until after a term of years, having been put in this form for the convenience of settling an estate [his brother Albert's]." Moreover, he protested, the firm "has capital of $500,000 over and above all its indebtedness of every kind whatsoever and . . . the partners have in addition to that, subject to attachment for debts of the firm an amount fully equal to that." The Bradstreet memorandum Houghton regarded as "the infamous plot," the emanation of one person who "first had influence enough with a Bank President to get him to throw out certain paper, and used the fact to coach the Agency, and then quoted the Agency as authority for that. This is the way Satan always does his work; but Satan is always conquered, and this Satan will be I have no doubt."[19]

Houghton, Mifflin's load of debt was one of Osgood's cards. Another he started to play in 1881 was royalties to authors.

Even though publishers insisted that courtesy of the trade had not been invented and adhered to for the sake of keeping authors' rates from increasing, writers had begun to regard the practice with jaundiced eye. The publishers' arguments that the system worked in behalf of both, that the house which had all a man's books would work them harder than it would had it to divide the interest with rivals, the plea that to reach the immortality of "Collected Works" would be easier were all in the hands of one house had begun to evoke suspicion. The publishers' most logical argument — that having invested money, time, and sympathy in the writer's early efforts, they deserved to share in the rewards of his maturity — fell on increasingly deaf ears. Publishers insisted, needlessly perhaps, that authors were free to seek where they could find; no courtesy was asked of them. However, even when negotiations were initiated by the author, gentlemen publishers consulted one another.

When George Parsons Lathrop offered his novel *Newport,* after its run in the *Atlantic,* to Charles Scribner, even as his firm had reported to Osgood Harte's advances a decade before, so now Scribner wrote Houghton, informing him that Lathrop had come to his house "entirely unsolicited," that his firm "refused to make any proposition until he assured us that his book would not be published by you in any case." Houghton replied good-naturedly that Lathrop had not been exactly frank. Houghton, Mifflin had offered 10 percent but, being doubtful of the book's sale, had suggested an exemption. Lathrop had already been angered by Houghton's terms for his *Atlantic* appearance and had written Aldrich, ". . . the history of one-sided concession & of beating down prices cannot go on indefinitely; that is certain." The proposal that a certain number of volumes in the first edition be royalty free had understandably increased his dissatisfaction and on his own initiative he had sought a new house. When Scribner's letter had arrived, Houghton, Mifflin was still debating whether or not to meet Lathrop's terms. Even though the question had not been decided, Houghton made no objection to the book's going to Scribner. He was pleased, he said, that it was to be under the imprint of a house which "knew how to treat its confrères in the Trade with courtesy."[20]

Houghton's conclusion was no idle compliment. Both he and Charles Scribner were being subjected to James R. Osgood's raiding. By any standard George Washington Cable was a Scribner author, discovered and developed by that house. By 1881 Cable, in addition to appearing frequently in *Scribner's Monthly,* had

had three books, *Old Creole Days, The Grandissimes,* and *Madame Delphine,* published by the New York firm. James R. Osgood's second company was in need of authors. Rather than negotiating directly with Cable and thus risking the trade's contempt for violation of its ethics, Osgood used George Waring, his traveling companion of 1878, as a cat's-paw. Without naming names, Waring inquired of Cable if he would be interested in changing publishers, suggesting that $3500 for serial rights with 5 percent on sales would be available. Cable notified Scribner, who met the terms. Osgood thereupon upped his bid for book rights only, promising 22½ percent in royalties, plus a $1000 advance. Scribner refused to be further baited and Osgood got the book, *Dr. Sevier.*[21]

Another author Osgood won from an established publisher by his siren song of 20 percent was Joel Chandler Harris, whose Uncle Remus stories in the Atlanta *Constitution* had attracted the attention of D. Appleton & Company in the late '70s. J. C. Derby, the former publisher, after his failure in the early '70s, had entered the employ of Appleton. At the end of 1879 he was sent south on a publishing mission, one of his responsibilities to stop in Atlanta to make a deal with Harris for his first book — *Uncle Remus: His Songs and His Sayings.* After Appleton published the book in 1880, Harris became a popular contributor to a variety of periodicals, appearing most frequently in the new *Century* magazine. On the formation of Houghton, Mifflin, Derby left Appleton to become literary scout and subscription agent for Houghton. In May 1882 Derby suggested that his new employers take steps to secure Harris. Houghton replied to the suggestion, "If Uncle Remus comes to us naturally we will welcome him cordially." However, he must be a free agent. If in his engagement with the *Century,* he had not reserved to himself the book rights, then permission from the "Century people" must be first secured. By this time Osgood with his 20 percent had entered the picture. *Nights with Uncle Remus* and *Mingo* came out under his imprint. Whether he consulted the "Century people" is not on record. Considering his treatment of Scribner and Houghton, Mifflin, it seems unlikely.[22]

Although Houghton, Mifflin, enclosing checks for royalties due, notified its authors that it had assumed the liabilities and publishing rights of Houghton, Osgood, inevitable confusion resulted, especially since Osgood in publicizing his new company expressed "the hope that 25 years experience in the successive firms of Ticknor & Fields, Fields, Osgood & Co., James R. Osgood & Co., and Houghton, Osgood & Co." would help his new firm to share in his inherited traditions. "What does it all mean?" Elizabeth Stuart Phelps asked Osgood, "and how can we do without you? And do you still publish? And which is the 'firm'? And how sorry — very sorry I am!" Such confusion while unfortunate was of minor import as compared to Osgood's determination to win for his list by promises of excessive royalties the authors he coveted. By January 1, 1881, Osgood's intention of violating the terms of the dissolution agreement had become manifest. With a show of reasoning, patently specious, he let it be known that he considered the January 1, 1881 date, which appeared only in the clause affording him favored discounts on Houghton, Mifflin books, applied also to the paragraph which stated that neither publisher would "seek by any influence" to secure authors from either house without mutual consultation and consent.[23]

The annuitants — Longfellow, Lowell, Holmes, Whittier, and Emerson — Houghton did not have to worry about. They had agreed to Osgood's assignment of their contracts to Houghton, Mifflin, contracts of his devising which he could no longer fulfill. However, heirs and executors did not consider themselves bound. Julian Hawthorne, who had sold out his interest in his father's copyrights to his sister Rose (Una had died), had kept the manuscript of *Dr. Grimshawe's Secret*. Osgood offered him an advance of $1000 plus 10 percent on the book for his services as editor. Although Houghton regretted losing, for the time being, Hawthorne's posthumous novel from the author's Collected Works, just at this time in preparation, he could take no exception. The royalty was not excessive, nor had Houghton, Mifflin approached Julian, possibly because at the very time of *Dr. Grimshawe's* appearance, the firm was considering a manuscript in Rose's possession, a preliminary study her father had made for *Grimshawe*. On publication of the Osgood book, after considerable debate, Houghton, Mifflin decided against issuing the earlier draft.[24]

The case of the Emerson-Carlyle correspondence was a different matter. Both Emerson and Carlyle had agreed in the early seventies that after their deaths, Charles Eliot Norton should edit their exchange of letters. Carlyle died in 1881, Emerson the following year. Houghton, Mifflin promptly got in touch with Norton, who agreed selections from the letters should appear in the *Atlantic,* that the firm should have the book. Almost at once, Osgood entered his bid of 20 percent and Norton, as agent for the Emerson family, felt he "had no choice but to take the best." He withdrew permission for selections from the Emerson-Carlyle letters for the *Atlantic* and gave Osgood the book. As with Hawthorne, Houghton, Mifflin at this time was preparing a collected edition of Emerson. On its appearance, by mutual agreement with his heirs, Emerson's annuity contract was abrogated.[25]

A number of living authors on Houghton, Mifflin's list not immobilized by annuity contracts had an understandable concern for immediate royalties. Henry James was one of these. Although he characterized himself as "a very bad bargainer . . . born to be victimized by the pitiless race of publishers," by 1880 he had acquired some of the arts of the market place. First, dissatisfied with royalty accounts from Macmillan, his English publisher, he offered *Confidence* to Chatto & Windus, an offer which was accepted. Next he learned the lucrative joys of simultaneous magazine publication by placing *Washington Square* with *Harper's Monthly* in this country and *Cornhill* in England. He was now in an excellent position to open negotiations for his next novel, *The Portrait of a Lady.* "To escape the bad economy of lavishing a valuable fiction on a single public," he demanded that the *Atlantic* "simultane" with *Macmillan's Magazine.* "I can always be your novelist if I can publish here also," James promised. He also felt secure enough to increase his rate to $250 an issue. Houghton, Mifflin was opposed to the so-called simultaneous scheme for periodical publication. To secure English copyright, the novel must appear first in England. This meant that *The Portrait of a Lady,* opening in the October *Macmillan's,* could not start in the *Atlantic* until November. Even by slow boat the English magazine would reach the United States before the *Atlantic* was in subscribers' hands. Still Houghton accepted James's conditions, and Macmillan, to win this author back, afforded an advance of £250 for serial rights. James anticipated realizing $5000 before his novel had finished its run.[26]

As Houghton had expected, *Macmillan's Magazine* reached this country before its opposite number of the *Atlantic* was ready and thus stole such thunder as *The Portrait of a Lady* might have provided his magazine had the English magazine not preceded it in the market. However, as a book it acted well, selling in four and a half months 4556 copies. On the strength of this success, James for his next *Atlantic* serial again stipulated simultaneous publication, increased his price to $300 a number, and asked for 20 percent on the book, stiff demands which at first Houghton refused to meet. However, when Aldrich, now editor of the *Atlantic,* was leaving for Europe in 1882, Houghton gave him "*carte blanche*" with James. Aldrich did his best, but his best wasn't good enough. Osgood was also abroad in the summer of 1882. All the *Atlantic* got was James's warmed over dramatic version of *Daisy Miller,* which would fill only three numbers of the magazine, the price $1000. Osgood had managed to sign James on at 20 percent. Houghton might have had the book rights to the *Daisy Miller* play, but he refused them because it was his determined policy not to compete with Osgood, who he believed was offering his authors "large advances in order to get them away." Those who "sold out to Osgood," he reluctantly allowed to go. He would not, he said, "pay two values" for them. Henry Holt considered a royalty of more than 10 percent "immoral." Houghton thought 20 percent poor business for both author and publisher.[27]

On January 1, 1883, James signed the first of a series of agreements with Osgood and thereby "mortgaged" his literary freedom. Under the terms of these contracts, James was to have 20 percent, except on the *Daisy Miller* play which was held at 15 percent up to 1500, then 20 percent. Further, James agreed for $4000 to provide a novel, and for an additional $2000, three shorter pieces,

Osgood to find magazine outlets. The *Century* got *The Bostonians,* the novel James had agreed to provide, but before it had completed its run, Osgood had failed. For at least a year before the event, Clemens had anticipated Osgood would "go bust." James, far from the scene, was denied such prescience. Shortly before his publisher's collapse, Houghton, Mifflin had accepted his *The Princess Casamassima* for the *Atlantic* at $300 a number, even though James had promised book rights to Osgood. Learning of Osgood's failure, James suggested that for $350 a number, Houghton, Mifflin could have the book rights. Houghton was not interested in Osgood's leavings.[28]

The author who suffered most acutely, psychologically anyway, during this contest between gentlemen was William Dean Howells. With the exception of his two years under Houghton, Osgood, when the *Atlantic* as well as his books had been published by one house, his position had been consistently anomalous. When Ticknor & Fields owned the *Atlantic* and he was assistant editor, his books were in the hands of Hurd & Houghton. In 1874 positions were reversed. Hurd & Houghton had purchased the *Atlantic,* of which he was now editor, but James R. Osgood was his publisher. In 1880, under the terms of the dissolution of partnership agreement, Osgood's rights in Howells' books became Houghton, Mifflin's. Howells respected Houghton; Osgood he cherished. According to Edwin Mead, Howells' cousin-by-marriage, Howells did not see the document but accepted Osgood's interpretation of the agreement because of "his entire confidence in Mr. Osgood's veracity."[29]

Throughout 1880 Howells continued as editor of the *Atlantic* with Houghton, Mifflin as his publishers. In January 1881, Osgood, in line with his interpretation of the dissolution of partnership agreement, offered to act as agent for Howells in placing his articles and fiction with the New York magazines until he had a periodical of his own, James R. Osgood & Company retaining book rights. Houghton reacted angrily to the news that he was once again to lose Howells' books and the author took the only possible step, writing to Osgood that he was withdrawing from their engagement "with the full knowledge that I can in nowise be legally affected by any disagreement between Mr. Houghton and you." To Houghton he wrote, "I have written to Mr. Osgood to say that I withdraw from my proposed engagement with him; and I have done this for the reason that I will not be made the battle-ground between you and him in your differences as to the interpretation of your agreement. I have no more right to question the sincerity of his construction of the contract than I have to question yours. All that I intend is not to be the occasion of trouble between you."[30]

Howells at this time gave no indication to Houghton that he anticipated resigning his *Atlantic* post. One reason he did not was that Osgood had talked of buying back the *Atlantic*. Perhaps he made an offer for it, but Houghton's correspondence at this time makes clear he hadn't the faintest idea of parting with the periodical. The day after he received Howells' letter, he wrote Aldrich, with whom he had obviously discussed the matter, "I hasten to tell you . . . I rec'd a letter from Mr. Howells, enclosing a copy of one to Osgood, withdrawing his acceptance of Osgood's offer. I am not without hope that we can still arrange matters, pleasantly all around, so that you can be editor of the Atlantic, and Mr. Howells remain writer for it, and continue to add his new books to our list."[31]

Houghton had not been altogether satisfied with Howells' work as editor. The *Atlantic,* he told Richard Grant White, lacked character. What it needed was a bolder tone. His Western trips had made him realize the possibility of a wider audience if the periodical dealt more vividly with the contemporary scene. Howells, for his part, was likewise restive. Although under Houghton's rule he had increasing freedom from the petty aspects of editing, his salary had not been raised. "Fifteen years' fret and substantial unsuccess" had brought him close to the breaking point. Praise of the magazine meant little to him; "blame galled" him. "The chance came to *light soft,*" he told Scudder, "and I jumped out." To make the jump took the good part of a month. On January 31, Houghton reported to Aldrich, suggesting he " 'drop in' when convenient . . . 'nothing in particular' " had happened, but he would "be glad to have matters in such shape that something could happen if neces-

sary." On February 2, Howells resigned his *Atlantic* post and reported to Osgood that he was now free to accept him as agent and
publisher.[32]

Howells' three-year contract with Osgood, as might be expected,
guaranteed 20 percent on each novel to be produced, at least one
a year, but only after 10,000 copies had been sold. To offset this
large exemption, Osgood was to pay Howells a weekly salary equal
to his *Atlantic* wage. All Osgood asked was one novel a year. That
completed, Howells was free to do any other writing he pleased.
For such extra production, Howells authorized Osgood as agent.
"The arrangement is ideal," Howells wrote his father, "and was his
own [Osgood's] proposition."[33]

The loss of Howells both from its list and as editor of the *Atlantic* coupled with reiterative rumors that Houghton, Mifflin was
in a shaky financial condition had serious repercussions. Howells'
defection seemed to substantiate the talk that Osgood was the injured party, that he was the publisher meriting loyalty, especially
since his was apparently the stronger house. Press releases as well
as his generous rates gave evidence of that. One particularly vi-
cious paragraph in circulation was that Howells retired because the
Atlantic had a deficit of $26,000. Nothing could have been further
from the truth. The *Atlantic*'s net profits from January 1880 to
April 1881 were slightly over $2600, hardly a sum to make the
Houghton, Mifflin partners throw their caps in the air, but still not
a deficit. At last the firm decided to try to set the record straight.
On April 18, 1881, "for the sake of removing a misapprehension or
confusion," it sent a circular to its authors detailing the steps by
which it had become their publisher and emphasizing that the new
James R. Osgood & Company "was absolutely unconnected with
the former firm bearing that title." The books, with a few exceptions, formerly published by the first James R. Osgood & Company
"are now published by Houghton, Mifflin & Company . . ." At the
time of separation, ". . . it was distinctly understood by all parties
that Houghton, Mifflin & Co., and they alone, were the successors
of Hurd & Houghton, and of James R. Osgood & Co., and their predecessors, Fields, Osgood & Co., Ticknor & Fields, and W. D. Ticknor," the circular read. To make its position clear, the firm quoted

from the dissolution agreement the paragraph embodying the principles of courtesy of the trade. Three days later, on April 21, Houghton left for England.[34]

The circular was addressed to authors; inevitably, however, one came to Osgood's attention. A week after Houghton had left the country, Osgood took space in the *Transcript* to defend himself against what he said was an implication of breach of faith on his part. He denied that either firm had the right to claim "title to the name, reputation or traditions of their predecessors . . . for these are the intangible articles, which cannot be transferred or assumed at will. Every successive firm must create and maintain its own traditions, and time alone can show upon whom, if upon anybody, the mantle of honorable traditions left by those houses will fall." He admitted the quoted clause setting forth trade courtesy to be correct, but asserted its force had ceased on January 1, 1881. He made no reference to the favored discount provision, the only section of the document in which that date appeared.[35]

In the absence of Houghton, George Mifflin and Azariah Smith, who even as Howells had come to Ticknor & Fields in 1866 and who understood Osgood, having himself under the name of "Fritz" written artful paragraphs for the newspapers, devised a reply to appear also in the *Transcript*. Houghton, Mifflin requested Osgood to submit "the whole document to our authors . . . or any other competent disinterested person . . ." Partisans of either side would then be free to reach their own conclusions. This Osgood refused to do, writing, "It cannot be a matter of concern to 'our authors,' except where an author may choose to hold himself responsible for the business conscience of his publisher." Thus James R. Osgood's honesty is impugned by default. Houghton, Mifflin considered the exchange sufficiently convincing to make a pamphlet of the various letters for distribution to its authors with the note: "As the foregoing pages contain all the communications which have taken place, or probably will take place, in relation to the contract between Mr. Osgood and ourselves as to soliciting each other's authors to change publishers, we have thought it advisable to send you the whole without comment."[36]

Some of Houghton, Mifflin's authors remained unconvinced.

On May 10, 1881, Bret Harte replied to a letter from Osgood, "I had received one of Houghton Mifflin Co's circulars and had detected a bad smell. I am rejoiced at your fumigating it in your reply, received this morning. D——m H. M. Co. anyway! By the way, of course, you hold my last copyrighted book . . ." Fortunately for Harte, Houghton, Mifflin held his last book as well as his earlier ones. Perhaps it was only natural that authors should side with Osgood. He was so genial and generous. Men in the trade judged the contest differently.

William Lee of Lee & Shepard was impressed by Houghton, Mifflin's "kind and magnanimous treatment of Mr. Osgood." "Of course," he said, "his personal friends would think he is all right in the matter, but everybody else must see the facts to be precisely as you have stated them." Houghton, Mifflin's behavior he thought dignified and restrained. "I think," he confided to Azariah Smith, "if Mr. Houghton had been here the expressions might have been a little stronger."[37]

To have been in the center of such a struggle must have been nerve-wracking for a man of Howells' delicate sensibilities. Even after the break, tension persisted. In spite of everything, Houghton hoped to keep Howells' friendship. He asked him for dinner. Here is a curious letter revealing more vividly than any other document the intensities engendered.

211 Tremont Street, Boston
February 17, 1881

Dear Osgood

I have just written a dispatch asking whether you would trust my judgment about accepting Mr. Houghton's dinner independently of you. The persons asked are Aldrich, Warner, Fields, Clemens, and four Boston newspaper men. I told Mr. Houghton at first that I should not come unless you were asked. We had a long talk, and he urged that this was his personal and private affair, by which he meant no reflection upon you whatever. I think I will get him to say this in writing or before Aldrich; and then if you approve, I will accept. I will if possible get him to agree to the transfer of my plates to me, and to the republication of my story where I like. I have not decided that I will go to the dinner, but my judgment now is in favor of it. Let me know what your feeling is.

Yours ever,
W. D. H.

Surely things had come to a fine emotional peak when a mature, distinguished author did not feel free to dine out without permission. Howells, the innocent, was the tortured one. The torture took its toll.

The story referred to in the letter was *Doctor Breen's Practice,* engaged for the *Atlantic* before Howells' resignation and destined for book publication by Houghton, Mifflin. The question of republication rights was not settled easily, but ultimately Osgood won because as Houghton wrote Howells, he would rather have his friendship than insist on rights which Howells could not "readily accede." Despite this assurance, Howells was so upset that he wrote Aldrich he was delaying cashing the firm's check for $300 for "A Police Report" because of a "certain displeasure" between Houghton and himself. He would rather have the article returned than cause the new editor of the *Atlantic* embarrassment. Aldrich felt no embarrassment. "A Police Report" appeared in the January 1882 *Atlantic.*[38]

When it came to work, Howells was "a stocky giant," capable of incredible hours at his desk. For fifteen years he had driven himself, producing not only an impressive series of books but also a monumental number of editorial pages. Month by month he had "hewed and pared" for the *Atlantic,* editing, revising, rewriting, and proofreading. His schedule shames the claims of a modern busy man. His release from editorial duty might have been expected to free him from the enervating strain of deadlines. Such was not to be. The "puissant" Osgood had placed his two-number *A Fearful Responsibility* with *Scribner's* and his next novel, *A Modern Instance,* with the *Century* to start in December, the month *Doctor Breen* was to end in the *Atlantic.* Osgood had also engaged him with the *Century* at $20 a page to write a series of illustrated articles on Italian cities, an engagement which would require a European trip.[39]

Inured to work though he was, Howells was not hardened to emotional and psychic strain. His spirit in 1881 was subjected to a variety of stresses. His talented daughter Winifred had been disturbingly, inexplicably ill. His Belmont house, Redtop, had proved unsatisfactory, a financial drain, especially since he had been unable to sell his Cambridge house. These tensions combined with those imposed by the power struggle of two gentlemen publishers exacted their toll. In the middle of November Howells took to his bed for five weeks "down with some sort of fever . . . the result of long worry and sleeplessness from overwork . . ."[40]

Howells, unlike his friend Clemens, apparently did not anticipate Osgood's failure, or perhaps he hesitated to desert his friend, who by 1884, the year his contract ran out, had published seven of his books. More work was engaged for, in preparation, or in mind. Then there was the possibility of a magazine devoted entirely to fiction, an idea which he and Osgood had often discussed. Although Boston was no longer the center of the universe for him, to live there still appealed. And so, after a year abroad, he renewed his engagement with Osgood, returned to Boston, and before long bought his house on the fashionable water side of Beacon Street. In the summer of 1884 he began writing *The Rise of Silas Lapham,* completing it in March 1885.

Two months later the papers carried the news of James R. Osgood & Company's failure. A note for "a considerable amount" which the firm "had confidently expected to renew" had been protested. "The pinch came," said the Boston *Evening Transcript,* "and there was but one way out," suspension of payment and an assignment for the benefit of the firm's creditors. Liabilities were first reported as $222,489.22. The committee investigating the company's affairs reduced this figure to something under $200,000. Included in the liabilities was $21,000 in unpaid royalties. Osgood's report of assets as $278,086.84 the committee also revised downward to a mere $100,000. The "immensely profitable" Heliotype Company, owned by Osgood and leased to James R. Osgood & Company was found sound — liabilities, $43,838.15; assets, $58,827.36. The committee exonerated the partners from any possible charge of unfair practice or "outside speculation . . . to the detriment of the business." However, it was discovered that each partner as an individual was in debt "for a considerable amount, mainly borrowed capital," and that each had "indorsed to some extent the commercial paper of James R. Osgood & Co." Osgood was offered the opportunity to reach a composition with his creditors and thus continue in business, but he was obliged to confess that to do so would require additional capital and that any attempt on his part to borrow "would prove fruitless." Apparently even Charles Fairchild, whose paper company was one of Osgood's largest creditors, had concluded that Osgood was a bad risk. On the recommendation of the committee, then, a new company was organized which would assume the obligations of Osgood's firm, paying 33⅓ cents on the dollar. Partners in this ill-starred association were Benjamin H. Ticknor, Thomas B. Ticknor, and George F. Godfrey. After seventeen years, under the title of Ticknor and Company an honored name reentered the annals of publishing.[41]

Osgood's public behavior in the five years of his second company's existence had given little evidence that he was operating on a shoestring and a short one at that. Each year he went abroad, in the firm's interest of course; in 1881, close on the heels of Houghton. There money melted away as he entertained as gaily and lavishly as ever. It melted away just as easily at home. His joyous generosity linked with his reputation for affording large advances and 20 percent royalties created the image of a prosperous publisher. In 1883, Howells in seeking to secure John Hay's anonymous *Breadwinners* promised that Osgood would offer "better terms than any other publisher will or can." Rumor indeed surpassed Osgood's own rosy estimates as to the strength of his firm, placing his assets as high as $400,000. In the public eye, his was a strong house. Authors joined with him were to be envied.[42]

One explanation given at the time for Osgood's failure was that he had at least $100,000 tied up in books that had not yet begun to earn their way, books such as *The History of the American Episcopal Church, The Memorial History of the County of Hartford,* and Justin Winsor's *Narrative and Critical History of America* in eight volumes, only two volumes of which had been completed. Another expensive, long-range undertaking was William F.

Poole's *Index of Periodical Literature*. Books such as these required substantial outlays before publication. For editorial work alone, Osgood owed Winsor $5000 and an equal amount must be paid before all the volumes were on the market. Ultimately such undertakings may pay for themselves and finally earn profits; time and reserve capital are essential for their being worked successfully. Yet money tied up in slow movers affords an insufficient explanation for Osgood's troubles, especially when his original stock in trade is considered. In the 1870s his catalogue included not only the New England great who had reached their meridian but also an oncoming group of young writers who were already making names for themselves. He had a balanced list which included books of many different types. He also had four periodicals. The fire of '72 and the panic of '73 took their toll, of course, but they likewise took their toll of other publishers — publishers who survived, or who failing were yet able to raise fresh capital, reorganize, and continue to make publishing history. Lee & Shepard, whom Osgood petitioned into bankruptcy in 1875, is a case in point. So is Louis Prang, who had taken Walter Smith's series of drawing books off Osgood's hands and had also taken on Osgood's partner John S. Clark. That firm, after a series of calamities, failed in 1884. However, Prang survived his receivership and was still on the publishing scene in 1895 to give employment to a young book designer from the Middle West — Bruce Rogers.[43]

The causes of business failures, as well as the ethics of businessmen, were clearly of concern to Howells as he developed the *Silas Lapham* plot. There is the dry, ghostly Milton K. Rogers, with his wildcat stock investments, his crazy patents, always dropping his bread butter side down. After Silas had forced him out of the paint business at the moment of prosperity, he did a land office business with some milling property he owned, but he just couldn't make money. "He'd run through Vanderbilt, Jay Gould, and Tom Scott rolled into one in less than six months, give him a chance, and come out and want to borrow money from you," Silas said when he himself was facing failure. Rogers had never achieved wealth. Osgood, in a sense, had had it thrust upon him, at least as far as his list was concerned. Moreover, he had been protected.

His creditors from 1873 on had been as indulgent as could be expected. He had had an opportunity to be advantaged by Houghton's possibly severe but nevertheless sound management. His "financial disintegration" had been "like the course of some chronic disorder . . . with continual reliefs, with apparent amelioration . . . it had its moments of being like prosperity . . ." It had been continual but not incessant. So Howells wrote of Lapham's ruin. But why should Osgood or Lapham have caught the disease in the first place? As James Bellingham, the man in State Street, explained it to his cousin young Corey:

> I suspect that a hopeful temperament and fondness for round numbers have always called him to set his figures beyond his actual worth. I don't say that he's been dishonest about it, but he's had a loose way of estimating his assets; he's reckoned his wealth on the basis of his capital, and some of his capital is borrowed. He's lost heavily by some recent failures, and there's been a terrible shrinkage in his values. I don't mean merely in stock . . . on hand, but in a kind of competition which has become very threatening . . . Then besides, Lapham has been into several things outside his own business, and, like a good many other men who try outside things he's kept account of them himself; and he's all mixed up about them . . . Whether he can be tided over his difficulties remains to be seen. I'm afraid it will take a good deal of money to do it — a great deal more than he thinks, at least. He believes comparatively little would do it. I think differently. I think that anything less than a great deal would be thrown away on him.

Lapham could not raise the large sum he required to avoid an assignment; neither could Osgood.

Houghton, Lawson Valentine, and Warren, finding Osgood's contribution to the partnership a heavy weight of promissory notes, not much less than his cheerfully estimated assets, may well have squeezed him out of their combination just as the national economy was recovering from a prolonged depression even as Lapham forced Milton Rogers out of the paint business. Given Osgood's conduct before and after the Houghton, Osgood partnership, what other course should responsible businessmen have followed? If

Menu drawn by Thomas Nast for the 1886 Delmonico dinner given in honor of Osgood before his departure for England as representative of the house of Harper at $10,000 a year.

in fact they did so, there is no evidence that any of them carried their act on their consciences as Silas Lapham unwillingly carried his. Nor did anyone suffer retribution, reasonable or unreasonable. All prospered, even Osgood. The house of Harper gave him a $10,000 a year job as its London representative. No one went back to begin "the world anew where he had first begun it," as Silas did in achieving his ethical genesis.

Howells believed a novel should follow its unmoralized way; yet *The Rise of Silas Lapham* during the writing became a sermon, a statement of the way men in business should behave. Lapham's behavior when he forced the incompetent Rogers out of the paint business at the moment of prosperity is contrasted with his behavior in adversity when he refuses to sell land he knows to be worthless. This is the rise of Silas Lapham, a conclusion as divorced from the reality of the business scene Howells was picturing as the novels of false sentiment he satirized in his subplot.[44]

In 1881 during the contest between these gentlemen publishers, Howells had taken to bed with a fever. In 1885, *Silas Lapham* completed but still running in the *Century,* he experienced a vast sense of emptiness. "His affairs prospering, his work marching as well as heart could wish, suddenly, and without apparent cause, the status seemed wholly wrong . . ." "The bottom dropped out," he told a friend. "Grave questions . . . compelling attention" refused "to be curtly dismissed." Some of these questions were perhaps related to the business scene he had been picturing contrasted to that in which living people were fulfilling their parts even as the novel marched to its exalted conclusion.[45]

Howells had imprisoned an ethical fiction in a novel. Houghton had done the same in a legal document for publishers' courtesy. Neither stood the test of the market place. And Osgood? Dubious as some of his business conduct was, he had achieved a niche in publishing history as the author's friend. He had shown that gentlemen publishers did not always follow their vaunted credo, that writers might find, if they sought, more generous masters than those who had discovered and developed them. What matter that Osgood could not pay the bills? Others would be on hand to foot the expense. Houghton, Mifflin would pay Winsor his $5000; at considerable loss to the author, Macmillan would pick up James. Ticknor and Company, hoping to retain Howells as one of its authors, afforded him the $7500 Osgood had guaranteed for 1885. For this the nascent firm secured *Silas Lapham* but not its author. On the urgent recommendation of Charles Fairchild, the house of Harper took on William Dean Howells, paying him an annual $10,000 for the exclusive right to his work.[46]

Houghton for his part while Osgood lapsed to insolvency had reduced his company's debt by over half a million dollars.[47]

XII

SUBSCRIPTION BOOKS AND LIMITED EDITIONS

DURING THE 1880s Houghton, Mifflin's dominant purpose was to reduce its indebtedness. The reduction in the first five years of the decade was spectacular (from $763,111.48 to $261,466.49), and in the year of Osgood's failure Mifflin was boasting that his firm was on "Easy Street." The process went on more slowly for the rest of the decade (from $207,231.94 in 1886 to $161,919.31 in 1890) and by contrast, these years were to Mifflin monotonous. To his sister-in-law, Houghton may have appeared to be living like a millionaire. However, as he more than once apologized to associates pressing speculative ventures, his management of his publishing acquisitions was conservative. His grim purpose was to make sure there would be no pieces of Houghton, Mifflin for Fairchild and Osgood ever to pick up. He achieved his purpose by following three major policies — acquisition of fresh partnership capital, reworking the lists inherited from Hurd & Houghton and Houghton, Osgood, and cautious investment in new writers.[1]

Four men were added to the roster of the original partners during the decade, and in 1893 Houghton's nephews, Alfred F. and Oscar Ready Houghton were also admitted to the fraternity. Another contributor to the firm's financial stability was Houghton's silent partner of some thirty years before, Edmund Hatch Bennett, now a judge and Dean of the Boston University Law School, who had $50,000 with the firm. The Hurd family also retained its investment in the house. The first to be added to the original Valentine, Mifflin, Houghton partnership was James D. Hurd, eldest son of Melancthon, who had come to work at the Press in 1882. Young Hurd's partnership lasted only three years (1884–1887), being cut short by his death. His capital contribution of $50,000 now became standard for successive partners. In 1888 three more names were added to the association — James Murray Kay, Thurlow Weed Barnes, and Henry Oscar Houghton, Jr.[2]

James Murray Kay, a Scot by birth and trained in a London banking house, had married a Maine girl, Mary F. Prentice, a school friend of Mrs. Houghton, at whose persuasion the Kay family located in Brookline. Kay, regarded as a financial "wizard" by his intimates, became treasurer. An interesting aspect of Kay's affiliation with Houghton, Mifflin was that he was brother-in-law of George F. Godfrey, the man from Maine who after Osgood's failure had provided the brothers Ticknor with $25,000 in partnership capital. A year after Kay joined Houghton, Mifflin, the house purchased the assets of Ticknor & Company at the time of its liquidation. Thurlow Weed Barnes had been a friend of Houghton's son when they had been Harvard students, Barnes, class of '76, Harry '77. At this time Houghton had taken an affectionate interest in Barnes. In the years following his graduation, Barnes served as associate editor of his family's paper, the Albany *Evening Journal,* and in 1883 Houghton, Mifflin undertook to publish as a subscription book the autobiography of his grandfather, Thurlow Weed, to which Barnes added a memoir. During the prolonged process of getting the two-volume *Life* completed and into the subscription market, the Houghton-Barnes friendship was renewed. Under persistent pressure, Barnes, after two years of debate, decided to resign his newspaper post and cast his lot with the Boston house. After a couple of years, finding the duties expected of him at Park Street uncongenial, he withdrew as an active partner but doubled his capital investment. By 1893, perceiving more lucrative opportunities for his money in New York, to Houghton's ill-concealed irritation, he severed his connection with Houghton, Mifflin.

Young Harry Houghton's admission to the firm was both logical and merited. Under Mifflin's tutelage, he had served an eleven-year apprenticeship at the Press. At first, he had been less attentive to drudgery than his father wished, but on his falling in love, the daily grind took on meaning. As a result his father found himself reading with satisfaction Mifflin's reports on Harry's sudden devotion to hard work. Harry's inspiration was Rose Gilman, daughter of Houghton's niece Stella and Arthur Gilman. Houghton approved the union and provided the means for the desired end by affording his son the required partnership capital.

When Houghton, Mifflin & Company came into being in 1880, Mifflin hoped that at last his wish to have both publishing and printing activities under one roof would be realized. According to his thinking, the Press should be the nerve center of the business. However, his wishes did not prevail. During its first summer, the firm continued to operate from its dismal rooms over Lee & Shepard at 47 Franklin Street, but by August new quarters had been located and Garrison reported to his sister:

> You will be gratified to know that Houghton, Mifflin & Co. have hired the old Woman's Club parlors at No. 4 Park St., & are to occupy them Sept 1st. I shall sit by a window commanding

Houghton, Mifflin & Company's main office at 4 Park Street in the 1880s.

that lovely view of the Common, & the sunsets mirrored in the Frog Pond, in the very room where our Conversation Club has so often held its fortnightly suppers & meetings, & where Father addressed the Woman's Club time & again; the last occasion, I think, being, the 43rd anniversary of the club, Oct 21, 1878. It is very pleasant to me to think of spending all my hours, waking & sleeping, in places which he knew & which knew him so well . . .[3]

Although the quarters were less spacious than those of Houghton, Osgood's in the once handsome Cathedral Building, Houghton had as much reason to be gratified as his confidential clerk. Some thirty years before, when he had come to seek his fortune in Boston, he had taken a room on Hancock Street on the northern side of Beacon Hill. Now his publishing offices were on the southern slope, occupying two floors of what had been to him in those long ago days the Josiah Quincy mansion. The rear windows of Park Street looked out on the Old Granary Burying Ground where, tradition had it, were interred, amongst other heroes of the Republic, the bones of the creator of Mother Goose. Houghton now had an historic list and an historic setting.

Mifflin's hopes for terminating the firm's New York activity were defeated by Valentine and Albert Houghton, both convinced that through efficient administration, business there could be increased to $50,000 if the Astor Place location were given up and a more fashionable address found. Under the terms of the partnership agreement, Houghton and Mifflin were active partners; Valentine was "not bound to devote any more time or attention to the business . . . than he may hereafter see fit to do." He found it fit to pay attention almost at once. Having located an attractive residence at 11 East 17th Street, he telegraphed, "I am ready for action, action!" No one else had ever pressed Houghton in this fashion. He agreed to the shift in location but opposed Valentine's proposal to enlarge the scope of the branch office by reintroducing retail selling. He feared such enlargement would result in unhealthy competition

with the parent house, placing the two very much in the position of a couple of quadrupeds who are bumming against each other, and neither getting very far.

Moreover [he wrote Valentine], an active sale of our books at retail would provoke all our retail customers in New York, and again react upon us, and prevent them from keeping such a good line of our books as they otherwise would. It seems to us that we had better plod on, and make the New York house a branch of the Boston house, holding it responsible to us for its doings, and trust to the natural growth of the business for its support.

In the interest of economy, he suggested the upper floors of the house be rented to transients at $1.50 to $2.00 a night. If this were done, both he and Mifflin could stay there when they came to New York. Houghton, Mifflin authors, too, might find the rooms convenient.[4]

Houghton, Mifflin's New York "book parlors," when they were opened on October 19, 1881, appeared to one reporter as luxurious as a private library. The walls were papered with a Pompeian design in light brown with a green frieze, and comfortable chairs in front of an open fire invited the book lover to sit and leaf through some of the handsomely bound books displayed on the broad cherry center table. One to catch the acquisitive eye was a Holiday Edition of Bayard Taylor's *Home Ballads* "bound in calf with birds-eye maple-wood sides so finely polished and finished that the grain was distinctly brought out."[5]

In the beginning Mifflin's fears about the New York branch were justified; up to 1886 it recorded small but persistent losses. Valentine, however, believed that by "a judicious stimulating of Capt. Albert," who would "inoculate his followers," the trend could be reversed. When his partners asked for his plan of action, he countered, "You know as well as I do that no fellow can define how he is going to fight and win a battle beforehand. And a good General would rather be shot on the spot than undertake to tell a careful committee how and what he is going to win." One part of General Valentine's battle plan was to do more in the way of attracting wealthy buyers to the display rooms. By now Houghton, Mifflin had ventured considerable sums in subscription books and limited editions and was pointing with pride to such clients as August Belmont, Nicholas Roosevelt, William Maxwell Evarts, T. A. Havemeyer, and a clutch of others. Valentine thought more of the carriage trade could be attracted to 17th Street if a few repairs were made.

> In regard to a new stoop — a better approach to the book parlor, I will only say, I heard a lady whom you esteem say that she hoped she never would have to climb those steps again. With this indictment, I leave it to you and Mr. Mifflin to decide what expressions you make, if any, to help Albert draw the Astors and the Stillmans and the Huntingtons and the New York Knickerbockers. Comprenez vous? What says Mr. Mifflin, what says Mr. Hurd, and last but not least, what says Mr. Houghton?

Beyond doubt the stoop was repaired, for in the following year the New York branch showed a small profit.[6]

Mifflin may have been grudging in approving repairs at 17th Street. No such hesitancy hindered expansion of the Riverside Press. In October 1886 work was begun on a new building for the Lithographic Department. Its completion afforded opportunity for various newspaper releases depicting the modern Riverside. Its "magnificent" 100-horsepower Corliss engine supplied more than enough power to drive 33 presses, 16 of them Adams, the remainder Hoe cylinder or job. Seven thread-sewing machines, each capable of doing the work of four girls, further increased efficiency of manufacture. The plant's 600 employees were now being given during the summer a half holiday with full pay on Saturdays. Within ten years the Savings Department had multiplied eightfold. A fire brigade of 65 workers was kept in constant training even though the plant was now fully equipped with a Grinnell automatic sprinkler system. With his well-equipped plant and loyal workers, Mifflin expected to be able to turn out books faster than the publishing department could give them to him. He was constantly in search of outside work to serve "as a balance wheel." Such work was essential, he told Houghton, "and in the face of almost ruinous competition [we] have worked up a good deal of new work from year to year." Included in the outside work was an order for a million advertising circulars for flour.[7]

Devoted as Mifflin was to the Riverside Press, he nonetheless was certain the major effort of the house should be to look out for and vigorously push the publishing product, for here lay the firm's major valuation and expense. Included in this expense were copyright obligations, a portion of which were to the annuitants, who whether or not they produced new books were assured their annual stipends, at least until the original Osgood agreements ran out in 1885 and 1886. It was up to the publishing side to rework the list in a way that would make the books of these writers justify the system by producing profits at least equal to what the annual return would have been had these writers been retained on the standard 10 percent royalty. To succeed in this purpose, the firm issued a variety of editions at prices to suit every purse. In 1886 complete collections of Longfellow's poems were to be had in at least nine different editions: the Cambridge, the Riverside, the Household, the Library, the Red-Line, the Family, the Diamond, the Subscription, and the Large-Paper, varying in price from the single volume Diamond at a dollar to the three-volume Subscription (prose included) bound in sealskin for $80. In addition to complete editions, single poems of the annuitants were given new interest by being issued in several illustrated formats. Their products were further worked by being cut up into quotations for calendars and birthday books.

Of the variety of editions produced for the annuitants, the most notable were the subscription, especially the limited editions de luxe, for it was in producing this type that Houghton indulged his love of fine bookmaking and it was under his tutelage that Mifflin learned a profitable market existed for the limited edition, the more limited the more lucrative. It was also during this time that Daniel Berkeley Updike served a twelve-year apprenticeship with Houghton, Mifflin before establishing his Merrymount Press in 1893. During these years also, the way was prepared for the unique achievements of Bruce Rogers and the Riverside Press in the early years of the twentieth century. In variety and range the work of Riverside in the 1880s "far outstripped anything that was being done in Britain at the same time." William Morris' Kelmscott Press was not established until 1891.[8]

Subscription distribution, a method especially adapted to a publishing venture requiring large financial outlay before the book could be marketed, had played a part in Houghton's schemes from the beginning. Although subscribers were not required to make payment until delivery of the book, the majority, having signed on the line, paid the charge. Thus the publisher was assured manufacturing costs before the book went into production. Two large Hurd & Houghton undertakings in this line were the American edition of Smith's *Bible Dictionary* and Edward Knight's *Mechanical Dictionary*. In preparation of the former, under the editorial supervision of the American Biblical scholars Horatio Hackett and Ezra Abbott, the firm invested $100,000. Work begun in 1867 was not complete until 1871. For ten years thereafter subscriptions were taken by *"specially appointed Traveling Solicitors."* After a decade of distribution in this manner, the volumes (there were four) were sold through the trade at a $5 reduction per set. Thus the work secured two markets, standard practice with publishers of subscription books. However, Houghton's were not of the type to be "dumped" on the trade within months, even weeks, of announcement they would be sold by subscription only, as was the habit of the cheap Hartford subscription houses, including the American Publishing Company.[9]

For the few subscription books issued by his house, Houghton anticipated two sources of revenue, subscription and trade. For Knight's *Mechanical Dictionary,* a third and unexpected source developed. Edward Knight, a United States patent attorney who for twenty-five years had served the Federal Patent Office, in 1868 signed an agreement with J. B. Ford & Company, specialists in subscription methods. Knight was to produce a two-volume dictionary to "embrace a terse, historical exposition of each topic treated, with descriptions of important appliances of mechanical and chemical science to manufacture . . . Especial attention" was to be devoted "to matters of such national importance as civil, military, steam and mine engineering and metallurgy." J. B. Ford & Company was one of the numerous publishing fatalities of the depression following the '73 panic. In 1875 Hurd & Houghton purchased the plates and publishing rights of Knight's *Dictionary* and subsequently negotiated a contract with Knight under which in lieu of a royalty he was to receive $4.00 a page on the final volume (the work had by now grown to four volumes) and for an additional $2228.14 was to assign his copyright in all volumes to his publishers. Thus by the time the work was completed in 1885, Hurd & Houghton were the sole owners of the *Dictionary*.

Before this, however, Roswell Smith of the Century Company had made overtures to purchase. Houghton was not interested. ". . . my plan," he told Smith, "is to get all I can out of the book in its complete form, and then make it up in other forms . . . and get a second harvest, which I am looking forward to as being a very rich one." He knew that Roswell Smith and the Century Company had desperate need of the rights to Knight's *Mechanical Dictionary*. Century had announced for publication in December 1882 the four-volume *Imperial Dictionary of Great Britain*, imported from Blackie & Sons of Glasgow. Unfortunately for Roswell Smith, the compilers of the *Imperial* had made "too-free use" of Knight's definitions and illustrations. Century had plans in train for an American revision of the *Imperial*, a revision which would ultimately result in the *Century Dictionary* at an eventual cost of $987,000. A minor part of the cost was an arrangement Century was obliged to make with Houghton, Mifflin. As Smith told Houghton, "If I ever did buy anything cheap from the time I began to get cheated in trading Jack Knives I do not know when it was." For the privilege of publishing the *Imperial* in the United States unimpeded by a lawsuit and of using Knight's definitions in the proposed *Century Dictionary,* Century paid Houghton, Mifflin $3000. In addition all illustrations taken from Knight must be paid for at the rate of 15 cents a square inch. Because of this tangle, publication of the *Imperial* in the United States was delayed from December 1882 until March 1883.

The *Bible* and *Mechanical Dictionary* had appeared first on Hurd & Houghton's list. Both were originally published for subscription distribution, graduating to the trade only after the first market had been exhausted. The firm followed the same pattern for a number of other books. However, in the 1880s the majority of Houghton, Mifflin's subscription editions reversed the pattern. Trade had the original market.

The first of these undertakings — a complete Longfellow — was initiated during the Houghton, Osgood association and volume one bears that imprint, volumes two and three, Houghton, Mifflin's. One reason for undertaking a sumptuous edition of Longfellow at this time was that in addition to being wooed and won by Harper for its *Monthly,* the poet had become increasingly irritated with Osgood as publisher, who he thought had treated him "cavalierly." The Centennial Edition of his *Complete Poetical Works* had been a misnomer; it was by no means complete. Furthermore, in an advertising blurb included in the book, Osgood had listed *Christus* and *Dante* as prose and had quoted the *Christian Intelligencer* as saying, "Indeed, his perception of, and power to eliminate that which is beautiful in all things is his greatest characteristic . . ." "Against one and all these things I seriously protest," Longfellow wrote Osgood. "Pray consider these things." In considering, Houghton, Osgood decided to bring out an edition of the poet which would surpass in elegance of dress and princely adornment any previous volumes devoted to an American writer.[10]

Originally issued in forty-five quarto parts at 50 cents each, the three volumes (or six for convenience of handling) might be had in a variety of bindings ranging in price from $30 to $80. In preparing the edition, the firm invested $60,000 in plates and illustrations, the latter numbering 600, thirty of them full page, all expressly prepared for these volumes. Passages selected by the poet were drawn from nature by some thirty-seven artists, among them Edwin A. Abbey, F. O. C. Darley, Mary Hallock Foote, Winslow Homer, Augustus Hoppin, and John La Farge. The three volumes were completed by the summer of 1883. By the end of the following year 50,000 subscribers attested the value of the work. Press comment was ecstatic. The volumes were judged "the finest specimen of bookmaking ever produced in this country," their illustrations, a high-water mark in wood engraving, the paper supplied by S. D. Warren & Company, the best "even their famous mills can produce." The entire undertaking was hailed as "an honor to the country."

Over the years, similar, although less monumental, subscription sets were issued for all the New England group. However, Houghton disliked the method of distribution. "The subscription business is bad enough at best," he said, "but it is the only way in which we can sell books of such magnitude as the Longfellow." Given the opportunity, he assured his friends, he would turn one of his own subscription agents out of doors.[11]

More congenial to his temperament was the limited edition. His first venture in this line had been in 1867 when he had published an edition of Dickens in fifty-five volumes, limited to fifty sets, and hand-printed on special paper. Even though the work was acclaimed one of "the handsomest . . . ever made in this country," only a few of the sets sold, "for [according to the *Critic*] the rage for luxurious book-making was not as great then as it is now." "Now" for the *Critic* was the 1880s. More and more Americans were becoming art conscious. Books were on the periphery of art; they even had speculative value purchasers discovered after they had bought Houghton, Mifflin's 1883 edition de luxe of Hawthorne limited to 250 at $6 a volume. The twelve-volume sets were promptly subscribed, many by shrewd booksellers, some said, and were shortly selling for $15 a volume. In subsequent editions de luxe, Houghton, Mifflin increased the number of sets, for Emerson and Longfellow to 500. Even so Emerson was fully subscribed before the first volume had begun printing, and when the English publisher Routledge requested a copy, Houghton was pleased to reply that all he could send him was the firm's stamped copy. The earnings of these editions must have gratified him too — the eleven-volume Emerson over $9000; the Longfellow over $10,000.[12]

One of the most distinguished undertakings in the line of limited editions was Houghton, Mifflin's commitment to publish Francis James Child's *English and Scottish Popular Ballads,* a vast elaboration of Child's ballad volumes in the *British Poets* series. An edition de luxe limited to 1000 in imperial quarto on extra laid paper in eight parts (it would eventually run to ten), to be numbered, the name of each purchaser recorded, was announced in March 1882, the American price $5 a part; the English and Continental, Henry Stevens as agent, a guinea. Child's royalty was 10 percent with no exemptions. In addition he was to have

fifty copies to give to libraries and individuals who had aided him
in his extensive and persistent search for unpublished ballads and
their numerous variations, oral or manuscript, in Scandinavia,
Germany, Spain, and France as well as the British Isles. On the
appearance of the first part at the end of 1882, reviewers were
unanimous in praise both of Child's scholarship and the mechanical execution of the volume. The typography, the paper, all the
externals of the quarto were declared to "challenge comparison
with the very choicest work of foreign presses." Riverside had
"never turned out a volume handsomer and in better taste . . .
The series will form a magnificent body of ancient English poetry,
beautifully published, and edited in the most scholarly fashion."
Lowell, who had helped and would continue to help Child in his
search, thought his friend's "enormous labour" had built "an im-
perishable monument."[13]

So detailed an undertaking was ideally suited to Houghton's
deliberate nature. His reiterated creed inscribed on his personal
bookplate *"Tout bien ou rien"* paralleled the scholar's search for
perfection. Had he been a prince instead of a merchant, his
patronage would have supported this type of bookmaking. He
would have understood Child's confession to Lowell after the first
volume had appeared. "The mass of matter was very oppressive
when I thought how little time might be left me, and if I had
not been afraid to wait, I would have pushed into the Slavic
territory and have forestalled some just criticism. But now I am
going on to finish the other seven parts as well as I can in the
shortest practicable time. I must not be careless, but must still
less be fussy." In spite of Child's resolve, "the shortest practicable
time" proved exasperatingly long to Henry Stevens, English agent
and expatriate Green Mountain Boy, to whose impatient inquiries
as to when succeeding volumes would be forthcoming, Houghton
replied, "This work goes very much too slowly to suit an American's impetuous nature, but there is no help for it. If a man will
delve in old ballads and old literature, we have to wait his time . . ."
Sales also proved deliberate. The eight volumes published by 1890
had averaged something under 500 each. The work would not be
completed until 1897. By then both scholar-editor and his pub-

lisher were dead. The "little time" left Child had been fifteen years. To George Lyman Kittredge, Child's pupil and assistant, the ten volumes of *English and Scottish Popular Ballads* were "one of the greatest monuments of learning ever erected by one man." They also bear testimony to the excellence in book design and manufacture of which the Riverside Press was capable. Another superb example, equal in scholarship and production to Child's *Ballads,* is Charles Sprague Sargent's fourteen-volume *Silva of North America,* its 740 illustrations by Charles Edward Faxon engraved on copperplate in Paris.

Although Houghton preferred books intended for reading rather than display, he was sufficiently aware of the taste of the times to undertake elaborate, illustrated editions of single works. In 1885 his firm realized the apotheosis of Victorian rococo elegance in book design with two publications, Oliver Wendell Holmes's *The Last Leaf* and F. Hopkinson Smith's *Old Lines in New Black and White.* Both these volumes were produced by methods used the year before in publishing Elihu Vedder's illustrated edition of Edward Fitzgerald's translation of the *Rubáiyát* of Omar Khayyám.

According to Vedder's recollection, when he approached Houghton in the spring of 1883 with a proposal that he illustrate the *Rubáiyát,* the publisher asked, "But who and where is this Omar?" Apparently, Houghton had been so absorbed in exploiting the Americans in his catalogue, he had overlooked this English paraphrase of a Persian poet which had first appeared in this country in an 1870 pamphlet edition of one hundred and which later Osgood had introduced to American readers just before he sought cover under the Houghton, Osgood aegis. Osgood's simple Red-Line edition had sold slowly. Under Houghton, Mifflin's management, it rode the wave of Vedder's success; the illustrations drew wide attention to the poem. Unaware of Omar, Houghton may have been; with Vedder's work he was familiar. Four of his drawings appeared in the firm's illustrated *Enoch Arden,* inherited from Ticknor & Fields via Osgood. In 1880 the *Atlantic* had reviewed favorably a Boston exhibition of Vedder's pictures. Included in the exhibition were illustrations of a verse of Omar's

and Thomas Bailey Aldrich's "Identity." These would be pass-
port enough for Vedder's proposal.[14]

The artist and the publisher were prompt in reaching an agreement, if not an understanding. Vedder's whirlwind personality
may well have defied Houghton's unhurried comprehension.
They signed a half-profits contract on March 31, 1883, and
Vedder returned to Rome and his studio, where he found it easy
"to imagine 'some buried Caesar bled.'" Working at white heat,
within three weeks he had worked out his general plan of fifty-six
designs embracing, indeed literally smothering, the one hundred
and one stanzas of the poem. The magnificent scale of Vedder's
conception was more than Houghton had anticipated. He indicated moderation but the artist refused to listen. This was to be
"the most remarkable [book] ever published in America," a record
of Vedder's artistic creed. "I do not intend the drawings to be
close illustrations of the text . . ." he explained. "They are accom-
paniments of the verses — parallel but not identical in thought."
He wished his drawings to be reproduced by American craftsmen
to "show that the progress we have been so liberal in bragging
about has a solid foundation." To protests that his plans were too
elaborate, too expensive, he retorted, "Of course, I expected it
would require money and lots of it — and I at least was prepared
to eat less and do something fine even if it only paid expenses
which I *did* think it would do. I still think so." An establishment
like the Riverside Press, he argued, should be prepared at least
once "to do itself proud." When Houghton, Mifflin suggested
some of his figures would be less open to criticism if they were
given a veil or two, Vedder exploded. His sketches were no more
undraped than the poem. "It must be borne in mind that I am
not illustrating Martin Tupper, nor for the matter of that Omar
Khayyám, but Elihu Vedder and 'such as I am I mean to be.' I
will also take care of the dignity of the work. I am sincerely sorry
there should have been any question of the sort and shall be more
so should you prove as firm in your opinions as I am for I have
decided irrevocably to stand by myself and retain the drawings."

Houghton believed a half-profits contract constituted a partnership. Since the author was bearing half the expense, his opinions

must be balanced against those of his publisher. Vedder won his points about his illustrations, but he yielded to Houghton, Mifflin's preference for phototypes rather than engravings. The process was complicated. Vedder had his drawings photographed in Rome. The photographs were sent to Boston, where phototypes were made. Then proofs were sent to Vedder for suggestions and changes before printing. In both the trade and limited editions the final versions were mounted on leaves of heavy plate paper, hinged on strips of linen, "making the book wholly obedient to the opening hand." The de luxe edition, limited to one hundred copies and selling for a like amount of dollars, was distinguished from the trade, which sold for a mere $25, by a larger page and the margin of each illustration was graced with a supplementary design. The volume was bound in full Levant morocco and lined in silk designed by the artist.

Houghton, Mifflin pulled out all its promotional stops in bringing Vedder's *Rubáiyát* to the public. In addition to placing attractive prospectuses in proper places, it staged exhibitions in Boston at the Art Club, in Chicago at the Art Institute, in New York at the Tile Club. By happy chance, Houghton himself was in Nashville and Cincinnati when exhibitions were held there. In Boston 2000 were in daily attendance during the week of the show. In New York "eminent artists," among them Saint-Gaudens, attended the opening night. So did Harper's Alden and Century's Gilder. Rumor had it that the originals could be had for $5000 and a movement was afoot to have them purchased by the Metropolitan Art Museum or the National Academy. Reviews of this publishing venture were rapturous. The publishers were praised for their painstaking care, "their judicious breadth of taste," "their wise liberality." "A new era in American art illustration" had arrived. Vedder was hailed as a more finished draughtsman than Blake; Doré by comparison was "course, vulgar, and material." The *Rubáiyát* illustrations revealed "striking demonic power" and "mystic spirituality." Even as Hawthorne, Vedder was "a true growth" of American soil. His art would survive the years. Today, Fitzgerald's translation still pleads its *carpe diem* in paperbacks and battered limp leather; Vedder's *Rubáiyát,* even in the trade edition, is kept behind locked cabinet doors in libraries.

Since Fitzgerald's version had no copyright protection, following Houghton, Mifflin's vigorous promotion, it was immediately reprinted by numerous houses. The newly founded Grolier Club, organized to unite booklovers and bookmakers, chose it for its second publication, issuing it in paper covers. Despite the competition of cheap editions (one sold for 20 cents), the firm continued to tote up sales for Vedder's version, introducing a $12.50 edition in 1886, a $5 one in 1894. Osgood's simple Red-Line at $1.00, benefited by men of longer purse and longer patience, remained a popular item in the Houghton catalogue for over forty years.

From the title page of Vedder's *Rubáiyát* on which was pictured a naked boy by a river watching paper boats, a colophon for the house was derived. Up to this time the general form of the Hurd & Houghton colophon had been used, an entwined H and M taking the place of the two H's, the triple partnership symbolized by three stars in the points of the shield. After James Hurd's admission to partnership, the three stars were outmoded. As a first step toward a new device, the firm asked Vedder to introduce the motto from Houghton's bookplate *"Tout bien ou rien"* in a scroll on the left hand of the boy. The result was too charmingly simple. ". . . it seems to me," Houghton wrote, "that if we could put in the center of this cut a glimpse of a river, a tree, the sun shining upon them, and in the distance a little old fashioned hand printing press, with this motto [*Tout bien ou rien*] in the side and top borders and 'the Riverside Press' in the bottom in Caxton we should get a design which would be especially adapted to our purpose, would be unique, and, if well done, would look well." Houghton's suggestions were executed by Sidney L. Smith, who elaborated Vedder's drawing beyond recognition, changing the wistfully naked youth to a middle-aged man in a loin cloth, seated under a gnarled tree of knowledge, piping paper boats toward a minute hand press. Lest any of the symbolism be obscure, a lamp of knowledge and the rising sun illuminate all, suggesting to a contemporary wit that Houghton, Mifflin & Company had to get up early "to catch the literary worm." In the years to come many

The origin of one of Houghton Mifflin's most famous colophons is Elihu Vedder's boy by the riverside from his *Rubáiyát of Omar Khayyám.* The second design, executed by Sidney L. Smith, follows minutely Houghton's suggestions for elaboration of the Vedder colophon.

variations would be played on the themes here presented. Few recall the sensitive face of Vedder's child.[15]

Another Osgood property that performed in a phenomenal manner under Houghton, Mifflin's management was General Lew Wallace's *Fair God,* published in 1873. This novel of Aztec life was an immediate success, selling more than 7000 within a year. For the rest of the decade sales declined in a normal fashion, averaging just over 100 up to 1880. In November 1880, Harper published the General's *Ben-Hur.* At first sales were less than spectacular — 2800 in seven months; a decline followed. In 1882 sales picked up sharply, averaging 300 a month. *Ben-Hur* was off on a chariot race. Each succeeding year broke the monthly average of the one before — 750 — 1200 — 4500, and so to the end of the decade when sales had reached 400,000. The yearly sales graph of *The Fair God* was parallel, although of course less sensational: 1881 — 318; 1882 — 591; 1883 — 968; 1884 — 1683; 1885 — 4665, for a total of 82,297 by 1890, earning $32,762.55 for Houghton, Mifflin, for Wallace, $12,244.55, a fair record for a seventeen-year-old. *The Fair God* never achieved the princely recognition of a limited edition. However, in 1898 it was honored with a two-volume Holiday Edition. The book might have achieved an even wider sale had Wallace been willing to have it appear in the Riverside Paper Series. Since he would not permit cheap editions of his works, not until after his death was his fiction open to the paperback market.[16]

The Riverside Paper Series, initiated in the summer of 1885, although it later came to include untried authors, in its first two years is a further example of Houghton, Mifflin's reworking its list. Old novels of Edgar Fawcett, W. H. Bishop, Holmes, Aldrich, Howells, and others, bound attractively in olive gray, rough paper covers with Vedder's boy by the river reproduced in soft green, were prepared for the market at 50 cents each. One purpose of this undertaking was to secure at least some of the readers being developed by the cheap reprints in George Munro's Seaside Library, Norman Munro's Riverside Library, Donnelley & Lloyd's Lakeside Library, Frank Leslie's Home and Fireside Libraries, John W. Lovell's Library, the Harper Franklin Square Library, and the tawdry productions of the American Book Exchange. Some of these paper-bound reprints of unprotected foreign material sold for as little as 3 cents a copy. Most of the fiction published in the Riverside Paper Series was American and copyrighted. Valentine was enthusiastic about the series, believing the greatest reward would be realized in the future. During a Southern trip in 1886, he wrote Houghton, "From the *very little* I have seen of the South, I am impressed with the feeling that 'paper covers' would pave the way for cloth, and make known the good things coming from the Riverside Press say in 96 . . . Atlanta is a *live city* & her sons will want some good bindings in the next generation if not this."[17]

Another reason for the introduction of the Riverside Paper Series was that in 1885 a change in the postal rates allowed periodicals to be mailed at 1 cent a pound. Books in cloth were charged at 8 cents. The Riverside Paper Series qualified as a periodical for it was to be issued weekly during the summer months.

There is no record of Houghton's opinion of the Riverside Paper Series, the huge subscription Longfellow, or the profusely illustrated single poems. He probably enjoyed the sound of dollars ringing in Houghton, Mifflin's coffers and he must have been pleased by the critical acclaim, but in the light of his affection for another series begun at this time, it is safe to assume that neither the cheap nor the elaborate editions represented his ideal book. His was a commercial institution committed to making money. In consequence his concept of perfection was in repeated conflict with the practical. "I am constantly confronted with this problem," he told Henry Stevens, "whether to do a book absolutely to suit my own taste, or modify my taste to suit the great public, who are the purchasers, elevating their taste, and making it conform to mine as far as possible. This, it seems to me, is the great problem of the present day, — adapting the best standards to modern demands."[18]

For Houghton, to compromise was to surrender, something he refused to do in producing the first edition (limited to 250) of his Riverside Aldines. In these compact, comfortable books he intended "to give the best which the printer's art in America can produce," his models the Renaissance Aldus Manutius and his nineteenth-century English disciple William Pickering of the Chiswick Press. The books were to affect no novelty, carry no ornament save the Aldus colophon of the anchor and the dolphin. Their beauty was to be in their proportion and in the fineness of the material. The page was to be clear and open, but would avoid extra "leading," that is, too liberal space between the printed lines. "Widely leaded pages," he thought, "are provincial, and specially American, and, like anything else that is padded, tell against the character of the book." The pages were to be uncut. "The fact is," he said, "if you allow a knife to touch a book after it has been folded and put in book form, you absolutely destroy its proportion forever and a day." The Aldines were to have paper titles and be bound in red cloth.

The authors he chose for the series were all Americans who, with the exception of Hawthorne and Thoreau, had many years of writing ahead of them. When Henry Stevens objected that those included, especially Charles Dudley Warner, did not merit so fine a dress, Houghton admitted that a group of three-hundred-year-old classics would be more appropriate. The trouble was, American publishing was too young to have acquired such a list of native writers. Time, he hoped, would vindicate his choice from the living writers in his catalogue — Aldrich, Warner, Lowell, Harte, Burroughs, and Sarah Orne Jewett.

Houghton was recognized by his contemporaries as having "revolutionized printing in America." In 1881 the *Publishers' Weekly* noted that work done at the Riverside Press twenty years before was now commanding exceptional prices at auctions. "Mr. Houghton," the *Weekly* said, "is *par excellence* the American printer . . ." By this time, however, the Riverside Press was not alone in creating notable books. One of its closest competitors was the press of Theodore De Vinne in New York, which was doing outstanding work for Scribner, Century, and the Grolier Club. At the Paris Exposition of 1889, Century won the highest award, a Diploma of Honor; Appleton, Lippincott, G. & C. Merriam, and Houghton, Mifflin took second places with gold medals. That Houghton influenced the art of the book in his generation is beyond question. De Vinne admitted his debt to the founder of the Riverside Press. Less generous in his acknowledgment was Daniel Berkeley Updike.[19]

Updike came to the house in the early months of its founding before the company had taken rooms on Park Street. After having served briefly as assistant librarian *pro tempore* in the gracious atmosphere of the Providence Athenaeum, he found the dreary Franklin Street offices depressing. Since he was twenty years old, he was something senior for the position of office boy secured for him through the kind efforts of a cousin. He didn't care for the work, the hours, or the pay. Another Houghton, Mifflin office boy, in his recollections, makes clear the reasons for Updike's misery.

> Juniors in the office arrived daily at half past seven. We did some of the janitor work, brought in the mail from the post office, made copies of out-going letters by pressing them into a large book after dampening its blank tissue-leaves. All of us, including the department heads, remained until six. But in summer we closed at five with a half-day on Saturday. All had a two weeks vacation with full pay. That was from $3 a week for a boy who had served less than a year up to sixty for veteran chiefs of the several departments.[20]

Although the newly invented typewriter was office equipment at Park Street from the beginning, letters both typed and hand-written were transferred to bound and indexed books by a laborious process:

> A waterproof, thin pasteboard, the size of the letter book, was laid under the page of the letter book. A brush was then dipped in a water pan, and run carefully back and forth over the page. A blotter was then placed on the page to absorb excess moisture. The . . . letter was then placed face down upon the sheet, another blotter placed above the letter, the book closed, run into a press operated by hand, the handle of which turned round and round until sufficient pressure was obtained. After two minutes had elapsed, the letter was removed . . . and placed upon the writer's desk . . . if the blotter did not absorb enough moisture, the letter would come out blurred and indistinct . . .

In later years, Updike recalled Houghton's manner as "hectoring." Many of the letters in the firm's 1880 letterbooks are blurred and indistinct. Possibly Updike was responsible for some of the blots. Houghton assumed in others a devotion to duty comparable to his own.

Even though he had worked only a few weeks, Updike had his two-week summer holiday. Once away from the horrors of Franklin Street and Houghton's "Old Testament presence," he made up his mind never to go back. Then came a flattering letter, promising shorter hours. During his vacation the firm had moved to its new location. Updike decided to return. The Quincy mansion he found more to his taste than the second floor of 47 Franklin and he was relieved shortly to graduate from office boy to the Advertising Department to work under the supervision of Azariah Smith, whose literary bulletins were generally regarded as the "best announcements of new books" in the trade. Updike was put to work first clipping newspapers, then in preparing copy, and finally working on catalogues, brochures, and fliers.

Houghton had definite ideas on advertising, as indeed he had on most publishing matters. In 1881 the firm allowed $30,391.29 for this department. By 1893, the year Updike left to establish his own press, the amount had more than doubled. "The publisher, in the last analysis, is neither printer nor bookseller, but advertiser. It is his business to make the author known," Scudder wrote in an article on "Authorship in America" in 1883. In the same year Houghton explained his advertising policies to the disgruntled Richard Grant White, who felt Houghton, Mifflin had not been "pushing" his books energetically. The house believed in his books because of their staying qualities, Houghton assured White, reminding him that those of his books which Hurd & Houghton had taken over from the Sheldons still continued to sell, and sell better than they ever had under the Sheldons. White should not judge Houghton, Mifflin on the basis of the number of newspaper notices his books received. "Notices in newspapers are read by very few people except the authors themselves and those specially interested . . . they are besides very expensive," Houghton explained. The firm only used press notices "to secure as far as possible the good will of the papers" and, of course, to keep authors happy. Direct mail advertising was the way to reach the public. Attractively designed fliers, prospectuses, brochures, and catalogues, all widely distributed was the technique Houghton favored to build business. "That our methods have been good is proved in the steady increase in the volume of our business since we adopted them," Houghton concluded. Scrapbooks of such publishing ephemera in the Houghton, Mifflin files bear testimony to the exceptional caliber of the work of the Advertising Department in the 1880s. In addition to routine lists, there are the handsome sample pages for the limited editions de luxe, catalogues of selected books — Western Authors, Children's Books, Educational Books, Law Books, and so on — fliers for the various series, and charming bookmarks used to announce new books. In assisting in the design of such advertising paraphernalia, Updike learned some of the rudiments of the craft to which he would later add distinction.

His work showed such promise that in 1886 he was offered a promotion. The promotion, however, meant that he must leave Park Street and work at the Riverside Press. Obviously, a knowledge of the mechanics of book production was essential for a young man who showed taste in design but whose "extravagant experiments" were proving expensive. Updike was ready to make the change, but his mother, who had come to Boston to make a home for him, persuaded him to turn down the opportunity. As a result Updike remained at Park Street to be paid compliments instead of increased dollars, even though William Gammell of Providence, pleading Mrs. Updike's "straitened circumstances," had used his influence to have her son's salary raised.

The plea that Updike should have more dollars because of his mother's indigence must have rung with a hollow sound in the ears of the Vermonter whose youthful experience had been with privation of a sharper kind. Twice during his employment Updike took European holidays with his mother, one of a year. The reason that his salary was not raised on request is not far to seek. Finally in 1891 another opportunity to work at the Press developed. Updike believed the opening was created for him because his work could be accomplished more efficiently at Riverside than at Park Street. He perhaps did not realize that his supercilious, critical presence in the Boston office was causing trouble.

In the late summer of 1891, Houghton went abroad. In his absence Mifflin supervised both the Press and the Boston office. In one of his frequent letters to his senior partner, Mifflin reported, "I am troubled oftentimes by the lack of harmony existing between the Advertising Department and the general selling department. There seems to be a separation . . . which works to not much better advantage than a separation in married life before it becomes an actual divorce. I am trying to restore the harmony which should exist, but with some of the materials it is not very easy work. I shall content myself with this general allusion to the difficulties of the subject, with which I know you yourself are familiar." Updike, on his transfer to Riverside, found himself as miserable as he had been at Park Street. Now thirty, he "languished to such an extent that after two years," he concluded, "it was not worth while to languish more" and handed in his resignation. Mifflin, who valued Updike's "unerring skill and good taste," saw him leave with genuine regret, a regret perhaps tinged with a sense of failure on his part. Both he and Houghton took pride in the long service, the rule rather than the exception, that their employees rendered. Some by now had served Houghton for over forty years. Loyalty he regarded as a reciprocal obligation.

In thanking the Riverside workers for a New Year's gift in 1890, he spoke from his heart.

> Some of you have been associated with me during the whole period of my business life, namely forty-one years, and many have been connected with the Firm for a long period of years. The interest which you have shown in the business and the ambition which you have shared with me to make it the first in the land have furnished me the greatest happiness of my life. We have tried to make your interests our own, and to share with you such prosperity as the business may have given us . . .
>
> I can only repeat, in acknowledgment of your kindness to me . . . that I am deeply grateful for the good feeling which you evinced. I also assure you that there is no interest and welfare in this world of so much importance to me as your interest and welfare . . . I trust our relations may long continue, and that each of us, while increasing our love and interest in the business, may increase our love and respect for each other.[21]

The occasion for the "elegant presents" his workers had given him was a New Year's party, at which the 600 employees of the Press and their families had gathered for speeches, feasting, and dancing, Thomas' Cambridge Orchestra and the Riverside Quartet providing the music. Authors were included in the party as well as workers. Both Dr. Holmes and Lowell addressed the group as naturally did Houghton, who recalled the early days of the Press when the force had been so small he could hold such parties in his home. He told of the success of the Riverside Press Savings Association, which for seventeen years, with one exception, had paid an annual dividend of 10 percent and of how he had gone to France to look into a similar profit-sharing plan and had reached the conclusion that Riverside's was superior. Mifflin, too, was called on for a speech and for his brevity was awarded hearty applause. "Really," he said, "I never made a speech in my life. I would rather take a licking than make a speech. I wish you a Happy New Year." But he was not spared the spotlight. James

Wilson, who had come from England to the Press in 1864, told of Mifflin's apprentice days, of how ruddy-faced, eager, and inquiring he was. "What do you do this for?" he would ask. "Well, why is this done? What would be the result if it wasn't done this way?"[22]

In his speech Houghton talked with pride of his profit-sharing plan and of the more recently organized Riverside Press Mutual Benefit Association. Certain other achievements he did not mention. To do so would have been inappropriate, but both Lowell and Dr. Holmes knew. The annual stipends of the annuitants had been raised: Lowell's to $2000, Holmes's to $4000, Whittier's to $3000, Longfellow's (for the benefit of his heirs since he had died in 1882) to $5000. Mifflin was aware of another triumph which his partner did not mention on New Year's 1890. Houghton, Mifflin's net indebtedness now stood at a mere $161,000.[23]

These achievements had been secured partly through the firm's vigorous reworking of its list in numerous varieties of editions. These editions, however, afford only a partial explanation. The catalogue listings had been increased during the decade from 1200 to 3000. Included in the list were new writers and books intended for use in schools and colleges.

XIII

VENTURES IN EDUCATION

ALTHOUGH HOUGHTON, MIFFLIN established an Educational Department in 1882, its share of the then eight-million-dollar textbook business was that of the lamb rather than the lion. However, because of contemporary acceptance of its editor-in-chief, Horace Elisha Scudder, as a philosopher of education, the school texts and supplementary reading books published by the house had an influence out of proportion to their number. That the firm figured at all in the purely textbook market was due to its good fortune in securing a Harvard mathematics teacher, Henry Nathan Wheeler, to head its new department.[1]

The 1880s, within the textbook industry, was a decade for revision. Facts had become obsolete, "methods at least obsolescent," the *Critic* noted satirically. "There is a 'felt want' . . . a 'progress of the time' . . . a 'spirit of the age' . . . This 'spirit of the age' is a wonderful thing. One year the alphabet is taught the regular way; next year the 'spirit of the age' requires that it be taught backward, and some new book will come out to show how to do it." In this "spirit of the age" Houghton, Mifflin decided to revise a number of its texts and reference books. Anne Charlotte Lynch Botta, in 1860, had produced for Derby & Jackson a *Hand-book of Universal Literature* in which, with the temerity of Hawthorne's scribbling women, she had surveyed the world's literature. In a closely packed book, she embraced man's written word. On Derby & Jackson's failure, Ticknor & Fields had taken up the book and by this line of descent it had come to Houghton, Mifflin, and Mrs. Botta was asked to bring the book up to date, a task she accomplished promptly, offering at the same time to produce a compact survey of American literature. The firm declined her offer because its own *Primer of American Literature* was at this very time being revised, a revision undertaken as the result of rumors that a rival epitome was about to be published by a Chicago house. Competition also inspired the updating of two other venerable Houghton, Mifflin texts — Andrews and Stoddard's Latin grammar and Warren Colburn's *Intellectual Arithmetic upon the Inductive Method of Instruction*.[2]

Ethan A. Andrews and Solomon Stoddard's *Grammar of the Latin Language* had been on the market since 1836. In schools around Boston it was a perennial standard. So much was it a part of the mental furniture of the day that Henry James in *The Bostonians* could picture a beastly little boy frustrated by the Latin language kicking at everyone and everything — his tutor, his mother, the Romans, *and* Messrs. Andrews and Stoddard. James might well have been astonished had he known that his offhand reference to Andrews and Stoddard was responsible for bringing to conclusion negotiations which had been in progress for revision. One of the Andrews heirs had been dilatory in making up her mind to accept Houghton's proposal. Reading *The Bostonians* as it ran in the *Century,* she was so charmed by the allusion to the *Grammar* in the July 1885 number that she wrote straight off to accept the firm's proposal. Henry Preble of Harvard was engaged to modernize the text, incorporating advances made in American classical scholarship since 1836. Because he rejected the English system of pronunciation, new plates were required and the firm invested $20,000 in manufacturing and putting the book on the market. In 1888, three years after the project had been initiated, Houghton, Mifflin was at last able to announce ANDREWS ET STODDARD DE GRAMMATICA LATINA LIBER EDITO AB HENRICO PREBLE . . . SUMPTIBUS ET TYPIS HOUGHTONII MIFFLINQUE ET SOCIORUM, BOSTONIAE, IN REPUBLICA MASSACHUSETTENSI. After fifty years the book had been given a second run.[3]

In his correspondence with the Andrews heirs (the Stoddard heirs had assigned their interest to Houghton, Mifflin), Houghton had emphasized their good fortune, and the firm's, in securing Henry Preble as reviser, writing, "his being a member of the faculty of Harvard College will be no detriment to the book." His faith was well founded. Henry Nathan Wheeler, so recently of Harvard's faculty, was proving himself a valuable addition to the house. He had just completed his revision of Colburn's *First Lessons: Intellectual Arithmetic upon the Inductive Method of Instruction* and was at work on his own *Second Lessons.*

Colburn's was an even more antique text than Andrews and Stoddard's, having been copyrighted in 1821. One reason for its durability was that it derived from classroom experience. In fact, Colburn maintained that his pupils, by their questions, had themselves made the book, and Timothy Carter, recalling the days when he had been with Cummings, Hillard & Company, first publishers of the text, spoke of the "custom work" the author had put into the book. "A compositor could not be kept upon the work," he told Houghton, "because the author kept proofs until his class had tried on every Lesson to be sure they were just hard enough & not to [sic] hard for the preceding preparation." Because of this graded approach from the simple to the complex and because the method was based on observation rather than abstraction, Horace Mann called Colburn's *Arithmetic* "the greatest educational book of the century." In 1856, Colburn's publishers boasted an annual sale of 100,000 in the United States, a figure increased by 50,000 by British sales. Such reports attracted competitors. By 1880 Colburn's yearly sales had dropped to 12,500.[4]

Revision of texts may have been in the spirit of the age; it was also essential if a house looked for a toehold in educational publishing, a department of the book industry in the 1880s less savory than others. The "big four" — Ivison, Blakeman, Taylor & Co., Van Antwerp, Bragg & Co., D. Appleton & Co., and A. S. Barnes and Company — dominated the field, spending as much as $200,000 annually on agents and "introduction accounts," allowing under this heading excessive discounts and accepting in exchange as part of the price books of rival houses. In defense of themselves despite cries of "trust," "monopoly," and "ring," the four companies formed a syndicate, its announced purpose "to combat the evils of dishonest competition," not to fix prices. Three years earlier, in 1881, the *Publishers' Weekly,* long distressed by evi-

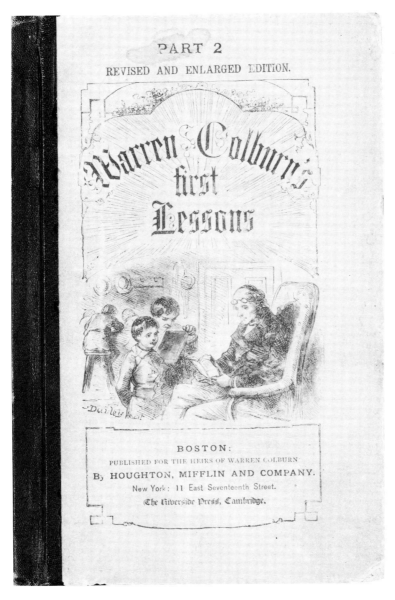

PART 2

REVISED AND ENLARGED EDITION.

Warren Colburn's
first
Lessons

BOSTON:
PUBLISHED FOR THE HEIRS OF WARREN COLBURN
By HOUGHTON, MIFFLIN AND COMPANY.
New York: 11 East Seventeenth Street.
The Riverside Press, Cambridge.

Front cover of Warren Colburn's *Arithmetic*. Houghton acquired
a half interest in the text from Colburn's heirs in 1862.

dences of corruption within this branch of the trade, had addressed a questionnaire to those involved, requesting information as to each firm's practice in regard to exchanges and discounts. Houghton, Mifflin had replied virtuously, "Our practice is very simple, merely to introduce our books where we can at wholesale. We do not exchange."[5]

Within the year conditions had altered. Rumor had it that Colburn was doomed, that this or that school was about to adopt a different text. The firm directed its agents to seek conferences with school committees and Wheeler went to work on his revision, bringing the problems up to date, especially those relating to prices and coins. He also introduced various teaching aids such as colored counters and materials with which the children could play at keeping store. The work completed, he went on the road, and Houghton in his travels also worked for the cause. Although the syndicate had assured rivals it would not attempt to supplant texts that had proved satisfactory to a school system, the work of the combine was evidenced almost at once. On a sales trip to Vermont, where texts which would be retained for five years were being adopted, Wheeler found that the big four had offered their books "on an even exchange, without any price whatever." Later when he went to Missouri, he discovered that the syndicate had that state in its control. To meet the competition Houghton, Mifflin offered 20 cents apiece for old Colburns plus a 15 percent discount on all orders for the revised edition in excess of ten. This was not enough and the firm decided to cut prices. The retail price of the revised Colburn was 35 cents. If old Colburns were traded, 10 cents would be the charge, a price four or five cents less than cost. The policy proved effective and Wheeler's revision sold 25,000 in its first year. However, for the rest of the decade, although the firm trumpeted the text as "in use in almost every state in the Union," sales dropped to an annual average of something over 13,000.[6]

In April 1890 the syndicate organized itself into a single company, its purpose "to do away with undue and costly competition." However, in a little over a month after its founding, an agent of the company was caught offering a member of the Washington

State Board of Education a bribe of $5000 if he would see that its contract was revised from an award of 28 percent to 80 percent of the state's textbook needs. For some years to come, rivals in the field were to be faced with this sort of competition. Even so, Houghton, Mifflin found that teachers were eager to introduce classics in all grades and Wheeler prophesied a brilliant future for his Educational Department. "The chances for our literature are grand," he boasted, "& they will grow better every year." That this was true was the result of Scudder's educational theories and the exceptional list of copyrighted American works in Houghton, Mifflin's catalogue.[7]

Scudder, on resigning his partnership early in 1875, had hoped to achieve financial security as a free lance in writing and lecturing. His independence was relative only. That same year, he cautiously yielded to Houghton's urging to give his afternoons to the interests of the firm for an annual $1200. This arrangement proving unsatisfactory from his point of view, he stipulated that any work he did for the house be paid for on a time basis. In 1882 he again submitted to Houghton's reiterated arguments, agreeing to work at Park Street for at least three hours a day. Then in the summer of the same year, on Aldrich's departure on a three-month European holiday, he assumed the responsibility of the *Atlantic* for $600. In 1884 he again took on Aldrich's editorial duties for the summer. In 1886 he once more took the *Atlantic* for three months and before August had run its course, he at last concluded to accept Houghton's proffered harness, agreeing to give substantially all his time to Houghton, Mifflin for a salary of $5000. His average annual income during these eleven years had been slightly over $4000. To keep on at "miscellaneous work with Black Care riding behind" had become a greater burden than he cared to carry. Under his new arrangement he was at liberty to come and go as he pleased, his contributions to the *Atlantic* would be paid for, and he was free to place articles with other periodicals, that is, if he could find the time. Houghton is reputed to have been a man of monumental temper. He was also one of prodigious patience, which more than once contributed to the realization of his stubbornly held purpose.[8]

More than Black Care influenced Scudder to accede to Houghton's relentless pressure. Mark Hopkins had taught him that he should use his gifts. He believed he had two, one literary, the other editorial.

> The organization which is included in the Riverside Press and the firm of Houghton, Mifflin & Co. [he argued] is one capable of exciting a strong influence on good literature in America. What if I, giving my mind to its business, so guide and form this influence as to make it more operative, more beneficent. What if I, from my singularly fortunate position, can be the cause of other people writing worthy books. I am not, I hope, over-confident, but I cannot avoid the fact that I am placed in a curiously powerful position. I can take the initiative in publishing schemes and I have a willing, ready though conservative, body of men to carry out these schemes. There is no doubt that if I am wise and devoted I can strongly affect literature in America . . . I hope I am not selling my birthright for a mess of potage![9]

During his eleven years of uncertain independence, Scudder had been remarkably productive. In his fine, clear, fluent script he had written seventeen books. His editorial work for the firm had been immense, including not only standards such as the works of De Quincey and Bacon but also the American Literature Series and the American Commonwealths Series. In addition he had worked closely with a variety of authors — with Marie Hansen Taylor on *Life and Letters of Bayard Taylor,* with Emma De Long in her editing of *The Voyage of the Jeannette: The Ship and Ice Journals of George W. De Long, Lieutenant-Commander U.S.N., and Commander of the Polar Expedition of 1879–1881,* and with Mrs. Agassiz in her work, *Louis Agassiz: His Life and Correspondence.* He also contributed sections or chapters to a variety of compilations, among them Bryant's *History of the United States,* Justin Winsor's *Memorial History of Boston,* and the Merriams' subscription edition of their dictionary. And all the while he was writing stories, essays, and criticism for a wide selection of periodicals in addition to the *Atlantic. Harper's, Scribner's, Appleton's, St. Nicholas,* the *Independent,* the *Nation,* the *Christian Union,* and a number of newspapers all printed Scudder contributions, his most favored subjects — American literature, history, and education. In 1877 he found himself on the Cambridge School Committee. ("I suspect HOH's hand in this," he told his wife.) That tour of duty concluded, he graduated in 1884 to the Massachusetts Board of Education. In the 1880s he was sufficiently prominent as an authority on literature and education to be offered two positions outside of Boston — a Williams professorship and direction of the Literary Department of Pulitzer's New York *World*. Both opportunities he turned down, even though Pulitzer assured him he could set his own terms. He preferred his Cambridge and Boston to $10,000. After all, in 1881 he had been elected to that select body of gentlemen, the Massachusetts Historical Society. In 1882 he was invited to give a series of Lowell Institute lectures. Further honors came to him in trusteeships of Williams and Wellesley.[10]

His widely circulated theories of education in the primary and secondary schools received recognition when he was invited to speak at the San Francisco meeting of the National Teachers Association in July 1888. In persuading Scudder, who was reluctant, to accept the invitation, Houghton pointed out that his recent articles had brought him to the van of educational theorists, that in going to California he would "have a great opportunity of preaching sound doctrine to the entire country." Scudder, for his part, regarded the invitation as a challenge which if met might organize the "spiritual forces of our schools."[11]

In one of the articles to which Houghton referred, "Nursery Classics in School," Scudder had warned, "Every year more is exacted of the school . . . Character must there be formed as well as mental habits . . . The notion of what constitutes education has not so much expanded as the notion of the place of education. The school-house is becoming the American temple; it borrows from the church and the family, leaving one dry and the other weakened." The school no longer may use the Bible as once it had done. However, "unless the definite end of enobling the mind through familiarity with literature of the spirit is recognized in our school curriculum, the finest results of education will be lost." Fortunately, literature of the spirit finds expression in the classics of all nations. If there were a Bill of Rights for children, one of its articles would be the freedom to enjoy "the stories which have grown smooth from being rolled down the ages of Indo-European peoples." One advantage of these stories from the childhood of the race is that since the stories are of no definite authorship, they may be retold in language which the child can understand and in listening to them or in reading them, his imagination awakened, his horizons enlarged, he ventures in the world of the spirit. Preparation for larger meanings has begun.[12]

These theories had found expression in Scudder's *Children's Book, The Book of Fables, Chiefly from Aesop,* and the *Book of Folk Stories,* the last published in 1887.

In that year hysterical talk about Americanism poisoned the air. The Chicago Haymarket riots had occurred the year before and the case of the alleged anarchists, condemned by the lower courts, was now before the Supreme Court. To many the cure for the malady which had caused the Chicago riots was instruction in Americanism. In an *Atlantic* article, "American Classics in School," Scudder had defined that illusive abstraction as a sense of continuity revealed in the country's "laws, institutions, art, character and religion," a revelation "expressed through art, and mainly through the art of letters." He believed a study of American classics would give young people a reasoned patriotism. He condemned the usual school readers as a "pitiful waste" of a young person's "growing mental powers." Too many of them were composed of fragments which presented "commonplace lessons in minor morals." A study of American classics need not lead to provincialism, for they are larger than their continent. "The windows of Longfellow's mind look east, and the children who have entered into possession of his wealth travel far," he wrote.

> The companion of Thoreau finds Concord suddenly become the centre of a very wide horizon. Irving has annexed Spain to America. Hawthorne has nationalized the gods of Greece and given atmosphere to New England. Whittier has translated the Hebrew Scriptures into American dialect. Lowell gives the American boy an academy without cutting down a stick of timber in the grove or disturbing the birds. Holmes supplies the hickory which makes one careless of the crackling thorns. Frank-

lin makes the America of a past generation a part of the world before treaties had bound the floating States into a formal connection with venerable nations. What is all this but saying that the rich inheritance which we have is no local ten acre lot, but part of the individual state of humanity? Universality, cosmopolitanism, these are fine words, but no man ever secured the freedom of the universe who did not first pay taxes and vote in his own village.[13]

This was the sound doctrine Houghton wanted preached to the assembled teachers in California, a doctrine which had already been embodied in Scudder's anthologies of *American Poems* and *American Prose*.

The success of these two volumes led to the inauguration in 1882 of the Riverside Literature Series, a project Scudder had had at heart for a number of years. Unabridged American masterpieces were to be made available to schools as cheaply as possible. Although the volumes were to be equipped with study aids, Scudder specified that the introduction, rather than being a surgical operation "upon the corpus vile," serve merely as an initiation in the biography of the writer, indicating his place in literature. Notes were to be few, their purpose to "gently remove obstacles" and "to open vistas" for the student. The series, which began with Longfellow's *Evangeline,* was clearly printed on cheap but opaque paper with reasonable margins. The small books, bound in pale green paper covers, sold for 15 cents. Although English classics came to be included in the series, in the first years concentration was on American authors. By the end of 1883 eleven titles had been published and sales totaled 34,530. Five years later, when Scudder went to San Francisco, the number had grown to thirty-nine and sales topped 100,000. The majority of the volumes were protected by copyright.[14]

Because Aldrich was again departing for Europe, Scudder was frantically busy in the weeks preceding his California trip. Once again the *Atlantic* was his responsibility for three months and now Houghton, who for a number of years had been dissatisfied with Aldrich's editorial work, tossed another problem in Scudder's lap. Would he consider taking "charge of all the literary affairs of the concern . . . *including the Atlantic*"? If he accepted the responsibility, Houghton, Mifflin would afford him an assistant. Just before he left for the West, Scudder dashed off a line to Mark Antony DeWolfe Howe, a young man in whom he had recently taken an interest and who had confided that after he had received his Harvard M.A., he hoped to find his future in a publishing house. Scudder suggested that if Howe would call at Park Street, Houghton would give him an interview.[15]

Scudder had crossed the Atlantic twice. His trip to San Francisco was his first experience of the continent west of Chicago. His reactions to the sights as he crossed the country were typical of any Eastern tourist. The squalor of the approach to Chicago shocked him, the spacious sweep of the Nebraska prairies startled. Denver had "a bright, joyous air . . . as though it knew its future and had no misgivings." The Rockies lacked the serenity of his familiar White Mountains; they were distorted and twisted, carrying tremendous "agony in their faces."[16]

Scudder, in addressing the large audience of teachers gathered from every state in the Union in the San Francisco Opera House on the morning of July 18, repeated the ideas of his *Atlantic* articles. However, perhaps because of his trip across the country, he placed his ideas in a frame of larger import. ". . . the social problems which confront us concern the most elemental conditions of society," he warned ". . . the relations of labor to well-being are to determine the final issue . . . The sight of material prosperity which has so wrought upon and inflamed Labor in Poverty has likewise struck upon the conscience of the nation . . ." More alarming, more insidious than the anarchic force is the "disintegrating force of disbelief resident in every part of the body politic." A nation which has lost faith in ideals, which "sneers at sacrifice and worships worldly success" will be destroyed from within rather than by foreign agents.[17]

The defense against cynicism on the one hand and anarchism on the other is instruction which will lead to spiritual power. "Nature is such an avenue, and we have not yet learned to place our school-houses in gardens as we one day shall . . ." Music and art also provide avenues, but "in literature, above all, is this spirit enshrined." The destiny of the nation is in the hands of the young. "... what that destiny is to be may be read in the ideals which the young are forming ... whether those ideals shall be large or petty, honorable or mean, will depend much upon the sustenance on which they are fed," Scudder cautioned.

Although in his San Francisco speech Scudder was concerned almost exclusively with what he called literature of the spirit, he was well aware of the importance of the literature of knowledge. He had himself just completed such a text, a *History of the United States of America*. One of the purposes of education, he believed, was to make good citizens. Patriotism (a spiritual essence in his view) derived from a sense of continuity, from an "identity with antecedent life," from a knowledge of the country's history and the men who had made it. His belief found expression in three Houghton, Mifflin series — the Men of Letters, American Statesmen, and American Commonwealths. The anticipated market for these, as with so many other of the firm's publications, was twofold — educational, as supplementary reading, and trade.

The least successful of the three was the American Commonwealths, Scudder the editor. The appeal was limited and the firm soon found that if a state were not "book oriented," sales were pedestrian. Perhaps another reason for the series' relative failure was Scudder's editorial policy. He wished a sympathetic rather than a critical treatment of the subject. Originally he had planned to do Massachusetts. On realizing he would not have the time, he commissioned Brooks Adams. Adams' study of his commonwealth lacked the circumspection Scudder wished, but since it was "an able book which will invite and receive attack," he recommended the firm publish it, but outside the series, a compromise which Brooks Adams accepted.[18]

The American Men of Letters was originated immediately after the break with Osgood in June 1880. James T. Fields agreed to act as editor for an annual $1500. In accepting the responsibility, Fields spoke of his "exceptional influence." He anticipated he would be of "inestimable" value to Houghton, Mifflin. However, all he had secured before death intervened in April 1881 was Scudder's *Noah Webster*. On Fields's death, Charles Dudley Warner, persuaded by Lowell's promise to do Hawthorne, accepted the editorial post.[19]

The American Men of Letters Series was clearly an imitation of Macmillan's English Men of Letters, reprinted in the United States by Harper, for which Henry James had written *Nathaniel Hawthorne*. James's analysis of Hawthorne was written primarily for an English audience bred with respect for social gradations. Although James gave high marks to Hawthorne's literary achievement, he fell afoul of many of his countrymen when he pictured him as "thoroughly American in all ways . . . in none more so than in the vagueness of his social distinction . . . He liked to fraternize with plain people, to take them on their own terms, and put himself, if possible, into their shoes." James regretted that Hawthorne chose such ordinary shoes when he might have worn those of his wealthy Salem contemporaries who "doubtless had pretensions to be exclusive." Hawthorne, James explained to his English readers, "had a democratic strain . . . and a relish for the commoner stuff of human nature." Moreover, Hawthorne was a thorough American in his "exaggerated, painful, national consciousness," in his "belief that other nations of the earth are in a conspiracy to undervalue" anyone from the United States. Hawthorne, James judged, was a provincial. He would have been a greater writer had he been more Europeanized, more cosmopolitan.[20]

To James's surprise and disgust, his effort to explain an American author to the English raised a storm of protest. Howells, in his *Atlantic* review of the book, predicted that in some quarters James would be "attainted of high treason." One quarter would certainly be in the office of Henry Oscar Houghton.[21]

On Houghton's agenda for his London trip of 1881 was a meeting with Lowell to secure his promise to write the life of Hawthorne. To that end shortly after his arrival, he gave an elegant breakfast at Verrey's in Regent Street. Lowell was seated on his right, the publisher John Murray on his left, a galaxy of representatives of other English houses round the board. Lowell some years before had told Longfellow he would like to write Hawthorne's life and he now agreed to Houghton's proposition. Although his duties of state prevented him from settling down to the task, for a number of years he encouraged Houghton to believe he would finally write the biography and the firm repeatedly announced the book as forthcoming. At long last in 1889, Lowell said he was ready to undertake the project provided Houghton, Mifflin would pay him $3000. His price was too high. Ultimately the assignment fell to George E. Woodberry, whose *Nathaniel Hawthorne* would appear in the Men of Letters Series in 1902, over twenty years after Houghton had initiated the project.[22]

Another writer whose life should have been one of the first in the series was that of Longfellow. Warner settled on Howells and was vastly put out to discover that Osgood's hold on Howells meant he must find another biographer. After Osgood's failure in 1885, Howells agreed to undertake the poet's life, but before he could fulfill his promise he had signed an exclusive contract with Harper. Not until after the turn of the century did the life of Longfellow appear in the Men of Letters, then written by the aging Thomas Wentworth Higginson.[23]

Despite these difficulties in arranging for biographies of some of its most revered writers (similar ones were encountered for Lowell and others), the American Men of Letters Series proved a satisfactory commercial undertaking, eventually reaching twenty-three volumes. That no living authors were treated reflects Scudder's theory of biography. For him time's perspective was essential. Death must set its asterisk before an author might move in the circles of the elect and there be judged.

This editorial policy governed the Statesmen Series as well. Houghton, Mifflin was as quick as any other house to whip out a campaign biography or a memorial, but men recognized as statesmen were those whom history had taken for its own. According to John T. Morse, the editor, the idea for the series was his. He had first tried to sell it to Henry Holt, but that publisher had turned it down because he assumed that American interest in history stopped with the Revolution and that therefore the proposal was commercially unsound. Houghton, on the other hand, responded enthusiastically to Morse's plan, giving him complete authority for the series, which was to "present a full and fair view of the history of the United States told through the medium of the efforts of the men who had shaped our national career."[24]

Charles Dudley Warner in planning the Men of Letters proceeded deliberately, arranging for only three volumes in his first year. "Mr. Morse, on the other hand," went "ahead with precipitancy." Before Garrison "could say Jack Robinson," he had arranged for ten biographies.[25]

Although Morse had autonomy in selecting the subjects and their writers, Houghton was so keenly interested in the project that he could not refrain from having some say in the matter. He it was who suggested that Theodore Roosevelt do Gouverneur Morris. He also insisted, over Morse's objection, on accepting Carl Schurz's *Henry Clay.* However, in the main Morse was architect, forcefully overriding objections to Andrew Jackson and John Randolph. Jackson, he maintained, was a brilliant subject. Although he had done "more mischief than all other presidents & statesmen put together . . . his influence was immense & lasting." As for John Randolph, he thought him "a most picturesque character whom everyone wants to know about." He was sure Henry Adams would produce an absorbing biography, that is, "if he ever finishes it." "As for Aaron Burr," Morse wrote Houghton, "I fully agree with you — and, to be candid, I do not expect or wish to see the volume come into the series. Mr. Adams suggested that he might like to write it, and I said 'yes' in order to induce him first to write Randolph. In fact the chances are largely that he will never send us the 'Copy' of Burr. I shall not press him for it."[26]

This disingenuous dealing with Henry Adams, who fulfilled his Randolph engagement promptly, was a mistake. The book was published in October 1882. In the same month Morse wrote Adams that Houghton had refused to accept Burr for the series "because Aaron wasn't a 'statesman.' Not bad that for a damned bookseller!" Adams jeered. "He should live a while at Washington and know our *real* statesmen." He was ready for another publisher and Osgood, always on the alert, indicated interest, but Henry Adams, perhaps recalling his experience as editor of the *North American Review,* declined his offer. Houghton was willing to publish Burr but not in the Statesmen Series. Henry was not as amenable as his brother Brooks. His Burr, he told Morse, had been written for the Statesmen. There it would appear or not at all, at least under Houghton, Mifflin's imprint. He did not "propose to be dictated to by any damned publisher." Houghton, for his part, did not propose to be ordered around even by an Adams. In his view, a traitor was not a statesman. Although Adams apparently showed his Burr manuscript to other publishers, it was never published.[27]

In 1885 two of the authors in this series, Allen B. Magruder and James K. Hosmer, were charged with plagiarism. Only one of the charges was correct. Hosmer's life of Samuel Adams in its initial form was too long and in the process of cutting, some of the footnotes were deleted. On the biography's appearance, the New York *Tribune* accused Hosmer of stealing from William Vincent Wells's *The Life and Public Services of Samuel Adams,* published in 1865. The *Tribune* noted that a similar charge had been leveled at Magruder's *John Marshall.* Hosmer's home paper, the St. Louis *Globe-Democrat,* elaborated the accusations and at the same time suggested that Houghton, Mifflin paid its editors and authors so little that competent men would not work for the firm. "As for publishers who lend their names to such deceptions, and solicit purchasers for books that they know or should know are not truthfully represented they cannot hope to escape serious criticism and the loss of a considerable measure of public respect and confidence."[28]

This was the type of newspaper paragraph Houghton, rightly or wrongly, attributed to Osgood, and in controlled anger he came to the defense of Hosmer, Morse, and his firm. In a letter to the editor of the *Globe-Democrat,* who had confessed that no one in his office had read the book, he pointed out that, although using the same sources as Wells had, Hosmer had reached very different conclusions. Morse he defended as an editor of energy and integrity. As for the bargains Houghton, Mifflin made with its authors, those were private affairs and had no place in criticism. Moreover, the reputations of those producing biographies for the series, among them Henry Adams, Henry Cabot Lodge, Sidney Howard Gray, and Daniel Coit Gilman, refuted the charge of incompetence.

The case of Allen B. Magruder's *John Marshall* was a different matter. Magruder had in fact used "words, & sentences, paragraphs & even pages" from his source, Henry Flanders' *Lives and Times of the Chief Justices of the Supreme Court of the United States,* and the book's publisher, Lippincott, threatened suit. Houghton was in a "terrible taking" over the matter, realizing that Flanders and Lippincott had his firm "by the throat." He dispatched Morse to Philadelphia with authority to compromise the matter as best he could. Morse was persuasive and both author and publisher agreed for $500 to let the matter drop. Morse was ready to assume the charge because of his responsibility as editor, but Houghton refused his offer. Although he found "the Magruder matter" "a source of great mortification, if not disgust," he did not blame his editor. "No man, no matter how careful, can protect himself or us from a fraud like this," he wrote. His firm alone would accept the consequences.[29]

Despite such difficulties, the Statesmen Series proceeded more regularly and promptly than the others. Sales for the five volumes of the first year averaged over 2500 each and new biographies were added year after year until the series numbered thirty-one.

At the time of the Magruder and Hosmer troubles, Houghton, Mifflin itself was being subjected to a series of exasperating raids on its proud list of New England authors. So effective had been its forwarding the cause of American literature in the schools that a new reader could hardly be in the running without selections from Longfellow, Whittier, Holmes, and the rest. The State of California, having decided to secure educational profits to itself, had undertaken to publish its own texts. The Superintendent of Public Instruction requested permission from Houghton, Mifflin for selections from its list free of charge; his excuse was that the material had been "so long and universally used in reading books and other publications as to seem public property." Moreover, he argued, such use would serve as an excellent advertisement for the house. Houghton, Mifflin was not interested in that sort of advertising. It insisted on a royalty in the interest of its authors as well as itself.[30]

At least the State of California, a novice in the business, had requested permission. Not so with the commercial house of Ivison, Blakeman & Taylor. In a series of readers edited by William Swinton (a "drunken reprobate," according to Garrison) appeared "choice selections" amounting to eighty pages from Houghton,

Mifflin authors. In reply to Garrison's protest, Ivison, Blakeman & Taylor, in "mortification," agreed to a royalty, suggesting at the same time that Houghton, Mifflin deny selections from its list to other publishers. To this condition the firm would not agree, and the question as to the amount of royalty due dragged on for months, Houghton, Mifflin finally accepting 1 percent on the retail price of all copies sold. At least the controversy had been kept from public notice. Houghton was a litigious man but he was also one of discretion.[31]

The less said about the New England writers' copyright protection, the better. Some of their works had already outrun their dates and others were on the verge of entering the public domain. Among gentlemen publishers "courtesy of the trade" had by now been extended to include American writers and their heirs. An author whose name had long been associated with a particular house was regarded as that publisher's property even though the United States Government no longer offered a shield against theft. Moreover, publishers usually continued to pay royalties, at least until competition from non-gentlemen made such payments commercially absurd. Newcomers to the trade like John W. Lovell, and some not so new, paid small heed to the custom. Certain houses even had agents in Washington searching copyright files, readying themselves to pounce once a work had entered the public domain. Perhaps no other publisher's list was as vulnerable as Houghton, Mifflin's. It would become more so with every passing year, unless new writers came to the house with equally durable goods.

The three series discussed had brought new names to the list but, with the exception of Henry Adams, none destined to take a place in the great succession either in sales or critical acclaim. What effect Scudder's San Francisco speech and his other writings on education had in creating a demand for American literature can only be surmised. A tangible result of his speech was a new author for the house. One of the people in his audience was a schoolteacher whose *Birds' Christmas Carol* had been privately printed and sold for the benefit of the kindergarten movement on the West Coast. Whether she showed the book to Scudder or sent

PARK STREET. 21 August 1888

MS. No. 2104   Received 20 August 1888
By Mr. Coolidge
Title: The Birds' Christmas Carol

Author: Kate Douglas Wiggin

Author's instructions:
Receipt of MS. acknowledged:
Submitted to H. E. S.
Reported by reader 20 Aug.
Character: A striking, well-written little
story, with elements of popularity in
it. I would recommend a few pictures, + board covers with lithographic design, so as to make it
50¢ worth.

Recommendation: To publish.
Report   approved   Aug. 23 188 8
Author advised   HOU
MS.

Reader's report for Kate Douglas Wiggin's *The Birds' Christmas Carol,* submitted by Scudder and approved by Houghton. The format for such reports was introduced by Scudder in September 1882. The same form, scarcely altered, is still in use.

it after him on his return to Boston is not clear, but by the middle of October she had signed a contract, Scudder having recommended the narrative as "a striking, well-written little story with elements of popularity in it." He suggested "a few pictures & board covers with lithographic design, so as to make it 50¢ worth." Houghton, after reading the story to his family, approved the recommendation and the book was rushed through the press so that it might be in time for the holidays. Published in November, before the end of the year *The Birds' Christmas Carol* was pushing 4000 in sales. Kate Douglas Wiggin had entered the Houghton, Mifflin stable. She would wear the firm's colors for many profitable years. Ultimately *Carol* would appear not only in a trade edition but also in an educational one as a supplementary reader.[32]

From the beginning of his printing-publishing career, Houghton had foreseen the rewards inherent in educational publishing. His partner George Harrison Mifflin was less sanguine of success in this department, confessing in 1891, "Before long I shall catch something of your enthusiasm over the prospects of the Educational Department. But, of course, it is a thing more in the future than for the actual present." What the future held was to be indicated by John Fiske's *History of the United States for Schools,* in preparation just at this time.[33]

That Fiske was asked to write a school history was due to a chance recommendation of Scudder's. He feared the house was about to jettison the jovial explicator, so he "threw into the caldron the notion" that Fiske might write a history for the Educational Department. Scudder did not wish the firm to lose a writer whose style he considered luminous, whose power of synthesis, whose perception of cause and effect made his books exceptionally readable. "Mr. Fiske," he said, "has a marvelous faculty for appropriating the best material and transforming it by his genius into the appearance of his own invention." He regarded him as a "capital generalizer."[34]

The reason Houghton, Mifflin was considering throwing Fiske overboard is not far to seek. For a decade he had been selling his work before it was done, taking advances for his promises to produce. Although his books on Darwinism and American history sold well and his 10 percent royalties were promptly paid, always he needed money. "Again comes the penniless author," he would write, or "I hope you won't set me down as an intolerable bore if I ask *once* more for an advance . . . The need is now, this week . . ." First it was $100, then $200, then $300, then $500. Finally, in 1889, Houghton, Mifflin arranged a contract under which the firm would pay him an annual $5000, Fiske agreeing to devote his entire time (with the exception of two months) to writing books, the copyrights to be assigned to Houghton, Mifflin, until they had earned his annual fee, royalties on his earlier books continuing. Within two years he was imperiously demanding a $2000 loan, a loan he expected would shortly be worked off by educational editions of four of his books — *The American Revolution, The Critical Period of American History, Civil Government,* and *The Discovery of America.* He also undertook to fulfill Scudder's recommendation that he write a school history. His *History of the United States for Schools* was on the market by August 1894 and within five years its sales surpassed a gratifying 129,000. So profitable was this venture in educational publishing that in 1897 Fiske's annual fee was raised to $12,000, then shortly to $15,000. Even this failed to meet Fiske's needs, harassed as he was by family illnesses and the building of a new house. By the end of 1900 Fiske's financial affairs had reached another crisis and he wrote his publishers that he would be in "serious trouble" unless he could "raise $15,000 within the next few weeks." He recognized that this amount would raise his debt to the firm to $41,000, that the advances he looked for in 1901 would run the figure up to $56,500, plus interest, but he was confident that his next volume *New France and New England,* combined with sales of a proposed subscription edition of his works, would earn $20,000 in royalties in 1901. By 1903, he was certain, his royalty returns would extinguish his debt. According to his analysis, Houghton, Mifflin could comply with his request "without incurring an atom of risk." In two years, 1898 and 1899, gross sales of his books had come to $125,000. He foresaw no diminution of this record in the years to come. His books, he boasted, were gilt-edged securities. Houghton, Mifflin was not so sure. Between the middle of December 1900 and the middle of

January 1901, it advanced him $5000. Beyond that it refused to go. Fiske died the following July leaving his debt to his publishers to be paid off by friends and heirs.[35]

Generally speaking, the Educational Department in the first two decades of its existence initiated few books of its own. Fiske's school history might qualify as one, even though the author was essentially a trade property. Another which is of interest because of its long life is W. H. Tillinghast's translation of Carl Ploetz's *Epitome of Ancient, Mediaeval, and Modern History,* accepted for publication in 1882. Today, under the editorship of William L. Langer, constantly revised, it appears in the Houghton Mifflin catalogue as *An Encyclopedia of World History.*

One of the reasons Houghton, Mifflin's Educational Department produced so few books that did not derive from its general publications is to be attributed to Scudder, who believed:

> The function of all education is to liberate one, to set him free from the limitations of his local and temporal condition . . . The distinction between an uneducated and an educated person is that the former is a serf, bound by his own petty experience, limited by his own constricted observation; the latter is freed from contemporaneity and knows that there are other standards than his own. In the process of education he learns of the relations of things and no longer knows things and persons in their isolation and separateness . . . He learns that there is a great whole, and that all his separate conceptions converge toward it.

He was convinced that even though a publishing house must be governed by sound commercial practice, "its highest calling" was "in defense of sound learning" and the encouragement of "pure literature," the mediums through which an understanding of the world's common humanity is achieved. Mifflin and Houghton supported their editor in his belief.[36]

XIV

THE TRADE IN THE 1880s

DURING THE FIRST TWO DECADES of Houghton, Mifflin's existence, there was no noticeable cleavage between its Educational and Trade Departments. Even though sales of both departments were merged in the final yearly accounting, there can be no doubt that Trade was responsible for the firm's growing reputation as a general publisher with a large and varied list distinguished by many outstanding publications, not the least of which were its periodicals.

In the year Hurd & Houghton acquired the *Atlantic,* Scudder had written in the *Riverside Bulletin:*

> What is it that renders the magazine form so attractive to the publisher? Its periodicity has something to do with it. He knows the value of the nimble sixpence, going through its agile performance twelve times a year, regularly. He appreciates, too, its value as an advertising agency. It carries his name like a flag everywhere it goes, and accustoms people to associating certain qualities with it; for the magazine rarely fails to symbolize the house from which it issues. That is, in fact, its great charm with the publisher. He is always wishing to impress his business upon the public mind, and though he may issue book after book, no single one quite expresses what he considers to be the character of his house, while the magazine with its flexibility, its power of presenting many sides, and its magisterial function of also accepting, rejecting, and criticising, becomes a very free exponent. It is indeed much more likely to reflect the character and taste of the house than of its editor, and most likely to succeed when it is a genuine representative of the concern whose name it carries . . .[1]

A house with as varied a list as Houghton, Mifflin's required more than a single periodical to represent it, and in the 1880s, in addition to the *Atlantic,* it published *Dwight's Journal of Music,* the *Boston Medical and Surgical Journal,* the *Reporter,* the *Andover Review,* the *Journal of American Folk-Lore,* the *United States Official Postal Guide,* and on the failure of Ticknor & Company in 1889, Osgood's *American Architect.* For a number of years the house was also exclusive agent for the *London Quarterly* and the *Edinburgh Review.* In 1883 Houghton came close to adding another magazine to this collection, one written specifically for the workingman.[2]

Houghton's interest in the project had been aroused by the Reverend Jonathan Baxter Harrison, who during Howells' regime had contributed a series of papers on labor to the *Atlantic.* In October 1878 his "The Nationals, their Origin and their Aims," in its detailing of thirty interviews with workingmen in three states had been dramatic enough to draw from Howells the comment, "It is astonishing, disheartening, and alarming. If those fellows get the upper hand, good-by Liberty! We shall be ground down by the dullest and stupidest despotism that ever was." As a step toward correcting the dangerous tendencies he perceived in Labor's condition, Harrison advocated instruction through a magazine which under the frosting of pictures and stories would carry information to the wage earner and his family on cooking, sanitation, education, morals, and politics.[3]

Harrison had first presented his idea to the Harpers whose house he discovered had "a decided dissent" from his views. He was therefore surprised to have Houghton seek him out at the Holmes breakfast in December 1879 to discuss the possibility of such a magazine. As usual Houghton's ideas about such an undertaking were positive and clear-cut. The periodical should be a weekly which would "bring out not only conditions as they exist, but in comparison with other times and countries, — everything, in fact, that would give the workingman a true picture of industrial conditions of production." It should be "a popular, high-toned, illustrated labor paper, with capital enough behind it to assure its success regardless of the subscription list . . ." It must in

Thomas Bailey Aldrich, editor of the *Atlantic Monthly*
from February 1881 to March 1890.

no way appear to patronize the worker; it must be edited from his point of view and concentrate on his interests. The undertaking must not savor of philanthropy in any way. However, to assure its success a guarantee of $100,000 was essential. He was ready to pledge $10,000 and hoped to raise similar amounts from other businessmen. To that end he arranged that Harrison talk with a number of his friends, among them S. D. Warren. These men were encouraging and Harrison prepared a prospectus.

While this was being debated, Houghton, Mifflin sent Harrison south to gather material for a series of articles. With Houghton's approval, Harrison also arranged to contribute letters to the New York *Tribune*. Houghton had not anticipated that Harrison's *Atlantic* articles would simply be a rehash of his *Tribune* letters. When this proved to be true, he felt cheated. "Confidence, you know, is a plant of slow growth," he wrote Harrison, "and when once destroyed is very hard to resuscitate. I have no desire to punish you or anybody, but the fact remains, nevertheless, that we have been deceived . . ." Harrison was no longer a candidate for editor of the proposed labor magazine. In his place Houghton secured the promise of Carroll D. Wright, who in 1885 would become first Commissioner of Labor, a post at that time under the Department of the Interior. In the end not only Harrison but also Houghton's business friends failed him. All he was able to raise in addition to his own pledge was $20,000. The abandonment of the project was a matter of regret to Wright, who judged Houghton a man "far ahead of his time." For discussion of politics including labor's problems, Houghton must depend on either the *Andover Review* or the *Atlantic,* neither of which would appeal to the audience he wished to reach. Nor was his new *Atlantic* editor one to explain to his comfortable readers the ferment of the time. Thomas Bailey Aldrich believed in "America for Americans."

Aldrich, before assuming command of the *Atlantic,* made "a thorough examination" of his "nerve and backbone." He thought he fully understood the demands of his office. He could not possibly have anticipated the picture succeeding generations would inherit from his enemies. Even his friends contributed to the image of a superficial, indolent editor. To them he was "a traveller returned out of an earlier century," a Herrick, a Lovelace, a Sidney, with "the swing and gaiety of a Cavalier," "a knight-errant riding through the forest of the world with songs on his lips and a wit as nimble as his sword." Hardly the man to edit a magazine whose high purpose in literature was "to leave no province unrepresented," in art to maintain a critical department "without any regard to prejudice," in politics "to keep in view the moral element which transcends all persons and parties."[4]

Howells was the first perhaps to limn the picture when he reported to John Hay that Aldrich was enjoying his editorial work. "He hates writing, you know, and he likes reading and talking, and he spends six hours every day at the office where I used to put in a scant afternoon once a week." Henry James was acid in his contempt. To him the new *Atlantic* editor was "the great little T. B. Aldrich," encompassed by a "queer impenetrable atmosphere of travel, luxury and purchase," and when Aldrich was prevented from going to Russia in 1884 because of an outbreak of cholera, he reported, "The Atlantic lately brought one Aldrich, that gilded youth, who edits periodicals from Brown's Hotel. As he appears to have everything the world can give, he is afraid he may have the cholera, so returns presently to his homes." In 1934 Berkeley Updike in his recollections of Park Street recalled Aldrich's talk as "a constant firework of witticisms," but credited "the impeccable scholarship" of the magazine to Susan Francis. The editors, he said, were "often indolent." Miss Francis had already frozen the image in her article "The Atlantic's Pleasant Days in Tremont Street," in the magazine's semicentennial number in November 1907. Here she pictured Aldrich as an "easy going editor" who "lived from hand to mouth." Although his inventory approached bankruptcy, he rarely solicited articles, having a "calm belief that excellent copy would come with each new month." His scintillating talk continually interrupted the serious business of ordinary toilers who must work for a living. In naming the authors of Aldrich's *Atlantic*, she created the impression that his contributors were indeed a thin lot — George Woodberry, Harriet Waters Preston, Rowland Sill, Richard Grant White, Mrs. Sarah Butler Wister, and of course the "Old Guard." Taking Miss Francis as his source,

Aldrich's office at 4 Park Street, of which Ferris Greenslet wrote, "Even in his editorial office Aldrich contrived to surround himself with the homelike comfort to which he was accustomed. He chose for his purpose a little back room at No. 4 Park Street, reached by a spiral stairway much resembling the pictures of Dante's *Purgatorio* with the terrestrial Paradise at its summit. Its windows overlooked that haunt of ancient peace, the Old Granary Burying-Ground, where, as he liked to say, lay those who would never submit any more manuscript. But any melancholy that might have arisen from the scenery was mitigated by an open fire of cannel coal, by a pipe . . . and by the constant attendance of his setter, 'Trip.' Once when Trip ate a sonnet, Aldrich asked, 'How did *he* know it was doggerel?' "

Ferris Greenslet, Aldrich's affectionate biographer, added the suggestion that Aldrich was "less accessible to new and unknown talent than Mr. Howells," an idea repeated in Mark Antony DeWolfe Howe's *The Atlantic Monthly and Its Makers*. Bliss Perry gently elaborated the tradition and Ellery Sedgwick in his *Happy Profession* gave the essence of these recollections when he characterized Aldrich as "talented, agreeable, and lazy."

In judging Aldrich's *Atlantic*, the majority agree that although he delegated editorial drudgery to others, he succeeded in giving the magazine "a notable unity of tone and distinction of style," the result of his "fondness for clear competent, workmanlike writing." He was himself a "fastidious composer and reviser" and expected as much from others. However, he thought of himself in this regard as less particular than his predecessor, exclaiming, "I wish I had anything like Howells' extreme nicety! Why, when he picks up a word for his purpose, he picks up the shadow with it." Even so, he once told Bliss Perry that he "set so high a value on distinction of style," he "would rather be disapproved of in beautiful prose than praised in slovenly English." What, one wonders, would have been his reaction to John Jay Chapman's estimate of him:

> These Aldriches who think style is the *means* of saying things well! How false is a philosophy of composition which admits that there is such a thing as beauty — as an end to be reached — and yet this simple proposition seems like a paradox — what better proof could we have of how thoroughly the plagiarists have overcrawled the world? "Use beauty-wash!" they cry — patent Italian sonnet-varnish — the only thing that has stood the test of time. Use the celebrated "Milton finish" for odes, epics and epitaphs — cures lame feet and rhymatism. Use the Petrarch burnisher — porcelain-lined, it secures fame. Use Shakespolio, Wordsworthene, and Racine — they never vary and are *"Reliable"* — Is it a wonder a man will not arrive anywhere if he spends all his life getting forward and backward over his style?

It is perhaps a truism that it's a poor editor who has no enemies. Some of these estimates of Aldrich are merited. Others are not. The charge that he maintained a low inventory is true, but the policy was a calculated one. An almost universal cause of complaint among authors in these years was the habit of editors to accept contributions and then to keep them for weeks, perhaps months, even years, before finding room for them in their periodicals. *Century* kept F. Marion Crawford's "Gods of India" for twelve years; *Scribner's,* a contribution of Scudder's for two. Henry James complained that various editors were condemning him "apparently to eternal silence" by not printing manuscripts in hand. John DeForest was profoundly discouraged when Alden

kept a novel of his for six weeks and then notified him if he wished
to appear in *Harper's* he would have to wait two years. The *Century*, he found, would not have space for years to come and the
Atlantic had three or four serials already engaged. "I shall be
driven to volume publication which at present is almost without
profit," he lamented to Howells, who was only too familiar with
the complaint. When he had assumed office as *Atlantic* editor, he
found that Fields had bequeathed him bushels of accepted contributions, "a load which he gradually lightened by counting each
manuscript dead when the author died." In line with the tradition, he left Aldrich "a half-peck" of similar accumulations, a
burden under which Aldrich refused to groan. Those which he
could not use in the foreseeable future he returned to their authors. Some, because of definite promises made by his predecessor,
he could not so treat. Howells had accepted Elizabeth Stuart
Phelps's six-number *Dr. Zay* but had delayed printing because of
the similarity of subject with his *Doctor Breen's Practice*. He had
promised her it would open the first volume of the 1882 *Atlantic*.
He had also taken for 1882 George Parsons Lathrop's *An Echo of
Passion* and had commissioned a full-length serial from William
Henry Bishop. Aldrich found himself loaded with fiction engaged
by Howells and he had to ask Mrs. Phelps to agree to a further
delay of four months. Such difficult overlapping Aldrich hoped to
avoid in his management of the magazine. He intended that the
editorial breadbox used for accepted manuscripts should be but
sparsely filled.[5]

Aldrich admired Howells, who had found time to be a novelist
as well as an editor. However, there may have been an element of
criticism in his remark, "No man shall say that I crowded him out
and put myself in." He intended to edit the magazine, he told
Stedman, not write for it. His contributions to the *Atlantic* during
his regime were few by intent. He hoped instead to find place in
other magazines. Under the terms of his contract, he had such
liberty, a freedom the Harpers denied Howells when in 1885 they
signed him on at an annual $10,000. Since Aldrich's salary was a
mere $4000, he merited Houghton's loose tether, including his
extended summer holidays.[6]

As soon as New York learned that Aldrich's contract with Houghton, Mifflin was not exclusive, both Alden of *Harper's* and Holland of *Scribner's* solicited articles, stories, or poems, the former offering $1500 for a series of papers to be made of his experiences during his proposed Russian trip. Aldrich went to Russia in 1882 and 1886 but no light papers on the Muscovites resulted. The suppressed horror of the country was too ominous for this stray from another century, the surface too raw for the play of his wit. The perpetual drunkenness of the average Russian defied the humor of this nineteenth-century Herrick. The national characteristics of brutality and crude cunning were for private description only, and he confessed to Edith M. Thomas that his Russian experience had proved a creative white elephant. A few poems were all he was able to produce. One of them, however, linked him oddly with the liberals of his time. In "Batyushka," the refrain of each verse is "God save the Tsar." The final stanza reads,

> Batyushka! . . . How his heart is cold!
> Wait till a million scourged men
> Rise in their awful might, and then —
> God save the Tsar!

The Tsar's literary censor obliterated the poem from every copy of *Harper's* that crossed the border, a paradoxical fate for a poet who would shortly write of the threat of anarchists ("these brutes," "the spawn and natural result of the French Revolution") to America's "Unguarded Gates."[7]

While it is true that two of the contributors who gave special distinction to the *Atlantic* during the years of his administration — Henry James and Sarah Orne Jewett — were nurtured and brought to prominence under Howells' considerate management, the charges that Aldrich did not seek contributions and was not accessible to new talent have no basis in fact as even a cursory look at his correspondence and the *Atlantic Index* will demonstrate. Names new to the *Atlantic,* some fresh caught in the editorial seine, others but five-inch trout on another's hook, star Aldrich's line, a line frequently played by Horace Scudder, Aldrich's editorial stand-in. Here appear Edward Bellamy, Mary Hartwell

Catherwood, Margaret Deland, Arthur Sherburne Hardy, Thomas Hardy, F. Hopkinson Smith, Alice French, Louise Imogen Guiney, Agnes Repplier, William Roscoe Thayer, Woodrow Wilson, Owen Wister, Olive Thorne Miller, Bradford Torrey, Edith M. Thomas, Rowland Sill, Bliss Carman, Frank Dempster Sherman, and prophetically Walter Hines Page and Bliss Perry. Few of these swam into the *Atlantic* estuary by chance.

Even though Aldrich at the start was overburdened by accepted manuscripts, especially fiction, almost at once he started to play his line. Aldrich repeatedly said the *Atlantic* would be nothing if it were not distinctively American, but one of his first editorial acts was to solicit a contribution from an English author. The necessary serial, James's *The Portrait of a Lady,* begun under Howells, would run through December 1881; William Henry Bishop's *The House of the Merchant Prince* through 1882. With Mrs. Phelps's *Dr. Zay* and Lathrop's *An Echo of Passion* for the same year he was sufficiently supplied. All these were of Howells' engaging. Every magazine editor wishes to impress his personality on his periodical. Moreover periodical readers of the '80s had an insatiable appetite for fiction. Perhaps recalling *Far from the Madding Crowd,* which had been running in his *Every Saturday* at the time of its demise and perhaps aware that Thomas Hardy had fruitlessly offered a novel to Howells, Aldrich inquired through Houghton's London agent, Henry Stevens, whether Hardy would contribute an eight-number story for 1882 to the *Atlantic.* Stevens sent his answer to Houghton, indicating that Hardy was delighted and that his first installment would be ready for the May *Atlantic.* The opening chapters charmed Aldrich and he liked the title *Two on a Tower.* He left for Europe in the middle of June content with his catch.[8]

Aldrich had nothing to do with the business arrangements. They were sufficiently unusual to be handled from the counting room. That department, because of its experience with *The Portrait of a Lady* and *Macmillan's Magazine,* would not agree to any more simultaneous publication in periodicals. Since Hardy under these conditions could not enjoy the fruits of dual payment, he asked £100 an installment, a figure arrived at, he explained, by "merely adding the sum that would have been paid by an English magazine to the price I should have received for advance sheets from America." Houghton, Mifflin met the price and Hardy agreed, since he was coming at a stiff rate, to assign the book rights royalty free, stipulating only "nominal" British publication to forestall English pirates. The first one or two chapters would be sufficient. *Two on a Tower* was no *Pickwick*. It had no scene like the trial which if unprotected would be lifted by a British tramp.

Houghton, Mifflin's securing of American book rights proved valueless. No sooner had the May 1882 *Atlantic* appeared than Henry Holt, since Osgood had sold him the rights to *Far from the Madding Crowd* and his house had therefore been the first to introduce Hardy to American readers between boards, reminded Houghton that under the rules of publishers' courtesy book publication should descend to him, agreeing however to pay Houghton, Mifflin 10 percent on sales. The arrangement did little to pay off the firm's investment. *Two on a Tower,* proving a sensation, was promptly pirated by John W. Lovell and others of his stripe and only negligible royalties accrued.

Aldrich returned from his first Russian trip in time for the sensation. According to Bliss Perry, Miss Francis, in the interest of Victorian decorums, during the summer of '82, "when Aldrich was studying vintages in Hungary," deleted "certain passages" from the novel. However, her editorial propriety was not enough to prevent public outcry. In its denouement the sad story of the frustrated Lady Constantine and her relatively low-born lover appeared to many both immoral and a fleer at religious orthodoxy, a stench in the nostrils of the righteous. According to the *Literary World,* *Two on a Tower* with its suggestion and innuendo "might better have been left unwritten and would much better be left unread — certainly by readers of the *Atlantic Monthly* . . ." However, that Hardy did not again appear in Aldrich's *Atlantic* must not be attributed to Victorian sensibilities as to sex and attacks on the Established Church. Aldrich continued to cultivate the author but no matter what the morals of the tale, Hardy's condition for his next offering — simultaneous publication with *Macmillan's Magazine* — was out of the question. Moreover, when Hardy suggested *The Woodlanders* as a serial for 1886, Aldrich had his fiction in hand. Henry James's *Princess Casamassima,* begun in September 1885, would run through most of the following year and William Henry Bishop's *Golden Justice,* commissioned by the editor, would be running concurrently.

As 1882 drew to a close, Aldrich had failed to secure his serial for 1883. Actually he had a sensation at hand but failed to recognize it. Arthur Sherburne Hardy, a young Dartmouth mathematics professor, had asked him to consider his *But Yet a Woman.* This American Hardy in 1882 was a literary unknown, and Aldrich rejected the manuscript, turning it over to Scudder.

No one in Houghton, Mifflin was enthusiastic about the novel. However, Alpheus Hardy, the writer's father, was a prominent Boston merchant and clipper ship owner. Reluctantly, the house agreed to publish the novel if the author would pay for the plates. The book was put in train and then one of those publishing mysteries occurred. Advance orders flooded Houghton, Mifflin. New York took the entire first edition, Boston half again as many. Houghton was puzzled. "To what this apparent success in the outset may be attributed, I am unable to say," he wrote Hardy's father. *But Yet a Woman* proved more than an apparent success. Within seven months it had sold well over 16,000. Aldrich was now ready to negotiate with Hardy for an *Atlantic* serial but he was too late. Other magazines had claimed the services of the season's sensation and even though Hardy professed "to feeling a stronger kinship with no. 4 Park Street, and to the desire to knock at that door before entering others," not until 1888 did Aldrich secure a Hardy serial for the *Atlantic.*[9]

Perhaps one reason that Aldrich did not recognize a circulation builder when he had one was that at the very moment Hardy had knocked at Houghton, Mifflin's door, Aldrich was negotiating for his 1883 serial with another astonishing young man, one accustomed to drawing rooms rather than classrooms, Francis Marion Crawford, the brilliant, exotic nephew of Julia Ward Howe and Sam Ward, the King of the Lobby. Crawford's first novel, *Mr. Isaacs: a Tale of Modern India,* had been written at Sam Ward's suggestion and through his influence published by Macmillan in both London and New York. Now Crawford was in Boston

staying with his Aunt Julia on Beacon Street. With him he had
the manuscript of his *Dr. Claudius*. Reversing Arthur Hardy's
procedure, he submitted his story for book rather than periodical
publication and Scudder recommended acceptance if only because
it was "a readable novel by a young man who has caught the public
attention." Aldrich requested the story for the *Atlantic* but the
author insisted it must appear as an entity. Houghton, Mifflin offered a $2000 advance on the book and a 10 percent royalty, for
American rights only; Macmillan, $2400 for both English and
American rights. Crawford accepted the latter offer, apparently
not realizing that Houghton, Mifflin's plan would allow him to
negotiate with an English publisher for a higher fee than the $400
Macmillan allowed him for the second copyright. Houghton, by
the way, did not object to simultaneous *book* publication. Indeed,
such a system he considered as affording as much protection for the
American writer and publisher as would be secured by International Copyright. Simultaneous magazine publication was an
entirely different matter.[10]

Although Crawford would not consider *Atlantic* appearance for
Dr. Claudius, Aldrich persuaded him to write a twelve-number
serial for $1200 with 10 percent on the resulting book, Houghton,
Mifflin to issue in the United States, Macmillan in London. Aldrich must have been astonished at Crawford's speed. Writing "at
the double quick, without turning a hair," he produced *A Roman
Singer* in less than two months. The novel would not begin its
Atlantic run until July, but Crawford was impatient to be off and
in May he left for London and Rome. By happy chance, Houghton
was also bound for Europe on the same ship, and during the crossing a firm friendship developed. Crawford agreed that Houghton,
Mifflin would have his next book in America and that he would
take care of the English rights. *A Roman Singer,* published as a
book in the spring of 1884, didn't quite equal Hardy's record
with *But Yet a Woman;* nonetheless, the sales were gratifying —
14,000 in a little over half a year. All indications were that an
enduring publishing association had been cemented. Aldrich secured Crawford's promise of an *Atlantic* serial for 1885 and Crawford announced in print that he would not listen to any proposal

except from the *Atlantic* because of his friendship for T.B.A. In a similar spirit of admiring affection, Houghton, Mifflin raised Crawford's royalty to 15 percent.

In the 1880s Europe was the place many of the American literary crowd were to be found and Aldrich, leaving Scudder in the editorial chair, went in search of them in the summers of 1882, 1884, 1886, 1888, and 1889. During his travels, at one time or another he talked with Clemens, Howells, Lowell, Bret Harte, Clarence King, John Hay, and Henry James. With the exception of Henry James, he had small success with the writers listed. He might have had Hay's *Breadwinners* but he would not accept the author's insistence on anonymity. Howells, he found, "sold to the Century" through Osgood, who also had James under mortgage. All he was able to report to Houghton during his first trip was that "After a great deal of diplomacy and Old Port, combined with several attacks on Henry James in his bath-tub, I have secured the dramatization of Daisy Miller for the *Atlantic*. I think it a great card. Whether the thing is good or bad in itself, it is certain to pique curiosity, and give us something to advertise."[11]

"Daisy Miller" proved a flop rather than a card and as a result the counting room refused to consider any more stories in dramatic form. Nevertheless Aldrich continued to court James and on his next trip secured the promise of *The Princess Casamassima,* but not the book rights. Those he had promised Osgood. *The Princess* proved longer than anticipated and Aldrich's long range plans for the *Atlantic* had to be readjusted to provide pages. *The Tragic Muse,* James's final serial under Aldrich, the author promised to keep to seventeen or eighteen pages an installment but warned that some numbers might rise to twenty. Engaged as a twelve-number contribution, James's buxom *Muse* before it was finished ran to seventeen. Since for both novels James received $15 a page, his prolixity was to his advantage. At least for *The Tragic Muse* Houghton, Mifflin got the American book rights at the standard 10 percent.[12]

One of Aldrich's triumphs in 1885 was a serial he secured from a relatively unknown writer. He needed two six-part stories for the first volume of the 1885 *Atlantic*. One he requested from Charles

Egbert Craddock, whom Howells had earlier introduced to *Atlantic* readers with four short stories. In the half-peck of accepted contributions which Howells bequeathed to his successor was the manuscript of a fifth. This Aldrich printed in June 1881. Subsequently, he accepted two more stories and persuaded the house to bring out a collection with the title of *In the Tennessee Mountains,* to be published in the spring of 1884. The book proved a critical success and Aldrich at once invited Craddock to write a six-number serial for 1885. *The Prophet of the Great Smoky Mountains* was the result, which by good chance took eight rather than six numbers and thus filled pages originally held for James, who at a late date found he would not have the opening chapters of *The Princess* ready for the July number as he had originally promised. Perhaps it was events like this that gave Miss Francis her impression of Aldrich's calm optimism.[13]

Aldrich and his firm were soon aware that the name Craddock was a pseudonym, and there was considerable speculation at Park Street as to the identity of this genre writer from Tennessee. The handwriting indicated a strong, dominant person. The heavy black holograph produced with a stub pen caused Aldrich to hope the writer had laid in a supply of ink for the winter so that the well's running dry would not be an excuse for delayed installments. He suspected the author to be a lawyer, the stories revealed such legal expertise. No one thought of a scribbling woman. Then on a March morning in 1885 Craddock dropped in at Park Street. Garrison reported the event to Houghton.

> We had a call from the author of In the Tennessee Mountains and the Prophet of the Great Smoky Mountains, and you will be surprised to learn that Charles Egbert Craddock, whose real name you are aware is M. N. Murfree, proves to be a young lady of 30 or 32 years of age. She called yesterday to see Mr. Aldrich, who was greatly taken aback by the revelation, and he subsequently invited her to dine at his house, and took her to see Booth in the evening. Mr. Howells and Dr. Holmes came to meet *him* and were astonished to find *her*.
>
> She is very bright and agreeable, and Aldrich is very well pleased with her. She is very lame, and is accompanied by her

sister. The two are staying at the Hotel Vendome and will be there six weeks, probably . . . Aldrich has already started a paragraph in the press, which will no doubt make a considerable sensation.

Sylvester Baxter, alerted by Aldrich, wrote a story for the *Herald*. Other newspapers took up the tale and Charles Egbert Craddock was the sensation of Boston's spring literary season. Scudder took the two sisters on an historic tour of the city, Mr. and Mrs. Mifflin gave a dinner for them, and the Houghtons persuaded them to spend a week at their Cambridge house. The two sisters were, of course, taken up by the widow of Charles Street and here Mary Noailles Murfree found a sympathetic friend in Sarah Orne Jewett, whose literary career in many ways paralleled her own. Both had begun their *Atlantic* careers under Howells and both had been guided to mature realization of their abilities under Aldrich's sympathetic direction. Miss Jewett said Aldrich taught her many lessons and that through his suggestions she found a path she might otherwise have missed. Miss Murfree was grateful to him both for his suggestions and his intervention with Houghton, Mifflin which secured her double the rates at which she had started as contributor. Both were running concurrently in the *Atlantic*. Sarah Orne Jewett's *Marsh Island* was the second six-number serial Aldrich had secured for the first volume of the 1885 *Atlantic*.

If fiction was what readers looked for in their magazines, Aldrich gave them their desire in ample measure. His 1885 record is impressive. In quality and quantity of American serials he was outclassed only by Gilder of the *Century*, who in 1885 was publishing Howells' *Silas Lapham*, Clemens' *Huckleberry Finn*, and the closing chapters of Henry James's *Bostonians*. However, the fare Aldrich supplied his readers did nothing to stay the *Atlantic*'s falling circulation. Gilder boasted in February 1885 that the *Century*'s was 210,000 and "still rising." No such trumpets were heard from Boston. Eighteen eighty-six opened with the *Atlantic* selling something over 10,000.[14]

Most fiction writers of the 1880s looked first for periodical appearance, then book publication. Crawford's refusal to "magazine" three of his novels was exceptional. Houghton, Mifflin's experience with his books, Arthur Hardy's *But Yet a Woman,* and Kate Douglas Wiggin's *The Birds' Christmas Carol* indicated that periodical publication was far from essential for commercial success. Two other novels published by Houghton, Mifflin in this decade also achieved their sales records without benefit of periodical appearance.

Margaret Deland, whose experience in literature so far had been in writing rhymes for Prang's Christmas cards, had come to Houghton, Mifflin in 1886 with a small volume of verse, *The Old Garden,* which the house reluctantly published. Sales proved to be greater than her "fair circle of friends" had seemed to assure. She at once began a novel, *John Ward, Preacher.* Six weeks before its publication in April 1888, Mrs. Humphry Ward's *Robert Elsmere* had been published in New York. The house of Harper might have had the American rights to Mrs. Ward's novel but Alden was unwilling to take on this protest against ecclesiastical formalism and the supernatural elements in the Christian faith. He refused the book because ". . . its purpose was antagonistic to the teachings of our Savior in vital points — especially as to his resurrection." To publish it "would be a greater injury" to his house "than to incur the imputation of immorality." Macmillan, less fearful of *odium theologicum,* gave the book to the American public. Sales were spectacular, the *Publishers' Weekly* estimating 150,000 in a year.[15]

Houghton's reaction to Mrs. Deland's *John Ward, Preacher* differed from Alden's to *Robert Elsmere.* Scudder in reporting on Mrs. Deland's manuscript wrote, "The book is a singular mixture of wasted power, graceful situations, acute observations, lofty sentiment and towering absurdity in the main theme. The story offends a healthy view of modern life. A hero so noble and saintly as John Ward would never have made so monumental a mistake." If he could have his way, he would advise the author to tear up her script and begin another. However, because he recognized the sales promise in this picture of a Presbyterian minister who carries his doctrines of foreordination, election, and eternal damnation to their inevitable conclusion in his effort to bring his dearly loved but free-thinking wife to an acceptance of hell, he recommended publication. One member of the firm demurred. "To deny eternal punishment would be very unpopular! Who would stand behind such a novel?" he asked. Mrs. Deland said she would. "Then," said Houghton, "I will stand behind you." And that was that. *John Ward* came out to be greeted by a critical cacophony of latter-day Calvinists, but the book sold over 27,000 in two years. Aldrich was prompt to request of Mrs. Deland an *Atlantic* serial for 1890.

The next novel to make records for Houghton, Mifflin without benefit of magazine appearance was Edward Bellamy's *Looking Backward,* published first in 1888 by Osgood's successors, Ticknor & Company. The book had performed well for that company, selling 35,000 in a year. However, Ticknor & Company itself was ailing. Branded by Osgood's mark of failure, the firm in five years had declined, to end finally in the hands of an assignee — Charles Fairchild. The company's plates, publishing rights, and goodwill were up for sale. Houghton, beyond doubt, took sardonic satisfaction in picking up the pieces of James R. Osgood & Company, the price — $70,000 cash down. Although by his Ticknor purchase Houghton secured certain books by authors already on his list, notably some of James and Howells, Scudder when told of the plan was downcast. All he could foresee was more work for him. The Ticknor list was loaded with mediocre novels. On him would fall the task of weeding the chaff from the wheat, of preparing the catalogue which would now number over 3000 titles. He it was who must study the list and decide what volumes deserved reworking, which newly acquired authors were worth cultivating. He thought the acquisition of little value, save perhaps for the Bellamy novel.[16]

Scudder had followed Bellamy's career with sympathetic interest ever since 1880 when Appleton had published *Dr. Heidenhoff's Process,* which he had found of exceptional power, full of realism and "uncommonly clever." *Miss Ludington's Sister,* published by Osgood four years later, inspired him to constructive criticism. He thought the conception highly original, "a piece of fine though extravagant imagination," he wrote in an *Atlantic* review, but

Bellamy "has begun a statue in marble, and left it on legs of clay. There is no excuse for this wanton misuse of high power. Hawthorne never would have been guilty of such an outrage, and yet in the earlier part of the story Mr. Bellamy comes nearer Hawthorne than any writer whom we have. Indeed, the more we look at the matter, the more our imagination gives way to a pity and the sense of personal loss." In 1886, while Aldrich was abroad, Scudder had accepted for the *Atlantic* Bellamy's *The Blindman's World* and when *Looking Backward* appeared he had reviewed it with lukewarm favor, finding somewhat wearisome the thin, ghostlike characters "who smile and talk on the exhausted air receiver of the twentieth century," and scarcely credible, the vision of an age to come when "the lion with his claws pared" will eat grass. However, he was moved by "the earnest cry for the peace of human brotherhood" — a cry which resounds through the book.[17]

The majority of Houghton, Mifflin's readers of the 1880s had demonstrated their taste for two antithetical types of fiction — the novel that took them out of the daily routine to lands of passion and times of high deed and the novel of controversy. *Looking Backward* in its basic concept — that property is the root of evil — provided controversy. It also provided escape, not to some far country or forgotten century, but into the future of the United States reconstituted as a cooperative commonwealth which science has equipped with labor-saving devices and various contrivances to fill the gentle citizens' lives with entertainment. Since both wealth and poverty have been eradicated, crime has vanished, and everyone loves everyone, a state devoutly to be wished for. In its wishing, the public, within two years of Houghton, Mifflin's acquisition of *Looking Backward*, had purchased 200,000 copies.

As Scudder had anticipated, the Ticknor purchase greatly increased his burdens. When he had agreed to give all his time to the firm, he had been promised a qualified assistant. To find one had not been easy. Scudder hoped for a young man whom he could train as his successor. His choice was the twenty-four-year-old Mark Antony DeWolfe Howe, but Houghton preferred to

find someone within his organization. He settled on Thurlow
Weed Barnes. Scudder was displeased. He found it an ungracious
task to instruct a partner in the duties of his office. He disliked
Barnes's lack of system and the way he "banged" manuscripts
about. Barnes liked the work as little as Scudder liked him and
in February 1890, he made his declaration of independence. He
was succeeded by the competent Herbert R. Gibbs, Williams 1872,
who had come to Riverside immediately after his graduation.
Some years later, he had taken time off for an M.A. at Yale.
Scudder, of course, was delighted to have a Mark Hopkins man as
his aide and he found himself initiating Gibbs "in the mysteries"
of his assignment "with great zest." Although Scudder had some
reservations, he thought perhaps this studious, methodical,
cautious young man might be the one to follow in his footsteps.
For a few months at least he had a sense of ease, even though he
knew from his frequent talks with Houghton that a crisis lurked
just around the corner.[18]

Despite Aldrich's achievement in maintaining a continuous
flow of American fiction in the pages of the *Atlantic*, Houghton
had grown increasingly displeased with him. He had become
convinced that Aldrich had no idea how to edit a periodical,
and when he said that, he was not thinking of Aldrich's fastidious-
ness in phrasing or his sense of syntax. Aldrich's serious errors in
tact with certain authors of the house were what drove Houghton
to consider replacement. In 1882, through Scudder's efforts,
Daniel Coit Gilman, then president of Johns Hopkins, had submitted "The Dawn of the University" for publication. Aldrich,
when President Gilman offered to review a book for a friend,
ungraciously declined the proposal. Gilman was angered and
withdrew his manuscript. Whether the withdrawal was connected
with Aldrich's brusque rejection or not, Houghton would so consider it. One of the functions of the *Atlantic* was to serve the
house. In his view, its editor had more than the periodical to
consider in his dealings with authors.[19]

In 1885, true to his promise, Crawford offered his *Zoroaster* for
the *Atlantic*. Aldrich complained he didn't want a novel set in the
fifth century before Christ. He would rather have one with a

Turkish setting. Crawford would have preferred to make arrangement with Houghton, Mifflin for *Zoroaster,* but Aldrich's rejection deterred him from taking up the subject with the firm. Moreover, he needed money at once, and so he accepted "Macmillan's large offer — £1250 in advance for the first 25,000 copies and royalty afterwards." "I am sorry," Crawford wrote Houghton, ". . . as I should be loth to have anything cross the friendly relations we have had — especially as you have put me under great obligations by your courtesy and kindness." Aldrich got his Turkish serial — *Paul Patoff* — and Houghton, Mifflin secured the American rights, but that was the last Crawford novel the firm would have. A breach had been made. Aldrich had lost the house a lucrative author.[20]

In 1889 an extract from Lowell's "How I Consulted the Oracle of the Goldfishes," destined to open the August *Atlantic,* somehow found its way to the Boston *Transcript* of June 24. The poem would no longer be a proud novelty for the magazine. Aldrich, on the eve of departure for Europe, pleaded innocence to Houghton's angry remonstrance. In the same year Aldrich declined two manuscripts; one submitted by Woodrow Wilson, the other by Harvard's President Eliot, an article commissioned by Scudder during his summer's vice-regency.[21]

Of the political articles appearing in the *Atlantic* during Aldrich's administration, two were provided by Woodrow Wilson. That they appeared was due to Scudder's efforts. For five years Scudder had been making a consistent effort to develop this new writer for both the house and the *Atlantic.* In April 1884 an unsolicited manuscript from the young graduate student at Johns Hopkins had arrived at Park Street. It was but a sample, three chapters only. If these indicated a book worthy of publication, Wilson promised to complete the work as soon as possible. Scudder found the chapters "a fruitful discussion of the practical working of our government," clear, fair-minded, and unhackneyed. Wilson, assured publication should his subsequent chapters be of the caliber of those already in hand, completed his *Congressional Government* by the following October and signed his contract, the standard 10 percent, in December. Sales were small, 1595 in the first year, but demand though minor was persistent, and by the 1920s after forty years on the market, the book had run through twenty-nine editions. The favorable reviews which it received on its appearance gave the future President of the United States early affirmation of his intellectual power and confirmed Scudder's judgment that here was literary promise worthy of cultivation.[22]

Almost immediately Scudder requested Wilson to do the volume on North Carolina for his Commonwealths Series, a request Wilson was forced to decline because of physical breakdown. ". . . any man would be sorry to be handicapped by precarious health, and any young man would be sorry to lose a chance to enter the 'Commonwealths Series' . . ." he wrote. Scudder was concerned and in 1886 on his return from Washington, where he had appeared before the Senate Committee on Patents in behalf of International Copyright, he stopped off in Baltimore to confer with this student of political theory in whom he saw such promise. Next he requested an *Atlantic* article. This Wilson supplied for April 1886 with his "Responsible Government under the Constitution." At the same time he decided to afford a trip to Boston to establish personal relations with his publishers. Mifflin he found surprisingly young, "brisk, clear-voiced, hearty, well-conditioned"; Houghton, "a tall, somewhat rugged, but genial gentleman of 65," who arranged he have a tour of the Press so that when his next book was ready, he could visualize the manufacturing process. His tour of Riverside over, he was off for a smart drive about Cambridge in Houghton's carriage so he could see "the homes of all the literary celebrities." The following evening, the publisher entertained his new author at dinner.

Wilson was well pleased with his Boston venture, especially since it afforded opportunity to develop further his warm relationship with Scudder, whom he felt free to consult on general and ambitious projects he had in mind, particularly a work on political philosophy. Later he wrote Scudder of his impatience and discouragement. Should he publish monographs or concentrate on the greater undertaking? "I don't know why I have presumed," he apologized. "Although you have shown no more interest in me, I suppose, than you show in any young man of sober and creditable literary ambition, I have somehow gotten it into my head that you will know better than most men how to understand and forgive an impertinence like this." Scudder advised that he conserve his energy, that he make haste slowly, advice which Wilson cherished. "It does me an immense amount of good to feel that I have won your friendship, and to receive such tokens of your interest in me and my work," he assured Scudder. And later, "I have had a score of times to thank you in my heart — and in my conversation with confidants — for the letter which you wrote me in '86 in answer to my outpour of confidence touching the work upon which my mind is set . . ." He called Scudder his "literary godfather," and promised the *Atlantic* would have first call on any articles he wrote.

Because of this cordial relationship, Aldrich's rejection of Wilson's contribution had no serious repercussions. The young man readily assented to Scudder's request for a second political article with "The Nature of Democracy in the United States." The case with Harvard's President Eliot was different. In the summer of 1889 while Aldrich was abroad, Scudder had suggested to Eliot that he prepare an article on Prescott. The manuscript arrived after Aldrich had returned from his holiday. Failing to check with Scudder on engagements made during his absence, he returned the article, delegating the task of writing the covering letter to Miss Francis. On hearing of this gross carelessness, Houghton was in a towering rage.[23]

Houghton, a hard man but just, must have acknowledged to himself at least Aldrich's editorial achievement in face of stiff competition from the New York magazines. In addition to keeping the *Atlantic* supplied with fiction, in a decade of poetic impoverishment, he had won the loyalty of two minor poets — Edith M. Thomas and Rowland Sill. The latter liked Aldrich's blue pencil. "I wish you had nothing to do but criticise my mss!" he wrote. If there were an opening at Park Street, he would like to come as Aldrich's editorial assistant. Considering the material available, Aldrich did as well as could be expected. "Our old singers have pretty much lost their voices, and the new singers are so few!" he complained to Stedman. "You can't make even statuettes out of butter."[24]

There were rhymesters aplenty. A sampling of Scudder's manuscript reports reveals their ability. Of Mrs. Marian Longfellow Morris' "Thoughts and Memories," he wrote, "A volume of wholly commonplace verse, which may have eased Mrs. Morris when she was tired but could not rest anyone else." Of "Destiny," by Allen Griffith, "Bloated bosh in verse"; of C. A. Young's "Poems," "Poetry of the Calliope order, tempered by an Indian war whoop. Mr. Young dances about in paint and feathers, but the paint is bought at the stores, and the feathers from a duster"; of Mark Trafton's "The Birch Canoe," "Doggerel verse, easily written, hardly read"; of Rupert Hughes's "A Drowsy Day," "If there is any real metal in this ore, there will have to be lots of fire to get rid of the coarse slag"; of Nina Picton's "At the Threshold," "A flight of imagination by means of paper wings"; of "Yttvise of the Albatross" by L. P. Brown, "Jim-jam poetry, written just before the attack made the author senseless."[25]

Such comments do not indicate great poetic genius on the threshold. Of course, there was Emily Dickinson and a few of her poems were being sent to magazines by her sister-in-law Susan, all to be rejected until 1890 when *Scribner's Magazine* accepted "Renunciation." If Susan Dickinson submitted a sample to the *Atlantic,* beyond doubt Aldrich returned it. In his judgment Emily's ideas tottered and toddled. Her lyrics were "versicles" whose "queerness" and "quaintness" would not save them from oblivion. Aldrich would have no part in deciding whether or not the firm should accept Mabel Todd and Thomas Wentworth Higginson's manuscript for the first series of Emily's *Poems.* Scudder, whose judgment Houghton considered infallible, must bear the blame for this rejection, if indeed there was a rejection. The firm's remarkably complete file of manuscript reports has none for Emily Dickinson. Since Scudder and Higginson were Cambridge neighbors, the decision may well have been an over-the-fence affair. However, Scudder's published comments give no indication that he "thought Higginson must be losing his mind to recommend such stuff," as has been alleged. He found the first volume one of "fragmentary richness," with shafts "of light sunk instantaneously into the dark abysm." "The perfect poem" seemed just beyond the reader's grasp. Furthermore, Scudder cooperated with Higginson in placing his "Emily Dickinson's Letters" in the October 1891 *Atlantic,* an article designed to promote interest in the second volume of Emily's poems, to be published by Roberts Brothers in November. In his criticism of this volume Scudder found "intellectual excitement" in "the quick contact with another nature." "We raise our objections, we rule out poem after poem. Yet we keep on reading, never sure but irritation will give way to delight. The lawless is sometimes more interesting than the lawful."[26]

Even had Houghton, Mifflin opportunity to consider officially Emily Dickinson's poems, the firm would understandably hesitate. Edith M. Thomas, enthusiastically recommended to Aldrich in 1881 by Helen Hunt Jackson, had appeared frequently in the *Atlantic.* By 1884 both Roberts and James R. Osgood were courting Miss Thomas with offers of book publication. Miss Thomas chose to stay with Houghton, Mifflin. In 1885 it published her *A New Year's Masque and other Poems*; two years later *Lyrics and Sonnets.* At the time a selection of Emily Dickinson's poems became available, Houghton, Mifflin was preparing to bring out Miss Thomas' *The Inverted Torch.* It was Helen Hunt Jackson who approached Roberts Brothers about Miss Thomas' first book. Roberts was interested, but graciously yielded to Houghton, Mifflin's prior right. Since Roberts, again through Mrs. Jackson's influence, some years before had approached Emily Dickinson with an offer of publication, inevitably Houghton, Mifflin, observing the ritual of the trade, would refrain from bidding. On learning of the commercial and critical success of Emily Dickinson's poems, Houghton would have no reason to find fault with either Scudder or Aldrich for a lost opportunity.

Houghton may have agreed with the New York *Tribune* that Aldrich's *Atlantic* gave too much space to literary criticism and in consequence lacked vigor, but he must have admitted that the organization of this department was outstandingly efficient. Aldrich's coterie of critics month by month produced page after page of intelligent, perceptive analysis of the literary scene. The chief burden of the department fell on Scudder, who was responsible for more of the formal criticism than anyone else; he also originated and continuously produced the sprightly "Books of the

Month," which in eye-torturing fine print closed each issue of the magazine.[27]

Aldrich's *Atlantic* within the limits imposed by the business administration was rich in reading matter. Houghton could hardly blame his editor for the magazine's ailing circulation. Although it is usually linked with the New York quality magazines as a competitor, in subscribers it was not. *Harper's Monthly* and *Scribner's Magazine* claimed over 100,000; the *Century,* over 200,000. After 1881 the Riverside Press figures for binding *Atlantics* remained less than 20,000, the nadir being reached in 1886. In that year Houghton, as he had done some years before in absorbing the *Galaxy,* attempted to give the magazine's circulation a boost. He opened negotiations with Clark W. Bryan, whose *Good Housekeeping* had been operating out of Holyoke for a year. Bryan was tempted to sell, but in the end concluded to move his offices to Springfield and there continue his venture. Others stood ready to buy the *Atlantic,* move it to New York, fill it with pictures, and thus make it a genuine threat to its three rivals. One of these was John Brisbane Walker. Houghton was unmoved by such propositions. Even though the magazine was running down financially, it was not for sale. Park Street enjoyed the prestige of the periodical.[28]

Although the *Atlantic* stood aloof from the circulation race, in bidding for authors it could not avoid competition. Writers gave lip service to the magazine's literary reputation; for dollars they gave more. Aldrich had little to say about these dollars unless the rate was standard. What that standard was defies analysis. Some contributors received as little as $6 a page; others bargained astutely for a scale comparable to that paid in New York. Moreover, the agent had entered the scene. Gilder of the *Century* might "wail piteously at the way Osgood was sucking his blood," but he paid the charge. In addition new competitors for authors' wares had started playing their parts. Syndicate artists, men who placed cheap, hackneyed fiction in newspapers throughout the country, had been around for some time. They had posed no threat to the quality. But now three men proposed to bring literature to the generality: Allan Thorndike Rice who, having revitalized the *North American Review,* was in search of new fields to conquer, Charles A. Dana of the New York *Sun,* and S. S. McClure, on the threshold of his extraordinary success story. These men promised authors large financial rewards and an ever expanding audience. If Houghton hoped to retain his distinguished contributors, he must at least approach New York rates. He refused to contend with Osgood on royalties. In managing the *Atlantic* he chose a different course.

He encouraged writers to set their own price. Using Dr. Holmes as an intermediary, he sent word to James Russell Lowell that while he did "not want to bid against other publishers," as long as Lowell wrote for the *Atlantic* money would prove no stumbling block. To Charles Dudley Warner, he explained:

> I wish you had set a price upon the articles ["On Horseback"] for the Atlantic, as that would have relieved me from any responsibility in the matter. How would $20.00 a page do? Our page contains less than 700 words, and is very much smaller than either the Century or Harper's page. I was aware of what Thorndike Rice is doing. He pays at the rate of $30.00 a thousand, and sells at the rate of $10.00 a thousand, and to papers that I think would cheapen the quality of authorship as good as yours. I am afraid also it would seriously affect the sale in book form. The highest price we have felt able to pay for the best articles in the Atlantic has been $15.00 a page, and my impression is that we have paid it to you among the first, if not the first of all, and there are only two or three writers who now receive it. Our ordinary price for first-class articles is $10.00 a page . . . I shall esteem it a great favor, if this price which I indicate is acceptable to you, if you will not mention it to others. When we raised the price to you before, we had claims made immediately from another party whose articles we did not prize so highly.[29]

Although neither Dana's nor Rice's grandiose syndicate schemes proved profitable in the long run, their effect was to raise authors' demands. Henry James boasted to friends that for his two contributions to Dana he had been paid "thousands." For "Pandora," a story of about 18,000 words, he received between $1100 and $1200, for "Georgina's Reasons," probably a like amount. Translating this sum to the *Atlantic* page measurement yields well over $40 a page. James at once warned Aldrich his *Princess Casamas-*

sima would cost $500 an installment, a price Houghton refused to meet. In many cases, however, he agreed to an author's request for an increase in rates.[30]

Helen Hunt Jackson won perhaps the highest payment of any writer other than Thomas Hardy during the decade. Although she protested that she didn't want to be thought "grasping," that she loved appearing in the *Atlantic,* that being read by the elite was part of the pay, that she liked her articles printed in solid type rather than having the "paragraphs served as entrees" in a banquet of pictures, would "Dear kind, Mr. Houghton" afford $400 for two articles on the West? The *Century* would pay her more. Since the articles, "A Midsummer Fête in the Pueblo of San Juan" and "Among Skylines" total about fourteen pages, she was asking over $28 a page. Houghton, enclosing a check for $400, replied, "I appreciate your value as a writer, but I do not remember that the Atlantic has ever paid so much for papers before, except in one instance, and in that case the writer said it was his life work, and he died before he finished it." In something over two years, Mrs. Jackson herself died of cancer.[31]

One lady to whom Houghton would not yield was Annie Fields. The situation was delicate; frequently resident at Charles Street was Sarah Orne Jewett. Houghton, Mifflin would have but the smallest regret in parting with Mrs. Fields. Losing Miss Jewett would be a very different matter. The ladies had few secrets from each other. Inevitably what was paid one was known to the other. Thus Miss Jewett wrote, "I hope I was not grasping about the verses? A.F. had $30 for last one in the Atlantic — At least I think she did." Mrs. Fields, for her part, wished to be on equal footing with her friend for prose. If "Going to Shrewsbury" may be taken as a standard, Miss Jewett was being paid approximately $13 a page at the end of the decade. Mrs. Fields valued herself at a comparable rate, but Houghton, Mifflin's counting room ranked her at $10 a page. She made an issue of her worth to the *Atlantic.* Unfortunately, Scudder reported the controversy to Aldrich.

Dear Aldrich

I have been waiting for a good opportunity to write you. Perhaps a row with Mrs. Fields gives as good an occasion as any. Here is the correspondence condensed.

(Mrs. Fields to Mr. Scudder)

When would you like the Charles Reade papers, which I promised Mr. Aldrich? They are ready.

(Mr. Scudder to Mrs. Fields)

I should be very glad to see them before the end of June.

(Mrs. Fields to Mr. Scudder)

Mr. Aldrich said I might have till the 9th of July.

(Mr. Scudder to Mrs. Fields)

Very well, then, do as you were told.

(soliloquy of Mr. Scudder)

Why does the woman ask me, if she knows already?

(Mrs. Fields to Mr. Scudder)

Here are the two papers, of 7–8 pp. each. The price of each is $150.

(Mr. Scudder after a conversation with HOH)

Before sending to the printer, let me ask if that is your final price. The publishers are unwilling to pay more than $10 a page. Unless Mr. Aldrich has agreed to pay your price. Also I should be glad to print the paper as a single long paper in the Sept. no. rather than divide it. Also I must ask you to revise some of your intemperate (and ungrammatical) expressions regarding International Copyright.

(Mrs. Fields to Mr. Scudder)

Mr. Aldrich did not in so many words agree to pay me $300, but he knows what I get from Harper. I object to having the paper printed in one piece. I won't have a line of my writing disturbed. Please show this letter to Mr. Houghton. He will do the right thing.

(Mr. Scudder to Mrs. Fields)

That's just what I did. He was the very man who told me not to offer more than $10. We have nothing to do with Harper's. The last price paid you for prose by the Atlantic was $10.

(Mrs. Fields to Mr. Scudder)

Send back the papers. Very Respectfully.

(Mr. Scudder to Mrs. Fields)

Here they are. Regrets.

(Historical criticism upon the correspondence)
The letters are models, upon Mr. Scudder's part of gentleness, suavity and consideration, on Mrs. Fields' of irony, suppressed anger and freezing scorn.

(My own conclusion)
I'm sorry not to print Reade's letters, some of which are quite interesting, and the Atlantic needs copy, but I am glad to escape the necessity of printing a long extract from the Pall Mall Gazette, and the illogical and ungrammatical comments of Mrs. Fields. The price of $300 was preposterous . . .

You may please yourself with thinking that you are the only one who has come out with a whole head of hair; my hair and Mr. Houghton's have gone.

Scudder's report was unfortunate because Aldrich and his wife were habitués of that salon of pet names on Charles Street, where reputations were demolished "with one silken, slipping word." Here Aldrich was the Duke; his wife, the Duchess.[32]

Long before Aldrich's gauche rejection of President Eliot's article on Prescott, Houghton more than once had talked seriously with Scudder of the possibility of his adding the *Atlantic* to his other duties, first in 1886 after Crawford had given his *Zoroaster* to Macmillan. Scudder did not wish to be found looking at Aldrich's boots and he "flatly refused to act as a committee to confer with Aldrich about the improvement of the editing." In December 1889, following the Eliot fiasco, Aldrich tendered his resignation, then withdrew it, then went off to Florida to think the matter over. Houghton was "at his wit's end to know how to dispose of Aldrich" and Scudder found himself a shuttlecock. "Here's a pretty how de do," he wrote in his diary. For the first six months of the new decade the *Atlantic* continued under Aldrich's direction. In May he announced his intention of again going to Europe for the summer, assuming Scudder would take over as he had in the past. Scudder refused. Finally in the middle of June, Aldrich made a clean break and Scudder wrote in his diary on June 17, 1890:

Yesterday Mr. Houghton told me that Aldrich had resigned the editorship of the Atlantic, and proceeded to speak of me in con-

nection with the work. I said, smilingly, you have not asked me
to take the place. No, he said, some things we don't ask. I believe I never asked Mrs. Houghton to marry me. I think it not
unlikely, for his habit of mind is so ineradicably indirect that I
can easily think of him talking an hour with Miss Manning, and
at the end of it, her finding herself engaged to him. I must take
him as he is, although his isness is rather trying at times . . .

All this is of minor importance. I am more stirred by the fact
that I am now invested, permanently, with the editorship . . . I
have known of the dissatisfaction of the firm for a long while, and
I am taking the magazine when it is running down financially
. . . My aim is to keep the magazine at the front of American literature, but I will not boast as the one who puts his armor off.
How strange it seems. Ten years ago when Howells left the Atlantic I was more disappointed than I like to remember at not being
asked to take his place . . . I do not think I am likely to make
lucky hits, but I think I can strengthen the magazine all along
the line, and my heart beats quicker at the thought of serving God
in this cause of high, pure literature.[33]

According to Mark Antony DeWolfe Howe, the *Atlantic* was
"the best editorial position in the gift" of the house. This gift
amounted to an annual saving for Houghton, Mifflin of $3000.
Aldrich's salary had been $4000. Scudder's on this appointment
was raised from $5000 to $6000. For the next three years the
editorial work on general publications as well as the magazine
would be carried by three people — Susan Francis, Herbert R.
Gibbs, and Horace Elisha Scudder. Houghton had solved the
nagging problem of joint command. The right hand would now
know what the left hand was doing.

The Trade, despite the pressure of Osgood's competition, had
had a remarkably successful decade. The Old Guard had remained faithful. So had a number of younger writers, notably
Sarah Orne Jewett and John Burroughs, and Aldrich himself had
produced two books and a new edition of his poems, clear refutation of his indolence. Moreover, a group of untried writers of
promise had been discovered and the *Atlantic*, its ailing circulation notwithstanding, had become a symbol of the house.

XV

DEATHS AND COPYRIGHTS

FOR HOUGHTON, MIFFLIN the closing decade of the nineteenth century was weighted with mortality. Moreover, the national economy was sick. In 1893 the country experienced panic and an ensuing depression as severe as any it had known. Houghton, Mifflin rode the troughs, but the national ailment left its mark. The company's net profits declined from $114,393.08 in April 1893 to $36,583.05 in 1896, the low for the period. Other firms less conservatively managed fell victim to the times, among them Samuel Clemens' Charles L. Webster & Company, Emily Dickinson's publisher, Roberts Brothers, and D. Appleton and Company. In 1899 the great house of Harper with liabilities of $5,265,271.00, J. P. Morgan & Company its largest creditor, was up for sale. In that year Houghton, Mifflin, with a total indebtedness of $474,261.17 and partnership capital of $1,319,227.65, recorded net profits of $59,077.10.[1]

At times it must have seemed to Park Street that death was indeed the dusty answer to years devoted to the creation of American standards. Between 1890 and 1900 more than twenty of its authors died, the most important, James Russell Lowell in 1891, Whittier in 1892, Oliver Wendell Holmes in 1894, and Harriet Beecher Stowe in 1896. The Old Guard was dying off; their copyrights were running out also. Protection at this time was for forty-two years, twenty-eight for the original copyright, fourteen for renewal. Any work published between 1848 and 1858 would enter the public domain between 1890 and 1900. Included would be various works by Hawthorne, Holmes, Mrs. Stowe, Thoreau, Longfellow, Lowell, and Whittier. More disturbing than expected expiration was the discovery that a number carried copyright notices open to challenge and that publishing tramps were on hand to take advantage of the opportunity.[2]

Lowell's death in 1891 introduced a series of contractual and copyright problems which required attention throughout the decade. Some years earlier, when Dr. Holmes had asked Lowell for his view of an afterlife, he had replied that he had always been treated like a gentleman and that he expected similar respect in the future. Could he have known of the struggle that was to ensue over his literary remains, he might have been less confident. It will be recalled that Osgood had put him on a ten-year annuity contract in 1876. When time for renewal approached, Garrison recommended that Houghton, Mifflin return Lowell to a royalty basis; his books were not earning the annual $1500. This Houghton was unwilling to do. Lowell was his ideal man of letters, one grounded in his country's history and service and at this very moment active in the fight for International Copyright. He had been associated with Houghton from the early days when, as editor of the *Atlantic,* from 1857 to 1861, he had skylarked along the Charles on his way to the Riverside Press to perform his editorial duties. Houghton thought if Lowell could find time to produce a new book (none had appeared since 1877), its publication would awake interest and stimulate sale of his earlier ones. Lowell obliged by getting together his "Democracy" and a number of other addresses. In reward, his annuity was raised to $2000. As before, subsequent books were guaranteed to Houghton, Mifflin, each to earn the standard 10 percent for six months and then to fall under the annuity. In the time remaining before his death, Lowell produced two more books, *Political Essays* and *Heartsease and Rue.* In 1890, Houghton, Mifflin prepared for his place on the library shelves of the nation by presenting his collected works in a Riverside Edition at $16.50, a subscription edition at $22.00 (Lowell called it *Edition de looks*), and a popular edition at $10.00. In addition three numbers of the Riverside Literature Series were preparing a new generation for reverent purchase of Lowell's *Works* in uniform bindings. Three of his early productions now entered the public domain, *The Vision of Sir Launfal,*

A Fable for Critics, and *The Biglow Papers,* first series. The firm readied new illustrated editions of these, thus attempting to secure public interest in its authorized Lowell books rather than in those of the tramps who, in the name of education and the general good, were now free to print these works without paying a cent to the still living author. Houghton, Mifflin took justifiable pride in its proprietary right to the productions of James Russell Lowell.[3]

Lowell had named Charles Eliot Norton as his literary executor. On hearing of the appointment, William James exclaimed, "The way that man gets his name stuck to every greatness is fabulous, Dante, Goethe, Carlyle, Ruskin, Fitzgerald, Chauncy Wright, and now Lowell! His name will dominate the literary history of this epoch." Recalling the position Norton had taken when he had preferred Osgood's offer for the Emerson-Carlyle correspondence to Houghton's, Park Street was apprehensive. In Houghton, Mifflin's favor would be the failures of Osgood and Ticknor & Company. Through the 1889 purchase of the latter's assets, the Emerson-Carlyle book had arrived on the Houghton, Mifflin list. So circuitous a route to security might be a persuasive argument. Still, Lowell was a public figure of more than literary prominence. On his death Garrison reported to Houghton:

> Mr. Scudder has written Dr. Holmes inviting him to contribute a poem on Mr. Lowell to the Atlantic . . . and he has also written to Mr. Norton, asking him to either contribute an article to the Atlantic, or to allow the Atlantic to use the paper which he may perhaps prepare for the next meeting of the Historical Society. He has also intimated that he hopes Mr. Norton is going to give the Atlantic some of Mr. Lowell's unpublished papers and letters. We of course feel quite uncertain as to what Mr. Norton will decide to do about the correspondence (the unpublished essays will naturally come to us), and I dare say that the Harpers have gone or will go for the Life and Letters through Mr. Curtis, and Macmillans may also try to capture them. I do not suppose that Mr. Gilder has been too modest either to put in his application.

This was on the eighteenth of August. Ten days later Garrison again reported on the Lowell question. He had just received a letter from Norton, who "declined to write an article for the

Atlantic, saying he does not like the fashion of talking about one's friends in public after they are dead." As for the Life and Letters, he had not made up his mind. Hardly had Garrison finished reading Norton's letter when James Ripley Osgood appeared in his office.[4]

Osgood, in the years since the failure of his second company, had been serving the house of Harper as London agent. With the approval of his employers in the fall of 1890, in anticipation of the passage of the International Copyright Law, he had organized a British publishing house with Clarence W. McIlvaine as partner. Although he continued to serve the Harpers, he was also once again in business for himself. In his conversation with Garrison, he complained of A. P. Watt, now Houghton, Mifflin's London agent, who seemed out of sympathy with Osgood, McIlvaine. Next he indicated interest in securing English rights to Mary Hartwell Catherwood's *The Lady of Fort St. John,* shortly to complete its *Atlantic* run. He said nothing about Lowell, but on the day of his call at Park Street, he dispatched a note to Norton, requesting English rights to Lowell's posthumous papers and asking if Norton was free to negotiate with Harper. ". . . when the question of terms arises you will find us ready to deal with it on your own basis. We will pay as much as any other firm — nay, more," he promised.[5]

Norton, having received Osgood's letter, wrote Houghton, Mifflin:

> It would seem very fitting that you, as the publishers of his [Lowell's] works hitherto, should also publish this and such other volumes of his writings as it may seem well to issue. But within the last ten days, I have had application from four of the most reputable publishing houses, to be allowed to publish these volumes, and each offering special pecuniary inducements. My duty in the case seems to be plain. I must (waiving other considerations which might in other circumstances have great weight) make that arrangement for publication which may seem to secure the largest pecuniary benefit for Mr. Lowell's heirs.

He suggested the house make a proposal. Houghton, Mifflin had no intention of bargaining for that which it regarded as legally its own, Lowell's essays and poems. "... our beloved mutual friend Charles Eliot Norton ... has gone off decidedly half cock," Mifflin fumed. He directed that a copy of the pertinent clause in the 1886 contract, defining the publisher's rights, be sent to Norton. In reply, Norton conceded Houghton, Mifflin was entitled to a book of essays, that and no more, writing, "As to such volumes as I may conclude to make from Mr. Lowell's manuscripts, and to publish at some future time, I am also clearly of the opinion that they are not covered by your contract. I should hope that you might publish them, but I should expect better terms . . ." The pale Cambridge aesthete, for all his contempt for his age and its god Mammon, as trustee knew his duty. If necessary Lowell's posthumous papers could wait book publication until the 1886 contract had run out.[6]

Some ten years earlier Houghton had refused to bargain against Osgood's 20 percent, but to lose Lowell's letters would be an error. They should make the concluding volume of his Collected Works. Since these were not covered by the annuity contract, Houghton, Mifflin gave Norton his choice — either half-profits or a royalty of 20 percent with an advance to be agreed upon. In the meantime Osgood had been deftly at work, calling on Norton to discuss terms. Would he accept an advance of $2500 from the house of Harper, £250 from Osgood, McIlvaine, with two-thirds of the profits on net sales, these profits guaranteed not to fall below what 20 percent of the retail price on all copies sold would amount to? A careful trustee could hardly fail to accept such largess, especially since he was to have for himself a sum sufficient to mitigate his distaste for "the fashion of talking about one's friends in public after they are dead." Norton agreed to write an article on Lowell for *Harper's Monthly*.[7]

Lowell's other literary remains could well wait book publication until the 1886 annuity contract had run its ten years. In the meantime they could be parceled out to periodicals at a neat return. Harper wanted the six lectures on the "Old English Dramatists" for its *Monthly* and in the name of publishers' courtesy, what about 20 percent on the resulting book? Armed with this offer, Norton suggested Houghton, Mifflin meet the price. Capitulation was better than legal contest. The book came out under the Boston imprint in the fall of 1892. Other periodicals clamored for posthumous scraps and Norton made the most of the market. *Scribner's* took "On a Bust of Grant" for $1000. Howells, now editor of the *Cosmopolitan,* promised the pay would be "as good as the best" for whatever Norton cared to submit. Richard Watson Gilder of the *Century* took his opportunity more coolly. When Norton offered Lowell's short sketch on Francis Parkman for $500, he replied that he "did not think it would be honest for him to ask the publishers to pay that price"; $150 he thought a more realistic value. Norton promptly accepted the reduction.[8]

Meanwhile Park Street was desperate. After Norton's refusal to write an article, Scudder sought Howells' cooperation. He too refused. Only then did Scudder bethink himself of Henry James, who accepted the invitation gladly, feeling, in contrast to Norton, there would be "a kind of piety in writing" a "loyal and affectionate tribute." He could not possibly have it ready, however, until time for the January 1892 number. At least the magazine would have Dr. Holmes's poem for the October number, but from Lowell, its first editor, it must have a posthumous product too. Norton offered a paper on Richard III provided the *Atlantic* would pay enough. Houghton was abroad. Garrison, Scudder, James Murray Kay, and Mifflin met in grand conclave. Garrison suspected that Gilder was considering the paper, that the *Century* people would pay $1000. Scudder suggested trying $500. Kay was "inexorable." The price was absurd. Houghton would never consider such highway robbery. Mifflin cast the deciding vote. Five hundred dollars it would be. "Poor Kay!" Scudder wrote in his diary, "he gets long letters from H.O.H. crowding him on finances, bulling him into cutting down expenses, and yet as Mifflin remarked, ten to one if he ruled now as he wanted to, H.O.H. would come down upon him and want to know what he was about meddling in matters he didn't know anything about! For twenty-five years Mifflin said I have been learning how to get along with H.O.H. but Kay is still in the depths of ignorance." Lowell's Richard III paper, an address originally delivered in Chicago in 1883, appeared in the December 1891 *Atlantic.*[9]

Houghton was not angered by the $500, but he was kept in a constant fury by the refined Norton's commercial gambits. Every Lowell matter must be taken up with him. In 1893 Woodberry was engaged to do the Lowell biography. Mysterious difficulties developed. Houghton suspected Norton but Norton blamed the delay on Woodberry's temperament and suggested Scudder or Mrs. Fields for the assignment. Two years later, Woodberry's contract was canceled and a new one drawn. Instead of the Lowell, he would do the Hawthorne so long promised by Lowell. More positive evidence of Norton's control showed up in another matter. Scudder sent off to the State Department for copies of Lowell's diplomatic papers, hoping to make an *Atlantic* article. Norton refused permission on the grounds that such publication would be antithetical to the interests of Lowell's heirs. George Putnam, a Lowell executor and lawyer, even accused Houghton, Mifflin of an "improper" act in having sought the papers. Houghton's blood pressure rose every time the problem came to his attention. He turned negotiations over to Mifflin. Finally in 1895 in anticipation of the 1886 agreement, a new contract was drawn. Lowell's heirs would have an annuity of $3500 and 10 percent royalties for six months on new books, Houghton, Mifflin retaining publication rights, except for letters and biographical material. The exception proved a continuing irritant. In 1901 when Scudder was writing his biography of James Russell Lowell, Colonel George Harvey, directing the affairs of Harper at J. P. Morgan's behest, notified him the charge for quotations from Norton's *Letters of James Russell Lowell* would be $10 a thousand words.[10]

By this time Norton had wearied of his Harper bargain. After the first fine flush of novelty the *Letters'* sales had diminished year by year, in 1901 reaching a low of seventy-four copies. In 1891 he had won $3750 in advances. After that, what the two-thirds net profits amounted to is problematical. Possibly Osgood's extravagant offer of 1891 was subsequently modified. According to Eugene Exman's recent history of the house, Norton won "the highest royalty ever paid by Harper's up to that time, 20 percent to 2000, and 25 percent thereafter," a significantly different contract from the one Osgood proposed, not very different from Houghton,

Mifflin's proposition. In any case, by the turn of the century, Norton, tired of his Harper bargain, readily acceded to Houghton, Mifflin's suggestion that steps be taken to secure the *Letters* for its various uniform editions of Lowell. Indeed, he couldn't see that the volumes had any value to Harper, sales had so fallen off. Colonel Harvey, however, liked those two odd volumes. For $500 and royalties to Norton, he would allow Houghton, Mifflin the *Letters* for its subscription editions only. James R. Osgood, though ten years dead (he had died in 1892), with all his failures had succeeded in this — except for the Elmwood and Autograph Editions, Houghton, Mifflin's uniformed drill of Lowell's collected works would never include the author's *Letters*.[11]

On his last visit to the United States, securing Lowell's literary legacy had been one among many of Osgood's objectives. Two other Houghton, Mifflin authors who must in the course of things also die were on his list — Whittier and Holmes. They were, however, living and administering their literary futures. Both politely rejected his offers, but both, aware of the uncertain threshold, were putting their affairs in order.[12]

Organizing death's remains is usually unpleasant. The simple Whittier left few loose ends. Well in advance he had sought his biographer, settling on his nephew-in-law Samuel T. Pickard, after a variety of more eminent men had proved unavailable. Because of his early association with William D. Ticknor, he had selected the company run by his sons as publisher, but the remnant of that company by the time of his death was facing bankruptcy. The biography came uncontested to Houghton, Mifflin, to be bound uniformly with the Riverside and Subscription Editions of Whittier's *Works*. At his death all was peaceful on the publishing front. So too was his funeral.[13]

The services were held in the garden behind Whittier's Amesbury house. Here Garrison and Scudder found their places. ". . . the scene was very striking. It was a lovely afternoon. Apple and pear trees hung their fruit above us and the sunlight broke through the branches. A table with a big Bible on it stood in front . . . Seats were arranged on the grass and the grapery was filled with people, while Barefooted Boys were clustered in an apple tree eat-ing apples. The speaking was not very impressive, but one thought chiefly of Whittier and this bright outdoor scene, his own last words — love to the world, and one listened to the sweet recitation of Eternal Goodness by a Quakeress."[14]

Dr. Holmes, even as Whittier, had prepared for the end. His son was to be his executor. On his frequent calls at Park Street in 1891, he talked of his biography. Finally, in 1892, he reported that because "a somewhat pressing proposal was made me by a literary gentleman to take my Life in hand," he had decided to write his autobiography. His life had already been "three times handled." He now thought he would see what he could do with it himself, and he promised he would not forget "the now venerable periodical which I rocked in its cradle between thirty and forty years ago." Episodes which might interest its readers, the *Atlantic* should have. Scudder was delighted by the prospect that under his editorship the magazine was to have excerpts from the doctor's autobiography.[15]

Dr. Holmes's relationship with his publishers had been a singularly happy one. In 1883 the firm had raised his annual stipend to $4000 for a five-year period, Houghton, Mifflin to have exclusive rights to all his literary productions. The doctor fulfilled his obligations generously with an impressive number of books, among them his life of Emerson for the Men of Letters Series, and for the *Atlantic* two serials and many single-number contributions. In 1888 at his own request his annual payment was reduced to $2500 because he was not writing regularly and could not in conscience take the larger payment. However, in 1890, after he had begun *Over the Teacups,* he wrote Houghton that he would like a new five-year contract at the old rate since he was once again writing regularly for the *Atlantic.* He had recently had an attractive offer from the *Forum,* but he assured Houghton, "You have been my publisher for a long time and I do not wish to listen to any outside temptations. My nature is a very loyal one, and (in Prior's words)

"I hold it both a shame and sin
To quit the good Old Angel Inn."

Holmes's annual fee was returned to $4000.[16]

Scudder's hopes for autobiographical contributions from Dr. Holmes were disappointed. His son the judge called at Park Street to forbid publication of any of his father's ramblings. Moreover, he requested that knowledge of his intervention be kept secret. "Evidently at home he shows more the infirmities of age than we perceive when he calls here," Garrison commented. Here was a delicate situation. The firm agreed not to press the doctor for his reminiscences. What should be done, however, if he actually presented a manuscript? To refuse publication to the man who had figured so importantly in the launching of the *Atlantic* would be difficult. The Holmes family, Garrison thought, was unduly exercised lest the doctor "exceed the bounds of taste." Nonetheless, the firm cooperated. Even though the doctor repeatedly announced that he was accumulating masses of notes, none of his recollections appeared in the *Atlantic*. The firm hoped the notes would be made available to Holmes's biographer. The judge dashed these hopes. His father ". . . left no autobiography which could be used," he told Houghton. His wife's nephew John T. Morse, editor of Houghton, Mifflin's Statesmen Series, would write the elder Holmes's life.[17]

In 1882 the *Nation* had noted that the files of the Library of Congress were open to all, that an investigator would find there many a faulty copyright entry. Certain publishers took the hint. Following Oliver Wendell Holmes's death in September 1894, three publishing tramps, Hurst & Company of New York, Donohue, Henneberry & Company of Chicago, and Henry Altemus of Philadelphia, announced forthcoming printings of *The Autocrat of the Breakfast-Table*. Houghton's anger could hardly be contained. The *Autocrat* had begun its run in the first number of the *Atlantic;* on its completion there, it had been copyrighted as a book in 1858. Houghton, Mifflin had taken care to renew the copyright in the doctor's name. Protection would not expire until 1900. The firm announced its intention to prosecute. The case of *Houghton, Mifflin* v. *Hurst* never reached the courts. In preparing for it, Rowland Cox, the firm's lawyer, discovered that "no copyright was secured by Oliver Wendell Holmes or Phillips, Sampson & Co., or any other person in any of said twelve numbers of the Atlantic Monthly containing said book, the 'Autocrat of the Breakfast-Table,' or in any part of said numbers." To advertise these defects would be to embolden other pirates. Both Judge Bennett and Rowland Cox advised the publishers "to withdraw as quietly" as they could.[18]

Judge Holmes, more interested in the law than in publishing profits, decided to make a test case of this facet of the domestic copyright law, choosing Rowland Cox as attorney. Hurst's *Autocrat* stated on its title page that it had been taken directly from the *Atlantic Monthly*. Since the chapters had not been registered, they were in the public domain. The only argument the Holmes side could present was that although the individual installments were free to all, the book was not, that Hurst had the right to reprint, but only in comparable sections. He had no right to gather the sections together as a book, that ". . . the twelve parts as parts of the continuous composition did not exhaust the rights of the author. There still remained the right to take a copyright upon the composition as an entirety." After being tried in the lower courts, where the Hurst contention of the right to publish the *Autocrat* was sustained, the case reached the United States Supreme Court in 1899. Here in affirming the decisions of the lower courts, Justice Brown said: "We have not overlooked the inconvenience which our conclusion will cause, if, in order to protect their articles from piracy, authors are compelled to copyright each chapter or installment as it may appear in a periodical; nor the danger and annoyance it may occasion to the Librarian of Congress, with whom copyrighted articles are deposited, if he is compelled to receive such articles as they are published in newspapers and magazines; but these are evils which can easily be remedied by an amendment of the law." In summary, "The serial publication of a book in a monthly magazine, prior to any steps taken toward securing copyright, is such publication of the same . . . as to vitiate a copyright of the whole book, obtained subsequently, but prior to the publication of the book as an entirety." The pirates, having received authority from the highest court in the land, made much of their opportunity.

In 1895, before the *Holmes* v. *Hurst* case reached the Supreme

Court, Houghton, Mifflin purchased Oliver Wendell Holmes's copyrights for $20,000 and Harriet Beecher Stowe's for $10,000. Since there was no longer reason for keeping the fact of defective copyright from public knowledge, the firm decided to bring to trial two similar cases, one involving Holmes's *Professor at the Breakfast-Table,* the other Mrs. Stowe's *Minister's Wooing.* Although Houghton, Mifflin did not expect a favorable decision, it appealed the decisions of the lower courts because it hoped by fighting "the 'pirates' to the last ditch," to dramatize the inequities of the existing law. In these cases Houghton, Mifflin appeared as proprietor of the *Atlantic* and owner of the Holmes and Stowe copyrights. The argument was that copyright in the magazine protected its contents. However, the Court held that ". . . the copyright of the Atlantic Monthly by Ticknor & Fields did not operate as notice of the rights of the author to any article therein appearing . . ." Subsequent entry under a different title, that is, of the contribution rather than the magazine, did not protect the work. Again Justice Brown apologized, saying, "It is exceedingly unfortunate that, with the pains taken by the authors of these works to protect themselves against republication, they should have failed in accomplishing their object; but the right being purely statutory, we see no escape from the conclusion that unless the substance as well as the form of the statute be disregarded, the right has been lost in both cases."[19]

This last opinion was rendered in 1903. In 1909 the Copyright Law was revised. Among the changes was a provision that "copyright upon composite works or periodicals shall give to the proprietor thereof all rights in respect thereto which he would have if each part were individually copyrighted . . ."[20]

Houghton expected loyalty from his authors. He returned the obligation in equal measure. In the 1880s Harriet Beecher Stowe's *Uncle Tom's Cabin* enjoyed an annual average sale of 30,000. Houghton thought the little lady deserved to be memorialized in a row of volumes in uniform bindings. Before that could be accomplished, she required something else. Today it would be called a cocktail party. In 1882, it was a garden party. Even though a number of her books were in the hands of another publisher, such an affair would mark her clearly as one of Houghton, Mifflin's own.[21]

This was to be a gathering for *Atlantic* contributors, but since Aldrich was off on one of his European trips, Houghton took care of the details almost singlehandedly. Governor and Mrs. Claflin graciously opened their Newtonville estate, The Elms. There was a tent, a collation, a string orchestra, carriages at the railway station, and, of course, speeches and poems. Houghton hoped to relieve the possible tedium with wine of some sort; however, Mrs. Claflin was polite but firm in denial. Even so the party was a success. The two hundred or more guests enjoyed the perfect June day and the lovely views from the tree-shaded lawn. "H. O. aquitted himself creditably, & Ward Beecher & Dr. Holmes fairly outdid themselves," Garrison reported. "Dr. Holmes's delivery of his clever poem was very spirited — he is a capital reader — and he added no little life & zest to the occasion. Trowbridge's poem was good, but the rest of the verses (by women) were worthless. Whittier's poem was excellent and well read by Frank Sanborn . . . & Mrs. Stowe's cheerful & happy little talk to us at the close, — the whole audience standing as she spoke — a pleasant ending; the optimistic remark with which she dismissed us being, — 'Be sure that whatever ought to be done will be done!' "[22]

One thing that "ought to be done" in Houghton's view was a collected edition. His firm had the best of Harriet in *Uncle Tom, Dred, The Minister's Wooing,* and a number of other books. But when Osgood succeeded Fields, she had transferred her business first to Roberts, then to J. B. Ford & Company. Houghton opened negotiations with Ford's successors, Ford, Howard & Hulbert, and in 1884 for $1000 secured the plates and publishing rights of *My Wife and I, We and Our Neighbors, Poganuc People, Little Pussy Willow, A Dog's Mission,* and *Queer Little People.* Houghton knew how to make them earn their purchase price. These combined with the other Stowe books on Houghton, Mifflin's list, *Uncle Tom* excepted, earned the author in the next ten years an average annual royalty of a little over $1000. *Uncle Tom's* average in the same period was over $2500. In 1892, in anticipation of the copyright's expiration, Houghton, Mifflin, to defeat the pirates, determined to saturate the market with editions ranging in price from 25 cents to $4. Hardly were plans in operation than an article appeared in the *National Advertiser* for March 1, 1892, asserting under the caption "A Remarkable Discovery," that *Uncle Tom's Cabin* had never been properly copyrighted. "It made a fortune for its publisher," said the *National Advertiser,* "and all this time it has been open to the world," exhibiting a fine disregard for the aging author. The *Advertiser* compounded the injury by asserting that Houghton, Mifflin had failed to renew its faulty copyright, that "for the last twelve years there has been no form or pretence even to copyright the book."[23]

Since many of the firm's records had been destroyed in the fire of 1879, among them apparently copyright certificates for Mrs. Stowe, it dispatched Wheeler to Washington to investigate. His search of the Library of Congress files confirmed Houghton, Mifflin's belief that there was not an iota of truth in the charge of failure to renew. However, the original copyright was in truth imperfect. Through a printer's oversight one installment (chapters 12, 13, and 14) had failed to state as then required, "Copyright secured by the author." Moreover, to an agent of the United States Book Company, the *National Era* appeared to have failed to deposit the copies required. It was this agent who had inspired the *National Advertiser's* article.[24]

Despite the knowledge that *Uncle Tom* had a minor copyright defect, Houghton, Mifflin determined to feign fight. Letters were dispatched to the *National Advertiser* demanding a retraction, to the *Publishers' Weekly,* the *Literary World,* and other journals, asserting the validity of the copyright. The firm promised to secure an injunction against anyone who published or sold any but its authorized editions. The threats proved effective. In 1892, *Uncle Tom's Cabin* earned Mrs. Stowe $6693.77. Four years later, the book free to all, royalties had fallen to a mere $696.56. The author was now in her eighty-fifth year and Houghton, Mifflin purchased her publishing rights.[25]

One of the major concerns of authors, publishers, and printers during the 1880s was International Copyright. Houghton supported practically every effort from the Harper proposal of 1878 to the Platt-Simonds Bill, finally enacted in 1891. His support entailed repeated trips to New York and Washington. So frequently was he away on these matters that his partisan wife wrote him in irritation ". . . the Copyright Bill might as well 'go to Guinea,' as to take you off on these sudden trips. And why couldn't one of those Scribners or Putnams or somebody else go on some of the expeditions occasionally, instead of staying quietly at home and voting that you should do all the work?" Houghton certainly did not do all the work, but as his correspondence with publishers and legislators reveals, he was remarkably active, especially in advocating simultaneous publication. Senator Jonathan Chace of Rhode Island, the chief architect of the bill that became law, said that of all the men who came to Washington in behalf of International Copyright, Houghton was the one with the clearest understanding of the operation and effect of the proposed legislation, that to Chace his "arguments in its favor were more important . . . than those of any other person, either author or publisher."[26]

The chief contention of opponents to various proposed measures was that royalty payments to foreign authors would increase the price of books and in consequence obstruct the nation's efforts to encourage learning. In 1886 James Russell Lowell effectively lanced this festering argument with his pointed epigram, "There is one book better than a cheap book, and that is one honestly come by." His widely circulated quatrain supplied partisans of the cause with an additional moral weapon.

> In vain we call old notions fudge
> And bend our conscience to our dealing;
> The Ten Commandments will not budge
> And stealing will continue stealing.

Henceforth the contest was not whether there should be International Copyright, but rather what provisions the law should include.

The Harper draft of a proposed treaty with England contained two recommendations that divided authors, publishers, and printers in controversy for ten years. The first was that a foreign author having published abroad should be allowed three months before bringing his book out in the United States. At the end of this period, if the work had not been published in this country, it would be free to anyone who cared to print it. The other recommendation was that books of foreign authorship be printed and bound in America; stereos and electros might be made abroad. With this latter provision, Houghton was in sympathy. To require stereo plates to be made here would work hardship, especially for manufacturers of dictionaries. "A duplicate set of plates, with one editorial supervision and one expenditure for the type setting, would make as good a book for the two countries as if the thing were done twice. Many such books would never be done at all if it were necessary to remanufacture the plates," he said. As a producer of tons of Merriam-Webster dictionaries, Houghton knew whereof he spoke. A touch of self-interest may be reflected in his statement. The Merriams had undertaken a vast revision of the 1864 dictionary. The Riverside Press would soon be bending all efforts to keep up with the demand for the 1890 *Webster's International*.[27]

As for the period of grace, Houghton would allow none. Such a concession would grant monopoly to English publishers. Their editions, imported, would absorb the market before an American house had an opportunity to try its hand with an English author. ". . . if we could have simultaneous publication all the other questions would settle themselves in time," he wrote Joseph W. Harper. No manufacturing clause would be necessary. However, he was sufficiently eager for International Copyright to sign the Harper draft submitted to the United States Government in 1880 under the title "Suggestions from American Publishers to the Department of State for an International Copyright Treaty approved by American Authors."[28]

This same willingness to yield a point if he could gain one characterized Houghton's support of ensuing efforts to secure International Copyright after the Harper plan came to nothing. In the end he won his argument for simultaneous publication but the manufacturing clause of the Platt-Simonds Bill was more restrictive than he thought necessary, requiring as it did home-produced stereos and electros as well as printing and binding. To the English, and the American devotees of Free Trade, the conditions of simultaneous publication and American manufacture were intolerably protectionist. Houghton would sacrifice the second but never the first.

In his 1888 speech before the International Copyright Association of New England, Houghton urged that effort be made to create public sentiment in behalf of the movement. Voters should be made aware that the passage of such a law would not increase the price of books, "that competition always made books and everything else cheaper than any other method." The effect of International Copyright would be to stimulate American authors for whose books a vast army of readers, forever replenished from the schools, waited. The number would increase in geometric progression. If indeed the English, because of lower labor costs, proved able to undersell the American product, he was certain that American publishers could win the game, not in price but in excellence. "The fact is that when an American sees anything better than he has had before, he will have it. I have never been troubled with the multitude of cheap books. People who buy a cheap book will throw it away soon, and come and buy the better book we publish, and they will keep it . . . My own feeling is that we should give a copyright to anybody, whether he be Hottentot, Jew, Englishman, Frenchman, German, or whatever he may be provided he will first publish that book in this country . . . I don't care a fig for any mechanical protection. I am willing to compete with any of them, but I want the freshest and newest books published here first . . ."[29]

When Houghton said he didn't give a fig for any mechanical protection, he probably spoke the truth. High tariff had become for him a natural right, he had been talking about it for so many years. At one time the *Nation* had a little mild fun over Houghton's reiterated assertion that Europeanization of America was inevitable if the existing duty on books were lowered. "All children are taught that vigilance is the price of liberty," the magazine observed, "but the maxim is open to the charge of vagueness, which could never be brought against Mr. Houghton's substitute that the price is a simple twenty-five per cent duty on books. Nothing short of twenty-five will do, it should be remembered. Ten or fifteen, or even twenty would be equally fatal, and we cannot afford to run any risk about freedom." Such gentle ridicule had no effect on Houghton. In his view, any reduction in tariff would ruin the American book industry. Readers would be overwhelmed with a flood of print awash with pernicious foreign philosophies. However, if good sense prevailed, the nation was safe and American typesetters need fear no reduction in wages.[30]

The Platt-Simonds Bill passed the House in December 1890. Its career in the Senate was tortuous, but at last on March 4, 1891, in the final hours of the Fifty-first Congress the bill secured the necessary votes. Henry Cabot Lodge rushed it back to the House for approval in its amended form. That body acting "favorably upon it he supervised its enrollment by the clerks in the otherwise deserted chamber, with the eerie light of the dawning sun creeping in the windows. Upon President Harrison's signature International Copyright became the law of the land. From now on foreign authors would be paid for their works if they accepted simultaneous publication and American manufacture.[31]

Dispatches announcing passage and the President's signature arrived at Park Street shortly after the business day had started. Houghton was in high spirits. He sent off notes to Lowell, Holmes, and other Houghton, Mifflin authors. Scudder wrote to James Bryce, "feeling it desirable to help a little in making a right sentiment in England." About noon Houghton proposed that his associates join him at a neighboring bistro for a glass of ginger ale. In the memory of one office boy that was "a shining hour . . . a real occasion when the partners went forth to celebrate, Houghton, Mifflin and Company, dignified and silk-hatted, moving slowly down the hill!"[32]

Following the passage of the bill, questions as to its effect on American publishing were general. Lowell, whose epigram and quatrain had crystallized the ethics of the question, confided to Scudder, "I have a good deal more practical sense than I generally get credit for, and I think the English make altogether too much fuss over the matter of printing in this country. To this country the bulk of the printing must come, whether they will or not, and this bill only anticipates the issue." Houghton thought its chief benefit would be a new stability in the trade. The policy of his house would be as before to give "its fullest attention to the cultivation of American literature, taking the English as incidental."[33]

Houghton soon found the English could not be taken as incidental. As successors to Ticknor & Fields, first American publishers of Robert Browning, Houghton, Mifflin regarded itself as the poet's authorized American publisher. In 1886 when it paid £100 for *Parleyings with Certain People,* Browning reaffirmed the firm's authority. In 1889 it paid another £100 for *Asolando.* Browning died on the day of publication. In administering his works in successive editions, Houghton, Mifflin felt it had played a large part in developing the American vogue for the poet. In 1894, when Macmillan's New York branch announced publication plans for a complete Browning, Houghton's anger was Homeric. He protested by letter, then went to New York. Macmillan's Brett, making "as many tergiversations as any circus rider," admitted that £100 was a large sum for *Asolando.* Nonetheless, his edition would go forward. After all, since the new International Copyright Law was not retroactive, none of Browning's work was protected, even his latest poem, so recently purchased. Many British writers, Brett told Houghton, now they were covered by American copyright, planned to seek new houses and sell their works a second time. Houghton's fury was difficult to restrain. He wrote off to A. P. Watt directing him to confer with Frederick Macmillan. The English publisher was adamant. Browning's collected works would appear under Macmillan's New York imprint.[34]

Watt at least could reassure Houghton about the majority of English authors. They had no plan to resell their works. "I unhesitatingly say that so far as I know, no author . . . has ever promulgated such a doctrine." Both Walter Besant and Rider Haggard had been "offered a very large pecuniary inducement" to leave Harper and have their works, copyrighted, come out under another aegis. Both refused. "So keen was Mr. Haggard's sense of honour that I afterwards on his account re-purchased from the Harpers the right to publish certain works of his, at a sum nearly approaching £1000. There was no copyright on any of these books,

and had Mr. Haggard wished to do so he could legally have followed the course suggested by Mr. Brett." English authors "would
treat with indignant scorn" so perfidious a plan. They "value too
highly the importance to them of the International Copyright Act,
and are too grateful to those like yourself who have been instrumental in passing it, to do anything . . . which would jeopardize it
and probably cause a return to the status quo ante."

Houghton's pleasure in the passage of the Platt-Simonds Bill was
further qualified. In the final days before its enactment, Senator
John Sherman of Ohio had entered the picture. Many years before (in 1872) Sherman, then in the House, had proposed that any
publisher be permitted "general reproduction and republication
of the works of any foreign author upon payment of five percent
royalty to the writer." Matthew Arnold effectively demonstrated
the impracticality of such a royalty scheme by picturing the poor
English author attempting to collect his "precarious and illusory
benefit" from a myriad of sources beyond the broad Atlantic. Sherman's proposal was lost in the shuffle. In 1891 he was a Senator
and a powerful one; his Anti-Trust Act had become law, one with
which the publishing fraternity would tangle in the not distant
future.[35]

In January Houghton, one of a delegation, had gone to Washington to check on the progress of the Platt-Simonds Bill. He returned to Boston confident International Copyright would soon
become law. On February 9 Senator Sherman introduced his
amendment which "authorized the importation of foreign editions
of books by American as well as foreign authors," in effect denial
of a publisher's limited, national monopoly of the right to copy,
assigned him by the author. The proposal, twice passed by the
Senate, was unacceptable to the House. On its third round in the
senior chamber it was defeated. To the liberal George Haven Putnam, "the whole episode was a noteworthy instance of slovenly and
hap-hazard legislation." Haphazard maybe, but a modification of
the Sherman amendment found its way into the bill as passed.
"Persons purchasing for use and not for sale" might import "at any
one time" two books of foreign manufacture, a minor exemption
but one open to wide abuse. Americans had shown themselves

skillful in evading the law. There was no reason to expect a change.

Importing and selling American works pirated abroad without permission of the copyright owner had always been against the law. Houghton believed the best way of enforcement was to stop such books at their port of entry. Customs officials, however, maintained no statute existed authorizing them to do so. In 1882, greatly exercised by "a little fellow out West" who was selling an English reprint of *Uncle Tom* for 10 cents, Houghton persuaded the Treasury Department to order Collectors of Customs to detain such illegal imports. He reported his success, which had cost him "a good round sum," $1000, to Clemens.

> I do not mean by this that I have had to pay anybody in the Treasury Department, but I have had to pay people who could command the attention of the Department.
>
> I believe, nevertheless, that this will do more towards stopping the importation of English reprints of American books than any appeal to the newspapers, or any suits of law which you and I may find necessary to institute, as it makes it the duty of the different Collectors to withhold these books until the permission of the owner of the copyright is obtained before entry. All that is needed now is a little practical attention on the part of your publishers, and you, who have been probably the greatest victim of this reprinting, may perhaps be able to smoke your pipe and drink your mug of beer in peace hereafter.

Vigilance was essential. How many English and Canadian reprints evaded Customs is impossible to estimate. In 1891 one George Whitney of Springfield attempted to import an English edition of *Stories from Uncle Tom's Cabin*. He said he thought the copyright had expired. Learning that it had not, he offered to pay Houghton, Mifflin a royalty. The firm refused to compromise. The books must be returned to England.[36]

The publishers who had done the most to secure the essential cooperation of the printers in securing passage of International Copyright felt betrayed by the importation exemption of the 1891 law. Joseph W. Harper told Houghton:

. . . I still feel sore over the shabby way in which you & Lippincott & Lea & W. H. Appleton & I were treated by some of our
publishing brethren in the Copyright business, where they actually voted to accept the Sherman Amendment & virtually vio-
late our agreement with the printers. I would like an autonomous
existence a little while longer — though perhaps eventually all
of us will come to some syndicate system or other, & be long-haired
philosophers with our printing offices at Brook Farm.

Speaking of threatened attempts on the part of the Copyright
League to break faith with the printers, Mr. Henry C. Lea . . .
said that the probable result of any attempt of the kind would be
the repeal of the whole measure. He added that the printers feel
rather keenly the contempt with which they have been treated &
will be quite ready to measure swords with their treacherous allies.
And this, I take it, is the way you continue to feel?[37]

Houghton, perhaps, did not reply to Harper's question. He
knew he must leave to future generations the large problems of
copyright which the Platt-Simonds Act had failed to solve. Mortality was crowding him; his concerns were becoming particular. One
month and a few days after International Copyright had been won,
Mrs. Houghton died; on May 5, Lawson Valentine went to his
reward; the following day Scudder, on his way to New York, was
stricken with erysipelas, an attack to be followed by pneumonia.
Houghton himself was troubled by an uncomfortable shortness of
breath and occasional but embarrassing narcolepsy. Here were
more than signs and portents. The institution he had created must
be prepared for another command. Each department within the
organization must be captained adequately. The New York office
was sailing smoothly under his nephew Albert F. Houghton's supervision. The Riverside Press, rattling away on Webster's *New
International* and the traditional standards, was organized for the
eventuality. On Houghton's death Mifflin would take his place.
Handsome Harry, his son, would follow Mifflin at the Press. To
ensure continuity, in 1893 his grandnephew Edward Rittenhouse
Houghton, fresh from Amherst, was taken on to be trained to step
into Harry's shoes. The Educational Department was expanding
under Wheeler's adequate direction (a Chicago office had been
opened in 1890) and the Subscription Department had a new and

vigorous manager in Charles S. Olcott. The loyal Garrison and the canny James Murray Kay clearly had years ahead of them. All was well save for the Trade Department and the *Atlantic*. Houghton clung to his idea that both should be under the direction of one man; however, even before Scudder had fallen seriously ill, it had become apparent that he must have more help than that afforded by Gibbs and Miss Francis. One man could not direct the magazine, search for new authors, prepare fresh editions of Dickens, Scott, Thoreau, and so on, as well as edit the Riverside Literature Series, the Commonwealths Series, the Cambridge Poets, and give unstinted assistance to the Educational Department.

Although the *Atlantic* was to remain with the Trade, it was agreed that a promotion manager was essential, a position promptly and effectively filled by another Mark Hopkins pupil—MacGregor Jenkins. The nagging problem was to find an editorial assistant, one who under Scudder's tutelage would eventually captain the *Atlantic*. As before, Houghton wished to find a person within his organization, one who had come up the ladder to the bridge. Houghton's estimate of men was still unerring. His choice was Francis H. Allen, a young man who had come to the Press in 1884. Allen was to serve the house for a full half century, for forty of those years as an editor whose particular concern was science, with special emphasis on nature writing, a type of book for which Houghton Mifflin has won particular distinction. However, young Frank Allen failed to impress Scudder who liked him but thought he lacked creative ability and the aggressive qualities required of an *Atlantic* editor if the magazine were even to hold its place in the increasingly competitive periodical field. Scudder sought "a young fellow who knew his generation," yet who would be sympathetic with the ideals and traditions of the firm. Between 1891 and 1895 many were considered; one or two served briefly. Because of their subsequent fame in letters a listing may be of interest: Edwin Emerson, Paul Reynolds, Gamaliel Bradford, Jr., Bliss Carman, Charles Townsend Copeland, Edmund Clarence Stedman, Royal Cortissoz, William Roscoe Thayer, and others of lesser note. These were the men Scudder pondered, but always he came back to his first choice — Mark Antony DeWolfe Howe, who had failed

of Houghton's approval in 1888, now apparently happily at work
on the *Youth's Companion,* a position Scudder had been instrumental in securing for him. Scudder had one reservation. "If he
did not stutter! I would gladly have him help me. But if he did
not stutter he would very likely not be an editor." But the young
man had "substantial qualities"; his five years with the *Companion*
showed that he could endure the tedium of editorial application,
but Howe was employed. The sands were running out. Another
illness, attacks of inexplicable deafness, and headaches reminded
Scudder of his own mortality. He hoped to have a sabbatical in
1895 before he burnt himself out. On April 1, 1893, he noted in
his diary:

> Mark Howe came to see if I would let him review some recent
> books of verse. We looked over my shelves and made up a pack-
> age for him. Then as the opportunity seemed given me, I fell
> into full talk with him over the place which I wanted him to fill.
> I tried to set forth all that was hard and irksome about the work
> and dwelt upon the severity of the discipline, yet I suspect that my
> own interest in the matter prevented me from being very disagree-
> able. At any rate the more I talked the more I could see the place
> attracted him. I cautioned him against feeling too sure and finally
> dismissed him with so strong a wish to have him come that I
> could almost think I should be the more disappointed of the two
> if he did not come . . .[38]

A little less than two weeks passed. Howe again reported at
Park Street. He had resigned from the *Companion;* Harper had
offered him a job; he wished to go to England for five weeks. Another seven days passed, during which Houghton gave Howe an
interview and fell asleep during a long stutter. The young man
was to have his holiday and begin work at the end of June. "Already my work seems lightened though I haven't got him yet,"
Scudder exulted.

During the summer, work went smoothly. Scudder perceived
his successor in this understudy and began making plans for nine
months in Europe in 1895; by then, he hoped, Howe would be
ready to assume full responsibility. In the end it was his understudy, not Scudder, who would have a European holiday. In April

1894 after nine months at his desk, the young man began having trouble with his eyes. His service thereafter was intermittent. Following a five- or six-week absence in the spring, he returned to Park Street for the summer; then his doctor ordered at least six weeks of rest. In November he departed once again for the other side. So far, Howe's tour of duty had not much relieved the sadly overpressed Scudder. In December '94, Howe became a "semi-detached" assistant, that is, he was to choose his own time with pay on an hourly basis. In March 1895, his eyes troubling him seriously, he told Scudder he must give up his work entirely. Scudder's anticipated sabbatical must be postponed, the search for an assistant renewed. Once again came the parade of names, interviews, trips to New York, and the like. Bliss Carman came as a temporary relief.

Mifflin in this last year of Houghton's life did what he could to spare his senior irritating yet essential detail. A far more brisk, impetuous, and impatient man than Houghton, he assured the harried Scudder that he was wholeheartedly behind him, that he recognized the necessity of his having an able assistant. However, Scudder must find his own man. There was urgency in his advice. Learning that Walter Hines Page had resigned as editor of the *Forum*, Scudder wrote to inquire whether he would be available as assistant editor for Houghton, Mifflin. He was, and Scudder went to New York for an interview. Although impressed by Page's force, he was assailed by doubts. Could this man run in harness with anybody? Further interviews were arranged and Scudder went to New Rochelle to meet Mrs. Page. Mifflin dined with "Scudder's friend." Page came to Boston and Houghton, even though he was now seriously ill, received him and did not fall asleep as of late he had been doing with increasing frequency. No man could in Page's dynamic presence. Houghton's estimate was unhesitating. He saw that Page was no man to sacrifice his own certain promise in service to the firm. He mistrusted "people who came in by the cabin window." The ladder was the way up. On July 31, Scudder wrote in his diary:

> In the evening I went down to see H.O.H. and had a long and decisive talk with him over Page. Decisive in that he left the

matter wholly to the rest of us, and I know the decision they have made. There was to me a certain solemnity in our talk. H.O.H. has been really unwell and felt his weakness, but he roused himself, for he felt not only the importance of the matter, but also that he had practically no voice, since he could not personally look into it, as he ordinarily would. Yet the business, the interests involved in the concern of H. M. & Co. — he cared for all this and was most earnest that *this* republic should suffer no hurt. It was clear that he was not over anxious about his personal estate; he was deeply concerned in the institution he had built up.[39]

Walter Hines Page accepted the position proffered a week later. On the afternoon of August 25, 1895, Henry Oscar Houghton died. He would never know how correct his judgment had been.

The funeral services for Henry Oscar Houghton were held in the Harvard Street Methodist Episcopal Church, Cambridge, where he had been Sunday School Superintendent for thirty years. Among his honorary pallbearers were Edmund Hatch Bennett, once his partner in H. O. Houghton & Company and now Dean of the Boston University Law School, Melancthon M. Hurd, his first partner in publishing, O. M. Baker of G. & C. Merriam, Theodore L. De Vinne of the De Vinne Press in New York, and William A. Bancroft, Mayor of Cambridge. Those attending the service included members of the Board of Aldermen and the Common Council of the City of Cambridge, a delegation of the Massachusetts Association of Master Printers, numerous representatives of the Boston trade, and employees of Park Street, New York, and the Riverside Press. Among the authors were Thomas Bailey Aldrich, John Fiske, William Dean Howells, Edmund Clarence Stedman, Kate Douglas Wiggin, and Arthur Gilman, once a salesman for Hurd & Houghton and now a regent of Radcliffe College. The simple ceremony included the singing of "Rock of Ages" and "Nearer My God to Thee." Among the many floral tributes were two that would have especially warmed Houghton's heart — seventy-two roses from his Sunday School class and, from his Riverside Press employees, a pillow of ferns, pinks, and roses with the motto *"Tout Bien ou Rien."*[40]

Press eulogies were inevitable following the death of a man who

On August 23, 1895, Henry Oscar Houghton, despite failing health, attended the christening of his first grandchild, Rosamond. In this picture, his daughter-in-law Rose, her child in her arms, sits beside him and his son is astride his horse, Dime. Two days later, the elder Houghton died.

was both publisher and public figure. The poverty of his origin, the days of his youth, his rise from journeyman to master printer to owner of a press to publisher were rehearsed. "His was a marked figure as he used to be seen walking out over the West Boston Bridge, often with Mr. Scudder, his day's work done, his cloth office bag under his arm — a man of grave and thoughtful habit, taking a long and slow and heavy step, and looking down as he walked, his mind full of the talk in which he was busy, or occupied with subjects from the scenes far away from him." His "large, broad conception of his business" had widened it into a profession. He was pictured as having a strong, rugged face, Scotch in aspect, "a granite face" of "power and invincible determination," a master of himself and life. His remarkable administration of the Riverside Press was the subject of special comment, his cooperative savings plan, the happy condition of his workers, his basic kindness,

his unpublicized generosity. Nothing less could be expected on the
death of so public a figure.[41]

The comments of his associates, not intended for general release,
help to reveal the man. Thomas Bailey Aldrich told George Woodberry, "Houghton had many very good points, but somehow I feel
less disturbed about his departure than I should feel about that of
a person less capable of looking out after number one in the next
world." Then perhaps recalling Osgood's failure, the depressions
of the past and the disasters of the present, "His shrewd business
instincts, however, were not things I ever objected to; he was a
safe man to deal with; he didn't wreck himself and everybody
else."[42]

Scudder commented:

> For thirty years now I have been associated with Mr. Houghton.
> In that time I have seen him under many conditions. I have often
> been sorely tried, and I doubt not I have tried him, but we have
> worked together and been stronger friends at the end then ever.
> He was a large-minded man and very far sighted. He was unself-
> ish too in a great sense, for strong, resolute and self-willed as he
> was he labored to build up what really has been an organism and
> to suppress himself in it. And he was a truly upright man and
> feared God.[43]

Garrison, who was Houghton's confidential clerk for twenty-five
years, wrote:

> He always respected my independence . . . Strong partisan as he
> was, he never attempted to influence or control the views or vote
> of any man in his employ . . . To none was he more generous
> & helpful in their hour of trouble than to those who had ill-used
> him, & while he could rarely conquer a prejudice against a man
> if he started out with it, & was often harshly unjust, he more than
> once atoned for it by stretching out a helping hand if the need
> came. His pride in his trade was genuine, & I never saw a trace
> of covetousness for wealth in him. His satisfaction in being a self-
> made man was devoid of vulgarity, & he was always careful to tell
> of those who had given him essential aid to his rise.
>
> The women authors all felt his personal kindness, consideration
> & sympathy, & gave him their confidence & strong friendship.

With stars like Lowell, Longfellow, Whittier & Holmes, he was rarely at ease, lacking the social graces & *savoir faire* and feeling his intellectual inferiority, but Whittier certainly liked him, & Dr. Holmes was the type of an author's loyalty to his publisher.[44]

George Harrison Mifflin paid his tribute to his senior partner four years before his death, writing when Houghton was traveling in the Near East in 1891.

> . . . your visit to Jerusalem will recall forcibly those days, when I was just beginning to realise what I must be doing when I got home — and was wondering what it would be, and whether it could amount to anything! And I want you to know from me in spite of any or all differences of view which may at any time have come between us or which may at any future time arise, it is to you I owe whatever constancy of aim or purpose I may have shown in connection with our business. The business has been in many ways such a source of happiness to me that I like to tell you this. And so along your Eastern Journey I shall have you doubly in mind both on account of old and present associations . . . I want only in this letter to thank you for your kind words and for the assurance of your affection, which is very dear to me. Goodbye again then, and may all good attend you.[45]

Henry Oscar Houghton had now gone on his western journey.

The partners of the firm during Mifflin's seniority. From left to right, seated, James Murray Kay and George Harrison Mifflin; standing, Albert F. Houghton, Henry O. Houghton, Jr., and Oscar R. Houghton.

XVI

THE FICTION BUSINESS

ALTHOUGH J. PIERPONT MORGAN, and a number of other bankers, restored confidence in the dollar by a loan of $62,000,000 to the Cleveland government in the summer of 1895, the country's economy did not regain its vitality until after McKinley's election in 1896. Publishing was perhaps less seriously affected in this depression than some other businesses, but naturally among Houghton, Mifflin authors and within the trade questions arose as to what would happen to the company now its founder and recognized driving force had been removed from the scene.[1]

Except to his immediate associates, George Harrison Mifflin was unknown. He had held no public office, had served on no committees, had made no pronouncements on International Copyright, discounts, or other large publishing questions. However, to all inquiries that came to his desk, the new head of the house was reassuringly confident. Business would continue as usual at both Park Street and the Press. Houghton "had prepared for his going as much as was possible." His capital was to remain with the firm. His son and executor Harry would now take charge of Riverside. So smoothly did the wheels run that at the first staff meeting following his death, Henry Oscar Houghton's name was not mentioned. Obsequies had been paid. Business was the order of the day.

Mifflin had turned fifty in May 1895. For twenty-five years he had served his senior loyally and well. He was now eager to leave his mark on the firm which had so long borne his name. Among his associates he was universally liked. "There could be no more delightful man to work with & under, & his prompt decisive ways are a contrast to Mr. Houghton's deliberate habits . . . no man is less opinionated than he, none more ready to hear & carefully weigh opposing views . . ." Garrison reported to his brother Wendell. His "energy & vim, and inspiring force" charmed the confidential clerk. Mifflin was both positive and aggressive. Garrison was sure cooperation throughout the ranks was inevitable. Scudder's evaluation was more guarded. Mifflin, he thought, would make a fine leader provided "his enthusiasms did not carry him out of the reach of reason." Responsibility, he hoped, would change his impetuosity to mastery and broad judgments. His instinctive modesty, indeed diffidence, had a certain charm. Experience in command should bring assurance. Although he was impatient, spontaneous, and avid for commercial success and although he lacked Houghton's large philosophy of publishing as part of the pattern of the nation, he was nevertheless meticulous in fine points of honor. He was also sympathetic to the problems of the individual. Mifflin hoped to give his various department heads more rein than Houghton had ever allowed.[2]

The Riverside employees at a party in celebration of Mifflin's birthday had presented him with a Dutch clock. To the delight of his affectionate audience, "Mifflin responded in a short characteristic explosion in which he said he loved the Press and was ready to live and die for Riverside." For a quarter of a century he had worked for his plant with infectious enthusiasm. Improvements had been frequent and by 1890 the old Cambridge Alms House Estate had been changed beyond recognition. The wooden tenement on the edge of the property had been torn down, the grounds enlarged and laid out in parklike lawns and driveways, and all buildings had been equipped with incandescent lights, a boon to the workers, who had suffered from the heat and fumes of gas illumination. In 1891 Mifflin reported to his senior partner, who was abroad, of his satisfaction in Riverside's "general tidiness," but "I cannot express to you how lonely I sometimes feel in going around to think you are not here to share the pleasure of the improvements . . ." To make vivid the new machines being introduced, he wrote with ardor of the recently acquired automatic feeders. "It is I think, without question the most wonderful machine in our establishment, feeding as it does these enormous sheets of paper, 35 by 48, more accurately than can be done by hand into the folding machine. The combination automatic feed and folder takes the place, I figure, of sixteen girls, and does the work with greater accuracy." The automatic feeder proving effective, two more were introduced, these for cylinder presses. Then there was a new folding machine that did 20,000 full-size sheets a day; the old hand-fed machine had folded but 7500. There were new sewing machines, two especially designed for the Webster *International* and also a new dry press machine, a cutter, and a hydraulic signature press, all marvels of invention. The typesetting machine proved difficult to master. The operators required prolonged training. At first they could do only 15,000 to 20,000 ems per day. "We are, however, gaining now daily, and are keeping an accurate account of exactly what the machine does day by day, and its expenses as compared with hand production. The showing, which was at first unsatisfactory . . . is improving, the result of the last day's work being 32,000 ems, — a saving over hand production of from 25 to 40%." Mifflin anticipated that eventually the typesetting machine would show at the very least a yearly $1200 profit as against the cost of hand labor, done primarily by girls at 33 cents per thousand ems.[3]

Delighted as he was with the miracles of automation and although Riverside's equipment included some fifty presses of various types, Mifflin was especially pleased with three second-hand Adams presses he had picked up for $500, a real bargain, he thought. These would be valuable for short runs. Houghton, Mifflin was proud of its catalogue of 3000 titles. Many of these books were in but occasional demand. Better to keep a work available than let it go out of print. The Adams presses could produce runs of 150 or 200 economically. Authors of dying books or of new ones with a limited market garnered minor copyright returns because of this policy. During the depression production of small editions of standards, for which there was always a demand, kept compositors, binders, and others on the payroll.[4]

In 1893 Houghton had confessed to Scudder that he sometimes regretted the enlargement of his printing interests to include the risks and responsibilities of publishing. "There was a little sadness in his tone as he reflected on what he might have done if he had stuck to his own trade of printing." John Wilson's University Press, a victim of the panic, would have fallen into his hands; his contracts with the Merriams, the American Tract Society, the Government, and other sources of rich revenue would have been enough. He would have been spared the essential but irksome details of tending restive, jealous, suspicious authors, the irritation and sometimes expensive litigation resulting from defective copyrights and piracy, the problems of distribution and the unpredictable fluctuations of the market, especially for new and possibly ephemeral books.[5]

Mifflin, on the other hand, in spite of his devotion to Riverside, was convinced that in publishing not printing lay the golden reward. He pointed out to Scudder that all John Wilson had had during years of work was a modest living. Thomas Niles, head of Roberts Brothers, in contrast, in 1894 had died a rich man, among his assets a first mortgage on Wilson's press. Mifflin expressed these views in 1896. He did not then know that Niles had failed to prepare for his exit the business which he directed, that in 1891 he had ordered the books of the firm destroyed, that his death so weakened Roberts Brothers that its failure was inevitable, that its assets would be purchased by Little, Brown in 1898 for an estimated $250,000.[6]

One of Houghton's basic publishing tenets had been to work over old material, especially in hard times. This principle served the house well in the depression following the '93 panic even as it had assured the house more than survival in earlier periods of financial stress. In April 1895 Mifflin was pleased to report, "The last half of 1894 pulled us well out of the hole in which we were placed by the panic and the succeeding twelve months." Although few new books appeared on the list, net profits were $84,000.63.

> This matter of new books comes up again and again in our several comparisons, and it is one which we must keep before us with unceasing vigilance, or the absence of new books will make itself seriously felt in time. Of course, there is a limit to what we can do in the way of making over old editions. We have not however,

by any means reached the limit . . . But we must keep a sharp lookout for new American writers . . . Our general sales feels [sic] the absence of new books more than any other part of the business, and in turn this reacts on the printing office and the bindery.[7]

Eighteen ninety-six was Mifflin's first full year of administration. He was determined it should be a banner one, depressed though the market might be. Many publishers cut down their lists. Not so Houghton, Mifflin. The *Literary World* greeted the firm's fall announcement ecstatically: "Think of it, a hundred and thirty volumes at one dump in these hard times! Standards and experiments, juveniles and those most problematical of literary risks — poems, biographies and sports, histories and novels, Phelps and Fields, James and Jewett, Harte and Hayes, Wiggin and Wilson, Thaxter and Thoreau, Bates and Burroughs, Lathrop and Lothrop, a pair of Harrises and a trio of Lowells — a long and brilliant procession most certainly. Stand by and see it pass."

Among the names listed no significant new authors appeared. There were however a number of fresh books which would prove worthy of the collected editions the firm was proud to provide loyal authors, some even which might eventually graduate from Trade to Education as examples of classic American literature: Lafcadio Hearn's *Kokoro: Hints and Echoes of Japanese Inner Life,* Henry James's *The Spoils of Poynton,* Sarah Orne Jewett's *The Country of the Pointed Firs,* John Burroughs' *Whitman: A Study,* and Woodrow Wilson's *Mere Literature.* But these were not the titles that set Mifflin's eyes sparkling, his boisterous laugh resounding through the offices at 4 Park Street.[8]

He had mastered Houghton's sound instruction in the value of standards, tool books, and school texts. Such would continue the core of the firm's list, but he wanted also books that would set people talking, books he could boast about. He realized his wish in a series of novels, each achieving remarkable sales for "a neat and Houghton, Mifflin book": In 1896 Elizabeth Stuart Phelps Ward's *A Singular Life,* F. Hopkinson Smith's *Tom Grogan,* and Kate Douglas Wiggin's *Marm Lisa;* in 1897 Paul Leicester Ford's *Story of an Untold Love;* in 1898 Gilbert Parker's *Battle of the Strong,*

F. Hopkinson Smith's *Caleb West*, Kate Douglas Wiggin's *Penelope's Progress*, and Mary Johnston's *Prisoners of Hope*. In two years or less, all these titles went over 10,000, some a long way over. The twentieth century came in with a bang. Within a few weeks of publication, Miss Johnston's second novel, *To Have and To Hold*, passed 135,000.

Mifflin might have had something to boast about in 1899 also, had Walter Hines Page been as willing as an Appleton editor proved to undertake a prodigious task of revision and cutting. Edward Noyes Westcott, a retired banker and invalid, even as he had tried it on a number of other publishers, had submitted his voluminous manuscript of *David Harum* to Park Street. The first reading fell to Miss Francis. She reported the tale as a character study of a "sort of rough diamond, who does good by stealth & blushes to find it fame, who is great in horse-trade, who chews a good deal of tobacco, & tells stories from his own experience, chapter after chapter, with some humor & a great deal of bad English." Page may have accepted Miss Francis' summary, but he threw his weight against publication on the grounds of the novel's "extraordinary and impractical" length; "to stand any chance of success," it would have to be cut by at least a quarter. Relying on his subordinates' opinions, Mifflin initialed the report. The manuscript, returned to its author, continued its rounds of publishers finally arriving at Appleton. Here the editor, realizing the possibilities of the story provided its focus were sharpened, undertook the pruning Page had perceived as essential. Thus benefited by editorial know-how, *David Harum* sold 500,000 in nineteen months. Mifflin, in a letter of mild rebuke, drew Page's attention to his editorial failure. "I find the book very much liked here in Boston . . ." he complained, "and I had a long talk with a lady last night about it, and she was very loud in its praise and could not understand how we could have allowed such a book to slip through our fingers. I myself have not read it, but I propose to do so, and am hoping that I dislike it and thus become reconciled to its loss."[9]

Houghton, Mifflin editors had made and would continue to make, inevitably, errors in judging manuscripts. In 1899 Scudder had damned Laura E. Richards' *Captain January* because it was "strained, affected, neither fish, flesh, nor foul." The book was finally published by Estes & Lauriat in the fall of 1890, but only after Mrs. Richards had tried "every reputable publisher" of her acquaintance. While it did not achieve the sales of the sensations of the decade, it developed a steady demand, selling 100,000 in eight years. Sixty years after publication its total was reckoned at 288,000. Other manuscripts reported on unfavorably and returned to their authors included Ambrose Bierce's stories, because their core was horror. They lacked the strength inherent in most tales of terror. Albert Payson Terhune's fiction was judged crude and breezy, "doomed to a short life and a quick burial." Clyde Fitch's narratives had no dramatic power. The incidents were hackneyed, the characters lifeless. Frank Norris' *Yvernelle: A Legend of Feudal France* (a long romantic poem) was immature. The author had no future.[10]

There were, of course, many submissions from authors whose names would never make literary history. Victor Pryor's "Uncle Sam's Cabins: the White Slavery of the North and West" was thrown out as "rubbish"; Frank Carleton Long's "A Man with a Sobriquet" must be "disinfected" before it could be read; George Harold's "One of the Least of These" was "a tale of shame unskillfully told." Some of the rejected authors took umbrage. One, William C. Dix, threatened to shoot Houghton, Mifflin's editor. Although finally sent to Danvers Insane Asylum, he continued to send excited letters and rambling manuscripts. For the poor man's sake, Scudder was sorry that he had been incarcerated; for his own he was relieved. A dead editor on the third floor of Park Street was not the kind of sensation Mifflin was after.[11]

Manuscripts of the sort Dix submitted took little time to evaluate. As Dr. Johnson observed, "It is not necessary to eat the whole ox to tell the beef is tough." Certain submissions were not so readily judged. Numerous readings and inter-office debates were required. The editor was not always the final arbiter. Scudder was eager to accept Owen Wister's *The Dragon of Wantley;* he thought it a glorious bit of fooling, but he qualified his recommendation by admitting the narrative lacked bite and the enduring qualities of satire. Houghton read the manuscript and vetoed Scudder's rec-

ommendation. Page wished the house to publish George Santayana's *The Sense of Beauty*, but he showed doubt of its commercial
value by suggesting it be taken on commission. Garrison voted
against the proposition. Bliss Perry found Upton Sinclair's *Prince
Hagen* fascinating because of its sincerity, idealism, and rapid development. However, he thought the author might be a fool or
crank. Mrs. Perry read the story and didn't like it at all. Mac-
Gregor Jenkins liked it and Ben Ticknor thought it might prove a
David Harum, but another reader condemned it absolutely. Mifflin read it and could reach no decision. Scudder, who was on vacation, was called on to interrupt his holiday and help the battery
of judges at Park Street. His vote was negative and the manuscript
was finally returned to Sinclair.[12]

Houghton, Mifflin's success in the fiction business with such
novels as *Story of an Untold Love* and *To Have and To Hold* was
by no means unique. The decade of the '90s, in spite of the depression, the Spanish-American War, and the bicycle craze, was
notable not only for the number of novels produced, but also for
such sales as the publishing fraternity had never before enjoyed.
There had been isolated books which achieved sensational sales —
Uncle Tom's Cabin, Ben-Hur, Looking Backward — but never
before had so many houses been washed by a Niagara of sales at one
time. Production increased remarkably in 1895. In 1894, 729
novels had appeared; the next year the total was 1114. This was
the decade of Barrie's *The Little Minister* and *Sentimental
Tommy*, of Anthony Hope's *The Prisoner of Zenda*, of Henryk
Sienkiewicz's *Quo Vadis?*, of Stephen Crane's *The Red Badge of
Courage*, of Charles Monroe Sheldon's *In His Steps*, of James Lane
Allen's *The Choir Invisible*, of Winston Churchill's *Richard Car-
vel*, and Charles Major's *When Knighthood Was in Flower*. Big
sellers did not ensure solvency, however. The house of Harper had
its share of popular fiction — Hardy's *Tess of the D'Urbervilles*,
Lew Wallace's *The Prince of India*, and Du Maurier's *Trilby*.
Nonetheless in 1899 its assets were up for bids, its largest creditor
the house of Morgan. In the following year D. Appleton found
itself in comparable trouble despite the sales of *The Red Badge of
Courage* and *David Harum*. According to the *Critic*, prosperity
had been the company's undoing.[13]

George Mifflin found such failures as those of Harper and Appleton melancholy object lessons. Unsound business methods were the root cause, in his view. Such publishing disasters colored his dealings with authors. Over and over again he argued, sometimes shrilly, that an author should stay with one house so that his books could be worked systematically and cumulatively. If indeed Park Street's rates were lower than those of New York, Houghton, Mifflin's literary traditions should not be lightly brushed aside. In New York, the methods of Wall Street obtained; the dollar dominated negotiations. In Boston, publishers were gentlemen. Some authors listened and were persuaded that to leave the good old Angel Inn was perhaps a sin. Others, less docile, deserted Park Street, always for the same cogent reason. The oats in another barn were served with a more lavish hand.

This was a time of extraordinary pay scales as well as sales. Robert Louis Stevenson was reported to be writing a series of letters from the South Seas for the New York *Sun* for $10,000. The *Bookman* announced that Kipling secured $12,000 for serial rights plus an advance of $15,000 for *Captains Courageous*, that Mrs. Humphry Ward won $18,000 from the *Century* for *Sir George Tressady*, that her total take from serial rights and royalties would probably come to $60,000. Lew Wallace was known to have asked $100,000 down for his *Prince of India*, a demand Harper compromised by assuring Wallace an annual $10,000 for ten years. Rumor had it that Scribner paid James Barrie $50,000 for *Sentimental Tommy*. Some of these stories were probably leaked intentionally. Authors would be attracted to a house with a reputation for generosity. Publishers' courtesy was no bar to an author's shopping around. "If all the stories with regard to prices paid successful authors of the present were true, our bankers would take to writing novels," the *Literary World* commented. Such bruited rewards made Houghton, Mifflin's rates seem picayune, especially to an author who had arrived. The worn argument that he should keep all his books with one house failed to persuade if he found another publisher who would pay him a couple of thousand more for serial rights and afford a large advance on a 20 percent royalty. To complicate matters, Harper and a number of other houses with periodicals had begun to make magazine acceptance conditional on book rights, a departure from the good old bookish ways that drove Mifflin into a spluttering rage.[14]

Of the novelists who gave Mifflin something to boast about, three were new; three had been associated with the firm for many years. The new ones were Gilbert Parker, Paul Leicester Ford, and Mary Johnston. The two men were strays, strangers in the Houghton, Mifflin stable, hoping for brighter ribbons than they had yet won. Parker had been given cordial welcome to the *Atlantic* in 1894, when he submitted "Three Commandments in the Vulgar Tongue." On his offer to write a serial for $2500, Scudder was delighted. He hoped also to secure the book, but Houghton, true to his understanding of trade courtesy, was reluctant. Since Appleton had recently published Parker, he would be advised to stay with that house. After its *Atlantic* appearance, the author's *Seats of the Mighty* came out under the New York imprint, to appear in the *Bookman*'s list of books most in demand in 1896. However, Parker, whose books were distributed among a variety of publishers, had begun to think of bringing them all together under one colophon. He inquired whether Houghton, Mifflin would take his next book. If all went well, perhaps he would settle down at Park Street. For his *Battle of the Strong* he asked $3000 from the *Atlantic* and 15 percent on the book, terms reluctantly granted. On the basis of the *Battle*'s sales, over 20,000 in less than three months, his next request was for $5000 and a 20 percent royalty. The firm seriously considered the proposition. In 1890 it had paid that much for Frank Stockton's *House of Martha*, which after its *Atlantic* run, in a year sold in excess of 4000. Gilbert Parker had proved he could win a far larger market.[15]

Negotiations were protracted. The author's condition that the *Atlantic* editor agree to publication without seeing the manuscript made the Park Street administration gag. In the old days, to accept a serial without seeing the text, to receive chapters seriatim, had been usual, at least for writers of established reputation. Under Mifflin's dispensation, to the fury of Mary N. Murfree and a number of others, this custom as far as possible was to be curtailed. The innovation was doomed to failure, but Mifflin for a time was determined to enforce it. After all, if an editor had only a general idea of the length of the serial, to plan his magazine for the year was difficult. Frank Stockton's *House of Martha* had proved too short; Henry James's *The Tragic Muse* had overrun its allotted space. Also the end might betray the beginning. It might be risqué, even as Hardy's *Two on a Tower* had proved.

Houghton, Mifflin need not have debated the matter. The firm didn't have a chance of keeping Parker. Harper offered him $10,000 for serial rights and a 20 percent royalty with a $5000 advance on publication. Ultimately, because the author wanted his books "under one banner in a uniform and definitive edition," he notified Park Street that the New York house was to be henceforth his official publisher.

Paul Leicester Ford was even more of a maverick than Parker. Although only thirty-one when he offered his six-part *Story of an Untold Love* to the *Atlantic,* he had already established himself as a historian and bibliographer of note and a novelist of promise. In 1894 Henry Holt had published his *The Honorable Peter Sterling,* a slow starter, but once on its way it sold well, so well that Ford was soon critical of Holt, who he claimed failed to keep the booksellers supplied with his book. When he sought out Houghton, Mifflin, the firm assured him he would have no reason to complain of its distribution.[16]

Ford came at a bargain price — 15 percent on the book and $1000 for the *Atlantic's* serial rights. *The Story of an Untold Love* sold 13,000 in its first year, almost 30,000 in two, and shortly Ford was claiming that his new publisher's distribution was as poor as Holt's. For his next book, he thought, he had better try another publisher. Mifflin made what he considered an exceptional offer — $2500 for serial rights, 15 percent on the first 10,000; 17½ percent up to 25,000; 20 percent thereafter, English rights to be secured. Ford held out for more. Houghton, Mifflin doubled its ante for serial rights. During negotiations the author had been shopping. Dodd, Mead outbid Park Street — $6500 and 20 percent. Paul Leicester Ford was out of the Houghton, Mifflin stable. The novel — *Janice Meredith* — sold 200,000 in three months, and the *Critic* reported that at one point for fifteen days, Ford was receiving $1000 a day in royalties. For the loss of *Janice Meredith,*

Mifflin consoled himself and his partners, "The fact is [he wrote] these authors have the most exorbitant ideas, and publishers seem perfectly willing to indulge them." Ford, he thought, had "handled his cards skillfully, not to say sharply. For my part, I think we are well rid of what might have proved an entangling alliance." The alliance would not have endured for long. In the summer of 1902 while *Janice Meredith* continued its gratifying sales, Malcolm Ford, a disinherited brother, shot Paul Leicester and then turned the pistol on himself.

The third writer new to Houghton, Mifflin was a Southerner and an unknown. When Mary Johnston's *Prisoners of Hope* arrived at Park Street, it was given a first reading by two young men new to the editorial staff; carried away by Mary Johnston's tale, they recommended it to Page. He too recognized its appeal, "reading paragraphs aloud and slapping the crisp manuscript to enforce his commendation." Miss Johnston was signed on at 10 percent, and Page, learning she had begun another romantic novel, made a point of calling on her in Birmingham on his next trip south. He brought back the incomplete manuscript of *To Have and To Hold. Prisoners of Hope,* without benefit of magazine appearance, had sold almost 5000 in its first year. Houghton, Mifflin offered 15 percent on the new novel and $3500 for serial rights. Before *To Have and To Hold* had completed its *Atlantic* appearance, in anticipation of New York bids for Miss Johnston's next novel, Mifflin saw to it that the author was given an appreciative extra $1000 as a Christmas gift, merited recognition of present and future popularity. The book, published in February 1900, by the end of August had sold over 200,000. It had also the pleasant effect of stimulating sales of *Prisoners of Hope.* From both her books the author had earned a tidy $52,529.72. By the end of the year *To Have and To Hold* was in its 275th thousand.[17]

Gilbert Parker and Paul Leicester Ford left Houghton, Mifflin because Harper and Dodd, Mead offered more money. After the success of *To Have and To Hold,* Mary Johnston too was wooed with New York offers of $10,000, even as Mifflin had anticipated. However, he was able to convince Miss Johnston that to keep her books under one flag was to her advantage even though all he would afford for her next novel, *Audrey*, was $7500 (a fancy price according to Garrison) and a graduated royalty — 15 percent up to 25,000, 20 percent thereafter. Since advance orders for the book were in excess of 100,000, both publisher and author were soon reaping their rewards.

Mifflin made remarkable efforts to keep writers long associated with the house content, contributing to their charitable causes and giving them the treatment royal when they arrived at Park Street. Complaint as to rates might well bring adjustment, even though Garrison protested, "These authors are ready to drink the life-blood of publishers." When Sarah Orne Jewett carped at the price she was paid for an *Atlantic* story, she was sent an extra $50. In Christmas notes, Mifflin gave cheering reports of sales; Miss Jewett's *Pointed Firs* was in its sixth thousand; Mrs. Fields's *Authors and Friends* in its fifth. But surely his most extraordinary gesture was hopping on his brand new bicycle for a spin to Newton Centre to cheer on the restive and repetitively complaining Elizabeth Stuart Phelps Ward. The trip was obviously worth the effort, for on his return he reported jubilantly, ". . . . it is much quicker coming from Newton down the hills and with the wind than vice versa and modesty alone prevents me from mentioning the time it took me. I will say however that thirty-five minutes is nowhere." Perhaps Mifflin's excursion is one explanation for a survey of booksellers which the New York *Times* shortly undertook in search of an answer to the crucial question, "Do bicycles hurt books?"[18]

Elizabeth Stuart Phelps, who having married in 1888 was now Mrs. Herbert D. Ward, had won Houghton's gratitude in 1880 by choosing to keep her immensely popular books with the new house rather than going with Osgood. She served the firm faithfully, producing with her facile pen at least fifteen books in as many years. Her *Singular Life,* published in October 1895, by December 1896 was in its 38th thousand. Inevitably, tempting offers came from New York. Although Mrs. Ward protested fondness for the "old fashioned way," her need for money outweighed her affection. Might she have an advance, she asked Mifflin, and at least 20 percent on her next book — *The Story of Jesus Christ*? She had heard William Dean Howells was getting more. He was obviously pros-

pering even though Houghton, Mifflin and Harper shared his
books. What would be the harm in her following a similar pattern? Mifflin replied in haste:

> We wish to do everything in our power to have you feel that it is
> to your interest to keep on in the "same old-fashioned way" as you
> term it. The "unattached" method is not all it appears to be on
> the surface. You speak of Howells getting for example 20 per-
> cent and being a "rolling stone." The first suggestion is I am sure
> a mistake, and I think Howells never made a more fatal false step
> than when he entered upon that fatal rolling stone policy. His
> books now simply don't sell, and he finds doors once so hospitably
> open now closed to him. I may say to you in strictest confidence
> that we recently had the offer of bringing together all his books
> for a final "definitive" Edition, which had it been made and sold
> by the methods we had in mind should have brought him in a
> permanent and steady income; but we declined the offer (though
> the copyright would not have been over half the sum you name)
> and this because owing to his methods, he has written himself out,
> has so scattered his works that he has killed the goose so to speak
> that "laid the golden egg!" He is almost the only one of "our
> authors" who thought he saw his interest in the "highest bid"
> policy, and the results in his case have been quite disasterous to
> his permanent place in literature and I believe also to his personal
> happiness.[19]

This letter, written in July 1897, the year of Howells' *The Land-
lord at Lion's Head,* failed to convince Mrs. Ward. On the evidence, the author had neither written himself out nor killed his
goose. An advance of $4000 and a 20 percent royalty proved more
persuasive. *The Story of Jesus Christ* and a number of other of
Mrs. Ward's books came out under Houghton, Mifflin's imprint,
but she continued critical and demanding. The firm's advertising
she thought too conservative. Mifflin was reluctant and cautious
in meeting her requests for advances. A break came in 1906.
Harper was to have her next book. Alden had written her, ". . .
under no circumstances will we publish now, a serial in our periodicals unless such serial is accompanied by book rights . . . We
make no exceptions to this rule."

Although Alden's policy was one followed by Houghton, Mifflin during the few years Page controlled the *Atlantic,* after 1900 Mifflin insisted his firm make no such restrictive demands. He recognized, however, that magazine appearance was a financial necessity for most writers. To his writers for whom the *Atlantic* had no space, and possibly no liking, he suggested serialization in such periodicals as *McClure's, Scribner's,* or the *Ladies' Home Journal,* "where this unpleasant question of coupled book and serial rights would not arise." If driven to negotiate with Harper, his authors should make clear that appearance in one of that firm's periodicals was not to be construed "as a possible entering wedge for severing . . . long and friendly relations" with Park Street.[20]

Mrs. Ward's criticism of Houghton, Mifflin's advertising was not an isolated case. Similar complaints will undoubtedly be found in the archives of all publishers. Houghton, Mifflin had been subject to such attacks from the beginning, but they came with increasing frequency after 1895 and the era of the "boomed" book. To many a writer, that the market for his book had been exhausted was incredible. All that was required was a little pushing; sales would then double. Neither the merits of the work nor the taste of potential readers entered his calculations. When Sarah Orne Jewett's *The Tory Lover* surpassed in sales those of any of her previous books, passing 12,000 in three months, she pleaded for more advertising. Mifflin protested that the company had already spent so much in that department that the firm's margin of profit had been reduced to the vanishing point. She countered by offering to contribute $500. Mifflin declined the offer. The firm itself would be willing to spend that amount if it would do any good. Five hundred dollars would be a drop in the bucket for the program she envisioned, nor would such a program reap the reward she anticipated.[21]

When his authors plagued him about advertising, they touched Mifflin on a sensitive spot. He had wanted something to boast about. His novelists had met his need. Advertising is a form of boasting. In 1881 this department reported an expenditure of something over $30,000; in 1895, over $67,000. For the fiscal year April 1900 to April 1901, the figure climbed to $98,770.94, the

peak for some years to come. Responsibility for advertising had
been largely Azariah Smith's, whom Mifflin regarded as "one of
the ablest in the business." However, because he'd been at the job
ever since 1856 when he joined Ticknor & Field's staff, Mifflin
feared that Smith was inclined to travel in well-worn ruts. He was
given as an assistant a recent Harvard graduate and new employee
— Roger Livingston Scaife. Houghton, Mifflin's advertising was
to be conducted "with the same care and thoroughness" that had
made the manufacturing department outstanding. Layouts were
to be studied with the same painstaking attention as that given
dummies. "What I want to do [Mifflin advised] is while giving
strength and vigor to our advertising to keep it free from methods
associated with patent medicine and Pears Soap, which some publishers seem to be striving to equal or surpass." He wished dignified announcements rather than "howling" spreads. He planned
to find out whether there was any perceptible relation between advertising expenditures and sales. Garrison embodied the results
of the firm's study of the problem in a letter to his nephew Oswald
Villard.

> This whole matter of newspaper advertising is one of the most
> puzzling & baffling with which publishers have to deal. There is
> almost no way of telling what benefit or return we get from any
> particular medium, & when we occasionally try a test advertis-
> ment in a single paper . . . the results seem absolutely *nil*. Again,
> tabulating the advertising cost on any particular book with pro-
> ceeds of sales, or the gross advertising of any particular year with
> the gross sales of that year, there seems to be no relation between
> the two. We have increased the advertising & seen the sales fall
> off; we have cut down the advertising & seen the sales increase.
> We have sometimes spent as much, sometimes as much again, on
> a book as the total receipts from sales, while another book has
> sold handsomely with little or no advertising. Last year's experi-
> ence was an eye-opener, when we came to our annual analysis of
> advertising & sales, & we are retrenching heavily & selling, I be-
> lieve, just as many books! I know that advertising is the life of
> the newspapers, but it may also be the death of the publishers
> if not done with consumate prudence & judgment. More & more
> we incline to believe that formal newspaper advertisements &

announcements are the least effective way of making a book go. Mouth to mouth praise counts far more. The personal interest of salesmen in large bookstores is of material value. I do not question that we have wasted from $10,000 to $25,000 annually in advertising for many years past.

For the following year (1901–1902) Houghton, Mifflin's advertising budget was reduced by over $23,000.[22]

One of Scaife's theories was that window displays were a quick and relatively inexpensive way to capture a reader's fancy. Descriptions and pictures of locally arranged retailers' windows could be sent to other outlets throughout the country as demonstrations in forwarding a particular Houghton, Mifflin book. He had opportunity to prove the effectiveness of his idea not only in the windows of local bookshops such as the Old Corner, but also at Park Street itself. In 1901 the firm undertook to operate its own shop.

For some years Mifflin had been considering moving his offices from Park Street to more modern and efficient quarters. One possibility was the new building next to the Athenaeum on Beacon Street. The proposal was looked on with horror by such old hands as Scudder, Garrison, and Azariah Smith. In the end the decision was to refurbish 4 Park and to extend the quarters by taking over the first floor, up to this time occupied by another tenant. To a "heathenish punster" the new bookroom, as the firm called it, with its ceiling-high black walnut bookcases, ebony center table and armchairs, and high walnut settles, suggested the place be called "Boston Blackwoods." At least on cold days an open fire crackled on the hearth and in any weather two graceful, arched windows permitted light and a satisfying view of the Common. These windows Scaife arranged for the opening of the shop on December 19, working until after midnight the day before. The result of his efforts quite "bowled over" Mifflin, who found the display "fascinating, simple, and effective." Opened in time to catch the last of the holiday trade, the room was crowded from morning to night. The head of the firm entered into the venture with characteristic enthusiasm, sometimes selling books himself, five dollars' worth on the first day, fifty dollars' worth four days later. The featured book in Scaife's display was Mary Johnston's *Audrey*.[23]

Roger L. Scaife's 1902 window display of Mary Johnston's *Audrey* in the new bookroom at 4 Park Street.

Cutting down on newspaper advertising, as Houghton, Mifflin now intended, was no way to keep authors happy. Many of them kept careful tab on the extent to which their books were being pushed. To a writer like F. Hopkinson Smith, news of Mary Johnston's handsome sales was infuriating. That his *Caleb West* had failed to approach her record even though it had been on the market two years was his publisher's fault. Mifflin, he believed, was ignorant of the fundamentals of his business. He was pocketing profits that should be spent in bruiting the works of F. Hopkinson Smith.

F. Hopkinson Smith, architect, engineer, and contractor, had become identified with Houghton, Mifflin in the 1880s as an illustrator. Not until he was forty-eight did he attempt authorship, and then at Scudder's suggestion he prepared a text to go with some of his travel sketches. In those days he had protested, "I sorter kinder look on you all as *my firm*. My object is not to get money out of you or myself or anybody else. If anybody thinks that let them try it on." When his *Colonel Carter of Cartersville* started its run in the *Century,* he wrote Scudder, "You were the first man who encouraged me to write and who understood what I was driving at. Had not your kindly words reached me . . . after the first part of 'Wellworn Roads' was laid on your desk I doubt whether I could have gone on with any degree of confidence in myself or the result. Now will you do some more Missionary Work for me? Will you read 'Carter' as it appears in 'The Century' and give me a prod now and then when I wander out of the road? Not a tickle, but a *prod.*"[24]

His next novel, *Tom Grogan,* also ran in the *Century,* but, as in the case of *Colonel Carter,* was published by Houghton, Mifflin. For the *Colonel,* Smith received 10 percent; for subsequent books, 15 percent. By 1894 his *Atlantic* page rate had reached $15. And it was his *Atlantic* rate which began the trouble. The *Century* had paid $1600 for *Tom Grogan.* Smith's demand from the *Atlantic* of $5000 for *Caleb West* (a six-number story) was "enough to paralyze any sober-minded publisher." Its appearance in the *Atlantic* would not increase the magazine's circulation, Mifflin was certain, and he wrote Smith, "The truth is, strictly between us, that few people read serials in the magazines. They appear for a double purpose. In the first place, they serve as announcement cards for different magazines, and in the next place they help out the authors in their cash receipts. But so far as we have been able to study the problem, no serial published in any magazine, certainly no serial published in the Atlantic, ever had any influence on the circulation of the magazine, whereas published in book form the sale has often been large and immediate." The firm's offer of $3000 Smith accepted. Persuaded against his better judgment that he should keep his books with one publisher, he even allowed Houghton, Mifflin another book, a collection of short stories, but that was the last. True, he suggested the firm publish *The Fortunes of Oliver Horn,* but his price was $10,000 for serial rights, 15 percent up to 25,000; after that his publishers must be content with a 20 percent commission. Mifflin protested that such terms would land his firm in receivership. Five thousand dollars was the limit.[25]

Smith had a grudge. Although *Caleb West* had sold 83,000

(50,000 in paper) in two years, he regarded Houghton, Mifflin's handling of the book a "dead failure." It should have passed 100,000. Moreover, after original costs had been met, an author of his reputation should have a larger share of the profits than his publisher. A New York publisher had told him that Houghton, Mifflin's profit per volume on *Caleb* was probably 34 cents. He figured the firm had realized from his nine books between $35,000 and $45,000. Reduce your profits to 30 cents a volume and spend $2000 in additional advertising, Smith advised.

This he claimed was to be the "new finance, — not the finance that has kept the men poor who really made the literature of our country and whose work today is really making the incomes of many of our publishers . . ."[26]

When Mifflin heard that at one of the Twelfth Night meetings of the Century Club, F. Hopkinson Smith had appeared in the dress of Kaiser Wilhelm, his long mustaches waxed to an upward turn, and in his speech of the evening had said, "I am a man of peace; I vant a piece of Morocco; I vant a piece of China; I vant a piece of every country that I have not the whole of alretty," his Boston publisher perhaps agreed.[27]

Although Smith transferred his business to Scribner, Houghton, Mifflin continued to publish the author's books already in its hands, finally putting all nine in a uniform edition. An office boy and future editor of the Boston house — Robert Newton Linscott — watching the boisterous greetings exchanged between publisher and author assumed a bond of fellowship; in reality the bond was less than contract deep. Linscott did not know what went on behind closed doors. Mifflin regarded Smith as cantankerously unpleasant. The banter between the two smelled acridly of money. Their arguments over royalties, percentages, and profits never ceased, profits which Mifflin asserted would "produce in the sinful a smile." Smith taunted in reply, "You're all right, George. You have a heart full of generous spontaneity . . . If I did not know you as well as I do I should think that after your good impulses had bubbled up your commercialism closed in around the nozzle and either strangled the bubble or else strained the outflow through the mesh of environment . . ."[28]

One source of dispute was Smith's share of the profits from a scheme for 25-cent reprints of four of his volumes to be done by the Regent Press at a 2½-cent royalty, Houghton, Mifflin and the author to share and share alike, standard practice in such deals. At first Smith refused to abate his royalties. Grosset & Dunlap, another reprint house, he considered "ghouls and scavengers." Their editions sold for 50 cents.

> Now comes along this last pirate, who knocks the stuffing out of all their prices . . . and then gets his fine work in on the author and pays him one and one-quarter cents. Thank God! that our debased currency does not go lower than a copper cent, bearing the inscription, "In God We Trust," so we probably have reached the bottom.
>
> And now, my dear George Mifflin, after you have educated the public into buying a first class looking book . . . how can you expect them to pay $1.35 for precisely the same thing, the only difference being that they get fresh vegetables for $1.35 and canned goods for 25¢.

On Mifflin's assurance that he might realize $2500 on the deal, Smith acceded to the arrangement. He did so, he said, only because his reduced circumstances had put him in the bread line. "I am awfully sorry for you," Mifflin retorted, ". . . I hate to think of your being short of food . . . I am going to pray for you, and I have no doubt that you will pray for yourself." Smith thought his publisher should do more than pray. "For instance something like this. 'Enclosed you will find two bread tickets, entitling you to one and a half ounces of bread. Present it at the back door of the kitchen at the Hotel Vendome at half past three o'clock on the 15th. Ask to see the Chef, and he will probably put a little butter on yours.' "[29]

Mifflin was diffident about his literary judgment, declaring to his associates that if he liked a book, they could be sure it would be "a dead failure." Even in matters of book design, the department of his enterprise on which he left an enduring mark, he was inarticulate. He would rather make the book than tell how to make it. His conduct of the commercial side of the business was unmarked by such timidity. Here he had complete confidence. He had loved figures ever since Houghton had put him to work under the head bookkeeper at the Riverside Press way back in 1868. In matters of finance he was certain of his path. He would not tolerate from anyone advice on how to run his business, least of all from authors. Ever since 1881 exact figures had been kept on each book published. In considering a new manuscript by an author already on the list, the Houghton, Mifflin administration frequently examined these records. An earlier book's performance had an influence on its successor's acceptance and the terms offered. An editor's commendation carried weight; so did the concise history of profit or loss. In one of his tirades against his Boston publisher, Smith had suggested that Mifflin report to him the firm's advertising expenditures, a request Mifflin probably ignored. Had he thought it expedient, he might have readily satisfied Smith's curiosity. The firm's profit on the $1.50 edition of *Caleb West* was 32 cents, not 34 cents. Between April 1898 and April 1899 the book secured a credit balance of $6229.73. Smith's copyright return for the same period was $6020.77. Advertising outlay came to $1188.91. Smith's new finance was not for Mifflin even though in his conservative bidding he lost such publishing bonanzas as *Janice Meredith*. Some authors were content with Boston ways, none more so than Kate Douglas Wiggin, and for good reason.[30]

Of the writers of popular fiction in the first years of Mifflin's administration, Kate Douglas Wiggin must have been the publisher's ideal. Once in a while she complained about rates, but usually she never asked what she was to be paid and generally was pleasantly surprised to receive more than she expected. She also was frequently critical of Houghton, Mifflin's advertising, but in the long run concluded that "old books can never be warmed up by newspaper advertising," "that until a book *is* a success, there is no use in spreading expensive advertising." Her first book, *The Birds' Christmas Carol,* had sold 250,000 in a dozen years and was on its way as a juvenile classic. Nor was the *Carol* false to its promise. With quiet regularity title followed title, one, *Penelope's Progress,* making the *Bookman's* list before the turn of the century. Her annual income from her books alone in 1901 had reached $6769.40. After the publication in October 1903 of *Rebecca of Sunnybrook*

Farm the figure jumped to $38,185.56. Although no subsequent book of hers sold as well as *Rebecca,* she continued to produce fiction that won a numerous audience, the most notable *Rose of the River* and *Mother Carey's Chickens.* Almost a quarter of a century after the *Carol's* appearance her earnings from all her Houghton, Mifflin books had reached the impressive total of $232,392.77. This figure does not include the interest earned by the money she left with the firm at 6 percent. Nor does it include sums she received for her *Atlantic* appearances. Here she achieved the status of being the highest paid of any of the magazine's contributors, at one time receiving $52 a page. She protested mildly when all the firm would afford for *Penelope in Ireland* was $2500. She could have secured $5000 in New York, she objected. Still, she thought, the *Atlantic* ought to have the story. When Harper offered her a tempting fee for serial and book rights for *A Little Moorland Comedy* (a collaboration), she acceded to Mifflin's urging that she allow him to place the story with Edward Bok's *Ladies' Home Journal,* Houghton, Mifflin to have the book rights. Such loyalty deserved reward.[31]

In 1917 the firm proposed a collected edition of her works, to be autographed and sold by subscription. Her response was one of surprised gratification that her publishers should consider putting her "not-immortal" writings in such permanent form. "Naturally," she wrote, "every author after 38 years would like to gather up & leave behind something complete & it appeals to me because I should like to 'edit' a little, & get brief but good things like 'The Old Peabody Pew' and 'Susanna & Sue' together, out of their gift bindings . . ." Once the undertaking was in train, she was troubled by the expense to the purchaser, the price ranging from $2.50 per volume in cloth to $100 in full levant. Edward Bok thought that was "going some!" So apparently did John Jacob Raskob; he afforded only $500 for the ten volumes in half morocco.[32]

Houghton, Mifflin in the years to come would have its share of popular fiction, but not until after the firm's incorporation in 1908 would there be such a run as had begun in 1896 to reach its peak in 1903. Mifflin had come to office at a particularly fortunate time for one who wished to brag. Novelists had appeared to answer his need. However, to assume their loyalty to a single house had become an anachronism. For fiction money was the touchstone. Mifflin might fume and argue; authors had become skillful shoppers. The dead were more comfortable companions. They did not complain about distribution, advertising, serial rights, advances, and royalties. Houghton, Mifflin could publish a new edition of Hawthorne's *The Scarlet Letter* and sell over 20,000 in a year, even though the novel had been on the market for half a century. Yet, the house could not live on the dead. Nor could it survive on the fiction business. New writers with promise of permanence — poets, essayists, historians, critics — were essential to the list. The *Atlantic* must prove the lure. Such was Mifflin's purpose.[33]

Riverside's light team which delivered galley proofs or advance copies to the post office until shortly before the First World War.

XVII

SCUDDER'S *ATLANTIC*

ALDRICH'S FORCED RESIGNATION from the *Atlantic* had sad consequences for his successor. The ex-editor, traveling in Europe during the summer of 1890, tried to forget "the unctuousness of the
spacious Mr. Houghton" and "the corrugated wisdom of the multi-
farious Scudder," but newspaper accounts of the change made
forgetfulness impossible, so many of them seemed to suggest that
such merit as the magazine had had during his administration was
attributable to Scudder. "Now, from March '81 to June 16, 1890,
neither Mr. Scudder nor anyone else was associated with me in
shaping the course of the *Atlantic Monthly*," he wrote George
Woodberry, requesting him to "drop a line somewhat to that effect
among the literary notes in *The Nation* ... I could easily straighten
out the thing if I were home: over here I am quite helpless."
Woodberry duly performed the commission. On August 28, the
following paragraph appeared in the New York periodical. "The
statement which we have observed in several well-informed papers
to the effect that the excellence of the *Atlantic* during the past
decade was in no small degree due to the new editor, Mr. Horace E.
Scudder, in the capacity of assistant, deserves correction. The *Atlantic* has had no assistant during this period. Mr. Scudder's collaboration extended no further than the routine oversight of the
issue of numbers, practically already prepared, during Mr. Aldrich's occasional vacations."[1]

The *Nation* notice failed to mollify Aldrich. On his return to
Boston in the fall, he undertook himself to set the record straight,
not through the press but in the drawing rooms of Beacon Hill and
Charles Street, murmuring, "What a world this is with Scudders in

it!" "Scudder," he quipped, "has about as much tact as a jelly-fish. Peccavi! — to the jelly-fish." He intended to have nothing to do with Houghton, Mifflin's "middle — ('fair to middling') — man." Sarah Orne Jewett learned the lesson but varied the innuendo. "What a strange world this is," she would say, zigzagging her hand, "full of scudders and things."[2]

Scudder could not understand what had clouded his pleasant twenty-year relationship with Miss Jewett. Aldrich, he thought, was his friend. Five times in ten years he had taken the *Atlantic* for the three summer months when Aldrich went abroad. Moreover, for the entire decade he had written the achingly burdensome department at the back of the magazine, called "Books of the Month." He admired Aldrich's bright humor. That Miss Jewett suddenly failed him, he attributed to Annie Fields, whose "Singing Shepherd" he had returned on the grounds that her price was more than the *Atlantic* could afford. For two years (1892–1893) to Scudder's requests for contributions, the ladies held themselves aloof. Finally, his repeated efforts to pour oil on troubled waters took effect. First, a cordial letter from Mrs. Fields, then Miss Jewett came to Park Street with a manuscript, a call followed by one from the widow of Charles Street herself, bringing an olive branch. "I am afraid that in bringing about this change . . . I may have been laying a trap for myself," Scudder noted ruefully. "Too much good will on her part!"[3]

The malice of Charles Street was subsequently taken up by other gentle Americans. Mark Antony DeWolfe Howe described Scudder as too filled with sweetness and light. As editor, he lacked initiative, being content "to take chiefly, and gratefully, what came to him." The inventory of the editorial breadbox he kept at starvation rations. Next, Ellery Sedgwick, a latecomer to Annie Fields's memento-laden rooms, in creating his own image as an inventive, vigorous editor, pictured Scudder's direction of the periodical as heavy-footed, a typical issue starting off "with an admirable paper on the Upanishads." As a result *Atlantic* subscribers numbered but 5000. "Ellery," he reported Scudder as advising, "one thing I have never done. I have never *invited* a contribution to the *Atlantic*. If it is offered, I receive it. If it is good, I print it." Sedgwick protested he "loved the old gentleman" who gave this curious advice. Love, of course, takes many forms. Scudder, who died in his sixty-fourth year, was in his early fifties when Ellery, a Harvard undergraduate (1890–1894), sought him out for advice on his literary future. Another story provoking careless laughter in the house of pet names on the water side of Charles Street ran, "Why is Horace Scudder greater than Moses? Moses dried up the Red Sea once only; Scudder dries up the Atlantic monthly."[4]

As a matter of record, the Riverside Press during the 1890s never bound fewer than 10,000 copies of the *Atlantic* a month. At the time of Aldrich's resignation the magazine was running down financially. By 1893, under Scudder's direction, it was showing a profit. Then came the panic, the depression, and Houghton's death. For the rest of the decade the periodical was published at a loss. Indeed, not until 1903 did it again figure on the profit side of the ledger. Beacon Hill and Charles Street, of course, were not the world nor even Park Street. The latter was satisfied with Scudder's efforts. Houghton considered the editing of the magazine better, more systematic, than it had been for years. Mifflin praised Scudder's *Atlantic* for showing renewed life and vigor. Appreciation came from other sources as well. Howells admired the January 1892 number excessively. By comparison, he said, other magazines were but Sunday newspapers published once a month. Its literary standards were of the highest. He especially applauded Scudder's courage in printing Walter Crane's "Why Socialism appeals to Artists." Neither Alden of *Harper's* nor Gilder of the *Century* would have dared run the article, he believed. Hamilton W. Mabie considered the magazine "catholic, vital and in touch with our life. After all," he wrote Scudder, "we cannot do much unless we are in touch with life around us. Anything is better than the aridity of dilettantism . . . the *Atlantic* is strong, varied, interesting; you will compel people to read it." After the magazine had been under Scudder's direction for four years, Edmund Clarence Stedman assured him, ". . . under your quiet administration, the old maga has picked up steadily." In May 1896 the *Literary World* declared ". . . the old 'Atlantic' was never more youthful, springy, and alert than it is today," and in January 1897 the same magazine found it

Horace Elisha Scudder, literary adviser and editor-in-chief
for general publications from 1864 to 1902, and editor of
the *Atlantic* from April 1890 to July 1898.

strong and rich. "If the *Atlantic* keeps on as it has been going of
late it will pretty soon put Mr. Scudder in the company of great
editors, if he is not there already." And in truth Scudder's achievements with the *Atlantic* were greater than has generally been recognized. Bliss Perry, at least, paid a portion of his debt when he
wrote of him, "He made fewer errors, I fancy, than any editor of
the *Atlantic,* but his hits were often credited to other players."
Scudder set himself the task of changing the focus of the magazine,
a purpose realized in his time. His plough broke the crust and
ploughed the field. He planted the seed. Others harvested the
praise.[5]

The *Atlantic* from its beginning had been a "miscellaneous"
periodical, its concerns — literature, art, science, and politics. Under Howells and Aldrich it had become increasingly preoccupied
with fiction and criticism. Scudder did not neglect these departments, but his purpose was to give more space in the *Atlantic* to
articles on contemporary, controversial themes. "Politics, as you
know," he wrote Wendell P. Garrison of the *Nation,* "is the last
item in the comprehensive title of the magazine, but I may almost
say that since I have had my hand on the magazine it has been the
first consideration in my mind." Any subject having "a direct bearing upon the public life of the country" he included under the
general heading of politics. He wished the magazine to be "strong
in the treatment of public affairs of immediate importance." It
must be above party lines, but questions of public concern could
be discussed if the discussion derived from principles rather than
the quotidian of political exigency. In requesting a paper from
Theodore Roosevelt on civil service reform, he explained, "I have
a very strong desire that the Atlantic should take its stand unmistakably on all the great public questions which confront our people, and should give forth no uncertain sound on the right side.
There is always a right side, and there are after all few questions
of importance which cannot be discussed independently of party
lines. Not merely principles but measures and I believe men can
be subjected to sound analysis, though in the case of men I admit
that a preliminary funeral is of great service."[6]

Few articles of this type came without advance planning and active search. Mark Antony DeWolfe Howe and Ellery Sedgwick's canard that Scudder lacked creative editorial initiative, that he waited for contributions to drop through the *Atlantic* mail slot, is belied by Houghton, Mifflin's letter books. He both planned articles and sought writers. ". . . the success of the magazine," he told Houghton, "depends largely upon the power of the editor to study the field and to have a distinct policy which should be discovered in the papers which he solicits rather than the volunteer ones which he accepts." Furthermore, like attracts like; once the new emphasis of the *Atlantic* was recognized, contributions in tune with his editorial purpose would arrive unsought.[7]

In seeking contributors, Scudder did much more than suggest a topic; in general terms, he frequently described the content. Theodore Roosevelt's review of Captain Alfred T. Mahan's *The Influence of Sea Power Upon History* in the October 1890 *Atlantic* led him to propose to Mahan a paper which would expand the suggestion of the book that the Pacific coast was defenseless. Would not the shifting center of maritime operations, once in the Mediterranean, now in the Atlantic, "pass in the distant future to the Pacific?" he asked. "Meanwhile would not the completion of a canal taken with the British movements at the terminus of the Canadian Pacific, and the Occidentalizing of Japan and the growth of Australia immensely quicken the process? and if this be so will not the Pacific coast of our country become a far more potent factor in our historical development than it has been, and is not Government bound to take steps for the protection of the frontier?" Mahan responded with his prophetic "The United States Looking Outward" and "The Isthmus and Sea Power."[8]

For a list of authors to whom Scudder wrote comparable letters with equally gratifying results, the firm's letter books must be consulted. The names most familiar to the contemporary ear are perhaps Charles W. Eliot, Wendell P. Garrison, Edwin L. Godkin, Albert Bushnell Hart, George Kennan (the uncle of the diplomat George F. Kennan and not to be confused with him), Abbott Lawrence Lowell, Theodore Roosevelt, and Woodrow Wilson. The articles won through his search range widely from the party programs of 1892 through New York's Tammany Hall, corruption in

Pennsylvania, gerrymandering (the politicians' secret weapon in his view), and the problems of minorities — the Negro, the American Indian, and immigrant citizens — to analyses of the operation of the Federal Government. Scudder himself wrote one of these articles, "The League as a Political Instrument," a statement of the creed and action of the independent voter.

Scudder was bound to get into some kind of trouble by this shift in the focus of the magazine. Houghton approved heartily of the change. He even agreed to Scudder's proposal that the magazine carry "a succession of brief unsigned papers, which shall be taken as expressing the judgment of the magazine in public affairs just as unsigned book reviews are taken as expressive of its judgment in literature." Moorfield Storey wrote the first paper, "The Political Situation." Scudder anticipated Storey's analysis would "bring down the wrath of Republicans," but he was eager to print it, provided Storey would change one sentence, one that would be "a red rag to every Blaine man." He conceded the paper could not be written without naming names, but he thought personal judgment should be avoided.[9]

The plan had been in operation some months when Houghton heard that Edward M. Shepard, a Democrat, had prepared a paper on the coming campaign. He protested. The *Atlantic* must not appear to be committed to any political party. Shepard's article and any more to come of a partisan nature must bear the author's signature. Other political articles, even though signed, troubled him. He objected to William Everett's "An Unpaid Debt," a paper on the French spoliation claims, because its purpose appeared to be "to expedite a job in Congress." He regarded the accusations of Henry Childs Merwin's "Tammany Hall," in which Richard Crocker was branded a thief, dangerous. Houghton, Mifflin's treasurer, James Murray Kay, warned of a possible libel suit. Nevertheless, Houghton finally gave his approval and the article appeared on schedule in the February 1894 *Atlantic*.[10]

Perhaps it was the fuss Park Street made over Merwin's article that led Scudder to turn down Jane Addams' paper on Pullman and the frightening strike of 1894. He was impressed by Miss Addams' skill and earnestness in stating "the principles of *social* morality in its relation to industrialism," but he mistrusted her analysis of Pullman's motives. Had she been fair? he asked. ". . . I cannot think the eloquence of the counsel for the weak should blind us to the judicial aspects of the case," he wrote. Also, ". . . since Mr. Pullman is a living man I should wish to proceed with the greatest caution in the Atlantic. Even capitalists are persons." A dead man would be safer game and there were plenty of those.[11]

Scudder thought ". . . the fair discussion of an historical situation which has in a measure its parallel today offers one of the best indirect modes of educating public opinion." In 1888 he had voted for Cleveland and in that election had observed that ". . . at least twenty-five thousand voters in the city of New York . . . did not care a rap who was elected President, provided they and their friends could keep their noses in the public crib . . ." This indifference, he believed, derived from people's ignorance of "the organic growth of the nation," of "its inheritance from other times and peoples." In consequence, the Atlantic carried many articles on historic figures and events of the past.[12]

One reason Scudder insisted the Atlantic discuss principles in the light of current events, rather than the events themselves, was the length of time which must elapse between the writing of the paper and its publication. If a contribution were received in the first week of April, for example, it could not appear until the June Atlantic; the May number had been closed on March 25. Scudder repeatedly urged on Houghton, Mifflin swifter publication techniques but without success. Since the immediate cause of an article might seem less imperative at the end of six or eight weeks, the give and take of controversy was practically denied the Atlantic. Occasionally, to circumvent this repressive condition, Scudder sought two articles on the same subject to be presented from opposing points of view. Sometimes he sent advance sheets of an article to men of differing persuasions, their comments to be printed in footnotes. Thus he hoped W. T. Harris' "The Education of the Negro" would excite argument. Especially he wanted the Negro's point of view. "Is there not one of force named Washington?" he asked Harris. Was there any "strong Southern congressman, one whose name would command attention?" In pursuit of this idea, he wrote to at least eight possible commentators. To execute such a plan took precious time from a schedule burdened with the general publications of the house as well as the magazine. Usually Scudder, because of the delay between the appearance of an article and a possible reply, advised those who didn't like what they found in the *Atlantic* to have their say in the *Nation* "while the article is still hot in the mouth." Scudder's *Atlantic* was replete with themes of political controversy. Conditions of manufacture denied it the stimulation of riposte.[13]

Another department in which Scudder made a radical departure from the methods of his predecessor was in critical papers and reviews. Aldrich had relied chiefly on a "capable coterie," Richard Grant White, George E. Woodberry, George Parsons Lathrop, Scudder, and Harriet Waters Preston. Richard Grant White had died in 1885. Scudder had no intention of continuing Woodberry, Lathrop, and Miss Preston in exclusive office. He would continue to call on them, but as he told the complaining Lathrop, "I am trying to widen the critical outlook, by depending less on two or three men." "It is very rare that I print anything which is volunteered," he explained to Miss Preston. "Almost everything done grows out of my sense of what is especially desirable and in accordance with a pretty distinct policy. It is written either by me or at my request." In developing the new critics who came to the *Atlantic* during his regime he hoped to impress on them his belief that ". . . the first and last function of criticism is to come face to face with the actual creation and to see it and it alone."[14]

Scudder wished to "depolarize" the *Atlantic* not only in criticism but also in articles of general interest. In pursuit of this policy he threw work in the way of a remarkable group of young men, all new to the *Atlantic* and in that sense at least his "discoveries." Among them were Mark Antony DeWolfe Howe, Irving Babbitt, George Pierce Baker, Gamaliel Bradford, John Jay Chapman, Charles Townsend Copeland, Royal Cortissoz, George Lyman Kittredge, William Vaughn Moody, George Santayana, Owen Wister, and from England, Havelock Ellis. Some spoke for the *Atlantic* in unsigned reviews and "Comment on New Books"; others wrote major articles over their own names.[15]

Although Scudder held the average serial novel in low esteem, his *Atlantic* continued to run them as an essential feature. He intended to use the magazine "both to test new writers and to grapple some of the old ones." He preferred a story of three or four numbers to longer fiction, but "Alas," he noted, "the evolution of the magazine writer has not yet produced the contributor who is satisfied with a few pages!" Better than the brief serial was the short story or sketch, something swiftly told in 5000 to 6000 words. Short short stories were what he wanted, he told Alice French. "Their concentration of effect is what readers are coming to like. A race of modern readers like ours educated upon . . . the scraps into which newspapers are degenerating is particularly caught with stories to be taken down with a gulp." He welcomed her Arkansas sketches because they were rooted in the soil and because their locale was *terra incognita* to his *Atlantic* audience. He thought his readers no longer demanded "a clear completion of the whole business," but rather found "an artistic satisfaction in an ending which was in effect the last statement of the dominant motif of the work."[16]

Many stories that came unsought he found too dismal, so concerned with "hard, grinding fate," so sordid, he could not bring himself to print them. He believed "that where vulgarity of nature is to be shown . . . a very little is required to show it." Thus he rejected contributions from Ambrose Bierce because his stories were "repulsive" and "coarse," "with the kind of vigor which requires coarseness to account for it." *Tales of Soldiers and Civilians* he found "uniformly horrible and revolting. Told with some power, and now and then with strokes of wonderfully vivid description, with plots ingenious in their terror and photographic in their sickening details, we must pronounce the book too brutal to be either good art or good literature. It is the triumph of realism, — realism without meaning or symbolism."[17]

In searching for fiction, Scudder did not wait for volunteer contributions any more than he did in conducting the other departments of the *Atlantic*. Sometimes his search called for more than letters of inquiry and office conferences. In 1892, for example, hoping for a story from George Washington Cable, he went to Northampton to spend two days listening to the author read an

untitled, unfinished novel. He performed a similar service for
Margaret Deland. His mission to Northampton failed to produce
an *Atlantic* serial. So did his letters of appeal to Clemens and Edward Bellamy. However, Paul Leicester Ford with his *Story of an
Untold Love* and Gilbert Parker with *The Seats of the Mighty* and
The Battle of the Strong, both authors Scudder "finds," brought
an element of excitement to the *Atlantic*'s pages that was in tune
with the temper of the times. And it was through Gilbert Parker
that Scudder came to know a brilliant young Englishman, John
Buchan, who would become an *Atlantic* contributor after Scudder
had resigned his post. The serial Buchan submitted at Scudder's
request, probably *The Half-Hearted,* was not suited to serial publication, Scudder decided, because the story was "one to read
swiftly with special reference to the denouement." However,
Houghton, Mifflin was pleased to publish the book.[18]

Scudder's attempts "to grapple" some of the old *Atlantic* contributors, in fiction at least, were circumscribed. Howells was denied
him because of his exclusive Harper contract. Sarah Orne Jewett
for the first years of his administration remained remote. When
she did come back, her price was so stiff — over $35 a thousand
words — the *Atlantic* could not afford to publish her as frequently
as Scudder would have liked.

> It is a disappointment to us [Scudder wrote] that the *Atlantic*
> should no longer, as once, have practically the exclusive publica-
> tion of your stories, but it is not difficult to see why this is no
> longer possible. The illustrated magazines in their fierce rivalry
> and their eagerness to avail themselves of the reputation of favor-
> ite authors are like buyers in an auction room bidding hard
> against each other, and I for one am heartily glad that authors
> are thus in a position to command higher prices. *The Atlantic*
> in a sense is out of this keen competition. It has its own field and
> proposes to cultivate it carefully. As the representative, in pur-
> pose at any rate, of the most stable and pure American literature
> it can ill afford to dispense with stories from you; it has no dis-
> position to part company with an honored contributor. We shall
> pay your prices as laid down in your letter; the only difference will
> be that we must content ourselves with less frequent publication.
> This is our loss, for you have no difficulty in placing your stories;

but I hope the day will be far distant when any volume of *The Atlantic* will fail to contain at least one story from your pen. I shall look forward with great pleasure for *The Only Rose.*

For his persistence and courtesy, in 1896 Scudder was rewarded with Sarah Orne Jewett's masterpiece, *The Country of the Pointed Firs.*[19]

Another honored contributor Scudder wished to grapple to his *Atlantic* was Henry James, whom he hoped to persuade to write short stories rather than serials. Houghton, Mifflin's counting room attributed the *Atlantic's* ailing circulation, in part at least, to the seventeen-number *The Tragic Muse,* agreeing with *Literary World* when the story failed to conclude in the April number as had been promised, "Life may be short, but there is no doubt that Mr. Henry James is long." Explaining that he had "as many serial sails set" as the *Atlantic* could carry, Scudder inquired in August 1890 whether James would contribute four single-number stories for the 1891 *Atlantic.* The stories should not be over ten to twelve *Atlantic* pages, at the very limit not more than 10,000 words. James was charmed to oblige, especially since Scudder's request arrived at the same time the September *Atlantic* containing Scudder's review of *The Tragic Muse* came to his hand. The review, James wrote, "brought tears to my eyes — giving me a luxurious sense of being understood, perceived, felt." He regarded Scudder, he said, "more as an acute than as a benevolent critic. Have you not achieved the miracle of suspecting there may be *meaning* in what one writes? I don't notice that anyone else ever has! As regards your proposal to send four short stories before 1892, I embrace it with enthusiasm. I am perhaps capable of sending you five." One, he added, would be a two-number tale.[20]

Scudder had been touched by James's warm response, but when the first story arrived at the end of October he found himself in a quandary. "The Pupil" would fill twenty-three and a half pages, not ten or twelve, nor could it be divided into two numbers. To do so would destroy its *"one* long rhythm," and James urgently promised if "The Pupil" appeared as a single number, his next story would indeed be held to ten *Atlantic* pages. Scudder, in his advertising prospectus for 1891, had announced James as a contributor. He had planned to have him appear in the January

number, but "The Pupil" was out of the question, not because
of length alone. With some misgiving Scudder wrote James, "I
am more or less under fire as the new editor and naturally I mean
that the *Atlantic* shall not suffer by my accession. To publish,
therefore, as the first of your contributions a story which from its
length will receive special attention, but which I cannot defend 'as
good as it is long' is to invite criticism both for you and for me
which I wish to avoid." In his reluctant judgment "The Pupil"
was structurally weak. Moreover, it was deficient in interest, pre-
cision, and effectiveness. "I hate to write all this, but I should hate
myself still more if I didn't," he concluded.

Scudder's rejection came as a shock to James. He believed he
"had done a distinctly happy thing" in "The Pupil." Even so, he
promised to send a shorter story to be called "The Servant." He
would send it, that is, if he didn't become "panic-stricken" when
he considered its possible fate. Scudder's judgment, he said, had
made him feel "nervous & insecure." And that was the last Scudder
heard from James for over three months. Finally, he ventured to
write. Where was the promised story? "Why this deathlike silence?" he asked. James replied in a letter remarkable for its disregard of an editor's province. After he had reread "The Pupil"
in the light of Scudder's comments, he had concluded he had not
been treated fairly. "I could *not* see that it was a performance that
the *Atlantic* ought to have declined," he wrote, "nor banish from
my mind the reflection that the responsibility in any case, as regards the readers of the magazine, the public, should, when it's a
question of an old & honorable reputation, be left with the author
himself. The editor, under such circumstances, may fairly leave
it to him — & I should not have shrunk from any account the
reader might have held me to." However, mollified by Scudder's
tactful concern, he promised to send soon a couple of tales. These,
he promised, he would do his "best to keep . . . really short."

Although James's best did not result in brevity, from now on
Scudder accepted with only minor criticism whatever James submitted. He did not wish to lose an author whose writing he deeply
admired and whose name had been so long associated with the *Atlantic*. "The Old Things" proved particularly difficult for the editor. Projected as a tale of about 15,000 words, Scudder announced

it as a single-number story. James found he could not accomplish his purpose in 15,000 words. Next it was promised as being completed in three numbers, finally in six. Even that was a false promise. "The Old Things" ran to 70,000 words and seven numbers. For Scudder's patience, Houghton, Mifflin at least secured the book, to be published in 1897 as *The Spoils of Poynton,* a title change resulting from one of the few comments Scudder ventured to make. He did not like the original title.

Sales of *The Tragic Muse* had not justified publication. In its first year it sold 897 copies and carried a debit balance on the firm's books of $435.05. Some seven years later through minor sales its debit had been reduced to $100.98. Why should Houghton, Mifflin want another slow moving James title? A new book, Scudder told James, would be the occasion for "furbishing the older books and making a more solid and imposing front." Save for *The Portrait of a Lady* few had profited the publisher but Scudder wrote, "we — I speak for myself and the firm — have been sincerely desirous that an American novelist of whom we are proud should continue to publish his books with the firm that first presented them, and is ambitious to be identified always with the permanent elements of American literature."

Others than James expected more pages in the *Atlantic* than the editor wished to yield. As Scudder explained to Ellen Olney Kirk, one of whose stories he hoped to "squeeze" into the June 1892 number, "I suppose if the editor of the Atlantic had been entrusted with making the world, he would have run his blue pencil through the Desert of Sahara and various circumpolar spots and fancied that he was improving the universe." The majority accepted necessary cuts with good grace. Some who didn't wrote amusing letters. John Jay Chapman, who in his early days had called Scudder his patron, gave him "carte blanche — that is, all the margin" for making his "wise & admirable corrections" in his "A Canto of the Inferno." Five years later when Scudder requested that a contribution be shortened Chapman wrote:

> Many thanks for my manuscript returned O Procrustes. I do now let loose my opinion — hold it no longer. The introduction is too long for a short praise, too short for a long praise, too condensed

for a general praise & too general for a condensed praise — and being as it is you do not like it —

Enough! O Gate Keeper. But know this — I will not change a hair of his head — not for the sake of getting him baptized by the pope with all the cardinals of Culture for sponsors. And for his clothes — I have magazines of figured dresses of all the approved patterns — all point device — with every cut of smock from the high lyrical collar to the spoon-fed bib — but they shall lie by their time, and the urchin shall go unbreeched — but for a rag or two of fine cloth he trails behind him.

And thou, Earth-judging ticket taker shalt return uninstructed to thy grave — for I will not — at this late hour unlock with the key of this rejection the great store houses of revelation — yours

Pantagruel.[21]

Some of the cuts Scudder requested were made not because of length but because of his sense of propriety and respect for individual privacy. Thus when Rose Hawthorne was preparing "Some Memories of Hawthorne," he explained:

I . . . found myself stopping now and then with a question whether the freedom of private correspondence justified printing. For example, your mother wrote very explicitly of your father's political enemies when he was removed from the surveyorship. Is it wholly wise to print Mr. Upham's name, Silsbee's and Devereux's? It was sixty years ago, but the families are as much alive as your father's! Pardon me also if I raise a shadow of a doubt as to the publication of all the intimacy involved in the relation of the three sisters at the time when your father was drawing near your mother. A shadow of a doubt, for I found it all delightful, but I was the sole reader in MS and I caught myself thinking of the printed page spread broadcast, and of the idly curious. The same shadow falls for me across the page of some of your mother's writing in the moment of her supreme happiness.

Scudder made similar requests for deletion when William Roscoe Thayer was editing the letters of Sidney Lanier.[22]

In matters of style Scudder had the reputation of being an exacting master, perhaps the most severe of his contemporaries. His ideal was one that was "strong . . . intelligible, compact, reserved, suggesting more than it carries." John Fiske's prose was of the type. He would perhaps allow his authors "a darling idiosyncracy" or two, but he wished them to avoid "newspaper slouchiness." A writer need not "be dull to be decorous," but "a sort of undress capering" distressed him. "Friskiness in treating the subject is not to be despised," he advised William F. Biddle, "but I wish you would make the article a little less free and easy. I am sure you can do this without transferring it into military uniform." The magazine as a whole must have consistency of tone. In pursuit of uniformity, he spent hours "reducing to shape the German-silver English of the Countess von Krockow," in "bettering the style" of this one and that. Percival Lowell hardly recognized his "Venus in the Light of Recent Discoveries" when it appeared and he wrote satirically thanking Scudder "for the March Atlantic with your article on Venus in it. I congratulate you heartily on it and almost wish I had written it myself." Most contributors, however, were happy to receive the "well-known 'Scudder polish.' "[23]

In 1895 when Scudder tapped Walter Hines Page as his assistant and possible successor, he was chiefly troubled as to the man's literary taste. He feared Page's long experience as a newspaperman in the West, the South, on the New York *World,* and the *Evening Post* might have watered his standards. He had no question of his integrity, but was there in him "a grain too much of the journalist, a grain too little of the litterateur?" he wondered. Although Scudder had increased the number of *Atlantic* articles of a political complexion, he regarded the fostering of literature as the magazine's highest function. Admittedly, Page had done a splendid job in his eight years with the *Forum,* wiping out its $20,000 debt and making it a paying proposition, boasting 30,000 subscribers. But in the *Atlantic*'s need for subscribers, it must not become the *Forum,* aggressively polemical. Although Mifflin hoped to make the periodical a flagship to boast of, he agreed with Scudder on this point.[24]

Page, his salary $5000, reported for work on September 5, 1895, his duties — book manuscripts, reading reports, and the search for new writers. Mifflin, uncertain of the dynamo he had bought, insisted Scudder countersign all reports. Scudder, however, sensing

Walter Hines Page, who came to the firm as assistant
to Scudder in 1895, was editor of the *Atlantic*
from August 1898 to July 1899.

Page's volcanic nature, planned that he should be more than assistant. He hoped Page would soon take the laboring oar on the *Atlantic*. After all, if his long planned sabbatical were to take place in 1896, Scudder must afford Page every opportunity to show he could carry both the periodical and the general publications of the house. The firm, especially Mifflin, must have confidence in its new man before Scudder could realize his cherished plan.[25]

To Scudder's dismay, Page proved to have a variety of ailments — bilious attacks, rheumatism, and a mysterious infection which kept him at home periodically. Scudder, in spite of his brilliant assistant, was "half in despair over the amount of unfinished work and the variety of duties that assailed" him. Moreover, when Page was his vigorous self, he was impatient of detail. Scudder had told Houghton that the *Atlantic* editor must go out among men, that letters of appeal were not enough. Before Page's arrival, Scudder had traveled as much as his heavy schedule would allow, but shy and self-effacing and subject intermittently to inexplicable attacks of deafness, he shrank from the responsibility. Now his assistant went off, and Scudder, though pleased at this release, was left to struggle with the office "anaconda." Soon it became clear that his sabbatical would have to be postponed if Page were to administer the *Atlantic* and the trade department as Scudder had done. Moreover, Page would himself require an assistant.[26]

Mifflin's approach to the *Atlantic* problem differed from that of Houghton, who in most of his projects had followed James Brown's early admonition. If an undertaking didn't pay for itself, get rid of it. This he had done with *London Society*, the *Riverside Magazine for Young People,* the *Reporter,* and the *Andover Review.* The *Atlantic* he retained, valuing its prestige rather than its money-making potential. In 1893, under Scudder's direction, it had showed a profit. Since then it had lost money. Mifflin was determined the magazine should be a commercial success. Page, he thought, might be the one to turn the tide even as he had succeeded in doing for the *Forum.* In 1896, the periodical lost $10,000 and Scudder offered to put the shaping of the magazine entirely in Page's hands. Mifflin refused to listen. Editor and subeditor must work as a team, Scudder holding the line for literature; Page pushing the publishing side — circulation, advertising revenue, and new writers.[27]

When Page had come to Park Street in 1895, the Riverside Press was binding close to 11,000 *Atlantic*s every month; two years later 13,000, by 1898 well over 14,000. Outside cash advertising had also increased from a monthly $1600 to almost $2500. Mifflin was jubilant. ". . . if we can increase the advertising patronage of the magazine," he wrote Albert F. Houghton, "our problem in relation to it is in a great measure solved." Jubilant, that is, until he examined the debit side of the ledger. The heavy expenses in pushing the magazine, in advertising, in meeting authors' competitive demands showed up on the firm's Profit and Loss sheets. Circulation had increased, but the *Atlantic*'s loss in 1897 was $13,000; in 1898, almost $16,500. Nonetheless Mifflin was determined to keep the *Atlantic*. Offers of purchase he tossed in the wastebasket.[28]

As time for Scudder's deserved leave approached (he was at last to begin his holiday in June 1897 on half pay), finding a young man to assist Page became imperative. He must be one who might eventually become a permanent member of the staff, for Scudder hoped on his return to have an emeritus position, acting solely as literary adviser, freed from routine office work. He looked forward to long, uninterrupted hours in his study when he could begin his life of Lowell.

The search began in earnest in January. As before Mark Howe appealed to Scudder, but the firm was doubtful. He might come at too high a price; he might not have fully recovered from his eye troubles. A younger man who would fill the bill more cheaply, one who would start fresh in his training seemed a better solution. Scudder settled on Ellery Sedgwick, who had done a bit of editorial work for him on a collected edition of Bret Harte and whom Scudder thought a "bright and merry fellow," with "literature born in him." Sedgwick was at work on the *Youth's Companion* in a position Scudder had been instrumental in securing for him. Charles Minor Thompson, an editor of the *Companion,* gave Sedgwick a good word, but warned he was "slow not so much in judgment as in execution." After Scudder had had a number of interviews with his protégé, he sent him Houghton, Mifflin's official invitation.

Ellery then had a conversation with Page and decided "the *Atlantic* raft" was too small for the two of them. In his letter of regret to Scudder, however, he said he thought it wiser for him to stay with the *Youth's Companion* for the time being. It was now May. Scudder's departure was only a month off. The situation looked "ominous." "If my place is not filled I shall be wanted very much indeed when I return and I shall find it hard to get my emeritus position," he worried. Fortunately, since in the end there is always an available man, before Scudder's sabbatical was over, the problem had been solved. William B. Parker, Harvard '97, had been transferred from subscription and advertising to serve under Page.[29]

As acknowledged editor of the *Atlantic,* Page held his position just one year, from July 1898 to July 1899. He was however acting editor twelve months earlier. In the second year of his control, *Atlantic* losses fell to a trifle under $6000 and Riverside was binding between 17,000 and 18,000 monthly. Cash advertising totaled $20,750. Mifflin thought the "Atlantic trick" had been mastered and he looked forward to the time when the full force of his new editor's management would show in added subscribers and increased advertising.[30]

Page made a number of changes in the *Atlantic*'s tone and content during his two-year administration. There would be no paper on the Upanishads for Page. He was impatient of the tenuous or mystical.

> . . . you may search the whole splendid development of literature which has expressed the activity and growth of the English race for more than a thousand years (and this is our peculiar inheritance) [he wrote a contributor] and you find nothing mystic in it. Such things as you find that are in any way akin to Walter Pater have been forgotten by the rough and energetic race to which we belong, — forgotten in favor of those concrete, fundamental, far-flung lines of active ideas which dominate us, and from which we cannot get away if we would. You see I am afraid to turn the *Atlantic,* even to the slightest extent, away from what seems to me its necessary development in absolute harmony with the bent and character of the American temper. Rossetti, Pater, Maeterlink —

none of these ever touched the English heart . . . By English of
course I mean American as well . . .

Because Page regarded literary criticism as mere "talkee-talkee,"
he dropped "Comment on New Books" and in larger criticism
selected books were taken as a topic of discourse rather than being
made specific objects of inquiry. This meant that many books
worthy of notice were disregarded. Scudder saw these changes take
place with regret, for he held the magazine's criticism an essential
part of its literary commitment. To his distress Page also made
the Contributors' Club an occasional rather than a monthly feature.[31]

Scudder's major concern, one shared by Mifflin, was that Page
would "Forumize" the *Atlantic,* that the dynamic and immediate
would outweigh the quiescent, that the periodical's pages would
offer too few islands for contemplation as the topical absorbed
more and more space. However, conditions of manufacture continued to make the daily event, unless discussed in the light of
larger principles, out of the question. One of Page's first acts on
being given increased authority in 1896 was to confer with Mifflin
and Harry Houghton at the Press. He considered the delay between receipt of an article and publication intolerable. The interval must be reduced to three weeks at most. Everyone agreed and
Page reported his triumph to Scudder, who was glad enough to
have a condition he had inveighed against ameliorated. He envied
the forceful drive of his assistant. The victory proved a paper one.
Years later, six to eight weeks, save for holding open the concluding pages of the magazine for a special article, was still the time
required.[32]

Page bore out Scudder's fears at least twice. The new *Atlantic*
editor did not share his senior's conviction that even though Henry
James's novels sold slowly, to have his name on the list and his
contributions in the *Atlantic* was an asset in associating Houghton,
Mifflin with "the permanent elements of American literature."
In 1898 when James submitted "In a Cage" for the *Atlantic,* Page
would have none of it. "A duller story I have never read," he protested. "It wanders through a deep mire of affected writing and
gets nowhere, tells no tale, stirs no emotion but weariness. The

professional critics who mistake an indirect and round-about use
of words for literary art will call it an excellent piece of work; but
people who have blood in their veins will yawn and throw it down
— if, indeed, they ever pick it up."[33]

In the same year, Page demonstrated the blood that ran in his
veins when, to signalize his support of the great little war against
Spain, he resurrected the cut of the American flag the *Atlantic* had
flown on its cover during the Civil War to symbolize its support
of Lincoln's purpose, the preservation of the Union. Its appearance in 1898 demonstrates Mifflin's conviction that the magazine's
editor must be autonomous. When a political article went against
Houghton's Republicanism, he sometimes acted the part of editor.
Except in establishing how much authors were to be paid, Mifflin
left the conduct of the periodical to those he had hired to do the
job. He was opposed to the war. He thought Congress had be-
haved "with shameful impatience," "even madness," and he telegraphed President McKinley to that effect. His opposition was sec-
onded by others at Park Street — Azariah Smith, Henry Wheeler,
and Francis J. Garrison, a devoted follower of his father in the
causes of the Negro, women's rights, and world peace. The opinions at Park Street were not isolated phenomena. To many Americans, the government's humanitarian wish to free an oppressed
people was beclouded by an imperialist drive and commercial
self-interest. Page considered such talk "twaddle." Driving Spain
out of Cuba was "a necessary act of surgery." He welcomed the
news from Manila which set "every statesman and soldier in the
world thinking new thoughts about us." ". . . we are brought
face to face with world wide forces in Asia as well as Europe,
which seem to be working . . . for one of the greatest changes
in human history," he said in the first number of the *Atlantic*
which flew the flag. Had Scudder been in control, the flag would
not have been flown. Less emotional than either Mifflin or Page,
he believed the test of his country's motives and skill lay in the
future. Her abilities in administration of her responsibilities
would tip the scales of justice, he hoped, but he also confessed that
he could not see clearly to the bottom of the question. ". . . the
water is so wide I can't quite make out Truth's feature." "War in

itself is a terrible thing," he said, "but war in some form, as far as we can see is a part of human development as long as good and evil are in conflict. You and I would use other weapons than gunboats, but gunboats sometimes make a shorter and more humane end to evils." The time to fly the flag would be when the liberated islands of the Philippines and Cuba had established stable governments of their own.[34]

Except for the flag, the *Atlantic*'s political and social position under Page's direction developed on lines already established by Scudder, many of the articles of 1897 through 1899 being written by men whom Scudder had long cultivated. Even Lord Bryce, a newcomer to the magazine, he had courted since 1884. "The Essential Unity of Britain and America," in the July 1898 *Atlantic* was in fulfillment of a promise Bryce had made to Scudder. One of Page's singular triumphs was obtaining a series of papers on our western national parks. The author, John Muir, was new, but Scudder in laying out plans for his *Atlantic* had looked for such contributions and in 1891 printed Alpheus Hyatt's "The Next Stage in the Development of Public Parks"; in 1893, Julius Hammond Ward's "White Mountain Forests in Peril." The statement that Page "broke the literary calm of the *Atlantic,* and thus gave the old magazine a new lease on life," is difficult to credit. Of course, he had the small war on his side. War has forever proved the good fortune of periodicals.[35]

One of Page's coups is of particular interest because of its consequences. In the fall of 1897, the *Atlantic* received a "Contributors' Club" from James M. Campbell of Lombard, Illinois. From this Page learned that Thomas Carlyle's sister Janet, now eighty-three, had been a Canadian resident for fifty years. He put the "Club" in the editorial breadbox and dispatched his assistant Parker to Toronto to secure such letters as Carlyle had written this favorite sister. By this time Janet (Mrs. Robert Hanning) had died, but Parker was successful in winning serial and book rights from her heirs. Only then did Campbell's "A Reminiscence of Carlyle" appear in the *Atlantic*. By this device, Page thought he had outwitted competitors. What was his surprise then to receive, after negotiations had been completed, a group of the very same letters edited by Miss Faith Fenton, submitted for *Atlantic* consideration through Paul Reynolds, once a Houghton, Mifflin employee, but now a New York literary agent! Almost at the same time S. S. McClure announced that some of Carlyle's letters to his sister Janet were to appear in his magazine. Charles Townsend Copeland was already at work editing the Houghton, Mifflin cache. Investigation proved that the faithless Fenton had been given authority by Mrs. Hanning's heirs to make extracts from the correspondence for a newspaper article. "To turn a penny on her own account," she had made complete copies and in New York had sold some to McClure. Of others she had made her article, which Reynolds had so innocently submitted to Page. The heirs were indignant, publishing a denial of Miss Fenton's rights in the *Critic* and requesting Houghton, Mifflin to take legal action to prevent publication by anyone other than the firm to whom their authority had been given. Resort to the courts was not necessary. Both Reynolds and McClure recognized Houghton, Mifflin's priority. In straightening out the matter, Page went to New York for conferences with both Reynolds and McClure. The Carlyle letters started their course in the September 1898 *Atlantic;* at the same time Page himself had started a new course. S. S. McClure would shortly remember this *Atlantic* editor and call for his help.[36]

In the spring of 1899, when Harper was unable to meet its creditors' demands, the house of Morgan, holding Harper bonds of $2,500,000, chose McClure to take over the failing publisher's empire. Two years earlier, McClure, wishing to couple book and periodical rights, had formed a publishing alliance with Frank Doubleday. *McClure's Magazine,* begun in the panic year, was now pushing 400,000 and the young firm of Doubleday & McClure was prospering, but if it were to take on Harper, more executive help was imperative. McClure invited his recent opponent in the Carlyle matter to join his firm, offering for his suzerainty "one or two kingdoms" of his vast dominion. Such an offer made Park Street seem a rabbit warren. To Mifflin, Page's announcement that he would resign in the summer of 1899 was worse than the torpedoing of the *Maine.* The war was over, the national economy was on the way up and so was the *Atlantic's* circulation. He had not expected the melancholy object lesson of Harper's failure to hit so close to home. In the emergency he could think of no one to turn to save Scudder.[37]

Scudder, on his return from Europe in June 1898, although he had not been granted his coveted emeritus position, had been relieved of the *Atlantic* and he looked forward to considerable freedom from office work. Many of his editorial tasks he hoped to accomplish in his own study. He was still to have charge of all trade publications, both new books and fresh editions of those already on the list. He was also responsible for the Riverside Literature Series, the Commonwealths Series, and the Cambridge Poets, for which he would do the Keats. Then in 1900 on the death of Charles Dudley Warner, the Men of Letters Series fell to him. As a further burden, Houghton, Mifflin's Educational Department called on him frequently not only for ideas for texts but also to establish contact with authors to write the texts he envisioned. However, he expected to organize his work so efficiently that he would have time for a memoir of Justin Winsor and his biography of Lowell. This "leisurely" schedule was more than once complicated by Page's absence from Park Street on business trips or because of sickness. Scudder found he had to be at his desk much more than he had anticipated, that he had to take *Atlantic* work home with him at night. To bear the brunt, however, he could now rely on Page's assistant, William Parker, the loyal Gibbs, and Frank Allen. He hoped in *Atlantic* emergencies to serve solely "as a court of last resort."[38]

On June 30, 1899, he made the following entry in his diary:

> We have come up for a full summer [to Chocorua] I trust, and my hope is that I may make a large beginning on my life of Lowell . . .
>
> I am a little alarmed when I consider how much else I have to do and that with considerable dispatch. For I am reading carefully the proofs of Hart's Chase [Albert Bushnell Hart had specified that Scudder assume this responsibility rather than John T. Morse, editor of the Statesmen Series]. I must prepare a volume of Sill's prose. I must read Trevelyan's Macaulay and arrange the letters for the final volume of Macaulay's Miscellanies and I am

very desirous of completing my little book of legends in time for publication this fall. Then there will be proofs to read as the books come back to me, there will be *mss* to read — I brought one with me — the necessary correspondence with the firm and the work involved in managing the inauguration of Miss Hazard [In his capacity as trustee of Wellesley College]. I must look back on this in October.

He didn't have to wait until October.

A week later he received "a pretty startling letter" from Mifflin telling him of Page's offer from McClure and requesting he return to Boston. Scudder was confident a replacement for Page could be found, but he dreaded "the induction of another man." Inevitably he would be required at the office. His hope for uninterrupted hours had gone glimmering. Reluctantly he returned to Park Street.

Conferences over the question of Page's successor were endless. Mifflin hadn't an idea. He relied on his senior editor for inspiration. Scudder suggested Henry Dwight Sedgwick, older brother of Ellery, lawyer, and *Atlantic* contributor; the novelist Arthur Hardy; then Abbott Lawrence Lowell. At the last name Mifflin "took fire." "The very man!" He could visualize the newspaper announcements. Another Lowell in the great succession. But this Lowell was abroad. A cable was dispatched. Two days later came the reply, "Appreciate offer, but cannot." Lines had already been laid to Henry Sedgwick, and off went Scudder to New York. Again, no go. The same with Arthur Hardy. Ten days had passed and nothing had been accomplished. Then to his elders came Mac-Gregor Jenkins, business manager of the *Atlantic* and Williams 1890. What about Bliss Perry? The name meant nothing to Mifflin; Scudder knew it well. Less than a month before, as trustee of Williams, he had sat on a committee that had judged the young man's father, Arthur Latham Perry, and for his tasteless even "insolent" book *Williamstown and Williams College,* had struck his name from the college catalogue.

Scudder also knew of the younger man. Bliss Perry was Williams 1881 and following his graduation he had taught English there. In 1893 Perry had transferred to Princeton. At that time Woodrow Wilson had sought for his brother-in-law, through Scudder, Bliss Perry's Williams position. Quite possibly the two men met at Princeton as well as at Williams. In 1896 at the time of her Sesquicentennial, when the College of New Jersey became Princeton University, Scudder had been awarded a Doctor of Letters there. At that time Scudder was a house guest of the Wilsons. In their three years at Princeton, Perry and his wife had become friends of the Woodrow Wilsons. Scudder would attach no bill of attainder to the son because of his father's book. Bliss Perry, like Scudder, was a Mark Hopkins man, one of the last. Scudder had every reason to hope that Perry's background and academic experience would make him sympathetic with his editorial and publishing ideals. Although he sometimes deplored the necessity, Scudder accepted the market place as an essential concomitant of the printed word. Within a commercial setting, to exert editorial persuasion in behalf of the artist and his work was a worthy purpose, he believed, in influence akin to that of the ministry and teaching. He trusted Bliss Perry would share his dedication.

A telegram was dispatched to Greensboro, Vermont, the Perrys' summer home. A reply came from Mrs. Perry. Her husband was off fishing and could not be reached for a week. MacGregor Jenkins set out for Vermont and Scudder returned wearily to Chocorua. Here two weeks later Perry reported for an interview, having been first to Boston. Two days later Mifflin summoned Scudder once again to Park Street. Perry had accepted the *Atlantic* editorship and must be instructed in the duties of his office. For the coming academic year Perry would be dividing his time between Princeton and Park Street, and he could not assume responsibility for the Trade Department for a year at least. Once again Scudder's emeritus position must be postponed. He hoped now to have in 1901 another summer in England, a winter in Italy.

Brave hopes, not different than those of other men as they look forward to retirement. But something was wrong. "I begin to fear I am growing old, and yet I am only sixty-one," he mourned. He had been in the habit of getting up at five-forty-five so that he could get in a couple of hours' work before the day began. A lame back, inexplicable fatigue, and unwonted nervousness made him decide to husband his strength. He changed his rising to quarter of seven. An attack of bronchopneumonia in January 1901 proved a blessing; the long convalescence gave him leisure to go over carefully his draft of Lowell and finally see the two volumes through the press. After that, frail as he was, he promised Mrs. Fiske to edit the projected twenty-four-volume subscription edition of her husband's works. This was a promise he could not fully keep. Before the end of the year it was beyond doubt that his disease, diabetes, would soon be fatal. He died January 11, 1902.

More than one memoir of Scudder's contemporaries refers to him and the work he did as hack. Such he was not. He had not submitted to the lash for money. Be it remembered that in 1886 he could have let himself out for hire to Joseph Pulitzer, salary unlimited. All that offer merited in his diary was an exclamation point. In 1864 he had made his choice, for him a happy one. He knew then that he was born to serve; he hoped in serving to have an ever expanding circle of influence. The penumbra of that circle prevails. *Non ministrari sed ministrandum.*

Next to the last entry in his diary reads, "In the afternoon had a call from Ferris Greenslet, who wants a position in the editorial department. Wrote Mifflin about him . . ." Scudder had an abiding faith in life's continuity, a belief that the present holds both past and future. Bliss Perry considered his interview with Scudder decisive. The dying editor's letter to Mifflin was equally so. Perry shortly invited Ferris Greenslet to serve under him. Scudder had worked for Houghton, Mifflin for almost forty years. Greenslet would serve the firm even longer. Scudder's *Atlantic* was to have a different destiny.[39]

XVIII

THE GENTLE READER

IN 1901 Houghton, Mifflin again turned down an offer for the *Atlantic,* this an anonymous one tendered through Walter Hines Page. Although the firm's annual report for the year recorded a loss of almost $10,000 for the periodical, Mifflin still had faith. MacGregor Jenkins, William B. Parker, and Bliss Perry would work a miracle.[1]

Page at the time of the offer was more or less on his own. S. S. McClure's scheme for securing the house of Harper to himself had collapsed. In December 1899, the former editor of the *Atlantic* had dropped in at Park Street to report the affair to Scudder.

> The Doubleday crowd had an option on the business. They had but to assume the debt and they could have the whole affair. But after looking into it for several weeks and trying in vain to fund the debt they found it was impossible to ascertain the whole extent of the difficulty, that the business was practically bankrupt, and so they retired. The assets had been enormously exaggerated, especially the plate-valuation and apparently no analysis was ever made. Page said he was two months trying to find out what it cost to make Harper's Weekly, and it was simply impossible.

Page had not been in the least cast down by the turn of events. Everything looked big to him; he and Frank Doubleday had deserted McClure to form a company of their own. Although Doubleday had no capital, he brought with him from Doubleday & McClure important publishing rights and the loyalty of certain authors. Page, however, was cock of the roost. He was no longer a hired man.[2]

One of Page's big plans was a periodical over which he would

have complete control. This he realized in his *World's Work*.
The first number appeared in November 1900. Page's anonymous
offer for the *Atlantic* came in May 1901. At that time he claimed a
circulation of 16,000, a wonderful showing, as Mifflin commented
dryly. As for the proposal to purchase, "My dear Page," he wrote,
"As you say it is indeed funny how many fellows there are who are
ready in these days to buy at wild prices almost any kind of property. So that I am not surprised that there is someone who is mad
enough to want to buy the Atlantic. But curiously enough the
magazine is not for sale but perhaps that is lucky for the fellow who
might like to buy it!"[3]

Who was the lucky fellow? Ellery Sedgwick, who had made up
his mind when he was a Harvard sophomore to one day own the
Atlantic, was now in New York and it was Page who secured for
him his editorial job of "reconstructing" the ailing *Frank Leslie's
Popular Monthly.* Page certainly did not need the *Atlantic* either
for prestige or circulation. By 1907 (the *Atlantic's* fiftieth year), the
World's Work had far outstripped the Boston periodical, claiming
a circulation of 100,000. In that year the *Atlantic* was more than
paying its way, showing a profit of something over $2000, with pos-
sibly 18,000 to 20,000 subscribers. In 1901, Ellery Sedgwick didn't
have the money to buy at a wild price. For the time being the *Atlantic* remained a Houghton, Mifflin property.[4]

Perry, of course, benefited from his inherited inventory, even as
Page had benefited from the plans and contacts Scudder had made
while he was in control. Mary Johnston's *To Have and To Hold*
began its run in the June 1899 number and for a few months "almost doubled" the magazine's circulation, or so a company release
boasted. Then in 1900 the new editor made a "lucky hit," securing
from ex-President Cleveland "The Independence of the Executive." Advance interest was keen. Mifflin was tingling with delight. The Riverside Press printed 40,000 copies of the June *Atlantic.* Fact failed to fulfill expectation. The American News
Company returned a full 10,000, and Garrison noted wryly that
Houghton, Mifflin had plenty of souvenir copies if anyone wanted
them. Possibly others returned advance orders too, for Perry in
his autobiography written some thirty years afterward recalled a
printing of only 23,000.[5]

Perry, more than any of his predecessors, deferred to the prejudices and preferences of his Gentle Readers. In a series of cozy editorial chats, he gave them "a survey of the editorial pantry and kitchen," seeking their sympathy and understanding of the host who must satisfy the tastes of the guests at the *Atlantic* table. The menu, he pointed out, was diversified. Diners need not savor every item on the bill of fare. The Gentle Reader for his part seems to have been an uneasy patron of the *Atlantic* board, directing "streams of sorrowful correspondence" to the editor, objecting to contributions offensive to his palate. These protests, coupled with MacGregor Jenkins' study of the *Atlantic* subscription list, made Perry aware of the changing nature of the magazine's readers. He thought it essential that his contributors consider this new audience.[6]

After accepting Henry James's "Maud-Evelyn" for the April 1900 number, he advised the author:

> I am tempted to add a word of suggestion about the new audience which the Atlantic is reaching nowadays. More than half of its circulation — which has been growing rapidly of late — is now west of the Mississippi, and there are more subscribers in Wisconsin than in any state except Massachusetts. I confess that I am not certain about the temper of this audience, but I know it differs markedly from the old Atlantic circle of readers. The *nuances* of "Maud-Evelyn" — to take a concrete illustration — will be quite lost upon a great many of our subscribers who are losing their heads over "To Have and To Hold." That cannot be helped, I suppose, and it ought not & will not prevent our printing an occasional story that is too subtle & delicate for "the general." But I think it will be well for you to bear this condition in mind when you are mulling over subjects & possible modes of treatment of the papers which you may from time to time do for us. Please don't think we are sufficiently "journalized" to prefer coarser to finer work . . . but it does seem to me essential to the effectiveness of an Atlantic paper nowadays that it should be constructed upon as simple and strong lines as possible.

In conclusion Perry graciously found "a delicious whimsicality" in his offering advice to an *Atlantic* contributor of James's experience. In fiction at least James was either unable or unwilling to benefit

Bliss Perry, editor of the *Atlantic* from August 1899
to July 1909, and from 1902 to 1909 editor-in-chief
of the Trade Department.

by Perry's suggestions. Two subsequent contributions, a short story, "The Faces," and an unnamed serial, proved unacceptable for the magazine. In returning the manuscripts Perry explained that James was a luxury the periodical could seldom afford. He did not confess that MacGregor Jenkins had "besought" him, "with actual tears in his eyes, not to print another story by Henry James, since he was trying desperately to persuade the American News Company that the *Atlantic* was not really a 'high-brow' periodical."[7]

Perry, even as Scudder, held the serial in low esteem and in 1906 tried the experiment of having none. Not a murmur came from the Gentle Reader. For 1907 he and his assistants decided to follow the same plan unless by chance a novel of unusual power came to their attention. Perry went off for a six-month sabbatical in June 1906 and Ferris Greenslet (William Parker had left editing for teaching the year before) was flattered to be left in charge. One of his first acts as deputy was to accept a critical paper from the English writer May Sinclair, who the year before had met with high favor when Henry Holt had published her novel *The Divine Fire*. In the course of his correspondence with Miss Sinclair about her essay, Greenslet learned that she had another novel in train. He requested the privilege of considering it. Following receipt of the manuscript, he was enthusiastic. The narrative *The Helpmate* had a "clean-lined structure," its texture was "vivid and dramatic." It was just the sort of serial the *Atlantic* needed. "It promises, I believe, to be a novel of as much popularity as distinction, — and that is saying a great deal," he wrote. Nevertheless, would Miss Sinclair make some changes? He feared that the magazine's "excellent audience" would be quick to take exception to the story's lack of "conventional reticence," especially in the opening chapter, which was indeed "dangerous . . . for the reader who must form his first impression of the story from a brief segment of it, the first chapter would I fear suggest that the novel is going to be a bit bizarre . . ." The scene that caused this consternation was a bedroom with clothes strewn about on the furniture and a man and his wife in bed. Please, couldn't the action be transferred to a more acceptable apartment?[8]

Miss Sinclair refused to allow any fear of the Gentle Reader's

propriety to traduce her sense of what was right for her story. Even
so Greenslet ventured to run it. "The result was cataclysmic . . .
subscriptions were cancelled by the score, chiefly from Boston."
However, the Gentle Reader beyond the Mississippi seemed to like
the dish. For every subscriber lost two were gained and "the magazine enjoyed the largest increase in circulation it had had in any
one year up to that time." The subeditor reported happily to the
author, "We continue to hear good things of 'The Helpmate,' one
of the latest being that Augustus Saint Gaudens . . . who has been
ill for two years and unable to endure reading of any sort, has been
having it read to him and liking it very enthusiastically." Even so,
Perry, on return from his sabbatical, found a pile of letters from
readers driven to the pen by dread that the staid *Atlantic* was on
course to corrupt American morals.

Perry's deference to his readers affected every department of the
magazine. They had objected to Page's curtailment of the Contributors' Club. Perry, convinced by letters of protest that it was the
most popular dish on the *Atlantic* menu, made it again a monthly
feature. His preference was for the bright, witty, and informal.
Because letters from subscribers persuaded him that many turned
first to this section, if he wished special attention called to a new
book, he recommended a Club rather than a formal review. However, in contrast to Page, he held criticism essential to the periodical's literary commitment. In later life, reviewing the *Atlantic*
volumes of his administration, he felt that in this department he
had perhaps disregarded the preferences of his readers. Since Ellery
Sedgwick chose to ridicule Scudder for running an article on the
Upanishads, that Perry also did should be noted. Yet in accepting
Paul Elmer More's "The Forest Philosophy of India," he worried.

> We cannot afford to print very many articles that seem remote to
> the interests of the average magazine reader . . . When we tried a
> series of articles on the philosophy of India some years ago, the
> experiment was disastrous. The very word Upanishads is one of
> ill omen in our circulation department to the present day because
> of the letters of protest that poured in from subscribers who care
> nothing about such subjects. We have had to abandon papers on
> Greek and Roman literature for the same practical reason.[9]

Perry's major change in presenting the *Atlantic*'s criticism was to introduce the signed or at least initialed review. The pontifical tradition of the "Atlantic speaks" article troubled him. The individual, not the periodical, its editor or its publisher, must be held responsible. However, in neither body articles nor the Contributors' Club would he allow riposte. To that extent he would stand behind his writers. "We have used extraordinary care to keep 'back talk' out of the pages of the magazine," he told Harriet Monroe. No space would be afforded to those who wished to make "personal protest against the judgment of the Atlantic's critics."[10]

Perry's prohibition against talking back irritated some Gentle Readers profoundly. Jesuits sought pages for reply to a slur on their colleges; Protestants were ready to take up the gauntlet when the tone of an article seemed Romanish; and on the appearance of John Burroughs' "Real and Sham Natural History," William Joseph Long and Ernest Thompson Seton, both Burroughs' targets, thought they had a right to speak in their own defense. The most energetic protests were entered by the Christian Scientists. In 1901 Eugene Wood, in "What the Public Wants to Read," ridiculed Mary Baker Eddy's literary style and in the spirit of levity talked of her three marriages. The faithful requested room for refutation. The privilege was denied. Then in 1904 Perry accepted a diagnosis of Christian Science, by a doctor, John Woolman Churchman. Perry thought the doctor had written his article with "care and sobriety," that he had rendered the *Atlantic* a service. He looked forward to printing the paper and gave it the lead position in the April number. This sober treatment of the subject proved more infuriating to the Scientists than had Wood's ridicule. They demanded opportunity for rebuttal, intimating the *Atlantic*'s benefit would be an increase in subscribers. Perry proved adamant and the Scientists complained to Mifflin, who proved as obdurate as his editor. Perry had been correct when he had said the *Atlantic* refused to allow back talk. The reason was a practical one. "Even if this custom were desirable, the way the magazine is printed makes it impracticable. It is now, for instance, the 18th of April. The May Atlantic is entirely printed; the June Atlantic went to Press nearly two weeks ago; the July and August numbers contain special features arranged for months ago, so that we have been obliged to tell many correspondents within the past week that September is now the earliest possible month for printing material not already planned for."[11]

These articles on Christian Science had unlooked-for consequences. The Riverside Press for years had been printing a number of important books for the Mother Church. Following publication of Churchman's "Christian Science," this business was removed from Riverside. However, "it so happened that there were certain details of the work calling for peculiar skill and experience," which the new printers lacked. They turned to the Press, now full up with other business. Harry Houghton consulted his senior partner. At considerable inconvenience, the firm agreed, without taking credit, to do the work assigned another. "Now in practice which showed the better Christian Science Spirit — those who profess or those who profess not?" Mifflin asked one of his troubled authors — Clara Louise Burnham, a devout member of the faith.[12]

Clara Louise Burnham had come to Houghton, Mifflin at the time of its Ticknor purchase. In the intervening years she had produced a series of popular books, among them *Miss Archer Archer,* which in less than a year sold over 8000. By this time Miss Burnham's books in the firm's catalogue numbered a dozen, each boasting a credit balance. Following the success of *Miss Archer Archer,* the author began to complain about Houghton, Mifflin's advertising and her returns. She threatened to change publishers. Her royalty was raised from 10 percent to 15 percent. In 1903 the Boston publisher D. Lothrop urged that she give him her next book.

> I told him [she wrote Mifflin] my mind was made up because our relations were of the most friendly and that it was your desire that I should remain with you, and that you had done everything to make me do so. He said it came to a question of bidding; but I told him my mind was made up. He asked me to let them know when I experienced a change of heart; and went away with evidently a poor opinion of my business ability . . .

On the heels of this offer from Lothrop came Churchman's article. Once again Miss Burnham considered taking her business elsewhere, fearing Houghton, Mifflin's imprint would injure the sale of her books. Mifflin assured her that such would not be the case. Conviction came when the royalty on certain of her books was raised to 20 percent. Miss Burnham continued loyal to Park Street.[13]

A consequence of a different order than loss of business at the Press or the threatened defection of a profitable writer was the advent of a new figure on the Park Street threshold. S. S. McClure, always on the alert for subjects of timely interest which he could present with his particular flair, used as one of his sources for guidance the quality magazines — *Harper's Monthly, Scribner's,* the *Century,* and the *Atlantic.* Possibly the minor furore over the *Atlantic*'s Christian Science articles influenced him in accepting a cumbersome and lengthy biography of the foundress. Its writing must be stringently revised, its facts checked. His choice for the major part of this task was Willa Cather. Her name was not unknown to Houghton, Mifflin. In 1899 Parker, in the name of the *Atlantic* editors, had returned her story "The Roots of Life" with "unusual reluctance and regret." He had especially enjoyed her fidelity in portraying Nebraska prairie country. More encouraging than reluctant rejection had been Ferris Greenslet's flattering review of her first book, *April Twilights,* a volume of poetry. Inevitably when she came to Boston on her Christian Science assignment, she sought out Houghton, Mifflin and the man who had given her serious critical recognition. To her "Boston meant Ferris Greenslet." For him she would prove one of the first stars in his brilliant galaxy of new writers acquired for his firm.[14]

Although Perry would not allow any talking back in his magazine, certain Gentle Readers could riposte without bothering to demand space in the periodical. In 1905 Rollo Ogden of the New York *Evening Post* proposed a series of "Letters to Literary Statesmen," in which the political opinions of certain public figures before they had assumed office would be compared with their words and actions after they had the reins in their hands. Perry thought the idea brilliant. The apostle of the strenuous life was to be the first subject. A "Letter to Theodore Roosevelt" appeared in the March *Atlantic*.[15]

When Roosevelt had come to the Presidential office after McKinley's assassination, the *Critic* had greeted his accession with "A Man of Letters in the White House." The new President, the youngest ever to hold that high office, was better known as an author than any of his twenty-four predecessors. A cultural renaissance was looked for. His contributions had appeared in numerous periodicals. His books were in the hands of various publishers. Houghton, Mifflin had two in its Statesmen Series — *Gouverneur Morris* and *Thomas Hart Benton*. Other volumes might be anticipated. Opposed though Mifflin had been to the war with Spain, he was nonetheless a Teddy Roosevelt fan. The President was a Houghton, Mifflin author, a Harvard graduate, and a Porcellian brother, reasons enough for enthusiastic loyalty. However, Mifflin's partisanship here did not weaken his support of the *Atlantic* and its editor.

Rollo Ogden's satire failed to amuse. Anger rather than laughter was the response from Washington. The two offending pages were torn from the White House *Atlantic* and Massachusetts Senator Lodge, also a Houghton, Mifflin author, was directed to make representations to the firm. An apology was expected. Perry obliged but at the same time tendered his resignation. Mifflin feared Lodge's wrath less (a "Letter" to him was scheduled for later in the year) than the loss of an editor who had made the *Atlantic* show a profit for two years in a row and who was well on his way to repeating the miracle in 1905. He asked Perry to relent; the firm, he protested, "did not wish in any way to influence" editorial decisions. As in the past, it would stand behind its editors no matter what the eminence of the Gentle Reader. Perry withdrew his resignation. He also canceled the epistle to Lodge.

More than Ogden's satiric "Letter" must have irritated Roosevelt in Perry's *Atlantic*. Under Page the magazine had been in tune with the spirit of San Juan Hill. Under its new editor the tone of the magazine changed. Perry approved the Hague Convention. He was a member of the American Peace Society, and when the Peace Congress met in Boston in October 1904, he saw to it that the *Atlantic* prepared for the event by running an introductory article, "World-Organization Secures World Peace." Other papers favorable to the movement followed. As for the war with Spain, Perry had been critical from its start. His attitude did not change when he became editor of the *Atlantic*. Readers of the magazine who paid no attention to shifts in editors must have been puzzled to discover that their periodical, which had so recently supported the expansionist policy of the country, in 1900 assumed an opposite stance. The war was over; there was no going back, but problems remained. In the turbulent Philippines, revolt and counter-revolt clouded the issue of annexation. Some of the articles of Perry's years have a hauntingly contemporary ring.

In an editorial "Give the Country the Facts," he demanded to know what was going on in the troubled islands. Three years had passed since the Battle of Manila Bay yet no responsible civil government had been established. "Absolutely irreconcilable statements" had emanated from generals in the field, committees of inquiry, party leaders, and the President. Were the so-called revolutionists in fact just a few Tagalogs, or were they perhaps representatives of a practically united people?

> We have spent a vast amount of money in this Philippine investment. If we have wasted it in the impossible task of trying to force our civilization upon an unwilling people, we cannot find out our blunder too soon . . . in our forcible annexation of a foreign territory there are involved certain ideals of liberty and self-government which are more important to the perpetuity of the United States than any sacrifice of treasure and life in a single generation . . . The homely truth is that we are . . . up to our knees in mud and water, and in no temper to listen to speeches.

Parents of those slain in the field had a right to know the truth.[16]

As for Cuba, sixty years before the Bay of Pigs, one of Perry's contributors wrote, "At no time in the recent history of Cuba has it been more difficult than now for the people of the United States to obtain a correct view of the conditions on that island . . . A continuation of the present conditions in Cuba will be possible for sometime to come without serious trouble . . . It will inevitably result in another intervention . . ." the only hope being, the author concluded, that a responsible Cuban government request the United States to annex the country.[17]

Perry's concern with his country's embroilment in the Pacific and the Caribbean found expression not only in articles of clear political intent but also in some literary contributions, movingly in William Vaughn Moody's "Ode in Time of Hesitation" and "On a Soldier Fallen in the Philippines." It even found its way into a review of Barrett Wendell's *A Literary History of America*, in which William Morton Payne wrote of the "late sinister departure from the consecrated traditions that have made this nation great." "Empty phrases about world politics and manifest destiny" would not gloss the evil. Many other articles in Perry's *Atlantic* reflect his interest in the world beyond the borders of the United States. He eventually concluded, however, that his effort had been wasted. Nothing could overcome his subscribers' indifference to international affairs; the temper of his readers was irrevocably isolationist.[18]

His prohibition against back talk did not mean that he avoided controversy or views opposed to his own. "I should be sorry to think [he told Godkin] that we could not publish an able and honest expression of political opinion by a close student of democratic tendencies because there would be some people who would not like it . . . I should prefer not to print articles that are merely obstructive or denunciatory, or that 'despair of the republic,' . . . If you can discover and point out any source of goodness in things evil, so much the better from our point of view." The *Atlantic* must present as sunny a surface as possible. In pursuit of pleasant controversy, Perry arranged for papers which would discuss topics from various angles. Not all such papers were specified in advance. When Jack London submitted "The Scab" uninvited, although Perry found the author's treatment one-sided because he had made no recognition of recent improvements in industrial relations, he accepted it for the *Atlantic* series on business ethics. Anticipating remonstrance from his sometimes cheerless readers, Perry in an introductory note gave assurance that London's radical article would be followed shortly by one perhaps more to their taste — John Graham Brooks's "Is Commercialism a Disgrace?" Another article of a liberal complexion was Vida D. Scudder's "Ill-Gotten Gifts to Colleges," a plea that educational institutions, and churches too, refuse the tainted money Rockefeller was now beginning to give to these supposed bastions of integrity. Other articles contained the yeast of the time, the intellectual's contempt for business because of revealed rapacity and unprincipled greed in high places.[19]

Perry printed such discussion with some trepidation. He was not troubled by the opinion of the publishers who held the purse strings of the *Atlantic*. The question was how much liberalism could the Gentle Reader digest. He knew for certain that an author far left of center would produce an upset. True, under Page the *Atlantic* had run Peter Kropotkin's "Autobiography of a Revolutionist," but Kropotkin, although an apostle of violence to whom revolution was "a peremptory necessity," was a scholar and a prince. On his American tour in 1901 the Lowell Institute welcomed him to its rostrum and Boston was glad to have him grace her drawing rooms. Emma Goldman, "Queen of the Anarchists" and manager of his tour, had no such prescriptive right. Like the prince she was a Russian; but rather than a patrician she was a Jew who had served a prison term for her part in an attempt on the life of Henry Clay Frick, and President McKinley's assassin claimed he had been inspired by her oratory. When in 1906 she inquired of Perry whether or not her contributions would be acceptable to him, he told her that his subscribers would be unable to read "in a dispassionate and unprejudiced manner an article signed with your name . . . We say this without the slightest wish to pass judgment upon your attitude toward social questions."[20]

In his autobiography Perry writes disparagingly of Houghton, Mifflin's use of the *Atlantic* as a feeder for its list, a curious stricture since this had been a long accepted role for magazines connected with publishing houses be they the *Atlantic, Harper's, Scribner's* or the *Century*. Newer magazines such as *McClure's* and *Munsey's* on their success led their owners to take on book publishing so that they would have something more to offer their writers than the ephemeral magazine page. The publisher even as his editor was interested in the taste of his readers. An author's trial run in the periodical might save the house expensive sacrifices in terms of unbought books to the faceless goddess called public preference. Perry's academic delicacy was violated by George

Mifflin's commercialism. To one who would "gladly teach" since big business had been so frequently demonstrated shady, all business was performed in the wrong temple by men of impoverished culture. Mifflin, although capable of making fine books, rarely if ever read one, so his editor maintained, a charge subsequently taken up by Ellery Sedgwick. Mifflin was no publisher-editor as was Henry Holt. Nothing delighted Mifflin more than the prospect of a best seller, and in the nature of things he read many books in manuscript if not between covers. Those he liked he frequently took home to read to his wife, but he was diffident about his literary judgments. Decision as to acceptance was the province of his editors. If the firm failed to welcome a burgeoning author, the fault lay with Perry or his assistants rather than with Mifflin or the other officers of the administration.

Since only 3 percent of all unsolicited manuscripts could find space in the *Atlantic,* rejected authors were legion. Among those rejected whose names are now prominent in the literary lists appear the Americans Amy Lowell, Willa Cather, Gertrude Atherton, John Erskine, Harriet Monroe, Upton Sinclair, and Theodore Dreiser and from abroad, Anne Douglas Sedgwick, Selma Lagerlof, Philip Gibbs, E. Phillips Oppenheim, Somerset Maugham, Blasco Ibáñez, and H. G. Wells. Ultimately, three of the ladies — Amy Lowell, Anne Douglas Sedgwick, and Willa Cather — through the tact and perception of Ferris Greenslet, would become identified with the house. The rest found other publishers to their purpose. One took satiric revenge.

H. G. Wells, through his agent James B. Pinker, approached Houghton, Mifflin in 1903, offering the firm his *Mankind in the Making* and the opportunity of becoming his American publisher. On the advice of Gibbs, Perry declined the opportunity. Since the thirty-seven-year-old author's books, a dozen or more, were scattered among a variety of houses, he didn't look like a sound publishing investment, especially since Gibbs judged him "only a minor writer of no larger promise." Three years later Wells crossed the Atlantic to discover America. When in Boston, he called at Park Street to offer "In the Days of the Comet." Again Gibbs reported unfavorably, judging that Wells, in this excursion into space, was reworking an old vein. The story, though "ingenious, plausible and readable," was not worth the requested $1000 advance.[21]

Shortly, in his *The Future in America,* Wells depicted Boston as having died from the neck up. Her cultural development had ceased in 1875, or thereabout. In the ensuing years she had committed the "scholastic error" of trying "to remember too much, to treasure too much." She had "collected herself into a state of hopeless intellectual and aesthetic repletion." Longfellow overburdened her. One night after a club dinner, probably the Odd Volumes, bored by the refined collectors of "toned and seasoned books" and limited editions, Wells went for a walk. "Somewhere about midnight," he reported, "I came to a publisher's window, and stood in the dim moon light peering enviously at piled copies of Izaak Walton and Omar Khayyám, and all the happy immortals who got in before the gates were shut. And then in the corner I discovered a thin, small book. For a time I could scarcely believe my eyes. I lit a match to be the surer. And it was *A Modern Symposium,* by Lowes Dickinson, beyond all disputing. It was strangely comforting to see it there — a leaf of olive from the world of thought I had imagined drowned forever." The following year, Perry extended *his* olive branch, accepting Wells's four-number "Socialism" for the *Atlantic.* In the end, however, because of difficulties in synchronizing dates with magazine appearance in England, the engagement had to be given up.[22]

As in H. G. Wells's case, many considerations other than the preferences of the Gentle Reader governed Perry's approving choice — space, articles on similar themes already engaged, price, publishing comity, and, of course, a writer's ineptitude. Usually unsolicited papers were returned with a covering form or noncommittal letter. The editors of the *Atlantic* were grateful for the contribution but it had proved "unavailable." An author who received more than such formal word had reason for gratification even though rejected. Through persistence some authors secured criticism not originally granted.

Perry, it will be recalled, had been eager to publish Upton Sinclair's *Prince Hagen* but had been overruled by Scudder. Undiscouraged, Sinclair next submitted an essay called "Review of Reviewing" and a novel, *King Midas.* When these too were returned he pleaded for criticism. In reply, Perry minced no words. Sinclair's article was painfully egotistical; he had violated taste in quoting from private letters Charles Eliot Norton and Barrett Wendell's opinions of Appleton and Scribner. Sinclair hadn't the faintest idea of the conditions under which periodical reviews were written. As for *King Midas,* it was "crude and hysterical, the less said about it the better." In concluding, Perry was kind, assuring Sinclair that he believed in his ability and that he was sure his work would eventually show great power. Even so, he subsequently declined the author's Civil War novel, *Manassas,* and a "very radical article" on industrial problems. His prophecy, however, was fulfilled. In 1906 Doubleday, Page published Sinclair's *The Jungle.* That novel placed sixth in the year's best seller list.[23]

Theodore Dreiser's failure to appear in the *Atlantic* has a revealing explanation and has nothing to do with space, price, or articles engaged. Before the turn of the century he had thrice approached the magazine unsuccessfully as a poet, but in 1900 three of his papers brought encouraging replies, although for one reason or another they proved "unavailable." Before the end of the year a fourth paper, one on Fall River, was accepted as part of an *Atlantic* series on cities. A $100 honorarium was dispatched, the paper set up. Then someone at Park Street made a discovery. A few sentences from Bliss Perry's letter to Dreiser of December 22, 1900, tell the story. ". . . we find that considerable portions of your paper have been taken almost verbatim from an article in the Forum for November 1894. We enclose a copy of parallel passages in order to remind you unmistakably of the extent to which you have used this article . . . We do not think it necessary to use many words in characterizing this deception which has been practiced upon us." Dreiser was asked to return his fee. He obliged after a second request.[24]

As a feeder for the list, Perry's *Atlantic* was less successful in securing new writers than that of any previous editor. He complained that his green Boston bag failed to produce a manuscript of "a second Keats or Charlotte Brontë." No second Longfellow or Hawthorne brought the shock of recognition. In fact, Houghton, Mifflin's list fed the *Atlantic*. Men and women long identified with the house and the magazine continued to contribute — John Fiske, Charles Eliot Norton, Thomas Wentworth Higginson, John Burroughs, Bradford Torrey, Henry James, Edward Everett Hale, John Townsend Trowbridge, Olive Thorne Miller, Sarah Orne Jewett, Kate Douglas Wiggin, and the Alices, French and Brown. More recent writers who had entered the list under either Scudder or Page include John Muir, Woodrow Wilson, Paul Elmer More, Irving Babbitt, Gamaliel Bradford, William Vaughn Moody, Josephine Preston Peabody, Havelock Ellis, and Lafcadio Hearn. Perry's "discoveries" who would produce books for the house were notable as professional men — teachers, doctors, ministers — Hugo Münsterberg, Le Baron R. Briggs, C. Hanford Henderson, John W. Foster, William Garrott Brown, Charles A. Conant, Samuel McChord Crothers, William Allan Neilson, and Sir William Osler. Of shining lights in literature alone there are but four new names — Edwin Arlington Robinson, with one poem, Jack London, John Buchan, and Mary Austin. This paucity of promise is mirrored in the *Atlantic*'s fiftieth anniversary number in Higginson's survey of fifty years of literature. Looking to the future and quoting Coleridge's requirements for writing a good book, he mourned, "but alas who is to fulfill them?"[25]

Some contributors to the *Atlantic* could not feed the Houghton, Mifflin list. They were already bound to other publishers. Two such were Edith Wharton and George Washington Cable, both in the Scribner stable. In accepting the latter's *Bylow Hill*, Perry made clear that his firm was not seeking book rights, that it was to the author's best interest to keep all his books with his present publisher. The *Atlantic* would make no offer that would appear to be an attempt to lure Cable from Scribner. Would $750 be satisfactory for the three-part story? Cable countered with a request for $1000. Houghton, Mifflin met the price even though the book would not come under its imprint.[26]

Of course if an author insisted on his dissatisfaction with his present publisher or if his books were held by a variety of houses, no such niceties entered into the negotiations. Lafcadio Hearn's was such a case. His first recognition as a commercially viable author, it will be recalled, had been given him by James R. Osgood. On the failure of Osgood's second company, Hearn's *Stray Leaves from Strange Literature* had gone to Ticknor and thus came to Houghton, Mifflin in 1889. In 1886 Hearn had offered his *Some Chinese Ghosts* to Houghton, Mifflin. But the firm failed to welcome him and the book was published by Roberts Brothers. Subsequently, encouraged and befriended by Henry Mills Alden, Hearn accepted Harper as publisher for three of his books. By 1890 he had become dissatisfied with his New York publishers and their magazine. In three years of frustrating effort, he had averaged less than an annual $500. He had come to hate their "vulgar" periodical and its "miserable" $20 per thousand words. It was edited on the "Procrustean system to hit the public with exactly a certain number of words." His text was abbreviated to accommodate illustrations, "the idiocies of a sign-painter." He concluded to break with Harper and again sought Houghton, Mifflin. At last he was accepted by both the house and the *Atlantic*. He was proud of the new imprint. Houghton, Mifflin, he regarded as "the Macmillans of America — beautiful printers, — and essentially a literature-firm." From 1891 through 1897 he appeared frequently in the *Atlantic* and four of his books were published by the house. Then suddenly his contributions stopped. He had been angered by an advertising biography which he regarded as an invasion of his privacy. For publishers he shifted first to Little, Brown, then to Macmillan.[27]

One day in late 1903 subeditor Greenslet going through the morning's mail came on "a portentous" straw-colored envelope, with "queer blue stamps" and smelling of sandalwood. Lafcadio Hearn, pleased by Paul Elmer More's *Atlantic* essay "Lafcadio Hearn: The Meeting of Three Ways," had returned to the Houghton, Mifflin fold. The author's royalty was raised from 10 percent to 12½ percent. Following Hearn's death in 1904, the firm, for the benefit of the author's widow, placed with other periodicals such manuscripts as the *Atlantic* could not use, brought out a posthumous volume, and presented the author with his ticket to immortality — a subscription edition. Ferris Greenslet gave enthusiastic encouragement to Elizabeth Bisland (Wetmore) as she prepared her *Life and Letters of Lafcadio Hearn* and *Japanese Letters of Lafcadio Hearn*. He also saw to it that various collections of Hearn's literary remains appeared. He recognized the author as "an authentic, if sub-calibre, genius," but he gave him Houghton, Mifflin's time-tested treatment for big names. Hearn's wife and son would be the beneficiaries.

That the *Atlantic* proved a lure to any writer and thus a feeder to the Houghton, Mifflin list must be attributed to its still "awful respectability." Its peers — *Harper's, Scribner's,* and the *Century* — paid better and had larger circulations. The *Atlantic*'s mean rate was $10 per 700 words for body articles, $8 for Contributors' Clubs. To fill his 144 pages, Perry was allowed a monthly budget of $1440, a sum that must have been more than once exceeded, for as in previous regimes exceptions were made for names of repute. James continued to command $15 a page. Lord Bryce was wooed with promises of $21 a page and Charles Eliot Norton was paid $1000 for his five-number "Letters of John Ruskin." Poetry was measured at $20 a page, but Edwin Arlington Robinson secured $30 for his "Calverley's." Generally fiction was purchased by the piece rather than the page, the figure varying from $120 for a short story by a tyro like Jack London to $350 for an old hand like William Dean Howells. The palmy days of the serial were over, at least for Houghton, Mifflin. Soon after the turn of the century Boston had given up bidding against New York at $5000 a round. F. Hopkinson Smith's new finance was not for George Harrison Mifflin. The amount paid to Mary Johnston and May Sinclair, $3500, appears to be the highest figure for a twelve-number contribution.[28]

Rates of this sort inhibited the *Atlantic*'s functioning effectively as a feeder for the list. So did Mifflin's reluctance to approve advances against royalties. He was opposed to the practice not only because of the financial chance which the firm must take in such an arrangement, but also because he felt it unhealthy for an author to be burdened with debts which could only be paid off by mining his intellectual treasure. The vein might run out, or unanticipated changes in the taste of the Gentle Reader might ring the death knell for an author whose first books had found favor. In spite of her popularity, he repeatedly advised Mary Johnston not to insist on one because ". . . it tends to create a strained relation between author and publisher." An overpayment would place her under moral obligation, perhaps difficult to fulfill. Stern advice perhaps, but Mifflin was as softhearted as he was hearty. Authors experienced in the ways of the house knew that if they could bypass his guardians — Perry, Francis J. Garrison, and James Murray Kay — the dragon in the inner sanctum would prove a paper one. Thus Mary Johnston finally secured an advance of $10,000 for *The Long Roll*. In this case Mifflin had no cause to regret her persuasion. The novel's earnings more than doubled $10,000 in the first year. Miss Johnston at the time had been a Houghton, Mifflin author for more than ten years. For her, reaching the top was easy. The new and untried were forced to accept the routine answers of those of lesser power. Jack London was one of these.[29]

London had sought the *Atlantic* in the summer of 1899 with "An Odyssey of the North." At that time he inquired whether Houghton, Mifflin would be interested in publishing a collection of his stories. Perry's assistant, William B. Parker, accepted "An Odyssey" provided the author would prune it of possibly 3000 words. He liked its vigor and "essentially healthy" quality. London's collection was taken for book publication in the spring of 1900. Hardly had word been sent than the firm received an anonymous and illiterate communication "from a party in California," charging that London's stories were stolen. Park Street was concerned. The Western charges would be difficult to check. Parker wrote the editor of the *Overland Monthly*, saying that because Houghton, Mifflin was "warmly interested" in Jack London, they would be grateful for confidential information as to his character. The *Overland's* reply proving satisfactory, London's collection of stories, *The Son of the Wolf*, was published in April 1900. It sold in excess of 2500 within a year and earned for its author a little over $400. The *Critic* in noticing the book declared that London had "jumped" Gilbert Parker's claim. ". . . what he has taken he will hold — if strength counts in the field of fiction . . . the days of the giants are not yet gone by." The author was prepared to call

Houghton, Mifflin his publisher, the *Atlantic* his magazine. He submitted three stories in rapid succession. All were turned down, even though Parker found "The Law of Life" vigorous and of excellent craftsmanship. The subject, unfortunately, was "forbidding," the effect "depressing." Perry's *Atlantic* must present a cheerful aspect. So the Gentle Reader dictated. Parker hoped, however, that he would have the pleasure of seeing another London story soon.[30]

That pleasure was to be S. S. McClure's, and Garrison presently noted sourly that the New York periodical had announced three London stories as forthcoming. He expected McClure, Phillips & Company would appropriate the author's next book, an accurate prophecy. London changed publishers because McClure had offered a generous advance. When Parker heard this and of London's pressing need for money, he wrote in distress:

> I am afraid we were somewhat blind in reading the letters that came with your stories for the Atlantic that were sent back, and I fear the house never knew your situation. They would, I am sure, have been glad to make you an advance on royalties of The Son of the Wolf if they had had any inkling of the real situation.
>
> For the rest, there can be no reflection upon you for giving your books to McClure's. I cannot help admiring their hearty generosity in the matter, and hope you have now left behind the rougher road.[31]

Although London continued to send stories and articles to the *Atlantic,* he was lost to Houghton, Mifflin and soon to McClure as well. George P. Brett of Macmillan had had his eye on this young, prolific writer. His firm would be glad to take him on. London, from his experience with Houghton, Mifflin, had learned he must be forthright in his demands for money. Would Macmillan guarantee him a monthly $150 for a year? With such assurance, he would produce possibly six books for his new publisher. Brett improved the proposition, offering an annual $1800 for two years. One book he was working on, London confessed, had been promised Houghton, Mifflin, a first look at it anyway. Brett forestalled a possible division of loyalty by offering outright purchase (no royalties) for $2000. *The Call of the Wild* came out as a Macmillan book in July 1903. Even though *The Son of the Wolf* earned London a mere $500 in two years, in the long run because it was under a royalty contract, it produced more for its author than his immensely popular *Call of the Wild*. Houghton, Mifflin, profiting by the author's sudden fame, even as the firm had done with Lew Wallace's *Fair God* after the appearance of *Ben-Hur,* reworked London's first book in successive editions so that by 1914, it had earned possibly $4000 or $5000 in royalties. For his books under royalty contract with Macmillan, London recommended that Brett imitate Park Street's technique.[32]

Rebecca of Sunnybrook Farm made 1903 a big year for Houghton, Mifflin. What a year it would have been had the firm also published *The Call of the Wild!* Mifflin's joy would have known no bounds. London loved *Rebecca,* by the way. "I would have quested the wide world over to make her mine, only I was born too long ago and she was born but yesterday," he wrote Kate Douglas Wiggin.[33]

Perry is something less than just when he suggests in his autobiography that Houghton, Mifflin rated *Rebecca of Sunnybrook Farm* of more value than Sarah Orne Jewett's *Country of the Pointed Firs,* that sales alone determined the firm's estimate. His choice of Miss Jewett to contrast with Kate Douglas Wiggin is misleading. Mifflin courted the favor of both ladies. The Wiggin books outsold the Jewett, but the latter were commercially successful, *The Country of the Pointed Firs* exceeding 7500 in its first two years and thereafter enjoying a continuing if modest sale, justifying publication in terms of profit as well as esteem. If, as he says, the weekly "Powwows" served him "as a Graduate School in Business Administration," it seems odd that Perry did not there learn that profitable books like *Rebecca* made possible venturing in new volumes of less assured popularity.[34]

Mifflin delighted in sales, but he was also dedicated to maintaining the reputation of his house as publisher of the best in American literature. This reputation could not be sustained by simply reworking the list or producing the facile novels of Clara Louise Burnham and Elizabeth Stuart Phelps Ward. Poets were imperative. In this department, Perry's *Atlantic* was a singular failure. The blame is not entirely the editor's. Longfellow, as Wells noted, was still the poet regnant. The Gentle Reader preferred his verse in library volumes. The second coming was not yet. In Perry's judgment Father John B. Tabb's voice was the best of the new. George Sylvester Viereck, with his Babylonian excesses, and "others of his class" were "only posturing in public." Word went around that the *Atlantic* had placed an embargo on poetry, and a Contributors' Club epitomized the editor's choice.

TO A BLANK SPACE IN A MAGAZINE

What's this! A half-page without anything on it!
Not even a quatrain, yet room for a sonnet!

How came it that such a space failed to get collared
By "Madison Clinton" or "Frank Dempster Scollard"?

A rather small space to exhibit much art in,
Then why not reserve it for "Edward S. Martin"?

Or, if it were thought they could put but a dab in
Then why not be courteous and let "John B. Tabb" in?

Now where was the agent of that babbling trio —
Ubiquitous "Elsa" and "Zona" and "Theo"?

Yes, somebody blundered — so careless, so reckless
To let any one of those mentioned go checkless!

But thank you, Sir Editor, for this brief space is
In Magazine Verse Land a charming oasis.

Far fairer than latter-day lyric or sonnet
Is this virgin half-page without a thing on it.[35]

Despite this poverty of poets, Houghton, Mifflin hopefully published a respectable list of living and therefore promising poets — Anna Hempstead Branch, Lizette Woodworth Reese, Josephine Preston Peabody, Abbie Farwell Brown, Florence Earle Coates, Louise Imogen Guiney, Edith M. Thomas, John Vance Cheney, William Vaughn Moody, Frank Dempster Sherman, Ridgely Torrence, Paul Elmer More, and Edward Arlington Robinson.

Whether published on commission or at the standard 10 percent only a few of these poets' volumes justified publication through sales. Commercial success in other departments made these ventures possible.

That Houghton, Mifflin published Josephine Preston Peabody was due to Scudder's dedicated efforts rather than to Perry's passion for noncommercial literature. In 1894 when he accepted "The Shepherd Girl" for the *Atlantic,* Scudder had given Miss Peabody her "patent to Poethood." In the years that followed, he quite lost his heart to this "quaint little creature," and he gave to her freely of his time and criticism. In her book, Scudder was a "genuine dear," whose "words of commendation and belief" gave her "beatitude." By 1900 in addition to *Old Greek Folk Stories* in the Riverside Literature Series, she had had two books of verse published, one, *The Wayfarers,* by Copeland & Day, the other, *Fortune and Men's Eyes,* by Small, Maynard & Company. In 1901 her five-act play *Marlowe* was ready. She hoped Houghton, Mifflin would publish it. Scudder, convalescing at Chocorua and busy on his *Lowell,* took time to write a detailed report to the firm and a special letter to Bliss Perry, requesting support of his recommendation to publish. Houghton, Mifflin, he confessed, "is at times very commercial," but "at others disposed to take the larger view, and it is our business, I mean distinctly yours and mine, to take every occasion to reinforce them in this latter mind. If we do not, who will? We cannot ignore the question of profit & loss, but even on commercial grounds I hope to put in a plea when I present the matter of Marlowe . . . I hope you can sustain me with a good conscience." In his manuscript report he argued for publication because "the house has made its position to a considerable extent through poetry, and it may be said to have some obligation toward this art . . . As a matter of policy, I believe a house that stands for the enduring in American literature should now and then make a venture of this sort. As a mere matter of advertising a book of genuine poetry has its value just as a Catalogue of Authors may. Probably it would be vain to seek a cash credit to that Catalogue." Scudder doubted that Josephine's ultimate place was with the immortals, but for the pleasure she was sure to give her own genera-

tion she deserved publication. Houghton, Mifflin should assume
the entire risk granting Miss Peabody 10 percent with no exemptions. *Marlowe* was published on Scudder's terms. The play
proved both a critical and commercial success and Josephine
Preston Peabody remained a Houghton, Mifflin poet until her
death in 1922.[36]

Edwin Arlington Robinson had no such advocate in Bliss Perry.
Robinson had come to Scudder's attention when, through his
uncle Edward Proby Fox (an employee at the Riverside Press), he
had submitted three prose sketches. Although Scudder found
merit in their "effort at telling something worth while" and in
their restraint, he did not recommend publication. Robinson was
encouraged, however, and in 1896 offered a collection of forty-four
short poems, hardly enough to make a volume. Scudder recognized the individuality of the poems, but their publication, he
was sure, would be unprofitable. Houghton, Mifflin's recent experience with volumes of verse had "been so very discouraging,"
he wrote, "that we cannot think it advisable to attempt a wider
circulation to Mr. Robinson's poetry than he is likely to secure
through friendly means." *The Torrent and the Night Before* was
printed by Riverside at the poet's expense, 312 paper-bound copies
for $52. The following year the small Boston publisher Richard
Badger brought out, probably at the author's expense, Robinson's
The Children of the Night. In 1902 having been twice refused
by Scribner, the poet approached Houghton, Mifflin with his
Captain Craig, which Perry, according to his autobiography, persuaded "the sceptical House" to publish. He does not add that
the decision was to do so only on a 15 percent commission, a decision readily understood in the light of Perry's manuscript report
in which he wrote:

> A volume of obscure verse, often eccentric & prosaic in character
> but with flashes of genius occasionally. It is the work of an inter-
> esting man, who is thought by his friends to be capable of real
> poetical accomplishment. They admit, however, the grave faults
> of this *Ms* volume & Prof. Kittredge agrees with me in thinking it
> less attractive than Robinson's last volume "Children of the
> Night," (Badger, 1899). The only ground of acceptance is the

faith of Robinson's friends and the possibility of a more popular
book later.

After *Captain Craig* was on the market it was advertised hardly
at all, nor did Perry take the trouble to have it noticed in the
Atlantic, a lack of push which astonished Henry Mills Alden of
Harper. He considered *Captain Craig* a distinguished piece of
work. "There is no volume of poems on any publisher's list for
1902–3 that compares with it," he wrote Perry. Robinson's later
and more popular books — Perry's argument for accepting *Captain Craig* — the poet gave to Macmillan.[37]

Perry claimed that his *Atlantic* was "engrossed with the lives of
men and women who are making America what it is and is to be."
Yet the overall impression created by the volumes of his administration is retrospective, undoubtedly because a number of anniver-
saries occurred between 1900 and 1909 — the centenaries of Emerson, Hawthorne, Longfellow, Whittier, and Holmes — and the
Atlantic's fiftieth birthday in 1907, the year of Thomas Bailey
Aldrich's death. All these events called for memorials, recollections, new editions, and publication of literary remains, excerpts
to be used in the magazine. Perry was proudest of persuading
the firm to undertake Emerson's journals in ten volumes and
Thoreau's in fourteen. "That, at least, was something worth
doing," he said. And indeed it was. Today such an undertaking
would be subsidized by a university press and run by a battery of
scholars and research assistants, with an ever ready Xerox for
handmaiden.[38]

Mifflin was ardent in supporting Perry's proposals, especially
the Thoreau. He persuaded his reluctant New York partners that
the journals provided a fine publishing scheme, that both prestige
and money would be the firm's reward. In contrast, Charles Eliot
Norton regarded the project sourly. "I am not sure that I am glad
to hear that Thoreau's manuscript journals are to be published
practically complete," he wrote Perry. "I think we have too much
of all our standard authors, and I would rather have the amount
of their work diminished than increased. There will have to be
an immense jettison of the cargo with which most of them are
starting their voyage down the River of Time." Very different
was Mifflin's reaction. He thought it "a little less than marvelous

that so much material should have been left in unpublished form."
Thoreau, he wrote the New York Houghtons, "should be our next
great author after Emerson." The journals must be printed in
full, "thoroughly edited with cross references to the books where
the material has been used in other forms by Thoreau." For this
task he chose the Houghton, Mifflin nature writer Bradford Torrey
and the firm's own Francis H. Allen. He was willing to pay the
manuscript's owner, E. H. Russell, either a 10 percent royalty or
a flat sum. Russell chose the latter — $3000 — the manuscript to
be returned intact after the firm had finished with it. These ventures and others like them in which Perry had a part, such as the
Bruce Rogers limited editions of Emerson's *Compensation* and
Hawthorne's *Mosses from an Old Manse,* even though they paid
for themselves, would hardly qualify as commercial in the ordinary
sense of the word.[39]

Perry's tactful direction of the *Atlantic* pleased his Gentle

Riverside Monotype girls about 1904. Monotype was the first method
of machine composition used at the Press, but for a number of years
after its introduction "the main part of the composition" continued to
be done by hand. By 1916, however, only ten percent of the work was
manually set, much of it by twelve elder compositors. Being unable to
change their ways, they would have been out of work had not Riverside
set aside alleys where they could follow their accustomed routine.

Readers and MacGregor Jenkins' advertisers sufficiently for the magazine to show a profit, with the exception of one year, from 1903 to the end of his administration, its biggest year being 1904 with a satisfying $8000 plus. In 1907 the periodical celebrated its fiftieth anniversary. For thirty-three years it had been published by Houghton's successive companies — Hurd & Houghton, Houghton, Osgood, and Houghton, Mifflin. All but twenty of its hundred volumes had been printed at the Riverside Press. All but its first two editors had been in Houghton's employ and had been given remarkable freedom in conducting the affairs of the magazine. The volumes of each regime bear the unmistakable mark not of the business that paid the bills but of the editors — Howells, Aldrich, Scudder, Page, and Bliss Perry.

Plans for the anniversary had been laid two years in advance. Perry wished all twelve numbers of the magazine to share in the jubilee, but the November number, issued around the twentieth of October, was to give the stellar performance. The world that October was in the grip of a money crisis and on October twenty-first the United States witnessed the beginning of a financial panic, one of the most severe in its history. Fifty years before, the first number of the *Atlantic* had appeared under similar conditions. In 1907, however, Mifflin could boast that had it not been for the newspapers he would not have known there was a crisis. His firm was thriving. Gross sales were well over $1,000,000, a figure steadily maintained since 1900. If pressed, he would have had to admit that net profits had declined from $60,000 at the turn of the century to $39,000; that the *Atlantic*'s profit of 1904 had not again been equaled and for 1907 it was only a little over $2000. Even so he had small cause for concern. Shortly after Houghton's death, the partners had agreed to set aside from their capital funds of over a million a yearly reserve, these moneys to meet without embarrassment any probable demands on the firm. This reserve in 1907 was over $400,000.[40]

In 1908 Perry, because he wished on his retirement "to leave some pleasant memorial of" his "service with the magazine and the House," dedicated his *Park Street Papers* "to George H. Mifflin Maker of Beautiful Books Whose Loyalty To High Standards Has

Upheld At No. 4 Park Street The Great Traditions Of Publishing And Whose Kindness Of Heart Has Endeared Him To His Associates." Mifflin was surprised and touched. However, a quarter of a century later, Perry in recalling his ten-year Graduate Course in Business Administration, asserted that he had found no inspiration in Park Street's methods. Scudder's commitment to artistic achievement within a commercial setting seemed to him quixotic. None of Perry's manuscript reports, or those of his assistants to which he gave his okay, reveal him to be an editor who insisted that merit be recognized at the sacrifice of profit. For him, in fact, there were no Great Traditions in publishing, at least at Park Street. "Messrs. Houghton, Mifflin and Company," he wrote, "were among the most upright and successful publishers in the United States, but I confess that I thought sometimes of the sermon which my old friend Dean Murray vowed he would preach some day upon the text 'Nothing damns like Success.'" His garments had been soiled by commercialism. He apologized to his God for having entered the house of Rimmon. He did so only as a servant bearing up the arm of his master. The ivied peace of the university was more to his temper. There he need not examine the waters which allowed him his scholar's shell of quiet. Four years after leaving Princeton, he had been gratified to be asked by Harvard's Eliot to take over Barrett Wendell's "English 28" for a year. Beginning in 1907 he would give half his time to Harvard, half to Houghton, Mifflin, relying on his assistants Susan M. Francis, Herbert R. Gibbs, William Booth (successor to William Parker), Ferris Greenslet, Frank Allen, and MacGregor Jenkins for details in administering the *Atlantic* and the Trade Department. By 1910 he would be secure in "the Cockpit of Learning," freed from the pressures of Circulation and Advertising, "those twin Deities of the magazine." At Harvard he would teach groups of "agreeable boys" the literature he loved, transforming them for a year or two, perhaps, into Gentle Readers.[41]

Before he won this freedom certain far reaching changes had taken place in the fortunes of the *Atlantic*.

TRIUMPHS IN EDUCATIONAL PUBLISHING

In 1900 when Ellery Sedgwick had sought Scudder's advice on whether or not to accept McClure's offer, his senior had thought him "so conservative and timid" that "the intellectual stir and excitement" of serving under the New York entrepreneur would benefit him. Since his literary instincts were sound, "to toss him into that pot and see how he boils" would be "for his own good." Even though Ellery had not accepted McClure's offer, he had had considerable boiling by the time he returned to Boston. For five turbulent years he had served as editor for *Frank Leslie's Popular Monthly,* changing its name first to *Leslie's Monthly* and then in 1905 to the *American Illustrated Magazine.* Within a few months he reduced the title to the *American Magazine.* During these years he had made investments in the periodical which were to yield him "one hundred cents on the dollar." This occurred in 1906 when the publishers of the magazine sold it to John S. Phillips, McClure's partner, and a group of skillful journalists — Ida Tarbell, Lincoln Steffens, Ray Stannard Baker, Finley Peter Dunne, and William Allen White. These purchasers assumed the *American's* debt, a rumored $400,000. Sedgwick's take on the transaction was between $16,000 and $17,000. Out of a job, he now accepted a post with McClure, whom he served for a year to their mutual dissatisfaction. Next, briefly, he worked as literary adviser to D. Appleton and Company. In his seven New York years he had found no employer to his liking. Even an offer from Henry Holt that he act as editor for a projected periodical failed to tempt him. The time had come for Sedgwick to launch his own raft. His 100 percent return on his *American* investment supplied some of the makings but not enough. He consulted three Houghton, Mifflin employees — Bliss Perry, MacGregor Jenkins, and Roger S. Pierce. He also secured promise of financial aid from Waldo Emerson Forbes, at this time assisting his uncle, Edward W. Emerson, in editing Houghton, Mifflin's Centenary Edition of Emerson's *Works*. Possibly Henry Holt was in on the deal too. At least after Sedgwick's company was formed, he was known about the office as its "patron saint."[1]

At any rate, Sedgwick, assured financial backing, in January 1908 sent Mifflin a proposal over which he had worked a fortnight. His labor bore fruit. To all previous offers for the *Atlantic* Mifflin had replied in effect, "The Atlantic is very near & dear to us and is not for sale at any price." In Ellery's letter, however, he found "certain intimations" which led him to invite "a frank and confidential talk." The letter was opportune. Perhaps Sedgwick had heard of plans for reorganization going forward at Park Street.[2]

Houghton, Mifflin was about to change from a partnership to a corporation. The reasons for such a move are not far to seek. Sickness and death continued to warn the house of the necessity. Mifflin himself had been made aware of his mortality when in 1899 he had been stricken with typhoid. Then, the day after Scudder's funeral in 1902, without warning, Azariah Smith died. In 1905 Oscar Ready Houghton's death and that of Henry Nathan Wheeler carried further portents, dramatically reinforced the following year by the sudden death of the founder's promising son Harry. As one of the heirs and executors of his father's estate, he had controlled the largest block of capital funds of any of the partners — his own $50,000 and the $700,000 plus of the founder. At Harry's death, Mifflin's partnership funds amounted to about half that of his senior partner; Lucy Valentine's, to one-fifth. The other partners, James Murray Kay, Albert F. Houghton, and his nephew Albert Houghton Pratt (admitted to the firm on Oscar Ready's death) had each contributed $50,000.[3]

Following Harry's death, Edward Rittenhouse Houghton, grandnephew of the founder, became head of the Riverside Press, where he had been learning the business since 1893. Although not an executor for either Henry Oscar Houghton's estate or

Harry's, he served as fiduciary to the founder's heirs — three daughters — Justine, Alberta, and Elizabeth, and Harry's widow Rose and her three children — Rosamond, Virginia, and a baby boy, another Henry Oscar Houghton. Four women and three children would hardly be advised to put all their eggs in one basket and carry it themselves as Henry Oscar Houghton had done. New capital was essential to compensate for any withdrawal of funds in behalf of these or other heirs which might seem the part of wisdom. All moneys must be protected from the liabilities characteristic of a partnership. Incorporation was the answer.

The firm, dropping a comma and an ampersand, became Houghton Mifflin Company, with capital of $1,150,000, George Harrison Mifflin president, Albert F. Houghton vice president, James Murray Kay treasurer. Its quick assets were reported as $938,000; the value of its manufacturing and publishing plant as $1,000,000. Shares had a par value of $100 and, in addition to those who already had money in the firm, five men had each subscribed for five hundred. Garrison had been offered the opportunity, but except for his house, $50,000 was "five times" his "world fortune," he confided to his sister. Ellery was also asked to become a shareholder but he preferred to secure the *Atlantic*. Those ready to venture, Edward Houghton, James Duncan Phillips, Stephen B. Davol, Roger Livingston Scaife, and George Harrison Mifflin, Jr., were known about Park Street and the Press as Mifflin's "bright young men." Of the 10,000 shares held for the partners of the parent firm, Henry Oscar Houghton's estate, before distribution to his heirs, remained the largest with 4684. Mifflin came next with 2410; then Lucy Valentine with 1056. The remainder was distributed among the estate of the founder's son, James Murray Kay, Albert F. Houghton, and Albert Houghton Pratt. The agreement for dissolution of Houghton, Mifflin & Company and the formation of the new corporation stated that the *Atlantic Monthly* was "not to be conveyed to said corporation as a part" of the old firm's "business and assets." Rather it was "to be sold to a corporation to be formed for the purpose for fifty thousand (50,000) dollars," payment, $35,000 cash, $15,000 in stock in the new company.[4]

Since change from a partnership to a corporation had preceded Harper's vividly remembered failure, Houghton Mifflin's announcement in April 1908 caused general alarm, especially because it was coupled with news of the *Atlantic*'s sale to Sedgwick. To many the sale suggested financial crisis. To all worried inquiries Houghton Mifflin was reassuring. Incorporation meant "stability of capital & permanence of organization, undisturbed by the death of any man or men." The new investors had "handsomely increased" available capital. Moreover, the men of the new directorate offered "the fresh blood so essential to the life & continuance of a great organization." Houghton's republic would suffer no diminution. The firm had never been "stronger, or so strong, financially & organically." As for the *Atlantic,* since the house held "a minority block of stock with special advisory powers," Garrison assured Oswald Villard, "it really remains with us, if no longer of us." The magazine under its new management would have greater editorial independence and an opportunity for increased "business push & exploitation." The arrangement was "an alliance, or partnership, between the house and the magazine, in which, while a certain important independence" existed, "the true interests of both" would "best be promoted." Perry was to remain for a year as adviser. "The Riverside prints; 4 Park Street issues; — but the Atlantic Monthly Company, not H. M. Co., publishes," Mifflin assured the troubled Richard Watson Gilder, "and this is exactly as I would wish . . . so its friends may rest easy." In its "literary achievements" and "commercial growth," the magazine, "in perfect truth," was "quite a lively proposition."[5]

Sedgwick in recounting his winning of the *Atlantic* denied any liveliness to the magazine. At the time of his purchase, according to his recollections its circulation was 13,500, or possibly 15,000. The magazine's annual deficit, "always expected and as readily realized," he put at $5000. Houghton Mifflin's records show Sedgwick's recollections to be less than precise. For the July 1908 number, the month the *Atlantic* came under his control, Riverside bound over 20,000 copies. In 1903 it had showed a profit of $8000 and managed to operate profitably each year thereafter except for a small loss in 1906. Although the figure had fallen to something over $2000 in 1907, the first quarter figures for 1908 gave promise of a better performance.[6]

From 1908 to 1917 Houghton Mifflin, through its minority holding of 150 shares of Atlantic Monthly Company stock and its advisory power, maintained interest in the periodical and Riverside continued to print the magazine. For a few years, relations between Sedgwick and the house were cordial. Authors recognized as Houghton Mifflin's continued to appear in the *Atlantic;* new writers winning Sedgwick's acceptance were pleased to call Park Street their publisher.

When Sedgwick had taken over the *Atlantic,* he attributed its low circulation to its being a "small fifth wheel" in a "cumbersome coach." The fifth wheel, for its revolutions, required "the individual devotion of a small and compact organization." This he had and under his lively direction, benefited by World War I and his country's entry in 1917, the periodical prospered, by 1918 achieving the largest circulation in its long history, something over 100,000. By this time the affiliation between the Atlantic Monthly Company and Houghton Mifflin had begun to creak. Running a fifth wheel had not contented Sedgwick. His company, still operating out of Park Street, entered into competition with Houghton Mifflin in a division of publishing which in recent years had come to occupy increasingly Park Street's attention — that of textbooks and supplementary reading for schools. His *Atlantic Classics,* drawn from the magazine's repository of essays and fiction, were designed for a similar market. For some years the *Atlantic* and Educational Department offices had been crowding each other for space. Sedgwick's periodic five-year lease lapsing in 1917, he took opportunity early the following year to move to a new location at 41 Mt. Vernon Street. By this time Mifflin's interest in his prospering Educational Department exceeded any commitment he may have had to the *Atlantic.* He agreed to relinquish all but ten shares of Atlantic Monthly Company stock and these might be had on demand. On the heels of this arrangement, Sedgwick transferred printing of the periodical to the Rumford Press of Concord, New Hampshire. When Mifflin died in 1921, the Atlantic Monthly Company called in Houghton Mifflin's remaining shares. The firm's association with the *Atlantic,* as printer from the magazine's birth (with the exception of James T. Fields's administration), as publisher from 1874, had come to an end.[7]

To many people inside and outside the house, this letting go of the *Atlantic* was a disappointing turn in the story of the house. Yet the parting comes as no surprise. Mifflin in his management of the business ever since his senior partner's death had prepared for it. He loved commercial success, but more than the ephemeral rewards of a *Rebecca of Sunnybrook Farm,* he looked for security. When finances were "easy" he tended to become "careful," fearful of tomorrow. Moreover, his preference was for the concentrated. In the Houghton, Osgood days he had hoped to have the entire publishing operation under a single roof. That hope had proved unattainable. Under his administration, however, with book sales showing an annual increase (from something over $900,000 in 1895 to over $1,000,000 in 1907), the scope of the firm's activities narrowed. In 1897 he sold off the Lithographic Department. This accomplishment made him want to put on "jubilee costume," the department had been such a "dreadful nuisance." In 1899 he rid himself of the firm's law books. With the sale of the *Atlantic,* he had reduced his publishing concerns to three — Subscription, Trade, and Educational. The Riverside Press was possibly relieved to be freed of the monthly pressure to get out the *Atlantic* in editions of ever increasing size.[8]

During Houghton's lifetime, Mifflin had not shared his partner's enthusiasm for educational publishing; that, he thought, was a thing of the future. By the turn of the century the future was with him. The firm's educational sales had increased from $75,566.15 in 1891 to $224,203.48 in 1900. The year before incorporation they were running neck and neck with Subscription's but trailing Trade's by almost $200,000. Within the next fifteen years the lead would be reversed. Educational sales would exceed those of Trade and Subscription combined. That this shift in balance took place in a house known chiefly for its general publications, especially literature, must be attributed to the foresight and energy of James Duncan Phillips and Stephen B. Davol, augmented within a few years by that of Franklin Sherman Hoyt.

When the Educational Department had been established in 1882, public school enrollment was about ten million. By 1920 the figure had more than doubled. In the years between, the demand for trained teachers led to an increase in the number of Normal Schools, the establishment of Schools of Education in numerous universities and frequent reappraisal of educational theory and practice. College enrollment also increased but less dramatically than that of the public schools. Henry Oscar Houghton had anticipated the rewards of educational publishing. Scudder and Wheeler had ploughed their furrow. The Riverside Literature Series and Colburn had been productive plantings. The new director perceived a broader field, a richer harvest.[9]

Houghton, Mifflin's 1899 catalogue reflected Mifflin's indifference to the possibilities of educational publishing. Of books designed solely for schools, John Fiske's *Civil Government* and his *History of the United States for Schools,* each with teaching aids and study questions, were the most outstanding. For the rest, the titles were long familiar — Colburn's *Intellectual Arithmetic upon the Inductive Method of Instruction,* Andrews and Stoddard's *Latin Grammar,* Riola's *How to Learn Russian,* Edward Robinson's *Hebrew and English Lexicon,* and Ploetz's *Epitome of Ancient, Mediaeval, and Modern History,* all Henry Oscar Houghton acquisitions. There were, of course, the various series but the majority of volumes in these had been prepared with a dual audience in view, the general reader at one price, the student at a lesser one. If, like the Riverside Literature Series, the books were designed for the schools, they nonetheless drew their content from the trade, their editors from the roster of that department's writers.

For two years following William N. Wheeler's death in 1905, administration of the Educational Department was shared by Phillips and Davol. Both had served under Wheeler, Davol mainly at Park Street, where he had been in charge during Wheeler's sabbatical in 1901, Phillips on the road securing adoptions and developing fruitful acquaintance with teachers and school administrators. The young men at once accomplished a significant change in the status of their department, its recognition as a separate entity with offices of its own next to those of the *Atlantic Monthly* on Park Street's

The directors of the Educational Department in 1905,
Stephen B. Davol and James Duncan Phillips.

third floor. Thus began the crowding which played a part in Houghton Mifflin's sacrifice of the *Atlantic*. The Educational Catalogue issued under Phillips and Davol's direction drew, as had earlier ones, from the Trade, but the number of books designed solely for schools increased. Among the new titles were Eva March Tappan's histories of English and American literature for grammar and high schools, W. F. Webster and Alice W. Cooley's Language Series (texts which related the study of English grammar and composition to that of literature), J. N. Larned's *History of the United States for Secondary Schools*, and Stephen Leacock's *Elements of Political Science*.[10]

Phillips and Davol were executives rather than editors or educators. Neither was trained in pedagogy; yet a revolution in American education was under way, as they soon found out when in 1906 John M. Tyler submitted his *Growth and Education*. His thesis was that the schools of the day thwarted and defied "nature's intent in the child's development," that because of this "the child's ultimate health and happiness" was imperiled. If Tyler were "right in half his conclusions" the educational system was "tumbling down as if built of cards." Neither Phillips nor Davol, even though aware of the work of John Dewey, G. Stanley Hall, and other philosophers of education, felt themselves competent to judge the book. They called on an outsider for an opinion, a step they found repeatedly necessary as fresh manuscripts arrived for consideration. Selecting school books required editorial techniques used only occasionally in the trade, where, except for tool books, editors and their readers were able to evaluate a script and guess at its probable sale. For textbooks consultation with authority was essential. Before publication was undertaken, Phillips must have an idea of the book's potential market, of the competition it would face, of its place in pedagogy's changing patterns, and of its accuracy. Among those whose advice he sought was Franklin Sherman Hoyt. In him Phillips found the man essential to his need, one prepared to measure the demands of the time, familiar with theory, informed about textbooks in actual classroom use, acquainted with school administrators and their problems.[11]

Hoyt represented a new breed of editor for Houghton Mifflin.

Franklin Sherman Hoyt, editor-in-chief of the Educational
Department 1907–1938, the third member of the triumvirate
whose vigorous direction made the department "the tail that
wagged the dog."

In choosing him, Phillips indicated the future he anticipated for the Educational Department. It was to play a major role in the educational revolution of the twentieth century.

Of New England roots, Franklin Hoyt, in his oration at the time of his graduation from Boston University in 1893, foreshadowed the career he was to follow; his subject — "Popular Education the Hope of Our Country." To be interested in education came naturally to him; his father had been a teacher for a time and had written textbooks, one published by Houghton's erstwhile friends, the Sheldons. Young Hoyt also nursed depressing childhood memories of one of his teachers, a martinet who had made life a misery for his charges by forcing them to memorize their reading lessons. He was a ready disciple of the philosophers of the new in modes of instruction and child training.[12]

Hoyt's fourteen years of teaching and school administration before he came to Houghton Mifflin had been characterized by experiment and innovation. Like John Dewey, he was certain that instruction should embrace a larger world than the classroom, that the social environment must be "accorded its rightfully supreme place in education." The child, if he were to learn, must have his interest invited. In one of his earliest positions, Hoyt tried the then novel experiment of taking his pupils on field trips, once to the local Gas Works so that his chemistry students could see some of their textbook principles in operation. At another school, harassed by unruly students, he introduced an academic "Roll of Honor," and disciplinary problems evaporated. Because of his energy and vision, Franklin Hoyt progressed rapidly as teacher and administrator, and in 1901 Indianapolis invited him to the post of Assistant Superintendent of its system, one of the most progressive in the country. Here he continued his experiments, establishing play centers for children where they could "scream and yell," introducing geometry in the seventh grade, and giving students high school credit for certain courses elected in their secondary school years.

Hoyt's early liberalism in educational experiment was subsequently given authority by graduate study which he undertook as time allowed, first at Yale, then at Columbia and its recently established Teachers' College, where he was awarded his A.M. in 1905. Here he became a participant in what has been called a "truly Copernican" shift in educational philosophy. The revolution had found earlier expression at the universities of Chicago, Michigan, and Stanford; but Columbia, because of its "hospitality to all major streams of progressivism in education," had become "the intellectual crossroads of the movement." Under the new dispensation, the child rather than the subject was to be the focus of curricula building. In the new century, the student, "his nature, his needs and his development" would be the teacher's concern.[13]

Nineteen seven was a year of decision for the thirty-four-year-old Hoyt. He was offered a college post in Ohio, Phillips pressed him to join forces with Houghton Mifflin, and D. C. Heath, the textbook publisher, bid for his services. The Heath offer was in excess of Houghton Mifflin's, but Hoyt felt the latter had prior claim because of his conversations with Phillips. In July he began his more than forty-year career at Park Street. However, his old school system did not forget him. In 1911, Indianapolis tried to win him back as Superintendent with an offer of $6000. Mifflin put an end to that temptation by advising he become a stockholder and director of the corporation. Hoyt, Mifflin knew, was a man he must bind to the firm, even as he had done with Phillips, Davol, Scaife, and Greenslet.[14]

Under the direction of the triumvirate of Phillips, Davol, and Hoyt, Houghton Mifflin's educational list not only expanded but also in some areas changed its formerly characteristic content, these changes reflecting, even anticipating, movements in educational theory and method. Between 1911 and 1921, the Educational Department issued 365 new titles. These few were faced with the competition offered by the thousands issued from 170 or more rival houses, some, like the American Book Company and Ginn, educational publishers only; others, like Macmillan and Holt, miscellaneous publishers even as Houghton Mifflin. Since the moneymakers in publishing are the durable texts, the triumvirate's wish must have been that some of their new items would prove as long lived as Colburn's *Intellectual Arithmetic on the Inductive Method of Instruction*. One which may possibly prove so came to

Hoyt's hand hardly a month after he had been in office — William Trufant Foster's *Argumentation and Debating*. For sixty years that text has appeared in the Houghton Mifflin catalogue. Others of similar promise would be numbered among the 365. Texts designed for the primary grades could hardly look for so long a life. Man's knowledge about the learning process was being continually enlarged. This enlargement required repeated changes in books designed for children. Yet even in this department, Hoyt struck a remarkably enduring series.

In 1911, the principle of graded reading already initiated in the *Riverside Primer,* Hoyt enlarged in a series of *Riverside Readers* designed to give the young selections from American authors appropriate to their ages from the first grade through the eighth. In the same year, he experimented with a new type of supplementary reader, an experiment prophetic of a general change in content of elementary education "away from literary masterpieces, prose and poem, toward reading materials better suited to children's interests." Lucy Fitch Perkins' *The Dutch Twins* began a series whose purpose was to instruct American children in their common humanity with those of other lands. The books were also intended to cultivate "in American born children an appreciation of the good qualities in their foreign born companions." In recommending publication of *The Dutch Twins,* Hoyt assured his firm that there was no other book like it in the field, that there was "a real demand for such a juvenile." He was correct. Eskimo, Scotch, Irish, French, Belgian, Japanese, and other twins to the extent of twenty-five followed the Dutch. Carefully researched and naïvely illustrated by the author, meticulously checked by Houghton Mifflin's naturalist editor Frank Allen, the books proved a continuing success.[15]

Many of the stories had their source in contemporary events. In 1914 Hoyt encouraged Mrs. Perkins to write *The Mexican Twins.* The United States was having an unpleasant time with that neighbor to the south and the yellow press, busy war mongering, was spreading "heated and fallacious rumors." Hoyt advised his author to present her picture "with as little shadow as possible." Information must be accurate, but children should not be burdened "with the tragedies of life." After the outbreak of war in Europe, Mrs. Perkins wanted to write a book about Belgian twins, but Hoyt thought the undertaking unwise. America was far from committed to the cause of the Allies. The prejudice "resulting from the war would make it impossible to use the book largely in the schools . . ." She would be advised to take a safer subject, something like the Cave or Spartan twins. However, in April 1917, his objection no longer held. America was at war. A book with a Belgian setting would now be timely. Could Mrs. Perkins complete the book soon enough for fall publication? In two months her first draft was in his hands. He was delighted. Even though individual German officers were indicated as arrogant and brutal, the hordes sweeping over Belgium were sufficiently gray. "The horror and sadness" of the narrative were muted. The joyous reunion of Janke and Mie Van Hove with their parents on the hearth of rich American relatives was entirely credible. America was the land of opportunity. Here all things were possible.[16]

Ferris Greenslet used to refer to the General Editor of the Educational Department as "the father of the twins." To the series Hoyt certainly stood *in loco parentis,* suggesting subjects, anticipating slips that would injure sales. Mrs. Perkins must not allow anything that would seem like "a slap at the Roman Catholics." Expressions which would offend the Jews must be avoided. Children must be treated with loving delicacy. To call one, even though Chinese, "Little Pig" would seem "lacking in respect and consideration." Such slips might adversely affect school adoptions. He doubted the wisdom of her undertaking *The Irish Twins.* He was afraid "that a story that was true to life in Ireland might offend"; the Irish were "so sensitive about their peculiarities." Fortunately, Mrs. Perkins skillfully avoided the pitfalls he anticipated. Her point of view proved "sympathetic and appreciative." The few changes he requested, she obligingly made. Indeed, as mother to the twins, Mrs. Perkins proved a docile helpmate; she obeyed her editor and he in turn readily gave her advice on her real children and her worries about money. At the time of the business gloom over the economy in 1920, she feared the race had been run for her twins. Hoyt was reassuring. Her copyrights were "as sound an in-

vestment as a gold bond." The success of her books would "rise
and fall with the tide of business expansion and depression," but
they had an assured popularity. No matter what happened, children's books would always be in demand, especially such as the
Twins.[17]

Although Houghton Mifflin's object in publishing the Twins
series was to place the books in the schools as supplementary readers, the firm's usual technique was to issue first a Trade edition.
A few months later the school one, aided by the publicity of the
first, would be on the market. In the majority of cases sales followed a similar pattern. In the first year or so, Trade's were
greater; then the relation changed and Educational sales led. Thus
The Dutch Twins, published by the Trade in October 1911, sold
over 4000 before the end of the year. In 1912, Trade led by a
trifle, but both editions sold over 3000. Thereafter Educational
sales mounted steadily, by 1920 going over 22,000 for that year
alone. Trade's sales, as in the beginning, were 4000.[18]

This was a decade of rising production expense. During World
War I and after, costs of book manufacture skyrocketed. According to James Duncan Phillips, who became Houghton Mifflin's
treasurer in 1915, the increase between 1915 and 1920 was at the
very least 100 percent. The cost of paper rose during the period
from just under five cents a pound to almost thirteen cents. In
consequence the price of books also increased, but at a rate in no
way comparable to rising manufacturing costs, for the *Twins* in
the Trade edition from $1.00 to $1.50, in the Educational edition
from 50 cents to 64 cents.[19]

The early success of the *Twins* made clear that they fulfilled a
need not met by the usual basal school reader. Before long Hoyt
initiated a series which rapidly supplanted the *Riverside Readers.*
Planned and executed by Emma Miller Bolenius, the books' school-
tested text and exercises had already proved their worth in courses
that were child centered in the new fashion. Hoyt recommended
publication enthusiastically. In his opinion, with the possible exception of the *Elson Readers* published by Scott, Foresman & Company, the Bolenius *Readers* were superior to anything on the
market. The series was at once extraordinarily successful. In-

troduced in 1919, the books sold over 150,000 the following year. In 1921 the figure more than doubled. Until the wind of theory set in another quarter, the Bolenius *Boys' and Girls' Readers* would prove a valuable publishing property. Contributing to their wide acceptance were detailed *Teachers' Manuals*. Here the program was laid out step by step, hour by hour, day by day. Among the teaching aids appeared diagnostic exercises and tests. In administering these the teacher could discover the individual need of her pupils. She could then conduct her class to satisfy varying levels of ability. The day of the Intelligence Quotient had arrived. In the introduction of the miracle of the IQ to assorted parents and the nation, Houghton Mifflin played a major role.[20]

In the educational pyramid, the largest purchasers of books are the primary grades. These sales, however, are in considerable measure determined by the educational philosophy promulgated at the apex. Teachers and students of teaching were eager for books on the theories and methods of the new time, as Hoyt discovered when in 1909 he published Frank M. McMurray's *How to Study, and Teaching How to Study*. It proved "a record breaker in sales," being taken up by "practically all state teachers' reading circles." To take advantage of this as yet hardly exploited market, he inaugurated two series — Riverside Educational Monographs and Riverside Textbooks in Education. For the first as editor and adviser he secured the services of Henry Suzzalo, for the second, Ellwood P. Cubberley, both friends of his Columbia days, and both, at the time of their appointments, of the Stanford University faculty. Cubberley was chairman of the Department of Education, Suzzalo in the Psychology Department. Their responsibilities were to judge unsolicited manuscripts appropriate to their series with special reference to competing texts and themselves to recommend authors and books. Their fees for books in the series were 3 percent up to 2000; 5 percent thereafter. For such books as they wrote themselves, 10 percent on the net price. Hoyt valued this Pacific coast connection and rightly so, for at Stanford unique experiments in education were in progress.[21]

Because of changes in educational thought and techniques, many of the books in the two series proved ephemeral, inevitably.

However, Cubberley produced a number that seemed destined to survive well beyond a generation — his own *History of Education* and *Public Education in the United States* and Lewis Madison Terman's *Measurement of Intelligence*. In recommending publication of Terman's book, Hoyt credited Dr. Cubberley with having watched its development for a number of years. It should be published, he thought, because it would "attract attention to the Riverside Textbooks in Education." Terman's book did much more than that. It affected the entire educational spectrum and introduced a new symbol to the American people.[22]

In *The Measurement of Intelligence,* Terman described his revision of the work of the French psychologists Alfred Binet and Theodore Simon in establishing an intelligence scale. By using Terman's tests accompanying his text, educators could now hope to determine the student's mental age in relation to his years. Published in 1916, the text and its accompanying tests and record booklets sold modestly. Then, after America's declaration of war in 1917, the United States Army, wishing "to weed out the grossly incompetent and to cream off the exceptional for officer training" secured a series of tests called Scale Alpha and Scale Beta. Terman's tests, known as the *Stanford Revision of the Binet-Simon Intelligence Scale,* were used in conjunction with the Alpha and Beta scales to determine the mental age of the country's warriors. The conclusions reached by analysts of the test results shocked the nation. "The average mental age of Americans was fourteen." Most of them "were uneducable beyond high school."[23]

The Army's use of the *Stanford Revision of the Binet-Simon Intelligence Scale* triggered a major controversy. Must the nation's youth be doomed forever to the prison house of its IQ? Would the democratic ideal of education for all turn the United States into a frightening "boobocracy"? Of the forty texts that appeared in the Riverside Textbooks in Education, none equaled Terman's in performance, none played a comparable part in shaping the schools. Although many testing techniques have since been devised, "Terman's Stanford Revision . . . with subsequent refinement, has remained the best known and perhaps most widely used individual mental test."

Hoyt's introduction of the Riverside Educational Monographs and Textbooks in Education was a departure from the established practice of the house. Long ago Houghton had advised the wisdom, in bad times, of reworking the list. Scudder, Wheeler, and Mifflin had repeatedly dotted the *i* in the founder's advice. In addition to the Riverside Literature Series, numerous others and a variety of anthologies embodied the principle. So did a flock of school editions of many books first published for the general reader. Hoyt followed this practice also. However, it was his innovations that contributed to the impressive growth of his department in these years. He had always loved the theater. His years at Columbia gave educational authority to his taste. In 1899–1900 that university established a chair of dramatic literature, the first in America, Brander Matthews as professor. Hoyt's recognition of the drama as a subject of growing secondary school and collegiate concern did much to add vigor and modernity to Houghton Mifflin's list of educational publications. A gratifying number of his acquisitions in this department would survive their generation.

The Trade had published Alfred Henniquin's *Art of Playwriting* in 1890 on Scudder's recommendation. He thought it "a pioneer" that would surely "attract considerable attention." Actually, the attention it attracted was negligible. Nothing in its performance suggested the theater as a profitable venture. Even so, Hoyt, heartily backed by Phillips, decided to give considerable space to dramaturgy and theatrical history. Among Houghton Mifflin books issued in this field before 1921 were Felix Schelling's *Elizabethan Drama,* Brander Matthews' *Development of the Drama,* Tucker Brooke's *Tudor Drama,* Ashley Thorndike's *Tragedy,* Joseph Q. Adams' *Shakespearean Playhouses,* and George Pierce Baker's *Dramatic Technique.* None of these has survived the years. Destined for greater longevity were the play collections: Brander Matthews' *Chief European Dramatists,* William Allan Neilson's *Chief Elizabethan Dramatists,* and Thomas Dickinson's *Chief Contemporary Dramatists.* Except for a few plays of Shakespeare, before Hoyt's day the Riverside Literature Series carried no drama. Under his administration a few were tried and it was thus that Thomas Dickinson and Joseph Q. Adams entered the Houghton Mifflin lists,

Dickinson offering to edit Goldsmith's *The Good-Natured Man* and *She Stoops to Conquer,* Adams editing Sheridan's *The Rivals.*[24]

When Dickinson was preparing his first volume of *Contemporary Dramatists,* Henry Holt, even though he was producing college texts, advised against the project. A sale of 2500 was all that could be expected. Hoyt, on the other hand, was certain that there was "a well defined and growing demand" in the colleges for such play collections. Such proved to be the case. Between 1915 and 1921 the First Series sold over 40,000. The Second Series, appearing in 1921, with an initial sale of 6000, gave fine promise for the future. Though the cost of getting the First Series on the market was high, over $12,000 including plates, manufacturing costs, and advertising, the book in its first year secured a credit balance of $3619.22 and returned its editor $3908.25 in royalties. Not all of the royalty belonged to Dickinson. From his 15 percent return, having secured permissions, he must pay the plays' proprietors. The task of securing rights was prodigious. Some of the authors were "cantankerous"; they feared sales of the anthology would injure sales of their plays published separately. One who was adamant in refusal was George Bernard Shaw. To allow one of his plays to appear in an anthology would be a disservice to Brentano's, his American publishers. Dickinson, he thought, had been naïve in agreeing to seek permissions from the plays' copyright owners. He was being exploited by Houghton Mifflin. Other writers proved more accommodating. Some settled for an outright payment, the highest $100, the rest for a half of 1 percent royalty. In the long run those who took the percentage rather than the flat fee reaped the greater reward. Nor did Dickinson consider himself exploited. In the next decade he undertook a Third Series of *Chief Contemporary Dramatists.*[25]

The modern theater proved its worth, at least at the college level, and few objections were offered to any of the plays Dickinson selected. However, his collection of short plays for schools was rejected because it catered to the "present ill-judged mania in the schools for new 'literature.' " The entire collection as reported by the reader, H. H. Webster, was "insipid, morbid, mystical poppycock." Ernest Dowson had better not be introduced to high school students. Dunsany's *A Night at an Inn* reeked "with gore." O'Neill's *Ile* was "a rough, inhuman play of the sea — full of oaths and profanity . . . It should never be printed for high school reading." Maeterlinck's *The Intruder* was "depressing and useless."[26]

In supplying literature for high schools Houghton Mifflin continued to rely on the Riverside Literature Series, which by 1900 had amply demonstrated its value as a publishing project. Constantly added to since its inauguration in 1882, at the turn of the century it numbered over 140 and enjoyed sales in the hundred thousands annually. Its content had received unsolicited testimony. In 1899, following a number of years of council in an effort to achieve standards and uniformity in the secondary school course, academic administrators reached agreement on minimum requirements for college entrance. Not long after, Houghton Mifflin fulfilled the student's need with *College Entrance Requirements in English for Careful Study*. Forty-six of the forty-nine items listed were included in the Riverside Literature Series. Clearly Houghton Mifflin need not depart far from its own backlog to supply the reading needs of high school students.[27]

During the first two decades of this century the Riverside Literature Series continued to add titles. None was calculated to satisfy the growing mania for the new noted by Webster. Some additions were by writers long familiar in the Trade catalogue, among them Sarah Orne Jewett, Thomas Bailey Aldrich, and William Dean Howells. More recent acquisitions of the Trade considered suitable for the series included such authors as Mary Antin, John Drinkwater, Sir Wilfred Grenfell, Helen Keller, John Muir, Josephine Preston Peabody, and Dallas Lore Sharp. Hoyt's particular hand appeared in the selection of plays introduced, but only Drinkwater's *Abraham Lincoln* could qualify as contemporary. The series also began to include numerous numbers related to the educational experience, Le Baron R. Briggs's *To College Girls and Other Essays* and *College Life*, and Charles W. Eliot's *The Training for an Effective Life*. Practical guidance items also were added, such as *New York State Education Requirements; Poems for Study, Revised to Meet Illinois State Course of Study; How to Teach English Classics;* and *Teaching English Classics in the Grammar*

Board of Directors, Houghton Mifflin Company, 1911
Front row: Roger L. Scaife, James Duncan Phillips, Albert F. Houghton, George H. Mifflin (President), James Murray Kay (Treasurer),
Nathan T. Pulsifer. Back row: Albert Houghton Pratt, George Harrison Mifflin, Jr., Francis J. Garrison (Clerk), Stephen B. Davol, Edward R. Houghton, Ferris Greenslet.

Francis J. Garrison, clerk of the corporation, was not a stockholder.
Although given the opportunity, he could not afford the investment.
Two other men in the line-up have not been presented in detail in the
text. Nathan T. Pulsifer, son-in-law of Lawson Valentine, represented
the interests of his widowed mother-in-law. Albert Houghton Pratt,
grandson of Albert G. Houghton, came to Houghton, Mifflin & Company in 1901. In 1917, he resigned from the firm. Later, having re-
married and taken his wife's name of Parma, he served as Curator of
Rare Books in the Library of Congress.

Grades. However, the majority of titles continued as from the beginning to be taken from English classics in the public domain or from the New England writers whose copyrights Houghton Mifflin either owned or controlled. By 1922 the series included over 300 different titles and sales were over a million annually.[28]

Number one, Longfellow's *Evangeline,* continued the most popular, its year of greatest sale, 1908 with over 64,000. By 1921, even though sales had fallen to approximately 36,000, *Evangeline* still led all the rest despite the fact that the poem had long since outlasted its copyright and was being published in competing editions by rival houses. So too with Whittier's *Snowbound* and Lowell's *Vision of Sir Launfal.* In 1908 each approached 50,000. By 1921 each had declined to 13,000 and 19,000 respectively. No other titles in the Riverside Literature Series equaled these records.[29]

A book's longevity is not necessarily a patent of its utility. Many forgotten items in the Riverside Educational Monographs and the Riverside Textbooks in Education served their temporal purpose. Their sales were satisfactory and they paid both author and publisher. Their greatest virtue, however, lay in the preeminence they gave to Houghton Mifflin as a publisher of books for teachers and students of teaching. By 1917, in this division Houghton Mifflin led the field. The success of these series Hoyt attributed largely to its editors. To meet the competition in other academic areas, he planned to secure editors equal in competence to Suzzalo and Cubberley. To have advisers for the various series had long been Houghton Mifflin's practice — Charles Dudley Warner for the Men of Letters, John T. Morse, Jr., for the Statesmen, Scudder for the Commonwealths Series, the Cambridge Poets, and the Riverside Literature Series. But none of these men were in the mainstream of education nor did they work closely with the authors they chose. Hoyt's editors would be in the academic swim, aware of existing texts and their faults. They would be men who could envision a classroom need, then select an author and supervise his book's development. In 1913, Hoyt turned his attention to the possibilities in history, securing as advisers William E. Dodd for American history, William S. Ferguson for Ancient, and James T. Shotwell for European. Of the three, none made a greater contribution in obtaining enduring texts than Shotwell, professor of history at Columbia. Under his direction Lynn Thorndike wrote his *History of Medieval Europe* and J. Salwyn Schapiro his *Modern and Contemporary European History*. Shotwell in his work with the firm was appreciative of its patience. He sensed it was in agreement with his "general principles of historical scholarship." Both editor and publisher were willing to move slowly, hoping ultimately to secure a text that would stand the test of time. Schapiro's book, contracted for in 1914, was four years in the making. It was worth waiting for; Schapiro's book, even as Thorndike's, is still carried in Houghton Mifflin's 1969 catalogue.[30]

Between 1907 and 1921 the Educational Department's triumvirate succeeded in radically freshening its list. Even so the catalogue was dotted with antiquities. Andrews and Stoddard had been dropped; so had Riola. But Robinson's 1834 *Hebrew and English Lexicon,* Anne Charlotte Lynch Botta's *Hand-book of Universal Literature* (on the market since 1863), and Carl Ploetz's *Epitome* (forty years young) were still there. So was Warren Colburn's *Intellectual Arithmetic,* but after one hundred years that particular sun was about to set. Hoyt himself (in collaboration with Harriet E. Peet) had prepared a series of arithmetics for the primary grades. Published in 1915, within five years the first three texts of the series had sold over 500,000. In 1920 Colburn's sold fifty-five. Henry Oscar Houghton's original investment in educational publishing was running out. However, the young men of the new directorate had made a spectacular start in providing for the future. Of the 365 titles added between 1911 and 1921, only eleven failed to pay for themselves. At the time Phillips reported this fact to the Board of Directors, he could not know that fifteen of the texts acquired under Hoyt's direction would survive the years, revised and freshened as required, to appear in Houghton Mifflin's current catalogue. Whether any will achieve Colburn's record remains to be seen. Perhaps they may at least equal the *Epitome*'s eighty-year run. That useful compendium, four times revised by William L. Langer, is now carried as *An Encyclopedia of World History*.[31]

No discussion of titles and their longevity can picture adequately the growth of the Educational Department in these first years. At the time of Houghton Mifflin's incorporation, its sales were something over $370,000, or 38.6 percent of the firm's total, and James Duncan Phillips wrote a group of his Harvard classmates of his directorship and of his particular interest in educational publishing, picturing Houghton Mifflin as

> a great business, a great big going concern full of life and activity and brimming over with human nature constantly changing and constantly presenting new points of view . . . My own personal end is the Educational Dept with three offices, three office managers, fourteen field agents, three editorial people, six cashiers and order clerks and some twenty odd stenographers not to mention packers and shipping boys . . . Outside the office there is the chance to look at the whole educational world as a field to be conquered and the opportunity to apply practically every idea which occurs to me without opposition and the full backing of a rich and vigorous concern. And best of all we are succeeding — the educational business is growing, it was never in better shape than it is today and it is on the right basis and cannot fail.[32]

Healthy as the department was in 1908, because Phillips intended his firm should have a larger share of the educational world he had set out to conquer, he prepared in 1912 a memorandum for Mifflin in which he demonstrated Houghton Mifflin's position in comparison with other publishers competing for the seventeen-million-dollar educational business of the nation. Of the twenty-odd companies in his list, the American Book Company led with $3,500,000; Ginn came next with $2,500,000; Macmillan third with $1,000,000. The rest were in the hundred thousands, Houghton Mifflin taking tenth place with $400,000. Phillips' goal was that his company should pass the million-dollar mark in sales. Possibly because he resented the generally held attitude within the firm that the Educational was a subsidiary of the General Department, he cherished a second ambition. He was determined that his department's sales should exceed those of the Trade.

By the end of 1921, the fortieth year of the Educational Department, he had achieved these stubbornly held purposes and a number of lesser ones. The Educational Department now had four offices, San Francisco having recently been added, and perhaps forty men in the field. Moreover, he had entirely revised the firm's accounting system (he had become treasurer in 1915); his object was to establish a clear division between all departments. "In former years the Trade and Educational Departments were merged in the general figures, and such separate showings as were made were merely divisions devised by each department, the Trade Department being the parent department from which the Educational Department sprang. Thus in former years the charges and credits were so mingled that many were inseparable."

The new system clearly defined the line and set up "an administrative overhead to take care of indivisible items which belong[ed] to the business as a whole." Phillips also undertook to educate his field force in "the best selling arguments and methods" for Houghton Mifflin's educational books "in comparison with competing texts." Under his and Hoyt's direction, the Educational Department followed the "conservative plan of publishing only books that promise[d] large sales" or that would promote an improvement in teaching. During a decade the department's new titles averaged about thirty-six a year.[33]

By these means, Phillips realized his two main goals. In 1921, of Houghton Mifflin's total sales of well over three million, the Educational Department, which now ranked fourth among its competitors, boasted sales in excess of $1,700,000 and within the firm it had outsold the Trade Department by $500,000. As important as its sales were its net profits, almost $350,000. Trade's by contrast were only $38,000, and Subscription's were only slightly over $5500. Education had become the most lucrative branch of the business.

XX

THE BUSINESSMAN AND THE CRAFTSMAN

BYSTANDERS witnessing George Mifflin's frequent angry explosions interpreted them either as "righteous indignation" or egocentric "roars and rages," the judgment depending on the observer's bias and the relationship in which he stood to Houghton Mifflin's chief. To some of the underlings he seemed a man always in a hurry, whose voice in his impatience, whether he were speaking over a wheezing telephone or talking urgently to the head cashier, rose to a shrill squeak. However, Mifflin's laughter was as ready as his wrath, and the fortunate were those who knew him intimately enough to savor both sides of his nature. For them, working at Park Street or the Press was a dramatic, almost theatrical experience. His excitement carried contagion. His joy in the firm's expanding business was catching.[1]

Mifflin had been at home in the nineteenth century. To him its clichés were of the stuff that made men. Despite his background of quiet affluence, he had worked in earnest, even as he had resolved to do in 1867 when he had chosen commerce as his career. Little that characterized the new century secured his acceptance or understanding. Houghton had not been one to admit dictation; neither was his pupil. Yet on all sides he was under direction. F. Hopkinson Smith was not alone in presuming to tell him how to run his business. Government and labor, as well as authors, were putting fingers in the printing-publishing pie.

On the morning after Roger Scaife had arranged his effective display of Mary Johnston's *Audrey*, Mifflin learned that a Boston Court Street newsdealer was advertising the novel for 95 cents. Later came word that in New York, R. H. Macy was selling *Audrey* for 96 cents, using Houghton Mifflin's announcement of the novel at $1.50 as part of its own "flaring" display. The item made "racy reading," but what, he exploded, was the American Publishers' Association going to do about holding the price line? Was no action going to be taken to cut off the department store's source of supply?[2]

Trade efforts in the 1870s at self-regulation in pricing and discounts had failed because individual houses such as James R. Osgood & Company had broken discipline. The revived Trade Sales, which the *Publishers' Weekly* had greeted so merrily in 1877, by 1891 had expired for good. Nonetheless price cutting persisted. Because of large discounts afforded throughout the trade, even small retailers sold their stock for less than the catalogue price. Only fools would pay more than $1.20 for a $1.50 book. Bargain hunters could secure a copy for less. Such chaos appeared to spell the end of independent booksellers. To combat book-butchers and department store bazaars, the majority of the trade at the end of 1900 organized the American Publishers' Association, its purpose to achieve a system of pricing and discounts that would be universally observed. Booksellers also united in the American Booksellers' Association. The two groups were to work together to maintain uniform prices throughout the country. No reduction in the publishers' announced "net" or list price, would be tolerated. Discounts to retailers on "net" price books were to be limited to 25 percent on one copy, 30 percent on five, 40 percent on 250 or more. After such a book had been on the market for a year, unless the publisher chose to repurchase, the retailer was at liberty to reduce the price. (Books not classified as "net," those which were out of copyright or had been on the market for some time, might still be sold to retailers at the old 40 percent to 50 percent discount.) Booksellers who cut prices on "net" books were to be blacklisted, their sources of supply denied. Because Macmillan and a few other publishers had objected, fiction was not included in the scheme.[3]

According to the liberal George Haven Putnam, the chief purpose of the publishers' and booksellers' associations was to save the bookseller from being driven from his trade by the ruthless

George Harrison Mifflin, partner in Houghton, Mifflin
& Company 1872–1908, president of Houghton Mifflin
Company 1908–1921.

price slashing of the department store moguls of whom Isidor and Nathan Straus, owners of R. H. Macy, were the most powerful. He denied, as did other publishers, that the APA's actions violated the Sherman anti-trust law. Each house within the association set its own price on its books, and competition between rivals was as keen as ever. Publishers, at least according to their lights, were not acting in restraint of trade. The system went into effect May 1, 1901.[4]

Mifflin was not sanguine of success, but he was willing to give the experiment hearty support. He warned his partners that in pricing new books, they must proceed with the utmost caution, else they would find themselves in "the hottest kind of hot water." "Net" prices must represent an actual reduction. Originally, Scudder's two-volume *Lowell* was to have been listed at $4.00. Now it must be priced at $3.50. In spite of Macmillan opposition, Mifflin advocated "net" pricing for fiction too. After Mary Johnston's *Lewis Rand* sold 100,000 at $1.40, others in the trade followed suit and by 1910 most publishers were listing their novels on the "net" basis. But by 1910 holding the price line had come in jeopardy.[5]

Macy's had refused to submit to this sort of dictation and accordingly had been blacklisted. By the end of 1902, through relentless, sometimes devious, means the APA had largely succeeded in cutting off the store's sources of wholesale supply. The Strauses filed suit under the Sherman Act. For eleven years suit and countersuit dragged tediously along. In December 1913 the United States Supreme Court found unanimously for the Strauses and ordered the APA to pay $140,000 in damages. For a keepsake, Macy's made a photograph of the check and framed it.[6]

Mifflin considered the conclusion of the case a "travesty of justice," but it did not surprise him. The law, he thought, "favors the scoundrel every time when the issue is between him and an honest man . . . there are so many safeguards established to protect a man from being improperly punished that a successful scoundrel can win almost every time when he knows just how far he can go within the limits of the law . . ." Putnam was equally intransigent. In his view the highest judicial authority in the land had given its blessing to predatory price cutting with the result that authors and publishers were "compelled to stand by while the property interest in their productions is undermined and book-sellers must accept the destruction of their means of livelihood . . ." He looked to the day when "one trade shall not be permitted for its own benefit to exploit and destroy the good-will value that has been created for the productions of another trade."[7]

To keep in touch with the APA, Mifflin relied chiefly on Albert Houghton. He hated going down to New York to attend meetings, more especially since events of absorbing interest were going forward at Riverside.

In erecting their new building in 1867 and in expanding the facilities of the Press in 1872, Houghton and his partners, Melanc-thon M. Hurd and Albert G. Houghton, had planned wisely. These three constituted the business entity known as H. O. Hough-ton & Company, owner of the Riverside Press, of which Houghton Mifflin, as its predecessors, was leaseholder. For over thirty years the plant had served the expanding business adequately. However, by 1895 need for additional space had become urgent. In selling off the Lithographic Department, Mifflin had taken the first step. Of the three partners in H. O. Houghton & Company, only Hurd was still living.

At the turn of the century he and the Houghton heirs agreed that expansion was essential if the anticipated demands of the future were to be met, and under Mifflin's direction major changes were initiated which would eventually almost double Riverside's capacity and result in the complex of buildings familiar today as the Riverside Press. First was a wing for electrotyping, then a sheet storage building, and an extension of the pressroom to accommo-date a number of new large cylinder presses. In 1889 Riverside had had thirty-three steam power presses, sixteen of them Adams, the remainder cylinder and job. By 1905, counting all kinds, the number had grown to sixty. Between two and three thousand tons of paper were required annually for their use. The next addition was for shipping and storage with space for two million books. In 1909 came an ultramodern building for composition and proofreading. A new bindery was badly needed; the old one on the third floor of the main building was hard put to handle the now usual daily production of 10,000 to 15,000 books. Plans were drawn, but construction was delayed by the outbreak of World War I.[8]

During the year that the composition and proofreading building was being built, Hurd, who had retired for reasons of health some thirty years before, came to Cambridge on a visit of inspection. Now a hale eighty-one with a magnificent thatch of white hair, he delighted Riverside's employees as he demonstrated his Alpinist's skill in negotiating ladders, Mifflin his exuberant guide. Together they examined the partly finished structure from top to bottom.[9]

In 1906 realization of these large plans for expansion faced possible interruption. The International Typographical Union, its membership grown from 2112 with 12 locals at the time of Riverside's first strike to 44,980 with 642 locals, determined to accomplish at least two of the objectives for which it had long been working — the eight-hour day and the closed shop. Since the compositors' strike of 1863, although "many" efforts had been made to unionize the Press, it had had little labor trouble. That such efforts failed has various explanations, one that precaution was taken to see that "walking delegates" were stopped at the gates.[10]

Once in the 1870s when Houghton was in Chicago, precautions failed and an organizer made his way to the shipping room. There he found a Negro working. Shortly, young Mifflin was astonished to be confronted by an unexpected apostle of discrimination. The delegate announced that if the person were not fired, he would call out the workers. Only momentarily was Mifflin nonplused. Even though he had served Riverside only a few years, he had become confident of his men's affectionate respect. "Call them out if you like," he said, and walked over to a rope that ran to the bell in the tower of the building, used normally to call all hands for fire drill. Two pulls and he requested the union representative to follow him to the fire escape outside his office. In the yard below, on the run, came the men and women of the Press, noisy at first, but hushed when it was clear fire was not the cause of the alarm. Then Mifflin made one of his characteristically brief speeches.

"Ladies and gentlemen, this man tells me that a Negro working for us must be dismissed or he will call a strike. Men, you may burn every one of these buildings down, but as long as there is a roof left under which he can work, he shall stay in our employment." The workers consulted for a minute or so, then one came forward. "All right, Mr. Mifflin, he can stay, we guess. Anything else you want?" The junior partner's gambit had worked and he withdrew in high good humor.[11]

Another reason Riverside had been spared labor trouble was that in the main its seven hundred workers were well paid and well treated. Deposits in their savings plan had grown from an initial $3000 to a sum in excess of $150,000. Six percent interest had been regularly paid even in depression times. The additional 4 percent on accounts of $100 to $1000 had been twice reduced, once to 3 percent, once to 2.88 percent. In one year only had the extra dividend been omitted. In 1883, under the guidance of Houghton, his employees established the Riverside Press Mutual Benefit Association, admission one dollar for men and indentured apprentices, fifty cents for women and girls, dues for the former ten cents a week, for the latter five cents. When sick or disabled, man and boy were to receive six dollars weekly; the opposite sex, three dollars. After thirteen weeks, payments would stop unless extended by a two-thirds vote of the Association. The females' assessments were nicely protected. They were to be used for sick benefits and death appropriations exclusively. The males' assessments paid for the running of the Association as well as their benefits. All were assured fifty dollars for a decent funeral or the comfort of relatives. The standard work week throughout book and job printing plants was fifty-four hours. Riverside's was fifty-two and a half, its workers having Saturdays after one to themselves. Its employment practice was open shop rather than non-union.[12]

The International Typographical Union's drive for the eight-hour day and closed shop had begun in 1905 with strikes in various cities. Inevitably, some publishers affected sought to place their business with Riverside. Such orders Mifflin refused because, as he told George Haven Putnam, Boston and Cambridge were on International's docket for February 1906. He must move with caution. His people were "loyal and trusting." This trust might

change were he to take work that came as the result of strikes elsewhere. New York had shown that open shops were liable to walk
out in sympathy with the unions.[13]

In Boston the strike took place on schedule. Across the Charles
the question hung in the balance. Three large presses were now
situated in Cambridge — Riverside, the University, and Ginn and
Company's Athenaeum, moved from Boston in 1896. On Monday,
January 29, 1906, the Cambridge Typographical Union held a
mass meeting. The chief speaker, James Duncan, of the American
Federation of Labor, assured his listeners that the eight-hour day
was in the line of progress, that enlightened management must inevitably accept labor's demands. Other speakers looking to the
future prophesied a time when the four-hour day would become
standard. The strike call stood for Thursday. On Wednesday night
the Cambridge Typographical Union held another mass meeting.
The three Cambridge presses had promised the eight-hour day,
not the closed shop, concession sufficient to win unanimous agreement from their employees. A telegram was dispatched to International headquarters protesting further controversy. Because
Mifflin had submitted to dictation, there would be no work stop-
page. In view of his background, training, and experience, his
private wrath needs no interpretation.[14]

The president of the Typothetae, the employing printers' trade
organization, estimated the eight-hour day would increase production costs from 18 to 25 percent. Members of his organization were
certain that charges to customers could not be sufficiently advanced
to cover the added expense. Publishers would seek printing establishments in foreign lands where labor's demands were less exorbitant. The death of an American industry was at hand, they
predicted gloomily.[15]

Because of its reputation for superior work, Riverside had always had customers other than Houghton Mifflin. Mifflin had
maintained the founder's standards in face of his clients' protests
over "costs, costs, costs!" In 1905 George French, a typographic
critic, noted in the *American Printer* the "uniform excellence" of
Riverside's product. Books manufactured there had dignity in design and execution. The Riverside Press had resisted "the tendency of the times to shirk responsibility and cheapen material and

processes. It uses good paper, it uses good ink, it sews the sheets honestly, it uses good glue; it gives all through the book a little better value than many publishers do . . . It costs a little more to make books this way — a cent or two a book — but the books are worth so much more to the knowing and particular reader." In labor's agitations Mifflin saw this reputation threatened; yet the eight-hour day was the better of two evils. A strike would prove costly in contracts, none dearer to him than the Merriam-Webster, now over forty years in the running.[16]

In 1900 the Springfield firm had issued a supplement to its 1890 *International,* adding 25,000 entries, and work was at once begun on the *New International* to be published in 1909. This would contain 400,000 entries, more than doubling those of its predecessor, all to be contained in one volume. When Mifflin had solved the manufacturing problems of the 1890 *International,* his men and women had been putting in a ten-hour day. Now he must get by on eight. Moreover, the tome was so large and cumbersome it presented obstacles which at times seemed insurmountable. Two of the "forwarders," the men who took the work from the sewers to lace in, round, and back and cover the volume, found the work so back-breaking they dropped from the ranks. No replacements were to be had in Boston and the Press advertised for help in New York and Philadelphia. Eventually all difficulties were solved and *Webster's New International Dictionary of the English Language* appeared on schedule. Charles Merriam and his firm both wrote to express appreciation of the miracle performed, saying "The excellence of the Riverside work has given to Webster one of its distinguishing merits in the eyes of the public. In our business dealings with you we have found an honor, a loyalty and courtesy which add to solid business satisfaction a personal gratification." The Springfield firm expressed a "confident hope and expectation that the connection between us may last for a long future. We trust and believe that the alliance of the Riverside, Webster and the Merriams will be perpetual."[17]

In yielding the eight-hour day Mifflin had preserved a contract which, while it would not be perpetual, would run for another fifty years and more. He also saved the day for an event of a personal nature which gave him enormous pleasure.

Harry Houghton turned fifty in February 1906. For him there was a celebration even as there had been for Mifflin eleven years before. He too was presented with a splendid clock with a silver plaque bearing an affectionate dedication from his workers. A description of the affair was released to the press as "evidence of the splendid feeling between Mr. Houghton and his employees." In his speech of gratitude, Harry Houghton looked forward to years of rewarding cooperation with the men and women of the Press. Shortly, his aspiration was snuffed out. In June Harry Houghton died of pneumonia.[18]

Mifflin's companionship with his junior had been a source of delight. Almost thirty years before, Henry Oscar had entrusted his son's business training to his youngest partner. Together, through their vivid curiosity and enthusiasm, they had maintained Riverside's esprit de corps. When the founder's death necessitated Mifflin's changing his base from Cambridge to Park Street, he was confident Harry would carry on in his tradition of excited participation. His own son, George Harrison Jr., was an artistic rather than an administrative type. After his graduation from Harvard in 1900, he had spent eighteen months abroad before coming to the Press to work in the Art Department. Three years after his father's death in 1921, he resigned from the firm. However, as a director he retained his interest in the company until 1939.

Edward Rittenhouse Houghton, the founder's grandnephew, and the one destined to succeed Harry as head of Riverside, had come to the Press in 1893 following his graduation from Amherst. His first job had been hauling paper in a handcart from a warehouse opposite Riverside to the pressroom across the street. Subsequently, under Harry's supervising eye, he had demonstrated his ability to master the intricate techniques of book production and in the years to come, under his conservative administration as successor to Mifflin as president of the company, both the publishing house and the Press would prosper. Moreover, it was he who in 1914 engaged young Henry A. Laughlin as a "$10-a-week odd man" and thus unwittingly chose the one who would follow him as president of Houghton Mifflin.[19]

Henry Laughlin's first interview with Edward Houghton repeated the pattern of Mifflin's with Henry Oscar forty-seven years before when the two had sat facing each other across a pine desk in the Old Corner Bookstore. Laughlin, in the spring of 1914 before his graduation from Princeton, had written Houghton Mifflin asking for a job. The firm replied that no position was available but suggested that if he were ever in the neighborhood, he call at Park Street. Not long after, the young man "chancing" to be in Boston, sought out Roger Scaife. There was indeed no opening in Boston, but Scaife suggested he go out to Riverside. He had heard that Houghton was looking for someone. The head of the Press was friendly enough. He needed a man all right, but he had his doubts about this Princeton product. After all, William Ellsworth of Century advised young men if they wanted to make money to go into steel, not publishing. Why should this one be seeking to reverse that sound advice? Edward Houghton had had a discouraging experience with a man of private means, his Amherst roommate who had tried working at the Press and who had quickly admitted defeat and thrown in the sponge. He advised this new applicant to go away and think the matter over. On the day England declared war on Germany, Laughlin was back and Houghton signed him on.[20]

For Mifflin, Edward Houghton's choice proved an unexpected gift. Here was a man with a heartiness and humor equal to his own. In him he found the rewards he himself had given to Henry Oscar Houghton — laughter, loyalty, and devotion to work. Like Mifflin, Henry Laughlin conveyed to others the magic of his excitement, the drama of the unexpected. When he went through the plant, every worker was on his toes. Over the years, he made it his business to know his men and women. In their illnesses, he took time to write, to send gifts, to call. His two years at the Press before he went off in 1916 to army service on the Mexican border proved tremendous fun. Under the experienced eye of Charles H. Roberts, superintendent of the Press since 1889, he began to learn the complicated mysteries of the ancient craft and its modern demands. Once a week at least this fascinating instruction was interrupted by the arrival of Mifflin, who would barely check in with Ned Houghton before he was off with Charlie Coolidge, who had served Riverside for over forty years and whose father had begun work for Houghton in 1852. Charlie usually carried a list of "shorts," out-of-stock titles, many of which might be on press or being bound. Mifflin, checking the list for due dates, would be violent about postponements, eager and impatient for delivery, but meticulous. A misspelling or a wrong title on the list were "a red flag" to him. Henry Laughlin found the whole operation entertaining.[21]

Another source of fascination to the new recruit was the "Studio," where during his first two years at the Press, he could watch Bruce Rogers, typographic genius of his time, at work on one of his masterpieces. Here too worked a senior pressman Dan Sullivan, whose skill Rogers found indispensable to his work.

Mifflin loved his best sellers, but Houghton had been his master. Tool books, textbooks, and standards must be the backbone of the business. A popular novel gave the firm ephemeral publicity. Long range undertakings like Child's *Ballads* and Sargent's *Silva of North America,* unsurpassed examples of scholarship and commerce fruitfully combined, had made the Riverside and Houghton Mifflin reputations and exemplified the firm's motto — *Tout bien ou rien.* The firm's back list supplied school books, anthologies, collected editions, publications for subscription only, and limited editions. In producing limited editions, Mifflin improved on his instruction.

The chief function envisioned for the bookshop Houghton Mifflin opened in 1901 was not display of its novels but rather exhibition of its fine bindings and typographic achievements. Here the Private Library Department arranged books in phalanxes — sets of Longfellow, Whittier, and Lowell, of Thoreau, Emerson, and Hawthorne. Here the prospective purchaser might examine examples of bindings, selecting from an array of brown, blue, red, and green to suit his inclination or his decorative requirements, the sumptuous gold tooling designed first by Philip Mason, later by Miss L. Averill Cole, who had trained under Jacobs of Brussels and Cobden-Sanderson of the Doves Bindery in England. Mifflin believed the work of his artisans at the Press who executed Miss Cole's designs compared "favorably with that done in London and Paris."[22]

One man clearly found the bindings to his taste. "A Boston

millionaire," George W. Weld, Mifflin reported in high glee to Albert, ordered sets totaling 112 volumes — Fiske in twenty-four, Hawthorne in twenty-two, Dickens in thirty-two, Lockhart in ten, Whittier and Holmes in twenty-four, all bound in full levant at $50 each. Weld's check for $5600 broke all records for the Subscription Department. The agent's commission came to $1000.[23]

Miss Cole was known especially for her elaborately inlaid bindings of individual works. Her *Marcus Aurelius* in full olive green levant with an interlaced inlay of gray green levant on both covers had won her first prize against two hundred competitors at an International Arts and Crafts Exhibition in Brussels. Her bindings might be seen and special orders placed at Houghton Mifflin's book rooms in both Boston and New York. Among the books displayed were Sir Philip Sidney's *Certaine Sonets* in full cream levant with wide inlaid borders in old rose and green and Auguste Bernard's *Geofroy Tory* in green levant with an inlaid panel of russet brown, the whole exquisitely tooled. These books were as beautiful inside as out, for their pages had been designed by Bruce Rogers.[24]

Bruce Rogers (or BR as he came to be known universally) had come to Boston from Indianapolis in 1895 after Louis Prang had acquired the Midwestern quarterly *Modern Art,* for which Rogers had been doing designs and illustrations. Once again Louis Prang supplied talent for Houghton Mifflin. Within six months of his arrival Rogers settled for regular employment at Riverside in preference to free-lancing and working for Prang. For the next four years he designed trade and subscription books and under the supervision of Azariah Smith devised advertising layouts and circulars. During this apprenticeship he acquired invaluable knowledge of book manufacture.

From the beginning of their association Rogers and Mifflin were congenial. They often talked of the ideal setup for perfection in typographic plan and finished book, agreeing that to achieve the ideal they must treat each volume individually, in a style appropriate to the author's intent and the spirit of the age to which it belonged. Their aim was not to imitate but to capture in original terms the essence of earlier times. They admired, with reserva-

Dear Mr. Smith
I like the general gray tone — not at all
too weak. With the several touches I have
indicated it will do beautifully — I'm
afraid you will think I am "fussy" though —
Yours truly
Bruce Rogers

Run outlines of
branches out to the
oval.

This side of plate
seems all weaker
than the other. Is
it only in the proof?

Leg just a little
too flat here

A little more
definite outline

shade this side of
base a little
Outline other side
a little more firmly

Am still a little
doubtful about the shade
here. Do you not
think it would look
better blank?

Outline the thigh
See touched proof.

Oct 12ᵗʰ 1903

In 1903 Sidney L. Smith devised a new colophon for the firm. This trial proof is of interest because it shows Bruce Rogers' penciled suggestions for changes. A further variation on this 1903 colophon includes Rogers' personal symbol of the thistle.

tions, the work of William Morris and his Kelmscott Press; they hoped to surpass in consistency of excellence the editions of the Grolier Club in New York and the Rowfant in Chicago. Mifflin gave the first hint of these ambitions when, in April 1899, he reported to Albert his scheme for a department to produce specially designed limited editions. He wished to reprint "a number of world-famous books of olden times which for one cause or another have become rare." There was to be no haste in production. Without regard to cost, the department would look "only to quality." Prices charged for the volumes were to assure profits on the venture. "I think that under Bruce Rogers' skillful treatment," Mifflin wrote his New York partner, "we can make books which will be as fine as anything produced either in this country or in England." Omar Khayyám's *Rubáiyát* was to be the first issue.[25]

As matters turned out, the *Rubáiyát* was second rather than first in what was to be called the Riverside Press Editions. Rogers wished to use some old type he had rescued as it was being trundled off to be melted down for its metal value. Because of the small quantity in good repair, only four or five pages could be set at one time. The type was then distributed and reset. To complete the *Rubáiyát* took an entire year. In the meantime, Rogers had prepared *Sonnets and Madrigals of Michelangelo Buonarrotti,* in type and design an outgrowth of a couple of pages for the *Georgics* he had made for an arts and crafts exhibition in 1898. The April 1900 publication of *Sonnets and Madrigals* was followed in July by that of the *Rubáiyát*. Both editions, limited to 300, were promptly taken up. Six months later Mifflin was boasting that the *Rubáiyát* was selling on the secondhand market at $4 to $6 above its publication price of $10. Some day, he gloated, Riverside Press Editions would become collectors' items, and would sell at many times their original prices.[26]

Mifflin's enthusiasm proved contagious. Scudder was full of suggestions for books appropriate to the series: Xavier de Maistre's *Voyage Autour de Ma Chambre,* Montaigne's *Essays,* a collection of Lowell's scattered antislavery papers, Izaak Walton's *Lives,* and Benjamin Franklin's *Autobiography.* Later Scaife recommended Thackeray's *Mr. Brown's Letters to a Young Man About Town* and Mifflin canvassed various of his friends for ideas, asking them to have "in mind buyers who prize finely printed books." Scudder's choice of the de Maistre volume fired Mifflin. In 1871 Hurd & Houghton had published the first English translation of the book. Now out of print, it was to be had only "at a high premium." This time, however, Mifflin wished to reprint following the French of the 1795 Turin edition. He recalled his time in Paris thirty-five years before when he had seen the *Voyage* displayed in every conceivable form: five-cent editions selling in the thousands, annotated school texts, and "so-called dainty and de luxe editions." The book's "wonderful qualities," which had "immortalized the author when so much else that was great in his day had utterly perished," justified the undertaking. Sometimes he was "well nigh in despair of making people understand" what he was "driving at." The paper gave him concern. It must be French, handmade, and of a certain quality and he suggested that interested importers make up three dummies from papers of different types. After months of experiment the little book was ready in an edition of 500 at $7.50. Mifflin was "quite raving" over it. He thought it "the best made book throughout ever issued from the Riverside Press . . . It would not have seemed to me possible," he wrote, "that such a bit of work in all details of paper, typography, press work, binding and general getup could have come from an American press." Bruce Rogers' work showed "perfect and restrained taste."[27]

Scudder's suggestion for the Montaigne had been accepted but this, a far larger project than those first undertaken, took four years to realize fully. Mifflin wanted to examine as many earlier editions as he could put his hands on. Then there was the troublesome question of editing and translating. Then what form should the volumes take? Rogers recommended folio and Mifflin was delighted. He thought the size would "lend itself to a typographical 'tour de force' . . ." The result would be "stunning." Rogers' new type, named for the author of the *Essays* and cut especially for him, he believed combined "many beautiful features." To a complaint from Albert, Mifflin fired off, "Of course, it's an experiment, but we must make experiments or else take a back seat . . . I believe in his [Rogers'] taste and judgment in such matters. I know of no one in the country who is today his superior."[28]

In its first two years Mifflin's new department produced thirteen limited editions; all, with the exception of Spenser's *Prothalamion and Epithalamion,* were promptly exhausted. The books received almost universal praise. They were admired for their "character, dignity, strength, virility, rather than beauty," for their originality within the bounds of taste. Of *A Report of the Truth Concerning the Last Sea Fight of the Revenge,* an imperial quarto, the New York *Tribune* commented, "If the publishers can do this they can do anything. They have nothing to fear from their English rivals."[29]

Rogers, no doubt, appreciated the praise, but he was not altogether happy in his situation. For an office, he had only the smallest of cubbyholes and whenever he went to supervise work in the composing room or pressroom, he felt like an intruder, sensing perhaps that more than one felt like Garrison, who had reported to . Mifflin on the progress of *The Log of the Mayflower,* "That has been going along at the snail pace of all the fancy jobs which our good friend Rogers superintends, and which are printed from homeopathic fonts of type which are in request at the same time for two or three other jobs . . ." Rogers also "disliked intensely the smell of printing ink and benzine"; the clatter of the presses with their ceaseless refrain of "double pneumonia, double pneumonia, double pneumonia" got on his nerves. He talked the matter over with Mifflin. He thought if arrangements more to his liking were not made, he would leave. Mifflin conferred with Albert and Harry. Persuaded by Mifflin's zeal, they agreed that Rogers must have a place of his own if he were to continue achieving his miracles. On July 30, 1903, Mifflin was pleased to notify Rogers that the plans of which they had talked were to be realized. "This 'Special Editions' field has presented peculiar attractions chiefly on account of the genius you have put into it," he wrote. "We have wanted that genius to have full and happy play, so far as it was in our power to guide it . . . I think in all these years we have sampled each other sufficiently to be sure how we each meet an emergency as it arises. So if you say amen to all this, we ourselves will say go ahead; and will do our best to make this a good life work for us both." Rogers was grateful for the firm's decision,

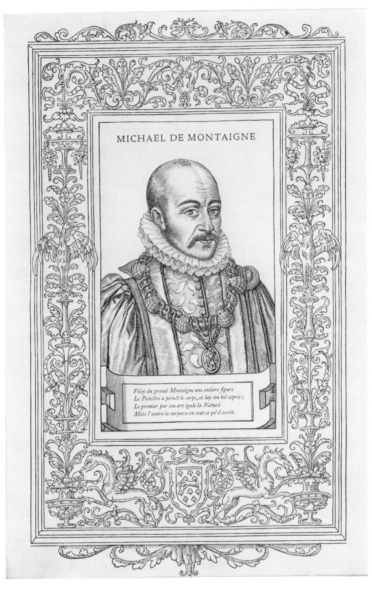

MICHAEL DE MONTAIGNE

Voicy du grand Montaigne une entiere figure
Le Peinctre a peinct le corps, et luy son bel esprit :
Le premier par son art égale la Nature
Mais l'autre la surpasse en tout ce qu'il escrit.

The Bruce Rogers edition of Montaigne's *Essays,* edited by George B. Ives and published in three folio volumes, was begun in 1902 and completed in 1904. The type, which was specially cut, was modeled on that designed by Nicholas Jensen. The frontispieces of the vol-

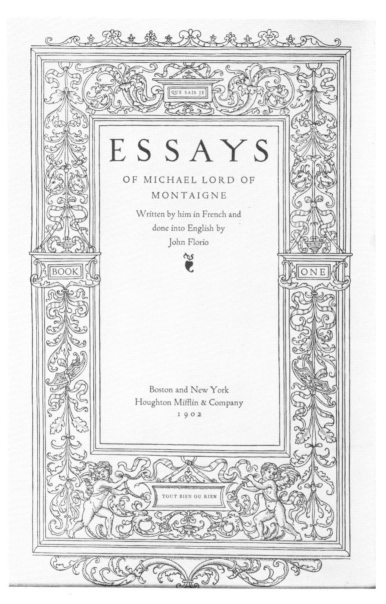

QUE SAIS JE

ESSAYS

OF MICHAEL LORD OF
MONTAIGNE

Written by him in French and
done into English by
John Florio

BOOK   ONE

Boston and New York
Houghton Mifflin & Company
1902

TOUT BIEN OU RIEN

umes, engraved on wood and set in a border based on designs of
Geofroy Tory, were of Montaigne, of Florio, and of Mademoiselle
de Gournay. The numbered sets, bound uncut in boards, with linen
back and paper label, were limited to 250 copies and sold for $120.

which he attributed primarily to Mifflin. In his letter of agreement, he wrote:

> It is seldom, I imagine, in the conduct of modern business, that an association of thorough business men, with a long record of practical and honorable success behind them and a certainty of its continuance in the future, is so ready to step aside somewhat from its natural course of production and to make substantial sacrifices for the sake of art. It is to me a remarkable and significant step toward what I believe will finally be the result in all lines of work — that the excellence of the product and the happiness of the producer in his work will be the ultimate aim of the manufacturer of any article which has any right to be made artistically.
>
> The ideal and the endeavor has of course been with you for a long time, and I take no credit personally for that fact, as it is the foundation primarily of all past success; but this new step marks, I think, a more definite and decided stand than any hitherto taken, in that it is a return to older and less commercial methods, and a reliance upon the men whose personality and skill shall give their product its excellence, rather than upon the exactness and speed and economy of machines, which after all turn out only a machine product.
>
> In so far as I have had a share in this step I am accordingly proud, and pleased to be the one to whom the opportunity comes. The fact of having the opportunity does away with all my doubts as to the advisability of continuing this work with you, which arose as I have said, only because I could not see my way clear to the accomplishment of my ideals. You have now done everything in your power to put aside the difficulties that surround me . . . I think I may safely promise that if success does not follow, it will be because of circumstances over which I have no control.[30]

The building chosen for Rogers was a part of the fireproof safe Houghton had constructed to secure his stereotype plates when he had rented the Cambridge Alms House Estate from Little, Brown in 1852. The structure suggested an antiquity greater than its years and was peculiarly suited to Rogers' ideal of returning "to older and less commercial methods." An open-timbered roof gave the small room an airy spaciousness. The bare brick walls were broken on the south by large, heavily mullioned windows, and on the north by an open flight of stairs ascending to a narrow balcony. The only ornament in the workroom was Rogers' broadside of the Declaration of Independence, considered "remarkable for the beautiful relation of its grays and blacks, the admirable handling of the letters to produce a uniform tone, and the dignified balance of the whole composition"; the only machines, some Adams hand presses. Here the designer was free to experiment with special types (two being cut to order for him), with tools for improving the letters, with inks and with papers of American, English, French, Italian, or Dutch manufacture. It was in this setting, which came to be known as the Studio, that Henry Laughlin watched Bruce Rogers and the elderly pressman Dan Sullivan creating the Riverside Press Editions.[31]

In 1904 the scope of the undertaking was enlarged by a new category called Special Limited Editions, and "Dr. Ferris Greenslet of the *Atlantic Monthly*" was announced as editor, his responsibility "to establish authoritative texts," providing editorial apparatus when necessary. One of the texts which absorbed Greenslet and which was to be the *"magnum opus"* for 1908 was a large folio of the *Divine Comedy* with Dante's Italian text and Charles Eliot Norton's translation on facing pages. Botticelli's designs, nearly one to every canto, were to serve as illustrations. In making up the book, FG was especially struck by "the almost chemical affinity" between the drawings and the text. Rogers had set a few trial pages in Montaigne when suddenly the *magnum opus* was abandoned, Charles Eliot Norton's death being offered as the reason.[32]

A more cogent one, perhaps, was the expense of the undertaking. The price of the folio was to be something over $100, a sum far in excess of that asked for any single volume so far published in the Riverside Press Editions. In four years the three-volume edition of Montaigne, limited to 250, had sold slowly. Ready purchasers had been found for the de Maistre and even for the *Song of Roland* at $25 and *Geofroy Tory* at $37.50. Over $100 for a single book was another matter. Houghton Mifflin was now incorporated and its president's enthusiasms must be weighed in the balance with the inclination of its directors.[33]

The Studio gave Bruce Rogers a degree of the freedom he

sought. Nonetheless the whole complex of the Riverside Press was an odd setting for a man who wanted "to be a tramp printer" and set up shop "with only a few types, a portable press, and a sketching pad . . . in a rural retreat at some converted mill." More was expected of him than special editions. As he had done from the beginning, he continued to design subscription and trade books, catalogues and leaflets. Across the yard from his Studio, the great clattering presses in the main building spewed out by the thousands his designs for Kate Douglas Wiggin's *Diary of a Goose Girl,* Mary Johnston's *The Long Roll,* Samuel McChord Crothers' *By the Christmas Fire,* and other works of varying degrees of artistic integrity. Following the firm's incorporation in 1908, he had hoped to be made a director. That possibility was negated in 1910 when Greenslet was tapped for that exclusive club. In April 1911, Bruce Rogers published his personal declaration of independence, announcing that after fifteen years he was leaving the Riverside Press's employ, but that through arrangement with the owners he was to be free to use the Studio and the types and ornaments which he had collected and designed under their aegis. He was at liberty to accept special commissions. The break became final in 1914. What Henry Laughlin watched with fascination was in reality the end of an era. Riverside special editions and other exceptional books would continue to issue from the Riverside Press; but Mifflin was now sixty-nine, and the excitement and drama of this unique marriage of art and commerce departed with Bruce Rogers.[34]

Of the close to sixty Bruce Rogers–Riverside Press editions, certain ones gave Mifflin particular pleasure. De Maistre's *Voyage Autour de Ma Chambre* recalled his youthful days in Paris. *The Poems of Maria Lowell,* with its "simple, high-thinking, honest" printing was an act of devotion to Houghton, who had printed the volume delicately and honestly himself in 1855. Rogers' varied techniques gave Mifflin repeated cause for exclamation: Boccaccio's *Life of Dante,* "printed on a hand press direct from types used for the first time," with its new woodcut of the poet based on his death mask; *Paul et Virginie,* the second of the series done in French, the first to use Didot type, the handmade paper skillfully stained by BR at the Press; the octavo *Theocritus* with its hand-engraved wood blocks, rough handmade paper, and superb title page; *The Familiar Letters of James Howell,* with its refreshingly different title page, yet perfect "in harmony with the general typographical treatment." Over this last, Mifflin exulted that Agnes Repplier, who had written the introduction, "went quite wild." The star of the group to him was *The Song of Roland,* its French Gothic type brought by Rogers from Paris, its quaint illustrations derived from the Charlemagne window at Chartres. In sending a copy to the printer J. Horace McFarland, he wrote:

> You will of course detect that it is an attempt to treat this bit of literature after the manner of the period of its issue. It is printed on a hand press from fresh type, and is unique in this, that with the exception of the illustrations (which of course are hand painted, as you will see) the color work was all printed at one impression so the register is faultless . . . this is the only book we have ever treated in this way. It was quite a funny operation to see the hand press form inked in the old fashioned way with different inks, and the sheet printed from the single impression. The book is in a further way interesting to me because the paper is of American make, which I do not think anyone would suspect.[35]

Mifflin was so proud of *The Song of Roland* that he sent a copy to President Roosevelt, his excuse apparently John Burroughs' *Atlantic* article in which the President had had a hand, "Camping and Tramping with Roosevelt." The gift led to a characteristic exchange of letters.

January 1, 1907

Personal

Gentlemen:

  Upon my word, I am paid three times over for that article by the receipt of your beautiful copy of The Song of Roland. Beautiful is the only word to describe it. It is awfully nice of you to have sent it to me. Incidentally, I am proud as an American that such a bit of work should be done in America.

with hearty regard,
Sincerely yours,
THEODORE ROOSEVELT

January 23, 1907

Personal

Gentlemen:

Would it be agreeable to you if I stopt at 4 Park Street on the morning of the 23d of February to look at some of your special editions like that Beautiful "Song of Roland" which you sent me? I am not an expert on these matters, but comparing that "Song of Roland" with other modern printing (notably with a very handsome edition of a great German book I have) it seemed to me far ahead, and almost like some of the very beautiful printing of books at the end of the Fifteenth Century. The other day I saw a Livy, tooled in Florence in 1476, which was so beautiful, altho so very expensive, that it really needed heroic self-denial for me not to purchase it.

Sincerely yours,

THEODORE ROOSEVELT

January 25, 1907

Dear Mr. President,

It will be altogether delightful to have you call at 4 Park Street on the morning of Feby 23, and we shall have the greatest interest in showing you all our Special Editions, and presenting to you our Mr. Bruce Rogers their designer. The writer further hopes to have the pleasure of meeting you at the Porcellian rooms the same evening.

Sincerely yrs,

HOUGHTON MIFFLIN CO.

January 26, 1907

Personal

Dear Brother unknown:

Three cheers! I did not expect to strike a Porc. Brother at the special edition exhibition, and now look forward all the more eagerly to it. Are you Brother Mifflin?

Yours,

THEODORE ROOSEVELT

January 29, 1907

Personal

Dear Mr. President,

Yes this is Brother Mifflin, but he never expected to live to see the day that a Porc Brother should be President of the United States — and Such a President!

Sincerely yrs,
GHM

February 23, 1907, was a red-letter day at 4 Park Street. A fire crackled on the hearth of this Boston Blackwoods, for it was bitter cold. The young men, not yet directors, lined the stair rail — Greenslet, Scaife, Davol, Phillips, Harrison Mifflin, and Edward Houghton. Mifflin, sartorially correct in black morning coat and striped trousers, was on the ready. Meanwhile, the crowds on the Common drifted away as the time for the President's appearance passed. His schedule had been thrown out of kilter. His train, the Federal, was an hour and seventeen minutes late. At last the clat-

During his Boston visit, President Theodore Roosevelt stayed with his Harvard classmate Sturgis Bigelow at 60 Beacon Street. Here he is shown leaving the Sturgis house for 4 Park Street.

ter of hooves and the yells of the shivering few outside warned of the President's arrival. Mifflin was in his element. Although the firm's public dinners of Houghton's day had long since been given up, he frequently entertained at his houses in Boston, Nahant, and North Andover. He was a skilled and gracious host.[36]

Outside 4 Park Street, the crowds grew as word spread that the President had arrived. People pressed against the fence of the Common and massed on Tremont and Beacon Streets as well. Mifflin would be the last person in the world to face willingly such a crowd and he suggested the President leave by the French windows which opened on the Old Granary Burying Ground at the back of the building. Roosevelt, however, was not yet ready for the graveyard. He left by the front door and obligingly turned glittering eyeglasses and shining teeth full face to waiting photographers. The people roared their approval. In his carriage at last, the President was followed by two Secret Service men, who jumped to the box, cautiously leaving a leg each free of the lap robe, ready in an emergency to spring to the President's side.

At a dinner in honor of the President at the Porcellian Club that evening, Mifflin would have further opportunity to talk with Roosevelt of their mutual interest in fine books. For others at Houghton Mifflin, memories of the President's morning visit to Park Street would be one of the highlights of their long service.

XXI

FG

FERRIS GREENSLET before he joined Houghton Mifflin had touched the hem of its garment, so to speak. In 1887, as a boy of twelve, while staying with an ailing uncle in Dansville, New York, he had met William Dean Howells. The former *Atlantic* editor took a liking to the slight, shy boy with a hesitant way of speaking, allowing him to read proof sent on by Harper and giving him a book inscribed "From his friend W. D. Howells." In 1893 when he was trying to make up his mind what college to choose, he went over the mountains from his home in Glens Falls, New York, to have a look at Williams. In the hack which he took from the station, he was struck by the good looks of another passenger. Eight years later, when he came to Park Street, he discovered his companion had been Bliss Perry. In the end, Wesleyan rather than Williams was his choice. At college, to his surprise, he found he "could walk a mile faster than any other member of the college body," and he became a star of the varsity walking team, an established track sport at the time. In a meet with Harvard, his rival on the stretch was James Duncan Phillips. In the contest Greenslet was the victor. In 1897, after receiving his A.B. from Wesleyan, he went on to Columbia. Here he worshiped at the feet of George Edward Woodberry, Houghton Mifflin author and acerbic friend of Thomas Bailey Aldrich. In 1900, his Ph.D. pocketed, he secured critical work on the *Nation*. The following year he called on Scudder to propose himself as a Houghton Mifflin editor.[1]

After Greenslet's call, Scudder wrote not only to Mifflin but also to Wendell Phillips Garrison. What had the literary editor of the *Nation* to say of the applicant, he asked. Garrison responded with what he considered "very disinterested" testimony. In his opinion, Ferris Greenslet would be "a valuable accession to any literary factory." His work for the *Nation* had shown "remarkable versatility"; his literary standards were balanced. His Columbia thesis on Joseph Glanville had resulted in a Macmillan book, which the *Nation* had reviewed favorably. Houghton Mifflin's gain would be the *Nation's* loss, Garrison concluded.[2]

Greenslet, as his autobiography makes so clear, was a fisherman by inheritance, instruction, and inclination. Before his call on Scudder in late November 1901, he had done a fair amount of casting in *Atlantic* pools. Gifted with an angler's patience, he knew it was "worth fishing a lot of water to get one good rise." Since his *Nation* engagement allowed him considerable freedom, he had time to write essays to submit to other periodicals. In the summer of 1900 he sent for Perry's consideration a paper on the seventeenth-century poet Crashaw. It was returned, but with reluctance. In November he tendered a paper on Giacomo Leopardi. This too was returned, but the editor's letter of regret inspired Greenslet to inquire if the *Atlantic* might have room for a critical examination of Stephen Phillips' *Herod*. Again, the answer was a disappointing no; a paper on Phillips had been previously engaged. Next he submitted his book on Walter Pater. By this time Greenslet's name was familiar at Park Street. Because of the caliber of the work, his Pater manuscript was given "special consideration," but the conclusion was not to publish. However, the letter of regret contained a suggestion that at some future time an editorial position might be available.[3]

With such encouragement, Greenslet came to Boston in the fall of 1901, accepting as stopgap employment a job at the Boston Public Library cataloguing Old French and Mediaeval Latin manuscripts. This task finished, he went to the Boston *Advertiser* as a literary columnist and shortly Perry accepted for the *Atlantic* his review of the *Dictionary of National Biography,* at the same time authorizing him to prepare a couple of additional reviews and a study of Jane Austen. As for the editorial position, that had not yet become available, but Perry's assistant, Parker, wrote confidentially, "As you are aware, we may soon have to contemplate a contingency more grave than that we had in mind when we first talked with you." Less than two months later, Greenslet found on his desk at the *Advertiser* a note from Bliss Perry asking if he would accept a position as subeditor of the *Atlantic Monthly*. Room was now available at Park Street. Scudder had died.[4]

Greenslet's progress within the firm was relatively rapid. Within five years he had achieved the title of literary adviser and following Perry's retirement in 1910 he was named editor-in-chief of the Trade Department. At about the same time, Roger Scaife divided with him his shares in the company and he was elected to the Board of Directors. Henceforth the two men regarded themselves as partners and so referred to themselves in their letters to authors. In the division of responsibility Scaife was charged with advertising and book format, Greenslet with contract negotiations, editorial supervision, and the soft answer that turneth away wrath. For the next thirty years Ferris Greenslet would be in large measure responsible for the content and character of Houghton Mifflin's trade list.[5]

Ferris Greenslet brought to Park Street a different spirit from that which had characterized the regimes of Scudder and Bliss Perry. To Mifflin he was "a gallant knight," a guardian of his inner sanctum capable of so phrasing denial that the petitioner retired almost content. His oblique humor, his Shandean nonsense, won ready response from the President of the Corporation, his peers, and his young assistants. Frank Allen loved to recall the private japes and capers of their green and garden days and regretted that Greenslet failed to evoke in his autobiography the flavor of their remembered merriment. "I should have expected to hear Mr. Mifflin's loud laughter ringing out now and then," he complained. Why hadn't he put down on paper the fun they had had with words? Why hadn't he told of his nickname, "the logodaedalist"? Because he radiated "some sort of ectoplasm," he was "fascinating" to the youthful Esther Forbes. He made daily drudgery a joy. Although he had on occasion a somewhat austere presence, about the office he soon came to be called FG. Others dubbed him "the Duke," possibly because of his biography of Aldrich, who had also answered to that name.[6]

Ferris Greenslet, who first came to the firm in 1902
as assistant editor of the *Atlantic*, served Houghton
Mifflin more than forty years as adviser, editor-in-chief
of the Trade Department, general manager of the
Trade Division, and director.

But Greenslet was no Aldrich. He had none of that poet's inclination for petty jealousy and back-biting. Nor did he share
Aldrich's feeling that "America was becoming the cess-pool of
Europe," to be ruled by "jail-birds, professional murderers, ama-
teur lepers . . . and human gorillas." FG was a humanist, not in
the Irving Babbitt–Paul Elmer More sense, but in the Baconian.
Man and all his works interested him. As a humanist he loved
the past as much as the present and found in Latin his delight,
especially in Virgil, whose language conveys "the sense of tears in
natural things." Of a scholastic, literary bent, he had however
none of the academician's condescension toward the market place.
His was a robust conscience. To make money out of literature
troubled him not a whit, and he soon mastered the language of
profit and loss, the metaphysics of overhead.[7]

Frank Allen was sorry FG's *Under the Bridge* had so few tales
about authors and their books. Enough had been left out to fill
a second volume, he protested. However, Greenslet was both re-
ticent and modest. To boast was not in him, save perhaps of a fish
or a dry fly. A number of his authors inveighed against Houghton
Mifflin, but rarely against its editor. Him they regarded with affection. Gamaliel Bradford, John Drinkwater, and John Buchan
dedicated books to him, and Mary Austin called a character in one
of her stories Greenslet because she wished a name that conveyed
a sense of life, "a little sharp and yet sound at the core like a winter
apple." Another reason that Greenslet cabined and confined his
memoirs was that in so doing, he was following the advice he gave
his authors, ". . . art, like surgery, is a purgation of superfluities,"
or in Michelangelo's precept, "The more the marble wastes, the
more the statue grows."[8]

FG preferred to meet a crisis in conference rather than by letter.
Unprepossessing in appearance, shy in speech, he yet had remarkable persuasive powers. Willa Cather at moments of decision preferred the mails, knowing that her editor might well divert her
from the course on which she had determined. His letters have
persuasive power too. They fulfill one of his tests of a manuscript.
Pricked anywhere, they bleed. To his authors he gave of himself.
Scudder had the reputation of applying his own polish to the

writer's words. Greenslet, save in objecting to a page agitated by adjectives, was less concerned with style. Even in matters of fact, he secured correction through question rather than assertion. His chief concerns were with brevity and consistency in both characterization and structure. Even though his comments might be adverse, to those writers whose works he valued, he almost always conveyed conviction of his buoyant belief in and enthusiasm for their work. With only one important author — Willa Cather — did he finally fail in this regard.[9]

Greenslet's pace was usually slow. Patience and pertinacity were as much a part of his editorial as piscatorial equipment. He waited for Anne Douglas Sedgwick for almost fifteen years, ten for *The Education of Henry Adams,* six for John Livingston Lowes's *The Road to Xanadu.* For each of these, and many others, he returned periodically to the streamside, interested, persistent, unhurried. Some like May Sinclair slipped his hook to try other publishers' richer pools.

In reviewing his life in publishing, Greenslet attributed Houghton Mifflin's failure to play a significant part in the literary renaissance of the twenties to the power of Boston's Watch and Ward Society. To explain to desirable new authors suppression of such books as *Elmer Gantry, Black April, The Sun Also Rises, Manhattan Transfer,* and *An American Tragedy* was difficult. The protracted and bitterly contested Sacco-Vanzetti case he considered another weight in the balance against Boston publishers. That Houghton Mifflin was fearful of publishing a book that might be banned in Boston is beyond doubt. A New York book blazoned as "Banned in Boston" might ride in triumph the tide of such gratuitous publicity, but Park Street's books were printed in Cambridge and published in Boston. Let one be prohibited and the entire edition would be subject to the police. "Our censors are the police and the police courts," Scaife told Radclyffe Hall. "They interpret the laws from the Statutes and they do not consider the work as a whole necessarily, but sentence by sentence." Houghton Mifflin would do the author poor service in publishing *The Well of Loneliness* even though it considered her novel "violently arresting" and "its grasp of the unusual human emotions" extra-

ordinary. In Boston, the police could effectively prevent its circulation anywhere in the United States, he feared.[10]

Added to this power of Boston's Watch and Ward and the local
police, other causes long operative kept new American writers from
approaching Houghton Mifflin. After all it usually takes more
than one published book for an author to realize his power, to find
his direction, to acquire a reputation. The flowering of the twenties had its roots in a revolution which had been going on for more
than a decade. Writers in that revolution Houghton Mifflin had
consistently refused to accept. As already noted, both Upton Sinclair and Theodore Dreiser had been denied Park Street's acceptance. Other young writers refused Houghton Mifflin's imprint
before 1920 include Vachel Lindsay, John Erskine, Max Eastman,
Louis Untermeyer, H. L. Mencken, Stark Young, Carl Van Doren,
William Rose Benét, Edwin Arlington Robinson (after the firm
had published his *Captain Craig*), and James Branch Cabell. Of
all of these Cabell was the most persistent, submitting within four
years five manuscripts, the last *The Cream of the Jest*, which was
declined as "A fantastic half-modern-half-archaic tale not likely to
succeed." By 1920 Houghton Mifflin's reputation for conservatism
had crystallized. Young writers destined to contribute to the brilliance of the dividend decade, as FG called the twenties, sought
other publishers than Park Street.[11]

That it had such a reputation should not be attributed entirely
to its editors-in-chief or its administration. The numbered manuscript reports, originated by Scudder in 1882, in 1902, the year of
his death, passed 10,000. During these twenty years, he more frequently than anyone else wrote the summarizing sheet which recommended acceptance or rejection. His tastes were those of a
delicately bred man of his time. He preferred the subtle to the
overt, the smiling aspect to the morbid. Although opposed to sensation for sensation's sake and considerate of individual privacy,
if a story or biography carried the seeds of reform, he believed it
should be published. Attached to his summaries might be extended analysis by one reader and additional comments by others.
Important publishing projects like the Thoreau journals, or
writers of repute new to the house, and authors whose books had

not yet paid for themselves were "powwowed," that is, taken up at the firm's weekly conference of department heads. If the summarizing sheet indicated agreement among the readers, usually that opinion governed the action taken. Many rejections were not powwowed, but received authority by being initialed by either Mifflin or his deputy. As has been seen in the case of *David Harum,* this initialing was at times routine. Following Scudder's death, Perry, even though he was now literary adviser, usually assigned preparation of the summary sheets to Herbert R. Gibbs, with the firm since its Hurd & Houghton days. Susan M. Francis, whose editorial experience had begun in the offices of James T. Fields, more frequently than anyone else wrote the detailed analysis. The lot of second reader fell to one or another of the younger men — Frank Allen, William Parker, William Booth, Roger Scaife, or Ferris Greenslet. Greenslet, after he succeeded Perry, although he wrote many, many reports himself, relied heavily on both Gibbs and Miss Francis for assistance.

Neither of these was prepared for the new times. Longfellow and Tennyson were their poetic ideals. Vachel Lindsay to them was "unpoetical" and "pretentious." In fiction they preferred a pleasant theme. The new realism violated their sensibilities. Novels with "unwelcome episodes of illegitimacy" were better left unpublished. If an author chose to write about a prostitute, he had no excuse unless he told his story "in such a way as to teach a wholesome lesson intensely, or to give an insistent warning." Both lacked Scudder's saving graces — humor and humility. To Gibbs, W. Somerset Maugham's *Loaves and Fishes* was "tiresome." Miss Francis judged the author as lacking in "brilliancy," "distinction," and "subtlety." Stultifying as the opinions of Gibbs and Miss Francis were, in the end the man on the bridge is the responsible person. It was Greenslet who vetoed Frank Allen's recommendation to publish John Masefield's *The Everlasting Mercy* and *The Widow in the Bye Street.* He found the poems "of strikingly individual quality," but doubted "their appeal to American readers . . . looking at Masefield's work as a whole," he wrote. "I don't believe it is quite promising enough to warrant taking these in face of a probable loss." In more than this instance his criteria were not those of the champions of the revolution going forward in New York. To him an adventure story "written with knowledge and atmosphere and in the King's English" was "a gift of the gods." In reading manuscripts he kept his eye on the object, the intended audience. The preferences of the literati played no part in his judgments. He believed "the only valid *raison d'etre* for the publication of anything is that it should have something to say to a reasonable number of unprofessional readers, a direct and immediate appeal to them." In 1915 he anticipated "that one effect of the greatest of wars" would be "to discourage the production of morbid and flippant literature and greatly to stimulate that of books dealing ably with the serious and permanent aspects of life." His publishing ideal was a balanced list, but in his understanding of balance, few writers who were to make the twenties notable found a place.[12]

A further deterrent to these writers in seeking Houghton Mifflin as publishers was Greenslet's four-year devotion to the Allied war effort. A generation disillusioned by the revelation that the printed word had proved a more devastating weapon in the arsenal of the Allies than it had for the Central Powers would scarcely seek a house known for its cooperation with Wellington House, the propaganda division of the British Foreign Office. By 1920 Wellington House and the United States Government's Committee on Public Information, with which Greenslet had also worked closely, had come under attack. One of the attackers was H. L. Mencken, whose manuscript of "The Battle of the Wilhelmstrasse" Greenslet turned down in 1917 because it was anti-British and said "a good many things which would perhaps better be left unsaid at the moment." During World War I, Houghton Mifflin published more than 100 titles related to the war, their distribution amounting to at least 1,500,000.[13]

The literary revolution had opened in 1908 with Mencken's article in the November *Smart Set* on "The Good, the Bad, and the Best Sellers." Here he excoriated writers with "the soul of fudge-besotted high school girls," who saw "the human comedy as a mixture of a fashionable wedding and a three alarm fire, with music by Frederic François Chopin," and produced saccharine,

Pollyanna novels. A dozen years later he was still fighting in the same sector. American letters, with an occasional exception, had not changed. "A timorous flaccidity," an "amiable hollowness," a "bloodless respectability," an "insipid correctness" continued to characterize the product. During these years Mencken had been beating his critical drum loud and hard for two Houghton Mifflin rejects — Theodore Dreiser and James Branch Cabell. His skill with assorted timpani had gained for these men a national reputation. In 1916 Dreiser's *The "Genius"* fell afoul of the New York Society for the Suppression of Vice. Mencken secured signatures on a petition of protest. Among the signers was Willa Cather. The following year Mencken rewarded her with his critical approval. In her work he caught Dreiserian echoes. Greenslet might well have been warned. Willa Cather was a Houghton Mifflin author.[14]

In fact he had been warned three years before. In 1914 Amy Lowell, his "General Grant of the poetic wilderness," had delivered herself to him on what was wrong with the house for which he stood. Houghton Mifflin had lost prestige, she told him, through publishing too many cheap novels. In doing so it had either lost or overlooked authors whose fiction might have helped to maintain the distinction the firm's list had previously boasted. In nonfiction also, Houghton Mifflin, she charged, was "far too prone to publish books by insignificant authors, allowing better men to slip through its fingers." The firm, once "the chief publishing house in America" had declined to second place, chiefly "through the fatal belief that the only great men are always dead, and that it is not worth while to bother about the younger authors as they are bound to be inferior." In poetry Hermann Hagedorn and Edwin Arlington Robinson had been lost to other houses. Nicholas Vachel Lindsay, "an extremely talented popularizer," "a gentleman so poor he would have jumped at any offer," Houghton Mifflin had not seen fit to encourage. For these reasons she was shifting her loyalty to Macmillan, publishers of "the largest amount of excellent poetry in the United States." Under Macmillan's aegis her name would be associated with those of Yeats, Masefield, and Tagore. Her motives were artistic, not commercial, she said.[15]

Amy Lowell, in her diatribe against Houghton Mifflin's second-rate novelists, cited Mary Johnston, Mary Roberts Rinehart, and T. Russell Sullivan. As for writers either lost or overlooked, her list was long and eclectic — Robert Grant, Edith Wharton, Margaret Deland, Mary E. Wilkins Freeman, Jack London, Thomas Hardy, H. G. Wells, Maurice Hewlett, Arnold Bennett, William De Morgan, May Sinclair, Anne Sedgwick, and Mrs. Humphry Ward. "Is it fair," Greenslet protested, "to line up against Houghton Mifflin all of the publishing plums?" He suggested the General was guilty of taking potshots. "Some of the authors you mention," he wrote, "have indeed left us; some of them have hinted that they would like to come back; some we haven't been altogether sorry to see go; some whose works we covet we have refrained from approaching owing to conditions of publishing comity." A number of the English writers Houghton Mifflin had been forced to forgo because of their prohibitive prices. As for Mrs. Humphry Ward, the firm had recently published her collected works to its "fiscal sorrow." Amy Lowell's second-rate novelists, he argued, were "indispensable on any well-balanced list . . . without their presence it is not always possible to publish more meritorious books of a less promising financial flavor. I can, however, honestly lay my hand across the cardiac region and assert that I have never consciously recommended a book on the ground of its popular appeal alone, or without thinking it good in its kind."[16]

Some of Amy Lowell's shots fell wide of the mark. Her comments on poets struck home. In the new century, the firm which boasted its Longfellows, Lowells, and Whittiers had done poorly, not because of a dearth of manuscripts. Since Greenslet remained poetry critic for the *Nation* through 1912, a plethora of poets stormed Park Street's doors. Its Editor-in-Chief knew what was happening on Parnassus, but one who considered George Woodberry an American Tennyson was hardly prepared to recognize the stirrings pregnant in a Vachel Lindsay. Contemporary verse he considered "a little fortuitous, a little factitious." Edward Arlington Robinson he thought dull; his mouth-filling phrases failed to stir the imagination. Woodberry, on the other hand, he valued as "almost unique" in his poetic aptitudes. He had "skilled mastery of the ancient resources of poetic art." His poems had "a purity of line, a sweetness of melody, a fineness of sentiment not to be found . . . in the work of any other among contemporary poets." In Greenslet's autobiography, the poets he recalled as creditable to the firm's lyric investment were Josephine Preston Peabody, Anna Hempstead Branch, Louise Imogen Guiney, and George Cabot Lodge, all Houghton Mifflin poets before he came to sit in judgment. Josephine Preston Peabody was a Scudder discovery. Louise Imogen Guiney had been writing for the firm since the eighties. Both Anna Hempstead Branch and George Cabot Lodge had appeared in Houghton Mifflin's catalogue during Perry's administration.[17]

Amy Lowell came to Houghton Mifflin at the suggestion of Josephine Peabody. Greenslet advised acceptance of *A Dome of Many-Colored Glass* not because he recognized promise in her poems but because he coveted for his firm her "extraordinarily interesting unpublished" Keats manuscripts "for which many publishers have been soliciting her." Taking her first book was simply an experimental cast and an inexpensive one. Because she did not want to embarrass Houghton Mifflin financially, Miss Lowell insisted on a commission contract. In the ensuing years of their association, Greenslet came to value Amy Lowell more for her personality than for her poetic abilities. Under her generalship, even after she had deserted Boston for New York, he maintained an important connection with her by publishing her anthologies of the Imagists. He also inaugurated the New Poetry Series in which appeared Conrad Aiken, Grace Hazard Conkling, Grace Fallow Norton, H.D., and John Gould Fletcher. The experiment proved abortive. After three years Houghton Mifflin concluded that poets, even in seventy-five-cent volumes, could not be made to pay for themselves and the experiment was given up. Had this not happened, the New Poetry Series would have included Archibald MacLeish, whose promise Greenslet did recognize and who would later become identified with the house.[18]

Amy Lowell's charge that Houghton Mifflin published too many cheap novels and as a result had lost position is curious. This was no new development. Novels which she would regard as second rate had been part of the stock in trade not only of Houghton Mifflin but also of its precursor Ticknor & Fields. In 1911, the year before she brought *A Dome of Many-Colored Glass* to Park Street, the house had published Kate Douglas Wiggin's *Mother Carey's Chickens,* Mary Johnston's *The Long Roll,* and Henry Sydnor Harrison's *Queed.* In the year of Amy Lowell's objection Mary Roberts Rinehart joined the stable. In 1916, the creator of Pollyanna, Mrs. Eleanor H. Porter, chose to run under Houghton Mifflin's colors.

Greenslet was proud of his discovery of Henry Sydnor Harrison, whose manuscript of *Queed* had been the rounds in New York before it arrived at Park Street. Despite its battle-scarred appearance, Greenslet was willing to give the tale a test. He found that "It bled!" As he read on "it bled some more." To him, the story was "strongly individual," with a vein of appealing "whimsical tenderness." Since it was Harrison's first novel, he advised it be "enthusiastically announced and moderately advertised." If its reviews were good, the advertising appropriation should be increased. "Rightly handled," the novel was "a safe venture." It might "prove to be very much more." Although the spring list had been closed, "within forty-eight hours, *Queed* was accepted and on it in a leading position." Harrison followed *Queed* with *V. V.'s Eyes* and then *Angela's Business,* each almost as popular as his maiden effort, and Greenslet declared "that the prospects sometime in the future of a collected edition of Harrison's works were better than those of any other of the younger American writers." Baltimore's "disturber of the peace" held an opposite view. To Mencken, Harrison's novels were "sentimental bosh — huge gum-drops for fat women to snuffle over." The people in *V. V.'s Eyes* were "preposterous," the novel's thesis "too silly to be stated in plain words." As for *Queed,* it was mawkish beyond bearing with its "vast drafts from 'Laddie' and 'Pollyanna' "; the hero was "a marionette without a toe on the ground."[19]

Nineteen fourteen must have been an unpleasant year for Ferris Greenslet. Hardly had he finished explaining his position on the publishing questions raised by Amy Lowell than a blast came from another Houghton Mifflin author. The exchange with Miss Lowell had been conducted as a private affair. This attack appeared in print.

Some years before, in August 1908, Charles Minor Thompson in an *Atlantic* essay had developed the point that honest literary criticism is impossible because of the common financial interests of book publishers, publishers of periodicals, advertisers, and authors. All enter into a "Silent Bargain." As a result the public is nurtured on an endless series of puffs. All criticism is based on handouts. "The publisher wishes his book praised, the publisher's advertising matter keeps the book-review publisher alive, and his money in turn, supports the critic." Consequently, American criticism is something less than honest. Thompson's article was couched in general terms. In 1914 in the *Yale Review*, Bliss Perry took up Thompson's thesis and developed it by naming names.[20]

Houghton Mifflin had just published Harrison's *V. V.'s Eyes*. "What does it signify to you or to me or to Literature," Perry asked, "that two tons of paper are being used in printing the advance orders of 'G. G.'s Ears,' or that the author of 'The Outside of the Platter' [Winston Churchill's *The Inside of the Cup*, published by Macmillan] has now read his last galley of proof and gone fishing?" Perry selected "Azariah Smith of Boston" as the inventor of this type of release. Azariah Smith, however, had been a

> high-minded gentleman who selected from advance sheets of the season's books published by his employers such passages and qualities as he could honestly praise. He had extraordinary deftness and tact, and when he could not praise, he was silent. But he produced without knowing it, an instrument demoralizing to the conscience and the critical sense. Everybody who knows the inside of a publisher's office has seen this instrument at work. Here is a clever boy, often college-bred, at his desk in the publicity department. Under the direction of the publicity manager, he prepares "reading notices" or "literary notes" of the books shortly to be published by his employers.

Because to read everything is impossible, he relies on the manuscript reports of the firm's readers and the advance instructions prepared for salesmen. (The Gospel According to Greenslet, some of the men on the road called it.) ". . . one-half to two-thirds of the 'book-talk' columns of most American newspapers are made up from paragraphs prepared in this fashion by publishers themselves." Since the publisher cannot put equal money on all his horses, he plays his hunches on one or two. ". . . the advertising copy prepared for the newspapers and magazines is an accurate indication of the relative cash value of the authors upon the publisher's list as the season begins." Later in the course these values may change. ". . . and then follows a tardy revision of advertising copy, a new distribution of adjectives and adverbs of praise." Since "we have no pure food law for magazines or books," traffic in butter is more honest than that in the word.[21]

The "clever boy, often college-bred" was, of course, Roger Scaife, who on first coming to Park Street had worked under Azariah Smith and who was now himself in charge of Houghton Mifflin's publicity with his own bright underling, Robert Newton Linscott. Angered by Perry's attack, Scaife protested:

> You know the game here at 4 Park Street, and you must realize that in order to maintain literary standards it is necessary to commercialize a part of the list, and that it would be impossible for us to publish some of the best books on our list were it not for the success of the popular books, some of which you may not personally care for.
>
> I wish . . . some plea could be made for publishers and the press who are trying to create new readers out of nothing, for some of these days these very readers will be in shape for your critical pages.[22]

Knowing the game at Park Street, Perry must also have been aware of the pressure authors exerted for publicity in their own behalf. None wished to be "damned with faint advertising." Those given the boom treatment were happy. Mrs. Porter was delighted with Houghton Mifflin's "splendid publicity campaign" for *Just David*. She had hesitated, she said, to shift from her *Pollyanna* publishers, L. C. Page & Company, to Park Street fearing she would be "buried" in Houghton Mifflin's "notable list." Scaife's releases had proved her fears groundless. She hoped her *David* would "show himself properly appreciative of all these hopes and dollars that are being lavished upon him." And so he did. Before publication, advance orders reached 100,000 and his creator received a check for $15,000. Houghton Mifflin had reason to be appreciative of Eleanor H. Porter. *Just David* made the best seller list in 1916. So did other of Mrs. Porter's novels for four successive years. Naturally she was pleased with her publishers and cheerfully confessed she was "chief of sinners when it came to optimism."[23]

Since Houghton Mifflin was now publishing between 150 and 200 titles a year, only a few could be given the Eleanor H. Porter type of campaign. For *Just David* the advertising appropriation was almost $4000, for *V. V.'s Eyes* over $6000. Authors whose sales could not be expected to approach those of Mrs. Porter or Harrison were sometimes less than pleased with Scaife's efforts in their behalf. One of the dissatisfied was Willa Sibert Cather, whose literary development Greenslet had nurtured ever since the day in 1907, when she had appeared at Park Street "fresh-faced, broad-browed," and "plain-speaking." After her return to New York, he had continued to cultivate her friendship, thus winning *Alexander's Bridge, O Pioneers!, The Song of the Lark,* and *My Antonia.* This last he recommended for the 1918 Pulitzer Prize. His recommendation failed of effect. The judges made the award to Doubleday's Booth Tarkington for his *Magnificent Ambersons.*[24]

Doubleday had been wooing Miss Cather ever since the critical success of *O Pioneers!* in 1913. Burton J. Hendrick, whom she had known in her McClure days, was now with Doubleday, Page. His stories of the surprising results his house was getting from slow-moving, intellectual novels made her feel envious. Hendrick's description of Doubleday's advertising techniques impressed her. She had been satisfied with Houghton Mifflin's efforts for *O Pioneers!,* she wrote Greenslet, but her next novel must be pushed harder. In two years *Pioneers* had sold a little over 4000. Properly handled, her new book, *The Song of the Lark,* should sell at least 30,000. She believed in her work. It was the best she had done so far, she exulted.[25]

FG hastened to drown out "Mr. Hendrick's siren song" with one of his own. Houghton Mifflin, provided it had "the goods," could "reach as large figures of sales as the Napoleons of Garden City," he assured Miss Cather. *Queed,* "which went in the front door of the Doubleday shop and left by the back," was a case in point. That novel had led the best sellers for almost a year. *The Song of the Lark,* though cut from a different bolt, was nonetheless "authentic stuff," so good it ought to be made better. The ending, he suggested, was not consistent with the beginning. An illuminating phrase or two might help the "low-browed reader's" understanding. His comments were tentative only; he did not ask that she follow them. Even though he found the novel's construction "peculiar," he was brimful of enthusiasm. As a convincing coda to his siren effort, he changed her contract. For *O Pioneers!* the royalty had been 10 percent up to 5000, 15 percent to 25,000, 20 percent thereafter. *The Song of the Lark* started at 15 percent, so also *My Antonia.* However, neither of the books achieved the sales Miss Cather had been led to expect in her conversations with New York publishers, and she became increasingly exasperated with Park Street.[26]

Her criticisms were numerous. Houghton Mifflin's charges for corrections were exorbitant. Its book format was unattractive; the page for *The Song of the Lark* crowded, the cover for *O Pioneers!* drab, the Benda line drawings for *My Antonia* too few. She wanted to issue a volume of short stories before *My Antonia,* but FG advised her to wait because publishing such a collection would be benefited by the appearance of her novel. Such a sequence would fit better in the general campaign for her work. In the end, however, Houghton Mifflin's half-hearted advertising was the basic cause for her alienation. On May 19, 1919, she wrote Greenslet a long indictment of Houghton Mifflin. Three New York publishers had approached her with offers of larger royalties and cash advances. One had outlined an appealing advertising scheme which made Houghton Mifflin's endorsement of her work seem timidly routine. Why hadn't the publicity department made use of some of the striking reviews of her book, Mencken's for example? Look at the way Knopf had advertised Hergesheimer's *Java Head.* Look at what Doubleday had done with Conrad. Did Houghton Mifflin believe in her work enough to increase its advertising appropriation for all her books, which should be presented as a unit because taken together they embodied unique features of our national life?

She doubted it. Cash advances and royalties were unimportant to her, she insisted. What she wanted was more originality in advertising and more than a casual indication that Houghton Mifflin was wholeheartedly committed to her work.[27]

Miss Cather in her letters to Greenslet so far had mentioned three houses as having offered her terms — Doubleday, Macmillan, and Century. Clearly, by now publishers' courtesy had become a pious myth. None of these, however, was to capture her. Six months after her letter of May 19, she sought out Alfred Knopf. That his house had been in her mind before she approached him is obvious. In 1916 she had inquired of Greenslet whether Knopf's advertised sales of W. H. Hudson's *Green Mansions* represented the truth. After the success of *Java Head,* she noted with gratification that Knopf in an advertising leaflet coupled her name with Hergesheimer's. Her illustrations chosen to indict Houghton Mifflin were his prizes, even Joseph Conrad, for it was Alfred Knopf, who during his apprenticeship at Doubleday, Page, had implemented Kipling's advice that the publishers proclaim their pride in Conrad's books.[28]

During the uneasy months that remained before Willa Cather transferred her business to Knopf, Greenslet did what he reasonably could to make her content. Houghton Mifflin went fifty-fifty with her on charges for extra corrections in *Antonia*'s proof because, he said, he recognized she was "not merely a fussy fiddler with proof"; she was not one of those who liked "to titivate in type rather than in type writing." Her next novel would start at a straight 20 percent and Scaife promised to arrange with Joseph Hergesheimer to write a *New Republic* study of her work. As for advertising, "the nub of her indictment," Greenslet patiently explained that Houghton Mifflin had in fact advertised her books collectively as well as separately, that the investment had far exceeded the usual 10 percent of receipts appropriated for the majority of books on the firm's list. For *Alexander's Bridge* the amount spent represented 38 percent; for *O Pioneers!* and *The Song of the Lark,* 20 percent. Indeed, the appropriation for the *Lark* had been so substantial that "under a strict system of accounting," the novel had not paid for itself. *My Antonia*'s slow sales were to be explained in part by its appearance so shortly before the Armistice. The excitement of that event had kept people away from the bookstores. Even so, by March 1919 *Antonia* had sold 6300. That it was destined to become an American classic, he was certain. Because he believed in it he had tried to secure British publication, but unfortunately, because it lacked popular appeal, eight English houses had declined it. When Heinemann, after a second look and a special appeal, finally accepted *My Antonia* he sent word through FG to Miss Cather that he did so "because of a sort of moral obligation to publish so distinguished a work." He expected to sell few copies.[29]

Greenslet's explanations, by letters and in interviews, were delaying action only. Miss Cather wished to follow *My Antonia* with another volume as soon as possible. She had two novels in mind, but neither would be ready for a year or more. A collection of short stories would serve to keep her name before the public. In 1916 she had requested that Houghton Mifflin buy from Doubleday, Page the plates of her 1905 *The Troll Garden;* she would like to have the book reissued. Greenslet considered the proposal "dubious." "The book has played its part," he thought, "and . . . it is probably better now to let the Cather collectors search for it in the second-hand shops and buy it at high prices." As for Miss Cather's proposal to bring out a volume of short stories in 1919, he urged her to send on the manuscript, but warned that war conditions might make publication out of the question. The Government was rationing paper and therefore publishers were limited as to the number of titles they might issue. In the face of this warning, Miss Cather withheld her collection. A year later, in December 1919, she notified Greenslet that Knopf was to bring out a new edition of her *Troll Garden*. However, she assured Greenslet that he would have her new novel "Claude," the title she had selected at this time for the book which would finally appear as *One of Ours*.[30]

In the end the collection of stories published by Knopf turned out to be not a new edition of *The Troll Garden* but rather *Youth and the Bright Medusa* in which five of the earlier stories reappeared. Greenslet all the while kept in close touch with his restive author, who frequently promised "Claude" was to be his. In mid-

December 1920 he dined with her in New York at the Brevoort. Knopf had done well with *Youth and the Bright Medusa,* she told him. His lively publicity had produced results. Even so, Greenslet was to have "Claude." Then on January 12, 1921, she announced that she had changed her mind. Because of Knopf's skill in promotion, she had decided to give him the book. However, she assured Greenslet, she had not broken with him. She was grateful to him for his early recognition of her skill and for his advice that she try her hand at a novel. Although Knopf was to have this one, she would still like to call Greenslet her publisher, she wrote, encouraging him to believe that after "Claude" had appeared she would come back to him.

This was no separation but a divorce and FG knew it. "Pax vobiscum!" he replied, "and best wishes for the prosperity of 'Claude.' As for me, I am planning to spend the evening reading the Book of Job . . . In the first mail this morning along came two pernickety, two very mean letters, of the sort that are the particular desolation of the publisher's life; the kind requiring extended, patient, long-suffering answers, a particularly trying affair when you are feeling more than usually short-suffering . . . Do, for heaven's sake . . . write me a pleasant letter. I need it!"[31]

After "Claude," properly presented as *One of Ours,* won the prize for which Greenslet had recommended *My Antonia,* chances that Willa Cather would return to Park Street went glimmering, especially since in the year she won the Pulitzer award ("a transaction comparable to the election of Charles W. Eliot to the Elks," Mencken thought), she realized over $19,000 in a single year from her two Knopf books. The loss of Willa Cather was one of the enduring regrets of Ferris Greenslet's publishing life.[32]

Willa Cather's and Amy Lowell's desertion of Park Street epitomizes the temper of the times. Always authors had found cause for seeking new houses, but never before had the exchange of publishing partners been so brisk. In Boston some came from another publisher to make Park Street their home. One of these was Eleanor H. Porter. Others like Mary Roberts Rinehart deserted their original publishers for Houghton Mifflin only to depart shortly for greater fame and fortune in New York. Still others in restless experiment left Park Street subsequently to return. Among these were Mary Austin, Gamaliel Bradford, John Muir, and Amy Lowell. Even Willa Cather, although she would always retain her Knopf identity, came back for a limited edition of her collected works, designed by Bruce Rogers to give it the weight of a "standard author." This exchange of partners was not confined to Boston. In New York, Edith Wharton left Scribner, her publisher for twenty-five years, later to return, and H. L. Mencken experimented briefly with a house other than Knopf's.

So repetitive became the exchange that Alberta Houghton, when she learned that some Knopf authors were being taken on by Houghton Mifflin, was moved to protest. "I am sorry to note the tendency to grab authors from other publishers. My father felt so strongly on this 'point' that I have hoped Houghton Mifflin could resist the temptation . . ." Roger Scaife reassured her that the firm was "no more in the habit now of attempting to pry away other publishers' authors than in the old days." Writers were simply more restless, more eager to make experiments than formerly, each believing he had a potential best seller if only his publisher would exploit it dramatically enough. The publisher's loss appeared to be the writer's gain. Once knowledge of his discontent or availability became gossip of the trade, he was up for bids. In these confusing patterns of exchange, the literary agent had come to play an important part.[33]

Houghton Mifflin seems to have been less irritated by the phenomenon of the agent than some other publishers, Henry Holt, for example who in 1916 found "American Literature in a Bad Way" because of literary agents who engaged books "two or three deep" before they were written and then hawked them about to the highest bidder, thus destroying the intimate, personal relationship which should exist between author and publisher. Houghton Mifflin had always relied on English agents for imports, and in the early Hurd & Houghton days J. C. Derby and others had performed comparable services in New York. These representatives, however, acted primarily in the interests of the publisher. (Derby was on a small salary and for a time had a desk in Houghton Mifflin's New York branch.) James R. Osgood, after his break with Houghton, clearly performed the function of agent for William Dean Howells and others. The agent as the writer's shopper at 10 percent for his effort is chiefly a twentieth-century development. To the author he frequently seemed essential as questions of first rights (serial and book) and secondary rights (syndication, cheap reprints, translation, theatrical, motion picture, and so on) became complicated and diversified.[34]

Park Street at least tolerated the agent. One of the leading ones, Paul Reynolds, had started his career with Houghton Mifflin. However, books that came in this manner represented possibly less than 6 percent of its new books, and to fulfill the province of agent free of charge, the firm established its own syndicate service. In addition, it undertook to oversee contractual arrangements for dramatic and motion picture sale. Most troublesome, as Houghton Mifflin's connection with the *Atlantic* became increasingly tenuous, was the author's demand for magazine appearance, especially as some New York houses continued to couple serial and book rights, the "King's gambit" Greenslet advised his men. They should deny it by seeking magazines independent of publishing houses. An agent was unnecessary. Free of charge, Houghton Mifflin would find an acquiescent outlet. When Anne Douglas Sedgwick wished to place *The Little French Girl,* FG submitted it first to Ellery Sedgwick for the *Atlantic.* Turned down there, painstakingly and patiently he sent it on to more than a dozen periodicals, always to have it returned. As a last move in the game, he turned it over to Paul Reynolds, who placed it with the unlikely *Forum* for $5000. Greenslet was the chess player. His retort kept Anne Douglas Sedgwick on his board. Within a year as a Houghton Mifflin book, her *Little French Girl* sold over 200,000.[35]

Amy Lowell, in accusing Greenslet of overlooking Miss Sedgwick, was uninformed and premature. In 1906 he had recommended enthusiastically her *A Fountain Sealed* as an *Atlantic* serial, only to be vetoed by Bliss Perry. Ever since, he had watched her literary development. In 1912 she placed ninth in the yearly best seller list. She was now a Century author and considerations of publishing comity forbade approach. In England in 1915, he visited her and her husband Basil de Selincourt and learned that she, like so many others, was restless. Her close friend at Century, Richard Watson Gilder, had died. She was working on a novel and open to suggestion. A vivid correspondence ensued but was interrupted by the de Selincourts' hospital service in France. At war's end the exchange of letters resumed and FG made clear he coveted becoming her publisher "on every ground, literary, commercial, and personal." She shortly made her peace with Century, and although Harper was also bidding for her, cast her lot with Houghton Mifflin. FG's perseverance had paid off. For Anne Sedgwick, so had Harper's bidding. Houghton Mifflin's contract gave her 20 percent and an advance determined by prepublication orders. This was for *The Third Window*. FG was convinced she was on the eve of doing her most enduring work.[36]

The relationship between editor and author was a happy one. This is not to say Miss Sedgwick wrote no letters of complaint. Women had long since taken Gail Hamilton's advice. Most of them were business women as well as writers. Some of Miss Sedgwick's letters were of the "pernickity" kind which forced FG to compose long explanatory letters, but in the end she accepted his advice, delaying, for example, her collection of short stories, *Christmas Roses,* until after *The Third Window* had won the market. "The whole philosophy of publishing," he told her, "is based on the principle . . . of putting the best foot foremost." FG's mastery of the game and his recognition of Anne Douglas Sedgwick's skill rewarded both author and publisher. Four times in the twenties under Houghton Mifflin's imprint, she appeared in the yearly best seller lists.[37]

FG attributed his loss of Willa Cather, in part at least, to World War I and his devotion to the Allied cause, a devotion which so absorbed his energies as to prevent him from giving her the editorial sympathy and encouragement essential to her temperament. His winning of Miss Sedgwick was likewise a byproduct of the war. The opening of his acquaintance with her came through their mutual friend George Trevelyan, whose *Life of John Bright* Houghton Mifflin had published and for whose visit to America in behalf of the Allies in 1915 Ferris Greenslet was the "prime mover."[38]

At the beginning of hostilities in August 1914, one estimate of United States favor was that perhaps 50,000 Americans were sympathetic to the Allied cause, but that out of "sheer ignorance . . . of what the vast and terrible conflict was all about," the rest remained to be persuaded. FG was one of the 50,000. Soon after the turn of the century, Mifflin had decided his house must establish firmer connections with British authors and publishers than it had so far enjoyed. To achieve his purpose, he chose FG as his emissary, sending him abroad in 1907, 1909, and 1912. These trips had prepared FG for 1914. One of his forebears, he liked to recall, had been characterized in verse as "happy Ferris" and had served as Messenger in Ordinary of Her Majesty's Chamber, Queen Elizabeth the First. His early reading had been largely in the English classics. The men who had made Britain's thousand-year history were as friends to him. He was prepared to like the living Englishman. He found him free of reported snobbery, friendly, outspoken, and sensible. In his meetings with British publishers, his sense of history and literature enriched his acquaintance. These were the sons of the mighty, the publishers of Scott, the Brontës, Darwin, Trollope, Browning, and Thackeray. Associations from his literate past peopled the rooms of Garland's Hotel, where he always stayed when in London, as they did also the streets of historic cities, the lawns of Oxford, and the backs of Cambridge. Through his diversions of walking and fishing, the English countryside, its rivers, its moors and hills and downs, was illuminated not only by the poetic past but also by the present as he made friends who shared with him his passion for the dry fly.[39]

Because many members of school committees were of the uncommitted majority, Hoyt, as has been noted, advised Mrs. Perkins to avoid the Belgians as a subject for one of her Twins books. In the interest of school adoptions, to wait on the event was the provident course, he counseled. The Trade, Greenslet thought, need not be so cautious. In his view, the publisher's job was to inform his countrymen, who must be made aware "of evil ambitions" loosed on the world. Should awareness lead to participation on the side of the Allies, so be it.

If any of Houghton Mifflin's Board of Directors held back from such commitment, before 1914 had come to an end, Greenslet had been able to persuade them such a course would be one of "enlightened self-interest." The career of Roland G. Usher's *Pan-Germanism* proved his point. From publication in February 1913 to August 1914, its sales had been under 1000. In the following five months the figure approached 100,000, sufficient evidence of the market for books on the European upheaval. Houghton Mifflin gave him authority to proceed and early in 1915 he left for England. In 1917 he made a second trip, arriving in London two days after the United States had broken off diplomatic relations with Germany. To be there just at that time was "an extraordinary experience for a visiting American," he reported. The lift of heart in the English was everywhere evident.[40]

Although the work of Wellington House, the British propaganda headquarters, was cloaked in secrecy, Houghton Mifflin's publishing connections were such that the emissary from Boston met the majority of those concerned with forging the word for the arsenal of the Allies. In charge of Wellington House propaganda designed for America was Gilbert Parker, now a knight, two of whose novels Houghton Mifflin had published in the 1890s and whose friendship Scudder had cultivated. Sir Gilbert's concern was not with the press but with books, Government publications, speaking engagements, and so on. One of Sir Gilbert's assistants was Hugh Sheringham, a fishing friend of FG's. Following Sir Gilbert's resignation in 1917 and the reorganization of the British propaganda effort, John Buchan, now a colonel, became director of Intelligence and Information in the Foreign Office. Wellington House was directly responsible to him. Friendship between FG and Buchan was natural; they had much in common. Both were of the same age and Buchan in civilian life held a position with the Scottish house of Thomas Nelson & Sons comparable to that of Greenslet's with Houghton Mifflin. Both were devoted anglers and loved the out-of-doors. Their meeting in 1917 was the beginning of a lifelong friendship and led to Houghton Mifflin's eventually becoming John Buchan's recognized American publisher.[41]

After America's Declaration of War, the United States Navy considered Greenslet's British connections important enough to offer him a London assignment but Washington suggested his post was on this side. He had been acting as a coordinator for the work of the Vigilantes, a private group of writers devoted to propaganda efforts. On the organization of the Government's Committee of Public Information under the direction of George Creel, some of the Vigilantes were called to serve on the Committee's Division of Syndicate Features. During 1917 and 1918, Greenslet was in frequent touch with members of the Creel Committee on this side, with John Buchan on the other.[42]

As with Wellington House publications, books deriving from the Creel Committee like Mary Roberts Rinehart's *The Altar of Freedom* and Ralph D. Paine's *The Fighting Fleets* served their immediate purpose and have been forgotten. So too with other manuscripts that came to FG's desk untainted by official inspiration but serving nonetheless as ammunition in this battle for men's minds. Such was the Reverend Abraham Mitrie Rihbany's *Militant America and Jesus Christ,* a book Greenslet described in a report to Buchan as proving convincingly "that Jesus would probably have been in khaki long before the first draft — probably in May 1915 after the *Lusitania,* very likely in August 1914."

FG never regretted his contribution to "the words that won the war" even though war's aftermath and the failure of the League of Nations were a bitter disillusion. On September 6, 1939, he wrote Buchan:

> How like a recurrent nightmare is the present war! It seems to take up just where the war we dealt with 25 years ago left off . . . I was studying yesterday, trying to analyze our publications during the last war, and the reason for their comparative success or failure . . . A good many of these . . . and those of the largest distribution, were Wellington House books, done at their charges. I don't think we shall want to operate that way again this time, but I would like to try to maintain the pre-eminence in the field which I think we achieved during the last war. Oddly enough, one of our World War books still continues to sell in modest volume, *A Treasury of War Poetry.* I am afraid, however, there won't be much poetry coming out of the present war.

Had it not been for the war, possibly Houghton Mifflin's fiction might have been more distinguished; yet from a commercial point of view the firm had little of which to complain. Eleanor H. Porter's novels made the annual best seller list for five years straight, a remarkable record. Equally remarkable was FG's selection from 1911 through 1920 of fiction which secured wide purchase. With the exception of 1914, one or more Houghton Mifflin writers appeared in the annual best seller list. Nineteen fourteen would not have been an exception had the *Publishers' Weekly* included nonfiction as a category. Usher's *Pan-Germanism* would then have placed somewhere in the running.

Much has been written about the novelists of the first two decades of this century and their readers who found in Pollyanna an escape from reality. Less notice has been taken of the growth of a reading public for books of nonfiction, a growth which FG had anticipated. Amy Lowell was unjust in her castigation of Greenslet and his house in this division of publishing. True, the "tea-party" essays of Samuel McChord Crothers and Agnes Repplier were popular items in the Houghton Mifflin catalogue, but writers who demanded more of their readers than a complacent smile were there also; others were about to appear. As essayists and critics — John Burroughs (now dean of nature writers), John Muir, Enos Mills, Havelock Ellis, Irving Babbitt, Paul Elmer More, Ralph Adams Cram, Cornelius Weygandt, John Livingston Lowes. As historians — Max Farrand, Samuel Stearns Davis, and Samuel Eliot Morison. As biographers — Henry Adams, Gamaliel Bradford, William Roscoe Thayer, Albert Beveridge, and on the threshold, Claude Bowers. The list is representative, not exhaustive. Some of these writers were carried not because they were profitable to the firm, but because their books gave Houghton Mifflin's list "substance and balance." Others, notably the biographers, contributed these qualities and more. A sale of 2000 qualified a book of this class as a success. If the figure passed 4000, both publisher and author had reason to throw their caps in the air. FG and his authors had numerous occasions for such celebrations. George Herbert Palmer's *The Life of Alice Freeman Palmer* sold over 16,000 in its first year; William Roscoe Thayer's *The Life and Letters of John Hay*, over 14,000, his *Theodore Roosevelt: An Intimate Biography*, over 23,000; Henry Adams' *Education*, over 11,000.[43]

In 1913 and 1914, as an experiment, the *Publishers' Weekly* introduced nonfiction as a classification in its best seller lists. In 1917, the division became standard. Houghton Mifflin authors, every time the category was available, placed somewhere in the list. The caliber of the volumes which won this distinction, especially after the war, is indicative of a reading public far different from that which had placed Mrs. Porter repeatedly in the fiction list. In 1919 her *Dawn* figured. In the same year as though in ironic counterpoint, *The Education of Henry Adams* led the nonfiction list. In 1920 Mrs. Porter's *Mary Marie* was number six on one side of the ledger. Thayer's *Theodore Roosevelt* was number four on the other. In 1921 Robert Lansing's *The Peace Negotiations* ran number six in nonfiction. Houghton Mifflin had no entry in fiction. Mrs. Porter had died. So had public passion for the glad girl. Sinclair Lewis' *Main Street,* under the imprint of the young firm of Harcourt, Brace, led the field. Even so FG had a slow starter running for him, though not an American. Rafael Sabatini, at 10 percent, had given him *Scaramouche.* Although it failed to place in the yearly lists, within twenty-five years its sales would top 500,000. Moreover, three times in the '20s other Sabatini novels would score as best sellers. FG's wish to publish books that would have "a direct and immediate appeal" to "a reasonable number of unprofessional readers" continued to be realized.[44]

So too his ideal of a balanced list. Houghton Mifflin's nonfiction won wide purchase from average readers. Further recognition came from the Pulitzer Prize Committee. In the year it denied Willa Cather's *My Antonia,* it selected *The Education of Henry Adams* for its biography award. In 1920 two Houghton Mifflin books were considered. In the end Albert Beveridge's *Life of John Marshall* nudged out Thayer's *Roosevelt.* FG's belief in public interest in the dead had in nowise proved the fatality Amy Lowell had declared it was.

This Miss Lowell had herself recognized. In 1920 she returned to the Park Street fold. For two years she had been repeatedly intimating to Greenslet that she was unhappy with Macmillan. Her six titles were selling well enough, initially something like 2300 and then a continuing annual sale of 500. Under her commission contract, she was making money. Macmillan, on the other hand, was carrying her books at a loss, and its president, George P. Brett, wished to abrogate her contract and put her on a 15 percent royalty, Macmillan to pay for the plates. The publisher would then be in the dictator's position, an unpalatable prospect to one of Amy Lowell's militant proclivities. She refused Brett's conditions and thereafter suspected him of deliberately obstructing the sale of her books. Finally in frustration she telephoned Greenslet to announce that Houghton Mifflin might have her next book and her earlier ones besides if it would meet her terms — either as before, publishing on commission, but raised to 20 percent, or a 20 percent royalty, she to own the plates. (Houghton Mifflin agreed to the royalty proposal.) She stipulated further that after Houghton Mifflin had spent a moderate amount on advertising, say $200, she be allowed to invest further amounts if she wished.[45]

Amy Lowell's return to Park Street proved for her a source of continuing satisfaction. She would hardly fulfill the portrait of an author if she had not found cause to complain about advertising and sales from time to time, but in the main because of Greenslet's tact, humor, and interest, she was kept content. On October 5, 1921, writing to her former editor, Edward C. Marsh, who had left Macmillan about the same time she had, she commented:

> I do not wonder that you left Macmillan. I am treated so differently at Houghton Mifflin's that it is a constant surprise to me . . .
>
> 'Legends,' which came out the very end of May with an edition of 2500 is reprinting, and 'Tendencies' is now in the press, which makes its fourth edition. 'Sword Blades' has also been reprinted, since I left Macmillan, for the fifth time. I never knew anything like the anxiety to do everything for me which they show. I have an entirely different contract now from what I had with you, in which certain stipulated advertising is done by them, and they assume all expenses of printing, etc. Can you believe it, they went way over their agreed amount of advertising and said they were glad to do it . . .

FG was, of course, delighted with the prodigal's return. For him it was one of the happiest events in his publishing life. The timing was opportune. Shortly before Miss Lowell's phone call he had received from Knopf a copy of Willa Cather's *Youth and the Bright*

Medusa. That he was to have Amy Lowell's *Legends,* her *Fable for Critics,* and finally the object of his first cast more than a decade before, her biography of Keats, perhaps compensated for his loss of Willa Cather. Knopf had benefited by Houghton Mifflin's years of investment in Willa Cather; Houghton Mifflin from Macmillan's in Amy Lowell. Both had secured personalities as well as publishing properties.[46]

On Amy Lowell's death, Greenslet felt that "a force of nature had been turned off." The years that he had "dealt with her, disagreed with her, fought, capitulated, made up, and smoked the cigar of peace with her without victory, to fight again; but with never a break in confident friendship" became for him cherished memories. For him she provided a "strong" note in his "daily symphony at Park Street." For younger workers like Esther Forbes, Greenslet's gifted assistant, Amy Lowell's presence irradiated routine work. In Greenslet's recollection only one other author — Albert Beveridge — compared with Amy Lowell in vividness and vitality. When death put a period to his association with these two, the "bountiful and damned decade" of the twenties became for him "a more drab affair" than it had been before.[47]

These first years of Greenslet's administration had noticeable effect on the firm's list. Always English writers had appeared there, but, in Houghton's phrase, these were incidental to the firm's focus on American authors. From now on, increasing numbers of British would publish in the United States under Houghton Mifflin's imprint. As custodian of works of dead Americans, the house was still preeminent. As guardian of burgeoning native talent, it had lost position. But in these years it had acquired the enviable reputation of backing a winner. From 1911 through 1921, twenty-one of its titles had appeared on the annual best seller lists and two of its biographies had won the recently established Pulitzer Prize. In rehearsing such a record, that all was not proceeding merrily comes as a surprise. Yet such was the case.

Laughter may have echoed through the editorial offices on Park Street's third floor, but on the second, where FG was known satirically as "The Author's Friend," whenever the Trade came to the attention of James Duncan Phillips, gloom prevailed. James Murray Kay had died. So had Francis Jackson Garrison. Mifflin, who was not well, rarely came to his office. The young men were in the saddle and they had stockholders as well as themselves to consider. The business was prospering. Book sales were over a million and net profits were in excess of $200,000. But Phillips didn't like the way the Trade was operating. Its methods he considered no better than those of a gambling casino. He'd rather try his luck at Monte Carlo. The risks were comparable, but the tables took less time and trouble. In 1920 he hired a firm of expert accountants. What he had long suspected was made evident. Because of rising costs all along the line, many a trade book when charged its share of operating costs, large sales notwithstanding, was losing money. Trade would never make any money, he said, until its policy was "decidedly revised." "The new books," he reported, "carry royalties which are higher than the profits of the business justify, whereas the old books have declined in their sales so far that the reprinting of them, in even small editions, costs so much that the manufacturing makes up more than is saved in royalty." The catalogue's 4000 titles must be reduced. So must royalties. New authors must be taken on at 10 percent.[48]

Greenslet assumed the task of persuading his 20-percenters to accept a cut. William Roscoe Thayer called FG "the most persuasive corkscrew" he had ever known. Certainly, almost every reluctant author yielded to his gentle pressure as he explained in delicately modulated phrases the mysteries of publishing finance. Mrs. Porter, on learning that on a sale of 20,000, Houghton Mifflin's profit was a minuscular 3 cents per volume was more than sympathetic. She was herself a Pollyanna girl. A royalty of 30 cents a copy instead of 38 cents would be quite acceptable. "I realize something of what the increased costs must mean to you," she wrote, "and of course I am glad to 'help out'; and I certainly hope that *Mary Marie* will bring you a little joy and profit before she — dies." Gamaliel Bradford appeared to be even more accommodating than Mrs. Porter. He suggested a reduction greater than the one proposed. Greenslet was overcome. "A suggestion from an author looking to a reduction in royalty is so admirable and epoch-making that my system has not yet recovered from the shock!" he wrote the author. The firm would not consider his generous gesture. Bradford's offer was gesture only. Almost at once, through Mark Antony DeWolf Howe, he requested the Atlantic Monthly Company to take over his books. Howe and Sedgwick were willing to consider the proposition, but advised Bradford to avoid mentioning the Atlantic Monthly Company in his negotiations with Houghton Mifflin. Bradford then told FG another publisher wanted to take him over, by this move putting Greenslet's persuasive powers to stringent test. Fortunately, they did not fail him. Bradford, who had been associated with the house since Scudder's time, remained with Park Street to produce *Damaged Souls,* his most popular Houghton Mifflin book.[49]

When Greenslet sailed for England in the spring of 1921, melancholy shadowed Park Street. Mifflin's illness had become serious and at the Riverside Press labor troubles were imminent. However, the angler from Glens Falls, New York, could take considerable comfort in his particular achievements. In the ten years and more of his administration, he had demonstrated his ability to pick winners in popular fiction. This success had not distracted him from his ideal of a balanced list. To give substance and distinction to Park Street's catalogue, he had many authors and at least two untried writers of promise were on his threshold — Claude Bowers and Esther Forbes. These years had taught him, particularly in his experiences with Willa Cather, Amy Lowell, and Gamaliel Bradford, that "authors come to regard their publishers as guide, philosopher, friend, banker, pawn-broker, nurse and recruiting sergeant," and that therefore "the peak of sound growth" in trade publishing, "is just short of the point where it ceases to be possible for the principals to keep in personal touch with their authors." To avoid passing the peak might prove difficult.[50]

XXII

EPILOGUE

AFTER THE COMPANY'S INCORPORATION, George Mifflin was forced to listen to more numerous voices than those of his usually acquiescent partners. More inclined to delegate responsibility than Henry Oscar Houghton had been, he could in his final years contemplate with satisfaction his preparation for Houghton Mifflin's perpetuation, at least at Park Street. Since 1908 business had almost tripled and a net surplus of over half a million dollars had been accumulated. Because of the skill and energy of his young men to whom he had been gradually assigning the reins, they could boast that their company had "a larger proportion of assets compared with its liabilities than almost any publishing house in America."[1]

Trade was safe in the hands of Greenslet and Scaife. Moreover, in 1899, Benjamin Holt Ticknor, Jr., grandson of William D., had come to work for the firm. Eventually, his achievements as sales manager for the Trade Department and as one of the directors of the company would become legendary. The Educational Department under the direction of the triumvirate, James Duncan Phillips, Stephen Davol, and Franklin Hoyt, had given more than token promise of its future. Phillips in his few years as treasurer of the company had amply demonstrated his conservative capacities. Furthermore, in 1919 the triumvirate had added to its sales force of the college division at $15 a week a young man just graduated from Harvard, William E. Spaulding, the son of Frank E. Spaulding, noted educator and author who at this time was superintendent of the city of Cleveland's schools. Mifflin perhaps anticipated that Edward Rittenhouse Houghton would follow him as president of the company. He could not know that Henry Laughlin in 1939 would succeed Houghton and that in 1957 Spaulding would succeed Laughlin. Had Mifflin had the gift of prescience, he would have been pleased to see that the company to which he had devoted his life was destined for a brilliant future under the guidance of these men. In 1921 Houghton Mifflin Company's present contained both the past and the promise of the years to come.

Mifflin's concern in his last years, however, was less for the future than for the present. The Riverside Press, though prospering, gave him cause for concern. Shortly after the Armistice of 1918, Edward Houghton had fallen ill. The plant was clogged with orders and labor troubles threatened. Opportunely, there came a letter from Henry Laughlin, who expected to be out of uniform in February 1919 and who hoped after a planned holiday to return to the Press. Mifflin took action at once, writing to Washington to secure Laughlin's earlier discharge and persuading the lieutenant to forgo his vacation. Thereafter, Mifflin, although confined to bed, conferred frequently with Laughlin about steps to be taken so that Riverside would be capable of meeting the demands to be made upon it. The war's benefit to publishers had been a vast increase in readers, an increase in which Houghton Mifflin had played a part, for in 1918 Hoyt had gone to France as an adviser on reading programs for our troops. The war's burden had been rising costs, a depression, and labor troubles.[2]

On March 22, 1921, Mifflin wrote Frank Doubleday, to whom he had been generous with time and advice when the Doubleday plant in Garden City was being built, that although he had not been downstairs for several weeks and was "still practically n.g." he still managed "to dig out a fairly good time." "Keep well and happy, and the Lord be with you," he said in farewell. Two weeks later he was dead.[3]

The funeral service for George Harrison Mifflin was held at the Arlington Street Church, the Reverend Paul Revere Frothingham officiating. Flowers had colored Henry Oscar Houghton's service and amongst those attending were many members of the trade. Music dominated Mifflin's service, the funeral marches of Beethoven and Chopin, the Dead March from Handel's *Saul*, the Allegretto from Beethoven's Seventh Symphony, the Adagio from his

Pathétique sonata. Houghton's honorary pallbearers had been chosen chiefly from his business associates, Mifflin's from his friends in private life, among them Dr. J. Collins Warren, Walter Hunnewell, Lord Camperdown, General Morris Schaff, Charles E. Stratton, and Frederic Amory. The ushers, headed by Roger Scaife, included such of the young directors as were in town and also friends and relatives — Charles Francis Adams, J. Lothrop Motley, Arnold W. Hunnewell, and Percy Crowninshield.[4]

Almost coinciding with the death of this nineteenth-century gentleman publisher, as Henry Holt for one characterized George Harrison Mifflin, occurred three events significant in the firm's history. One epitomized an ideal of the days that had gone; the other events presented Mifflin's successors with characteristic twentieth-century problems.

In March 1921, John Burroughs, the archetype of the publisher's author, died. Since 1871, when Hurd & Houghton had published his *Wake-Robin,* he had remained loyal to the house. Sometimes restive, perhaps, he had always been convinced that his best interests would be served by keeping his books under one imprint. Houghton Mifflin, for its part, demonstrated its appreciation of his allegiance in his annuity contracts. His first, of $500 in 1894, was based on an analysis of his royalty returns for the preceding ten years, which came to $4187.98. In 1899, his annuity was raised to $750; in 1907 to $1500; in 1912 to $2000. By 1918 Burroughs' books had ceased to approach in earnings this annual $2000. Nevertheless the stipend was continued until his death. In his lifetime he enjoyed three collected editions — the Riverside, the Autograph (both limited), and the Riverby. For some years to come, his place in the schools was assured through titles in the Riverside Literature Series, the Riverside Library, and other educational editions. After his death, he would have posthumous publication and a devoted biographer to keep his name in public memory. The Burroughs–Houghton Mifflin association had been nearly perfect, at least from the publisher's point of view. Burroughs had been neither shopper nor bargainer.[5]

Others held to a different creed. Since its acquisition of Ticknor & Fields's list in 1878, Houghton Mifflin had published Annie

Fields's books. Two of them, *Authors and Friends* and *Orpheus,* had been designed by Bruce Rogers. For the latter her own ideas had been thoroughly impractical, but BR had been able tactfully to modify "them to a proper form," producing "a rather stylish page," Garrison grudgingly admitted. She was always treated with deference, even though at times she proved difficult. After the turn of the century, Ferris Greenslet was among the young men of her coterie, a guest at both Charles Street and Thunderbolt Hill, her summer house. In conversations with him, Mrs. Fields made clear that Mark Antony DeWolfe Howe was to have her collection of literary memorabilia from which he would make a book or books. She also made clear that she expected these books to be published by Houghton Mifflin. Following her death in 1915, Greenslet and Scaife conferred frequently with Howe on plans for the first book, but because Howe had a number of other irons in the fire, his *Memories of a Hostess* was slow in reaching a stage where definite publishing plans and propositions could be made.[6]

In 1919, Ellery Sedgwick enlarged the book publishing phase of his enterprise, and he invited Howe to serve as editor and vice-president of his Atlantic Monthly Company. Between Howe and Houghton Mifflin no contract had been drawn, but Scaife and Greenslet assumed they had a "gentlemen's agreement," that no matter what happened, *Memories of a Hostess* was to be theirs. When they learned that such was not to be, that Sedgwick, not Houghton Mifflin, was to have the book, they were outraged and said so in no uncertain terms. "It doesn't seem to us that your connection with the Atlantic Monthly Company, and its subsequent emergence into book-publishing in any way vacates this understanding," Greenslet wrote. "Had there been a written contract it certainly would not do so. Why should it, when there was a mutual understanding, which from our point of view at least, was equally secure?" Then offering 15 percent on 2000, 20 percent thereafter with an advance on publication, Greenslet concluded, "But quite apart from the question of sales and profits, I hope that when you think the matter over, you will agree with us that the book really belongs to Park Street rather than Arlington Street."[7]

In spite of Houghton Mifflin's generous offer, Howe refused to change his mind, his defense being that Mrs. Fields's assignment "fully authorized" him to use her papers to "his best advantage." This was a matter of business only. The Atlantic Monthly Company's proposition was such that Howe could only feel "it fair to every interest involved" that he accept it. Ellery Sedgwick had put in practice a lesson he had learned in his New York years, a lesson he recorded in *The Happy Profession*, that "at the heart of the competitive system is a wild and whirling center, where dog eats dog, and throats are cut with suavity and dispatch."[8]

Many years before, James T. Fields had carelessly relied on an unwritten understanding. At that time Gail Hamilton felt cheated, and her *Battle of the Books* was the result. This time the publishers felt cheated. As gentlemen of commerce, they refrained from public comment. Before the private controversy over *Memories of a Hostess* had been concluded, Mifflin was beyond temper. Had this not been so, the explosion of his Homeric anger would have echoed through Park Street once again, especially if knowledge of this derogation of publishing ethics (as he would have considered it) had been coupled with another event of which he had forewarning. The printers of New England were on the march again. Because of the postwar depression, wages had been cut throughout the industry. The day before Mifflin died, the workers at Riverside struck in demand not only for restitution of their former wage but also for the forty-four-hour week. In London, Greenslet receiving the cabled news perceived an ironic connection between labor's forward drive and the death of "a paternalistic employer of the old order."[9]

Somewhat later, in preparing a memorial of George Mifflin for the Century Club, Greenslet drew a more rounded and vivid portrait of the man he had worked with for twenty years.

> His personality was of an extremely — even at times boisterous — vigour. The loud shout of laughter, the splendid explosion of righteous indignation, were characteristic of him in his prime. I shouldn't say that he had eccentricities in the unpleasant sense of the term. He had a liking for assuming the leading place in a conversation worthy of any Centurion. His talk was good, full of ripe experience and humor. It was made vivid by a marked gift

of dramatic imitation. I should say that perhaps his most distinctive and amiable quality was a certain boyishness that persisted in him to the end; an exuberance and delight in the little events and achievements of every day that his associates found always extremely stimulating.[10]

An enduring union of two people is cause for perpetual wonder, none for more than this partnership between Henry Oscar Houghton, product of northern Vermont's rugged soil, and George Harrison Mifflin, heir to the quiet affluence of Philadelphia and Boston; the former, deliberate, astute, relentless; the latter, boisterous, exuberant, impulsive; both instinct with affection for those tested and found true. Houghton was given to public pronouncements and community service; Mifflin avoided the limelight whether political or philanthropic. Both were ardent in behalf of their own workers but imperious in rejection of dictation by organized labor. Both were high tariff men, proud to be called conservative, whether as publishers or private citizens.

In this partnership was none of the petty jealousy that colored James T. Fields's attitude toward William D. Ticknor, none of the distrust that characterized the Fields-Osgood union. Houghton was forever impressed by his junior's "wonderful persistence." He never ceased to marvel that the gilded youth whom he had discouraged in 1867 had so applied himself that in time Mifflin's succession as senior partner was beyond question. The younger man, proud as he was of Houghton Mifflin's growth during his administration, always paid his debt to his senior; Henry Oscar Houghton had given a meaning to his life it might not have had. For this gift George Mifflin held his partner in loving respect.

Their combined lifetimes spanned almost a century. Because of this union, a business born in a poorhouse on borrowed money had prospered in spite of wars and financial panics. In times of depression many small publishing houses had been swept away by the economic tides and at least two of the greatest had been forced to reorganize. Houghton Mifflin, in contrast, only in its earliest Hurd & Houghton years had failed to show an annual profit. As important as its profits was its reputation for integrity. To this reputation Mifflin, in his devoted support of Bruce Rogers, had added a unique jewel to the emblem of the house. Moreover, since incorporation, Riverside's capacity had been practically doubled and in 1920 book sales were over three million, net profits in excess of $200,000.[11]

Houghton in securing the stereotype plates and publishing rights of Crocker & Brewster established a succession in educational publishing that dates from 1818; in his acquisition of the Ticknor & Fields list, one in American letters dating from 1832. Houghton Mifflin is proud of its descent from the Old Corner Bookstore. Its administration of that trust has benefited authors, their heirs, readers, and the firm as well. There are other dates of equal pride: 1852 for the founding of the Riverside Press, 1864 for Hurd & Houghton, and 1880 for Houghton, Mifflin. Houghton laid a firm foundation for his house. To build on that foundation had been Mifflin's task. In persuading his partners to incorporate, he had done more than secure fresh capital. He had assured the permanence of the firm. To his young men, the new directors whom he persisted in regarding as partners, he bequeathed his publishing creed, "ever to be mindful of the old while ever searching for the permanent in the new." This ideal combined with Henry Oscar Houghton's motto *Tout bien ou rien* is part of the heritage of those who today direct the fortunes of the house.[12]

NOTES

BIBLIOGRAPHY

NOTES

THIS HISTORY is based primarily on Houghton Mifflin Company's extensive records, which include numerous items from its precursors — Hurd & Houghton, Ticknor & Fields, Fields, Osgood, James R. Osgood & Company, and Houghton, Osgood as well as those of Freeman & Bolles, Bolles & Houghton, and H. O. Houghton & Company, owner of the Riverside Press from 1852 to 1921. While the majority of documents cited are deposited in the Houghton Library in Harvard University, the firm has retained certain indispensable papers. These include manuscript reports (stored at the Riverside Press), various financial statements, historical summaries, and other miscellaneous items (retained at its Boston office at 2 Park Street), and files of noncurrent Memoranda of Agreement (stored at its Burlington, Massachusetts, plant). Letters of a contractual nature such as Longfellow's of June 26, 1846, to William D. Ticknor, cited in chapter IV, note 5, and Elizabeth Peabody's of March 7, 1869, to Fields, Osgood, quoted in chapter VI, note 17, are frequently preserved with these Memoranda.

Of the firm's large deposit in the Houghton Library, its letter books have been of the greatest importance. The first of these material to this account is a private letter book of Ticknor & Fields, Fields, Osgood, and James R. Osgood & Company, which begins in September 1866 and concludes in November 1878. This series of letter books, which is incomplete, ends in July 1916. Thereafter modern carbon flimsies in the firm's files have supplied me with essential information. Since most of the Houghton Mifflin letters quoted or cited are taken from these sources, they are usually copies rather than originals. These letters are supplemented in part by the firm's files of correspondence, in part by various manuscript collections in the Houghton Library, notably those of Thomas Bailey Aldrich, Henry O. Houghton, William Dean Howells, Henry James, Jr., Henry Wadsworth Longfellow, Amy Lowell, Charles Eliot Norton, Henry M. Rogers, Horace Elisha Scudder, the Villard family, and George Edward Woodberry.

In addition to the letter books, other bound volumes of the firm's records on which I have relied are its payroll books, cost-books, account books, private journals, and copyright accounts. Of particular interest are its publication records under the headings of "Sales," "Earnings," and "Showings." Also helpful have been its collection of catalogues and its scrapbooks of publishing ephemera which include advertising fliers, prospectuses, news releases, and newspaper clippings.

Of the many periodicals published by Houghton Mifflin Company or its precursors, those I have most frequently consulted are the *American Architect,* the *Andover Review,* the *Atlantic Monthly,* the *North American Review, Old and New, Our Young Folks,* the *Riverside Bulletin,* and the *Riverside Magazine for Young People.* Other magazines which have been essential to my research are the *American Literary Gazette,* the *Athenaeum* (London), the *Bookman,* the *Century,* the *Critic, Harper's Monthly,* the *Independent,* the *Literary World* (Boston), *Macmillan's Magazine* (London), the *Nation,* the *Publishers' Weekly* (abbreviated in my notes to *PW*), and *Scribner's Magazine.* Unique among the many newspapers searched is the *Protective Union,* a weekly, published by the Boston Printers' Union from December 1, 1849 to November 9, 1850. The abbreviation Als means "autographed letter signed."

Among legal documents consulted, the richest in information for my purpose, even though a number of pages are missing, is that of *Sheldon et al.* v. *Houghton,* Equity Case No. 3–30 in the U.S. Circuit Court for the Southern District of New York, a copy of which I secured from the National Archives, Washington, D.C.

CHAPTER I

1. In 1894, Houghton, in a speech to the Citizen's Trade Association of Cambridge, gave the following account of the beginning of the printing industry in the United States.

A clergyman by the name of Glover left England with a printing press, two or three workmen, and his family, for this country in 1638. He died on the passage, and the press was set up in January, 1639, in the house of the first president of Harvard College, Henry Dunster. This president was a man with an eye to the main chance, and he secured possession of the press by marrying the widow of the man who started from England with it . . . Some years afterwards, when the son of this widow had grown up, he brought suit for recovery of the press. The president filed an account current in which he debited himself with an inventory of the press amounting to fourteen hundred and odd pounds sterling. He credited himself with his wife's board and several other incidental expenses, which looked very much as if he wanted to make as good an offset as possible. The difference between the two accounts mounted to about one hundred pounds, for which the president acknowledged himself debtor. The matter seems to have been taken out of the court and put into the hands of arbitrators, but there is no record of the president paying over to the heirs the amount adjudged against him. Some time after the receipt of the first press another was sent over by some society instituted for propagating the gospel among the Indians of this continent, and this press also fell into the hands of the president of the college, and the Indians are still unconverted. President Dunster also seemed to have great political influence, for he had a law passed that all the printing executed in the colonies should be done in Cambridge . . . Stephen Daye was apparently an employee of the president. He was not a successful printer. He did not know how to spell or punctuate, or do a great many things that printers are expected to do. He was soon dismissed from the office . . . In my judgment Mr. Daye was not in any sense the first printer. The first printer was Dunster. Although he did not set up type . . . he was the controlling power of the press, and so far as a man who marries a printing press, and has control of it, can be called a printer, Dunster was that printer.

Quoted in *The Cambridge of Eighteen Hundred and Ninety-Six,* edited by Arthur Gilman, pp. 332–33.

2. Henry Nathan Wheeler to H. O. Houghton, August 31, 1891. Wheeler was head of Houghton, Mifflin's Educational Department 1882–1905.
3. Except as noted, details in this chapter on Houghton's ancestry, childhood, and early maturity are taken from Horace Elisha Scudder's *Henry Oscar Houghton,* ch. I, II, III, and *The Descendants of Capt. William Houghton 1774–1863 and Marilla Clay 1780–1858.* W. D. Love, compiler.
4. "Sons of Vermont Pay Tribute to Mr. H. O. Houghton at the Riverside," Boston *Journal,* February 15, 1894.
5. Albert G. Houghton to Justin Houghton, July 23, 1836.
6. Scudder, *Houghton,* p. 4, quotes a reminiscence of Houghton's in which he recalled riding on the furniture wagon and helping to "drive the cows which we had to take with us." On the other hand, Neziah Wright Bliss, Bradford neighbor and college classmate of Houghton, credits the family with a single cow. Bliss to Scudder, May 30, 1896.
7. Boston *Journal,* February 15, 1894. For this and the following paragraph see also Daniel C. Houghton to Maria Houghton, December 12, 1836.
8. H. O. Houghton to Maria Houghton, December 12, 1836; Daniel C. Houghton to his father, January 26, 1837.
9. William Houghton, Jr., to his father, February 6, October 27, 1837, to his mother, August 30, 1837; H. O. Houghton to his mother, November 4, 1837; Justin Houghton to his father, October 27, 1837.
10. J. C. Derby, *Fifty Years Among Authors, Books and Publishers,* p. 271; H O. Houghton, Journal, November 12, December 19, 1839.
11. H. O. Houghton, MS, n.d.
12. Julian Ira Lindsay, *Tradition Looks Forward,* pp. 139, 162.
13. Quoted in Lindsay, pp. 151, 175.
14. H. O. Houghton, Records of Freshman, Sophomore and Junior Examinations, verified by transcripts of Houghton's record sent me by T. D. Seymour Bassett, University of Vermont Archivist. Bliss, quoted in Scudder, *Houghton,* p. 24, says twenty-four graduated. My figure of twenty-one comes from Bassett's transcript.
15. Boston *Journal,* February 15, 1894.
16. Quoted in Lindsay, pp. 182–83.
17. Notes from the Minutes of Phi Sigma Nu sent me by T. D. Seymour Bassett.
18. "Ought Farmers and Mechanics to go through College," H. O. Houghton MS, n.d. Perhaps Houghton was only abreast of his times rather than in advance of them. In 1841, Alden Partridge, president of Norwich Univer-

sity, Vermont, proposed to Congress that funds realized from the sale of public lands be used to support public colleges. Carl R. Woodward, "The Heritage of a Country-Bred Statesman," *New England Galaxy*, V, 37–46.

19. H. O. Houghton to his parents, February 6, 1845, October 20, November 19, 1846; James B. Dow to Messrs. Metcalf & Co., October 15, 1846.

20. H. O. Houghton to his parents, March 22 and 30, 1847. The elder Wilson died in 1868. In 1879, his son, aided by Charles Wentworth, bought the University Press from Welch, Bigelow & Co., its owners since 1859.

21. H. O. Houghton to his parents, July 7, 1847.

22. H. O. Houghton to his parents, October 13, 1847, May 15, September 2, 1848; Derby, pp. 272–73.

23. Details for this paragraph have been taken from the series of Houghton's letters to his parents already cited.

24. Hellmut Lehmann-Haupt, L. C. Wroth, and R. G. Silver, *The Book in America*, pp. 58–69; George A. Kubler, *A New History of Stereotyping*, passim.

CHAPTER II

1. Freeman & Bolles Journals, 1834–1840 and 1841–1849.

2. November 16, 1848, quoted in Scudder, *Henry Oscar Houghton*, pp. 53–54. Little & Brown, founded in 1837, changed its title to Little, Brown and Company in 1847. Little, Brown, *One Hundred and Twenty-Five Years of Publishing 1837–1962*, p. 6.

3. Memorandum of notes, January 1849.

4. Albert G. Houghton to H. O. Houghton, no month, 13, 1848, promises $600 from Mrs. Tyler; David Scott to H. O. Houghton, April 25, April 30, May 30, 1849. Scott's contribution of $600 was delayed in transit. Rufus Haywood to H. O. Houghton, March 26, 1849, promises $500 in a demand note before May 1. Scudder, *Houghton*, p. 55, and Derby, p. 275, suggest Haywood's contribution came at the last moment and was unexpected.

5. George A. Stevens, *New York Typographical Union No. 6*, pp. 195–210. According to the December 1, 1849, issue of the weekly *Protective Union*, in Boston there were 156 journeymen working 12 hours, 7 days a week at an average salary of $9.25. Three hundred twenty-five journeymen working 10 hours, 6 days a week, averaged $6.00. The figure of 8000 ems per day comes from the Boston *Herald*, August 21, 1851. Stevens gives the average as 5000. See also "Early Organizations of Printers" by Eihelbert Stewart in *Labor Bulletin*, 1905, II, 857–1042.

6. *Protective Union*, December 1, 1849; Stevens, p. 423.

7. *Protective Union*, December 1, 1849; Boston *Daily Evening Traveller*, May 1, 1849; Bolles & Houghton Payroll.

8. H. O. Houghton to his parents, January 12, October 1, November 19, 1849; Boston *Daily Evening Traveller*, November 21, 1849.

9. H. O. Houghton to his parents, February 18, 1850, quoted in Scudder, *Houghton*, p. 56; Boston *Daily Evening Traveller*, November 24, December 20, 1849. On December 22, *Protective Union* denied the "Disgraceful

Outrage," and the union offered a reward for "any information which may lead to the conviction of any member or members of the Boston Printers' Union, who have been connected with the outrage alluded to."

10. *Protective Union*, June 8, 1850; Stevens, p. 440; Scudder, *Houghton*, p. 73; H. O. Houghton to his parents, February 18, 1850.

11. May 12, 1851.

12. Bolles & Houghton Memorandum, July 1, 1851. The item "available cash" is composed of "on hand cash say 700 & M. R. R. Bond 1000" and net profits of $1023.92.

13. Lucius R. Paige, *History of Cambridge*, pp. 221–22; Cambridge *Chronicle*, January 25, February 1, 1849.

14. Memorandum of Agreement, December 5, 1851; Boston *Herald*, December 30, 1851.

15. Scudder, *Houghton*, note, p. 65, gives the payroll for April 10, 1852, as $575.22. My larger figure is taken from the Riverside Payroll Book under the date April 24, 1852. Bolles & Houghton Account Book, March 22, 1851. Stevens, p. 211, says it was "fairly common" in these years for employing printers to pay their help every two weeks.

16. H. O. Houghton and Company Account Book, October, 11, 13, 1852; Memorandum of Agreement, December 5, 1851, with endorsements of transferal from Houghton & Haywood to H. O. Houghton & Company, signed by Rufus Haywood, Edmund H. Bennett, H. O. Houghton, and Little, Brown, May 10, 1852.

17. "Platform, etc. of the Printers' Literary Union of Cambridge," 1853.

18. Memorandum of Agreement, September 10, 1855; bill from Little, Brown, six notes $8708.55, July–December 1858, settled by work done, January 29, 1859; another for $550, payable in five months, December 29, 1859.

19. *The Bookmakers' Reminiscences and Contemporary Sketches of American Publishers from the New York Evening Post 1874–1876*, pp. 25–29, consulted in the offices of *PW* through the courtesy of the late Frederic Melcher. Houghton's copy of Maria Lowell's *Poems*, bound in red morocco, with his crest stamped in gold on the back, is now in the Berg collection of the New York Public Library.

20. Scudder, *Houghton*, pp. 70–71. The *Athenaeum*'s praise is quoted in Ray Nash, *Printing as an Art*, p. 21.

21. George W. Van Vleck, *The Crisis of 1857 in the United States*, pp. 78–79; Edward Sanford Martin, *The Life of Joseph Hodges Choate*, I, 201–2; *PW*, September 27, 1873, p. 310; Memorandum of Agreement, September 30, 1857. Joseph Henry Harper in *The House of Harper*, p. 137, says of the 1857 crisis, "As a matter of business precaution, although not compelled to do so by actual circumstance, Harper & Brothers thought it wise to make an assignment of their business, and placed their affairs nominally in the hands of two of the sons, John W. Harper and Joseph W. Harper, Jr. This arrangement was only in name, and in no way injured the credit of the House." The statement as to the Harper suspension comes from the *PW* cited above.

22. Octavius Brooks Frothingham, *Theodore Parker*, p. 464.

23. J. C. Derby, *Fifty Years Among Authors, Books and Publishers*, p. 673;

The partnership agreement between H. O. Houghton and his brother Albert of September 30, 1857, was canceled by mutual consent on May 20, 1858. For a history of the University Press see *Bookmakers,* pp. 105–7.

24. Memorandum, November 1859, of books stereotyped by H. O. Houghton & Company for Phillips, Sampson; Copy of report of works in progress at the Riverside Stereotype Foundry belonging to Phillips, Sampson & Company, October 14, 1859; H. O. Houghton & Company memorandum, 1860 [no day or month], on Phillips, Sampson & Company (insolvent).

25. Little, Brown bill, April 1, 1859, settled May 11, 1859.

26. M. D. Wight, *A Memorial of O. W. Wight, A. M., M. D., Sanitarian, Lawyer & Author;* Scudder, *Houghton,* pp. 74–75; Derby, p. 276.

27. Memoranda of Agreements, March 7, April 20, June 18 (with endorsement, October 8, 1861), September 15, 1860; O. W. Wight to H. O. Houghton, June 13, 1860; H. O. Houghton to Wight, May 7, 1861; *Sheldon et al.* v. *Houghton,* Equity Case no. 3–30 in U.S. Circuit Court for the Southern District of New York, Exhibit D (copy provided me by the National Archives and Record Service, Washington, D.C.)

28. *Bookmakers,* pp. 25–29; *PW,* M. M. Hurd obituary, December 7, 1912.

29. Memorandum of Agreement, December 18, 1862; M. M. Hurd to H. O. Houghton, June 26, 1863.

30. Memorandum of Agreement, December 14, 1863.

CHAPTER III

1. Unless otherwise noted, information on Noah Webster and his dictionaries in this and the following paragraphs comes from Robert Keith Leavitt's *Noah's Ark,* pp. 1–68, Harvey R. Warfel's *Noah Webster: Schoolmaster to America,* pp. 287–377, and William Draper Swan's *The Critic Criticised, and Worcester Vindicated.* For H. O. Houghton's meeting with Webster see Horace Elisha Scudder, *Henry Oscar Houghton,* p. 7, and J. C. Derby, *Fifty Years Among Authors, Books and Publishers,* p. 272.

2. For "high protective tariff in thought," see Scudder's MS "American Literature," 1875, II, 29.

3. *American Literary Gazette,* November 15, 1865, p. 45; *PW,* February 17, 1877, pp. 192–93.

4. *Atlantic,* V (May 1860), 631–36.

5. *Atlantic,* XIV (November 1864), 642–44; Leavitt, p. 60.

6. Raymond Kilgour, *Messrs. Roberts Brothers: Publishers,* pp. 17–21. On custom or courtesy of the trade see also George Haven Putnam's *International Copyright,* p. 46, which states, "It was the understanding on the part of the publishers of this group [the legitimate, respectable publishers] that when one house had introduced an English author to the American market, his undertaking with that book or with later books by the same author, were not to be interfered with."

7. Warren S. Tryon and William Charvat, eds., *The Cost Books of Ticknor and Fields,* pp. xxiii, 473.

8. James Russell Lowell, *Letters,* ed. Charles Eliot Norton, I, 290. See also

p. 281 for Lowell's description of a winter walk to the Press. Horace Elisha Scudder, *James Russell Lowell*, I, 451.

9. Warren S. Tryon, *Parnassus Corner*, pp. 255–56; James C. Austin, *Fields of the Atlantic Monthly*, pp. 386–87.

10. James Russell Lowell, *New Letters*, ed. M. A. DeWolfe Howe, p. 99; Scudder, *Lowell*, I, 444; Frank Luther Mott, *A History of American Magazines*, II, 391; M. A. DeWolfe Howe, *The Atlantic Monthly and Its Makers*, p. 34.

11. Tryon, p. 267.

12. Daniel Jefferson of Little, Brown to H. O. Houghton, n.d.

13. Riverside Press Payroll Book, 1860–1863.

14. *Sheldon et al. v. Houghton,* Exhibit A & Schedule F; Extracts of letters received from H. O. Houghton by the Plaintiffs, January 9, April 28, May 6, 1863.

15. Ibid., June 13, 1863.

16. For this and the following paragraph on Dickens' works published in America, see Herman LeRoy Edgar and R. W. G. Vail's "Early American Editions of the Works of Charles Dickens," *Bulletin of the New York Public Library*, XXXIII (May 1929), 302–19, and *American Literary Gazette*, April 15, 1867, pp. 348–49, April 29, 1867, pp. 5–6, May 15, 1867, p. 15, August 15, 1870, p. 237; Eugene Exman, *The House of Harper*, p. 56. According to the *American Literary Gazette* of April 15, 1867, Dickens' earnings in twenty-five years from Harper amounted to over $60,000.

17. Daniel Jefferson to H. O. Houghton, October 21, 1865. The publishers listed are Harper; Getz, Buck & Co.; Wiley, Carey & Hart; Lea & Blanchard; James A. Dux; Hickley, Swan & Brewer; Redfield; F. A. Brady; Clark, Austin & Maynard; Peterson; Sheldon; Miller; Bradburn.

18. *Sheldon et al. v. Houghton,* Schedule F. In 1859 Harper paid Dickens £1000 for *Tale of Two Cities*. For *Great Expectations* (1860–1861) and *Our Mutual Friend* (1864–1865), £1250. *American Literary Gazette,* April 15, 1867, pp. 348–49.

19. Lemon, Fields & Co., to H. O. Houghton & Company, bill July 1859 and letter, February 5, 1864.

20. Scudder, *Houghton*, pp. 70, 72; Tryon, pp. 177, 228–29; H. O. Houghton MS, n.d.; "Dress in Books," *Riverside Bulletin*, February 15, 1871, p. 5.

21. *American Literary Gazette*, April 1, 1864, p. 374.

22. Memorandum of Agreement, March 1, 1864; Hurd & Houghton 1866 Grand Balance Sheet; Tryon, p. 278.

23. *American Literary Gazette*, April 1, 1864, p. 393, May 2, 1864, pp. 33, 38, May 16, 1864, p. 58.

CHAPTER IV

1. Warren S. Tryon, *Parnassus Corner*, pp. 54–59; Caroline Ticknor, *Hawthorne and His Publisher*, pp. 13–21; Memoranda of Agreement, July 14, 1832, April 1, 1833, October 16, 1834; Bill of Sale, March 12, 1834.

2. Tryon, p. 209. For Henry James's "titular screen," see *Atlantic*, CXVI (July 1915), 23.

3. Tryon, pp. 212–13.
4. Ticknor, *Hawthorne*, pp. 53–55.
5. Ibid., p. 119. According to an inventory of George S. Hillard, Administrator, Hawthorne's estate amounted to $28,034.61. Of this amount, $724.73 went for sundry bills; Sophia received $9103.30; Una, Julian, and Rose, $6068.86 each, On June 26, 1846, Longfellow wrote William D. Ticknor:

> Dear Sir,
> I have been reflecting upon your offer for the Poems, yesterday: and I confess that with all the good-will in the world, I cannot bring myself to be satisfied with it. I really do not think you offer enough. My own offer I think much nearer the mark, I proposed that you should give me 22½ c. per volume, you say 15. If you will make it 20 c, I will be satisfied. This is the utmost I am willing to do: and I must say that I think you will have a very good bargain of it at that. Please let me hear from you as soon as possible.

To underline the bargain, Longfellow added a p.s. "Both Bryant and Halleck receive from Harpers twenty-five cents per copy on their poems; which is twenty-five percent on the retail price." At the bottom of the page appears a penciled note, "Agreed to July 14, 1846, W.D.T." Emerson, Whittier, Holmes, and Lowell all dealt with the senior partner when they transferred their allegiance from other publishers to Ticknor & Fields. Nor was Longfellow alone in winning high rates. Lowell was secured to the house by a similar royalty. Once writers had been won, Fields was the man to keep them content. Thus it was he to whom Lowell appealed when he heard that Oliver Wendell Holmes was unhappy about his *Atlantic* rates and was threatening to "carry his wares to a better market." (James C. Austin, *Fields of the Atlantic Monthly,* p. 72.) Fields lost no time in calling on the Doctor, noting in a hasty scrawl on the very day of Lowell's appeal (March 1, 1861), "I have this day arranged the following tariff of prices with Dr. Holmes for his contributions to 'The Atlantic.' For Prose $10 pr, page of Essay articles etc.; not *serial* stories, $50 for Poems. The Serial Stories, same terms as formerly, pd. pr. Autocrat, Professor etc. J.T.F."
6. Tryon, pp. 231–32; Edgar Johnson, *Charles Dickens: His Tragedy and Triumph*, II, 1088–89.
7. Tryon, pp. 277–78.
8. Horace Elisha Scudder, *Henry Oscar Houghton*, pp. 82–84; *American Literary Gazette*, April 2, 1866, p. 299.
9. Ibid., November 15, 1864, p. 34; H. O. Houghton, MS speech, n.d. Possibly Houghton also bought at this time some English copper-face or Bell type. However, see chap. XXI, note 30.
10. Charles Dickens to H. O. Houghton, May 4, 1864; *American Literary Gazette*, April 15, 1867, p. 6, pp. 348–49, August 1, 1867, p. 186.
11. Ibid., May 16, 1864, p. 45.
12. Memorandum of Agreement, December 9, 1864; Ticknor, *Hawthorne*, p. 16.
13. *Bookmakers,* pp. 105–7; Scudder, *Houghton,* p. 42; Tryon, pp. 268, 404,

note 39; Memorandum of Agreement, July 29, 1867; Fields, Osgood & Co., November 17, 1870, to J. H. Beal, President Second National Bank, Boston. The bindery proved a successful operation, within two years returning to the three investors $10,000 each, the amount of their original outlay.

14. *Bookmakers*, pp. 111–12.

15. George Haven Putnam, *Memories of a Publisher, 1865–1915*, pp. 2–3; *American Literary Gazette*, September 1, 1864, p. 269, December 15, 1864, p. 109; Memorandum of Agreement, July, 1864. The Putnam firm was reconstituted on January 1, 1867.

16. Memorandum of Agreement, January 20, 1865. At the expiration of the contract, this edition of Cooper was taken over by Appleton, Houghton having had an analysis of the copyright status made by the Library of Congress. Sixteen of the copyrights had expired; seventeen more would expire within the decade. United States of America Library of Congress, Washington, May 8, 1871, to Hurd & Houghton. See also W. A. Townsend Scrapbook, pp. 2–13.

17. O. W. Wight to Hurd & Houghton, February 1, May 2, 1864; James Spedding to H. O. Houghton, January 20, 1865, April 23, 1867.

18. *Sheldon et al.* v. *Houghton,* Schedule G, H, and Exhibit A; Memorandum of Agreement, December 27, 1861; Felix O. C. Darley to Houghton, September 3, 1862; Extracts of letters received from H. O. Houghton by Sheldon & Co., November 27, 1865. (The letters are dated from January through April 1863); Houghton's proposed letter to the Sheldons has no date.

19. Except as noted all information on *Sheldon et al.* v. *Houghton* is taken from my photostatic copy of the transcript of proceedings.

20. Copies of James T. Fields's affidavits, although missing from the above, are in Houghton Mifflin's files.

21. Boston *Journal*, November 7, 1865.

22. For my general impressions of Joseph Hodges Choate, I am indebted to Edward Sanford Martin's biography of him already cited; for those of William Maxwell Evarts to Charles L. Barrows' *William M. Evarts* (Chapel Hill: University of North Carolina Press, 1941).

23. Evarts, Southmayde & Choate, December 23, 1865, to George Hale [Houghton's Boston attorney] and receipted bill, January 1, 1866.

24. *PW*, April 19, 1879, pp. 470–71.

25. London *Athenaeum*, January 7, 1860, p. 19, January 14, 1860, p. 52.

26. Fields to Dickens, September 18, 1866; Dickens to Fields, October 16, 1866, printed in Austin, pp. 380–81.

27. *American Literary Gazette*, January 1, 1867, p. 167, January 15, 1867, p. 191, February 1, 1867, p. 217, April 1, 1867, p. 335.

28. Carl J. Weber, *The Rise and Fall of James Ripley Osgood*, pp. 73–74; Tryon, pp. 304–5.

29. *American Literary Gazette*, April 15, 1867, pp. 348–49. Tryon, p. 305, says that Ticknor & Fields agreed to pay Dickens "10 percent on the retail price of every volume sold." The plain Diamond sold for $1.25; the illustrated for $1.50. See Ticknor & Fields Copyright Account Book for the 2 d royalty and the 5000 exemption.

30. *American Literary Gazette,* May 15, 1867, p. 37, June 1, 1867, p. 84.

31. Tryon, p. 308; *The Letters of Charles Dickens,* ed. Walter Dexter, III, 115–16, 531; *American Literary Gazette,* August 1, 1867, p. 186.

32. Dickens, *Letters,* III, 555–56, 559.

33. December 3, 1867.

34. Johnson, III, 1096; Dickens, *Letters,* III, 644; Ticknor & Fields Copyright Account Book; Joseph Henry Harper, *The House of Harper,* p. 262.

35. October 27, 1868. *The Western Bookseller,* December, 1868, p. 9.

36. Tryon, pp. 331–32.

37. Dickens, *Letters,* III, 522.

38. Ibid., p. 750.

39. Fields, Osgood to Dickens, January 3, 1870; James R. Osgood to Ben H. Ticknor, February 11, 1870.

40. Fields, Osgood to Dickens, March 8, 1870; Harper, *Harper,* p. 263; Dickens, *Letters,* III, 777.

41. Mott, *American Magazines,* II, 386, says, "Osgood tried to get *Edwin Drood* for *Every Saturday* but Harper got it and paid for it; nevertheless *Every Saturday* printed it, too. Tit for Tat." Harper, *Harper,* p. 263, implies that his firm paid for *Edwin Drood.* Nevertheless, the correspondence cited clearly indicates that Fields, Osgood paid Dickens £1250 for advance sheets of *Edwin Drood.*

42. July 19, 1869 to Osgood and John Spencer Clark, the third partner in Fields, Osgood.

43. May 28, 1869, to Osgood and Clark.

44. n.d. [1869] to Osgood; June 1, 1869 to Osgood and Clark. For details on Mrs. Stowe's "The True Story of Lady Byron" and its sequel see chapter VII, pp. 179 ff.

45. August 7, August 24, September 22, 1869, to Osgood and Clark.

46. Fields to Tennyson, December 5, 1869, January 28, 1870; Tryon, pp. 358, 360, 362.

CHAPTER V

1. Net Losses: 1866 — $7712.91; 1867 — $45,757.87; 1868 — $2934.68; 1869 — $24,919.17. Net gains: 1870 — $8,754.82. Hurd & Houghton Grand Balance Sheets. The first Grand Balance Sheets available for H. O. Houghton & Company begin in 1868, when the net gains were $28,282.32. In 1869 they were $34,861.44; in 1870, $19,638.20.

2. Memorandum of Agreement, January 1, 1866.

3. Charles C. Little to H. O. Houghton, November 21, 1866, April 1867; *American Literary Gazette,* January 15, 1868, p. 176, May 1, 1868, p. 6.

4. Ibid.

5. Program "Riverside Dedication by Employees at the New Buildings, Tuesday Evening, December 31st, 1867"; *American Literary Gazette,* June 15, 1867, p. 101.

6. Edward Stanwood, *American Tariff Controversies in the Nineteenth Century,* II, 152; *Riverside Bulletin,* November 15, 1871, p. 42; John Osborne Sargent to H. O. Houghton, October 24, 1866, January 17, 1867;

Scudder to James A. Garfield (draft), n.d.; *American Literary Gazette,* March 15, 1866, pp. 271, 275, April 2, 1866, p. 299, May 1, 1866, p. 5, January 15, 1867, p. 192.

7. Horace Elisha Scudder, *Henry Oscar Houghton,* pp. 92–94.

8. Unidentified newspaper clipping. *The Western Bookseller,* December, 1868, pp. 8–9, reported that Hurd & Houghton ceased publishing *London Society* in December 1867 because "it was found very soon that the arrangement would not work, inasmuch as the magazine could not be kept back but was sold here at a lower price than heretofore, thus interfering with the regular profits."

9. Scudder, Diary, March 17, June 9, 1865.

10. Horace Elisha Scudder, *Life and Letters of David Coit Scudder,* pp. 1–78.

11. Ibid., pp. 67–68.

12. Frederick Rudolph in his *Mark Hopkins and the Log: Williams College, 1836–1872,* p. 51, cites Washington Gladden as remarking on the number of Williams alumni serving as newspaper editors. Rudolph's list, given in a footnote, includes William Cullen Bryant, editor of the New York *Post.* Since Bryant was at Williams only one year (1810–1811), before Mark Hopkins' day, I have omitted his name, but have added editors of magazines. Gladden served as religious editor of the *Independent* for five years, then as editor and associate editor of Edward Fiske Merriam's *Sunday Afternoon.*

13. Scudder, *Houghton,* p. 86; June 28, 1858.

14. Scudder, *David Coit Scudder,* p. 29; Scudder to Charles Scudder, June 28, 1858.

15. Ibid.

16. September 26, 1860.

17. Ibid.

18. Information in this and the following paragraph comes from Scudder's Diaries and Joseph Henry Harper, *The House of Harper,* p. 219.

19. Scudder Diaries, 1862, 1863, and 1864, for this and the following paragraph. Scudder was too busy to write the article on children's literature for Norton, so the assignment was given to Thomas Wentworth Higginson.

20. *The Galaxy,* established by W. C. and E. P. Church in 1866, was taken over by the Sheldons in 1868. The first *Putnam's* ran from 1853–1857, and was reconstituted in 1868. Frank Luther Mott, *A History of American Magazines,* II, 428. "Singular fossil" was Charles A. Bristed's epithet for the *North American;* "megatherium" was James Russell Lowell's. Mott, *American Magazines,* II, 243; Lowell, *Letters,* I, 335.

21. *Youth's Companion,* II (May 30, 1828), 4.

22. Scudder, *Houghton,* p. 90.

23. Scudder, Diary, November 11, 1865. Swinburne called his publisher, James B. P. Payne of Maxon & Co, "that pellet of decomposed dung." *The Swinburne Letters,* ed. Cecil Y. Lang, I, 187.

24. William D. Howells, *Literary Friends and Acquaintances,* p. 102; *Life and Letters of William Dean Howells,* ed. Mildred Howells, I, 95–98.

25. June 9, 1866.

26. Scudder to his sister Jeanne, May 11, 1866, and his Literary Journal, August 2, September 18, 1866.

27. For verification of the facts and quotations in the following section on the *Riverside Magazine* the four volumes of the periodical and Scudder's two notebooks devoted to the business of the magazine should be consulted. Scudder frequently used a kind of shorthand in these notebooks, transcribing parts of important letters as well as noting daily details of his editorial administration. In quoting, I have expanded the shorthand into normal English. More specific citations will be found in my article, "Horace Elisha Scudder and the *Riverside Magazine for Young People*," *Harvard Library Bulletin*, XIV (Autumn 1960), 426–52.

28. *The Andersen-Scudder Letters*, ed. Waldemar Wastergaard, pp. 3–8, 14–15; *PW*, June 13, 1874, p. 558.

29. February 5, 1867.

30. Sarah Orne Jewett, *Letters*, ed. Richard Cary, pp. 17–19; Scudder to Miss Jewett (envelope addressed to Miss Alice Eliot), November 26, 1870.

31. December 21, 1866.

32. *American Literary Gazette*, October 1, 1867; Scudder, Literary Journal, January 22, 1868, August 27, 1868.

33. *Our Young Folks*, III (December 1867), 765; *Scribner's Monthly*, I (December 1870), 212.

34. *Riverside Bulletin*, September 1, 1873, pp. 29–30.

35. Fields to Charles Eliot Norton, March 12, 1869, to Osgood and Clark, August 7, 1869; Henry Adams, *The Education of Henry Adams*, p. 234; Edward Everett Hale, Jr., *The Life and Letters of Edward Everett Hale*, I, 97–119.

36. *Andersen-Scudder Letters*, p. 77; George Harrison Mifflin to H. O. Houghton, May 27, 1870.

37. Scudder to H. O. Houghton, May 28, 1870. In this letter Scudder proposed an illustrated magazine which would draw on the resources of Boston's new Fine Arts Museum for subjects. (Houghton was one of the founders of the Museum.) If the periodical were concerned with matters of fact rather than speculation and concentrated on American subjects, he anticipated a minimum of 10,000 subscribers.

38. Scudder, Notebook, Private, January 15, 1871; Scudder to Harriet and Vida Scudder, January 1, 1871.

39. *American Literary Gazette*, June 1, 1870, p. 73; Memorandum of Agreement, January 1, 1871; Jno. S. Blatchford to H. O. Houghton & Company, March 6, 1871; Scudder to Harriet and Vida Scudder, January 1, 1871.

CHAPTER VI

1. Except as noted, facts about George Harrison Mifflin's family, his growing up, and his early years with Hurd & Houghton are taken from two Mifflin manuscripts, "The Life of Doctor Charles Mifflin" and "An Account of the Beginnings of the Houghton, Mifflin Company," begun September 1914, finished October 1916. This last document which Mifflin recorded in shorthand, will be cited hereafter as "An Account." Other sources used are H. O. Houghton to G. H. Mifflin, October 30, 1878, G. H. Mifflin to

H. O. Houghton, November 9, 1891, and a series of letters written me by Mifflin Frothingham, G. H. Mifflin's nephew.

2. G. H. Mifflin to Benjamin Milles Pierce, September 13, 1867. I am indebted to Dr. Max Fisch of the University of Illinois for calling my attention to the Mifflin letters in the Pierce Collection in the Houghton Library, Harvard University.

3. G. H. Mifflin to Pierce, July 3, 1867.

4. G. H. Mifflin to Pierce, March 19, 1870.

5. Hurd & Houghton and H. O. Houghton & Company Grand Balance Sheet for 1872.

6. Francis Jackson Garrison to Fanny Garrison Villard [Mrs. Henry Villard], March 30, April 8, June 17, 1866, January 13, 14, 1868, January 11, 1872. W. P. Garrison to Scudder, February 6, 1871. Although W. P. Garrison did not become editor of the *Nation* until 1881, he had been in reality managing editor from its founding in 1865. Mott, *A History of American Magazines,* III, 344.

7. *American Literary Gazette,* March 15, 1871, p. 202; *Old and New,* VI (September 1872), 339.

8. F. J. Garrison to Fanny, May 21, August 12, 1872; to W. P. Garrison, May 26, 1872.

9. William Dean Howells, "The Man of Letters as a Man of Business," *Literature and Life,* p. 2.

10. Fields, Osgood to Harriet Beecher Stowe, June 8, 1869. Although Fields told Miss Dodge that information about his authors' contracts was confidential, in this letter to Mrs. Stowe, the firm reported Miss Dodge's earnings from 1863 through 1869. Augusta Dodge, ed., *Gail Hamilton's Life in Letters,* I, 412; Gail Hamilton [Mary Abigail Dodge], *A Battle of the Books,* p. 215.

11. Ibid., pp. 12–15; Fields, Osgood to Harriet Beecher Stowe, June 8, 1869.

12. Ticknor & Fields to Miss Dodge, September 8, 1868; Hamilton, p. 95; Dodge, II, 611–12.

13. Ticknor & Fields and Fields, Osgood to Miss Dodge, September 14, November 9, 20, 28, December 21, 1868, January 1, 7, 25, February 11, April 21, 1869. Also Hamilton, pp. 66, 76, 98, 107, 111, 113, 116, 122–36, 139, 153; Dodge, *Life in Letters,* II, 630. Miss Dodge to T. W. Higginson, February 12, 1869.

14. Hawthorne's original royalty rates are stated in the August 13, 1868, letter as *The Scarlet Letter,* 15 percent; *Twice Told Tales.* 2 vols., 10 percent; *Mosses from an Old Manse,* 2 vols., 10 percent; *Marble Faun,* 15 percent; *Snow Image,* 10 percent; *Wonder Book,* 10 percent; *Tanglewood Tales,* 10 percent; *Blithedale Romance,* 15 percent; *Seven Gables,* 15 percent; *Our Old Home,* 15 percent.

15. Ticknor & Fields to Mrs. Hawthorne, August 28, 1868. Sophia Thoreau, Henry David Thoreau's sister and heir, provides another notable example of the fixed sum arrangement. In 1863 for *Excursions* she was allowed 10 percent on the retail price of all copies sold. Thereafter she accepted 12½ cents, 250 copies being exempt, for *The Maine Woods, A Yankee in Canada,* and a new edition of *A Week on the Concord and Merrimac*

Rivers. For *Cape Cod* and *Letters,* with no exemptions, she was also allowed 12½ cents. On a new edition of *Walden,* now selling for $2, she was allowed 15 cents. Memoranda of Agreement, September 1, 1863; May 2, 1864; March 20, 1865; September 3, 1866; December 1, 1867.

16. Ticknor & Fields to Mrs. Hawthorne, August 28, 1868.
17. Elizabeth P. Peabody to Fields, Osgood & Company, March 7, 1869; Randall Stewart, "Mrs. Hawthorne's Financial Difficulties, Selections from Her Letters to James T. Fields, 1865–1868," *More Books,* XXI (February, September, 1946), 43–52, 254–63; Hamilton, pp. 229, 233–34.
18. Fields, Osgood to Mrs. Stowe, June 8, 1869, and to Anna Dickinson, May 31, 1869.
19. Hamilton, pp. 245–47.
20. Fields, Osgood to Mrs. Stowe, June 8, 1869; Hamilton, pp. 285–88.
21. Memorandum of Agreement, November 12, 1869; Dodge, *Life in Letters,* II, 643–44, 645–46, 657.
22. Hamilton, pp. 4–6.
23. *PW,* November 14, 1872, p. 518, September 18, 1875, p. 464.
24. Scudder to his sister Jeannie, November 26, 1871.
25. *Riverside Bulletin,* August 15, 1871, p. 29, September 15, 1872, pp. 33–34.
26. Ibid., February 15, 1871, pp. 5–6, April 15, 1871, p. 14.
27. Ibid., May 15, 1871, p. 17.
28. Ibid., August 15, 1872, pp. 29–30.
29. Ibid., June 15, 1872, pp. 21–22.
30. Ibid., April 1, 1873, pp. 9–10.
31. F. J. Garrison to Fanny, November 27, 1873.

CHAPTER VII

1. Fields to Osgood and Clark, August 24, 1869; Memorandum of Agreement, December 12, 1870.
2. James Russell Lowell, *Letters,* ed. Charles Eliot Norton, II, 34; *American Literary Gazette,* October 1, 1866, p. 246, August 15, 1871, pp. 229–31; Carl J. Weber, *The Rise and Fall of James Ripley Osgood,* p. 117; Warren S. Tryon, *Parnassus Corner,* p. 360.
3. Fields, Osgood to J. H. Beal, November 17, 1870; Chapter 232, Commonwealth of Massachusetts, An Act, April 30, 1869.
4. Memorandum of Agreement, April 7, 1869; *American Literary Gazette,* June 1, 1871, p. 58.
5. Frank Luther Mott, *A History of American Magazines,* III, 180–90; *Literary World,* IV (September 1, 1870), 49.
6. Memorandum of Agreement, May 30, 1873; *Jubilee Days,* Chemical Engraving Company, June 17–July 2, 1872, last four pages, unnumbered.
7. Osgood to Walter Smith, March 11, 1872.
8. Osgood to Gilbert & Rivington, April 26, 1872; to E. H. Huntington, March 12, 1873; to B. T. Dwight, August 29, 1872.

9. Memorandum of Agreement, February 10, 1873; *PW*, Christmas number 1877, p. 608; *The American Bookseller*, April 1, April 16, June 1, 1877, pp. 191, 238, 328–29.

10. *Atlantic*, XXXIII (April 1874), 508–9; *PW*, February 22, September 6, 1873, pp. 197, 243, March 21, 1874, p. 296; Osgood to The Heliotype Company, November 3, 1874, and to N. D. Leggett, Commissioner of Patents, September 17, 1873.

11. Boston *Journal*, November 22, 1865; Augusta Dodge, *Life in Letters*, I, 469; Hamilton, pp. 51–56.

12. Tryon, p. 290, gives a summary of *Our Young Folks* editorial arrangements which differs in detail from mine. However, see Dodge, *Letters* II, 260; Fields, Osgood to E. S. Phelps, December 11, 1869, and the citations in note 13.

13. Trowbridge to Lucy Larcom, January 6, 15, 1873; Osgood to Trowbridge, April 2, 1874; John Townsend Trowbridge, *My Own Story*, pp. 317–18.

14. Clark to T. W. Higginson, September 21, 1869; Osgood to Roswell Smith, November 22, 1873.

15. Ferris Greenslet, *The Life of Thomas Bailey Aldrich*, pp. 18–69.

16. Aldrich to Osgood, June 2, 1865. Possibly the periodical was the *Galaxy*, "born of a divine discontent with the *Atlantic Monthly*," which came into being the following year. Mott, *American Magazines*, III, 361. However, I have found no evidence that Hurd & Houghton had any part in the founding of the *Galaxy*.

17. Greenslet, *Aldrich*, p. 76; Ticknor & Fields, Ledger Private. Weber, *Osgood*, p. 65, dates Osgood's letter as November 16. On the evening of that day, Aldrich was at the Fieldses' who were giving "a little dinner party" for Gail Hamilton [Mary Abigail Dodge]. Dodge, *Life in Letters*, I, 528.

18. Greenslet, *Aldrich*, p. 84, 99; W. D. Howells to Aldrich, March 21, 1869, August 11, 1871; Richard Grant White to H. O. Houghton, January 17, 1866.

19. Osgood to W. L. Thomas, October 14, November 17, 30, December 11, 21, 1869.

20. Osgood to Chambers Bros., November 12, 17, 21, 1870; *American Literary Gazette*, June 1, 1871, p. 60.

21. Fields to Charles Reade, October 8, 1866; Osgood to Reade, June 9, 26, September 17, October 3, November 10, 1868, January 2, 1869, November 18, 1871; Malcolm Elwin, *Charles Reade*, pp. 185–90, 216, 219, 222–23.

22. Osgood to G. H. Lewes, June 30, July 31, September 30, November 10, 1871; to Trübner, November 10, 1871; to Fletcher Harper, November 14, 1871. Eugene Exman, *House of Harper*, p. 62, gives the price Harper paid for *Middlemarch* as £120. However, Mr. Exman kindly rechecked the records available to him for me and reported that the price paid was in fact £1200. At the time he was writing his history, he did not know of the Osgood-Harper deal and so wrote that *Middlemarch* was "snatched away [from Osgood] by Harper's."

23. Elinor Howells to Anne Howells Fréchette, November 23, 1871. Quoted by permission of William White Howells, as are all subsequent unpublished Howells letters. Permission for further publication must be secured

from either William White Howells or the Harvard College Library. In
January 1871, Osgood had raised Aldrich's salary to $3000. Ticknor &
Fields, Ledger Private.

24. Henry Adams, *Letters*, ed. Worthington Chauncey Ford, I, 185, 194; Osgood to Adams, October 13, 1870; to Lowell, October 22, 1870.

25. Harold Dean Cater, *Henry Adams and His Friends*, pp. 46, 53; Howells, *Letters*, I, 172.

26. Mott, *American Magazines*, II, 505, III, 323; George Haven Putnam, *George Palmer Putnam*, p. 362. Mott, *American Magazines*, II, 430, gives the circulation as 1500, a misprint, I believe, since his source is the preceding Putnam reference.

27. Forrest Wilson, *Crusader in Crinoline*, p. 444.

28. Ibid., pp. 451–57; Memoranda of Agreement, April 2, 1862, March 25, 1863; Fields to Mrs. Stowe, October 30, 1864. In this letter Fields offered Mrs. Stowe $3000, or $250 a month, for her contributions to the *Atlantic* and *Our Young Folks* during 1865. From 1866 through 1869, she received $10,000. Annie Fields, *Life and Letters of Harriet Beecher Stowe*, p. 326.

29. Joseph S. Van Way, "Nook Farm," *The Stowe, Beecher, Hooker, Seymor Day Foundation Bulletin*, I, 15–20.

30. Harriet Beecher Stowe, "The True Story of Lady Byron's Life," *Atlantic*, XXIV (September 1869), 295–313; Wilson, pp. 535–51. Wilson's thesis is that Mrs. Stowe told her "unsavory story" to proclaim "to the world the glamorous, stupendous fact that she . . . had been friend of Byron's wife and widow, the sharer of most intimate secrets." He exposes her error in claiming in *Lady Byron Vindicated* that a review of Guiccioli's book in the July *Blackwood's* caused her to write the article, stating, "Harriet's business correspondence shows by a dated letter that she had placed her manuscript in Osgood's hands as early as June 23, 1869. She could not possibly have seen the July *Blackwood's* much before the middle of July." He exonerates James T. Fields, as do many others, for any responsibility in allowing the article to be published. Fields's letter to Osgood, quoted in the next paragraph, shows Fields knew all about Mrs. Stowe's article well before it appeared. Quite possibly Mrs. Stowe did not see the *Blackwood's* article, although if the magazine's production schedule was similar to that of the *Atlantic*, it would have been out by the middle of June. Moreover, Fields, who was in constant communication with his Boston office, may well have sent advance sheets of the review, or at least gossip about it. For further details on press reactions to "The True Story of Lady Byron's Life," see Frank Lentricchia, Jr.'s "Harriet Beecher Stowe and the Byron Whirlwind," *Bulletin of the New York Public Library*, LXX (April 1966), 218–28.

31. James C. Austin, *Fields of the Atlantic Monthly*, pp. 293–94; Mildred Howells, *Life in Letters of William Dean Howells*, I, 150; Fields to Osgood and Clark, August 7, 1869.

32. *Macmillan's Magazine*, XX (September 1869), 396; Osgood to Mrs. Stowe, August 24, 1869; *Athenaeum*, September 11, 18, 25, 1869, pp. 336, 370, 404. The attacks continue for the rest of the year. The London *Echo* reported that Mrs. Stowe received £250 from *Macmillan's* and a like amount from the *Atlantic*. *American Literary Gazette*, October 1, 1869, p. 333.

33. Fields to Osgood and Clark, October 10, 1869; Howells, *Letters,* I, 150.
34. William H. Ellsworth, *A Golden Age of Authors,* p. 46.
35. Austin, p. 369; Fields to Bret Harte, March 12, May 7, September 3, 30, 1870; Osgood to Harte, December 27, 1870, January 10, 1871; G. W. Carleton to Osgood, November 21, December 31, 1870, January 3, 6, 11, 1871.
36. Osgood to Harte, March 8, 1871; *American Literary Gazette,* April 1, 1871, p. 226; Francis Bret Harte, ed. *The Letters of Bret Harte,* p. 12.
37. Osgood to Harte, July 18, August 25, 1871, January [1872]; Ticknor & Fields, Ledger Private.
38. Howells, *Letters,* I, 159–61.
39. *American Literary Gazette,* May 1, 1871, p. 4; Howells, *Letters,* I, 30.
40. Ibid., pp. 121, 125; Howells to Hurd, November 16, 1866, February 18, September 5, 1867.
41. Howells, *Letters,* I, 105, 126, 127, 146–47.
42. Osgood to Hurd & Houghton, May 31, 1871; Scudder to Howells, September 28, 1871; Memorandum of Agreement, March 1, 1872.
43. Memorandum of Agreement, November 1, 1871.
44. Flier of Boston Publishers and Booksellers, January 12, 1835.
45. B. H. Ticknor to Mr. Spalding, August 28, 1871; Julian Hawthorne to Osgood, April 20, 1871.
46. Osgood to Gedge, Kirby & Millet, December 18, 1874; Tennyson to Osgood, September 17, 1872.

CHAPTER VIII

1. "How We Put Out Our Fires," *Our Young Folks,* III (October 1867), 624–30.
2. John V. Morris, *Fires and Firefighters,* pp. 239–40, 253; Russell H. Conwell, *History of the Great Fire in Boston,* p. 194; *American Literary Gazette,* April 15, 1871, p. 226.
3. Augusta Dodge, ed., *Gail Hamilton's Life in Letters,* II, 690; F. J. Garrison to Fanny Garrison Villard, October 30, 1872.
4. Morris, p. 255.
5. Ibid., pp. 254–58; Conwell, p. 53, says the building was only four stories. Arthur W. Brayley in his *Complete History of the Boston Fire Department,* p. 271, gives the time of the first alarm as seven-twenty. Moses King in his *King's Hand-book of Boston,* p. 18, puts the value of property destroyed at $85,000,000. The Boston Auditor's Report for 1872–1873, p. 7, gives the time of the alarm as seven-fifteen, and sets property damage at $75,000,000.
6. F. J. Garrison to Fanny, November 13 and 20, 1872.
7. *Old and New,* VII (January 1873), 1; Conwell, p. 235.
8. Osgood to Trübner, November 15 and 22, 1872.
9. *PW,* June 7, 1873, pp. 550, 556; Auditor's Report, Boston, 1872–1873, p. 9; Osgood to E. H. M. Huntington, March 12, 1873; *PW,* April 26, 1873, p. 415; Weber, pp. 140–44.

10. Osgood to E. L. Godkin, November 20, 1873; Laura Stedman and G. M. Gould, *The Life and Letters of Edmund Clarence Stedman,* I, 490.

11. Memorandum of Agreement, November 20, 1873; *Littell's Living Age* to Hurd & Houghton, September 8, 14, 1874; *PW,* February 21, 1874, p. 189; Ferris Greenslet, *Life of Thomas Bailey Aldrich,* p. 107.

12. Memorandum of Agreement, December 1, 1873; Mifflin, "An Account"; see also James Duncan Phillips, "The Riverside Press," *Cambridge Historical Publications,* 1927, XIX, 22. Phillips, Houghton Mifflin treasurer 1915–1921, vice president 1921–1942, says, ". . . it is a curious fact that although it [the *Atlantic*] was published for thirty years by Houghton Mifflin Co., it was owned by Mr. Houghton and Mr. Mifflin personally, not by the firm, and was sold by them to the Atlantic Monthly Co. in 1908." I have found no evidence in support of this statement. Both purchase and sale are carried in the general accounts of the firm.

13. *PW,* July 17, 1874, p. 48; Howells to J. M. Comly, December 12, 1873, to Aldrich, January 20, 1874; Mildred Howells, *Life in Letters of William Dean Howells,* I, 30.

14. Howells to Aldrich, March 24, 1874, January 30, 1875.

15. Hurd & Houghton Ledger, 1873–1875; Harte to Howells, September 8, 1874. However, Houghton, Osgood and Houghton, Mifflin & Company published Harte's books.

16. Howells, *Letters,* I, 247; Leon Edel, *Henry James: the Conquest of London,* pp. 246, 261.

17. H. W. Preston to Howells, May 22, 1876; Memorandum of Agreement, December 1, 1873; Edel, *James: London,* p. 199; William M. Baker to Howells, April 15, 1873.

18. Henry Nash Smith and William M. Gibson, ed., *Mark Twain–Howells Letters,* I, 3, 22, 24, 26.

19. H. O. Houghton Company to Clemens, February 6, 20, 1875; Hamlin Hill, *Mark Twain and Elisha Bliss,* pp. 89, 189, note 54. I am indebted to Mr. Hill for arranging to have the two Houghton letters in the Mark Twain archives at the University of California photocopied and sent to me. Although these letters are in Scudder's hand, the signature is Houghton's.

20. Smith and Gibson, I, 90–92.

21. H. O. Houghton & Company Cost-book. Cost-book figures refer to the number of copies bound. The number sold was, of course, less. Frank Luther Mott, *A History of American Magazines,* II, 505, gives 20,000 for 1874.

22. *Atlantic,* XLII (October 1878), 475–87.

23. *Atlantic,* XXXIV (November 1874), 637; H. O. Houghton & Company Cost-book; Mott, *American Magazines,* III, 6.

24. Smith and Gibson, I, 156.

25. *Atlantic,* XLII (August, September, October, 1878), 238–40, 242–44, 374–76, 497–98; *Atlantic,* C (November 1907), 597.

26. Memorandum of Agreement, December 21, 1877; W. C. and C. P. Church to H. O. Houghton & Company, December 22, 1877; W. C. Church to H. O. Houghton, November 3, 1877. Mott, *American Magazines,* III, 378, gives 7000 as the *Galaxy's* circulation at the time of its sale.

27. W. H. Bishop to Howells, November 20, 1877.
28. L. N. Richardson, "Rutherford B. Hayes and Men of Letters," *New England Quarterly*, XV (March 1942), 110–41. The text of Houghton's letter appears on p. 108.
29. Smith and Gibson, I, 155–56.
30. G. P. Lathrop to Howells, July 4, 1877; Scudder, Diary, January 20, 1875; Howells, *Letters*, I, 254; Smith and Gibson, I, 24.
31. H. O. Houghton & Company to S. R. Crocker, December 17, 1874; *PW*, December 19, 1874, p. 671.
32. *The Literary World*, V (January 1875), 120; Samuel Roland Crocker, editor and founder of the magazine, was Bowdoin 1855. Osgood was the class of 1854. *American Bookseller*, VI (September 2, 1878), 243.
33. Smith and Gibson, I, 51–54.
34. Ibid., p. 55. Arthur Gilman, "Atlantic Dinners and Diners," *Atlantic*, C (November 1907), 650–51; Boston *Daily Evening Transcript*, December 17, 1874; New York *Tribune*, December 18, 1874; Howells, *Letters*, I, 199. The manuscript for Howells' speech is in Houghton Mifflin's files. I am indebted to George Montiero for discovering that the *Tribune* in reporting the dinner included Howells' speech.
35. *Harvard Library Bulletin*, IX (Spring 1955), 145–80.
36. Seating plan for the Whittier dinner.
37. Boston *Daily Evening Transcript*, December 18, 1877; Derby, pp. 281–82.
38. Samuel C. Webster, *Mark Twain, Business Man*, pp. 112, 158, 200–1; Charles Fairchild to Howells, April 6, 1877.
39. James R. Osgood & Company, Notes Payable, January 1, 1877; Mifflin, "An Account."
40. *The American Bookseller*, February 15, 1878, p. 141.

CHAPTER IX

1. "In the end James R. Osgood failed, though all his enterprises succeeded. The anomaly is sad, but it is not infrequent. They were greater than his powers and his means, and before they could reach their full fruition, they had been enlarged to men of longer purse and longer patience." William Dean Howells, *Literary Friends and Acquaintances*, p. 121.
2. James Ford Rhodes, *History of the United States*, VIII, 104–5.
3. For this and the following two paragraphs: *PW*, July 13, 24, 1875, passim. Ben Ticknor and William Lee represented their respective firms at the Convention. Carl J. Weber, *Rise and Fall of James Ripley Osgood*, p. 150, says Osgood was in attendance also. However, his name does not appear in the list of those present which is printed in *PW*, July 24, 1875, p. 242.
4. For this and the following paragraph: Raymond L. Kilgour, *Lee and Shepard: Publishers for the People*, passim; J. C. Derby, *Fifty Years Among Authors, Books and Publishers*, pp. 517–34; *PW*, October 3, 1872, p. 340, April 4, 1875, p. 359, February 27, 1875, p. 239; Anna Mary Wells, *Dear Preceptor*, p. 239; Shepard memorandum, n.d.; Osgood to Spalding, September 2, 1875. In this letter to Spalding, Osgood gives his claim

against Lee & Shepard and Lee, Shepard & Dillingham as "about $75,000." The actual amount was $76,238.77. Osgood & Company to Charles T. Dillingham, October 6, 1875 and Memorandum of Agreement with Edwin Fleming, October 23, 1875.

5. Mifflin, "An Account"; Memorandum of Agreement, January 13, 1874; Osgood to Welch, Bigelow, October 12, 1874; Memoranda of Agreement, December 8, 1874, January 1, 1875.

6. Osgood to Spalding, March [1875]; to Isaac T. Burr, September 4, 1875. A number of Shepard's notes which follow are written in pencil in obvious haste.

7. *PW*, September 5, 1875, p. 404; Memorandum of Agreement, August 30, 1875, signed by S. D. Warren & Co., Rice, Kendall & Co., Welch, Bigelow & Co., Welch & Co., Rand, Avery & Co., S. W. Wilder, H. O. Houghton & Co., Hurlburt Paper Co., J. & B. Crosby & Co., Macdonald & Sons, H. P. Co., and Thomas Y. Crowell.

8. For this and the five following paragraphs: *PW*, September 4, 1875, p. 405, September 25, 1875, pp. 509, 511-13, October 2, 1875, p. 538, October 9, 1875, pp. 561, 564, October 23, 1875, pp. 662-63, November 6, 1875, p. 710; Osgood to Charles Dillingham, October 6, 1875, October 13, 1875 and to F. O. J. S. Bazin, October 13, 23, 1875.

9. *PW*, August 7, 1875, pp. 279-80, September 4, 1875, p. 405, September 11, 1875, pp. 433-34, October 23, 1875, p. 663, January 29, 1876, pp. 110-11, 123, February 5, 1876, p. 170, May 27, 1876, p. 709; Osgood to A. W. Lovering, September 28, October 18, 1875.

10. For this and the following three paragraphs: *PW*, July 31, 1875, p. 249, September 18, 1875, p. 462, September 25, 1875, p. 500, October 16, 1875, p. 628, October 23, 1875, p. 652.

11. For this and the following five paragraphs: *PW*, March 4, 1876, pp. 285, 317, April 1, 1876, pp. 434, 436-37, 441, January 20, 1877, p. 60; James R. Osgood & Company, *Auction Catalogue*, March 28, 1876; Osgood to H. O. Houghton, July 9, 1875, March 21, 1876; Memorandum of Osgood's Plates, n.d.; W. D. Howells to W. C. Howells, September 9, 1877; S. D. Warren & Company, note on demand, April 3, 1876; Memorandum of Agreement, October, 10, 1876; Osgood & Company to Geo. A. Leavitt & Company, February 11, 1876. Leavitt's usual commission was 7 percent. However, for this auction he demanded and got 9 percent.

12. *PW*, April 15, 1876, p. 499.

13. For this and the following paragraph: *PW*, July 1, 1876, pp. 12-13, 20-21, 24, 73; John A. Pollard, *John Greenleaf Whittier*, p. 272.

14. *PW*, July 8, 1876, p. 130, August 12, 1876, p. 326.

15. Pollard, p. 266; Memorandum of Agreement, January 15, 1867; Osgood & Company to Whittier, October 1, 1872, August 12, September 20, 1873.

16. Memoranda of Agreement, January 1, 1876, May 1, 1877; B. H. Ticknor to J. R. Lowell, July 7, 1876; Osgood & Company to W. H. Forbes, November 5, 7, 1875. Emerson's Agreement contains a bankruptcy clause. Also, since he owned the plates for his books, he was to receive 15 percent during an eight-month royalty period.

17. For this and the following paragraph: Memorandum of Agreement, September 29, 1866 (in this Longfellow agreed to an annual $1000 on his

Poems); Sam Ward to Longfellow, December 27, 30, 1873, February 11, 27, 1874; Osgood & Company to Longfellow, February 11, 1874, April 26, 1875; Longfellow's Journal; Memorandum of Agreement, January 1, 1875; John Mills Alden to Longfellow, June 15, 1875; Fields to Longfellow, July 1, 1875. Osgood suspected Sam Ward rather than Fields as having arranged the deal. Ward to Longfellow, July 2, 1875.

18. For this and the following three paragraphs: *North American Review*, CXXIII (October 1876), 463, 478–79, CXLIX (July 1889), 115–17; Henry Adams, *Letters*, I, 266, 267, 300; Osgood to Henry Holt and B. H. Ticknor, October 28, 1876; Frank Luther Mott, *A History of American Magazines*, II, 249; Memorandum of Agreement, December 30, 1876; Henry Holt, *Garrulities of an Octogenarian Editor*, pp. 288–89; Ernest Samuels, *The Young Henry Adams*, pp. 283–89. Samuels, on the basis of an interview with James Duncan Phillips, attributes control of James R. Osgood & Company to Houghton. On the evidence, Charles Fairchild of S. D. Warren & Company seems the more likely candidate.

19. John Wilson bought the University Press early in the following year. *PW*, April 19, 1879, p. 472.

20. Grand Balances for Hurd & Houghton and H. O. Houghton & Company, 1874; W. E. Spaulding to F. S. Hoyt, July 13, 1942; *American Bookseller*, May 15, 1877, p. 293.

21. For this and the following two paragraphs: Mifflin, "An Account"; *American Bookseller*, February 15, 1878, p. 141; Memorandum of Settlement, May 6, 1878; Articles of Agreement, January 1, 1878.

CHAPTER X

1. Insurance claim for $19,593.67; *PW*, January 19, 1878, p. 66; W. D. Howells to W. C. Howells, January 13, 1878.

2. *The American Bookseller*, February 15, 1878, p. 141; *PW*, February 9, 1878, pp. 169–70; H. O. Houghton & Company, Liabilities, April 1, 1879.

3. For general information on the Exposition see the five-volume *Reports of the United States Commissioners to the Paris Universal Exposition 1878*. Also *PW*, January 26, 1878, p. 85, March 9, 1878, p. 270, and *Exposition Universalle de Paris 1878, Catalogue of the Collective Exhibit of the American Book Trade*.

4. Fields to Osgood, July 28, 1869; Carl J. Weber, *Rise and Fall of James Ripley Osgood*, p. 167, is in error in saying Aldrich was abroad in 1878. The summer of that year he spent in Swampscott. Smith and Gibson, I, 233. His first European tour was in 1875; his next in 1879. Ferris Greenslet, *The Life of Thomas Bailey Aldrich*, p. 137. For Edward's employment by Houghton, Osgood, see the firm's Private Journal.

5. American Publishing Company to Houghton, Mifflin & Company, December 21, 1896; Houghton Mifflin to Houghton Mifflin, January 6, 1916; Memorandum of Agreement, June 2, 1878.

6. Andrew D. White, *Autobiography*, I, 516; Francis Bret Harte, *The Letters of Bret Harte*, pp. 78–85.

7. Weber, pp. 160–70; Harte, *Letters*, pp. 156, 161.

8. Houghton, Osgood, Private Journal.

9. H. O. Houghton to Mifflin, March 29, 1878; *PW*, May 25, 1878, p. 503.

10. H. O. Houghton to Mifflin, March 30, 1878; Memorandum of Agreement, August 14, 1880; *PW*, October 5, 1878, pp. 414–16, October 12, 1878, p. 447, October 19, 1878, p. 475, December 7, 1878, p. 779.

11. For this and the following three paragraphs: *PW*, July 24, 1875, pp. 226–42 and pp. 196–97, June 1, 1878, pp. 526–30, June 8, 1878, p. 554; Donald Marquand Dozer, "The Tariff on Books," *Mississippi Valley Historical Review*, XXXVI (1949), 73–96.

12. Scudder, notebook "American Literature, 1875," III, 16–17, "American Literature, 1876," II, 33–34.

13. Scudder, unpublished "Literary Life," n.d., p. 22.

14. James A. Garfield to Scudder, May 29, 1871; Scudder to Garfield, unfinished draft, n.d.

15. H. O. Houghton to Mifflin, October 30, November 1, and 6, 1878.

16. Mifflin, Report, August 21, 1879; *PW*, July 26, 1879, p. 87; Leavitt, p. 73.

17. *PW*, September 28, 1878, p. 384, October 5, 1878, p. 416, April 19, 1879, p. 472, August 16, 1879, p. 173, September 6, 1879, pp. 276–77.

18. Houghton, Osgood, Copyright Book.

19. *PW*, January 31, 1880, p. 85.

20. Smith and Gibson, I, 276, 281–83.

21. J. C. Derby, *Fifty Years Among Authors, Books and Publishers*, pp. 283–85.

22. J. A. Warren, *A History of S. D. Warren Company*, p. 32. *The Reunion Book of Harvard Class of 1858* gives day of retirement as September 1, 1880. On the same day Fairchild entered the firm of Lee, Higginson. For accounts of the Holmes Breakfast see Derby, pp. 285–88, *Atlantic Supplement*, June 1880, and Arthur Gilman, "Atlantic Dinners and Diners," *Atlantic*, C (November 1907), 653–55.

23. *The American Bookseller*, January 1, 1880, pp. 5–6; Boston *Advertiser*, December 29, 1879; Weber, *Osgood*, p. 174; *American Architect and Building News*, VII (January 3, 1880) 1.

24. *PW*, January 31, 1880, pp. 86–87.

CHAPTER XI

1. Howells to Anne Howells Fréchette, March 17, 1871; Edwin H. Cady, *The Road to Realism*, pp. 204, 235, 243. Quotations in this chapter from William Dean Howells' *The Rise of Silas Lapham* are taken from the Random House, Inc., Modern Library edition, 1951.

2. Mildred Howells, *Life in Letters of William Dean Howells*, I, 366. Houghton's former office at the Riverside Press has been redecorated since this was written and his rolltop desk has been removed.

3. *PW*, May 8, 1880, p. 480.

4. H. O. Houghton to Lawson Valentine, September 7, 1882.

5. Mrs. Albert G. Houghton to H. O. Houghton, September 12, 1882.

6. Houghton, Osgood & Company, Liabilities, 1878–1879; H. O. Houghton to Judge Ray, August 17, 1882. See also Houghton's letter to his nephew

Oscar R. Houghton, August 2, 1882, in which he says, "I do not think it wise to take large risks with doubtful men."

7. *Christian Union,* May 14, 1891, pp. 627–28, 649; Lyman Abbott, *Reminiscences,* pp. 340–42.

8. Mifflin, "An Account"; Mifflin to H. O. Houghton, January 13, 1886; Houghton, Osgood & Company, Liabilities, 1878–1879; Co-partnership Agreements, April 1, 1880, February 28, 1882; Houghton, Osgood & Company, Private Journal; *Fifty Years of Publishing,* Boston, Houghton Mifflin Company, 1930, p. 4.

9. Mifflin, "An Account"; Boston *Daily Evening Transcript,* May 1, 7, 1880; *American Bookseller,* May 1 and 15, 1880, pp. 370, 417; *Literary World,* May 22, 1880, p. 173.

10. Assignment of Copyrights, May 11, 1880; "Note to Our Authors," May 5, 1881.

11. Roswell Smith to Osgood & Company, September 18, 1873.

12. Mifflin, "An Account"; *Literary World,* January 15, 1881, p. 30; *PW,* January 22, 1881, p. 63; Carl J. Weber, *Rise and Fall of James Ripley Osgood,* pp. 176–77.

13. Samuel C. Webster, *Mark Twain: Business Man,* pp. 147–48, 195, 243–44; Smith and Gibson, *Mark Twain–Howells Letters,* I, 349; Clemens to Osgood, March 7, 1881; Osgood requested 7½ percent on the first 50,000, 5 percent thereafter. Osgood to Clemens, April 5, 1882. This letter carries the following endorsement: "Osgood asks change of % — which I agree to, reversing it to 5 percent on 50,000, & 7½ afterward." The Memorandum of Agreement, April 10, 1882, also gives 5 percent on 50,000, 7½ thereafter. I am indebted to Hamlin Hill for arranging to have photocopies of Osgood's letters to Clemens and the Memorandum of Agreement sent to me from the Mark Twain archives at the University of California.

14. Clemens to Osgood, March 26, n.y., and December 21 [1883]; Smith and Gibson, I, 468; Webster, pp. 236, 242–46, 248, 250, 254, 261, 293–96, 300, 303, 304, 321.

15. Osgood to Clemens, December 8, 1883 (photocopy).

16. Lafcadio Hearn to Houghton, Mifflin & Company [December 1882], January [1883], February 7, 1883, and [April 1883]. Hearn's undated letters are stamped with date of receipt. MSS Record Book, 1880–1882. In 1885, Houghton recommended Hearn to the Merriams as "a well equipped scholar," with an "accurate knowledge of etymology," "well versed in erudite knowledge, and acquainted with various languages." H. O. Houghton to Messrs, G. & C. Merriam & Company, April 15, 1885.

17. Clara Barrus, *Whitman and Burroughs,* p. 205; C. E. Stedman to Aldrich, September 7, October 18, 1881; John Hay to Douglas O'Connor, May 27, 1882; *Letters of John Burroughs,* ed. Clara Barrus, I, 238.

18. Mifflin, "An Account"; Valentine's assignment was reported in the New York *Times,* December 24, 1882. On December 26, 1882, Houghton wrote the Merriams, "When Alonzo Follett failed some time ago, he had negotiable papers amounting to $90,000 in his hands, which he actually stole. Mr. Valentine promptly put himself into a condition to meet these liabil-

ities and one of his ways was to temporarily sell out to his partners his interest in the varnish business, which is very profitable, to enable him to avail himself of its credit to raise the necessary means to buy off these liabilities which is now being rapidly done, and none of these have been dishonest. He has not drawn any money from our business, and does not propose to do so . . ." Valentine's affairs so prospered that he was back in his reorganized company, now incorporated, by 1886.

19. H. O. Houghton to Arthur Macy, March 24, June 26, 1882; to L. Valentine, June 19, December 26, 1882; to M. M. Hurd, December 30, 1882; to J. C. Derby, April 3, 1883; to Judge Jameson, May 19, 1885; to Henry Stevens, May 21, 1885.

20. Donald Sheehan, *This Was Publishing*, p. 58; H. O. Houghton to Charles Scribner, November 8, 1883; G. P. Lathrop to Aldrich, November 2, 1882.

21. Arlin Turner, *George W. Cable*, pp. 111–12; Weber, *Osgood*, pp. 179–80.

22. Grant Overton, *Portrait of a Publisher*, p. 66; J. C. Derby, *Fifty Years Among Authors, Books and Publishers*, pp. 434, 437–38; H. O. Houghton to Derby, May 25, 1882; Joel Chandler Harris to H. O. Houghton, April 16, 1889.

23. Houghton, Mifflin & Company to H. James, May 1, 1880; Weber, *Osgood*, p. 176.

24. Memorandum of Agreement, May 3, 1882. What the two sketches had in common was that both dealt "with a young American who is entitled to the succession of estates in England, and introduces legends of a Bloody Footstep." H. O. Houghton to C. J. Mills, October 9, 1882. *PW*, August 26, 1882, p. 231, recommended publication "as showing his [Hawthorne's] method of building his romances . . ."

25. C. E. Norton to Aldrich, May 30, 1882; to H. O. Houghton, June 26, August 3, 1882; H. O. Houghton to W. H. Forbes, September 7, 1882.

26. Leon Edel, *Henry James: the Conquest of London*, pp. 398, 402; Henry James to Howells, June 17, August 19 [1879].

27. Houghton, Mifflin & Company, Book Journal; H. James to Houghton, Mifflin & Company, November 23 [1881]; H. O. Houghton to Aldrich, June 19, 1882; Leon Edel, *Henry James: the Middle Years*, p. 40; H. O. Houghton to Derby, May 25, 1882; to M. M. Hurd, December 20, 1882. On September 12, 1883, Houghton wrote Charles Dudley Warner, "As far as I know, no reputable publisher, excepting Osgood, pays for ordinary books of this kind more than ten percent . . . it has only been brought up in cases where Osgood competes. When the question has been made a condition of our continuing to publish for an author we have refused to increase his copyright."

28. Memoranda of Agreement, January 1, April 13, June 1, 1883; James to Houghton, Mifflin & Company, May 23, 1885.

29. Azariah Smith to H. O. Houghton, May 27, 1881.

30. Howells, *Letters*, I, 293; Howells to H. O. Houghton, January 10, 1881.

31. Howells to J. M. Comly, May 16, 1881; H. O. Houghton to Aldrich, January 12, 1881.

32. R. G. White to Aldrich, September 16, 1883; Howells, *Letters*, I, pp. 294–95; Howells to Osgood, April 17, 1881.

33. Howells to W. C. Howells, February 13, 1881. Three of Howells' novels,

A Woman's Reason, Indian Summer, and *The Minister's Charge,* arranged for under the 20 percent, 10,000 exemption plan had not passed that number by 1922. B. H. Ticknor to Ferris Greenslet, May 3, 1922.

34. *PW,* March 19, 1881, p. 309; "A Note to Our Authors." Generally, Houghton, Mifflin's Profit and Loss Sheets do not separate the firm's periodicals. However, the one for January 1880 to April 1881 does.

35. "A Note to Our Authors."

36. Ibid., A. Smith to H. O. Houghton, May 27, 1881.

37. Ibid.

38. H. O. Houghton to Howells, September 10, 1881; Howells to Aldrich, September 1881.

39. Laura Stedman and G. M. Gould, *Life and Letters of Edmund Clarence Stedman,* I, 478; Cady, p. 243; Howells, *Letters,* I, 367.

40. Ibid., p. 303.

41. *PW,* May 9, 16, 23, June 6, 13, 20, 1885, pp. 565, 591, 669, 690, 712–13; Boston *Daily Evening Transcript,* May 5, 1885; *Literary World,* May 16, June 13, 27, 1885; Weber, *Osgood,* pp. 222–23 and 228–29.

42. Howells to John Hay, August 30, 1883.

43. Boston *Daily Evening Transcript,* May 7, 1885.

44. William Dean Howells, *Literary Friends and Acquaintances,* p. 118.

45. Cady, p. 243.

46. Edel, *Middle Years,* p. 145, says James received not a penny of the $5000 Osgood had collected from the *Century* for *The Bostonians,* that Ticknor & Company offered him $4000 but subsequently withdrew its offer. Possibly the reason for this is that James sold to Macmillan not only the English rights, which Ticknor & Company had restored to him, but also the American rights as well as the English to his next novel.

47. Houghton, Mifflin Company, Grand Balance Sheets.

CHAPTER XII

1. Mifflin, "An Account"; Grand Balance Sheets.

2. For this and the following paragraphs on the various partners: H. O. Houghton to L. Valentine, March 18, 1882; Memoranda of Agreement, April 1, 1884, April 1, 1888; *The Firm of Houghton, Mifflin and Company,* p. 21; interview with Mrs. H. W. Burgess, James Murray Kay's daughter; H. O. Houghton to F. W. Seward, March 14, 1884; T. W. Barnes to H. O. Houghton, October 28, December 12, 1886; *Journal of Education,* XXIX (February 7, 1889), 6; Memorandum of Agreement, February 5, 1890; T. W. Barnes to H. O. Houghton, February 5, 1890, February 1, 9, 1894.

3. F. J. Garrison to Fanny Garrison Villard, August 1, 1880.

4. Albert F. Houghton to H. O. Houghton, March 7, 1881; "A Card," 1881; Mifflin to H. O. Houghton, February 17, 1881; H. O. Houghton to Valentine, September 12, 1882.

5. *PW,* October 22, 1881, p. 520.

6. Houghton, Mifflin & Company, Profit and Loss Sheets; Valentine to H. O. Houghton, June 9, 1886; Prospectus for *The Voyage of the Jeannette,*

The Ship and Ice Journals of Lieutenant Commander George W. De Long, edited by his wife Emma De Long.

7. For this and the following paragraph: *The Firm of Houghton, Mifflin and Company,* pp. 26–28 and 36–37; Mifflin to H. O. Houghton, July 20, October 5, 1886; Cambridge *Tribune,* November 17, 1888.

8. Ruari McLean, *Modern Book Design from William Morris to the Present Day,* p. 17.

9. For this and the following paragraphs on Knight's *Mechanical Dictionary: Riverside Bulletin,* January 16, February 5, 1871, pp. 3, 8; Prospectus for the American Unabridged Edition of William Smith's *Dictionary of the Bible;* Memoranda of Agreement, April 28, 1868, November 26, 1875, October 29, 1879, February 23, 1884; H. O. Houghton to Roswell Smith, December 8, 1882; Roswell Smith to H. O. Houghton, December 9 and 16, 1882; *The Critic,* III (January 27, 1883), 33.

10. For this and the following paragraph on the subscription Longfellow: *Complete Poems of Henry Wadsworth Longfellow,* Centennial Edition; Longfellow to Osgood, June 26, 1876, to Fields, January 24, 1877; *PW,* April 12, 1879, pp. 441–42, May 3, 1879, p. 512; leaflet for Longfellow Subscription Edition, December 2, 1884.

11. H. O. Houghton to Charles Allen, January 17, 1883.

12. *Critic,* III (April 14, 28, 1883), 172, 197; *PW,* May 12, 1883, p. 544; Houghton, Mifflin & Company, Book-Earnings; H. O. Houghton to Edmund Rutledge, October 19, 1883.

13. For this and the following paragraphs on Child's *Ballads:* Memorandum of Agreement, January 16, 1883; Prospectus for *The English and Scottish Ballads;* H. O. Houghton to Henry Stevens, May 4, 1885; *Scholar-Friends: Letters of Francis James Child and James Russell Lowell,* ed. M. A. DeWolfe Howe and G. W. Cottrell, Jr., pp. 51–52; Houghton, Mifflin & Company, Book-Earnings; *Atlantic,* LI (March 1883), 404–8 and LII (December 1896), 737–42.

14. For this and the following paragraphs on Vedder: Elihu Vedder, *The Digressions of V,* p. 407; Vedder to J. B. Millet, n.d.; to Houghton, Mifflin & Company, November 17, 1883, November 30, 1884, fragment, n.d.; Garrison to Mifflin, May 14, 1884, to H. O. Houghton, February 24, 25, March 16, 1885; *The Critic,* V (November 15, 22, 29, December 26, 1884), 230–31, 251–52, 263, 275; *Literary World,* XVII (November 27, 1886), 427; *Atlantic,* XLV (June 1880), 843, LV (January 1885), 111; leaflet for "What the Critics Say of the Rubáiyát"; Announcement for the Autographed Edition de Luxe; Prospectus for the Trade Edition.

15. *The Firm of Houghton, Mifflin and Company,* pp. 22–23; H. O. Houghton to Kenway, March 4, 1884; Cambridge *Tribune,* November 17, 1888.

16. Osgood & Company, Copyright Book; Houghton, Mifflin & Company, Book-Earnings; Irving McKee, *"Ben Hur" Wallace: the Life of General Lew Wallace,* pp. 122–26, 169–74.

17. Valentine to H. O. Houghton, April 7, 1886; *PW,* June 26, 1880, p. 666.

18. For this and the following paragraphs on the Aldines: H. O. Houghton to Henry Stevens, May 4, 1885, to C. E. Stedman, July 8, 1885; leaflet for "The Riverside Aldine Series."

19. *PW*, September 25, 1881, p. 400, August 17, 24, 1889, pp. 195, 213.
20. For this and the following paragraphs on Updike: Daniel Berkeley Up-dike, *Notes on the Merrymount Press*, pp. 5–9; Allen J. Jacobs, "Publishing in the 90s," *The Living Church*, September 21, 1938, p. 264; John Barnes Pratt, *Personal Recollections*, pp. 10–11; Houghton, Mifflin & Company, Profit and Loss Sheets; *Atlantic*, LI (June 1883), 810; H. O. Houghton to R. G. White, January 20, 1883; Houghton, Mifflin & Company to W. Gammell, November 17, 1883; Mrs. E. B. Updike to H. O. Houghton, October 9, 1886; Mifflin to H. O. Houghton, November 23, 1891; *PW*, September 24, 1881, p. 400.
21. Printed letter "To My Associates and Fellow-Workers at the Riverside Press, and the Allied Offices of Houghton, Mifflin & Co.," bearing H. O. Houghton's signature, January 30, 1890.
22. Cambridge *Chronicle*, January 1, 1890.
23. Memoranda of Agreement, Longfellow, January 1, 1885; Lowell, January 1, 1886; Whittier, May 28, 1885; Holmes, December 1, 1882. Emerson's annuity contract had been abrogated at the time his heirs and Norton gave the Emerson–Carlyle correspondence to Osgood. See chapter XV for a temporary reduction in Holmes's annuity at his request.

CHAPTER XIII

1. *PW*, February 9, 1884, p. 175.
2. *Critic*, I (October 22, 1881), 292; Garrison to H. O. Houghton, June 24, 1884; Houghton, Mifflin & Company, "Literary Bulletin," September 1884, p. 6.
3. *Century Magazine*, XXX (July 1885), 436; H. O. Houghton to Andrews, February 25, 1885; Mrs. E. C. Ortiz to H. O. Houghton, July 7, 1885; H. O. Houghton to Mrs. Ortiz, July 10, 1885; *Journal of Education*, February 7, 1889, p. 90; Houghton, Mifflin & Company, leaflet, 1888; *PW*, July 21, 1888, p. 109.
4. Houghton, Mifflin & Company, leaflet, May 1884; T. H. Carter to H. O. Houghton, May 3, 1894; Charles Carpenter, *History of American School Books*, p. 141; Houghton, Mifflin & Company, Book Journal.
5. *PW*, February 9, 1884, p. 175; Pratt, p. 17; *PW*, February 26, 1881, p. 227. Thomas B. Lawler in *Seventy Years of Textbook Publishing*, p. 95, says there were five big textbook houses but does not name them. Ginn, sixth largest, refused to join the syndicate.
6. Garrison to H. O. Houghton, August 26, 28, 1882, January 19, 1885, to Mifflin, June 24, 1884; Houghton, Mifflin & Company 1884 contract form, leaflet, 1885, and Book Journal. The old Colburn continued to sell, 3000 in the first year of the revised edition.
7. *PW*, July 20, 1889, pp. 46a–46b, April 26, 1890, p. 557, June 14, 1890, p. 793; H. N. Wheeler to Houghton, Mifflin & Company, April 27, 1893, to Mifflin, May 22, 1897.
8. Scudder, Record of Literary Work, Copyright Accounts, Journal Private, II, August 13, 1882, and January 3, 1886.

9. Ibid.

10. Scudder to Grace Scudder, November 20, 1876; Diary, March 24, 1886.

11. Scudder, Journal Private, II, October 30, 1887.

12. *Atlantic*, LIX (June 1887), 800–3.

13. *Atlantic*, LX (July 1887), 85–91.

14. Houghton Mifflin Company, *Fifty Years of Publishing*, pp. 4–6; Scudder to R. G. Moulton, May 27, 1894; Mifflin to Albert F. Houghton, April 8, 1897; Houghton, Mifflin & Company, Book Journal; Claude M. Fuess, *RLS.: Its Fortieth Anniversary*. Scudder's first title for the series was "American Classics for Schools" and under this designation in February 1882 appeared a collection of Longfellow's poems. Following Houghton, Mifflin's organization of its Educational Department in the same year, Scudder changed the name to the Riverside Literature Series. No. I, Longfellow's *Evangeline*, appeared in the spring of 1883.

15. Scudder, Diary, June 18, September 18, 1888; M. A. DeWolfe Howe to Scudder, August 1, 1888. During Scudder's absence in California, Howe went to Park Street for an interview. However, Houghton was not impressed and not until 1893, at Scudder's repeated urging, did Howe win the desired appointment.

16. Scudder, Journal of a trip to California, Summer 1888.

17. For this and the following paragraph: "The Place of Literature in Common-School Education," *National Educational Association Journal Proceedings and Addresses* Session of the Year 1888, Topeka, pp. 57–80. With some omissions, Scudder's speech appeared in the *Atlantic*, LXII (August 1888), 223–30.

18. Garrison to H. O. Houghton, March 18, 1895; Scudder to W. C. Webster, November 6, 1893; MS report 1316.

19. Fields to H. O. Houghton, June 28, 1880; Memorandum of Agreement, June 18, 1881; Garrison to H. O. Houghton, June 14, 1881.

20. Henry James, *Hawthorne*, pp. 45–46, 148.

21. *Atlantic*, XLV (February 1880), 282.

22. *Literary World*, XII (June 18, 1881), 216; A. Smith to H. O. Houghton, May 31, 1881; H. O. Houghton to C. D. Warner, May 2, 1883, October 25, 1884; Garrison to H. O. Houghton, October 23, 1884; H. O. Houghton to James R. Lowell, June 25, 1885; Scudder, Diary, November 26, 1889.

23. Garrison to H. O. Houghton, June 14, 1881, October 23, 1884; *PW*, April 10, 1886, p. 501. Scudder was eager to do Longfellow's life, but Houghton felt it would be poor public relations to let his editor-in-chief have such a plum. Before Higginson received the assignment a number of others were considered, Charles Eliot Norton among them. Scudder, Diary, May 1, 1891, February 2, 1892.

24. John T. Morse, Jr., "Incidents Connected with the American Statesmen Series," *Proceedings of the Massachusetts Historical Society*, LXIV (October 1930–June 1932), 370–88.

25. Garrison to H. O. Houghton, June 3, 1881.

26. Morse, in his account of the American Statesmen Series (See note 24), p. 381, says the assignment of Gouverneur Morris to Roosevelt was made at Henry Cabot Lodge's request. However, Morse, in a letter to Garrison,

May 9, 1887, wrote, "Following a suggestion of Mr. Houghton's I have asked the Hon. Theodore Roosevelt to write the Life of Gouverneur Morris." In the same account, pp. 385–88, Morse says of Henry Adams' Aaron Burr, ". . . I think that I may safely allege . . . that I never heard of any such undertaking by Mr. Adams." His letter to Houghton of April 30, 1881, seems to belie this statement.

27. Henry Adams, *Letters,* I, 341; Ernest Samuels, *Henry Adams: the Middle Years,* pp. 206–7, writes, "Whether he [Morse] . . . having unintentionally encouraged him, got cold feet when he saw what Adams had done to Burr, remains an open question." The question appears to be no longer open. Samuels is in error, of course, when he identifies Osgood as "another member of the Houghton firm."

28. For this and the following paragraph: New York *Daily Tribune,* May 29, June 15, 1885; Garrison to H. O. Houghton, June 26, 1885; H. O. Houghton to J. B. McCullah, editor of the *Globe-Democrat,* July 2, 1885.

29. For this and the following paragraph: Garrison to Morse, March 2, 1885; Morse to H. O. Houghton, March 5, 1885; Houghton, Mifflin & Company to T. & J. W. Johnson, March 9, 1885; H. O. Houghton to Morse, September 29, 1883.

30. Houghton, Mifflin & Company to Wm. T. Welcher, July 18, 1886.

31. Garrison to H. O. Houghton, May 29, June 1, June 27, September 4, 1883.

32. MS report 2104; Memorandum of Agreement, October 15, 1888; Ellsworth, p. 97; Kate Douglas Wiggin, *My Garden of Memories,* 1933, pp. 162–63, 178–79.

33. Mifflin to H. O. Houghton, July 10, 1891.

34. Scudder, Diary, December 1, 1891; *Atlantic,* LV (May 1885), 719, LX (January 1889), 122, LXVIII (September 1891), 429, LXIX (March 1892), 410.

35. There are many letters in Houghton, Mifflin's files and letter books related to Fiske's financial troubles. The following references give the main outlines of the story, I believe. Howells to H. O. Houghton, April 9, 1880; Garrison to H. O. Houghton, January 2, 1883, February 23, 1884; Fiske to H. O. Houghton, October 13, 1886, September 13, 1887; Memorandum of Agreement, January 1, 1889; Fiske to H. O. Houghton, December 1, 1890, December 1, 1894, and to Mifflin, July 13, 1896; Garrison to A. F. Houghton, December 6, 1897; Memorandum of Agreement, December 20, 1897; Mifflin to A. F. Houghton, December 29, 1900; Fiske to Houghton, Mifflin & Company, January 17, 1901. Fiske's statement of gross sales for two years was somewhat in excess of the actual figures which were for 1898, $99,723.45, for 1899, $131,236.92. E. C. Robinson to Mifflin, December 13, 1900. On April 22, 1901, Fiske wrote his lawyer Richard Stone an inaccurate and intemperate letter in which he said, "In point of fact I owe much to the late H. O. Houghton, not to his friendship or benevolence, but to his discernment. He saw that money was to be made through me and that my circumstances were likely to make me submit to a hard bargain. Such a bargain, worthy of Scrooge himself, was our contract of 1889, taking away my copyright and giving me a pittance of $5000 a year." Mifflin, on being shown the letter, wrote to Fiske on April 30, 1901:

At each step in the past we have met your increasing demands as far as seemed to us consistent with a sound business policy, and at times have yielded to you more than seemed wise to some of us. You know that in 1889, Mr. Houghton would have preferred a copyright to a salary basis; on general principles he believed that an author should have a continued interest in his writings, and in your case he felt that the result of a new venture in the school book line was problematical. But you said you must have a salary, and the amount of the salary agreed upon between you and him was as large as then seemed prudent to us. Afterwards, when it was found that the copyright plan would have been more profitable to you, we released you from your contract and credited you with all the royalties from the beginning. In this voluntary act of ours, which gave you thousands of dollars, you see only proof of our shamelessness. Had the school book experiment not been a success, and had we lost money by it, we doubt you would have reimbursed us for our loss. This we could not have claimed and should not have expected."

36. Scudder, MS of address to the Cambridge Theological School, October 1, 1882; "A Minor University," *Riverside Bulletin*, April 1, 1873, pp. 9–10.

CHAPTER XIV

1. *Riverside Bulletin*, September 1, 1873, pp. 29–30.
2. *Dwight's Journal of Music* ceased in 1881. Houghton published the *Reporter* from 1877 to 1888; the *Andover Review* from 1884 to 1893. The firm dropped *The United States Official Postal Guide* in 1886. The *Journal of American Folk-Lore* appeared under Houghton, Mifflin's imprint from 1888 to 1910. At the time the firm acquired the *American Architect,* it also took over *Poole's Index to Periodical Literature,* first published by Osgood in 1882.
3. For this and the following paragraphs on the proposed labor journal: Howells to Charles Eliot Norton, September 4, 1878; J. B. Harrison to Norton, September 4, December 18 and 23, 1879, January 8, August 3, 1881; H. O. Houghton to J. B. Harrison, January 11, 1883; Horace Elisha Scudder, *Henry Oscar Houghton,* pp. 103–7.
4. For opinions of Aldrich in this and the following paragraphs: Ferris Greenslet, *Life of Thomas Bailey Aldrich,* pp. 141–60; Mildred Howells, *Life in Letters of William Dean Howells,* I, 312; Lillian W. Aldrich, *Crowding Memories,* pp. 260–61; Daniel B. Updike, *Notes on the Merrymount Press,* pp. 160–69; Susan M. Francis, "The Atlantic's Pleasant Days in Tremont Street," *Atlantic,* C (November 1907), 719 ff.; Bliss Perry, *Park Street Papers,* pp. 160–69; Ellery Sedgwick, *The Happy Profession,* p. 174; Scudder, Note-Book, Private, II, October 3, 1882; Virginia Harlow, *Thomas Sergeant Perry,* p. 302; Henry James to Howells, July 31 [1884], September 29, 1888; M. A. DeWolfe Howe, *John Jay Chapman and His Letters,* p. 86; Aldrich to Bliss Perry, October 27, 1903.
5. Leon Edel, *Henry James: the Middle Years,* pp. 242–43; *Critic,* XXIV

(May 5, 1894), 301; Scudder to Houghton, Mifflin & Company, September 11, 1881; Howells to J. M. Comly, May 16, 1881; Howells, "Recollections of an Atlantic Editorship," *Atlantic*, C (November 1907), 603; M. A. De-Wolfe Howe, *The Atlantic Monthly and Its Makers*, p. 84; Howells, *Letters*, I, 299–300.

6. Greenslet, *Aldrich*, p. 141; Houghton, Mifflin Company, Journal Private.

7. J. G. Holland to Aldrich, May 28, 1880, April 7, 1881; J. M. Alden to Aldrich, February 12, 1880, October 10, 19, 1882; Aldrich to G. E. Woodberry, May 14, 1892; *Harper's Monthly*, LXXVII (June 1888), 127; *Critic*, XVI (June 7, 1890), 284.

8. For this and the following paragraphs on Thomas Hardy: Carl J. Weber, "Thomas Hardy and his New England Editors," *The New England Quarterly*, XV (December 1942), 681–99; Thomas Hardy to Houghton, Mifflin & Company, May 17, 1882; Houghton, Mifflin & Company to Hardy, May 25, 1882; Aldrich to Henry Stevens, December 28, 1881; Hardy to Aldrich, January 13, 1882; Memorandum of Agreement, June 7, 1882; Holt, pp. 207–8; Bliss Perry, *And Gladly Teach*, p. 168; *Literary World*, XIII (December 16, 1882), 168; Hardy to Aldrich, November 27, 1885.

9. A. S. Hardy to Hurd & Houghton, September 22, October 10, 27, 1877; MS report 110; A. S. Hardy to Aldrich, October 8, 1883, September 29, 1886, April 25 [1888]; H. O. Houghton to Alpheus Hardy, January 13, April 20, 1883; Houghton, Mifflin & Company, Book Journal. In 1878, Lippincott had published Arthur Hardy's *Francesca of Rimini*, a poem, after it had been turned down by Howells for the *Atlantic* and by Hurd & Houghton as a possible book. More recently (1881) both D. Van Nostrand and Ginn, Heath & Company had published two of his mathematical texts. *But Yet a Woman*, having been reprinted in the Riverside Paper Series, by 1886 had sold 30,000. A. Smith, interview in the *Mail and Express*, July 17, 1886. Although Houghton, Mifflin published Hardy's next novel, *Wind of Destiny*, Aldrich did not get it for the *Atlantic* even though Houghton urged Hardy to give it to him.

10. For this and the following paragraphs on Crawford: John Pilkington, *Francis Marion Crawford*, pp. 39–80; MS report 124; Houghton, Mifflin & Company, Book Journal; F. Marion Crawford to Aldrich, August 31, November [?] 1883; *Literary World*, XV (April 19, 1884), 135; Garrison to H. O. Houghton, October 23, 1884; Crawford to H. O. Houghton, May 7, 1884. Crawford applied for the post of editorial assistant to Aldrich, his price $5000. Crawford to Aldrich, July 5, 1884.

11. Howells, *Letters*, I, 319; Aldrich to Scudder, July 23, August 25, 1882, to H. O. Houghton [September 1882].

12. James to Aldrich, April 29, 1886, May 27 [1886], March 3, 1888; Memorandum of Agreement, February 11, 1890; Edel, *The Middle Years*, pp. 119, 163, 264. At James's page rate of $15 for the *Princess*, when his installments measured between twenty-three and twenty-four pages, he received $350. When it became apparent that the *Princess* would require fourteen rather than twelve numbers, James suggested he not be paid for the extra pages. Houghton, Mifflin preferred to pay him and he wrote

Aldrich, "Also I shall appreciate Messrs. H. & M. paying me — as they are so good to offer — for such extra pages as there may be after past deficiences are made up." That is, he had been overpaid at the page measurement for some of his installments. Through an error of either James D. Hurd or Garrison, he was sent $350 more than he had earned and was asked to return the draft, and on October 8, 1886, he wrote the company, "I understand of course perfectly your measurement of the amount of payment represented by my 14 instalments — & that this payment ended properly with the 13th. I didn't understand it when the draft arrived — that is, the draft itself seemed proof of the contrary. But pray control the impetuosity of your clerks, so that agreeable surprises may not — for your contributors — turn out to be delusions."

13. For this and the following paragraphs on Mary N. Murfree: Edd Winfield Parks, *Charles Egbert Craddock,* pp. 100–21; MSS reports 156, 358; M. N. Murfree to Aldrich, November 22, 1883, May 30, September 30, 1884, December 14, 1885; Memoranda of Agreement, April 2, 1884, April 15, 1884, September 29, 1884; Garrison to Mifflin, May 21, 1884, to H. O. Houghton, March 4, 1885; S. O. Jewett to Aldrich, July 23, 1890.

14. R. W. Gilder to Howells, February 18, 1885; Houghton, Mifflin & Company, Cost-book.

15. For this and the following paragraph: MSS reports 1226, 1344, 1752; W. E. Gladstone, " 'Robert Elsmere' and the Battle of Belief," reprinted from the *Nineteenth Century,* Buffalo, n.d., p. 16; *PW,* February 9, 1889, pp. 205, 208; Margaret Deland, *Golden Yesterdays,* pp. 143–88, 215; J. M. Alden to Howells, August 31, 1888.

16. Houghton, Mifflin & Company, Private Journal; *PW,* April 13, 1889, p. 547; *The Critic,* XIV (April 13, 1889), 189 and (April 27, 1889), 213; "The Firm of Houghton, Mifflin and Company," 1889, pp. 42–45. Thomas B. Ticknor came to work for Houghton, Mifflin at this time. Benjamin H. Ticknor continued to direct the affairs of Ticknor & Company for the benefit of the assignees for the next five years, then on November 8, 1894, Charles Fairchild wrote Houghton, "Mr. B. H. Ticknor is fairly stranded. Can't you make use of him? The affairs of his 'firm' are so far wound up that he will have little or nothing further to do for me. I know you will give him a place if you possibly can." So it was that two of William D. Ticknor's sons came to work for Houghton, Mifflin. Charles Fairchild had left Lee, Higginson & Company in January 1894 in debt to that firm. In the same year he established the Wall Street house of Charles Fairchild & Company. Henry Lee Higginson to Charles Fairchild, October 3, 1894, and the *Newport* [Rhode Island] *News,* July 10, 1910.

17. For this and the following paragraph on Bellamy: *Atlantic,* XLVI (December 1880), 826, LIV (September 1884), 416–17, and LXI (June 1888), 841; Frank Luther Mott, *Golden Multitudes,* 169. On August 26, 1886, Bellamy wrote Scudder thanking him for his criticism, saying that, "As regards your stricture upon Miss Ludington's Sister . . . if I were to rewrite the story it is quite possible that I should remodel it something as you suggest." In a New York *Tribune* interview on June 11, 1891, Houghton claimed sales had passed 400,000. "It is one of the largest sales of modern publications.

Yet the book is equalled and surpassed, from a literary and artistic point of view, by many publications which have not reached a tenth of its sale." He attributed the book's popularity to the current uncertainty of readers about the country. By the end of this narrative in 1921, sales approached 500,000. B. H. Ticknor to Ida M. Tarbell, January 22, 1927. Henry A. Laughlin in "An Informal Sketch of the History of Houghton Mifflin Company," 1957, p. 5, claims sales of over a million. *Looking Backward* is still in the Houghton Mifflin Catalogue.

18. Scudder, Diary, October 22, 1886, September 22, 1889, January 4, February 7, 17, 1890; Note-book Private, II, June 9, 1889. Others considered for the job include Berkeley Updike and Mason Hammond.
19. Daniel Coit Gilman to Scudder, December 17, 1882; MS report 83.
20. Crawford to H. O. Houghton, April 11, 1885. Scudder, when he became editor of the *Atlantic* took Crawford's *Don Orsino* for 1892 at $8.50 a page. The novel was also to appear in *Macmillan's*, but the English publisher promised this time that his periodical would not reach this country until after the *Atlantic*'s appearance, that is, not before the twentieth of each month. Garrison to H. O. Houghton, September 29, October 14, 1891.
21. Aldrich to H. O. Houghton, June 25, 1889; W. Wilson to Scudder, July 24, 1889 [copy]; Scudder, Diary, December 16, 1889.
22. For this and the following paragraphs on Woodrow Wilson: Houghton, Mifflin & Company, Book Journal; Memorandum of Agreement, December 3, 1884. Unless otherwise noted, all Wilson letters are copies. Wilson to Houghton, Mifflin & Company, April 4, 1884, to Scudder, March 4 Als and April 9 Als, 1885, May [12] Als 1886, July 10, 1886, January 1, 1887, March 31, and December 23, 1889, and February 7, 1891. Scudder, Diary, January 1, April 23 and 24, 1886; Ray Stannard Baker, *Woodrow Wilson*, I, 268–70. Here Wilson describes Aldrich also. "Saxon in colouring, briskly executive in manner, pithy and interesting in matter." In 1889, Scudder, as a Williams College trustee, suggested Wilson for a chair, a post Wilson could not accept because Princeton was about to create a professorship in his field.
23. Scudder, Diary, December 16, 17, 18, 1889.
24. Rowland Sill to Aldrich, July 30, November 16, 1885; Greenslet, *Aldrich*, pp. 146, 156.
25. MSS reports 1789, 1986, 2257, 2373, 3054, 3590, 3592.
26. For this and the following paragraphs on Emily Dickinson: *Atlantic*, LXVII (January 1891), 128–29, LXIX (January 1892), 143–44, and (February 1892), 277; Roger Burlingame, *Of Making Many Books*, pp. 272–73; Millicent Todd Bingham, *Ancestors' Brocades*, note p. 51; *The Letters of Emily Dickinson*, ed. Thomas H. Johnson, III, 769; Helen Hunt Jackson to Aldrich, March 15, April 19, August 19, 1881; Edith M. Thomas to Aldrich, February 13, September 11, 1884. Charlotte Lynch Botta had also recommended Miss Thomas to Houghton, Mifflin, describing her as of "rare genius." February 11 [1881]. Anna Mary Wells, *Dear Preceptor: Life and Times of Thomas Wentworth Higginson*, p. 278, suggests that Houghton, Mifflin was not interested in publishing Emily Dickinson because "Celia Thaxter was now beyond her fifteenth edition and they had

no need of another woman poet." That the firm was publishing Miss Thomas appears to invalidate the reasoning. Miss Thaxter, on the firm's list since the 1870s, had by now become a standard and involved no risk. Higginson was paid $100 for his October 1891 article; he objected saying he wanted $150, that the *Forum* would have paid him $175. Garrison sent him an additional $50 and notified Scudder "at what figure the Colonel estimates himself." Garrison to H. O. Houghton, September 29, 1891. In 1897 when Walter Hines Page was acting editor of the *Atlantic* during Scudder's absence abroad, he turned down five of Emily Dickinson's poems: "Nature is Sometimes Like a Child" and "The Saddest Noise," submitted by W. J. Rolfe, and "Dawn in Venice," "The Lash," and "Love and Pity," submitted by Emily's niece Martha Gilbert Dickinson. MSS Record Book. Perhaps from these rejections grew the myth that Houghton, Mifflin turned down the opportunity to publish a volume of Emily Dickinson's poems.

27. "Books of the Month" began in January 1881; in January 1891 the name of the department was changed to "Comment on New Books." Other members of the critical corps were Richard Grant White, who died in 1885, George E. Woodberry, George Parsons Lathrop, and Harriet Waters Preston. The last in a letter of August 9, 1882, asked Aldrich for regular employment at an annual $600. However, she suggested that perhaps Aldrich should say no. She felt the *Atlantic* ought to be stronger, ". . . there is too much woman's work in it already," she concluded. The *Tribune*'s charge of lack of vigor appeared on April 22, 1884.

28. H. O. Houghton to Mifflin and James D. Hurd, August 13, 1886; T. W. Barnes to H. O. Houghton, June 12, 1889; Houghton, Mifflin & Company Cost-books. Frank Luther Mott, *A History of American Magazines*, IV, 360. See also IV, 482 for John Brisbane Walker's purchase of the *Cosmopolitan* after his failure to secure the *Atlantic* and IV, 717, where the *Atlantic*'s circulation for 1887 is given as 12,500. In that year Riverside's monthly binding figures averaged over 13,500.

29. John T. Morse, *Life and Letters of Oliver Wendell Holmes*, I, 221–22; H. O. Houghton to C. D. Warner, February 17, 1885. What Osgood made from his services as agent is far from clear. However, Robert Grant in his *Fourscore: an Autobiography*, p. 126, records that Osgood for three of his novels paid him $3500 each and that the first of these Osgood sold to the Century Company for $5000, "which left him fifteen hundred dollars to the good besides any profit he might make on the sale of the book itself."

30. Charles A. Dana to Howells, June 9, 1884. This letter gives the amount paid for "Pandora." See also Edel, *The Middle Years*, p. 119.

31. H. O. Houghton to Helen Hunt Jackson, September 16, 1882; Helen Hunt Jackson to Aldrich, October 16, November 23, 1882.

32. S. O. Jewett to Aldrich, April 3 [188?] and Friday afternoon [188?]; Scudder to Aldrich, n.d.; Margaret Deland to Mrs. Aldrich, April 2, 1895. On July 24, 1890, Miss Jewett wrote Scudder, "the House has paid me fifteen dollars a page or thereabouts, on acceptance, in these later years . . ." Sara Orne Jewett, *Letters*, p. 65.

33. Scudder, Diary, October 22, 1886, September 18, 1888, March 19, 25, Sep-

tember 22, November 12, December 19, 30, 1889. Scudder's Diary for 1890 includes many references to Aldrich and the *Atlantic* and should be consulted passim for further details.

34. Scudder, Diary, June 16, 1890; M. A. DeWolfe Howe, *The Atlantic Monthly and Its Makers,* p. 91.

CHAPTER XV

1. Houghton, Mifflin & Company, Profit and Loss and Grand Balance Sheets; Peter Lyon, *Success Story: the Life and Times of S. S. McClure,* p. 162. Eugene Exman, *House of Harper,* p. 181.

2. Other Houghton, Mifflin authors who died during the decade were Jane Goodwin Austin, 1894; M. M. Ballou, 1895; Edward Bellamy, 1898; Frank Bolles, 1894; Anne C. L. Botta, 1891; Edwin Lassetter Bynner, 1893; Francis James Child, 1896; Rose Terry Cooke, 1892; Christopher P. Cranch, 1892; Lucy Larcom, 1893; George Parsons Lathrop, 1898; Samuel Longfellow, 1892; James Parton, 1891; Nora Perry, 1896; W. W. Story, 1895; Celia Thaxter, 1894; Justin Winsor, 1897.

3. Scudder, Diary, October 27, 1891; Garrison to H. O. Houghton, February 28, 1885; Memorandum of Agreement, January 1, 1886; James Russell Lowell, *Letters,* II, 416.

4. Van Wyck Brooks, *New England: Indian Summer,* note, p. 240; Garrison's letter to Houghton of August 28, 1891, describes Osgood as ". . . . a pretty sick man, thinner and older than when he was here last, and while a touch of lumbago of which he complained may be sufficient to explain this, I cannot help feeling that the trouble is deeper-seated."

5. Carl J. Weber, *Rise and Fall of James Ripley Osgood,* pp. 247–48; Charles A. Madison, *Book Publishing in America,* p. 70; Osgood to Norton, August 28, 1891. Osgood subsequently declined the Catherwood novel. Garrison to H. O. Houghton, September 18, 1891.

6. Norton to Houghton, Mifflin & Company, August 29, September 12, 1891; Mifflin to H. O. Houghton, September 5, 1891.

7. Houghton, Mifflin & Company to Norton, September 14, 1891; Osgood to Norton, September 15, 1891. When Garrison learned that Harper had secured the letters, he wrote Houghton, October 14, 1891, "J.R.O. has certainly relieved us of any obligation to show him special courtesy with our new books."

8. Norton to Houghton, Mifflin & Company, December 5, 1891; Garrison to H. O. Houghton, December 11, 1891; Norton to Howells, December 19, 1891; Mildred Howells, ed., *Life in Letters of William Dean Howells,* II, 19; Scudder, Diary, December 28, 1891.

9. Garrison to H. O. Houghton, September 9, 1891; H. James to Scudder, September 10, 1891; Garrison to H. O. Houghton, October 16, 1891; Scudder, Diary, October 14 and 15, 1891.

10. Scudder, Diary, November 26, December 2, 1892, February 4, April 17, June 21, September 19, 1895; Memoranda of Agreement, August 24, 1893, October 6, 1893, June 21, October 6, 1895; Scudder to Norton, November

18 and 25, 1892, to George Putnam, December 2, 1892; Harper & Brothers to Scudder, May 17, 1901.

11. Norton to Houghton, Mifflin & Company, March 14, 1902; Mifflin to A. F. Houghton, April 11, 1902; Mifflin to Norton, January 20, 1903; Exman, *House of Harper,* p. 179.

12. Weber, *Osgood,* p. 258; Thomas Franklin Currier, *A Bibliography of Oliver Wendell Holmes,* ed. Eleanor M. Tilton, p. 429.

13. Caroline Ticknor, *Glimpses of Authors,* pp. 76–79; Garrison to H. O. Houghton, July 8, 1891.

14. Scudder, Diary, September 10, 1892.

15. Holmes to Houghton, Mifflin & Company, January 2, 1892.

16. H. O. Houghton to Holmes, August 21, September 11, 19, 1882; Holmes to H. O. Houghton, June 21, 24, 1890.

17. Scudder to Judge Holmes, September 16, 1891; Garrison to H. O. Houghton, October 14, 1891; Scudder, Diary, November 3, 10, 1894; *The Critic,* XXIV (June 2, 1894), 377, XXV (September 1, 8, 13, 1894), 148, 161, 246.

18. For this and the following paragraph: *The Nation,* XXXV (October 19, 1882), 327; Garrison to A. F. Houghton, November 12, 1894; Houghton, Mifflin & Company, Boston, to Houghton, Mifflin & Company, Chicago, November 19, 1894; Houghton, Mifflin & Company to H. Altemus, November 21, 1894, to Rowland Cox, November 26, 1894; H. O. Houghton to Wm. A. Munroe, May 18, 1895; Supreme Court of the United States, October Term 1898, no. 124, Brief in Behalf of the Appellant, Oliver Wendell Holmes, Jr., pp. 4–5; *United States Reports,* Vol. 174, October Term 1898, pp. 82–90.

19. Assignment of Copyrights, February 12, 1895; Mifflin to Charles B. Perkins, January 14, July 13, 1896; *United States Reports,* Vol. 190, October Term 1902, pp. 260–66; Houghton, Mifflin & Company to Rowland Cox, May 13, 1897.

20. *Copyright Enactments,* Washington, Copyright Office, Library of Congress, 1963, p. 66. However, if after twenty-eight years, the copyright in the periodical is not renewed (which is frequently the case), "each poem, story or the like . . . must have its initial copyright renewed . . . if the item is not to enter the public domain and be free to all." Norman Holmes Pearson, "Problems of Literary Executorship," *Studies in Bibliography,* V (1952–1953), 3.20.

21. *PW,* January 17, 1891, p. 46.

22. H. O. Houghton to Mrs. Claflin, May 1882; Garrison to Fanny Garrison Villard, June 18, 1882.

23. Memorandum of Agreement, November 22, 1884; Garrison to H. O. Houghton, September 29, 1891; Houghton, Mifflin & Company, memorandum of average Stowe copyrights, 1886–1895.

24. A. S. Wheeler to Houghton, Mifflin & Company, March 16, 23, 1892.

25. Houghton, Mifflin & Company to National Advertising Company, March 24, 1892, to Charles Beaman, April 20, 1892, to *PW,* May 5, 1892; *Literary World,* XXIII (May 21, 1892), 187; memorandum of average Stowe copyright.

26. Mrs. Houghton to H. O. Houghton, February 23, n.y.; H. O. Houghton to

A. P. Watt, November 10, 1894. In addition to quoting Senator Chace's praise of him, Houghton told Watt that he withheld his support of the manufacturing clause until he found that the printers were so powerful the law would not pass unless their demands were met.

27. H. O. Houghton to the Hon. J. Chace, March 15, 1884.

28. H. O. Houghton to J. W. Harper, February 8, 1884; *PW*, December 18, 1880, pp. 835–36, December 25, 1880, pp. 856–59.

29. *PW*, January 21, 1888, pp. 74–75, January 28, 1888, p. 182.

30. *Nation*, XXXV (August 31, 1882), 166.

31. John A. Garraty, *Henry Cabot Lodge*, p. 125.

32. Scudder, Diary, March 4, 1891; Allen Jacob, "A Publisher's Office in the '90's. Four Years at Four Park Street, Boston," *Zion's Herald*, July 26, 1950, p. 699.

33. Scudder, Diary, March 5, April 3 and 7, 1891.

34. For this and the following paragraph: H. O. Houghton to Watt, November 10, 1894; Watt to H. O. Houghton, November 30, December 5, 1894; Smith Elder to Houghton, Mifflin & Company, December 9, 1886; Browning to Houghton, Mifflin & Company, June 15, 1887.

35. For this and the following paragraph: Aubert J. Clark, *The Movement for International Copyright in Nineteenth Century America*, pp. 104, 170–71; G. H. Putnam, *The Question of Copyright*, 1891, pp. 182–83.

36. *PW*, August 26, 1882, pp. 230–31; H. O. Houghton to the Hon. H. L. Dawes, August 1, 1882, to Henry Stevens, August 22, 1882, to Charles A. Ray, October 20, 1882, to Samuel Clemens, November 21, 1882; Garrison to H. O. Houghton, August 11, 1891. Whitney's effort to import was made in August, some months after International Copyright had gone into effect.

37. J. W. Harper to H. O. Houghton, October 16, 1891.

38. For this and the following paragraphs on Howe: Scudder, Diary, September 26, 1892, April 13, 1893; Helen Howe, *The Gentle Americans*, pp. 65–68. Mrs. Howe says, "This trip [that of November 1894] was taken for the simple purpose of spending one day with Fanny Quincy," his future wife. Scudder on August 15, 1893, defined in his diary his assistant's duties. "Howe is to have the details of the Atlantic, the reading of such Atlantic or book mss as I give him, the letters returning such rejected mss as he reads, work on comment [Comment on New Books], some of the indexing." During Howe's numerous absences, Frank Allen did his work. After he became "semi-detached" and later, Scudder threw various reviewing and editorial jobs his way. The Comment on New Books, *Atlantic*, LXXVI (July 1895), 137, on *Letters of Emily Dickinson* is Howe's. Here he questions the wisdom of publishing "the many intimacies of her offhand notes," and finds it "worth a passing remark that the strained mannerisms reach their height in the letters asking literary advice." Scudder's diaries for the 1890s are largely concerned with the *Atlantic* under his and Walter Hines Page's administration and should be consulted passim for details.

39. Scudder, Diary, July 18, 1895.

40. Boston *Globe*, August 27, 1895; Boston *Post*, August 30, 1895.

41. *Literary World*, XXVI (September 7, 1895), 280–81; Margaret Deland, "A Representative Publisher," *Outlook*, CLVII (November 2, 1895), 700–1.

42. Aldrich to Woodberry, August 27, 1895.
43. Scudder, Diary, September 1, 1895.
44. Garrison to W. P. Garrison, September 8, 1895.
45. Mifflin to H. O. Houghton, November 9, 1891. After Houghton's death Mifflin told Scudder that Houghton "never knew when he was defeated. He did not know at the last that Death was getting the better of him." Scudder, Diary, November 12, 1895.

CHAPTER XVI

1. Mifflin to Kate Douglas Wiggin, August 30, 1895, to Elizabeth Stuart Phelps Ward, November 14, 1895; Scudder, Diary, September 3, 1895. Mrs. Wiggin, after the death of her first husband, in 1895 married George C. Riggs. However, in footnotes, text, and files, she appears as Kate Douglas Wiggin, since that is the name by which she is remembered.
2. Garrison to W. P. Garrison, September 1 and 8, 1895. For Scudder's evaluation of Mifflin see his diaries from 1890 on.
3. Scudder, Diary, April 27, 1895; Garrison to W. P. Garrison, March 9, 1890; Mifflin to H. O. Houghton, July 10, 30, August 25, September 14, December 5, 1891. Mifflin's birthday, May 1, was celebrated at the Press on April 27. The clock given him by his employees is now in the office of Morgan Smith, present head of the Riverside Press.
4. Mifflin to H. O. Houghton, December 5, 1891.
5. Scudder, Diary, April 3, 1893.
6. Ibid., March 12, 1896; Raymond L. Kilgour, *Messrs. Roberts Brothers Publishers*, pp. 260–69, 279–81.
7. Mifflin to H. O. Houghton, April 5, 1895.
8. *Literary World*, XXVII (September 19, 1896), 301–2.
9. MS report 6685; Mifflin to Walter Hines Page, March 4, 1899; William H. Ellsworth, *A Golden Age of Authors*, p. 185; Grant Overton, *Portrait of a Publisher*, pp. 79–80; Frank Luther Mott, *Golden Multitudes*, pp. 202–3.
10. For *Captain January*, MS report 2447, *Literary World*, XXIX (March 5, 1898), 78, and Raymond L. Kilgour, *Estes and Lauriat*, p. 123. For Bierce, MS reports 3640 and 3947, for Terhune, MS reports 5167 and 6168, for Fitch, MS reports 2750 and 2783, for Norris, MS reports 3171 and 5325.
11. MS reports 2958, 2939, 3738, and 4559.
12. MS reports 3451 and 5480; Bliss Perry to Upton Sinclair, August 7, 16, and 20, 1901, to Scudder, August 16, 1901.
13. *Critic*, XXXVI (April 1900), 352, note.
14. *Bookman*, IV (October 1896), 95 and (September 1896), 7; *Literary World*, XXVII (November 14, 1896), 380; *PW*, August 12, 1899, p. 239.
15. For this and the following paragraphs on Gilbert Parker: Scudder to Parker, January 6, September 4, 1894; Parker to Scudder, November 10, 1894; Scudder to Parker, February 12, 1897; Houghton, Mifflin & Company to Mifflin, April 10, 1900; Parker to Mifflin, May 21, 1900, January 2, 1909; Houghton, Mifflin, Showing on Books Published April 1, 1898 to April 1, 1899. Parker began his negotiations for a uniform edition to be

done by Houghton, Mifflin in 1897. Later Appleton was to be his publisher. His transfer to Harper came in 1909. For Houghton, Mifflin's new policy of seeing the complete MS before acceptance, Mifflin to Mary N. Murfree, November 23, 1896.

16. For this and the following paragraph on Paul Leicester Ford: Garrison to Mifflin, January 24, 1898; Scudder, Diary, February 27, December 5, 1895; Mifflin to A. F. Houghton, March 10, 1898, August 25, 1898; F. Hopkinson Smith to Mifflin, May 2, 1900; Houghton, Mifflin & Company, Showing on Books Published April 1, 1897 to April 1, 1898, and Book Sales; *Critic*, XXXVI (February 1900), 115.

17. For this and the following paragraph on Mary Johnston: Burton J. Hendrick, *The Life and Letters of Walter H. Page*, I, 56, 61–62; Garrison to Mifflin, August 31, September 18, 21, 1900, to Mary Johnston, February 21, 1902; Mifflin to Lawrence Abbott, December 10, 1900; Houghton, Mifflin & Company to Mary Johnston, December 20, 1899; Memoranda of Agreement, February 23, 1898, August 4, 1899, May 22, 1901; Houghton, Mifflin & Company, Book Sales. Before Miss Johnston's *To Have and To Hold* had come to hand, Page had under consideration as his *Atlantic* serial an unnamed story by Joseph Conrad offered through Doubleday & McClure, who had purchased for £250 the American rights to *The Rescue, Heart of Darkness*, and *Lord Jim*. Page to H. W. Lanier, February 2, 1899; Peter Lyon, *Success Story*, note, p. 159.

18. Garrison to Mifflin, September 25, 1897, to S. O. Jewett, September 27, 1897; Mifflin to S. O. Jewett, December 21, 1896, to Herbert D. Ward, June 3, 1896; *PW*, June 20, 1896, p. 1008.

19. For this and the following paragraph on Mrs. Ward: Mifflin to Mrs. E. S. P. Ward, November 15, 1895, December 15, 1896, July 2, November 16, 1897, July 6, 1904; Mrs. Ward to H. O. Houghton, November 1, 1889, to "My dear Publishers," May 25, June 6, 1906. In her letter of May 25, Mrs. Ward pleaded that a long illness had forced her to accept the Harper offer.

In no sense do I wish or mean to take from the old House anything that I can serialize without doing so. Every magazine of importance in New York makes (now) publication a condition of serialization. I find no exceptions. The fact is perfectly well known in the trade, and, as for the public, it, as Thackeray said, 'is a jack-ass,' and never will know or notice who publishes any book. No possible harm can accrue to *you* — from my doing what almost all other authors do — while *I* am relieved of very grave financial anxieties, for a while, at least.

Everybody knows that authors must serialize, or starve these days.

Although the 1897 plans for Houghton, Mifflin to do a collected edition of Howells came to naught, negotiations were reopened in 1902, but agreement on details again proved impossible, and in 1905 Howells notified Mifflin that Harper was to do a Library Edition, Houghton, Mifflin to have a 5 percent royalty on the Howells books on its list. Howells to Mifflin, October 21, 1902, May 15, 17, 1905. In the end this Harper edition of Howells was far from complete, amounting to only six volumes.

20. Mifflin to Kate Douglas Wiggin, July 8, 1903, to Alice Brown, March 27, 1903; Houghton, Mifflin & Company to Alice Brown, April 24, 1908; Page to H. W. Lanier, February 2, 1899, to James B. Pinker, September 7, 1897; Stephen Crane, *Letters*, ed. R. W. Stallman and Lillian Gilkes, p. 185, note 48.
21. Mifflin to S. O. Jewett, December 5 and 7, 1901. Miss Jewett had made a similar offer in connection with *Marsh Island* in 1885. S. O. Jewett to A. Smith, Friday n.d. Her offer was not unique. Walter Hines Page in his *Publisher's Confession,* p. 51, tells of an author who contributed $1000 to the cause.
22. Houghton, Mifflin & Company, Profit and Loss Sheets; Mifflin to R. R. Bowker, October 29, 1901, to Scudder, October 7, 1901, to Lawrence F. Abbott, December 7, 1901; Garrison to Oswald G. Villard, October 9, 1901.
23. Scudder, Diary, March 22, 1897; Mifflin to A. F. Houghton, December 19 and 23, 1901; Boston *Times,* January 9, 1902; Boston *Advertiser,* February 14, 1902. On Scudder's suggestion, in 1898, Houghton, Mifflin extended its quarters by taking over the second floor of 3 Park Street. In May 1901 the New York address of the firm changed from Astor Place to 85 Fifth Avenue.
24. F. H. Smith to Houghton, Mifflin & Company, n.d. [1887], to Scudder, November 7 [1890].
25. Scudder to F. H. Smith, January 29, 1895; Garrison to A. F. Houghton, October 14, 1896; Mifflin to Smith, November 28, 1896, November 20, 1897; Smith to Mifflin, May 2, 1900.
26. Ibid.
27. Ellsworth, pp. 86–87. Ellsworth claims that R. W. Gilder "actually started" Smith on his career by encouraging him to write *Colonel Carter of Cartersville* for the *Century.*
28. Interview with the late Robert Newton Linscott; Mifflin to Smith, March 12, 1906; Smith to Mifflin, February 28, 1906.
29. Mifflin to Smith, March 2 and 5, 1915; Smith to Mifflin, March 3, 4, and 6, 1915.
30. Scudder, Diary, January 7, 1891; Mifflin to Lawrence F. Abbott, October 21, 1897; Houghton, Mifflin & Company, Book Journal and Showing on Books Published between April 1, 1898 and April 1, 1899.
31. Kate Douglas Wiggin to R. L. Scaife, May 4, 1920, July 14, 1922; Garrison to Mifflin, September 18, 1900; Houghton, Mifflin & Company to Mrs. Wiggin, December 21, 1901; Mifflin to Mrs. Wiggin, July 8, 16, and 20, 1903; Houghton, Mifflin & Company, memorandum of Mrs. Wiggin's income from her books 1889–1912, and Showing on Books From Publication to April 1, 1904. On June 19, 1895, Garrison reported to Houghton an amusing instance of Mrs. Wiggin's loyalty. "She is having a good time in Venice, in a Venetian family [he wrote] along with the Huttons and Warners and as the place had become known as 'Harper & Bros,' in consequence of their being there, she had chalked H. M. & Co. over her door to show what house she belonged to."
32. Mrs. Wiggin to R. L. Scaife, March 12 [1917]; Edward Bok to Mrs. Wiggin, September 24, 1917.

33. In these years Houghton, Mifflin published many novels in addition to those discussed, most of them selling better than average. The number of women in the list is striking, among them, Jane Goodwin Austin, Alice Brown, Clara Louise Burnham, Mary Hartwell Catherwood, Margaret Deland, Mary Hallock Foote, Blanche Willis Howard, Mary N. Murfree, Eliza Orne White, and Adeline D. T. Whitney.

CHAPTER XVII

1. Aldrich to G. E. Woodberry, July 22 and 28, 1890; Woodberry to Aldrich, September 12, 1890; *Nation,* LI (August 28, 1890), 170.
2. Aldrich to Woodberry, March 17, 1892; Robert Underwood Johnson, *Remembered Yesterdays,* p. 392.
3. Scudder, Diary, October 25, 1890, September 28, October 16, November 13, 1894; Scudder to Mrs. J. T. Fields, October 25, 1890.
4. Interviews with the late M. A. DeWolfe Howe. See also his *The Atlantic Monthly and Its Makers,* pp. 88–92; Ellery Sedgwick, *The Happy Profession,* pp. 154–55, 174. Sedgwick, p. 154, says that while he was still at Harvard, Page "took the magazine into his vigorous hands." Sedgwick graduated in 1894 and then went to teach at Groton for two years. Page did not come to Houghton, Mifflin until the fall of 1895. Burton J. Hendrick, *The Life and Letters of Walter H. Page,* I, 54, says in writing of the electric effect Page had in the staid offices of Park Street and on the *Atlantic,* "One of its editors had been heard to boast that he never solicited a contribution; it was not his business to be a literary drummer!" I assume Hendrick got his information from Sedgwick. A more unlikely Scudder statement is difficult to imagine.
5. Houghton, Mifflin & Company, Cost-books and Profit & Loss Sheets; H. O. Houghton to Garrison, June 2, 1891; Mifflin to H. O. Houghton, July 17, 1891; Hamilton W. Mabie to Scudder, June 7, 1891; Edmund C. Stedman to Scudder, May 1, 1894; Scudder, Diary, June 17, 1890, December 31, 1891; *Literary World,* XXVII (May 16, 1896), 158 and XXVIII (January 9, 1897), 14; Bliss Perry, "The Arlington Street Incarnation," *Atlantic,* CL (November 1932), 518; Houghton, Mifflin & Company, Cost-books. Houghton, Mifflin did not release circulation figures. However, publishers who did included not only paid subscribers, but also newsstand sale and the "necessary free list," that is, copies to advertisers, contributors, and so on. Thus the *Outlook* in 1904 with 91,000 paid subscribers claimed a "bona fida" circulation of over 110,000. Lawrence F. Abbott to Mifflin, December 28, 1904. Mott's figures, Frank Luther Mott, *A History of American Magazines,* II, 511, note 60, differ from those of the Cost-books.
6. Scudder to W. P. Garrison, June 30, 1891, to Theodore Roosevelt, June 30, 1891, to H. O. Houghton, August 10, 1891.
7. Ibid.
8. Scudder to Captain A. T. Mahan, August 27, 1890.
9. Scudder to Moorfield Storey, November 4 and 24, 1891.
10. Herbert R. Gibbs to Scudder, September 6, 1892; Scudder to H. O. Hough-

ton, January 7, 1891; James M. Kay to H. O. Houghton, n.d. Scudder cautioned Merwin to avoid libel; nevertheless he wanted the article to have sting. He hoped Tammany would ban the *Atlantic* and thus provide some free advertising. Scudder to H. C. Merwin, October 1893, January 4, 1894.

11. Scudder to Mrs. H. M. Wilmarth, April 18, 1896.

12. Scudder, "Recent American History," *Atlantic*, LXIII (January 1889), 117; Scudder to General J. D. Cox, March 21, 1895. Scudder also voted for Cleveland in 1892.

13. Scudder to Miss Helen Zimmen, March 12, 1894, to Henry Wood, January 5, 1891, to Dr. W. T. Harris, December 18, 1891, to N. S. Shaler, May 12, 1893.

14. Ferris Greenslet, *The Life of Thomas Bailey Aldrich*, p. 147; Scudder to George P. Lathrop, October 14, 1890, to Harriet W. Preston, March 24, 1894; Scudder, Rowfant Lecture 1892.

15. Scudder to Barrett Wendell, March 9, 1892, to W. C. Lawton, February 23, 1894.

16. *Atlantic*, XLIV (December 1879), 804; Scudder to Alice French, August 4, 1890, to H. O. Houghton, August 10, 1891; Scudder, Diary, February 25, 1891.

17. Scudder to Mrs. Margaret Collier Graham, November 1, 1893; MS Reports 3640 and 3947; *Atlantic*, LXX (July 1892), 136.

18. It is worth noting that Scudder, after he had relinquished command to Page, sought an *Atlantic* serial from Buchan. The correspondence indicates that the two men met in London, where Gilbert Parker offered Scudder use of his chambers. In September 1898 Page had turned down Buchan's *The Lost Lady of Old Years*. In the following month Scudder opened his negotiations. W. B. Parker to Paul Reynolds, September 12, 1898; Scudder to Buchan, October 28, November 14, 1898, March 18, May 20, June 21, 1899.

19. Scudder to Sarah Orne Jewett, September 27, 1893. In January 1893, Miss Jewett submitted and Scudder printed a Contributors' Club on Phillips Brooks's funeral. Jewett, *Letters*, p. 80.

20. For this and the following four paragraphs on Henry James: Scudder to James, August 20, October 30, 1890, February 19, June 9, 1896; Scudder, Diaries, September 9, November 20, 1890, March 13, 1891; James to Scudder, August 30, October 5, October 27, November 10, 1890, March 4, May 21, 1891; Houghton, Mifflin & Company, Showing on Books Published from April 1, 1890 to April 1, 1891 and Showing on Books Published to April 1, 1896 That Have Not Paid for Themselves. *Literary World*, XXI (March 29, 1890), 109. Mifflin thought the *Tragic Muse* had dealt a "pretty heavy blow" to the *Atlantic*. James was given a 15 percent royalty on the *Spoils* but was refused his requested advance of £150. Houghton, Mifflin scheduled publication for October 24, 1896, but after James reported the October date would conflict with Macmillan's schedule for *The Other House*, publication was moved forward to February 13, 1897. James had hoped *Spoils* would be out in time to catch the Christmas trade, but since Macmillan asked a three-month interval between the two books, this was impossible. James to Houghton, Mifflin & Company, September 26, 1896.

21. Scudder to Ellen Olney Kirk, April 6, 1892; John Jay Chapman to Scudder, September 17, 1890, October 8, 1891, August 28, 1895.
22. Scudder to Mrs. Rose Hawthorne Lathrop, April 29, 1896, to W. R. Thayer, March 7, 1894.
23. Eben Greenough Scott to Scudder, April 15, 1892; Scudder to Mrs. Mary McNeil Scott, February 7, 1893, to William Everett, April 30, 1895, to F. P. Coyle, January 28, 1891, to W. F. Biddle, October 1, 1895; Scudder, Diary, October 20, 1891; W. F. Biddle to Scudder, May 25, 1896; Percival Lowell to Scudder, February 27, 1897. On January 12, Lowell had written Scudder, "No proof needed except proof that you are satisfied."
24. Scudder, Diary, July 16, December 2, 1895; Burton J. Hendrick, *Life and Letters of Walter H. Page*, I, 49.
25. Scudder, Diary, July 26, October 10, 1895.
26. Ibid., November 9, 1895, April 10 and 18, 1896. Scudder's Diaries for the years Page was with Houghton, Mifflin contain frequent references to his assistant's ailments.
27. Houghton, Mifflin & Company, Profit & Loss Sheets; Scudder, Diary, April 27, May 6, 1896.
28. Mifflin to A. F. Houghton, October 22, 1898; Houghton, Mifflin & Company, Profit & Loss Sheets; Scudder, Diary, March 22, 1897.
29. Ibid., January 22, 1893, January 1, March 7, April 26, May 4, 1897; Sedgwick, p. 155.
30. Houghton, Mifflin & Company, Profit & Loss Sheets; Mifflin to A. F. Houghton, March 12, 1900; MacGregor Jenkins to Mifflin, March 12, 1901.
31. Page to Anna McClure Sholl, January 4, 1899; Scudder to E. P. Evans, March 22, 1897.
32. Scudder, Diary, May 7, 1896; Scudder to T. R. Lounsbury, July 15, 1899.
33. MS report 6743.
34. Mifflin to Mrs. H. D. Ward, April 1, 1898, to President McKinley, April 2, 1898; Garrison to Mifflin, May 9, 1898; Scudder to Vida Scudder, June 27, 1898, to George L. Fox, September 12, 1899; *Atlantic,* LXXXI (June 1898), 725, 727; Hendrick, I, 62–63.
35. Frank Luther Mott, *A History of American Magazines*, IV, 44.
36. Garrison to Scudder, May 12, 1898, to Mifflin, May 14, 1898; Page to S. S. McClure, July 8, 1898; *Atlantic,* LXXXI (June 1898), 284–86; *Critic,* XXXII (May 14, 1898), 335 and (June 11, 1898), 387–88.
37. Peter Lyon, *Success Story*, pp. 162–63, 167. Page was to have a salary of $15,000 and a share in the business. Scudder, Diary, July 10, 1899.
38. For details of the search for a new editor in this and the following paragraphs: Scudder, Diary, June 19 and July 10 through August 10, 1899; W. Wilson to Scudder, May 19, 1893; Bliss Perry, *And Gladly Teach*, pp. 160–65.
39. Scudder, Diary, November 21, 1901. Shortly after Scudder's death, Aldrich, who had long since forgotten his petty jealousy, wrote Mifflin to suggest the firm bring out a volume or two of Scudder's uncollected papers. Aldrich to Mifflin, January 22, 1902. *Peccavi.*

CHAPTER XVIII

1. The title is taken from Samuel McChord Crothers' "The Gentle Reader," *Atlantic,* LXXXVI (November 1901), 654–63. According to *The Critic,* XLVIII (March 1906), 200, Crothers' book of the same title rivaled in popularity *The Autocrat of the Breakfast-Table.* Houghton, Mifflin & Company, Profit & Loss Sheets.

2. Scudder, Diary, December 14, 1899. See also *Literary World,* XXX (December 9 and 23, 1899), 437–38, 452.

3. Mifflin to Page, May 6, 1901.

4. Sedgwick, p. 87; Frank Luther Mott, *A History of American Magazines,* III, 512, IV, 783. *American Magazines,* II, 511, footnote gives 25,000 as number of *Atlantic* subscribers, but see Houghton, Mifflin & Company, Cost-books and Profit & Loss Sheets.

5. W. B. Parker to Perry, April 2, 1900; Mifflin anticipated an edition of 50,000, Mifflin to Albert F. Houghton, March 31, 1900; Garrison to Mifflin, June 1900; Bliss Perry, *And Gladly Teach,* p. 174.

6. "On Reading the Atlantic Cheerfully," *Atlantic,* LXXXIX (January 1902), 1–4; "Number 4 Park Street," *Atlantic,* XCI (January 1903), 1–5; "On Catering for the Public," *Atlantic,* XCIV (January 1904), 1–5, all reprinted, with some changes, in Perry's *Park Street Papers. The Bookman,* XXVIII (January 1909), 477, in noticing the volume spoke of Perry's "editorial effusions," his "obsequious" tone, characterized by a kind of "anxious amenity."

7. Perry to Henry James, October 31, 1899; Perry to James B. Pinker (James's agent) October 3, 23, and 26, November 15, 21, and 27, 1899, March 26, 1900; Perry, *And Gladly Teach,* p. 178.

8. Perry to Clara E. Laughlin, May 28, 1906; FG to May Sinclair, June 15 and 22, July 12, August 30, September 28, 1906, March 8, 1907. For this and the following paragraph, see also Ferris Greenslet, *Under the Bridge,* pp. 97–98, and Bliss Perry, *And Gladly Teach,* pp. 194–95. In their autobiographies both Greenslet and Perry perhaps exaggerate the effect of *The Helpmate.* At least Greenslet was not intimidated by the Gentle Reader. He sought but failed to get Miss Sinclair's next novel. FG to Otto Kylmann, March 7, 1908. In 1912 he secured her *The Three Brontës* with an option on her next novel. In recommending publication, he wrote, "Miss Sinclair has of course been hawked about a good deal by her agents, and has been published in this country by Henry Holt, Harpers and the Century people. I have reason to believe that she would be glad to find a permanent abiding place . . ." By 1914 FG was confident that through his "delicate efforts" Miss Sinclair was about to enter Houghton Mifflin's stable with her *Three Sisters.* He was certain that by this time the author had "sufficiently learned the lesson of the disastrous effects of the over advance." He thought "the psychological moment" had come, that she would "see the true light." Houghton Mifflin repeated its standing offer of 15 percent up to 10,000, 20 percent thereafter. Miss Sinclair held to her terms, an advance and 20 percent, demands Houghton Mifflin declined to accept. MS reports A6909, A9277, and 9278.

9. Perry to Mrs. J. M. Parker, September 9, 1899, to Paul Elmer More, June 6, 1906; Perry, *And Gladly Teach*, p. 178.

10. Perry to Harriet Monroe, April 15, 1904.

11. Perry to Alfred Farlow, April 18, 1904; *And Gladly Teach*, pp. 170–71; *Park Street Papers*, pp. 31–37. In *And Gladly Teach*, Perry attributes the article to Philip H. Churchman. It is however signed John W. Churchman and Perry's letters of acceptance, one containing a check for $125, are so addressed.

12. Mifflin to Clara Louise Burnham, October 17, 1904.

13. Clara Louise Burnham to Mifflin, October 19, 1903; Houghton, Mifflin & Company, Showing on Books; Memoranda of Agreement, February 19, 1897, February 23, 1899, June 1, 1903, 20 percent on *The Right Princess* and *Jewel*, on *Jewel's Story Book*, 20 percent after a sale of 25,000. "We have further stipulated, however, that if she shall give any of her future books to another publishing house, the rate of royalty on the three books above named shall revert to 15 percent . . ." Garrison to Houghton, Mifflin & Company, February 20, 1906. Fifteen percent up to 25,000 then 20 percent became the standard contract for the many books Miss Burnham continued to produce for Houghton Mifflin.

14. E. K. Brown and Leon Edel, *Willa Cather*, pp. 134–35; W. B. Parker to Willa Cather, December 16, 1899. On May 21, 1907, FG wrote to Will Irwin, then on McClure's staff, "I hope the Eddy campaign is going every way to your satisfaction. Not the least gratifying aspect from our angle is the necessity which it occasions of Miss Cather's presence in Boston."

15. For this and the two following paragraphs see Perry, *And Gladly Teach*, pp. 183–85 and *The Critic*, XXXIX (November 1901), 401–9.

16. *Atlantic*, LXXXVII (March 1901), 424–26.

17. J. D. Whelpley, "Cuba of To-day and Tomorrow," *Atlantic*, LXXXVI (July 1900), 45–52.

18. *Atlantic*, LXXXVII (March 1901), 416; Perry, *And Gladly Teach*, p. 179.

19. Perry to E. L. Godkin, November 27, 1899, to Jack London, October 26, 1903; *Atlantic*, XCIII (January 1904), 54 and LXXXVI (November 1900), 675.

20. Barbara W. Tuchman, *The Proud Tower*, pp. 70–74, 81–83, 106, 109; *Atlantic* Editors to Emma Goldman, January 18, 1906. This letter although written in the name of the *Atlantic* Editors is in Bliss Perry's hand.

21. MS reports A532 and A2606; Houghton, Mifflin & Company to H. G. Wells, May 2, 1906.

22. H. G. Wells, *The Future in America*, pp. 226–36; *Atlantic* Editors to Paul Reynolds, May 11 and 15, 1907. According to Garrison, Wells, in picturing Houghton, Mifflin's display window, "drew on his imagination for his facts" when he "struck a match at midnight . . . & saw certain books there which never were there." Garrison to Oswald G. Villard, October 7, 1906. Houghton, Mifflin did not publish Lowes Dickinson's *A Modern Symposium*.

23. Perry to Upton Sinclair, December 28, 1901; Sinclair to Perry, December 1, 1903, June 6, 1904.

24. Perry to Theodore Dreiser, March 21, May 9, May 23, 1900. This last letter accepted the author's proposed paper on the Growers Association of California providing he keep it to 3 or 3½ pages or between 2100 to 2400 words. The article proved unacceptable and was returned to Dreiser on August 1, 1900. For the Fall River article see Perry to Dreiser, December 22, 1900 and Houghton, Mifflin & Company to Dreiser, February 26, 1901. When Dreiser finally returned the $100, he added $4 for interest. Houghton, Mifflin returned the $4. This early instruction in standards of intellectual integrity fell on barren ground. Twenty-eight years later, the author was taken in a similar deceit. This time his publisher — Horace Liveright — failed to catch the plagiarism before publication. *Dreiser Looks at Russia* was largely cribbed from Dorothy Thompson's *The New Russia*. Again parallel passages were used to prove the charge. W. A. Swanberg, *Theodore Dreiser*, pp. 343–46.

25. Perry, *And Gladly Teach*, p. 174; Thomas Wentworth Higginson, "Literature," *Atlantic*, C (November 1907), 612.

26. Perry to G. W. Cable, February 27, March 2 and 6, 1901.

27. For this and the following paragraph see Lafcadio Hearn to Houghton, Mifflin & Company, n.d. but stamped as received March 19, 1886. This letter indicates that Hearn first offered the stories to Ticknor. Scudder to Hearn, January 17, 1891; *The Japanese Letters of Lafcadio Hearn*, ed. Elizabeth Bisland; Elizabeth Stevenson, *Lafcadio Hearn*, pp. 177, 204–5, 298; FG, "Lafcadio Hearn," *Atlantic*, XCIX (February 1907), 261, also Ferris Greenslet, *Under the Bridge*, p. 80. Bliss Perry to Paul Elmer More, October 6, 1904, to Henry M. Alden, May 17, 1905; FG to Mrs. Charles W. Wetmore (Elizabeth Bisland), July 10, 1906; Memorandum of Agreement, September 8, 1903. For *The Romance of the Milky Way*, Houghton, Mifflin offered Hearn's widow 15 percent or a lump sum of $5000, "no royalty above that sum to be paid if a piratical edition appears." Contract Book, June 7, 1905. Hearn, originally an English citizen, had become a Japanese citizen in 1896; therefore there was a question about his American copyright protection. Stevenson, pp. 278–82. Hearn's earnings from Harper stand in sharp contrast to those of Thomas Bailey Aldrich, who in 1891 earned in two months $1700 from five or six poems in the *Century* and five in *Harper's* and who boasted that the former paid him $75 per 1000 words, the latter $100. Aldrich to William Dean Howells, February 3, 1892, to Perry, April 4, 1902.

28. Perry, *And Gladly Teach*, p. 181. "*The Atlantic* does sometimes pay special rates but seldom exceeds $10–$12 a page." W. B. Parker to Paul Reynolds, May 11, 1900. Perry to same, June 29, 1900. Some body articles as well as Contributors' Clubs were paid for at the $8 rate. Perry to Paul Reynolds, May 11, 1900; Perry to James B. Pinker, October 3, 1899; Houghton, Mifflin & Company to Charles Eliot Norton, June 2, 1904; Perry to James Bryce, December 6, 1899; Editors of the *Atlantic* to E. A. Robinson, March 9, 1907; W. B. Parker to Jack London, October 25, 1899; *Atlantic* Editors to May Sinclair, August 1, 1907.

29. Mifflin to Mary Johnston, January 25 and 28, 1907, May 26, 1908; Book-Earnings 1911; Memorandum of Agreement, February 27, 1911. Perhaps

one reason Mifflin agreed to Miss Johnston's request was that following *Audrey,* she produced in 1904 a best seller (*Sir Mortimer*) for Harper.

30. W. B. Parker to London, July 24, 1899; Garrison to Mifflin, November 13, 1899, July 20, 1900; W. B. Parker to the Editor of the *Overland Monthly,* November 21, 1899; Houghton, Mifflin & Company, Showing on Books; *The Critic,* XXXVII (August 1900), 100 and 162; Parker to London, March 1, 1900, turns down "The Dignity of the Dollar." Perry to London, March 20, 1900, returns his Yukon story with reluctance; Editors of the *Atlantic Monthly* to London, May 3, 1900, send back "The Law of Life." London offered his collection of stories to Macmillan as well as Houghton, Mifflin. *PW,* October 1966, p. 21.

31. W. B. Parker to London, March 14, 1901.

32. *Letters of Jack London,* ed. King Hendricks and Irving Shepard, pp. 129–35, 139–43, 149–51, 440.

33. Kate Douglas Wiggin, *My Garden of Memories,* p. 353.

34. Perry, *And Gladly Teach,* pp. 181–82; Houghton, Mifflin & Company, Sales.

35. Perry to Father Tabb, July 11, 1907; Frank Dempster Sherman to FG, September 11, 1905; *Atlantic,* XCVII (May 1906), 720.

36. MS report 9123; Scudder to Bliss Perry, July 27, 1901; Josephine Preston Peabody, *Diary and Letters,* ed. Christina H. Baker, pp. 19–94; Scudder, Diary, April 2 and 4, 1894.

37. Scudder to E. P. Fox, February 4, 1897; Emery Neff, *Edwin Arlington Robinson,* pp. 51, 57; MS report 9502; H. M. Alden to Bliss Perry, February 9, 1903; Memorandum of Agreement, March 22, 1902; Roger Burlingame, *Endless Frontiers,* pp. 251–57. Madison, p. 196, is in error in crediting *Captain Craig* to Scribner. That house in 1905, under pressure from President Theodore Roosevelt, took over from Badger *The Children of the Night.* Five years later Scribner brought out Robinson's *The Town Down the River.* In 1915 Robinson became a Macmillan author and that house brought out a revised edition of *Captain Craig.* Charles Beecher Hogan, *A Bibliography of Edwin Arlington Robinson.*

38. Perry, *And Gladly Teach,* p. 186, and *Park Street Papers,* p. 31.

39. Mifflin to A. F. and O. R. Houghton, April 8, 1903; Norton to Perry, May 18, 1903; Contract Book, May 11, 1903.

40. Houghton, Mifflin & Company, Memorandum of Sales, 1886–1907; Profit & Loss, and Grand Balance Sheets.

41. Perry, *And Gladly Teach,* pp. 182, 235.

CHAPTER XIX

1. Scudder, Diary, January 7, 1900; Sedgwick, pp. 136–37, 145–46; Frank Luther Mott, *A History of American Magazines,* III, 512; *Putnam's Monthly,* IV (June 1908), 374; Charles Madison, *Book Publishing in America,* p. 232; MacGregor Jenkins to Bliss Perry, June 26, 1908.

2. Ellery Sedgwick, *The Happy Profession,* p. 156; Mifflin to Sedgwick, January 9, 1908.

3. Houghton, Mifflin & Company, Grand Balance Sheets. The partners also

carried special accounts exempt from partnership liability. In 1908 these special accounts totaled $208,091.87.

4. Ibid.; James Murray Kay to Messrs. Bradstreet's, June 1, 1908; Garrison to Fanny Garrison Villard, April 5, 1908; Memorandum of Agreement, March 13, 1908. Sedgwick, p. 156, says he was offered a junior partnership. To the end of his life, Mifflin regarded his young men as partners rather than directors.

5. Garrison to O. G. Villard, April 10, 1908; FG for Mifflin to R. W. Gilder, April 9, 1908.

6. Sedgwick gives the first figure in his autobiographical sketch for the Fiftieth Anniversary of the Harvard Class of 1894; the second in his *The Happy Profession*, p. 156; Houghton, Mifflin & Company, Cost-books and Profit and Loss Sheets. The April 1, 1906 to April 1, 1907, Profit and Loss Sheet, shows a loss of $609.10 for the *Atlantic*, that for April 1, 1907 to April 1, 1908, a profit of $2264.11.

7. Sedgwick, p. 154; Atlantic Monthly Company, advertising letter, October 21, 1918; Memoranda of Agreement, April 26, 1917, April 24, 1919; Atlantic Monthly Company to Houghton Mifflin Company, October 1, 1921. The Atlantic Monthly Company moved to its present Arlington Street address in 1920.

8. Mifflin to M. M. Hurd, February 16, 1898. In this letter Mifflin sees "special promise" in the Educational Department. Memorandum of Book Sales, 1886–1907; J. D. Phillips, Memorandum of Sales, 1902–1910; Mifflin to James Murray Kay and Thomas Ticknor, September 4, 1897; Memorandum of Agreement, July 10, 1899.

9. Houghton, Mifflin & Company, Memorandum of Book Sales, 1886–1907 and Educational Book Showings; *Abstract of the 14th Census of the United States,* p. 404.

10. Houghton Mifflin Company, *Fifty Years of Publishing,* pp. 11–12.

11. MS reports A2619 and A3135. Hoyt was asked for his opinion of Eliza R. Bailey and John M. Manly's speller. He found points to approve, but considered Longmans, Green's *The Alexander Spelling-Book,* already adopted by Indiana, superior. Houghton Mifflin subsequently published *The Bailey-Manly Spelling Book,* the authors having revised their manuscript in line with Hoyt's suggestions.

12. For the content of this and the following paragraph, see Franklin S. Hoyt's Journal, passim.

13. Lawrence A. Cremin, *The Transformation of the School, Progressivism in American Education,* 1876–1957, pp. 5, 103, 170–75.

14. F. S. Hoyt's Journal.

15. MS report A6213. See also "The Quest for a Content in Education" in Newton Edwards and Herman G. Richey, *The School in the American Social Order,* pp. 538–39.

16. F. S. Hoyt to Mrs. Perkins, May 19, August 5, 1914, January 12, 1916, April 11, June 5, July 13, 1917. World War I created large problems for Hoyt. Mrs. Ella Lyman Cabot, cousin of Amy Lowell and wife of Dr. Richard Cabot, who wrote such best sellers for Houghton Mifflin as *What Men Live By,* in 1914 had been engaged to write *A Course In American*

Citizenship. The text was authorized by the School Peace League. After this country's Declaration of War the text required revision; it was "very seriously handicapped by the pro-German and pacifist material" included. Certain states had passed laws "requiring the daily study of patriotism in the schools." Hoyt asked that the title be changed to "A Course in Citizenship and Patriotism" and that any reference to the School Peace League be dropped. Mrs. Cabot agreed. Even so her revision was not acceptable. The text still left the impression that it was animated "by ideals that existed before the war." The author's effort, Hoyt believed, should be in support of the present war because its successful conclusion would "make such warfare impossible for the future." Once again Mrs. Cabot followed her editor's advice. Her text was ready shortly before the Armistice of 1918. Hoyt to Mrs. Cabot, January 27, 1914, April 10, 1918.

17. F. S. Hoyt to Mrs. Perkins, November 12, 1920, January 24, 1921; R. L. Scaife to Mrs. Perkins, March 8, 1921; Ira Rich (Trade editor) to Mrs. Perkins, April 5, 1935; MS report A8221. Lucy Fitch Perkins' appearance on the Houghton Mifflin list provides a provocative link with long forgotten publishing events. As a young woman she had worked for Louis Prang, who it will be recalled had purchased from James R. Osgood in 1875 the publishing rights to Walter Smith's series of art books, that series which Osgood had once thought would put him in the first boat in educational publishing. Lucy's job was to make outline drawings for coloring by third grade students. Following her marriage to Dwight H. Perkins, a promising Chicago architect, she retired into happy domesticity. The depression of 1893 drew her back into commercial life. Once again she worked for Prang, her illustrations appeared in *St. Nicholas,* and she had a number of juveniles published by McClure, Stokes, Century, and others. In 1911, Century, seeing a portfolio of her drawings of Dutch children, encouraged her to prepare a text, promising to publish her book. Desiring to make the most of the possibilities, she showed her work to other publishers, among them Hoyt, to whom she had a letter of introduction. All bid for the unwritten book. She accepted Hoyt's offer not because it was better than the others, but because, of the general publishers competing for her work, Houghton Mifflin had the largest Educational Department. MS report A6213 and Eleanor Ellis Perkins, *Eve Among the Puritans: a Biography of Lucy Fitch Perkins,* passim.

18. F. S. Hoyt to Mrs. Perkins, March 12, 1918; Houghton Mifflin Company, Sales.

19. For increases in costs of manufacture see reports of the Manufacturing Department to Houghton Mifflin's Executive Committee, October 15, 1915 through February 11, 1921.

20. MS report B4257; Emma Miller Bolenius, *First Grade Manual: a Help-Book for Teachers,* pp. iii–iv. *Fifty Years of Publishing,* pp. 17–18; Houghton Mifflin Company, Sales.

21. MS reports B1573 and A7800; F. S. Hoyt's Journal.

22. MS report B1567.

23. For this and the following paragraph, see Cremin, p. 188, Boyd H. Bode, *Modern Educational Theories,* pp. 310–27; Edwards and Richey, p. 611.

24. MS reports 2887 and A3942; Houghton Mifflin Company to Joseph Quincy Adams, December 19, 1916; Houghton Mifflin Company, Sales.

25. Houghton Mifflin Company, Sales and Book Showings; J. D. Phillips to Thomas A. Dickinson, March 9, 1917; Dickinson contract summary, n.d.; G. B. Shaw to Wm. Lyon Phelps, December 30, 1919 [Copy; original in Beinecke Library, Yale University]; H. H. Webster to Dickinson, March 9, 1921.

26. MS report B8135.

27. Houghton, Mifflin & Company, Educational Catalogue, 1906.

28. *Fifty Years of Publishing*, p. 6; Houghton Mifflin Company, Catalogue, 1922; Claude M. Fuess, *R.L.S.: Its Fortieth Anniversary*, p. 10.

29. Houghton Mifflin Company, Sales; FG to Richard Henry Dana (III), November 8, 1921, says, "In 1920 there were, in the American market, one hundred and ten editions of Longfellow's collected and individual poems, bearing other imprints than that of Houghton Mifflin Company." Longfellow's heirs at this time were drawing an annuity of $2000, even though in 1920 sales had amounted to only $852.67. The annuity contract was to run out on January 1, 1922. Houghton Mifflin gave the heirs the choice of returning to a royalty basis or of accepting a reduced annuity of $1000. The heirs settled for the annuity, which was renewed in 1925 to run for three years. In 1928, the heirs sold their rights to Houghton Mifflin Company for $1800. Richard Henry Dana (III) to FG, January 11, 1922; FG to Charles E. Stratton, February 18, 1925; FG to Charles E. Stratton, February 13, 1928.

30. Stephen Grant, "Development of the College Department of Houghton Mifflin Company, 1908–1940," p. 4; MS report B1377; J. T. Shotwell to F. S. Hoyt, September 25, 1920.

31. Houghton Mifflin Company, Sales; Executive Committee to the Directors, Houghton Mifflin Company, October 25, 1921. Books not mentioned in the text which have survived the years: Guitteau and Webster, *The Constitution of the United States;* Tappan, *The Story of the Greek People* and *The Story of the Roman People;* Foerster & Stedman, *Writing and Thinking* (1922 title *Sentences and Thinking*); Rand, *Modern Classical Philosophers*.

32. Memorandum of Educational Figures, 1901–1920; J. D. Phillips to "Dear Fellows," August 30, 1908.

33. For this and the following paragraph, Annual Report of the Executive Committee, February 1922; Reports of the Educational Department for the years ending December 31, 1920 and December 31, 1921.

CHAPTER XX

1. Interview with the late Robert Newton Linscott, in Houghton Mifflin's employ from 1904–1944, as messenger, office boy, bookkeeper, advertising manager for the Subscription Department, advertising manager for the Trade Department, and finally as a Trade editor. See also his posthumous "Speaking of Books: $3 a Week as a Start," *New York Times Book Review,*

February 6, 1966, pp. 2, 20. Linscott's recollections of Mifflin are unpleasant. For a convincing sketch from an opposite view, see FG to A. D. Noyes, secretary of the Century Club, December 15, 1921, quoted in chapter XXII, pp. 179–80.

2. Houghton, Mifflin & Company, Boston, to Houghton, Mifflin & Company, New York, February 27, 1902; Mifflin to A. F. Houghton, November 21, 1901, March 17, 1902.

3. "The Prices of Books," *The Dial*, XXX (March 16, 1901), 179–81. For an excellent exposition of the APA, net prices, and the Macy controversy see Donald Sheehan, *This Was Publishing*, pp. 222–37. The *PW* is replete with items on the subject. For a concise summary see its reprint on February 12, 1916, pp. 552–55, from the *Quarterly Journal of Economics*, of H. R. Tosdale's "Price Maintenance in the Book Trade."

4. "Fixed Prices and the Law," *PW*, November 16, 1912, p. 1637; G. H. Putnam, "A Publisher's Defense," *The Independent*, LXIII (November 1907), 1242–47. Putnam wrote, "The publisher has never been asked to fix the price of his book at one dollar or two dollars; but there has been a co-operative endeavor to maintain the price of a book set by a publisher, through the trade method of discounts."

5. Mifflin to Albert F. Houghton, October 10, 1901, enclosing "A Word of Warning," from the *Dial*, XXXI (October 1, 1901), 227–29; Mifflin to Edward A. Ditmar, September 17, 1903; Robert Sterling Yard, *The Publisher*, p. 20.

6. Ralph M. Hower, *History of Macy's of New York*, p. 356.

7. Mifflin to R. N. Pulsifer, September 2, 1903; George Haven Putnam, *Memories of a Publisher*, pp. 397–98.

8. *The Firm of Houghton, Mifflin and Company*, p. 33; *The Riverside Press*, pp. 3–24; Houghton, Mifflin & Company, *Portrait Catalogue*, p. 218; Houghton Mifflin Company, *Fifty Years of Publishing*, p. 31. John Coolidge Hurd, grandson of M. M. Hurd, in a letter to me, January 3, 1963, says, "When my grandfather M. M. Hurd and H.O.H. divided the business, M.M.H. kept the plant, and it was rented by H. O. Houghton & Co." I have come on no evidence that Hurd and H.O.H. ever "divided the business"; furthermore a Houghton, Mifflin & Company Memorandum of Agreement with H. O. Houghton, M. M. Hurd, and the estate of A. G. Houghton dated November 13, 1889, is for a twenty-year lease of the Riverside Press. Moreover, Henry A. Laughlin in his *Informal Sketch of the History of Houghton Mifflin Company*, p. 6, says "It may interest you to know that The Riverside Press property on the Charles River was still owned by the heirs of the Hurds and the Houghtons when I joined the business in 1914 and was bought from them after that (following Mr. Mifflin's death) by the issue of preferred stock."

9. John Coolidge Hurd to me, January 3, 1963.

10. Riverside's first strike occurred in 1849–1850. The earliest figures I have found for ITU membership are for 1853 in George E. Barnett, *The Printers*, p. 375; for the 1906 figure, ibid., p. 376; Mifflin to G. H. Putnam, January 17, 1906.

11. Mifflin Frothingham to me, November 13, 1963.

12. Houghton, Mifflin & Company, Grand Balance, 1905; Nicholas Paine Gilman, *Profit Sharing Between Employer and Employee,* pp. 321–22. Morgan K. Smith, head of the Riverside Press, to me January 26, 1967; Constitution of the Riverside Press Mutual Benefit Association, n.d.; Barnett, p. 156. Century Company also had a profit-sharing plan in which a portion of stock was earmarked for the employees, they to receive the income, which in some years amounted to $20,000.

13. Mifflin to George Haven Putnam, January 17, 1906.

14. Boston *Daily Evening Transcript,* February 1 and 2, 1906; Cambridge *Chronicle,* February 3, 1906.

15. Barnett, pp. 341–42.

16. *Riverside Bulletin,* October, 1905. See *PW,* September 14, 1912, p. 715, for an attack on printing establishments with lower standards, "Books so slapped together that they hold only as long as they are being sold are on a moral par with blowhole armor and rotten life preservers."

17. *Nation,* XXCIX (November 4, 1909), 434–35; G. & C. Merriam Co., to Mifflin, March 8, 1910; Mifflin to Charles Merriam, March 9, 1910.

18. Because Harry Houghton's birthday fell on Sunday the eighteenth, he was presented with his clock on the afternoon of Saturday the seventeenth at his home. On the following Tuesday all the machinery at the Press was shut down for fifteen minutes while Harry spoke to the workers. The Houghton genealogy, William DeLoss Love II, *The Descendants of Capt. William Houghton,* p. 52, gives August 14, 1906, as the date of Harry's death. However, *PW,* June 23, 1906, p. 1722, gives June 14.

19. Interview with Henry A. Laughlin, *Saturday Review of Literature,* May 9, 1948.

20. Laughlin interview; Ellsworth, *A Golden Age of Authors,* p. 13.

21. Interviews with Laughlin and Edward Artesani, former supervisor of the Riverside Press Bindery. Houghton and Haywood payroll, 1852.

22. *PW,* April 25, 1908, p. 1460; Houghton, Mifflin & Company, *Portrait Catalogue,* p. 238.

23. Mifflin to A. F. Houghton, October 11, 1901.

24. *PW,* March 5, 1910, p. 1135. For other Bruce Rogers books bound by Miss Cole see the Boston *Globe,* March 10, 1912.

25. Mifflin to A. F. Houghton, April 6, 1899; Mifflin to Philip S. Moxon, February 4, 1901.

26. Bruce Rogers in his *Pi,* p. 8, says that the type for the *Rubáiyát* had been bought in England by Houghton in the 1860s. However, Ray Nash in "Notes on the Riverside Press and B. D. Updike," reprint from *Dem Guterberg-Jarbuch,* p. 330, suggests that the type had been in use at the Riverside as early as 1858. Possibly the type was some that James Brown brought back from Europe and which Houghton acquired following Brown's death in 1855? Ralph Bergengren, "Art and Craftsmanship in the Printing of Books," *Outlook,* XC (September 26, 1908), 203; Mifflin to Lawrence Abbott, November 24, 1900.

27. Scudder to BR, November 14 and 16, 1900; Scudder to Charles Eliot Norton, June 27, 1901. In this letter Scudder drew Norton's attention to BR's work, giving a list of titles so far produced. Norton was at first op-

posed to a collection of Lowell's antislavery papers. Norton to Scudder, July 5 and 13, 1901. W. B. Parker to Scudder, September 25, 1901; Mifflin to A. F. Houghton, February 27, March 8, 1901, to Walter L. Harden, March 9, 1901, to Houghton, Mifflin & Company, March 14, 1901, to E. R. Graham, August 21, 1901.

28. Mifflin to A. F. Houghton, July 24, August 23, 1901.

29. Houghton, Mifflin & Company, Scrapbook.

30. Garrison to Mifflin, July 31, 1900; Rogers, *Pi*, pp. 112–13. BR's letter to Mifflin is dated July 31, 1903. For a picture of BR in his Riverside cubbyhole see Rogers, *The Work of Bruce Rogers: Jack of All Trades, Master of One,* facing p. 6.

31. Bergengren, p. 203; *Portrait Catalogue,* p. 240. Since many of Houghton Mifflin's records were stored in the Studio when I first began my work on this history, I have spent hours in the building. The majority of these records have since been transferred to the Houghton Library, Harvard University.

32. *Portrait Catalogue,* p. 240; FG to Arthur Symons, December 19, 1906; Prospectus, "Bruce Rogers & A. Colish announce the publication of *The Divine Comedy of Dante Alighieri*," 1954.

33. Houghton, Mifflin & Company, Sales.

34. Frederic Warde, *Bruce Rogers: Designer of Books,* p. 19; Laughlin interview.

35. Mifflin's letter to McFarland, January 4, 1908, contains comments on other Rogers books in addition to those quoted. The comment on *The Poems of Maria Lowell,* however, comes from Bergengren, p. 206. Mifflin apparently sent McFarland all the books listed in his letter, including the *Song of Roland* with Roosevelt's letters enclosed. This copy is now owned by the Harvard Porcellian. I am indebted to Charles R. Rheault, Jr., Manufacturing Manager of the Riverside Press, for copies of the Roosevelt letters.

36. For this and the following paragraph, Boston *Daily Evening Transcript,* February 23, 1907; Park Street, MS, n.d.; Mifflin Frothingham to me, November 27, 1963.

CHAPTER XXI

1. For details in this and the following paragraphs on FG's life before he came to Park Street see his *Under the Bridge,* pp. 41–70. Henry Oscar Houghton [IV] told me the story of the walking match between Phillips and FG.

2. Wendell P. Garrison to Scudder, November 22, 1901.

3. Perry to FG, August 23, November 20, 1900; W. B. Parker to FG, December 1, 1900; H. R. Gibbs to FG, June 22, 1901. FG's *Walter Pater* was published by McClure, Phillips & Co., 1903.

4. W. B. Parker to FG, December 6, 1901; Perry to FG, December 9, 1901.

5. Houghton Mifflin Company, Stockholders' Book, 1909–1911, p. 7. Scaife, as well as FG, secured many books for Houghton Mifflin.

6. Mifflin to Mary Johnston, July 29, 1908; Francis H. Allen to FG, June 22, 1943; Esther Forbes to FG, n.d.; conversation with Edward Weeks.

7. Aldrich to George E. Woodberry, May 14, 1892; FG, *Bridge*, pp. 45, 53.

8. Mary Austin to FG, October 28, 1915; FG to Ellis P. Butler, July 15, 1918. Greenslet the grocer appears in Mary Austin's "The Lovely Lady."

9. Willa Cather to FG, May 19, 1919.

10. FG, *Bridge*, pp. 177–78; Scaife to Radclyffe Hall, June 5, 1929. Mencken in reporting to Dreiser, May 27, 1921, the activity of the "Comstocks," said, "A publisher who takes any unnecessary chances is not brave, he is simply silly." *Letters of H. L. Mencken*, ed. Guy J. Forgue, p. 222.

11. MSS reports A4003(Lindsay), A2799, A3361(Erskine), A5917(Eastman), B3232(Mencken), B1993(Young), B3208(Van Doren), A5063(Benet), A6644, A7547(Robinson), A7493, A7494, A9421, A9565, B1782(Cabell), A6489(Untermeyer).

12. MSS reports A4003(Lindsay), A602(Selma Lagerlöf), A2349(Maugham), A814(Prosser Hall Frye), A7020(Masefield); FG to Buchan, July 24, 1918; to Amy Lowell, October 24, 1919; *PW*, July 13, 1915, p. 338. Miss Francis' report on Madison Cawein (MS 8089) typifies her poetic taste. In this she wrote that she had read Cawein without profit for fifteen years, ". . . though I know that when Mr. Howells was dethroning the great poets and setting up small ones in their places, he spoke kindly of Cawein, while disparaging Tennyson . . . To my thinking, Mr. Cawein has a Southern luxuriance of words, no artistic training, and only a moderate amount of thought."

13. FG, *Bridge*, p. 137; MS report B3232.

14. William Manchester, *The Disturber of the Peace*, pp. 43, 93; H. L. Mencken, *Prejudices: Second Series*, pp. 14–18, and *A Book of Prefaces*, p. 69.

15. FG, *Bridge*, p. 129; Amy Lowell to FG, May 7, September 29, 1914; Memorandum of Agreement, May 21, 1912; Foster Damon, *Amy Lowell*, p. 303.

16. FG to Amy Lowell, May 8, October 1, 1914.

17. *Nation*, XCV (December 19, 1912), 588–89; *Atlantic*, XCIII (March 1904), 421–25; FG to Amy Lowell, October 22, 1917; FG, *Bridge*, p. 128. As a Pulitzer poetry judge (1920–1926), FG objected to the committee's award to Robinson in 1925 for *The Man Who Died Twice*, which he found "duller than usual." FG to Wilbur Cross, April 28, 1925.

18. MSS reports A7305(A. Lowell), B3541(MacLeish).

19. MSS reports A6115 and A7528; FG, *Bridge*, pp. 126–27; H. L. Mencken, *Prejudices: First Series*, pp. 138–39. Carl R. Dolmetsch, in his *The Smart Set: a History and Anthology*, p. 22, says Henry Holt's editor Witter Bynner, having read Harrison's "Rhoda Gaines, M. A." in the January 1907 *Smart Set*, requested the author to do a book for Holt and that *Queed* was the result. Dolmetsch is in error in saying that Holt published the novel. FG apparently did not read *The Smart Set*. His MS report says, "We can find no record of the author's ever having published anything before either in magazine or in book form."

20. "Honest Literary Criticism," *Atlantic*, CII (August 1908), 179–90.

21. "Literary Criticism in American Periodicals," *Yale Review*, New Series, III (July 1914), 635–55. Interview with John Chipman, salesman for Houghton Mifflin Company in the late 1920s.

22. Scaife to Perry, June 26, 1914.

23. Eleanor H. Porter to FG, March 16, April 27, 1916. All information on best sellers in this and succeeding paragraphs comes from Alice Payne Hackett, *70 Years of Best Sellers 1895–1965*.

24. Houghton Mifflin Company, Book Showings; FG to Willa Cather, January 14, June 5, 1919; FG, *Bridge*, p. 116.

25. Willa Cather to FG, March 28, 1915.

26. FG to Willa Cather, March 30, April 5 and 29, 1915; Memoranda of Agreement, March 29, 1913, April 16, 1915, January 25, 1918.

27. For criticisms other than those set forth in her letter of May 19, 1919: Willa Cather to FG, June 30 [1915], November 24, 1917, May 30, 1919, December 28, 1919, January 7, 1920. Her fury with Robert Newton Linscott for the ineptness of one of his replies to her comments on his advertising copy was such that she inquired of FG ironically whether a post in the State Department wouldn't be more suited to his talents.

28. For Miss Cather's account of her transfer to Knopf see "Portrait of the Publisher as a Young Man" in *Alfred A. Knopf Quarter Century*, pp. 9–16. Also Alfred A. Knopf, "Publishing Then and Now, 1912–1964," *PW*, November 23, 1964, pp. 20–26. Miss Cather says, "I first went to Alfred Knopf in the early spring of 1920." However, her letter announcing Knopf was to have her *Troll Garden* to reissue is dated December 28, 1919. Moreover, FG in a letter to her dated January 31, 1920, refers to Knopf as "your other publisher."

29. FG to Willa Cather, May 19, 1919.

30. FG to Willa Cather, October 4 and 27, 1916, September 16, 1918; Willa Cather to FG, December 2, 1918; December 28, 1919.

31. FG to Willa Cather, January 14, 1921. Others in Houghton Mifflin appear to have been more sanguine than FG. At least Scaife assured his salesmen on June 27, 1922, that although Miss Cather had let Knopf have *One of Ours,* he expected Houghton Mifflin would have her next book.

32. H. L. Mencken, *Prejudices: Fourth Series,* p. 292; Edith Lewis, *Willa Cather Living,* p. 115. "Alfred Knopf told me that Willa Cather told him her real reason for leaving Houghton Mifflin was that FG addressed her by her first name, which offended her personal dignity." (Henry A. Laughlin in a note to the author.)

33. Alberta Houghton to Roger Scaife, June 16 [1926]; Scaife to Alberta Houghton, June 22, 1926.

34. *PW*, January 29, 1916, pp. 332–33.

35. Stanley Unwin, *The Truth About a Publisher,* note, p. 264; FG to Anne Douglas Sedgwick, December 10 and 21, 1923, April 30, 1925.

36. FG to Anne Douglas Sedgwick, July 11, 1925, April 30, May 8, October 22, 1915, April 19, 1919; Anne Douglas Sedgwick to FG, June 9, August 26, 1919.

37. FG to Anne Douglas Sedgwick, November 7, 1919. Sedgwick best sellers in the twenties: *The Little French Girl,* 1924 and 1925; *The Old Countess,* 1927; *Dark Hester,* 1929.

38. FG to Anne Douglas Sedgwick, April 30, 1915; George Trevelyan to FG, May 21, 1915.

39. James Duane Squires, *British Propaganda at Home and in the United States from 1914 to 1917*, p. 43; FG, *Bridge,* passim.
40. FG, *Bridge,* pp. 135–37; FG to Henry Cabot Lodge, May 11, 1917. Lodge replied to FG on May 12, "I can imagine . . . the feeling in England after our break with Germany. I can tell what that feeling must have been by my own, for I have been laboring for this result for two years."
41. Squires, pp. 16–41; FG, *Bridge,* pp. 157–59.
42. FG, *Bridge,* p. 163; FG to Buchan, May 10, 1917; James R. Mock and Cedric Larson, *Words that Won the War,* pp. 109–11.
43. Houghton Mifflin Company, Book Showings.
44. Hackett, *Best Sellers,* is in error in attributing *Dawn* to Gene Stratton Porter and in assigning Thayer's *Roosevelt* to Scribner. Charles A. Madison, *Book Publishing in America,* p. 256, says *Scaramouche* sold 600,000 in its first year. The correct figure is 26,350. Houghton Mifflin Company, Book Showings. By 1965 in paper back and hard cover it had sold 1,584,-793. Hackett, p. 21.
45. FG report to Houghton Mifflin Company (October 1920).
46. On September 30, 1920, FG wrote Willa Cather that he had heard from Knopf that her new book was being mailed to him.
47. FG, *Bridge,* pp. 129, 185; FG to Claude Bowers, October 14, 1931.
48. Houghton Mifflin Company, Profit and Loss Sheets; J. D. Phillips to N. T. Pulsifer, March 24, April 22 and 29, 1922; FG to Sir Wilfred Grenfell, May 21, 1932.
49. W. R. Thayer to FG, June 26, 1916; FG to Eleanor H. Porter, March 3, 1920; Eleanor H. Porter to FG, May 7, 1920; Gamaliel Bradford, Jr., to FG, February 19, 1921; FG to Bradford, February 21, 1921; M. A. DeWolfe Howe to Bradford, April 21, 1921; FG to Bradford, April 25, 1921. A characteristic FG letter on the subject is one of February 27, 1923, to Joel Chandler Harris:

> A very notable instance in the relation between a reasonable royalty which doesn't cramp the publisher of his operations, is seen in the great success in this country of the books of Rafael Sabatini. Although he has been offered as high as 30% by certain publishers desirous of securing his name on their lists, he has, with the agreement of his agent, taken 10% from us with quite extraordinary results, both in respect to his new books and in respect to certain older books, [which] after having been published in this country by Lippincott and sold less than 1000 copies each, have just been reissued by us and reached sales running from ten to twenty thousand copies. It is not the rate of royalty in the contract, but the size of the annual check that counts.

50. FG to John Buchan, September 30, 1939.

CHAPTER XXII

1. James Duncan Phillips, "Educational Figures, 1901–1920" and "Memorandum in regard to the History and Progress of Houghton Mifflin Co." [1921].

2. Laughlin interview; Hoyt Diary, [August] 1918.

3. *PW*, April 16, 1921, p. 1180. See also April 9, 1921, pp. 1125–26 for further appreciation of Mifflin.

4. Boston *Daily Evening Transcript,* April 8, 1921.

5. Memoranda of Agreement, January 1, 1894, February 10, 1912, including endorsements indicating increases. In 1906 Burroughs offered to carry the costs of making his *Bird and Bough* (a collection of verse), but Houghton, Mifflin refused to accept his offer. Garrison to Burroughs, February 23, 1906. In 1918 Burroughs, pleading "the high cost of living and dying," asked that his annuity be increased from $2000 to $4000 or $5000. Burroughs to FG, October 12, 1918. FG replied, October 14, that sales could not justify such an increase, that if Burroughs wished, Houghton Mifflin was willing to return him to a standard royalty contract.

6. Garrison to Mifflin, October 19, 1896, July 31, 1900.

7. FG to M. A. DeWolfe Howe, November 28, 1921.

8. Howe to FG, December 7, 1921 (on this letter Scaife scrawled in anger, "This is the limit."); Sedgwick, p. 90.

9. FG to John Buchan, April 7, 1921.

10. FG to A. D. Noyes, secretary of the Century Club, December 15, 1921.

11. Houghton Mifflin, Annual Report of the Executive Committee, February 1922; Houghton Mifflin Company, Profit and Loss Sheets.

12. Mifflin, interview in the New York *Sun,* December 6, 1913.

BIBLIOGRAPHY

Abbott, Lyman. *Reminiscences.* Boston: Houghton Mifflin Company, 1915.

Acklom, Morely. "The Rise of the House of Dutton," *Seventy-five Years of Publishing.* New York: E. P. Dutton & Company, Inc., 1927.

Adams, Henry. *The Education of Henry Adams.* Boston: Houghton Mifflin Company, 1918.

_____. *Letters of Henry Adams, 1858–1891; 1892–1918,* ed. Worthington Chauncey Ford. Boston: Houghton Mifflin Company, 1930; 1938.

Adams, Marian Hooper. *The Letters of Mrs. Henry Adams, 1865–1883,* ed. Ward Thoron. Boston: Little, Brown and Company, 1935.

Aldrich, Lilian W. [Mrs. Thomas]. *Crowding Memories.* Boston: Houghton Mifflin Company, 1920.

Alfred A. Knopf Quarter Century. Copyright Elmer Adler, 1940.

The Andersen-Scudder Letters, ed. Waldemar Wastergaard. Berkeley: University of California Press, 1949.

The Atlantic Index, 1857–1888. Boston: Houghton, Mifflin & Company, 1889.

The Atlantic Index Supplement, 1889–1901. Boston: Houghton, Mifflin & Company, 1903.

Auditor's Report. Boston, 1872–1873.

Austin, James C. *Fields of The Atlantic Monthly: Letters to an Editor, 1861–1870.* San Marino (California): Huntington Library, 1953.

Baker, Ray Stannard. *Woodrow Wilson: Life and Letters.* Garden City: Doubleday, Page & Company, 1927, vol. I.

Barnett, George E. *The Printers: a Study in American Trade Unionism.* Cambridge: American Economic Association, 1909.

Barrus, Clara. *Whitman and Burroughs.* Boston: Houghton Mifflin Company, 1931.

Bennett, George N. *William Dean Howells: the Development of a Novelist.* Norman: University of Oklahoma Press, 1959.

Bikle, Lucy Leffingwell Cable. *George W. Cable: His Life and Letters.* New York: Charles Scribner's Sons, 1928.

Bingham, Millicent Todd. *Ancestors' Brocades.* New York: Harper & Brothers, 1945.

Blank, Jacob (compiler). *Bibliography of American Literature.* New Haven: Yale University Press, vol. I, 1955; vol. II, 1957; vol. III, 1959; vol. IV, 1963.

Bode, Boyd H. *Modern Education Theories.* New York: Random House, Inc., Vintage Books. First published by The Macmillan Company, 1927.

Bolenius, Emma Miller. *First Grade Manual: a Help-Book for Teachers.* Boston: Houghton Mifflin Company, 1923.

The Bookmakers' Reminiscences and Contemporary Sketches of American Publishers from the New York Evening Post, 1874–1876. Office of the Publishers' Weekly, n.d.

Bowker, R. R. *Copyright: Its Law and Its Literature.* New York: Office of the Publishers' Weekly, 1886.

Brayley, Arthur W. *A Complete History of the Boston Fire Department.* Boston: John P. Dale & Co., 1899.

Brooks, Van Wyck. *New England: Indian Summer, 1865–1915.* New York: E. P. Dutton & Company, Inc., 1940.

Brown, E. K., and Leon Edel. *Willa Cather.* New York: Alfred A. Knopf, Inc., 1953.

Burlingame, Roger. *Endless Frontiers: the Story of McGraw-Hill.* New York, McGraw-Hill Book Company, 1959.

————. *Of Making Many Books.* New York: Charles Scribner's Sons, 1946.

Burns, Wayne. *Charles Reade: a Study in Victorian Authorship.* New York: Bookman Associates, 1961.

Burroughs, John. *Letters,* ed. Clara Barrus. Boston: Houghton Mifflin Company, 1925.

Butler, Robert Ernest. "William Dean Howells as Editor of the Atlantic Monthly." Ph.d. dissertation, Rutgers University, 1950.

Cady, Edwin H. *The Road to Realism.* Syracuse: Syracuse University Press, 1956.

The Cambridge of Eighteen Hundred and Ninety-Six, ed. Arthur Gilman. Cambridge: Printed at the Riverside Press, 1896.

Carpenter, Charles. *History of American School Books.* Philadelphia: University of Pennsylvania Press, 1963.

Cary, Richard. *Sarah Orne Jewett.* New York: Twayne Publishers, Inc., 1962.

Cater, Harold Dean (compiler). *Henry Adams and His Friends.* Boston: Houghton Mifflin Company, 1947.

Cather, Willa. *Not Under Forty.* New York: Alfred A. Knopf, 1936.

Charvat, William. *Literary Publishing in America, 1790–1850.* Philadelphia: University of Pennsylvania Press, 1959.

Clark, Aubert J. *The Movement for International Copyright in Nineteenth Century America.* Ann Arbor: University Microfilms, 1960.

Coffin, Charles Carleton [Carleton]. *The Story of the Great Fire, Boston November 9–10, 1872.* Boston: Shepherd and Gill, 1872.

Conwell, Russell H. *History of the Great Fire in Boston November 9 and 10, 1872.* Boston: B. B. Russell, 1873.

Copyright Enactments. Washington: Copyright Office, Library of Congress, 1963.

Crane, E. M. *A Century of Book Publishing, 1848–1948.* New York: D. Van Nostrand Company, Inc., 1948.

Crane, Stephen. *Letters,* ed. R. W. Stallman and Lillian Gilkes. New York: New York University Press, 1960.

Cremin, Lawrence A. *The Transformation of the School: Progressivism in American Education, 1876–1957.* New York: Random House, Inc., Vintage Books, 1961.

Currier, Thomas Franklin. *A Bibliography of Oliver Wendell Holmes,* ed. Eleanor M. Tilton. New York: New York University Press, 1953.

Damon, Foster. *Amy Lowell.* Boston: Houghton Mifflin Company, 1941.

Deland, Margaret. *Golden Yesterdays.* New York: Harper & Brothers, 1941.

Derby, J. C. *Fifty Years Among Authors, Books and Publishers.* New York: G. W. Carleton & Co., 1884.

Dickens, Charles. *The Letters of Charles Dickens,* ed. Walter Dexter. Bloomsbury: The Nonesuch Press, 1938, vol. III.

————. *The Speeches of Charles Dickens,* ed. K. J. Fielding. Oxford: Clarendon Press, 1960.

Dickinson, Emily. *The Letters of Emily Dickinson,* ed. Thomas H. Johnson. 3 vols. Cambridge: Belknap Press of Harvard University Press, 1958.

Dodge, Augusta, ed., *Gail Hamilton's Life in Letters.* 2 vols. Boston: Lee and Shepard, 1901.

[Dodge, Mary A.] *A Battle of the Books, Recorded by an Unknown Writer, for the Use of Authors and Publishers . . . Edited and Published by Gail Hamilton.* Cambridge: Printed at the Riverside Press, 1870.

Dolmetsch, Carl R. *The Smart Set: a History and Anthology.* New York: Dial Press, Inc., 1966.

Doran, George H. *Chronicles of Barabbas.* New York: Rinehart & Company, Inc., 1952.

Dozer, Donald Marquand. "The Tariff on Books," *Mississippi Valley Historical Review,* XXXVI (1949), 73–96.

Edel, Leon. *Henry James: the Conquest of London.* Philadelphia: J. B. Lippincott Company, 1962.

————. *Henry James: the Middle Years.* Philadelphia: J. B. Lippincott Company, 1962.

Edgar, Herman LeRoy and R. W. G. Vail. "Early American Editions of the Works of Charles Dickens," *Bulletin of the New York Public Library,* XXXIII (May 1929), 302–19.

Edwards, Newton and Herman G. Richey. *The School in the American Social Order.* 2nd ed. Boston: Houghton Mifflin Company, 1963.

Ellsworth, William H. *A Golden Age of Authors.* Boston: Houghton Mifflin Company, 1919.

Elwin, Malcolm. *Charles Reade.* London: Jonathan Cape, 1934.

Exercises in Celebrating the Two Hundred and Fiftieth Anniversary of the Settlement of Cambridge. Cambridge: Charles W. Sever, 1881.

Exman, Eugene. *The Brothers Harper.* New York: Harper & Row, 1965.

————. *The House of Harper.* New York: Harper & Row, 1967.

Exposition Universalle de Paris 1878: Catalogue of the Collective Exhibit of the American Book Trade. Cambridge: Riverside Press, 1878.

Fadiman, Clifton. "A View from the Fiftieth Year," *Fifty Years* [Alfred A. Knopf]. New York: Alfred A. Knopf, Inc., 1965.

Fields, Annie. *Authors and Friends.* Boston: Houghton, Mifflin & Company, 1896.

Fields, James T. *Biographical Notes and Personal Sketches* (A Memorial Volume). Boston: Houghton, Mifflin & Company, 1882.

Ford, James L. *Forty-Odd Years in the Literary Shop*. New York: E. P. Dutton & Company, Inc., 1921.

Freeman, Frank N. *Mental Tests: Their History, Principles and Applications*. Boston: Houghton Mifflin Company, 1939.

Frothingham, Octavius Brooks. *Theodore Parker*. Boston: James R. Osgood & Company, 1874.

Fuess, Claude M. *R.L.S.: Its Fortieth Anniversary*. Boston: Houghton Mifflin Company, 1922.

Garnett, Richard. "The Late Henry Stevens, F.S.A.," *Essays in Librarianship and Bibliography*. Library Series, vol. V. London: G. Allen, 1899, pp. 325–39.

Garraty, John A. *Henry Cabot Lodge*. New York: Alfred A. Knopf, Inc., 1953.

Gilman, Arthur. "Atlantic Dinners and Diners," *Atlantic*, C (November 1907), 650–55.

Gilman, Nicholas Paine. *Profit Sharing Between Employer and Employee*. Boston: Houghton, Mifflin & Company, 1889.

Gladden, Washington. *Recollections*. Boston: Houghton Mifflin Company, 1909.

Gladstone, Hon. W. E. " 'Robert Elsmere' and the Battle of Belief." Reprinted from the *Nineteenth Century*, Buffalo, n.d.

Grannis, Chandler B. *What Happens in Book Publishing*. New York: Columbia University Press, 1957.

Grant, Robert. *Fourscore: an Autobiography*. Boston: Houghton Mifflin Company, 1934.

Greenslet, Ferris. *The Life of Thomas Bailey Aldrich*. Boston: Houghton Mifflin Company, 1908.

————. *The Lowells and Their Seven Worlds*. Boston: Houghton Mifflin Company, 1946.

————. *Under the Bridge: an Autobiography*. Boston: Houghton Mifflin Company, 1943.

Gregory, Horace. *Amy Lowell: Portrait of the Poet in Her Time*. New York: Thomas Nelson & Sons, 1958.

Gross, Gerald. *Publishers on Publishing*. New York: R. R. Bowker Company, 1961.

Growoll, Adolph. "American Book Trade History." 13 volumes of clippings. Office of the Publishers' Weekly.

Hackett, Alice Payne. *70 Years of Best Sellers, 1895–1965*. New York: R. R. Bowker Company, 1967.

Hale, Edward Everett. *Memories of a Hundred Years*. New York: The Macmillan Company, 1902.

Hale, Edward Everett, Jr. *The Life and Letters of Edward Everett Hale*. Boston: Little, Brown and Company, 1917.

Harding, Walter. *The Days of Henry Thoreau*. New York: Alfred A. Knopf, Inc., 1965.

Harlow, Virginia. *Thomas Sergeant Perry*. Durham (North Carolina): Duke University Press, 1950.

Harper, J. Henry. *The House of Harper.* New York: Harper & Brothers, 1912.
————. *I Remember.* New York: Harper & Brothers, 1934.
Harte, Francis Bret. *The Letters of Bret Harte,* ed. Geoffrey Bret Harte. Boston: Houghton Mifflin Company, 1926.
Hearn, Lafcadio. *The Japanese Letters of Lafcadio Hearn,* ed. Elizabeth Bisland. Boston: Houghton Mifflin Company, 1910.
Heath, D. C. *An Address Delivered before the School Book Publishers' Association, 1899.* New York: Printed for Private Circulation, 1900.
Hendrick, Burton J. *The Life and Letters of Walter H. Page.* Garden City: Doubleday, Page & Company, 1922, vol. I.
Higginson, Thomas Wentworth. *Carlyle's Laugh and Other Surprises.* Boston: Houghton Mifflin Company, 1909.
————. *Cheerful Yesterdays,* Boston: Houghton, Mifflin & Company, 1898.
————. *Letters and Journals,* ed. Mary Thacher Higginson. Boston: Houghton Mifflin Company, 1921.
————. *Old Cambridge.* New York: The Macmillan Company, 1899.
Hill, Hamlin. *Mark Twain and Elisha Bliss.* Columbia: University of Missouri Press, 1964.
Hillard, George S. *Memoir of James Brown.* Boston: Privately printed by H. O. Houghton & Company, 1856.
Hogan, Charles Beecher. *A Bibliography of Edwin Arlington Robinson.* New Haven: Yale University Press, 1936.
Holt, Henry. *Garrulities of an Octogenarian Editor.* Boston: Houghton Mifflin Company, 1923.
Houghton, Mifflin & Company. *A Catalogue of Authors whose Works are Published by Houghton, Mifflin and Company. Prefaced by a Sketch of the Firm, and Followed by Lists of the Several Libraries, Series, and Periodicals. With Some Account of the Origin and Character of these Literary Enterprises.* Boston: 1899.
————. *Fifty Years of Publishing.* Boston: 1930.
————. *The Firm of Houghton, Mifflin and Company, Publishers, Boston, New York, Chicago, and London.* Cambridge: Riverside Press, 1889.
————. *Of the Making of Books and the Part Played Therein by the Publishing House of Houghton Mifflin Company.* Boston: [1921].
————. *A Portrait Catalogue of the Books Published by Houghton, Mifflin and Company with a Sketch of the Firm, Brief Descriptions of the Various Departments, and Some Account of the Origin and Character of the Literary Enterprises Undertaken.* Boston: 1905–1906.
————. *The Riverside Press.* 1911.
Howard, John Raymond. *Remembrance of Things Past.* New York: Thomas Y. Crowell, 1925.
Howe, Helen. *The Gentle Americans.* New York: Harper & Row, 1965.
Howe, Julia Ward. *Reminiscences, 1819–1899.* Boston: Houghton, Mifflin & Company, 1899.
Howe, M. A. DeWolfe. *The Atlantic Monthly and Its Makers.* Boston: Atlantic Monthly Press, Inc., 1919.
————. *John Jay Chapman.* Boston: Houghton Mifflin Company, 1937.
————. *Memories of a Hostess.* Boston: Atlantic Monthly Press, 1922.

————. *A Venture in Remembrance*. Boston: Little, Brown and Company, 1941.

Howe, M. A. DeWolfe, and G. W. Cottrell, Jr., eds. *Scholar-Friends: Letters of Francis James Child and James Russell Lowell*. Cambridge: Harvard University Press, 1952.

Howells, Mildred, ed. *Life in Letters of William Dean Howells*. 2 vols. New York: Doubleday, Doran & Company, 1928.

Howells, William Dean. *Literary Friends and Acquaintances*. New York: Harper & Brothers, 1902.

————. *Literature and Life*. New York: Harper & Brothers, 1911.

————. *My Mark Twain*. New York: Harper & Brothers, 1910.

————. *The Rise of Silas Lapham*. New York: Random House, Inc., Modern Library, 1951.

Hower, Ralph M. *History of Macy's of New York, 1858–1919*. Cambridge: Harvard University Press, 1943.

James, Henry. *Hawthorne*. New York: Harper & Brothers, 1879.

Jenkins, MacGregor. *Literature with a Large L*. Boston: Houghton Mifflin Company, 1919.

Jewett, Sarah Orne. *Letters of Sarah Orne Jewett,* ed. Annie Fields. Boston: Houghton Mifflin Company, 1911.

————. *Letters,* ed. Richard Cary. Rev. ed. Waterville (Maine): Colby College Press, 1967.

Johnson, Edgar. *Charles Dickens: His Tragedy and Triumph*. 2 vols. New York: Simon and Schuster, Inc., 1952.

Johnson, Robert Underwood. *Remembered Yesterdays*. Boston: Little, Brown and Company, 1923.

Johnston, Johanna. *Runaway to Heaven*. Garden City: Doubleday & Co., Inc., 1963.

John Wiley & Sons, Inc. *The First One Hundred and Fifty Years*. New York: John Wiley & Sons, Inc., 1957.

Joost, Nicholas. *The Dial, 1912–1920*. Barre (Massachusetts): Barre Publishers, 1967.

Kaplan, Justin. *Mr. Clemens and Mark Twain*. New York: Simon and Schuster, Inc., 1966.

Kilgour, Raymond L. *Estes and Lauriat*. Ann Arbor: University of Michigan Press, 1957.

————. *Lee and Shepard: Publishers for the People*. Hamden (Connecticut): Shoe String Press, Inc., 1965.

————. *Messrs. Roberts Brothers: Publishers*. Ann Arbor: University of Michigan Press, 1952.

King, Moses. *King's Hand-book of Boston*. Cambridge: Moses King, 1883.

Knopf, Alfred A. "Random Recollections of a Publisher," *Proceedings of the Massachusetts Historical Society,* LXXIII (January-December 1961), 92–103.

Kramer, Sidney. *History of Stone and Kimbal and Herbert F. Stone and Herbert F. Stone and Company*. Chicago: N. W. Forgue, 1940.

Kraus, Michael. *The United States to 1965*. Ann Arbor: University of Michigan Press, 1959.

————. *The United States Since 1865.* Ann Arbor: University of Michigan Press, 1959.

Kubler, George A. *A New History of Stereotyping.* New York: J. J. Little & Ives Company, 1941.

Latham, Harold S. *My Life in Publishing.* New York: E. P. Dutton & Company, Inc., 1965.

Laughlin, Henry A. *An Informal Sketch of the History of Houghton Mifflin Company.* Boston: [Houghton Mifflin Company], 1957.

Lawler, Thomas Bonaventure. *Seventy Years of Textbook Publishing.* Boston: Ginn and Company, 1938.

Leavitt, Keith. *Noah's Ark.* Springfield (Massachusetts): G. & C. Merriam, 1947.

Lehmann-Haupt, Hellmut; L. C. Wroth; and R. G. Silver. *The Book in America.* New York: R. R. Bowker Company, 1952.

Lenticchia, Frank, Jr. "Harriet Beecher Stowe and the Byron Whirlwind," *Bulletin of the New York Public Library,* LXXX (April 1966), 218–28.

Letters to Macmillan, ed. Simon Nowell-Smith. New York: The Macmillan Company, St. Martin's Press, 1967.

Lewis, Edith. *Willa Cather Living.* New York: Alfred A. Knopf, Inc., 1953.

Lindsay, Julian Ira. *Tradition Looks Forward.* Burlington: University of Vermont, 1954.

Little, Brown and Company. *One Hundred and Twenty-five Years of Publishing.* Boston, 1962.

Lodge, Henry Cabot. *Early Memories.* New York: Charles Scribner's Sons, 1913.

London, Jack. *Letters of Jack London,* ed. King Hendricks and Irving Shepard. New York: Odyssey Press, 1965.

Love, William DeLoss, II (compiler). *The Descendants of Capt. William Houghton 1774–1863 and Marilla Clay.* Berkeley, California: Privately printed, 1953.

Lowell, James Russell. *Letters of James Russell Lowell,* ed. Charles Eliot Norton. New York: Harper & Brothers, 1893.

————. *New Letters of James Russell Lowell,* ed. M. A. DeWolfe Howe. New York: Harper & Brothers, 1932.

Lyon, Peter. *Success Story: the Life and Times of S. S. McClure.* New York: Charles Scribner's Sons, 1963.

McGrane, Reginald Charles. *The Panic of 1837.* Chicago: University of Chicago Press, 1924.

McKee, Irving. *"Ben Hur" Wallace: the Life of General Lew Wallace.* Berkeley: University of California Press, 1947.

McLean, Ruari. *Modern Book Design from William Morris to the Present Day.* London: Faber & Faber, 1958.

————. *Victorian Book Design.* London: Faber & Faber, 1963.

Madison, Charles A. *Book Publishing in America.* New York: McGraw-Hill Book Company, 1966.

Manchester, William. *The Disturber of the Peace.* New York: Harper & Brothers, 1951.

Mann, Dorothea L. *A Century of Bookselling.* Boston: The Old Corner Bookstore, 1928.

Martin, Edward Sanford. *The Life of Joseph Hodges Choate.* 2 vols. New York: Charles Scribner's Sons, 1920.

Mencken, Henry L. *A Book of Prefaces.* New York: Alfred A. Knopf, Inc., Pocket Book, 1917.

————. *Letters of H. L. Mencken,* ed. Guy J. Forgue. New York: Alfred A. Knopf, Inc., 1961.

————. *Prejudices.* New York: Alfred A. Knopf, Inc., First Series, 1919; Second Series, 1920; Third Series, 1922; Fourth Series, 1924.

Meyer, Adolphe E. *An Educational History of the American People.* New York: McGraw-Hill Book Company, 1957.

Mitchell, Edward P. *Memoirs of an Editor.* New York: Charles Scribner's Sons, 1924.

Mock, James R. and Cedric Larson. *Words that Won the War: the Story of the Committee on Public Information, 1917–1919.* Princeton: Princeton University Press, 1939.

Morgan, Charles. *The House of Macmillan.* London: Macmillan & Company, 1944.

Morgan, Charlotte E. *The Origin and History of the New York Employing Printers' Association.* New York: Columbia University Press, 1930.

Morris, John V. *Fires and Firefighters.* Boston: Little, Brown and Company, 1955.

Morse, John T. *Life and Letters of Oliver Wendell Holmes.* 2 vols. Boston: Houghton, Mifflin & Company, 1896.

————. "Incidents Connected with the American Statesmen Series," *Proceedings of the Massachusetts Historical Society,* LXIV (October 1930–June 1932), 370–88.

Mott, Frank Luther. *Golden Multitudes: the Story of Best Sellers in the United States.* New York: Macmillan Company, 1947.

————. *A History of American Magazines.* 4 vols. Cambridge: Belknap Press of Harvard University Press, 1957.

Nash, Ray. "Notes on the Riverside Press and B. D. Updike." Reprint from *Dem Gutenberg-Jahrbuch,* 1960.

————. *Printing as an Art: a History of the Society of Printers 1905–1955.* Cambridge: Harvard University Press, 1955.

Neff, Emery. *Edwin Arlington Robinson.* New York: William Sloane Associates, 1948.

Nolte, William H. *H. L. Mencken: Literary Critic.* Middletown (Connecticut): Wesleyan University Press, 1966.

Norton, Charles Eliot. *Letters of Charles Eliot Norton,* ed. Sara Norton and M. A. DeWolfe Howe. 2 vols. Boston: Houghton Mifflin Company, 1913.

O'Connor, Richard. *Bret Harte.* Boston: Little, Brown and Company, 1966.

Orcutt, William Dana. *In Quest of the Perfect Book.* Boston: Little, Brown & Company, 1926.

Overton, Grant. *Portrait of a Publisher.* New York: D. Appleton and Company, 1925.

Page, Walter H. *A Publisher's Confession.* Garden City: Doubleday, Page & Company, 1923.

Paige, Lucius R. *History of Cambridge*. Boston: H. O. Houghton & Company, 1877.

Parker, Wyman. *Henry Stevens of Vermont*. Amsterdam: N. Isael, 1963.

Parks, Edd Winfield. *Charles Egbert Craddock*. Chapel Hill: University of North Carolina Press, 1941.

Peabody, Josephine Preston. *Diary and Letters*, ed. Christina H. Baker. Boston: Houghton Mifflin Company, 1925.

Pearson, Justus R. "Story of a Magazine: New York's *Galaxy*, 1866–1878," *Bulletin of the New York Public Library*, LXI (May–June 1957), 217–37, 281–302.

Pearson, Norman Holmes. "Problems of Literary Executorship," *Studies in Bibliography*, V (1952–1953), 3–20.

Perkins, Eleanor Ellis. *Eve Among the Puritans: a Biography of Lucy Fitch Perkins*. Boston: Houghton Mifflin Company, 1956.

Perry, Bliss. *And Gladly Teach*. Boston: Houghton Mifflin Company, 1935.

————. *Park Street Papers*. Boston: Houghton Mifflin Company, 1908.

Phillips, James Duncan. "The Riverside Press," *Cambridge Historical Publications*, XIX (1927), 15–31.

Pilkington, John. *Francis Marion Crawford*. New York: Twayne Publishers, Inc., 1964.

Pollard, John A. *John Greenleaf Whittier*. Boston: Houghton Mifflin Company, 1949.

Powell, Leona M. *The History of the United Typothetae of America*. Chicago: University of Chicago Press, 1926.

Pratt, John Barnes. *Personal Recollections*. New York: A. S. Barnes and Company, Inc., 1942.

Pulsifer, W. E. *An Argument Against State Publication*. n.p., n.d.

————. *A Brief Account of the Educational Publishing Business in the United States*. Atlantic City: 1921.

Putnam, George Haven. *George Palmer Putnam*. New York: G. P. Putnam's Sons, 1912.

————. *International Copyright Considered in Some of Its Relations to Ethics and Political Economy*. New York: G. P. Putnam's Sons, 1879.

————. *Memories of a Publisher, 1865–1915*. New York: G. P. Putnam's Sons, 1915.

————. *The Question of Copyright*. New York: G. P. Putnam's Sons, 1891.

Reid, Wemyss. *William Black: Novelist*. New York: Harper & Brothers, 1902.

Reports of the United States Commissioners to the Paris Universal Exposition, 1878. 5 vols. Washington: Government Printing Office, 1880.

Rhodes, James Ford. *History of the United States*. New York: The Macmillan Company, 1917, vol. VIII, 1877–1896.

Richardson, L. N. "Rutherford B. Hayes and Men of Letters," *New England Quarterly*, XV (March 1942), 110–41.

Rogers, Bruce. *Pi*. Cleveland: The World Publishing Company, 1953.

————. *The Work of Bruce Rogers: Jack of All Trades, Master of One*. A Catalogue arranged by the American Institute of Graphic Arts and the Grolier Club of New York. New York: 1939.

Rogers, Bruce and A. Colish. "Announce the Publication of *The Divine Comedy of Dante Alighieri.*" New York: Bruce Rogers and Press of A. Colish, 1954.

Rudolph, Frederick. *Mark Hopkins and the Log: Williams College, 1836–1872.* New Haven: Yale University Press, 1956.

Samuels, Charles E. *Thomas Bailey Aldrich.* New York: Twayne Publishers, Inc., 1965.

Samuels, Ernest. *Henry Adams: the Major Phase.* Cambridge: Belknap Press of Harvard University Press, 1964.

————. *Henry Adams: the Middle Years.* Cambridge: Belknap Press of Harvard University Press, 1958.

————. *The Young Henry Adams.* Cambridge: Harvard University Press, 1948.

Scudder, Horace Elisha. *Henry Oscar Houghton.* Cambridge: Riverside Press, 1897.

————. *James Russell Lowell.* 2 vols. Boston: Houghton, Mifflin & Company, 1901.

————. *Life and Letters of David Coit Scudder.* New York: Hurd & Houghton, 1864.

————. *Men and Letters.* Boston: Houghton, Mifflin & Company, 1887.

————. *Noah Webster.* Boston: Houghton, Mifflin & Company, 1882.

Sedgwick, Anne Douglas. *A Portrait in Letters,* ed. Basil de Selincourt. Boston: Houghton Mifflin Company, 1936.

Sedgwick, Ellery. *The Happy Profession.* Boston: Little, Brown and Company, 1946.

Sergeant, Elizabeth Shepley. *Willa Cather: a Memoir.* New York: J. B. Lippincott Company, 1953.

Shaw, Ralph R. *Literary Property in the United States.* New York: Scarecrow Press, Inc., 1950.

Sheehan, Donald. *This Was Publishing.* Bloomington: University of Indiana Press, 1952.

Sledd, James and Wilma R. Ebbitt. *Dictionaries and That Dictionary.* Chicago: Scott, Foresman & Company, 1962.

Smith, Clarke. *The Life and Letters of James Abram Garfield.* 2 vols. New Haven: Yale University Press, 1925.

Smith, Henry Nash. "That Hideous Mistake of Poor Clemens's," *Harvard Library Bulletin,* IX (Spring 1955), 145–80.

Smith, Henry Nash and William M. Gibson, eds. *Mark Twain–Howells Letters.* 2 vols. Cambridge: Belknap Press of Harvard University Press, 1960.

Smith, Janet Adam. *John Buchan.* Boston: Little, Brown and Company, 1965.

Sobel, Robert. *The Big Board: a History of the New York Stock Market.* New York: The Free Press, 1965.

Squires, James Duane. *British Propaganda at Home and in the United States from 1914 to 1917.* Cambridge: Harvard University Press, 1935.

Stanwood, Edward. *American Tariff Controversies in the Nineteenth Century.* Boston: Houghton, Mifflin & Company, 1903, vol II.

Stedman, Laura and G. M. Gould, eds. *The Life and Letters of Edmund Clarence Stedman.* New York: Moffat, Yard & Company, 1910, vol. I.

Stevens, George A. *New York Typographical Union No. 6: Study of a Modern Trade Union and Its Predecessors.* Albany: J. B. Lyon Company, 1913.

Stevens, Henry. *Recollections of Mr. James Lenox of New York and the Formation of His Library.* London: Henry Stevens & Sons, 1886.

————. *Who Spoils Our New English Books.* London: H. N. Stevens, 1884.

Stevenson, Elizabeth. *Lafcadio Hearn.* New York: The Macmillan Company, 1961.

Stewart, Eihelbert. "Early Organizations of Printers," *Labor Bulletin,* II (1905), 857–1042.

Stewart, Randall. "Editing of Hawthorne's Notebooks," and "Mrs. Hawthorne's Financial Difficulties, Selections from her Letters to James T. Fields, 1865–1868," *More Books,* XX (September 1945), 299–315 and XXI (February and September 1946), 43–52, 254–63.

Stowe, Charles E. *The Life of Harriet Beecher Stowe.* Boston: Houghton, Mifflin & Company, 1891.

Stowe, Harriet Beecher. *Life and Letters of Harriet Beecher Stowe,* ed. Annie Fields. Boston: Houghton, Mifflin & Company, 1898.

Strong, Theron. *Joseph H. Choate.* New York: Dodd, Mead & Company, 1917.

A Study of the History of the International Typographical Union, 1852–1963. Colorado Springs: Executive Council, International Typographical Union, 1964, vol. I.

A Summary Summing of the Charges, with Their Refutations on Attacks upon Noah Webster, LL.D., Made by Mr. Joseph E. Worcester, Mr. Sherman Converse and Messrs. Jenks, Hickling, and Swan. Springfield (Massachusetts): Geo. & Chas. Merriam, 1854.

Swan, William Draper. *The Critic Criticised, and Worcester Vindicated.* Boston: Swan, Brewer and Tileston, 1861.

Swanberg, W. A. *Theodore Dreiser.* New York: Charles Scribner's Sons, 1965.

Swift, Lindsay. *Literary Landmarks of Boston.* Boston: Houghton, Mifflin & Company, 1903.

Swinburne, Algernon. *The Swinburne Letters,* ed. Cecil Y. Lang. New Haven: Yale University Press, 1959, vol. I.

Swinnerton, Frank. *Authors and the Book Trade.* New York: Alfred A. Knopf, Inc., 1932.

Tennyson, Charles. *Alfred Tennyson.* New York: The Macmillan Company, 1949.

Thayer, John Adams. *Astir: a Publisher's Life Story.* Boston: Small, Maynard and Company, 1910.

Thayer, William Roscoe. *Letters of William Roscoe Thayer,* ed. Charles Downer Hazen. Boston, 1926.

Thomas, Lately [pseud.]. *Sam Ward: "King of the Lobby."* Boston: Houghton Mifflin Company, 1965.

Thomas Young Crowell, 1836–1915. New York: Thomas Y. Crowell Company, 1926.

Thwing, Charles Franklin. *A History of Education in the United States Since the Civil War.* Boston: Houghton Mifflin Company, 1910.

Ticknor, Caroline. *Glimpses of Authors.* Boston: Houghton Mifflin Company, 1922.

————— *Hawthorne and His Publisher*. Boston: Houghton Mifflin Company, 1913.

Tilton, Eleanor M. *Amiable Autocrat: a Biography of Dr. Oliver Wendell Holmes*. New York: Henry Schuman, 1947.

Tooker, Frank L. *The Joys and Tribulations of an Editor*. New York: The Century Company, 1923.

Trowbridge, John Townsend. *My Own Story*. Boston: Houghton, Mifflin & Company, 1903.

Tryon, Warren S. *Parnassus Corner: a Life of James T. Fields*. Boston: Houghton Mifflin Company, 1963.

Tryon, Warren S. and William Charvat, eds. *The Cost Books of Ticknor and Fields, 1832–1858*. New York: Bibliographical Society of America, 1949.

Tuchman, Barbara W. *The Proud Tower*. New York: The Macmillan Company, 1966.

Turner, Arlin. *George W. Cable*. Durham (North Carolina): Duke University Press, 1956.

Unwin, Stanley. *The Truth About a Publisher*. New York: The Macmillan Company, 1960.

————— . *The Truth About Publishing*. Boston: Houghton Mifflin Company, 1927. New York: The Macmillan Company, 1960.

Updike, Daniel Berkeley. *Notes on the Merrymount Press and Its Work*. Cambridge: Harvard University Press, 1934.

Vanderbilt, Kermit. *Charles Eliot Norton*. Cambridge: Harvard University Press, 1959.

Van Vleck, George W. *The Crisis of 1857 in the United States*. New York: Columbia University Press, 1943.

Van Way, Joseph S. "Nook Farm," *The Stowe, Beecher, Hooker, Seymor Day Foundation Bulletin*, I, 15–20.

Vedder, Elihu. *The Digressions of V*. Boston: Houghton Mifflin Company, 1910.

Wagenknecht, Edward C. *Longfellow: a Full-Length Portrait*. New York: Longmans, Green, 1955.

Warde, Frederic. *Bruce Rogers: Designer of Books*. Cambridge: Harvard University Press, 1926.

Warfel, Harry R. *Noah Webster: Schoolmaster to America*. New York: The Macmillan Company, 1936.

Warren, Charles. *Bankruptcy in the United States History*. Cambridge: Harvard University Press, 1935.

Warren, J. A. *A History of S. D. Warren Company*. Westbrook (Maine): S. D. Warren Company, 1954.

Weber, Carl J. *The Rise and Fall of James Ripley Osgood*. Waterville (Maine): Colby College Press, 1959.

————— . "Thomas Hardy and his New England Editors," *New England Quarterly*, XV (December 1942), 681–99.

Webster, Samuel C. *Mark Twain: Business Man*. Boston: Little, Brown and Company, 1946.

Weeks, Edward and Emily Flint, eds. *Jubilee: One Hundred Years of the Atlantic*. Boston: Little, Brown and Company, 1957.

Wells, Anna Mary. *Dear Preceptor: the Life and Times of Thomas Wentworth Higginson.* Boston: Houghton Mifflin Company, 1963.

Wells, H. G. *The Future in America.* New York: Harper & Brothers, 1906.

White, Andrew D. *Autobiography.* New York: The Century Company, 1905, vol. I.

Wiggin, Kate Douglas. *My Garden of Memories.* Boston: Houghton Mifflin Company, 1933.

Wight, M. D. *A Memorial of O. W. Wight, A.M., M.D., Sanitarian, Lawyer and Author.* Cambridge: Riverside Press, 1890.

Wilson, Forrest. *Crusader in Crinoline.* Philadelphia: J. B. Lippincott Company, 1941.

Woodward, Carl F. "The Heritage of a Country Bred Statesman." *New-England Galaxy,* V (Spring 1963), 37–46.

Yard, Robert Sterling. *The Publisher.* Boston: Houghton Mifflin Company, 1913.

INDEX

INDEX